Grid Technology for Maximizing Collaborative Decision Management and Support:
Advancing Effective Virtual Organizations

Nik Bessis
University of Bedfordshire, UK

INFORMATION SCIENCE REFERENCE

Hershey · New York

Director of Editorial Content: Kristin Klinger
Senior Managing Editor: Jamie Snavely
Managing Editor: Jeff Ash
Assistant Managing Editor: Carole Coulson
Typesetter: Sean Woznicki
Cover Design: Lisa Tosheff
Printed at: Yurchak Printing Inc.

Published in the United States of America by
         Information Science Reference (an imprint of IGI Global)
         701 E. Chocolate Avenue, Suite 200
         Hershey PA 17033
         Tel: 717-533-8845
         Fax: 717-533-8661
         E-mail: cust@igi-global.com
         Web site: http://www.igi-global.com/reference

and in the United Kingdom by
         Information Science Reference (an imprint of IGI Global)
         3 Henrietta Street
         Covent Garden
         London WC2E 8LU
         Tel: 44 20 7240 0856
         Fax: 44 20 7379 0609
         Web site: http://www.eurospanbookstore.com

Copyright © 2009 by IGI Global. All rights reserved. No part of this publication may be reproduced, stored or distributed in any form or by any means, electronic or mechanical, including photocopying, without written permission from the publisher.

        Product or company names used in this set are for identification purposes only. Inclusion of the names of the products or companies does not indicate a claim of ownership by IGI Global of the trademark or registered trademark.

Library of Congress Cataloging-in-Publication Data

Grid technology for maximizing collaborative decision management and support : advancing effective virtual organizations / Nik Bessis, editor.
        p. cm.
  Includes bibliographical references and index.

  Summary: "This book presents research on building network of excellence by effectively and efficiently managing ICT-related resources using Grid technology"--Provided by publisher.

  ISBN 978-1-60566-364-7 (hbk.) -- ISBN 978-1-60566-365-4 (ebook)
  1. Information technology--Management. 2. Computational grids (Computer systems) 3. Shared virtual environments. I. Bessis, Nik, 1967-
  T58.64.G75 2009
  658.4'038--dc22
                            2008042439

British Cataloguing in Publication Data
A Cataloguing in Publication record for this book is available from the British Library.

All work contributed to this book is new, previously-unpublished material. The views expressed in this book are those of the authors, but not necessarily of the publisher.

Editorial Advisory Board

Maozhen Li, *School of Engineering and Design, Brunel University, UK*
Tatiana Bouzdine-Chameeva, *Bordeaux Business School, France*
Wen-Yang Lin, *National University of Kaohsiung, Taiwan*
Iain Phillips, *Loughborough University, UK*
Antonio Puliafito, *University of Messina, Italy*
Alain Roy, *University of Wisconsin-Madison, USA*
Richard O. Sinnott, *University of Glasgow, UK*
Yong Yue Yong, *University of Bedfordshire, UK*

List of Reviewers

Vassiliki Andronikou, *National Technical University of Athens, Greece*
Nick Antonopoulos, *University of Surrey, UK*
Eleana Asimakopoulou, *Loughborough University, UK*
Mehmet Aydin, *University of Bedfordshire, UK*
Tatiana Bouzdine-Chameeva, *Bordeaux Business School, France*
Marina Burakova-Lorgnier, *University of Montesquieu Bordeaux IV, France*
Yun-Heh Chen-Burger, *University of Edinburgh, UK*
Gordon Clapworthy, *University of Bedfordshire, UK*
Rogério Luís de Carvalho Costa, *University of Coimbra, Portugal*
James Dooley, *City University, UK*
Marco Fargetta, *Catania University, Italy*
Genoveffa (Jeni) Giambona, *University of Reading, UK*
Rania Lavaki, *University of Montesquieu Bordeaux IV, France*
Maozhen Li, *Brunel University, UK*
Dayou Li, *University of Bedfordshire, UK*
Wen-Yang Lin, *National University of Kaohsiung, Taiwan*
Anton Minko, *OKTAL, France*
Kashif Munir, *King Fahd University of Petroleum and Minerals, Saudi Arabia*
Navonil Mustafee, *University of Warwick, UK*

Peter Norrington, *University of Bedfordshire, UK*
Iain Phillips, *Loughborough University, UK*
Antonio Puliafito, *University of Messina, Italy*
Alain Roy, *University of Wisconsin-Madison, USA*
Paul Sant, *University of Bedfordshire, UK*
Ahmet Sayar, *Indiana University, USA*
Richard O. Sinnott, *University of Glasgow, UK*
Rob Smith, *Newcastle University, UK*
Yong Yue, *University of Bedfordshire, UK*

Table of Contents

Section I
Grid Technology for Collaborative Decision Management and Support

Chapter I

Enjie Liu, University of Bedfordshire, UK
Xia Zhao, University of Bedfordshire, UK
Gordon J. Clapworthy, University of Bedfordshire, UK

Chapter II

Giuseppe Andronico, Istituto Nazionale di Fisica Nucleare, Italy
Roberto Barbera, University of Catania, Italy & Istituto Nazionale di Fisica Nucleare, Italy
Marco Fargetta, Consorzio COMETA, Italy
Emidio Giorgio, Istituto Nazionale di Fisica Nucleare, Italy
Salvatore Marco Pappalardo, Consorzio COMETA, Italy
Diego Scardaci, Istituto Nazionale di Fisica Nucleare, Italy

Chapter III

Vassiliki Andronikou, National Technical University of Athens, Greece
Dimosthenis Kyriazis, National Technical University of Athens, Greece
Magdalini Kardara, National Technical University of Athens, Greece
Dimitrios Halkos, National Technical University of Athens, Greece
Theodora Varvarigou, National Technical University of Athens, Greece

Section II
Social Aspects in Grid Environments

Section III
Grid Services for Advancing Virtual Organizations

Detailed Table of Contents

Section I
Grid Technology for Collaborative Decision Management and Support

Chapter I

Enjie Liu, University of Bedfordshire, UK
Xia Zhao, University of Bedfordshire, UK
Gordon J. Clapworthy, University of Bedfordshire, UK

At the heart of the Grid technology is the concept of resource sharing, which includes computers, storage, and networks. Grid currently appears to be the most suitable technology to support this type of future development. Web Services are the key technology in Grid infrastructure. This chapter presents a case study of a Web Services design and implementation to allow medical data in differing formats to be stored in a standardised form and to expose algorithms from existing applications that manipulate these data sets as online service objects. The aim is to explain the key concerns in service design and development using a real-world application as a case study. By reading this chapter, the reader should gain an overall understanding of how a service-oriented Grid application can be designed and implemented.

Chapter II

Giuseppe Andronico, Istituto Nazionale di Fisica Nucleare, Italy
Roberto Barbera, University of Catania, Italy & Istituto Nazionale di Fisica Nucleare, Italy
Marco Fargetta, Consorzio COMETA, Italy
Emidio Giorgio, Istituto Nazionale di Fisica Nucleare, Italy
Salvatore Marco Pappalardo, Consorzio COMETA, Italy
Diego Scardaci, Istituto Nazionale di Fisica Nucleare, Italy

Grid computing allows for the creation of e-infrastructures providing computational power and information storage capabilities needed both by present and future research centres around the world. Although the value of Grids is recognised by its early users, many companies, which would benefit from the adoption of this new paradigm, are still waiting claiming that Grid technologies are still not well-established and continuously evolving. A company usually takes a risk when it adopts a technology before its standardisation because if the technology subsequently demonstrates to diverge from (de-facto) standards then the investments can be partially lost and, additionally, switching to the new standard technology will probably be more expensive. In this chapter the authors present a couple of approaches which allow existing Grid infrastructures to evolve, by including newer Grid middleware, and consequently preserve the investment made on the infrastructure. The capability to evolve reduces current problems of Grid implementation (especially the lack of standards), so it makes Grid adoption by business companies and research centres painless.

Vassiliki Andronikou, National Technical University of Athens, Greece
Dimosthenis Kyriazis, National Technical University of Athens, Greece
Magdalini Kardara, National Technical University of Athens, Greece
Dimitrios Halkos, National Technical University of Athens, Greece
Theodora Varvarigou, National Technical University of Athens, Greece

The Grid has the potential to make a significant advance beyond the Internet, by turning it from a passive information medium into an active tool for creating and exploring new knowledge. Nowadays, this potential is becoming a reality and is emerging to Next Generation Grids (NGG) thanks to the far more cost-effective and universally applicable technology. Taking into consideration that Grids started delivering benefits to their adopters, this book chapter focuses on providing a business–technical presentation of two potential NGG applications, from two competitive and highly dynamic markets, including complex collaborations, which have shown rapid growth over the past decades; the supply chain management and the Cargo Transportation Logistics. We present a set of NGG components, the adoption of which in the aforementioned application domains addresses efficiently a set of technical issues ranging from performance to dynamic negotiation, and tackle the main trends and challenges in the corresponding business sectors.

Gayathri Nadarajan, University of Edinburgh, UK
Areti Manataki, University of Edinburgh, UK
Yun-Heh Chen-Burger, University of Edinburgh, UK

The infrastructure of Grid is approaching maturity and can be used to enable the utilisation and sharing of large scale, remote data storages through distributed computational capabilities and support collaborations and co-operations between different organisations. Grid can therefore be suitably used to support the creation and running of a Virtual Organisation (VO). However, to assist the smooth operation of VOs, robust computational and storage facilities alone are not sufficient. Appropriate rich business infrastructure must also exist. In this chapter, the authors consider business process frameworks that utilize semantics-based business process modelling (BPM) technologies, and they illustrate the multidisciplinary nature of our approach by applying them to three different fields: Supply Chain Management, Business Intelligence and Knowledge Management, and Intelligent Video Analysis. The authors aim to show that these three application areas that incorporate semantics-based BPM methods could be used to support developing Grid applications, and to subsequently support VOs.

Chapter V

The computational grid offers services for efficiently scheduling jobs on the grid, but for grid-enabled applications where data handling is a most relevant part, the data grid kicks in. It typically builds on the concept of files, sites and file transfers between sites. These use a data transfer service, plus a replica manager to keep track of where replicas are located. The authors of this chapter consider a multi-site, grid-aware data warehouse, which is a large distributed repository sharing a schema and data concerning scientific or business domains. Differently from typical grid scenarios, the data warehouse is not simply a set of files and accesses to individual files. It is a single distributed schema and both localized and distributed computations must be managed over that schema. Given this difference, it is important to study approaches for placement and computation over the grid data warehouse and this is their contribution in this chapter.

Chapter VI

This chapter focuses on the collaborative use of computing resources to support decision making in industry. Through the use of middleware for desktop grid computing, the idle CPU cycles available on existing computing resources can be harvested and used for speeding-up the execution of applications that have "non-trivial" processing requirements. This chapter focuses on the desktop grid middleware BOINC and Condor, and discusses the integration of commercial simulation software together with free-to-download grid middleware so as to offer competitive advantage to organizations that opt for this technology. It is expected that the low-intervention integration approach presented in this chapter (meaning no changes to source code required) will appeal to both simulation practitioners (as simulations can be executed faster, which in turn would mean that more replications and optimization is possible in the same amount of time) and the management (as it can potentially increase the return on investment on existing resources).

Section II
Social Aspects in Grid Environments

Genoveffa (Jeni) Giambona, University of Reading, UK

Nicholas L. J. Silburn, Henley Business School, UK

David W. Birchall, Henley Business School, UK

Flexible and remote working is nowadays becoming more and more widespread. In particular, virtual team working is growing rapidly. Although virtual teams have attracted the attention of many researchers, until recently little investigation had been carried out specifically on what impact trust – a key element in favouring cooperation among team members – has on the performance of such teams. In our opinion Grid computing, through the collaborative nature of the technologies employed, provides an opportunity to build trust through the sharing of common resources and the enabling of rich communications.

Rob Smith, Newcastle University, UK

Rob Wilson, Newcastle University, UK

A Virtual Organisation (VO) or Virtual Enterprise is a loosely-coupled group of collaborating organisations, acting to some extent as though they were part of a single organisation. This implies that they exhibit some properties of a conventional organisation without actually being one. In practice, this involves overcoming organisational boundaries, which tend to make collaborative working difficult. The authors propose that this is a socio-technical problem, requiring both a technical (software) infrastructure and a sociological approach to building, deploying and operating the VOs supported by it. This joint approach can help to overcome some of the problems associated with collaborative working, ranging from poorly coordinated activity, to ineffective problem solving and decision-making. We describe a socio-technical approach to building and operating VOs in highly dynamic environments and present two factual scenarios from the chemical and health industries. We describe a platform supporting such VOs, which was developed as part of the EPSRC e-Science Pilot Project GOLD.

Marina Burakova-Lorgnier, University of Bordeaux 4, INSEEC Business Schools, France

The aim of this chapter is to appreciate the need for and propose some thoughts on modelling trust–control dynamics for communities that use grid technology. It takes the viewpoint that members within a grid-based community require a trust framework that brings together and takes into account both social and technological approaches to trust. It also emphasises the importance of the simultaneous analysis of trust and control in their co-development. In line with the duality perspective that considers trust and control as independent yet interrelated dimensions, trust is explored in its relation to control. Control is examined as a multi-dimensional phenomenon that includes personal, formal and social scopes. The analysis of trust appeals to its cognitive and affective dimensions. The model introduced also takes into account the mediating role of psychological ownership in the trust–control dynamics. Specifically, shared psychological ownership is singled out as a new explanatory variable of this dynamic.

Section III
Grid Services for Advancing Virtual Organizations

Chapter X

Lu Liu, University of Leeds, UK
Nick Antonopoulos, University of Surrey, UK

A Virtual Organisation in large-scale distributed systems is a set of individuals and/or institutions with some common purposes or interests that need to share their resources to further their objectives, which are similar to a human community in social networks that consists of people having common interests or goals. Due to the similarity between social networks and Grids, the concepts in social science (e.g. small world phenomenon) can be adopted for the design of new generation Grid systems. This chapter presents a Small World architecture for Effective Virtual Organisations (SWEVO) for Grid resource discovery in Virtual Organisations, which enables Virtual Organisations working in a more collaborative manner to support decision makers. In SWEVO, Virtual Organisations are connected by a small number of inter-organisational links. Not every local network node needs to be connected to remote Virtual Organisations, but every network node can efficiently find connections to specific Virtual Organisations.

Chapter XI

James Dooley, City University, UK
Andrea Zisman, City University, UK
George Spanoudakis, City University, UK

This chapter describes a framework to support runtime service discovery for Grid applications based on service discovery queries in both push and pull modes of query execution. The framework supports six different types of trigger conditions that may prompt service replacement during run-time of grid business application, and evaluates the relevance of a set of candidate services against service discovery queries. The chapter also describes the language used to express service discovery queries and the three types of fitness measurement used to evaluate the candidate services against these queries. Both synchronous (pull) and asynchronous (push) mechanisms for service discovery are presented and shown to be complimentary in dealing with all six service discovery trigger conditions. The work is illustrated through examples.

Chapter XII

Nik Bessis, University of Bedfordshire, UK

Much work is under way within the Grid technology community on issues associated with the development of services to foster collaboration via the integration and exploitation of multiple autonomous, distributed data sources through a seamless and flexible virtualized interface. However, several obstacles arise in the design and implementation of such services. A notable obstacle, namely how clients within a data Grid environment can be kept automatically informed of the latest and relevant changes about data entered/committed in single or multiple autonomous distributed datasets is identified. The view is that keeping interested users informed of relevant changes occurring across their domain of interest will enlarge their decision-making space which in turn will increase the opportunities for a more informed decision to be encountered. With this in mind, the chapter goes on to describe in detail the model architecture and its implementation to keep interested users informed automatically about relevant up-to-date data.

This chapter demonstrates how Grid technology can be used to support intelligence in emergency response management decision-making processes. It discusses how the open Grid service architecture and data access integration (OGSA-DAI) specification services can facilitate the discovery of and controlled access to data, resources and other instrumentation to improve the effectiveness and efficiency of emergency response tasks. A core element of this chapter is to discuss the major limitations with information and communication technology (ICT) in use when a natural disaster occurs. Moreover, it describes emergency response stakeholders' requirements and their need to seamlessly integrate all their ICT resources in a collaborative and timely manner. With this in mind, it goes on to describe in detail a Grid-aware emergency response model as the practice to maximize potential and make the best of functionality offered by current ICT to support intelligence in emergency response decision-making.

Geographic information is critical for building disaster planning, crisis management, and early-warning systems. Decision making in geographic information systems (GIS) increasingly relies on analyses of spatial data in map-based formats. Maps are complex structures composed of layers created from distributed heterogeneous data belonging to the separate organizations. This chapter presents a distributed service architecture for managing the production of knowledge from distributed collections of observations and simulation data through integrated data-views. Integrated views are defined by a federation service ("federator") located on top of the standard service components. Common GIS standards enable the construction of this system. However, compliance requirements for interoperability, such as XML-encoded data and domain specific data characteristics, have costs and performance overhead. The authors investigate issues of combining standard compliance with performance. Although their framework is designed for GIS, the authors extend the principles and requirements to general science domains and discuss how these may be applied.

Foreword

The services that make up a Grid environment provide a distributed infrastructure for dynamic resource sharing and problem solving across multiple organizational boundaries, which effectively provides a virtualized wide-area distributed system. Overall, the Grid is about resource sharing, which includes computers, storage, networks, and other devices. Sharing is always conditional and based on factors such as trust, institutional policies, negotiation, and potentially how payment should be considered. The Grid concepts and ideas have now moved away from the world of joining high-performance computing (HPC) systems together to more generalized systems based on a service-oriented architecture that can provide infrastructure for a range of applications. The Grid infrastructure provides support for coordinated problem solving, which is beyond a simple client/server paradigm. Here we may be interested in combinations of distributed data analysis, computation, and collaboration. The Grid also includes dynamic, multi-institutional virtual organizations; these overlay and advance classical organizational structures, and may be large or small, static or dynamic.

A diverse range of applications are now being executed on the Grid. At one end of the spectrum are simple applications that may use a client/server paradigm, and at the other end of the spectrum, increasingly complex applications are being developed and executed. An example is workflows that may need to use a sophisticated distributed pipeline of services to fulfil their needs. Popular applications include HPC-based grand challenge problems that are computationally or data intensive and high-throughput ones that need to spawn hundreds of thousands of tasks in parameter sweeps. Newer applications include those that enable collaboration between distributed partners. This type of application can provide both collaborative support and facilitate decision management for shared projects.

Foreseeing future trends in technologies is an almost impossible task. Since its conception in the mid-1990s, the components and technologies that make up the Grid have changed radically, and even today they are still evolving, with "Cloud Computing" becoming a pervasive contender for the same space. This book brings together a collection of papers from researchers who are exploring the technologies that enable virtual organizations for a range of purposes, but most importantly, they are implementing ideas that further the means of undertaking collaborative processes. Overall, the work discussed in this book provides an interesting compilation that will allow readers to understand the state of the art of *Grid Technology for Maximizing Collaborative Decision Management and Support: Advancing Effective Virtual Organizations.*

Mark Baker
University of Reading, UK

Mark Baker *is a research professor of Computer Science in the School of Systems Engineering at the University of Reading, UK. Mark's interests are related to the research and develop of middleware to support parallel and distributed applications. Currently Mark is involved in projects involving resource monitoring, P2P messaging and registries, a Java-based parallel messaging system, virtual research environments and wireless sensor networks.*

Preface

Computer-based developments over the last four decades have facilitated managers with numerous collaborative tools to support operational, tactical, and/or strategic level of enquiries within the environment of an organization. In relation to managing decisions, the use of collaborative decision and management support systems has evolved over the years through developments in computational science including databases, data warehouses, data mining, data visualization, intelligent agents, artificial intelligence, and neural networks. One of the purposes of these technologies is to provide managers as decision makers with a holistic view of the situation under enquiry.

Managers in commercial and other organizational environments often find the effective and efficient utilization of Information and Communication Technology (ICT) resources quite a challenging decision-making process, but frequently a very supportive mechanism for sustaining and creating a competitive advantage.

Recent studies in relation to networking and resource integration have resulted in the new concept of Grid technology, a term originally coined by Ian Foster in 1995. Grid technology has been described as the infrastructure and set of protocols that enable the sharing, integration and collaborative use of networked computer-based distributed heterogeneous resources (hardware, applications, data and instrumentation) between the multiple organizations that own those resources.

During the last five years, scientists have almost exclusively used Grid technology for their own research and development purposes. Lately, the focus is shifting to more interdisciplinary application domains that are closer to everyday life, such as medical, business and engineering applications. Hence, the Grid concept as a paradigm has an increased focus on the interconnection of resources both within and across various and differing collaborative organizations. This book will ensure that Grid technology shall be of the fullest interest to decision makers seeking collaborative decision management and support by advancing effective virtual organizations.

WHAT IS A VIRTUAL ORGANIZATION?

In the last few years, the Internet has revolutionized the way we work and do business. In both commerce and academia, this has led to market globalization, which in turn has led us to experience an enormous increase in competitiveness between organizations.

In response, a number of organizations have vanished, others have started to collaborate, and some have chosen to shrink by offering more specialist services. In most instances, collaboration is the key for those surviving organizations (service providers), as they realize that a customer (service consumer) is mostly looking for the front-end of a completed package that is either a final product or service. As a note here, collaboration refers to the back-end process (from a consumer point of view) in which more than one organization share their competencies and work together towards the achievement of a mutual goal; that is to say, the final product or service. The growing trend of collaboration between organizations is also due to the fact that organizations are realizing that their goals are more demanding; they involve higher level complexity tasks and their resource capabilities may be inevitably limited in an environment of continuously rising standards and challenges. On the other hand, it is reasonable to think that there is a greater possibility of a more complete final product to be encountered, and earlier, if its development approach incorporates the input from more than the sum of the development parts.

Current ICTs are capable of supporting collaborative activities in cyberspace. These cyber-enabled collaborations involve the emergence of multiple organizations that function as one unit through the use of their shared competencies and resources for the purpose of one or more identified goals. It is important to note that a single organization collaborating in cyberspace may have as many unit functions – within the same or a different cluster of collaborative organizations – as the number of their identified goals. This cluster of collaborative organizations functioning as a unit towards an identified goal lasts for the lifetime of the identified goal. The fact that such collaboration is happening in cyberspace and that it has a transient life labels it as a virtual organization.

Thus, the enabling features (access to aggregated, distributed heterogeneous data, combined and parallel computational power, storage and instrumentation) offered by Grid technology have the potential to push the boundaries of and strengthen the aforementioned collaborations via a more informed (access to a greater horizon) and timely (quicker, on demand) collaborative support and therefore, provide more opportunities for advancing virtual organizations (VO).

With regard to collaborative decision-making, a VO utilizing Grid technology aims to facilitate managers with the ability to analyze and utilize data and instrumentation drawn from multiple pools encompassing registered distributed and heterogeneous (re)sources in a far more convenient and collaborative manner. It is anticipated that Grid technology will facilitate informed decision making – by enabling timely access to a larger number and range of resources – in a way that managers and their teams will be able to carry out parallel and/or combined tasks of increased complexity far more quickly through one or many interconnected, separable or inseparable collaborative VOs. Using Grid technology, a VO is also equipped with the combined competencies offered by the organizations involved. Competencies also refer to the distinct expertise and understanding each organization owns for the particular domain they serve.

In the context of this book, a VO utilizing Grid technology refers to the one which incorporates the combination of all those qualities (resource and competencies) as a whole, which each individual organization brings into the partnership. The quality of seeking results from a multi-perspective point-of-view, enabling a multidisciplinary, interdisciplinary and trans-disciplinary approach offers a greater chance for a far more informed, timely and complete end result to be encountered.

THE PURPOSE OF THE BOOK

The book aims to build a network of excellence in effectively and efficiently managing ICT-related resources using Grid technology. Its mission is to introduce both technical and non-technical details of Grid technology and its implications to the VOs involved, demonstrating its feasible and applicable arrangement within business and other organizational IT infrastructures.

It thereafter deepens its focus by highlighting strengths, weaknesses, opportunities, and threats when Grid technology is deployed – in a collaborative manner – within a commercial or other organizational setting. This is achieved by: presenting current and past implementations based on stabilized standards, as well as conceptualizing applicable practical opportunities. Contributions pay particular attention to presenting topics that are diverse in scale and complexity, as well as written by and for a technical and non-technical audience to suit different reading styles.

Specifically, the goal of the book is to educate readers by demonstrating how Grid technology has and could be applied to serve as the vehicle to maximize decision management and support across organizations in a far more effective and efficient virtual collaborative setting. The book prompts further development for best practices in identifying opportunities and provides future direction for innovative and applicable adoption of Grid technology in the area.

WHO SHOULD READ THE BOOK?

The content of the book reflects the interests of a broad audience as it offers state-of-the-art information and references for work undertaken to the challenging area of utilizing Grid technology for maximizing collaborative decision management and support. The book provides a rich source for both technical and organizational practices with regard to adopting Grid technology to advance effective virtual organizations.

The projected audience ranges from those currently engaged in to those interested in joining inter-disciplinary and trans-disciplinary collaborative work utilizing ICT.

In brief, this book will be of highest value to a specialist audience including industry leaders, consultants, managers, practitioners, researchers, academics, and advanced undergraduate and postgraduate students working in the area of Grid technology. It will also be of high value to those wishing to embark in joining partnerships for producing collaborative interdisciplinary work utilizing Grid technology as the method to understand their domains in a far more complete way. Non-specialist audiences include postgraduate students, researchers, and academics from non-computing disciplines such as information systems, social science, business, and management.

ORGANIZATION OF THE BOOK

Fourteen self-contained chapters, each authored by experts in the area, are included in this book. The book is organized into three sections according to the thematic topic of the chapter. Thus, it is quite possible that a paper in one section may also address issues covered in other sections. However, the three sections reflect most of the topics sought in the initial call for chapters.

Section I, "*Grid Technology for Collaborative Decision Management and Support*" includes six chapters. This section introduces concepts and principles of Grid technology such as distributed computation and resource-sharing using Web services, middleware, and applications. These cover state-of-the-art methods and techniques for collaborative decision management and support across various organizational settings. In addition, some chapters present scenarios and approaches on how these methods and techniques could be further improved. As such, they underpin future development and implementation of relevant services.

Section II, "*Social Aspects in Grid Environments*" includes three chapters. This section elaborates the social aspect of sharing knowledge with, and entrusting other organizations, in a Grid environment. The content of this section is particularly valuable to those whose concerns keep them from participating in a virtual organization partnership using Grid technology. It pays particular attention to issues related to the understanding of socio-technical aspects of trust and control between virtual teams and organizations.

Section III, "*Grid Services for Advancing Virtual Organizations*" includes five chapters. This section goes beyond and builds upon current theory and practice, providing visionary directions on how Grid technology could be used in the future to the benefit of various organizational settings. It discusses the wide implications of Grid technology as to advance virtual organizations. As such, it provides latest thinking, practices, and conceptual models in utilizing Grid technology prompting further development for best practices in the real-world by identifying opportunities to support innovative and applicable services as to advance virtual organizations.

A brief introduction to each of the chapters follows.

In **Chapter I**, *Building Service-Oriented Grid Applications*, by Enjie Liu, Xia Zhao, and Gordon J. Clapworthy, presents a case study of a Web services design and implementation to allow medical data in differing formats to be stored in a standardized form and to expose algorithms from existing applications that manipulate these data sets as online service objects.

Chapter II, *Sustainable and Interoperable E-Infrastructures for Research and Business*, by Giuseppe Andronico, Rpbertp Barbera, Marco Fargetta, Emidio Giorgio, Salvatore Marco Pappalardo, and Dego Scardaci, discusses the approaches on how a company can alleviate the risks when it adopts a technology before standardization. Their approaches allow existing Grid infrastructures to evolve, by including newer middleware, and consequently preserve the investment made in the infrastructure.

In **Chapter III**, *Scenarios of Next Generation Grid Applications in Collaborative Environments: A Business-Technical Analysis*, Vassiliki Andronikou, Dimosthenis Kyriazis, Magdalini Kardara, Dimitrios Halkos, and Theodora Varvarigou, focus on two emerging Next Generation Grid (NGG) applications, which serve complex collaborations. These have shown rapid growth over the past decades and include the supply chain management and the Cargo Transportation Logistics competitive and highly dynamic markets.

In **Chapter IV**, *Semantics-Based Process Support for Grid Applications*, Gayathri Nadarajan, Areti Manataki, and Yun-Heh Chen-Burger consider business process frameworks that utilize semantics-based business process modeling (BPM) technologies. They illustrate their multidisciplinary approach by applying them to three different fields: Supply Chain Management, Business Intelligence and Knowledge Management, and Intelligent Video Analysis.

In **Chapter V**, *Placement and Scheduling over Grid Warehouses*, Rogério Luís de Carvalho Costa and Pedro Furtado consider a multi-site, Grid-aware data warehouse, which is a large distributed repository sharing a schema and data concerning scientific or business domains.

In **Chapter VI**, *Leveraging Simulation Practice in Industry through use of Desktop Grid Middleware*, Navonil Mustafee and Simon J.E. Taylor focus on the collaborative use of middleware for desktop Grid computing, like BOINC and Condor. The chapter discusses the integration of commercial simulation software together with free-to-download Grid middleware so as to offer competitive advantage to organizations that opt for this technology.

In **Chapter VII**, *Trust, Virtual Teams and Grid Technology*, Genoveffa (Jeni) Giambona, Nicholas L.J. Silburn, and David W. Birchall discuss what impact trust – a key element in favoring cooperation among team members – has on the performance of virtual teams. The chapter explores the opportunity to build trust through the sharing of common resources and the enabling of rich communications.

In **Chapter VIII**, *The Socio-Technical Virtual Organisation*, Rob Smith and Rob Wilson discuss the problem in which several collaborating organizations act as though they are part of a single conventional organization. They present two factual scenarios from the chemical and health industries to illustrate the types of problem such systems are susceptible to and the utility of a socio-technical approach in overcoming them.

In **Chapter IX**, *Modeling Trust-Control Dynamics for Grid-Based Communities: A Shared Psychological Ownership Perspective*, Marina Burakova-Lorgnier discusses the need for, and proposes some thoughts on, modeling trust–control dynamics for communities that use Grid technology. The chapter proposes a trust framework that brings these together by taking into account both social and technological approaches to trust.

Chapter X, *Small World Architecture for Building Effective Virtual Organisations*, by Lu Liu and Nick Antonopoulos discusses the similarity between social networks and Grids, and that concepts in social science can be adopted for the design of New Generation Grid systems. The chapter presents an architecture which enables VOs working in a more collaborative manner to support decision makers.

In **Chapter XI**, *Runtime Service Discovery for Grid Applications*, James Dooley, Andrea Zisman, and George Spanoudakis describe a framework to support runtime service discovery for Grid applications based on service discovery queries in both push and pull modes of query execution. The framework supports six different types of trigger conditions that may prompt service replacement during runtime of Grid business application, and evaluates the relevance of a set of candidate services against service discovery queries.

In **Chapter XII**, *Model Architecture for a User Tailored Data Push Service in Data Grids*, Nik Bessis presents a model architecture and its implementation which allows clients within a data Grid environment to be kept automatically informed of the latest and relevant changes about data entered/committed in single or multiple autonomous distributed datasets. The chapter argues that an OGSA-DAI push architecture will enlarge the decision-making space, which in turn will increase the opportunities for a more informed decision to be encountered.

Chapter XIII, *Using Grid Technology for Maximizing Collaborative Emergency Response Decision Making*, by Eleana Asimakopoulou, Chimay J. Anumba, and Dino Bouchlaghem, discusses the major limitations with the ICT currently in use when a natural disaster occurs. The chapter then describes a Grid-aware emergency response model as the practice to maximize potential and make the best of functionality offered by current ICT to support intelligence in emergency response decision-making.

In **Chapter XIV**, *Unified Data Access/Query over Integrated Data-Views for Decision Making in Geographic Information Systems*, Ahmet Sayar, Geoffrey C. Fox, and Marlon E. Pierce focus on decision-making using Geographical Information Services (GIS), which increasingly rely on analyses of distributed heterogeneous spatial data in map-based formats. The chapter presents distributed service architecture for managing the production of knowledge from distributed collections of observations and simulation data through integrated data-views.

I hope you find this book an inspirational read.

Nik Bessis
University of Bedfordshire, UK

Acknowledgment

It is my great pleasure to comment on the hard work and support of many people who have been involved in the development of this book. It is always a major undertaking but most importantly, a great encouragement and somehow a reward and an honor when seeing the enthusiasm and eagerness of people willing to advance their discipline by taking the commitment to share their experiences, ideas and visions towards the evolvement of collaboration like the achievement of this book. Without their support the book could not have been satisfactory completed.

First and foremost, I wish to thank all the authors who, as distinguished scientists despite busy schedules, devoted so much of their time preparing and writing their chapters, and responding to numerous comments and suggestions made from the Editorial Advisory Board, the reviewers, and myself. I trust this collection of chapters will offer a solid overview of current thinking on these areas and it is expected that the book will be a valuable source of stimulation and inspiration to all those who have or will have an interest in these fields.

My sincere thanks go to Professor Mark Baker, University of Reading, who wrote the foreword and to all the members of the Editorial Advisory Board who provided excellent comments, expert help and continuous support. These are some of the very same people who are creating these scientific changes. We have been fortunate that the following have honored us with their assistance in this project: Professor Tatiana Bouzdine-Chameeva, Department of Information, Decisions and Management, Bordeaux Business School; Dr. Maozhen Li, School of Engineering and Design, Brunel University; Professor Wen-Yang Lin, Department of Computer Science and Information Engineering, National University of Kaohsiung; Dr. Iain Phillips, Department of Computer Science, Loughborough University; Professor Antonio Puliafito, Department of Computer Engineering, University of Messina; Dr. Alain Roy, Department of Computer Sciences, University of Wisconsin-Madison; Professor Richard O. Sinnott, National e-Science Centre, University of Glasgow; and Dr. Yong Yue, Department of Computing and Information Systems, University of Bedfordshire.

Special gratitude goes to all the reviewers and some of the chapters' authors who also served as referees for chapters written by other authors. Among those, I would like to particularly mention Dr. Rania Lavaki, University of Montesquieu Bordeaux IV; Anton Minko, OKTAL; Dr. Eleana Asinakopoulou, Loughborough University, Dr. Marina Burakova-Lorgnier, University of Montesquieu Bordeaux IV, and colleagues from the Department of Computing and Information Systems, University of Bedfordshire, including Dr. Paul Sant, Dr. Mehmet Aydin, Dr. Dayou Li and Peter Norrington for their most critical comments.

This work also would not have been possible without the support of the Head of Department, Professor Carsten Maple, and other colleagues in the Department of Computing and Information Systems at the University of Bedfordshire.

Last but not least, I wish to gratefully acknowledge that I was fortunate to work closely with an outstanding team at IGI Global. Julia Mosemann, Kristin Roth, Lindsay Johnston, Kristin M. Klinger, Megan B. Childs, and Jan Travers were everything someone should expect from a publisher: professional, efficient, and a delight to work with. Thanks are also extended to all those at IGI Global who have taken care with managing the design and the timely production of this book.

Finally, I am deeply indebted to my family and fiancée for their love, patience and support throughout this rewarding experience.

Nik Bessis
University of Bedfordshire, UK

Section I
Grid Technology for Collaborative Decision Management and Support

Chapter I
Building Service–Oriented Grid Applications

Enjie Liu
University of Bedfordshire, UK

Xia Zhao
University of Bedfordshire, UK

Gordon J. Clapworthy
University of Bedfordshire, UK

ABSTRACT

At the heart of the Grid technology is the concept of resource sharing, which includes computers, storage and networks. Grid currently appears to be the most suitable technology to support this type of future development. Web Services are the key technology in Grid infrastructure. This chapter presents a case study of a Web Services design and implementation to allow medical data in differing formats to be stored in a standardised form and to expose algorithms from existing applications that manipulate these data sets as online service objects. The aim is to explain the key concerns in service design and development using a real-world application as a case study. By reading this chapter, the reader should gain an overall understanding of how a service-oriented Grid application can be designed and implemented.

INTRODUCTION

In bioinformatics experiments related to *in silico* modelling, huge sets of data at different physical scales, and frequently from different sources, are created. Algorithms to process these data will often have been developed by researchers in dif- ferent institutions; some of them will be newly created but others will have been in long-term use. Models are becoming more complex, often involving teams of researchers working at different locations, each possibly specialising in only one aspect of the overall problem, so the demands for resource sharing and high-performance comput-

Copyright © 2009, IGI Global, distributing in print or electronic forms without written permission of IGI Global is prohibited.

ing, which is often available only at a distant site, are growing.

It remains a huge challenge to share and manage the distributed data, algorithms and computational resources and provide a suitable environment within which users can perform their tasks. Unless users can work in this environment in a familiar way that requires little change from their previous practice, there is likely to be resistance to the change and poor user take-up.

To provide support for users' activities, it can be valuable to build a digital library infrastructure that allows clinicians and researchers not only to preserve, trace and share data resources, but also to collaborate at the data-processing level.

This chapter describes the implementation of the digital library as a service-oriented Grid application, based on work in a project funded by the European Commission – LHDL: the Living Human Digital Library. We shall briefly introduce Grid technology including the data grid middleware used in the project, then describe Service-Oriented Architecture (SOA) and Web Services technology. Finally, we describe the LHDL project, including its overall design and the main concerns for the implementation. We also explain the reasons for choosing the particular technology and tools, with the aim of sharing our experiences with the reader.

To summarise, the overall objectives of the chapter are to:

- Provide an overview of relevant aspects of Grid technology.
- Describe the features of a digital bioinformatics library based on Grid and Web Services.
- Explain in detail a Web Service design and implementation that can be used for the Grid.
- Share experiences related to building such an application.

GRID TECHNOLOGY

In this section, we briefly describe Grid technology, its key features and its evolution. We then introduce a general Grid architecture, and summarise the resources that are provided by Grid. Finally, we survey Grid middleware and data Grid middleware.

Introduction

As expressed by Foster and Kesselman (1998) and later refined in Foster et al. (2001), the Grid concept is encapsulated by 'coordinated resource sharing and problem solving in a dynamic, multi-institutional virtual organisation'.

In the commercial world, IBM defines a Grid as 'a standards-based application/resource-sharing architecture that makes it possible for heterogeneous systems and applications to share, compute and store resources transparently.' (Clabby, 2004)

According to the Expert Group Report (2003), the Grid evolved through several phases, beginning as a means of sharing computing resources. Data sharing, and the use of special devices such as scientific instruments and medical equipment, were added later. The combination of the first generation of Grid with Web technology led to generic Grid services.

The focus later shifted to knowledge sharing and collaboration between organisations, while maintaining the security requirements of each individual. The knowledge Grid facilitates data mining across the Internet. It requires techniques for abstracting heterogeneous data, creating metadata, publishing, discovering and describing data in the Grid.

Grid Architecture

As an aid to understanding the role played by Grid middleware, we first introduce the overall Grid architecture (Figure 1), which typically contains four main layers: network, resource, middleware and applications (Asadzadeh et al., 2004; http://gridcafe.web.cern.ch/gridcafe/index.html).

The *network layer*, or grid fabric layer, acts as the physical infrastructure and provides connectivity to the grid resources, such as computers and networks. Networks are the essential underlying hardware and link different computer nodes as part of the grid to form one huge grid computer.

The *resource layer* consists of the grid resources that link to the network, such as computers, storage systems, specialised resources, and so on. The computation resources include supercomputers, clusters, servers and ordinary computers, which run various operating systems. The storage systems include different types of databases, archives, heterogeneous resources, etc. The specialised resources include sensors, telescopes and satellites that can transmit real-time data to computation sites or store them in the storage.

The *middleware layer* includes software that organises and integrates resources in the grid. The middleware can be separated into two levels. The functionality of the *core middleware* is akin to the operating system on a PC and offers services such as remote process management, co-allocation of resources, storage access, information registration and discovery, security and aspects of Quality of Service (QoS). The *user-level*

middleware utilises the interfaces provided by the low-level middleware to provide higher-level abstractions and services, including the application development environment, programming tools and resource brokers for managing resources and scheduling application tasks for execution on global resources.

The *application layer* includes all applications that utilise the grid resources to fulfil their requirements, including applications in science, engineering, business, finance, etc., as well as portals and development toolkits to support the applications. This layer is also known as the serviceware layer because it includes all common services that perform mostly application-specific management functions such as billing, time logging, and others.

Resources Provided by Grid

Grid technology enables people to share information, computational power, data storage capacity and instruments. A Grid is a collection of machines, resources, members, donors, clients, hosts, engines, which may be sited at different geographical locations and work in any combination. The two main resources that Grid provides are computation power and storage capacity.

Computation Power

The most common resources provided on the Grid are the available processors, which can vary in speed, architecture, software platform, and other associated factors, such as memory, storage, and connectivity.

Initially, the Grid was envisioned as a way to share large computer facilities by sending jobs to be executed at remote sites at which there were more powerful computers or computers with spare processing capacity. This kind of Grid usage was referred to as a computational Grid. However, large jobs are often data intensive; it may then prove more efficient to move the jobs to where

Figure 1. Grid architecture (Adapted from Asadzadeh et al., 2004)

Application Layer	
Middleware Layer	User-level Middleware
	Core Middleware
Resource Layer	
Network Layer	

the data resides, to avoid moving large volumes of data across the network. Thus, the Data Grid was introduced for applications that produce and consume large volumes of data.

Storage Capacity

The second most common resource used in a grid is data storage. Storage management is an important enabling technology for large-scale scientific investigation. Having to deal with multiple heterogeneous storage and file systems is a major bottleneck in managing, replicating, and accessing files in distributed environments.

A Data Grid provides integrated view of data storage; it is a grid computing system that deals with the controlled sharing and management of large amounts of distributed data. Each machine on the grid usually provides some quantity of storage for grid use, even if only on a temporary basis. Storage can be memory attached to the processor or it can be secondary storage – hard disks or other permanent storage media.

Storage capacity can be increased by using multiple machines with a unified file system. An individual file or database may span several storage devices and machines to overcome the maximum file-size restrictions that are often imposed by particular operating systems. A unified file system can also provide a single uniform namespace for grid storage, thus makings it easier for users to reference data residing in the grid, without regard to its exact location.

The computational grid and data grid are often combined to achieve better performance.

Grid Middleware

In this section, we shall survey the most popular Grid middleware. In the next section, we shall describe some middleware for the Data Grid, as that is relevant to the development described later in the chapter.

The Globus Toolkit (http://www.globus.org/) is an open source software toolkit for building Grid systems and applications that came from an R&D project involving the Globus Alliance and many others worldwide. It includes software for security, information infrastructure, resource management, data management, communication, fault detection, and portability. It is packaged as a set of components that can be used, independently or together, to develop applications. This is the main middleware and is used increasingly by developers. The latest version is Globus v4.

In 2002, the Open Grid Services Architecture (OGSA) emerged; this extended the Globus concept and technologies. OGSA is a community standard with multiple implementations. OGSA provides a framework, and users can define a wide rage of interoperable, portable services.

Legion was originally an R&D project at the University of Virginia; the software was commercialised by a company called Avaki, which was acquired by Sybase in May 2005. Sybase Avaki for Data Grids (http://www.sybase.com) is a complete packaged data-grid solution that provides a seamless, transparent and single unified view of data for computer grid applications. Avaki for Data Grids is scalable and secure and makes data provisioning, integration and access simple. Avaki automatically manages the required data needs of the application, such as access to relational databases, file systems or Web Services.

OMII-Europe (http://omii-europe.org) is an EC project to source key software components for Grid applications and to ensure that these can interoperate across heterogeneous Grid middleware platforms. OMII-Europe is an Open Systems project that endorses both the use of open standards and open source. OMII-Europe has chosen particular open standards for the Grid that it believes are essential for interoperability across global resources. The emphasis is on *re-engineering* software components rather developing new technology.

GLite (http://glite.web.cern.ch/glite/) is the next-generation middleware for grid computing developed by the EC-funded EGEE (Enabling Grids for E-sciencE) project, which aims to provide a seamless Grid infrastructure for e-Science. The distribution model is to construct different services ('node-types') from these components and ensure easy installation and configuration on the chosen platforms. GLite middleware is currently deployed on hundreds of sites as part of EGEE.

Data Grid Middleware

The aim of Data Grid is for users to store their data at various physical locations and be able to access them using only a logical filename or attributes rather than needing to know the exact physical location of each file.

In this section, three widely used Data Grid middleware are surveyed, namely: Storage Resource Broker (SRB), Open Grid Service Architecture – Data Access and Integration (OGSA-DAI), and Storage Resources Manager (SRM).

SRB (Rajasekar et al., 2003) is a data grid middleware software system that was produced by the San Diego Supercomputer Center (SDSC). It has been adopted widely and in different domains, such as Biomedical Information Research Network (BIRN) (http://www.nrirn.net/), TeraGrid (http://www.teragrid.org/), Real-time Observatories Application and Data management Network (ROADNet) (http://www.roadnet.ucsd.edu), etc.

As illustrated in Figure 2, SRB is implemented as a comprehensive client-server distributed data-management federated environment. It consists of three main components: storage systems, SRB servers and clients.

SRB manages both data and metadata. A federated system must have at least one master server connected to the Metadata Catalog (MCAT) that has services to facilitate brokering and attribute-based querying. Optional server agents can be added on behalf of the SRB server to manage each type of storage system. Storage systems store data collections in various formats such as database systems (e.g., DB2, MSSQL,

Figure 2. The SRB federation structure (Adapted from Rajasekar et al., 2003)

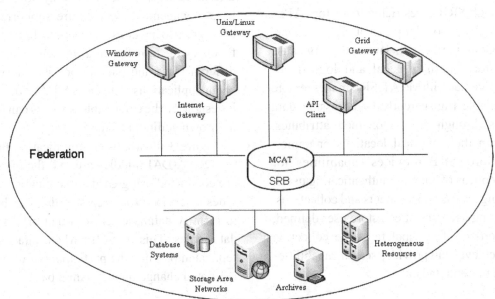

Oracle, and Sybase), archives (e.g., HPSS, SCSI tape, and DMF), heterogeneous resources (e.g., NT server, FTP, and HTTP), and so on. Different client interfaces are available for conveniently accessing all data resources within the federation as well as for supporting the management and collaborative (and controlled) sharing, publication, replication, transfer, and preservation of distributed data collections.

One example SRB data-access scenario can be performed as follows: 1) the SRB server/agent authenticates the user/application by checking their information against the MCAT; 2) the MCAT finds the location of the data object and SRB checks the user request against permissions stored in the MCAT; 3) the SRB server/agent contacts users with the result of their request; 4) the SRB server/agent communicates with the user through a port specific to this client session.

SRB allows the organisation of data from multiple heterogeneous systems that have been formed into easily accessible logical collections. In the SRB architecture, one partner normally owns/controls the SRB data. It would be suitable for domain-oriented digital data collection and would facilitate the central management of data resources; however, it may not scale well across domain collaborations.

Although SRB is restricted to custom APIs, it supports most popular types of user interface, such as Command client, Java and C. Because MCAT stores both physical and logical addresses, together with MCAT, SRB makes remote files available transparently by accessing data resources through queries on their attributes, rather than their physical locations or names. Furthermore, SRB provides capabilities for storing replicas of data, for authenticating users, controlling access to documents and collections, and auditing accesses; it can store user-defined, application-specific metadata at the collection and object level and provides search capabilities based on these metadata.

OGSA-DAI

The Open Grid Service Architecture (OGSA) (Foster et al., 2002) is a service-oriented framework defined by a set of standards being developed within the Global Grid Forum (GGF). OGSA is an informational specification (*de facto* standard) that aims to define a common, standard and open architecture for Grid-based applications. The goal of OGSA is to standardise almost all the services that a grid application may use, for example, job and resource management services, communications and security.

A fundamental OGSA concept is the Grid service. The Open Grid Service Infrastructure (OGSI) specification defines the interface, behaviour, and conventions that control how Grid services can be created, destroyed, named and monitored. OGSA specifies a Service-Oriented Architecture (SOA) for the grid that realises a model of a computing system using Web Services as the underlying technology.

Open Grid Service Architecture – Data Access and Integration (OGSA-DAI) (http://www.ogsadai.org.uk/) is a middleware product which supports the exposure of data resources, such as relational or XML databases, on grids. Various interfaces are provided and many popular database management systems are supported. The software also includes a collection of components for querying, transforming and delivering data in different ways, and a simple toolkit for developing client applications. The OGSA-DAI middleware is designed to be extendable, so users can provide their own additional functionality.

Figure 3 illustrates communication flows of the OGSA-DAI middleware. All the operations are conducted using Grid authentication. It provides a service group registry that can be used to identify database services that offer specific data tables. This is useful when databases are replicated or when the particulars of where data is located change on a dynamic basis.

Figure 3. The structure of OGSA-DAI (adapted from http://www.globus.org)

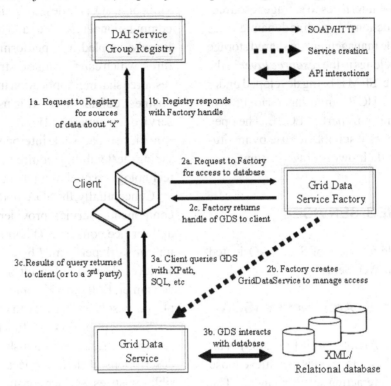

Once a specific database service is identified, an OGSA-DAI data service factory can be used to establish a database service instance that the client can then connect to directly to perform operations on the data of interest. The data service factory ensures that the database service itself is well managed. The database service then receives and responds directly to client transactions.

OGSA-DAI integrates a Metadata Catalog Service (MCS), which provides metadata storage and basic Grid authentication mechanisms. Moreover, it has an OGSA-DQP (http://www.ogsadai.org.uk) extension that provides a service-based distributed query processor. It supports the evaluation of queries over collections of potentially remote relational data services.

The OGSA-DAI middleware takes advantage of service-oriented computing. Extra functionalities can be added conveniently in the SOA style, such as Web Services. It is mainly used for integrating relational and XML databases. It may be inefficient to use it to manage huge collections of heterogeneous resources.

MCS stores logical metadata attributes and handles that can be resolved by a data location or data access services. With the involvement of Grid Data Service (GDS) and MCS, OGDA-DAI allows clients transparent access to databases from any grid resource. Furthermore, it has the capability for fine granular authorisations, data integrity and end-to-end security. Developers can embed their own application-specific activities by providing their own XML schema and implementation that can be used by the GDS engine.

SRM

In general, Storage Resource Manager (SRM) (http://sdm.lbl.gov/srm-wg/) is a middleware component that manages the dynamic use of a storage resource on the Grid (Shoshani, 2003).

SRMs provide interfaces to storage resources and advanced functionality such as dynamic space allocation and file management on shared storage systems. SRM belongs to the *resource layer* in the Grid architecture. SRM is being developed under the Worldwide LHC Computing Grid Project (WLCG), which is now part of EGEE. The open specification makes it suitable for use by institutions to adapt to their own storage systems.

SOA AND WEB SERVICES

Here, we provide a review of Service-Oriented Architecture and Web Services.

Service-Oriented Architecture (SOA)

Service-Oriented Architecture (Erl, 2005) is an architectural style whose goal is to achieve loose coupling among interacting software agents. The idea of SOA departs significantly from that of

object oriented programming (http://webservices.xml.com). SOA is a design for linking business and computational resources and has open-standard, loosely-coupled and platform-independent features, which can facilitate distributed computing, resource sharing, application interoperability and business collaboration. It is used on-demand by service consumers and represents an opportunity to achieve broad-scale interoperability while providing the flexibility required continually to adapt technology to evolving business requirements.

Conceptually, the SOA model comprises three components: service provider, service registry and service consumer (Figure 4). A service is a unit of work performed by a service provider to achieve a desired end result on behalf of a service consumer. Both provider and consumer are roles played by software agents on behalf of their owners. Service providers hide functionalities through service interface and publish machine-readable descriptions of their services in publicly accessible registries. Service consumers discover those

Figure 4. Service-oriented architecture (Adapted from Erl, 2005)

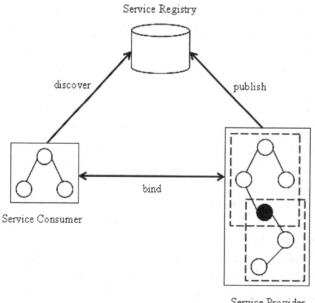

services by querying the registry, and bind to the selected services dynamically.

Web Services

According to W3C (http://www.w3c.org/), a Web Service is a software system designed to support interoperable machine-to-machine interaction over a network; SOA combined with Web Services technologies form the basis for building a Grid infrastructure (Asadzadeh, 2004). Web Services, as one instantiation of SOA, have the property of being loosely-coupled, open-standard, language- and platform-independent.

"Loosely-coupled" implies that service providers can modify backend functions while retaining the same interface to clients; the core service functions are encapsulated and remain transparent to clients.

"Open-standard" ensures the viability of collaboration and integration with other services. The resources over the Web are made accessible through an XML-based programmatic access. The solution provided by Web Services is agnostic to the platform, the vendor tools and the development environment and, at the same time, builds on widely utilised Web technologies (HTTP, SMTP, FTP, XML).

Language and platform independence enables services to be developed in any language and deployed on any platform. A Web Service can be invoked remotely, and its key benefit is the cross-platform and cross-programming language interoperability of the distributed computing model. In today's network environment, the users are all connected via the Internet, but individually, they have their own systems, which may be Unix, Linux, Windows, etc. The software language they are using may be C, C++, Java, C#, etc.

There are two main styles of Web Services: REST (Fielding, 2000) and SOAP (Simple Object Access Protocol). REST was first introduced by Roy Fielding to describe the web architecture. A REST web service is based on the concept of a "resource", which is anything that has a URI. REST is an architectural Style, not a Standard. Many Web Services, such as book-ordering services, search services, are REST-based Web Services.

When creating a REST-based Web service, first identify all of the conceptual entities that you wish to expose as services, then create a URL for each resource. Resources are clarified according to access features: whether clients can merely receive a representation of the resource, or whether they can also modify (add to) the resource. REST is designed to reveal data gradually – it uses hyperlinks to expose more details. Data are specified by a schema, and services are invoked by a WSDL file, or simply an HTML file.

A SOAP web service is the most common and most frequently marketed form of web service. The current implementation of SOAP-style Web Services mainly utilises XML technologies and obeys W3C-defined standards. WSDL (Web Service Description Language) is commonly defined in a machine-processable format by the service provider for invoking the service. SOAP, typically via HTTP, is adopted as the message transfer protocol between requester and provider. UDDI (Universal Description, Discovery and Integration) is used for service registration and discovery.

AN EXAMPLE APPLICATION

In this section, we shall describe the implementation of a service-oriented Grid application in the EC project, **The Living Human Digital Library (LHDL)**, with which we are involved. LHDL is used as a case study, though we point out that the final design/implementation will not necessarily be exactly as here, as LHDL was still on-going when this was written.

We first give the background of LHDL with its overall architecture, then discuss the reasons that Grid technology was chosen in it. Then, we describe the design of Web services in LHDL, the reasons of creating them and our approaches to web clients and the metadata management. Finally, we provide a detailed description of issues involved in the design and implementation.

The Overall Design of the LHDL Project

The Living Human Project (LHP) (Viceconti et al., 2006; Viceconti et al., 2007a) aims to create an *in silico* model of the human musculo-skeletal apparatus which can predict how mechanical forces are exchanged internally and externally, at all scales, from the whole body down to the protein level. As part of LHP, LHDL will build a digital library infrastructure in which users can create, share and update the data and algorithms constituting the LHP.

LHDL supports two types of resource: data and operations:

- *Data resources* are digital artefacts that represent the anatomy, the physiology, the pathology of a certain body, or of a region of it, at a particular spatial and temporal scale. They can be the result of measurements (Natural Data, e.g. set of spatial points obtained by digitising certain features of the body anatomy during dissection) or of calculations (Synthetic Data, e.g., the polygonal surfaces that limit the volume of a certain bone, computed from the medical images).

- *Operation resources* are procedures that generate new resources, usually by performing calculations that involve existing data resources. They can be used to represent the procedural knowledge that transforms one or more data resources into another via calculation, or to represent predictive models of physical events relevant for aspects of the physiology or pathology.

The implementation adopted is a common multi-layer design architecture (Figure 5); there are 3 main layers: Grid, Services and Clients.

At the bottom grid layer, data-grid middleware SRB and OGSA-DAI, mentioned in Section 2.5, are adopted to manage binary data and metadata resources, respectively. Large sets of binary medical data can be stored in a distributed way at different sites within the project federation. The SRB middleware is used to organise and integrate these resources into one unified collection across the network, regardless of the backend storage implementation at each site. Domain-specific metadata related to each data resource are stored in a relational database that can be accessed through the OGSA-DAI middleware.

The user-level Web Services layer is built on top of the two core items of data-grid middleware; it conveniently exposes the underlying data management function to client applications and integrates with other systems. It also hides the backend complexities from the clients and allows flexibility for distributing functions within communities, thus enhancing the opportunity for collaboration with other applications through the Internet.

Details of core services will be described later in the chapter. Four main types of service have been designed and implemented:

- **Storage services** act as interfaces to the SRB Data Grid for storing and retrieving binary data objects.
- **Community services** serve as interfaces to access metadata resource managed by OGSA-DAI database grid.
- **Execution services** provide the main medical data simulation and visualisation algorithms; they include translation services that import data in third-party formats into the digital library and express them in standard format or export data from the digital library in another format required by the user.

Figure 5. System structure for the LHDL

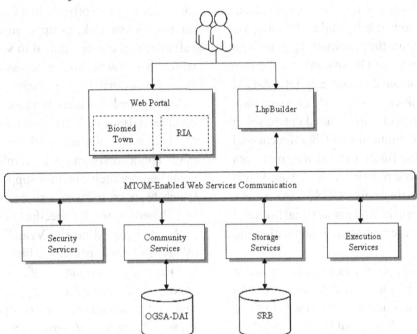

- **Security services** provide authentication and authorisation functions.

At the client layer, it is demanding to build web clients that allow users to access the application without location restrictions. From the users' perspective, the fewer technical requirements and software installations, the better, so web browser clients with a rich user experience would be a good solution.

Grid Technology Used in LHDL

The key point of the Grid is resource sharing, which includes computers, storage and networks. In LHDL, grid technology is used to build a digital library which can preserve large collections of medical modelling and visualisation data and to allow medical data-simulation and visualisation algorithms to be shared within the research community.

The data can be several Gigabits in size, and datasets may become even bigger in the future,

from trends identified in the medical modelling domain. It is important to keep these data collections secure, manageable and traceable. As mentioned previously, the Storage Resource Broker (SRB) Data Grid is designed not only to manage large binary objects but also to provide uniform interfaces to access the data resource. Our implementation adopts SRB to preserve and access large binary data in the library. Collaborating partners within the LHP domain can store their data at their own sites using different storage systems. The central Storage Resource Broker within the federation can access all data resources from one unified interface.

Because huge sets of data may be created by different applications and stored at different locations, it would be impractical to search the data resources without any knowledge of the data. It is essential to record information relating to the data, such as the owner, creation, types, etc., in an easily managed manner.

In the LHDL implementation, the knowledge information is defined by domain users as metadata. Metadata are designed to be stored externally in the database, which facilitates efficient searching compared to embedded metadata definitions in Data Grid. To handle the potentially large amount of metadata, we adopt OGSA-DAI middleware to access and manage the databases. OGSA-DAI can hide the back-end complexity of connection to databases and bridge distributed databases in heterogeneous communities. It is efficient and convenient for the future extension of metadata management into semantic ontology-based Grid applications. Furthermore, OGSA-DAI allows databases to remain behind institutional firewalls and supports certificate-based authentication and authorisation.

In biomedical applications, there is a trend for existing applications to share their resources and collaborate, or even integrate, with others. In some emerging areas, such as the multiscale modelling required for physiome research, such integration is essential, and this results in a quantum leap in the level of computing resources required to resolve the problems being investigated. These algorithms generally require high-performance computing facilities. Grid computing initially emerged as a paradigm for distributed resource exploitive computation, so computational-grid middleware is needed to allow the services to cooperate. However, in this chapter, we concentrate on the Data Grid.

Multimod Application Framework (MAF)

The aim of the execution services in LHDL is to make desktop operations found in the Multimod Application Framework (MAF) (Viceconti et al., 2007b) available as Web Services over the Internet. To aid a deeper understanding of the motivation and implementation, we first provide some background information about MAF before going into details of the implementation.

MAF is a framework for the rapid development of biomedical applications. Research has shown

that the medical community is much more willing to accept new software that is tightly focused on a particular task, as opposed to generalised software that can be applied to varied tasks but which, because of this, has a less directed interface. Unfortunately, the market need for each individual task is rather limited, so there is no commercial motivation to produce such software. MAF provides a framework that can support many applications simply by combining components appropriately and thus supplies a means by which bespoke software can be created rapidly and cheaply to meet a specific need.

MAF is based on the Visualisation Toolkit (VTK) and other specialised libraries. A generic MAF application is made up of components which control data entities and application services. The application services can be distinguished as *Views*, *Operations*, *Interactions* and *Interface Elements*. To demonstrate the use of Web Services, we mainly focus on the transfer of MAF *Operations* into services.

MAF operations can be categorised as follows:

- Translate
  - o Import
  - o Export
- Create
  - o Standard VME
  - o Procedural VME
- Modify
  - o Metadata
  - o Dataset
  - o SpaceTime
- Measure
- Custom

Translate operations include Import and Export. Their main function is to convert between different data types and VMEs. Import/Export Operations are the most important services as they ensure that the LHDL is open in terms of data formats, as any format can be translated to/from a VME via these WS.

Create Standard VME operations create, from scratch, VMEs that are worth transforming into Web Services. In contrast, the *Create Procedural VME* operations create VMEs with user-defined procedures, which makes no sense in the context of Web Services. In the current MAF implementation, the *Create Parametric Surface* operation is a procedural operation, and when transformed into a service, it should be converted into a *Create Standard VME* operation that creates a new surface VME, such as a sphere, cylinder or plane.

When a VME is fully tested and ready for other researchers to use, it is "published". If we accept that Web Services will work only on published VMEs, which cannot be modified, all *Modify* operations will involve the transfer of the original VME, the execution of the operation, and the creation of a new VME, that is, a modified version of the original one. This should apply to all three sub-categories; indeed, pure metadata modifications will not be performed by the Execution Web Services, but rather by the Community services.

Measure operations do not alter the VME to be measured, which remains unchanged; they take as input the VME to be measured, and return as output a text string to be sent to the presentation layer directly.

Custom operations solve very special problems, like opening with the right application a so-called external VME, which is a VME that wraps a file created by another application. In general, they should not be targets for Web Services.

Implementation of the Core Services

Although, in theory, data and procedures are separated in the LHDL implementation, for consistency we enable users to make their datasets or algorithms available to the rest of the research community in similar way. The concept of Virtual Medical Entities (VMEs) (Viceconti et al., 2007b) was introduced to store and transfer data

objects in a unified **metadata** plus **binary data** format. Meanwhile, service resources have been established that wrap each algorithm into a standardised Web Service object, which can be posted to the library, just as for a data object.

Four main types of services are defined in the project. This section will focus on the major services designated within the Community, Execution and Storage services and the flow among them (Figure 6).

Building the Services Using a Web Services Approach

This section focuses on implementation at the application level, rather than innovative core Grid infrastructure. The aim is to demonstrate common procedures, based on the project background, to develop applications services that are used in the Grid environment.

Web Services provide a standard means of interoperating between different software applications running on various platforms and/or frameworks. Web Services also represent a proven technology for building applications for the Grid. In LHDL, we built a service layer on top of the Grid middleware layer to expose functions to client applications.

In terms of algorithms and procedures, an important aspect of the project is to develop a service framework for sharing algorithms and utilising computing resources within the clinical research communities. The implementation is to cope with the dynamic aspects of a digital library that provides as content, not only data, but also simulation services, collaborative work services, interactive visualisation services, etc.

Researchers will be able to visualise and interact with the data resources, and may generate new data resources via a series of operations. In addition, an individual researcher who has developed a new algorithm for analysis, processing or simulation will be able to integrate it easily within this framework, and have it wrapped and

Figure 6. Core services in LHDL

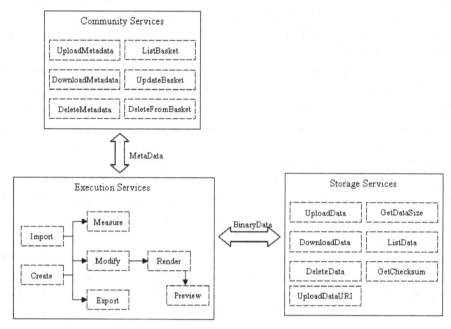

exposed as a service that other researchers or other applications can invoke remotely to process their data.

The Web Services approach will bring the following benefits to the project:

- Hiding back-end Grid complexities from client applications.
- Enhancing opportunities to collaborate with other organisations not only on data and algorithms but also on different computation resources.
- Facilitating the sharing of data resources: a set of import/export services will store and transfer data in a standard format.
- Facilitating the sharing and validation of algorithms: key algorithms from the existing MAF will be exposed as online services in order to share data and algorithms within the clinical and research communities.
- Providing Internet media to satisfy various application platform requirements: clinicians and researchers will not need to

download tools to test their data against algorithms.

Execution Services

Execution Services are at the core of exposing algorithms and procedures as services. They are implemented in C++, in the standard SOAP Web Services format. All data resources to be processed are downloaded in two parts: metadata from OGSA-DAI through Community Services and binary data from SRB through Storage Services. Similarly, all newly created data resources from Execution Services are uploaded as metadata and binary data through the Community Services and Storage Services, respectively.

According to the Execution services functional behaviour and metadata definitions, 6 main groups of services are defined, namely *Import, Export, Create, Modify, Measure* and *Preview*.

Import/Export Services are important for standardising the different formats of data within LHDL. Import Services convert third-party data formats, such as STL, VTK, VRML, DICOM, etc., into VMEs which are stored in MSF (Multimod Standard Format) for future processing. Export Services translate library data from the VME back into user-preferred file formats. Via these services, users can upload their own data into the LHDL user sandbox in a standard format and exchange them with other community members.

Create Services provide interfaces to build standard data resources from scratch. These could include *Create Parametric Surface* and *Create Reference System* services. These data objects can then be exported from LHDL to other visualisation software.

Modify Services take an input data resource, execute certain algorithms on it, then produce new data, e.g., from volume data, calculate the boundary between two regions and generate the isosurface representing that boundary.

Measure Services take a data resource as input, measure them using certain algorithms then return the results, mainly in text format, e.g. *Volume Measure* service inputs a surface type of data and computes the volume and area value of the surface, as well as the Normalised Shape Index (N.S.I). The data being measured remains unaltered.

In consideration of remote rendering and future system flexibility, Preview Services are designated as either *Render Services* or *Presentation Services*. Render Services take a data resource and renders it as an image stream. This may be passed to the Presentation Services to display the final image.

Community Services

Community Services offer functions not only for accessing metadata files through OGSA-DAI but also for basket management. Each metadata file records knowledge of its data resource. In the digital library, data resources from the public sandbox can be accessed by adding them to the user's basket.

UploadMetadata Service accepts metadata created by the Execution Services or the LhpBuilder application and stores them in the database. Each metadata resource also serves to identify the whole data resource.

DownloadMetadata Service takes requests with a data-resource identifier from the Execution Services or client applications and downloads the metadata from the database to the execution server or the client application machine.

DeleteMetadata Service take requests with a data resource identifier from the client application to delete a metadata file from the database.

ListBasket Service lists all the data resources in the user's basket. Once the user selects a data resource from the public sandbox and adds it into his/her basket, *UpdateBasket Service* receives this request and stores the information in the database. *DeleteFromBasket Service* deletes the relevant data resource from the user's basket.

Storage Services

Storage Services provide functions to access binary medical data from SRB; they are implemented in C++ as standard SOAP Web Services.

UploadData Service copies a file from the local computer to the remote data storage. For data created by Execution Services, the binary data are copied from the Execution server to the remote SRB. The service exploits MTOM technology (Message Transmission Optimisation Mechanism) (http://www.w3.org/TR/soap12-mtom/) to move large-volume data. If the name of the file to be uploaded is undefined, the service creates a default progressive name (Data_n). If the name of the file to be uploaded is the same as the data on the SRB with dimension zero, the service overwrites the data. The service returns a structure with checksum value and the name of the file uploaded.

DownloadData Service downloads a file to the local computer. It returns a designated data structure that is used by the client operation to create the local file. If the request came from Execution Services, the file is downloaded to the Execution Server. This service also exploits MTOM technology to move large data.

DeleteData Service removes a file or a collection from SRB; when a collection is removed, all of its contents are removed.

UploadDataURI Service creates an empty file on SRB with a default progressive name (Data_n) and returns its file name/URI. The file name will be used as an input parameter of the UploadData Service.

GetDataSize Service returns the dimension (in bytes) of a file stored on the SRB. *ListData Service* returns a list of files contained in the SRB, with the domain to which the user belongs. *GetChecksum Service* returns the Checksum value of data stored in the SRB.

Application Clients

This section will describe two approaches to building web clients in this application.

Biomed Town Web Client

As the name suggests, this web client is built in the Biomed Town (http://www.biomedtown. org/) virtual community web site, which acts as a portal for information related to biomedical research; it also hosts a number of biomedical research projects.

Figure 7 illustrates the sequence for a user request for a *Modify* service, which is a type of Execution Service. Data resources are stored as metadata (in XML format) and binary data in OGSA-DAI and SRB storage, respectively.

Once users log into the LHDL through Biomed Town, they can search the data resources via Search Services and retrieve the binary URI of the resource they require. The user may then ask for a list of the available execution service resources that can take this dataset as input and submit it to one of them. During the processing of

the Execution Service, the whole data resource is downloaded from the metadata databases and the SRB. A new data resource is thus created on the Execution Server after invoking the service. The Execution Services then upload the new binary part back to the SRB and the new metadata to Community. The user may also find a new data resource in their sandbox.

Rich Internet Application Client

From a consideration of the end-user experience, the overall accessibility and a straightforward invocation of Web Services, we adopted Adobe Flex (http://www.adobe.com/products/flex/) technology to build the web client as a Rich Internet Application (RIA) (Loosely, 2006). This approach brings several benefits:

- **User-friendly interface experience:** With RIA technologies, web clients can perform as a rich desktop application.
- **Convenient user access:** A Flex application is available across multiple platforms and is compatible with most modern web browsers such as IE and Firefox; this is important in a restricted environment such as a clinical institution.
- **Invocation of direct Web services:** A Flex application uses asynchronous messaging mode – after receiving the user's requests from the interface, the application invokes the Web Services, and the results are returned to the user immediately without extra clicking.
- **Reduction of network traffic:** Callbacks are used in RIAs, thus no extra click requests are required to obtain results from the server.

The current RIA client allows domain users to accomplish the main data-processing workflows. For instance, users export a surface as an STL file from some third-party software, upload and transform it into a standard data resource, deci-

Figure 7. Submission flow of modify service

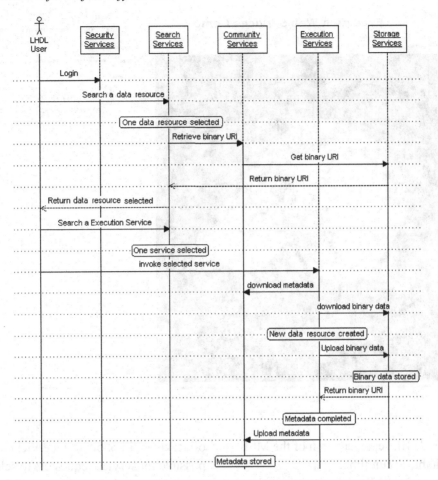

mate it to a pre-defined value, preview it with a certain camera render setting, then download the result in STL and port it back to their software. The workflow is controlled mainly by the users.

Figure 8 shows a snapshot of the Flex client. We currently call the main view area a preview panel as we merely render the 2D snapshot images, without mouse click interaction. Through the function menu located at the top of the page, the users can import/export data, execute certain operations, such as extract isosurface, decimate surface, etc, and preview the surface data-type as a JPEG image. The ControlBar panel lists the VMEs, allows the user to rotate/zoom the rendered result and provides an interface for input

for certain operations. The VME panel lists the main properties of the VME selected, such as name, type, boundary, etc.

Metadata Management

Metadata can be described as information about information; it plays an important role in service searching, so we explain it further here. In LHDL, metadata are applied not only to data resources but also to services.

Metadata for data resources are defined by domain users within the community. They are stored inside the VME and can be represented as either *TAG items* or *Attributes*, each of which

Figure 8. Web services RIA client

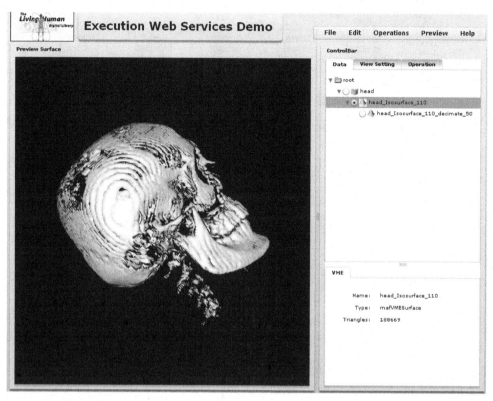

is stored in the XML representation of the MSF file and is editable at run time.

A TAG item is XML information with a name, a timestamp and textual information. It can be defined by the user at runtime, so we do not have a predefined number of these TAGs. Attributes are defined through a lower-level class which specifies the structure of the metadata, so the information structure is predefined at programming time, but the contents can be edited at runtime. In the LHDL project, we anticipate that ultimately ontology keywords will be based on TAG metadata that can be dynamically added to and edited for the VME.

Metadata also plays an important role in machine-to-machine service communications. Services with the same interface definitions may represent completely different functions, so it is essential to document the function and behaviour of services. Explicit service metadata makes it possible for service requesters to select and bind services dynamically. Moreover, it can extend the basic SOA model to discover services that match the requester's requirements both functionally and semantically.

In LHDL, service metadata are stored in the database in a similar way to the data resource metadata. Service metadata are defined by domain users and software engineers, together. They currently include knowledge such as service type, algorithm versions, benchmark testing, etc. The information can also help to preserve the traceability of data created by processing services.

Security

Security is hugely important in any application. Although the Grid infrastructure itself employs security solutions within, it is desirable also to secure at the application level.

The Web Services implementation described above is based on SOAP. When SOAP messages travel over the Internet they can be viewed or modified by attackers, as SOAP was not designed with security in mind. It was intended that secure messaging would be developed as an extension to the SOAP standard.

There are several options available for securing SOAP messages: Since they are transmitted using HTTP, SSL/TLS can be implemented on the server to transmit them over HTTPS. The **XML Encryption** and **XML Signature** security standards developed by W3C allow signing and encryption of XML content, the basic format for all Web Services messages. **WS-Security** extends the SOAP standard describing a mechanism for using XML Encryption and XML Digital Signature to secure SOAP messages. In the current implementation, self-signed HTTPS is being used.

As Web Services deployed on the Internet are available to all users, a trust model has to be formed between service providers and requesters. LHDL has adopted Shibboleth (http://shibboleth. internet2.edu/) to secure communication with trusted communities. Shibboleth makes use of SAML (http://xml.coverpages.org/saml.html) to exchange assertions on Authentication and Authorisation. SAML allows:

- Web Single Sign-On
- Attribute based authorisation
- Web Services to be made secure

In the current implementation, Shibboleth has mainly been implemented on the Storage server. Further implementations will be undertaken on the Execution and Community service server.

Implementation Issues

In a real-world system, the selection of the "best" approach is not always straightforward, as many issues, often application-specific, have to be considered. If the technology does not provide a global solution, we may need to break down the problem into different cases and use the most suitable for each, individually. We believe that this situation is fairly common at the current state of technology.

Development Environment

Microsoft's .NET (http://msdn2.microsoft.com/ enus/netframework/) and Sun's J2EE (http://java. sun.com/javaee/) are two popular Web Services development and deployment frameworks among a large number of service platforms. There are already many in-depth articles comparing them and, in theory, both could have been used in LHDL. However, consideration of the re-use of existing C++ code and the implementation of Web Services based on MAF applications, led us to adopt the .NET platform, so the main Execution Web Services were developed in Microsoft Visual Studio .NET.

Using the Existing MAF Code

It is logical to make as much use of existing MAF code as possible. However, there are many problems associated with this. We would like to share our experiences here, since we believe that similar issues exist in many other projects.

Most MAF Operations are based on an event-driven mechanism and have calls to onEvent, OpRun, etc. These will not work in a WS environment, because WS cannot interact with input such as std::cout, wxMessageBox, Dialog, etc. The Web Services should use off-screen rendering since the client side cannot see what is displayed on the server-side screen. User dialog messages and on-screen rendering will not work and will cause unpredictable access violation errors in WS.

Hence, MAF cannot be easily merged with WS, due to its original design. The same problem will probably appear even if we change to another platform, as Web Service applications are different from applications with dialogs and buttons.

Ultimately, we decided to extract the necessary code from the MAF package and adopt it for WS use. This approach may also work with transforming other highly interactive applications to WS.

Data Transfer

Another problem is how to transfer the large amounts of data associated with the graphics-rich nature of this application. The user has to input a large file containing the data to be processed and the resulting processed data is also often huge.

For data transfer from client to server, and *vice versa*, there are four cases:

- The operation returns text (e.g. the result of a volume calculation) that we do not need to make persistent, and thus has only to be returned to the Caller.
- The operation returns text that should be added to the metadata of the stored VME.
- The operation returns a binary object that must be returned to the Caller but not made persistent (e.g. the JPG file containing the computed image).
- The operation creates a new VME in the LhpRepository, or modifies an existing one.

We could implement all four cases, but in some the volume of data to transfer is not large.

To avoid large data transfer, we can allow the renderer always to generate a VmeImage, store it in the user's Sandbox, and return only its URI to the Caller. The image can then be downloaded and displayed independently, avoiding a large amount of data transfer during the interaction.

In cases where we need to transfer data, but not a large amount, we choose Base64. Base64 will generally not work on the uplink side (client to server) because the file describing the model is generally large and Base64 coding will further increase the size by 1/3. Using parallel FTP, gridFTP is a good option; the client side uploads the file to the server only once, and the server keeps it (while probably adding some expiry control, e.g. the server will delete it in 2 hours no operations requested on it).

The server performs operations based on the model stored and the operating instructions sent from the client. However, if the whole procedure needs to be interactive, the server should return an image after each operation (such as extract isosurface), using off-screen rendering. JPEG files are relatively small and thus suitable for transfer via the Internet. Base64 will not be a problem to encode the data used by WS file transfer.

Overall Implementation

The implementation of Execution Web Services has focused on extracting core operation code from MAF and reusing it. As MAF is written in C++, the Execution Services have been developed with C++ in the .NET environment.

In the conceptual service flow design, a service has an open communication channel to the next service; it writes data at the producing service end and is consumed at the client service end, similar to a socket connection.

However, MAF mainly uses VTK libraries to which, by their nature, data have to be loaded from a local file. (Charters et al., 2004) showed that no implementation to support this socket type of Web Services protocol currently exists. One cannot use a socket connection because each service may have to communicate through firewalls that would, in many instances such as for patient data, block such connections.

The problem has been overcome by downloading the remote output to a local directory, so VTK can then load the data from a local file, though this is not ideal as the remote process should have completed before the service using VTK can begin. The first service returns, as its result, a URI –the input for the following service.

As the URI of the output file is returned before writing the output is completed, the client service may not read all of the data contained within the file if the rate of data output is slower than the rate at which the data is being read. In this situation, a SOAP exception may be thrown, as the underlying process has not completed. A blocking I/O mechanism could solve this problem, but no work-around for this has yet been found (Charters et al., 2004).

The services implementation also needs to consider the scalability of transferring very large amounts of data across the network. Methods have to be investigated for obtaining large amounts of data from the service end; currently files are compressed in ZMSF format prior to transfer between services. Meanwhile, MTOM (Message Transmission Optimisation Mechanism) is being investigated for transferring data to/from storage.

CONCLUSION

Using an EC project for illustration, this chapter introduced relevant concepts of Grid technology, including Grid middleware with a focus on Data Grid middleware. The main part of the chapter then explained the practical issues of implementing Grid services.

Detail was included to provide the reader some experience in terms of real application development. The chapter also discussed technical issues encountered during the design and implementation of the case study to share the knowledge gained from that experience. Not all the issues will apply in every case, but the authors believe the insights will assist developers generally across many subject areas.

For further development of the system described, we note that the focus is on providing data and the applications built using SRB and OGSA-DAI. However, for future applications, a single server may not be sufficiently powerful to provide swift output. If it is desired to process the data using computational Grid services, and build the applications on middleware, such as Globus, changes will be needed to the existing services, for example, separating the exposing layer and the system processing layer so that processing tasks can be undertaken by different processors.

Further, the current client system can be improved by using Web Services orchestration/choreography technologies, such as BPEL (Business Process Execution Language), to build service workflows according to the user's requirements. This would give the user greater flexibility to use the available services provided by the digital library and orchestrate/choreograph them as required.

ACKNOWLEDGMENT

The work described was partially funded by the European Commission within the project LHDL: the Living Human Digital Library (IST-2004-026932). Some development was undertaken by other partners in the consortium, based at Istituto Ortopedico Rizzoli and at Cineca (both in Bologna, Italy), and we thank them for their contribution.

REFERENCES

Asadzadeh, P., Buyya, R., Kei, C. L., Nayar, D., & Venugopal, S. (2004). *Global grids and software toolkits: A study of four grid middleware technologies*. Technical report, University of Melbourne, Australia. Retrieved July 3, 2008, from http://arxiv.org/ftp/cs/papers/0407/0407001.pdf

Charters, S. M., Holliman, N. S., & Munro, M. (2004). *Visualisation on the grid: A web services approach*. Third UK eScience All-Hands Meeting, Nottingham, UK.

Clabby, J. (2004). *The Grid report, 2004 edition.* Clabby Analytics. Retrieved July 3, 2008, from http://www-03.ibm.com/grid/pdf/Clabby_Grid_Report_2004_Edition.pdf

Erl, T. (2005). *Service-Oriented Architecture: Concepts, Technology, and Design.* Crawfordsville, Indiana: Prentice Hall PTR.

Expert Group Report (2003). *Next generation grid(s), European Grid Research 2005-2010.* Retrieved July 3, 2008, from ftp://ftp.cordis.europa.eu/pub/ist/docs/ngg_eg_final.pdf

Fielding, R. T. (2000). *Architecture styles and the design of network-based software architectures.* Unpublished doctoral dissertation, University of California, Irvine, USA.

Foster, I., & Kesselman, C. (Eds.) (2000). *The Grid: Blueprint for a new computing infrastructure.* San Francisco: Morgan Kaufmann.

Foster, I., Kesselman, C., & Tuecke, S. (2001). The anatomy of the Grid: Enabling scalable virtual organisations. *International Journal of High Performance Computing Applications, 15*(3), 200-222.

Foster, I., Kesselman, C., Nick, J., & Tuecke, S. (2002). *The physiology of the Grid: An open grid services architecture for distributed systems integration.* Open Grid Service Infrastructure WG, Global Grid Forum, June 2002. Retrieved July 3, 2008, from http://www.globus.org/alliance/publications/papers/ogsa.pdf

Loosely, C. (2006). *Rich Internet Applications: Design, measurement, and management challenges.* Keynote Systems. Retrieved July 3, 2008, from http://www.keynote.com/docs/whitepapers/RichInternet_5.pdf

Rajasekar, A., Wan, M., Moore, R., Schroeder, W., Kremenek, G., Jagatheesan, A., Cowart, C., Zhu, B., Chen S., & Olschanowsky, R. (2003). Storage Resource Broker – Managing distributed data in a Grid. *Computer Society of India Journal, Special Issue on SAN, 33*(4), 42-54.

Shoshani, A., Sim, A., & Gu, J. (2003). Storage Resource Managers – Essential Components for the Grid. In A. Shoshani, A Sim, & J. Gu (Eds.), *Grid Resource Management: state of the art and future trends.* Norwell, MA, USA: Kluwer Academic Publishers.

Viceconti, M., Taddei, F., Petrone, M., Galizia, S., Van Sint Jan, S., & Clapworthy, G. J. (2006). Towards the Virtual Physiological Human: the Living Human Project. Paper presented at *7th International Symposium on Computer Methods in Biomechanics and Biomedical Engineering (CMBBE 2006)*, Antibes Cote d' Azur, France.

Viceconti, M., Taddei, F., Van Sint Jan, S., Leardini, A., Clapworthy, G. J., Domingue, J., Galizia, S., & Quadrani, P. (2007a). Towards the multiscale modelling of the musculoskeletal system. In *Y. González & M. Cerrolaza* (Eds.) *Bioengineering Modeling and Computer Simulation*, CIMNE, Barcelona, Spain.

Viceconti, M., Zannoni, C., Testi, D., Petrone, M., Perticoni, S., Quadrani, P., Taddei, F., Imboden, S., & Clapworthy, G. J. (2007b). The Multimod Application Framework: A rapid application development tool for computer aided medicine. *Computer Methods and Programs in Biomedicine, 85*(2), 138-151.

Chapter II
Sustainable and Interoperable E-Infrastructures for Research and Business

Giuseppe Andronico
Istituto Nazionale di Fisica Nucleare, Italy

Emidio Giorgio
Istituto Nazionale di Fisica Nucleare, Italy

Roberto Barbera
University of Catania, Italy, &
Istituto Nazionale di Fisica Nucleare, Italy

Salvatore Marco Pappalardo
Consorzio COMETA, Italy

Marco Fargetta
Consorzio COMETA, Italy

Diego Scardaci
Istituto Nazionale di Fisica Nucleare, Italy

ABSTRACT

Grid computing allows for the creation of e-infrastructures providing computational power and information storage capabilities needed both by present and future research centres around the world. Although the value of Grids is recognised by its early users, many companies, which would benefit from the adoption of this new paradigm, are still waiting claiming that Grid technologies are still not well-established and continuously evolving. A company usually takes a risk when it adopts a technology before its standardisation because if the technology subsequently demonstrates to diverge from (de-facto) standards then the investments can be partially lost and, additionally, switching to the new standard technology will probably be more expensive. In this chapter we present a couple of approaches which allow existing Grid infrastructures to evolve, by including newer Grid middleware, and consequently preserve the investment made on the infrastructure. The capability to evolve reduces current problems of Grid implementation (especially the lack of standards), so it makes Grid adoption by business companies and research centres painless.

Copyright © 2009, IGI Global, distributing in print or electronic forms without written permission of IGI Global is prohibited.

AN INTRODUCTION ON RESOURCES EXCHANGE APPROACH

The global market requires an effort from companies and research centres to continuously improve the quality of products and services. This improvement is possible only through a huge research activity having the goal of investigating new products and production innovations. An important part of this research activity consists of design and simulation of new products and services performed by means of the most powerful computational tools that companies can afford.

Moreover, the global economy creates additional challenges for companies because they have to face the problem of operating around the world and around the clock (i.e., twenty-four hours a day, seven days a week). For that reason modern companies require systems able to handle the information flow among different locations and monitor the situation in real-time, in order to set up an efficient management process.

However, in modern business, setting up a powerful and efficient IT infrastructure requires a big investment for companies in terms of both money and people. In fact, in order to properly manage the workload produced by company activities a large powerful hardware equipment and complex software are necessary. This kind of IT solutions can speed up the company growth process very much as well as its incomes but very often they are composed by really expensive components to be continuously upgraded. Moreover truly qualified employees are mandatory to administrate and maintain such complex systems, requiring additional costs for company balance. That is the reason why a wrong choice in this field could turn in a huge loss for the company.

Therefore, an efficient IT infrastructure, scaling up and down to fit requirements deriving from company activities, and maintaining an affordable cost, plays a key role for the success of modern companies. In this context Grid computing (Foster & Kesselman, 2003) is nowadays emerging as the most promising technology because it grants IT infrastructures to provide the power and flexibility needed by companies.

The word *Grid* identifies an innovative computational approach, defined in the mid '90s, which enables geographically distributed communities, named *Virtual Organisations* (VOs), to dynamically share CPU power and storage with the aim of avoiding resources under exploitation and overload. Therefore, companies can access resources just when really needed, either by paying for the time they effectively use the resources or compensating that by allowing others to access their own resources when unused (or underused). The resources exchange approach allows for the building of huge IT infrastructures able to supply the CPU power and the storage capabilities needed by companies and requiring a very limited increment of IT costs.

Although Grid is commonly considered to be the best solution to implement a flexible IT infrastructure, many cultural and practical problems limit its usage up to now. The former are related to companies' difficulties to adopt new technologies that deeply modify the infrastructures running the company business. The "scare" of new technologies grows for Grid since it requires sharing of IT infrastructure with further organisations and consequently putting it out of control. As an example, common users are often concerned about the confidentiality of data stored on remote resources. Actually, the Grid community is developing additional components in order to support the privacy of data allocated on shared resources (Scardaci & Scuderi, 2007) and grant a sufficient level of QoS - Quality of Service - on the resource usage so company can be confident that their needs will be properly satisfied. Other cultural problems, such as the general aim to apply as few changes as possible to business and production systems, must be considered.

The cultural problems could be overcome after the successful adoption of Grids from very important and relevant companies which will set good examples for the others. Unfortunately, there are still practical problems discouraging IT managers to adopt the Grid paradigm. Among them, the continuous evolution of Grid standards and the extreme fragmentation of the Grid community, producing different implementations which are not compatible/interoperable to each other, are the most relevant limitations to spreading this technology to business companies (De Roure & Surridge, 2003). In fact, companies willing to adopt Grid have to make investments in order to change their infrastructures and train employees but, unfortunately, they have also to accept the risk of wasting time and money since the supported Grid middleware can easily change in a very short period of time. Furthermore, in order to take advantage of Grid, many partners have to share the same infrastructure and this requires they use the same, or at least a compatible, *middleware*, meaning the software layer between resources and applications. In other words, the middleware is the level of Grid stack providing uniform and transparent access to resources. In this scenario it is obviously not valuable for a company an investment in using a middleware which has been discarded by its partners. In fact, the lack of other companies willing to share resources will turn in having no competitive advantage from use of Grid. Therefore, the choice of the middleware to be used is crucial and a wrong decision could produce a deleterious impact on the company economy. Indeed, middleware interoperability is the main issue that companies have to face after the set up of a Grid infrastructure and the problems concerning interoperability are sufficient to justify the behaviour of companies waiting for stronger and more widely adopted Grid standards. Actually, the advantage of using a Grid infrastructure is the chance to dynamically share resources among members of a Grid in order to establish VOs which are working on specific projects. In this context the term *resource* is as general as possible and specifies any kind of computing en-

tity, from CPU to records in a database or special tool collecting data. However, in order to share resources, companies and/or research centres must support the same middleware. Consequently, if a company decides to deploy a middleware which is not supported from its (current and future) partners, the possibility to use additional resources when required can be very limited. Moreover, since middleware are still evolving, after a given middleware is selected for the IT infrastructure and a different one will become a standard, the current investment in terms of both know-how and infrastructure set-up is then wasted.

THE STATE OF THE ART OF GRID MIDDLEWARE

Currently, a number of Grid middleware, both commercial and not, are under development all around the world. Although there are official Grid standards promoted from many companies involved in Grid technology, those have a quite limited support from middleware developers, which adopt new standards very slowly, so current middleware are generally not compatible and interoperable with each other. In this very dynamic scenario, where different communities evolve autonomously, it is extremely important to understand who is doing the best job and is able to drive future developments of Grid standards. Therefore, trying to determine which middleware would be a good choice for his/her company, a manager has to consider that middleware supported by big infrastructures and having large communities will probably be able to continuously improve their features better than others, because of the bigger impact those communities could have on standard organisations. Fortunately, middleware belonging to very big communities are a little number although they are still evolving and the size of underneath communities periodically changes. As a result, it is impossible to detect the most creditable middleware for the future. At the current status of the art, all of them have similar possibility to become the kernel of a universal Grid.

Additionally, depending on aims of the project involving the developers, they had to reach different goals for their respective middleware (i.e., security, data management, high performance computing, etc.). For that reason, it is impossible to identify the middleware that in general best fits all the projects a company could be involved in, especially for future ones which are probably still unknown at the moment of the choice of the middleware.

The list of middleware a company could use nowadays, considering the available level of support, includes, but is not limited to: gLite (http://glite.web.cern.ch/glite), UNICORE (http://www.unicore.eu/), Globus (http://www.globus.org/), Condor (http://www.cs.wisc.edu/condor/), and OMII-UK (http://www.omii.ac.uk/). Those middleware are generally not fully interoperable with each other so, after one of them is selected, the IT infrastructure is limited by the necessity to join organisations supporting the same middleware. Consequently, the current choice will influence every future project.

Therefore, in the highlighted scenario, IT managers will really benefit from introduction of resource sharing tools and techniques, very useful for companies deploying incompatible middleware. In fact, those solutions allow connection of owned infrastructures to new Grids without relevant impact on users and, consequently, preserve the current investment. Since middleware are not mature and drastic changes are still possible, just a limited number of research activities took place on interoperability, but there are already several approaches that should be considered.

This chapter focuses on two experiments solving interoperability problems: multi middleware integration (Wang, Scardaci, Yan, & Huang, 2007) and co-existence (Barbera, Fargetta, & Giorgio, 2007). Those experiments, led in different contexts and having different goals, show new approaches

for connection of infrastructures which are based on different middleware. Despite the different target, the side effects of both experiments are represented by new reference models useful to anyone who need to make infrastructures interoperable in a short time and simultaneously limiting efforts and saving past investments on infrastructure.

A WIDER LANDSCAPE: CURRENT ACTIVITIES ON MIDDLEWARE INTEROPERABILITY

As previously described, Grid interoperability is a big issue for current Grid infrastructures. Therefore, several research activities and a working group focusing just on that issue have been established to take care of the problem and figure out some possible solutions. In this section we now analyse the outcomes of some of these activities which are valuable with the approaches followed in this chapter.

The reference working group for the Grid interoperability is the "*Grid Interoperation Now Community Group*" (GIN-CG) (https://forge.gridforum.org/sf/projects/gin) of the Open Grid Forum (http://www.ogf.org/). The aim of this group is to provide solutions for the interoperability of specific elements by producing feedback and indications for both standardisation groups and software providers.

The target of GIN-CG is a true interoperability based on common and shared standards. This is a quite slow process requiring a big effort from middleware developers having to re-engineer their software in order to use new/different components. However, current results are promising because many middleware are converging on standards promoted by GIN-CG. As an example, the majority of middleware developers are integrating (or thinking to do in a quite short period) a common authentication mechanism based on VOMS (Alfieri et al., 2005) and, in the close future, XACML

(Moses et al., 2005). However, the activity of CIN-CG, concerning mainly new standards and less current features and functionalities, is much more important for middleware developers than for early adopters because outcomes of CIN-CG activities cannot be applied to current infrastructures and consequently are not immediately valuable for end users. Thus, solutions allowing integration between current and future middleware are more relevant for organisations which are currently introducing the Grid technology in their infrastructures.

Among the solutions providing integration of existing, and perhaps future, infrastructures approaches based on high-level interfaces and workflow engines are the most significant, for their ability to hide the middleware differences to users. A relevant example is the P-GRADE portal solution for the interoperability (Kacsuk, Kiss, & Sipos, 2008). P-GRADE is a Grid portal (Kacsuk & Sipos, 2005) enabling users to submit jobs to Grid infrastructures through a (quite) simple Web Interface. Additionally, users can build job workflows to be run from the portal, so to perform complex allocations exploiting the power provided by the huge number of resources available on a Grid just with a single submission process instance. An interesting capability of P-GRADE is the possibility to build a workflow in which individual jobs can be submitted on separate Grid infrastructures running different middleware in a totally transparent way from the user point of view. The only requirement for the user is to be authorised to submit on the infrastructures which are selected by the workflow engine. The differences among all the middleware are automatically handled by the portal, so users have just to know how to use the portal, ignoring all Grid details behind.

The P-GRADE approach is definitely useful both for users and their respective companies because the interoperation issue is confined inside the web portal and no problems will be made visible to the user when a new infrastructure has to be integrated. However, there are several drawbacks to such an approach. Current implementation of P-GRADE integrates support for several middleware. Nevertheless, if a company wants or has to work with a middleware which is not already supported, a big effort is required in order to include the related support features in P-GRADE, making the P-GRADE quick adoption difficult for a single company.

Moreover, P-GRADE does not include any uniform authorisation/authentication schema which is agreed among all the middleware. Each user has to be identified and authorised on every middleware through its own security solutions/methods, because the portal is located on a different level than security in the Grid protocols stack and cannot take into account such a problem. Therefore, the authorisation mechanism becomes more complex due to the fact that respectively authorising the partner infrastructure is not yet sufficient in this landscape. That can obviously make the security management process very difficult and more error prone.

Many other approaches addressing interoperability problems, similarly to P-GRADE, build higher level components responsible of the interaction with middleware and provide at the same time a common interface to end users. Those high level components are generally web applications (like P-GRADE), meta-schedulers (Elmroth & Tordsson, 2005) or other additional components. Notwithstanding the component designed to perform the integration of the different Grid middleware, the drawbacks highlighted for P-GRADE are not avoidable without some actions to be undertaken at lower levels.

BUILDING AN INTEROPERABLE INFRASTRUCTURE

The section *Introduction* presents the problems an IT responsible has to handle when he/she wants to join or create a Grid infrastructure in order to improve the overall infrastructure through resources sharing. These problems concern the difficulties to select the most suitable Grid model as well as the related middleware to realise a valuable and efficient infrastructure both for present and future projects. To help the IT responsible in the understanding of how his/her infrastructure could evolve in the future, this section introduces two possible approaches showing how a Grid infrastructure can join other infrastructures running different middleware. These approaches, discussed in more details in the next two sections, have already been successfully applied to real Grid infrastructures.

Before discussing infrastructure evolution, it is important to analyse the main features identifying the middleware so to understand the better choice for the initial implementation of the infrastructure. Fortunately, current middleware have sensible differences, so each of them is more suitable for a specific context and users can easily find the best solution fitting their specific requirements.

The following analysis is restricted to the most used middleware, even though this is not a real limitation because a true project, especially in the business scenario, cannot rely on experimental software, since it has not been tested enough and comes out with the lack of big communities which could fix problems when arising. So, we will mainly concentrate on gLite, Globus, UNICORE, Condor and OMII-UK middleware. These middleware have differences in many components such as *Job Allocation, User Authentication and Authorisation, Information System* and *Data management*. An IT manager has to focus on several specific problems to determine the best solution for its organisation.

The first element to be considered is the scalability for a satisfying number of resources and the support for a large distribution with resources spread in many sites. Actually, if a company/organisation needs a huge number of resources distributed over many sites, a multi level scheduler component is a fundamental feature for the involved Grid middleware. The higher logical level of this scheduler, named meta-scheduler, should be able to co-ordinate all the resources. Meta-scheduler is the core of the infrastructure because the quality of the whole infrastructure depends from its behaviour. Generally, a middleware includes a meta-scheduler component or at least some mechanisms to attach it externally. As an example, gLite provides a component, named "Workload Management System *(WMS)*", which is responsible of the higher level scheduling process. The WMS is a centralised service that can be replicated in many instances. The WMS, to be able to schedule jobs, has to know the end-point of available resources, namely the *Computing Element (CE)* in gLite terminology. Differently, Globus does not include any meta-scheduler but it is able to work with an external one like CONDOR-G, although recently there is an effort to include the *"GridWay"* meta-scheduler (http://www.gridway.org/) as a default option.

Alternatively, for a small scale Grid made of few sites/resources, users may have a list of resources to be manually selected during job submission. As an example, UNICORE middleware provides users with a client which downloads the list of resources (statically or dynamically generated) and shows them in a tree so users can analyse the resources set and select where to run their jobs.

However, it should be also considered that an increment of scheduler levels increases system complexity since it requires more effort to manage the infrastructure and reduces the efficiency. Therefore, the IT responsible has to predict the size of the infrastructure, which may strictly depend on the collaboration with its business partners. A optimal estimation of the infrastructure size is a very important issue in middleware selection process. Moreover, he/she should try to keep the infrastructure as simple as possible in order to minimise the effort needed in implementing and managing it. However, infrastructure must also be flexible enough in order to avoid additional components and/or investment for future enlargement in a valuable period.

A further issue to pay attention to when selecting a middleware is the security model. Many companies and organisations have users security rules implemented through specific software infrastructures. Hence, the new Grid infrastructure has to support at least the same rules and security level of the existing infrastructure. Currently, the majority of middleware have a security model based on X.509 certificates to identify users and policies defining the resources access. This model is strong enough for the majority of companies, so the problem could be more related to secondary aspects than security, such as single sign-on through Grid and non-Grid components, policy flexibility and so on.

In this context the differences among middleware are smaller since they are built on similar models. However, if a company has special requirements, it has to understand which middleware can be easily customised by introducing a different security model, better integrated with an already existing one. This should be evaluated for each case because there is not a common requirement but it is important to mind that more sophisticated middleware are generally more difficult to customise. Consequently, in many contexts companies have to evaluate the better solution between modifying the middleware to comply with the underlying security infrastructure, and changing the security model in spite of training employees to new procedures will be necessary.

In addition to the above issues, there are many further considerations to account as fundamental in order to select a Grid middleware and set-up the proper infrastructure. However, after a good analysis made with Grid experts, middleware fitting the company/organisation requirements better than others can be determined. The real problem, difficult to handle, which is the focus of this chapter, is the infrastructure evolution. It happens every time a change requires the infrastructure includes, or be included by, other infrastructures adopting different middleware.

The first approach solving the previously described evolution problem is based on the work made in the context of the ICEAGE (http://www. iceage-eu.org/) project. In this new approach, the basic idea is that different middleware do not necessarily need to communicate to each other in order to enable resources sharing among different infrastructures. The really important aspect to focus on is that resources belonging to an infrastructure managed by a middleware have to be made able to accept jobs when they are submitted with a different middleware. Therefore, the resources access is made by installing the different middleware components on every resource exploiting the ability of a resource to be shared by several components. In the following section the middleware co-existence will be shown in more detail and the problems faced to install/configure/maintain the new wider infrastructure will be highlighted.

The second approach to the problem is based on a solution allowing the interconnection of different Grid infrastructures through the set up of an additional component on the bound of two different Grid middleware. Middleware may have very heterogeneous architectures and interfaces, and thus they cannot communicate without the help of some external components. These components have to transform requests coming from a given middleware in requests compatible with the other one. Any type of request that can be addressed, such as job submission and control, data management and transfer, have to be taken into account. Moreover, described components have to provide the compatibility between the different middleware authentication and authorization processes, and assure an efficient way to share status information of resources available in their respective infrastructures. They are designed to make different middleware interoperable and assembled into a unique entity, namely the Gateway, acting as a *bridge* between the involved infrastructures. Therefore, IT managers can install a Gateway to enable interoperation between their best-fitting middleware and other grid infrastructures spread in the world.

In order to increase efficiency and limit impact on middleware architecture, the Gateway has to be designed taking into account basic aspects such as modularity, high throughput and scalability. Modularity makes the Gateway able to integrate all components needed to assure interoperability between different middleware. High throughput is another fundamental requirement because of the critical role of the Gateway which acts as a bridge among infrastructures. In fact, the Gateway could represent a bottle-neck for the system in consideration of the huge quantity of jobs might go through it. When necessary, a Gateway can be replicated between the same infrastructures guaranteeing throughput and load balancing.

An example of the Gateway has been deeply studied in the context of the EUChinaGRID project (http://www.euchinagrid.org/). This solution interoperating two specific middleware, gLite and GOS (http://vega.ict.ac.cn/), involved in the two big infrastructures of EGEE and CNGRID (http://www.cngrid.org/), will be described with more detail in a later section.

At a sharp look the importance of QoS in Grid computing is absolutely clear. Despite of the huge dimension of a classical Grid infrastructure, thinking that QoS could be considered a secondary aspect with respect to the Job Submission Service or the Data Management and Transfer Services would be absolutely wrong. The demonstration of the fundamental role of QoS concept lays in the efforts spent in continuously re-engineer and optimise middleware components in several projects (i.e., see the numerous releases of gLite in last years) as well as in all of the activities related to researches applied to service quality issues which has been performed in last years. In fact, since earlier Grid middleware releases, several groups have spent lots of work in developing and deploying two typical features respectively known as *Advanced Reservation* (Foster, Roy, & Sander, 2000) of resources and *Resources Ac-*

counting (Piro, Guarise, & Werbrouck, 2003). The former aims to find out an optimal solution to the problem of properly scheduling jobs execution in advance limiting overlapping on large sets of resources through early reservation. The latter sets up a bookkeeping system, called *Accounting System* tracing resources usage per user in order to calculate the bill corresponding to resource consumption due to user's request computation through a proper pricing policy directly depending on several static and dynamic factors. Those two features are part of, and influenced by, the QoS granted to users. Moreover, a big discussion is being done nowadays on Service Level Agreement (Andreozzi, Ferrari & al., 2005) to be subscribed between users communities or VOs and Grid Service Providers. When Grid technology will be mature enough the behaviour of every Grid infrastructure as well as the resource pricing policies will be driven by an economical process, very similar to the demand and offer process determining price of goods on the market.

Accessing an efficient IT infrastructure, granting enough QoS for production process, in a environment in which computational power demand continuously increases in time would traduce in a considerable save of money for the company.

MIDDLEWARE CO-EXISTENCE

The *middleware co-existence* is the result of the work done in the ICEAGE project which was aimed to deploy an infrastructure supporting the most widely used grid middleware. The main goal of ICEAGE project was to improve the Grid education methodology, by supporting activities such as providing materials and guidelines for educators and curricula developers. So, a Grid infrastructure had to be provided by the project as a standard environment where students could test new tools they had learned. Since the project was not related to a specific Grid technology, the provided infrastructure was required to support as many existing middleware as possible. Although several separate infrastructures, one per middleware, could have been set up, that demonstrated to be less advantageous for technical and economical reasons with respect to a unique infrastructure, shared among the different middleware which were going to be supported, since it does not require resources duplication. This new approach, shown in Figure 1, has been named *middleware co-existence* (Barbera et al., 2007).

The idea of the co-existence approach arose from the consideration that the majority of widely used middleware stacks do use the same components. As an example, the batch system finally executing user jobs and, partially, the security model can be easily shared. Given an already-deployed Grid infrastructure supporting a single middleware, installing just *add-ons* related to other middleware will reduce required efforts. In fact, some components are reused and do not need to be installed from scratch every time. From this perspective, co-existence can be seen as the simplest approach to integrate different middleware on a single infrastructure.

The batch system, in the Grid context called *Local Resource Management System (LRMS)*, is the part of the Grid infrastructure which is deputed to execute users' computational requests, commonly known as *jobs*. Those requests are remotely submitted according to the specific middleware instance. A front-end, usually a standalone machine, is the first element of a typical batch system architecture, namely *master node*, which accepts external requests. Then several machines act as slave elements, where computations are executed. Jobs are handled through one or more queues, having different priorities, and then executed according to the batch system scheduling policies and the load of slave nodes. As previously said, most of the middleware can share the same batch system and be able to execute jobs through it.

For this purpose Torque/MAUI (http://www. clusterresources.com/pages/products.php) has been chosen. It is one of most widely used batch systems and easily configurable as a LRMS for different middleware. Starting from a batch system already configured to accept jobs from gLite 3.0, necessary additional components has been added in order to accept jobs from Globus, UNICORE, and OMII-UK too and execute them

Figure 1. A multi-middleware infrastructure based on co-existence (Adapted from Barbera et al., 2007)

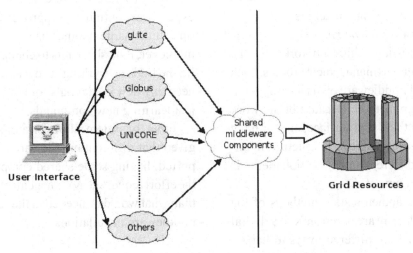

through the same Torque. No particular issues or incompatibilities among these different middleware components were found. Each of them has been installed separately and configured for jobs execution through Torque. For the batch system nothing changes when jobs are submitted using several middleware despite of a unique one. Nevertheless, different queues have been configured allowing dynamical scheduling priorities on the different middleware supported.

A different level of integration was necessary for Condor case. Unlike the other middleware we discussed, Condor is also a batch system able to execute incoming requests by itself. Unfortunately, not all the supported middleware could configure Condor as LRMS. Therefore, Condor was installed on parallel with Torque/MAUI. So, all middleware jobs requests were finally executed by Torque, but Condor ones directly executed by Condor itself. It is worth noting that no incompatibilities have been found, and the two batch systems can well co-exist sharing the same resources.

Providing an uniform interface to students has been simpler by far. In fact, gLite clients are grouped on a single machine, called *User Interface* (UI). Hence, other middleware (including Condor) related clients were just added to, and configured on, the same gLite UI, without particular problems. Minor issues only, regarding environment variables settings, were found and easily solved. So, different middleware clients do well co-exist on a single machine within this *multiple-middleware infrastructure*.

Another interesting unification work was done for security credentials management process. Each of the supported middleware owns its proper users authentication method. Because of the work already done on the User Interface, and with the aim to uniform access to the infrastructure, maintaining several different authentication methods would have been unuseful.

Although the authentication methods of the supported middleware are based on X.509 digital certificates, they have different ways to handle keys. While gLite, Condor and Globus use proxy certificates, UNICORE and OMII-UK implement a key store based system. Willing to not change radically authentication methods, the compromise adopted was to provide scripts able to convert from one format to another, both for user and machine credentials.

Moreover, scripts were responsible to make users enabled by one supported authentication model enabled by others too. That was easily doable in Globus and gLite cases, since they use a similar authentication model, and differ only in the way how remote users are mapped onto local accounts. Harder was the work done for the key store based methods, because they needed a way to synchronise the key systems between each other.

After this short overview of techniques adopted to let these five different middleware co-exist, the benefits and disadvantages of such an approach are now discussed. In a scenario where different infrastructures, initially supporting different middleware, and thereafter adopting a co-existence approach, there is the clear benefit that an increased amount of resources is available to users of all of the infrastructures. In another scenario, not too different from the previous one, in which the infrastructures supporting the middleware have to be designed from ground, the clearest benefit is that the set of potential users of such an infrastructure is immediately extended. The expert user continues to approach the infrastructure in the same manner he/she already knows; moreover, if he/she wants to change middleware, he/she finds everything ready, and does not even need any new credentials for authentication, but just learning new commands.

From the system administrator's point of view, given that different middleware have to be supported, having some shared components lowers the effort requested by management activity much than what would be needed in the case of separate middleware installations.

These advantages can be exploited wherever the need of supporting different middleware is real.

Instead, the drawbacks of such an approach are in the difficulty into making too different components to interoperate. As an example, information and monitoring systems provided by different middleware are very different and require an additional effort which has not been spent during the ICEAGE project due to the limited time coverage. Both systems should be improved and uniformed, so that resources usage could be monitored and reported uniquely. By doing that, users and resource brokers would have a realistic picture to better schedule usage of resources and do not have to refer only to the fraction of resources used by a single middleware.

GATEWAY

The work performed to achieve interoperability between gLite, the Grid middleware of the EGEE infrastructure, and GOS, the Grid middleware of the CNGRID infrastructure, in the context of the EUChinaGRID project will be now discussed. The EUChinaGRID project is an initiative, co-funded by the European Commission, aiming to extend the European Grid infrastructure for e-Science to China and to facilitate scientific data transfer and processing in a first sample of scientific communities which already set up strong collaborations between Europe and China.

gLite and GOS middleware adopt very different architectures and for this reason a *Gateway*-driven approach has been adopted to make them interoperable. The role of the Gateway is to translate requests coming from one middleware into requests compatible with the other.

The actual Gateway design has been performed by taking into account the ambitious aim to develop a generic Gateway interoperating several different middleware. So the Gateway architecture has been defined in a generic way, granting modularity and providing general solutions to interoperability problems. After that, some specialized modules have been created to make the two middleware involved in the project interoperable.

As said above, the main design principles of a Gateway are modularity, high throughput and scalability. A modular design of an interoperability-dedicated component usually consists of several independent blocks such as data staging, script parsing, authentication and authorization, and all of them could be modified according to the infrastructures/middleware the Gateway interconnects/makes interoperable. High throughput is fundamental since the gateway is between two or more different infrastructures so thousands of jobs may go through it every day. Moreover, different instances of the Gateway can be deployed and configured in order to connect to the infrastructures running the middleware involved. In this way, the gateway approach also guarantees the scalability of the system.

In this component design activity, two patterns, Inversion of Control (IoC) (http://martinfowler.com/articles/injection.html) and Staged Event Driven Architecture (SEDA) (Welsh, Culler, & Brewer, 2001), have been adopted to ensure modularity and high throughput. IoC is adopted as the way to instantiate and manage lifecycles of different atomic modules. The SEDA model was also adopted to assemble different atomic modules into pipelines for different purposes.

Figure 2 shows the conceptual architecture of the Gateway. It basically consists of three different components: thread pool, scheduler and pipeline. The pipeline is assembled at runtime. A fixed number of threads are allocated in advance and maintained in the thread pool. The scheduler will obtain an idle thread from the thread pool when it actually executes a batch job.

Figure 2. Conceptual architecture of the Gateway

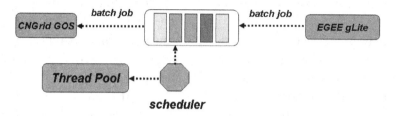

Authentication and Authorization

The cross-domain security issue seems to be one of the most relevant challenges in the design of the Gateway. The Gateway has to provide mechanisms to integrate authentication and authorization functionalities of the different middleware involved.

Two different possible security modules have been defined in the gateway. The first module is the Identity Mapping Service and the second module is the Security Token Service.

The Identity Mapping Service is used to map users' identities between heterogeneous identity management infrastructures, such as EGEE and CNGrid. Consider to have two infrastructure A and B, each one deploying a different middleware. When users of the A infrastructure try to use some services belonging to the B infrastructure, those services map the original credential of the users to a new credential using a format which is understandable in the B infrastructure.

The Security Token Service is used to centrally store security tokens (a standard security credential; i.e., for GOS an username and password pair, whereas gLite requires a valid GSI proxy) in order to allow users from different domains to retrieve the corresponding tokens when necessary, as defined in the OGSA-BES (OGSA Basic Execution Services) specification (https://forge.gridforum.org/sf/projects/ogsa-bes-wg). The Security Token Service is compliant with the WS-Trust Specification. Figure 3 shows the conceptual architecture of the Security Token Service.

Job Management Service

In order to allow Grid users to use computing and storage resources of different infrastructures, the Gateway must have the capability to forward batch jobs received from one Grid infrastructure to the other. The forwarding process should be transparent to the end user.

The Job Management Service ties with many other modules such as data management module, resource information discovery and selection module, authentication and authorization module, and so on. So, implementing the job management service in the gateway is a quite complex task.

The following issues have been focused: requests conversion in the Gateway including job description language; identification of the steps needed to allow job submission mechanism of each middleware to submit jobs to another middleware.

Although OGSA-BES has defined a standard job submission interface and the JSDL (http://www.ogf.org/documents/GFD.56.pdf) is chosen as the standard job description language, proprietary interfaces are widely deployed and it is difficult and impractical to replace them immediately. Then, a block to convert one job description language to another has to be deployed in the Gateway.

Allowing a job submission mechanism belonging to a specific middleware to submit a job to a computing resource related to another middleware is a very complex task. This problem has been solved by making components of an infrastructure

Figure 3. The security token service in the Gateway

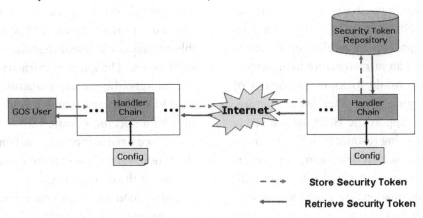

Figure 4. Role of the Gateway in the job management service

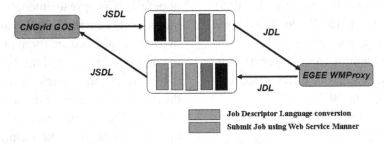

see each Gateway instance as a separated computing resource. Then, the Gateway will forward all the received jobs to the other infrastructure instead of processing it locally. To perform this task, the Gateway must implement a block containing a job submission mechanism properly modified to forward job to another infrastructure.

Figure 4 depicts the role of the Gateway, interconnecting EGEE and CNGRID infrastructures, in the job management service.

Data Management System

Hybrid solutions for data movement could have strong impact on performances, especially when an intermediate element such as a gateway is used. The solution of focusing on a point-to-point data transfer seems to be feasible. The usage of managed resources and their APIs (such as SRM, SRB) should help.

As a general solution for data management, interfaces compliant with the *Storage Resource Manager* (SRM) (http://sdm.lbl.gov/srm-wg/) have been adopted. This kind of interface acts as a higher level bridge above the low level transfer protocols in order to setup an effective and transparent data exchange service. All end users can use a series of uniform commands provided by the SRM client to access the storage resources.

Information and Monitoring Services

The process of discovering resources and their statuses is fundamental to reach a real interoperability between two middleware since an effective resource selection mechanism relies on a good knowledge of the current status of the resources.

The Berkeley Database Information Index (BDII) (http://agrid.uibk.ac.at/wpa2/bdii.html), service developed by the EGEE project, and adopted in gLite, is a flexible and effective information service. For this reason, it has been used to develop the process of publishing resource information from an infrastructure to another.

When a user would to know the status of resources belonging to another infrastructure, which does not support the BDII, he/she sends a request for querying resources' information to some gateway instance. By developing a customer-defined provider procedure which interfaces with GIP (Generic Information Provider), the Gateway connects to remote Grid nodes using the SSH protocol and extracts the information in a *GLUE schema*-compliant way (Andreozzi & al., 2005) from the resources (such as CPU load, memory usage, batch system status, etc).

In this way, users coming from different Grids could use the same method to query resources information based on the BDII.

OUTLOOK

The approaches described in previous sections show viable solutions to integrate infrastructures based on different middleware, with no, or at least limited, change required in the user experience, in a relatively short period and with low effort. This allows IT managers to invest in Grids getting benefits for their organisations without running the risks due to a not yet standardised technology.

Moreover, the value of these approaches can be valuable inside a single project and is not necessarily related just to the integration of infrastructures.

Current projects running on Grid technology are supported by different partners deploying a distributed infrastructure based on a specific middleware. In this model, all partners and their relative resources are constrained to that middleware. Nevertheless, there are many situations where a partner would support/use a different middleware because that features a better use of

resources or users are already familiar with the different middleware rather than with the one just selected for the infrastructure or whatever valuable reason could encourage the use of another middleware. Thus, a new infrastructure can use the highlighted approaches to set up multi-middleware VOs where users and resources are not tied up with a specific middleware. Thus, VOs can grow more easily since new participants have no restrictions on resources management, with a big benefit for the community.

Finally, considering a longer time period, when the standards for the Grid will evolve and the Grid technology will become really mature and hopefully widespread among companies around the world, the current middleware could converge to just one middleware (or many "*identical*"), so the interoperability will not be a big problem in the future. As an example, it is possible to look at the *internet* technology where initially there were many communication protocols but after a while the *TCP/IP* become the de-facto standard and the only one which is currently used. However, the IT history shows how adoption of standards and interoperation are not strict requirements for the success of a technology, so for the future two scenarios are possible: either all middleware implementations really support the standard or the standards will not be really integrated in the middleware which will evolve autonomously, likely with more effort on interoperability. In both scenarios the approaches shown in previous sections could be valuable and successfully employed to improve interoperability.

Actually, if the middleware evolves with a lazy support for standards, like today where the level of support to standards is not very high and quite different among the various existing middleware, the interoperability will remain a problem for future Grid infrastructures. Therefore, approaches based on multi-middleware co-existence and/or gateways, such as the ones presented above (or their evolutions), remain the best solution to rapidly and easily address interoperability issues.

On the other hand, Grid standards could gain strong support from the global community and middleware developers will certainly and integrally be compliant to them. So it would be quite reasonable to state that, after a while, all middleware will probably implement the same functionalities, i.e. the ones described by the standards. Since in Grids there are no limitations on the kind of resources and on the way they should operate, a Grid infrastructure could include resources needing special functionalities not supported by standards (i.e., special sensors producing data for an experiment could require specific functionalities for their tuning). Those special functionalities would require specific components to be exploited. Similarly, there could be common resources, such as CPU or storage, having features not supported by standards and that the users would exploit. In these conditions, the above approaches could be useful because they allow to support middleware with different features. Thus, the middleware can remain standard compliant and the *extra* features can be included in an ad-hoc middleware added to the infrastructure by means of gateways or through the co-existence in a way very similar to the highlighted approaches.

Therefore, independently of the Grid middleware evolution and the size of the infrastructure, IT managers can be confident that by using the approaches shown in this chapter their Grid infrastructures can easily evolve including new resources and/or joining with other infrastructures. Moreover, users will be able to use resources without changing the tools they already know and still maintaining the ability to totally exploit every available resource. So the investment for the infrastructure is really valuable for the future.

SUMMARY AND CONCLUSION

Grid computing allows for the creation of an e-Infrastructure providing present and future research centres with computational power and information storage capabilities they need. Although the value of Grid is recognised worldwide, the lack of truly supported standards makes Grid widespread adoption hard in consideration of the risk of either partly or totally loosing the investment made on a technology which is still under evolution. In this chapter we introduced two approaches for interoperability which are able to ensure existing Grid infrastructures to evolve and also to preserve the investments made.

A huge effort has already been spent on activities related to Grid middleware interoperability. The Gateway and Co-existence based solutions are, respectively, the results of some of those activities demonstrating how practical and cultural problems listed in earlier sections can be solved through granting resources sharing and overall infrastructure improvement. The goal is nowadays to further improve the implementations of interoperability approaches by taking care of studying how to extend valuable results obtained. That cannot be done without considering the experience gained from other similar activities.

Directions to be considered for the extension are:

- Reaching a better integration level with emerging standards.
- Extending results already available in order to achieve a deeper coverage of the interoperability issues. This will imply paying attention to a larger set of points not yet covered and providing a day-by-day improving interoperability level.
- Extending the set of *interoperable middleware*.
- Providing feedback concerning new solutions to standardisation organisations.

Interoperability among Grid middleware having different architectures is not a trivial task and can be reached at different levels. The first levels of interoperability are intended to supply users with the possibility of submitting their jobs from one infrastructure to the other and vice-versa also providing the capability of controlling submitted jobs from the initiator. A further level concerns the achievement of the full interoperability between Grid middleware. That is not easy. In fact, job submission and control, output retrieval, data management, data interoperability, etc. should be taken into account and properly managed.

The final level of interoperability is intended to be achieved by implementing interoperable services so that the user does not need to care about the middleware, but just access the services from whatever available portal, in a transparent and ubiquitous way.

The approaches described in this chapter are good starting points to move towards full interoperability. At the moment of writing this book, several projects are studying or proposing new solutions to achieve the full interoperability. Some of them plan to work on the Gateway-based approach, that could be easily improved by increasing the level of abstraction of its components in the multi-middleware interoperable environment, an efficient job submission and control ensuring process. Also promoting the resource interface abstraction process as well as providing efficient and widely valuable shared Authentication and Authorization models should be necessary steps on the path to full interoperability.

The Co-existence approach represents the quicker solution to fulfil the needs of existing infrastructures. It ensures fast answers to production and research requirements by being able to set up a flexible infrastructure in a very short time, and providing new functionalities without requiring additional knowledge to users.

Finally, continuously paying attention to the standardisation process is mandatory for who is taking care of middleware interoperability issues. Standardisation activities are just at the beginning in Grid landscape but, as said, they might have a big impact on future Grid development also influencing middleware interoperability. Seen

the high complexity of Grid infrastructure, a stack layers service-based approach is quite possible for the upcoming standards, which would describe level related services and corresponding interfaces. Developers might create components immediately compatible with every compliant middleware, also focusing on efficiency and performances. That could be an important step toward the fully interoperation level. Additionally, a dramatic enhancement of the global Grid system performances and overall QoS could be obtained, also providing a positive feedback for companies, research centres and newcomers willing to adopt Grid technologies.

Once this process is activated, companies will get back further benefits represented by working in a very efficient infrastructure where the risks discussed in Introduction section are lowered by the continuous improvement process which will be instantiated. That way, in the medium-long term, the risk of loosing investments made for infrastructures can continuously decrease determining an opposite growth of the company level of trustfulness in Grid solutions. That would allow for the creation of new opportunities for all the involved actors through collection of capitals coming from new investments in Grid applications made by old partners and newcomers.

The route to complete integration of Grids into business, production, and research infrastructure passes through interoperability issues. It is still a hard path to follow but advantages are clearly visible and already recognised by the global community.

REFERENCES

Alfieri, R., Cecchini, R., Ciaschini, V., Dell'Agnello, L., Frohnere, Á., Lőrentey, K., & Spataro, F. (2005). From gridmap-file to VOMS: managing authorization in a Grid environmen. *Future Generation Computer Systems 21*(4), 549-558. Elsevier.

Andreozzi, S., Burke, S., Field, L., et al. (2005). *GLUE Schema Specification version 1.2*. Technical report. Available at: http://infnforge.cnaf.infn.it/glueinfomodel

Andreozzi, S., Ferrari, T., Ronchieri, E., & Monforte, S. (2005). Agreement-Based Workload and Resource Management. In *Proceedings of the First International Conference on e-Science and Grid Computing* (pp.181-188). IEEE Computer Society.

Barbera, R., Fargetta, M., & Giorgio, E. (2007). Multiple Middleware Co-existence: Another Aspect of Grid Interoperation. In the *Third IEEE International Conference on e-Science and Grid Computing* (pp. 577-583). Bangalore, India.

De Roure, D., & Surridge M. (2003). Interoperability Challenges in Grid for Industrial Applications. *Proceedings of Semantic Grid Workshop at GGF9*. Chicago, USA.

Elmroth, E., & Tordsson, J. (2005). An interoperable, standards-based grid resource broker and job submission service. Paper presented at *First IEEE International Conference on e-Science and Grid Computing*. Melbourne, Australia.

Foster, I., & Kesselman, C. (2003). *The Grid 2: Blueprint for a New Computing Infrastructure*. San Francisco, CA, USA: Morgan Kaufmann Publishers Inc.

Foster, I., & Roy, A., & Sander, V. (2000). A Quality of Service Architecture that Combines Resource Reservation and Application Adaptation. In the *8th International Workshop on Quality of Service (IWQOS)*. LNCS, Springer-Verlag.

Kacsuk, P., Kiss, T., & Sipos, G. (2008). Solving the grid interoperability problem by P-GRADE portal at workflow level. *Future Generation Computer Systems, 24*, 744-751. Elsevier.

Kacsuk, P., & Sipos, G. (2005). Multi-Grid, multi-user workflows in the P-GRADE Grid Portal. *Journal of Grid Computing 3*(3-4), 221-238. The Netherlands: Springer

Moses, T., et al. (2005). *eXtensible Access Control Markup Language (XACML), Version 2.0*. OASIS Standard. Available at: http://www.oasisopen.org/committees/tc_home.php?wg_abbrev=xacml

Piro, R. M., Guarise, A., & Werbrouck, A. (2003). An economy-based accounting infrastructure for the datagrid. In *Proceedings of Fourth International Workshop on Grid Computing*. IEEE.

Scardaci, D., & Scuderi, G. (2007). A Secure Storage Service for the gLite Middleware. In the *Proceedings of third International Symposium on Information Assurance and Security* (pp. 261-266). Manchester, United Kingdom: IEEE Computer Society.

Wang, Y., Scardaci, D., Yan, B., & Huang, Y. (2007). Interconnect EGEE and CNGRID e-Infrastructures through Interoperability between gLite and GOS Middlewares. In the *Third IEEE International Conference on e-Science and Grid Computing* (pp. 553-560). Bangalore, India.

Welsh, M., Culler, D., & Brewer, E. (2001). SEDA: an architecture for well-conditioned, scalable internet services. *SIGOPS Operating Systems Review, 35*(5), 230-243.

Chapter III
Scenarios of Next Generation Grid Applications in Collaborative Environments:
A Business–Technical Analysis

Vassiliki Andronikou
National Technical University of Athens, Greece

Dimitrios Halkos
National Technical University of Athens, Greece

Dimosthenis Kyriazis
National Technical University of Athens, Greece

Theodora Varvarigou
National Technical University of Athens, Greece

Magdalini Kardara
National Technical University of Athens, Greece

ABSTRACT

The Grid has the potential to make a significant advance beyond the Internet, by turning it from a passive information medium into an active tool for creating and exploring new knowledge. Nowadays, this potential is becoming a reality and is emerging to Next Generation Grids (NGG) thanks to the far more cost-effective and universally applicable technology. Taking into consideration that Grids started delivering benefits to their adopters, this book chapter focuses on providing a business–technical presentation of two potential NGG applications, from two competitive and highly dynamic markets, including complex collaborations, which have shown rapid growth over the past decades; the supply chain management and the Cargo Transportation Logistics. The authors present a set of NGG components, the adoption of which in the aforementioned application domains addresses efficiently a set of technical issues ranging from performance to dynamic negotiation, and tackle the main trends and challenges in the corresponding business sectors.

Copyright © 2009, IGI Global, distributing in print or electronic forms without written permission of IGI Global is prohibited.

INTRODUCTION

Although initially designed to cover the needs of computational-intensive applications (Foster, Kesselman, & Tuecke, 2001; Leinberger & Kumar, 1999), Grid technology of nowadays aims at providing an infrastructure that can also service the needs of the business domain. Advanced infrastructure requirements combined with the innate business goals for lower costs and higher income are driving key business sectors such as multimedia, engineering, gaming, environmental science, among others towards adopting Grid solutions into their business. The various entities in the value chains pose different requirements with each one benefiting in a different way. Software vendors and solution integrators need to proceed with the "gridification" of their current applications so that the integration of them in Grid environments is feasible. Service providers pose strict requirements ranging from manageability to accounting and billing. The final success of this business orientation of Grid technology however will primarily depend on its real adopters; the end users who demand transparency, reliability, security and easiness-to-use. Especially in the case of business collaboration systems, the main focus of all parties involved in the collaboration is on lowering the costs and automating and standardizing communication as well as making the upgrade and maintenance processes less complex.

This shift from Science Grids to Business Grids resulted in advanced requirements in Service Level Agreement (SLA) management, data management, Grid portals (as interfaces) and Virtual Organizations (VO) management among others combined with re-prioritization of the non-functional requirements of the systems with security, reliability and scalability climbing the higher stairs in the hierarchy.

In the meanwhile, collaborative business processes nowadays are still being conducted through traditional means of communication such as fax, phone and e-mail. Even strategic partners with a significant market share and a complex network of partners rely on these means for a part of their transactions. And although electronic communication methods offer some form of automation and have proven to comprise much faster and cheaper ways for information exchange, they still require manual processes on both ends and they are far from providing automated and standardised communication among partners. In fact they suffer from a number of problems including human errors in manual entry of information, information loss, delayed information exchange, complex or limited information sharing, high cost of infrastructure (especially when offering improved reliability through replication mechanisms and supporting duplicate systems and providing security and complex collaborations) and the great effort required to integrate their internal systems to existing solutions.

The vision of Next Generation Grids (NGG) is mainly the development of an infrastructure for enabling new businesses and offering new business opportunities and new ways of work and collaboration through the support of three important business needs posed by the globalization of the world markets; agility, flexibility and robustness (Next Generation GRIDs Expert Group, 2006). More specifically, NGG focuses on delivering an economically viable and efficient infrastructure which will offer the commercially effective use of resources to participating organisations, simplicity of access to and use of Grid technologies and underlying Quality of Service (QoS) mechanisms (Tserpes, Kyriazis, Menychtas, & Varvarigou, 2008) and the levels of security and privacy required for confidence boosting. The aforementioned mechanisms are expected to allow the wider adoption of the proposed infrastructure both to the business and industry world as well as to the government domain, the consumers and the public.

Following the evolution in the Grid domain and the current approaches in NGG, as it is presented in this chapter the adoption of Grid solutions in the area of collaborative environments offers the ability to access, process and analyse real-time or 'near' real-time business data combined from different, distributed and heterogeneous data sources (including historic data and an extended range of data warehouses) and hence accelerate and improve the result of decision making. Moreover, it provides increased data re-use through the establishment of data federations allowing involving the same data in more than one projects without need for transfer and flexibility in scaling environmental changes.

This chapter aims at presenting and analyzing both from a technical and a business perspective two NGG Applications within strongly Collaborative Environments and highly competitive and emerging markets; Supply Chain Management (SCM) and Cargo Transportation Logistics (CTL). More specifically, work in this chapter shows how the NGG concepts and technologies can be applied within two globally emerging markets the business analysis of which has highlighted the great need for reliability, robustness, flexibility, availability and real-time operation – strong requirements partly or totally not met with current solutions. Initially, background information for each of these business sectors and definitions of the main terms are provided, followed by a scenario description for each sector presenting the main roles of the collaborations established and their participation in the collaborative environment. After the technical requirements for each scenario are presented, a set of NGG components addressing the most demanding technical needs related to each area is analysed. The technical analysis of these two scenarios is followed by a business analysis focusing on the business need of the Grid solutions proposed and the benefits stemming from the latter. During this analysis the business model found proper for enterprises to use when adopting the proposed Grid solutions is presented and the resulting Grid value chains are described. Finally, the main concerns

and challenges are briefly discussed and future research opportunities are suggested, whereas the business future trends are presented.

BACKGROUND

In the following paragraphs we briefly describe two business sectors with strong collaboration requirements: the Supply Chain Management (SCM) and the Cargo Transportation Logistics (CTL), which are analyzed from a business and technical perspective later on in this book chapter.

Supply Chain Management

Supply Chain Management comprises the integration of both internal and external business processes within the supply chain. The effort of the Council of Supply Chain Management Professionals (CSCMP) to produce an SCM definition resulted in "the planning and management of all activities involved in sourcing and procurement, conversion, and all Logistics Management activities. Importantly, it also includes coordination and collaboration with channel partners, which can be suppliers, intermediaries, third-party service providers, and customers." (Grant, Lambert, Stock, & Ellram, 2006, p. 46)

Initially product delivery was limited to the development of not much accurate planning of demand, then the product manufacturing and the stocking of finished goods at warehouses. The introduction of SCM systems comprised a significant step towards the inter-enterprise communication and thus enabled improved collaboration among different partners in the SCM offering increased productivity, inventory reduction, improved inventory and shipping rates among others (Anderson & Lee, 1999).

Focusing on improving collaboration and communication across enterprises, SCM has improved the way business works. Any SCM business – regardless of the specific sector it serves, such as pharmaceutical goods, food, toys or software – includes a labyrinthine materials and services network requiring prudent and efficient management for its smooth and successful operation. This network may involve hundreds of suppliers, distributors, manufacturers, importers, exporters, wholesalers, warehouses and customers during its day-to-day operation processing or submission of multiple orders depending on their role, with each side aiming at cutting costs, increasing efficiency and consolidating operations; in other words, controlling expenses (Epicor, 2005). Its primary goal is three-fold: inventory reduction, transaction speed increase through real-time (or near real-time) data exchange and sales increase by implementing customer requirements more efficiently.

The previous generations of SCM focused on MRP/MRPII (Material Resource Planning) automation, ERP (Enterprise Resource Planning) integration and APS (Advanced Planning and Scheduling) functional optimisation. With the market demanding flexibility, faster results, and lower software costs and moving towards a non-linear nature with complex collaborations and stronger needs for synchronisation, the evolution to next-generation SCM with demand-supply synchronisation comprising one of its primary features became essential (i2, 2005).

Cargo Transportation Logistics

The ship chartering for cargo transfer comprises an essential and critical process in an evolving, competitive and highly dynamic market. In fact, the major transportation mode of international trade is seaborne shipping (Christiansen, Fagerholt, & David, 2002). Cargo providers and aggregators are competing for better offers, while ship owners have to adapt to each market's particularities in order to optimise the cost/quality rate. The diversity of the provided services (the type of procurement is depended on a wide range of factors, such as the season, the ship type, the

region, the current requirements and demand, etc) is pinpointing the need for the dynamic orchestration of the involved systems and networks. This diversity is intensified by the non-static nature of fleets as their size and composition may change over time, whereas ships of various types, sizes, cost structures and other ship features may exist within a shipping company fleet. Moreover, the globalization of the shipping industry is creating processes on ship and cargo routing that must be completed independently, but at the same time must be treated in a single, coherent way from the ship-owner's perspective. And what is more, in their effort to remain profitable and increase their market share many shipping companies proceed with bringing their fleets into a pool and operate them together. In other words, in the field of ship-based CTL collaborations may exist even among partners sharing the same role within the network intensifying this way the complexity of this collaborative environment. The characteristics of this market include the need for dynamic assessment of trust and confidence level against its members.

And what is more, the presence of competing harbour agents representing groups of transporters, who in turn may have economic or physical dependencies, makes the situation even more complicated. Dynamically composing SLAs may solve the issue of the plethora of possible combinations but current integrated systems lack the capability to semantically represent these dependencies. Furthermore, the procurement of spare parts and other goods that a ship needs at a given point of time has a strong influence on decisions such as the next ship destination. These decisions are costing (and respectively making) money, thus, outputs of multiple disciplines related to shipping must be taken into account. However, regardless of the great variations in fleet size and mix of shipping companies that may exist, the key objective of the shipping companies remains common; **the optimal utilization of their fleets**. Another aspect of this objective is the *design of* *the optimal fleet.* In fact, shipping companies have to combine and analyse a large set of data including different types of ships and cargos, their cost structures, demand for shipping services, representative routes for cargo transfer with their cost and time consumption among others. Towards this objective the issues of routing and scheduling are of great importance.

The term routing according to (Ronen, 1993) refers to the assignment of sequences of ports to be visited by the ships, whereas scheduling refers to the temporal aspect of routing including all the timing of the different events on the route of a ship. More parameters may be variable and need to be determined. For example, when taking into account environmental conditions as well (such as ocean currents or heavy weather) cruising speed and bunker fuel consumption may be influenced and thus be taken into accounting when deciding on routing. In other words, the problem extends to also deciding on the route between two ports, and in fact it comprises a shortest path problem in the presence of obstacles.

Based on the above, the need for an environment in which such markets can flourish, fostering the healthy competition between cargo providers and the ship owners is becoming increasing, whereas it will allow the members of this market to dynamically assess the confidence level against each other enabling as well the dynamic consuming of their services from the ship-owners.

BUSINESS–TECHNICAL ANALYSIS OF COLLABORATIVE GRID SCENARIOS

Collaborative Grid Scenarios

Supply Chain Management Scenario

Overview

This section aims to present an SCM scenario taken from the pharmaceutical sector. Currently some initial efforts towards adopting a Grid solution within an SCM Collaborative Environment are being made through the FP6 European project BEinGRID (BEinGRID Project, 2008), which deals with a series of business experiments aiming at adopting Grid solutions in a wide range of business sectors, one of which is the SCM in the pharmaceutical sector. These efforts resulted in a successful case study and a 'Grid e-procurement' set of services offered to different stakeholders within the SCM through a customized portal (BEinGRID Consortium, 2008). The scenario as depicted in Figure 1, examines the collaboration scheme among the various parties involved in the supply chain from the corporate manufacturing companies to the retailer (i.e. local pharmacies and warehouses). The Pharmaceutical SCM scenario provides a unique testbed for studying the assets and challenges associated with the introduction of NGG applications in Collaborative Environments.

Roles

The main stakeholders involved in the Pharmaceutical SCM scenario are outlined below:

- **Supplier – pharmaceutical company:** The Supplier entity represents the supplier of one or more product categories to one or more retailers. The Supplier reviews and adjusts all orders placed by Retailers according to a number of factors (such as stock, seasonal demand, order forecasting, etc) and assigns the delivery of goods to the distributor that serves the area the retailer is in. In addition, the Supplier must ensure that a sufficient quantity of products is always in stock by ordering additional items from the manufacturer whenever the Distributor notifies them of a shortage in a specific product. Finally, another basic operation performed by the Supplier is the mid and a long-term forecasting of orders and sales both for reporting and decision-support reasons.

Figure 1. Typical SCM scenario

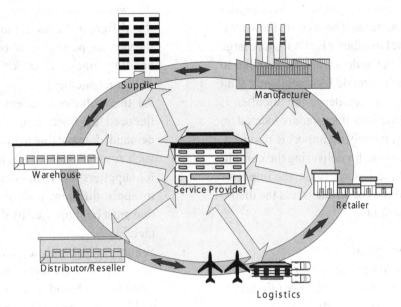

- **Retailer – pharmacy, warehouse:** Representing the Customer of the Supplier and being responsible for ordering products to replenish their stock in order to cover customer demand.
- **Distributor:** Representing a company in between of Suppliers and Retailers and being responsible for storing Supplier's stock and delivering it to the Retailers. A Supplier may collaborate with one or more Distributors, one or more per area. When the stock of a specific product falls below a specific threshold, the Distributor is responsible for notifying the Supplier in order to replenish stock.
- **Manufacturer:** Representing the company that manufactures the pharmaceutical products. The company receives orders from the Supplier and in case it is based on the same country as the Supplier, also delivers them directly to the Distributor.
- **Importer:** Representing the company responsible for importing pharmaceutical products from a Manufacturer based on

foreign soil. This company deals with all procedures related with importing products from Manufacturers located at a different country from the Supplier's (e.g. clearance, transportation) and is also responsible for delivering the products to the Distributor.

Scenario Description
On a regular basis the Retailer evaluates stock availability and decides what products need to be purchased in order to keep up with customer demand. The Retailer then selects the products needed to be purchased from their Suppliers and submits the order. The Supplier, based on the Retailer location and past transactions, selects a Distributor and assigns them the order.

According to product demand and stock availability, which is communicated to them by the Distributor, the Supplier adjusts the submitted orders and based on this information also decides upon the production speed. The aforementioned process is performed periodically until the point of delivery, when all pending orders need to be finalised. The Distributor is then responsible for shipping the final orders to Retailers.

When the distributor detects shortage to a product, they inform the Supplier. The Supplier will then request additional items from the Manufacturer. Since the Distributor is able to store large amounts of products, orders from the Supplier to the Manufacturer are made less frequently than the ones made by the Retailer to the Supplier. If the Supplier and the Manufacturer are located on the same country, namely no import is required, the latter is responsible for delivering the items to the Distributor directly. Otherwise, the Importer will handle the import of products and the distribution to the Distributor.

Technical Requirements

Utilising NGG concepts to the previously described scenario a set of technical requirements arise that are discussed hereafter:

- Provided that the cost of information loss or delay (due to network or hardware problems or heavy workload during rush hours) in an SCM can have great impact on the relations among collaboration parties (e.g., lost material order from Supplier to Manufacturer or lost product order from Retailer to Supplier) and that an order may be submitted to the system at any time during the day, a reliable infrastructure is required. Thus, *fault-tolerant mechanisms* need to be established with the main priority being on *data reliability.*

- Given that *timely communication of information* is required for the successful operation of the established collaborations in the SCM (e.g., low inventory levels should be known to the warehouses and the supplier promptly so that production is adjusted properly and demand is satisfied), data exchange – regardless of their format – among interested parties must be performed without any delay.

- Load balancing and effective scheduling of the application services so that system operates efficiently during rush hours and is able to serve a great number of users.

- Efficient *SLA monitoring and evaluation mechanisms* are required for monitoring the different SLAs established between the varying parties in the collaboration and handling unexpected occurrences during order management.

- As this collaborative environment is influenced by fluctuating factors (seasonal demand, demand due to unexpected factors such as a new flue, etc), it must be possible for suppliers and manufacturers to be able to apply different *policies* – a capability that must be supported by the Grid environment.

- *Security, trust, privacy and identity management* also comprise major challenges that have to be addressed in the dynamic and complex collaborative environment in the SCM. As enterprises are reluctant to share their data due to fears for information disclosure to other parties and/or data theft, trust, informational privacy and security comprise strong requirements for an SCM Grid solution.

Transportation Logistics

Overview

The scenario that will be presented and analysed in the following sections refers to seaborne activities and their logistics. There are three modes of operation in shipping: industrial, tramp, and liner (Christiansen, Fagerholt, & David, 2002), which are not mutually exclusive. The presented scenario will not focus on a specific mode but will cover various aspects of cargo transfer and ship chartering.

The aforementioned scenario is not limited to the application provision but on a complete value chain that allows the collaboration of its members in an advantageous way that enables a set of NGG features to be applied. In the following paragraphs, we will start with a general scenario description and proceed with the presentation of its high-level technical requirements (a detailed description of the solution offered by NGGs is included in the Technical Description section).

Until recently companies used to rely on their own resources in order to provide their services in an efficient and effective way. However, as markets grow and competition increases, many companies from a wide variety of sectors – one of them being transportation logistics – were forced to proceed with significant changes in the business procedures and models. In the case of Cargo Transportation Logistics in particular, many shipping companies nowadays perform collaboration efforts with competitors that suit their interests in order to be able to improve service provision, maintain or even extend their customer base, increase profitability and efficiency. To this direction, trusted shipping companies bring their fleets into a pool and operate them together each of them with a different collaboration degree and personal goals. Based on that, the ships of a ship owner do not only refer to the ships that he owns but also to the ones that he is able to operate based on their agreements.

When deciding upon the ships to be used for the cargo transportation and the route the selected ships should follow, a set of factors must be taken into account. The type, the size and the location of the cargo and the requested date of delivery along with ship specific information (such as size, capacity, type and cost) and harbour information (such as port fees and availability) as well as current demand comprise the most important ones. As such collaborations become more complex and wide for competitiveness and profitability reasons and fleet size increases, making such a decision comprises a complicated and time consuming operation. Using, thus, a Decision making mechanism that is able to provide decision support on the routing of the ships and the delivery constraints of the cargo proves to be a valuable tool for the further evolution of cargo transportation logistics.

Roles

Based on the above, we present a conceptual figure (3) of the scenario along with the flow of information. This scenario consists of four main roles including:

- **Ship owner:** Representing the actor that owns/operates the ships and which provides the corresponding ship information to the Decision making Mechanism.
- **Cargo aggregator:** Representing the actor that provides information regarding the cargo that will be transferred with various types of ships.
- **Service provider:** Hosting a Decision making mechanism, which is a mechanism that takes into account the aforementioned information from the ship owner and the cargo aggregator and defines the optimum mapping of cargo to ships and the corresponding routes with sequential cargo transfers.
- **Cargo provider:** Owning the cargo and requesting for its transportation to a specific destination.

Scenario Description

The process is initiated by the Ship Owner who requests information about the routing of the ships that he operates. The Ship Owner provides a set of parameters to the Decision making mechanism such as the ship's type, initial location, region of serving, requirements, dates of delivery, cargo type of serving, transportation cost, etc. At the same time, the Cargo Aggregator enquires data from the Cargo Providers regarding the type and the size of the cargo, its location and possible dates of loading and delivery and range of transportation costs. There has to be mentioned that the Cargo Aggregator enquires information from the Cargo Providers since it is not the company owning the cargo but can be seen as a placeholder for the information regarding the location and the type of the cargo. The information from both sides is fed into a Decision making mechanism at the

Figure 2. Typical CTL scenario

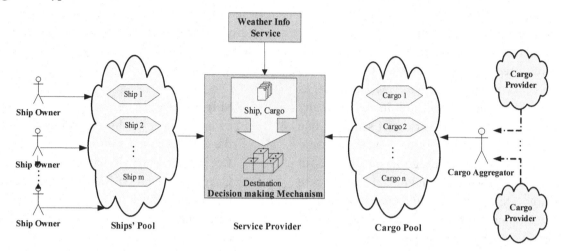

Service Provider's side which combines and processes it in order to provide the aforementioned routing information to the Ship Owner. At this point the set of parameters the Decision making mechanism is provided with may be enriched with weather forecast information and current and scheduled status of fleet, aiming at the optimal size and mix of the fleet as well as selecting the intermediate course between two ports based on weather conditions.

A key point in this scenario refers to the presence of competing harbour agents that represent groups of transporters, who in turn may have economic or physical dependencies. The latter raises an issue of major importance regarding the trust and confidence of information since for example a ship owner would not like to publish cost and type of cargo information to cargo providers that are competing or have the aforementioned dependencies.

Technical Requirements

Supporting the scenario that was briefly described in the previous section and applying Next Generation Grids' features to it requires the pursuit of a number of aspects that need to be addressed. These aspects are summarized as follows:

- The Decision making application should run as a service with various *fault-tolerance mechanisms* in cases of failure. It should be feasible to run on a distributed collection of resources (self discovered and managed) that can (self) tolerate faults.

- The application (Decision making mechanism) provider can also play the role of the infrastructure provider. Nevertheless in distributed environments, such as Grids, these roles can be distinguished. The latter poses requirements regarding application *deployment "on the fly"* to specific resources following functional & non functional specifications.

- The application services have to be *load balanced, managed, scheduled, maintained* and provided in a reliable way.

- Given the fact that this scenario refers to ships, the aspect of mobility has also to be examined and a set of mobile services and devices should be offered in a *seamless and transparent* way.

- *Trust, confidence and identity management* are major challenges that have to be addressed in the dynamic and complex environment in seaborne activities.

- *Dynamic composition of SLAs* is needed in order to address the issue of possible combinations of cargo transport from different cargo providers or unexpected changes in a ship's initial routing.
- This collaborative environment should also allow different *policies* to be applied by the ship owners / operators. Depending on the market status the ship owners may change their policies (e.g. in terms of costs) and therefore the corresponding services of a Grid environment are required in order to make the latter feasible.

In the Technical Description we propose a set of components along with their architectural orientation in order to tackle the technical issues raised by this scenario and enable the adoption of it in any heterogeneous and especially a Grid environment.

Technical Description

Supply Chain Management

As presented above, NGGs offer a set of functionalities that can prove beneficial for the SCM business sector. As describing all the Grid-related aspects of this scenario is out of scope, this section will focus on describing the most important NGG services related to the data management operations. These services were intentionally selected as data comprises the most important resource in the SCM environment, whereas data management comprises a research area with many open issues which however are critical for business applications, such as data replication.

Data Replication Management

Data replication management deals with the creation, registration and management of exact copies of data sets or a part of them with closely related issues comprising replica access and synchronization (Venugopal, Buyya, & Ramamo-

hanarao, 2006). Given the dynamicity of the Grid environment a flexible data replication solution is required. More specifically, the main SCM-related features that need to be taken into account when designing and implementing a data replication management service for the SCM include the *geographical dispersion* of the partners in the supply chain as well as the *great number of users* of the SCM services, the *different roles* and *levels of participation* in the SCM, the large amount of *information exchanged* during daily operation services and the need for *real-time operations* (e.g., order submission, order processing, inventory levels check). These requirements can be translated into the following SCM-related data replication features:

- *Dynamic and automated replica creation and placement* of the most *popular* data; the term 'popular' refers to data that have been accessed many times within a predefined time window (e.g., within the past month). Examples of such data in our scenario include parts of product catalogues of commonly ordered medical products or pending orders' information. The decision for the location of the new replica can be based on a number of factors including:
  - o Geographic distribution of requests to this data; the location preferable is the one closer to the 'area' from which most requests are made.
  - o Available disk space at the target machine
  - o Cost of replica maintenance
  - o Current and expected replica creation requests (*prioritisation*)
  - o Network connection, etc
- *Dynamic replica retirement*; policies are required which will determine when a replica should be deleted; In our scenario, seasonal demand (e.g., due to spring allergies) may significantly increase the order submission requests to the system for some medicine.

Based on the mechanism described above, this will lead to the automatic creation of new replicas for the catalogue information related to these medicines since they considered to be 'popular'. When demand falls to the normal levels for these medicines, the purpose the new replicas were created to serve does not exist any longer and they are deleted. Choosing which replicas will be deleted and when may depend on a number of factors including:

o   Low number of requests to that replica

o   Current and expected replica creation requests which would benefit from replacing the current one.

o   Available disk space at the hosting machine

o   Cost of maintenance makes it unaffordable, etc.

• *Automated real-time replica synchronisation*; as one of the main features of the SCM environment is real-time operation with orders requiring to be processed as soon as possible and notifications of events such as low levels of inventory requiring to be communicated without delay to the interested parties, replica consistency comprises a requirement of high importance. Although work has been done on replica consistency (Guy, Kunszt, Laure, & Stock, 2002; Ranganathan & Foster, 2002; Takizawa, Takamiya, Nakada, & Matsuoka, 2005) real-time solutions – whenever available – significantly lack of performance or fail to operate in real-time. Especially when it comes to database replication, the real-time synchonisation of transactions creates great overload (periodic/lazy synchonisation misses the real-time feature – an essential requirement in the SCM). Apart from network related and database related solutions, an efficient way to achieve real-time operation of the system without compromising the validity

of the data shared among interested parties is to introduce *prioritisation* during replica synchonisation. Choosing the order with which the replicas will be updated (*update prioritisation*) based on a number of factors such as replica popularity, hosting machine capabilities, network bandwidth, etc and redirecting requests to the updated replicas until all replicas have been synchonised can help avoid the excessive overload caused by the great number of data transfering and transaction communication performed for every data/replica update.

The above lead to an NGG Data Replication Management service with *Quality of Service (QoS)-awareness* being its main feature. Although QoS-awareness reinforces the load balancing and the fault tolerance benefits of data replication (requests are redirected to the most 'appropriate' replicas both from the current and expected load as well as from the reliability perspective respectively), still the parameters constituting it should be very carefully considered and selected, so that their monitoring and management doesn't overbalance the performance and afordabilty benefits of the data replication management service.

Cargo Transportation Logistics

As described in the "Business–Technical Analysis of Collaborative Grid Scenarios" section of this chapter, the advantages offered by NGGs can serve the Cargo Transportation Logistics (CTL) scenario. In the following paragraphs we present specific NGG concepts and describe the use of NGG services that can be applied to the CTL scenario. There has to be mentioned that other services offered by NGG environments can also be applied to this scenario. However, we describe the ones of major importance: Dynamic SLAs and Dynamic Policies. Prior to this, we present the Registry component that allows for the storage and later retrieval of pieces of information (in this case SLAs and Policies) in NGG architectures.

Registry

As already mentioned, a registry (Hasselmeyer, 2006) is used to store information for later retrieval. This information may refer to services, security tokens, service level agreements, policies and workflows; while in most cases a registry stores only one kind of information (it could as well store multiple ones). In the transportation logistics scenario, different kinds of registries have been deployed to store different kind of information: services, SLAs and policies. However, a registry is not a single component but consists of different sub-components as follows:

- A storage component, which is used to store the information that registered within the registry.
- A query engine service that allows queries (usually XQueries) to be applied to the stored set of registrations based on the supported query language(s), which are an XML form of SQL (e.g., OWL, RDF) (Baraka, 2004).
- A registry service that acts as the interface to the main registry components that were described above. Therefore, it is a front-end to the registry's functionality.

Based on the registry's description, man can register, update, remove and query on the registry for pieces of information.

Dynamic Service Level Agreements & Policies

Possible combinations of transport both in terms of the transported cargo and of their origin (different cargo providers) as well as unexpected changes in a ship's initial routing require Service Level Agreements to be composed, negotiated, evaluated and monitored in a dynamic way. Each Service Provider (SP) composes SLA Templates (Ludwig, Keller, Dan, King, & Franck, 2003; Wustenhoff, 2002) which are used in order to

negotiate with the users / customers and finally signs the SLAs. These templates include all the terms of an SLA and their main difference is that they are not agreed between the two parties and therefore signed yet.

Furthermore, each SP has a set of policies (Policy Templates). Based on the business model that is applied to the customers of a SP, the latter deploys different policies. In this scenario, policies play a critical role since depending on the market status (e.g. ship owners may change the advertised cost of a transport depending on the cargo and / or the cargo aggregator), a SP may change the policies associated to the SLAs.

In general, policy templates compose a trigger, a condition and a set of actions. The trigger value determines the condition under which a policy will be evaluated. If a policy is evaluated, the condition is considered to determine if the set of actions should be executed and the corresponding actions to be performed. These actions are also defined in the policy templates. A SP may create a set of management policy templates and associate them with SLA templates. There has to be mentioned that a policy template may be applicable to zero or more SLA templates.

When an SLA is signed using a specific SLA template, as a result of an SLA negotiation process, the set of policy templates that are associated with the SLA template are retrieved from the Registry and instantiated by a component: namely Evaluator.

Further on, Figure 3 presents a simplified component model including the major components for the TL scenario (Supervisor, Evaluator, Registry), along with a brief description of them, that enable the provision of the aforementioned features. These components and their architectural orientation follow the NGG design and interaction rules.

Taking into consideration that the main role of the scenario is the SP offering the Decision making mechanism for the Cargo Transport, SLAs have to be signed between the aforementioned SP,

Figure 3. Component model

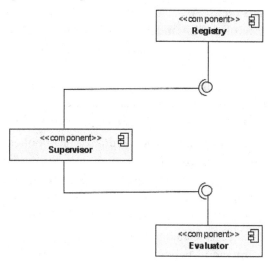

the Ship Owners and the Cargo Aggregators. In order to sign these SLAs the following components are used:

- Supervisor component, which is triggered in order to perform an SLA enactment. The first action of the Supervisor is to obtain all policy templates that relate to the SLA from the SLA template (the SLA Templates are stored in the Registry). Using policy templates the Supervisor finalises the resource set and management policies required to operate and manage the service.
- The Evaluator is configured by management policies that are triggered by events forwarded to the Evaluator. Triggering of these policies may cause actions to be performed.
- The Registry that stores SLA templates and policy templates.

With the use of these components in the Cargo Transportation Logistics scenario the SLAs that are signed between the Ship Owner and the Service Provider (offering the decision making mechanism) are associated with policies which may dynamically change based for example on

the "behaviour" of the Ship Owner (e.g. delivery delays) and which also have an effect on the Cargo Aggregator through the SLAs that are signed between him and the Service Provider. In the example of the delivery delay the corresponding policies will be triggered and the performed actions may include a discount on the agreed cost for this transfer. NGGs with dynamic SLAs and policies offer the required functionality in order to achieve the latter.

Business Analysis

In a world economy that globalisation and competitiveness comprise two of the major driving forces, companies – as they striving for achieving profitability maximization, increasing or maintaining their market share and enabling long-term competitive advantage – are focusing their efforts on improving the bottom line; raising revenues faster than costs. Especially in the supply market these new trends are also translated into rising commodity costs and more complex collaborations among interested parties. Thus, SCM and CTL become two areas were great technological and business advances are required in order for companies to follow the current market trends. The main concern of both of these markets relies on the physical movement of goods. In fact in both sectors one of the main objectives is the minimisation of the order management cycle time both for profitability issues as well as due to the perishable nature and the restricted on-the-shelf lifetime of some goods.

Supply Chain Management

Based on the above and the specific features of the SCM market, in this business sector effort must be put on two directions; management of purchases of direct materials and handling of administration costs as well as costs associated with less strategic tasks. The latter comprises a critical factor for the long term successful and profitable operation of the company, since focusing effort on the actual product is required for meeting constantly rising customer expectations requiring variations of existing products, quicker market launching of new ones and reduced order cycle times (Aberdeen Group, 2006). Moreover, partners participating in the supply chain (suppliers, warehouses, manufacturers) aim at minimizing revenue. In order for companies in the supply chain to achieve the above, they have to prove to be adaptable, innovative, scalable and fast in adopting new trends as well as in processing their tasks.

The rapid growth of large multi-billion dollar markets is not an easy task to accomplish, but according to a new study from analyst firm ARC Advisory Group (Group A. A., 2007) the supply chain execution (SCE) market will actually achieve that. In fact, according to this study the worldwide market for SCE is expected to grow at a compounded annual growth rate (CAGR) of 9.9 percent over the next five years. More specifically, the market was $4.6 billion in 2006 and its forecast for 2011 is over $7.4 billion.

According to Aberdeen Group (2006) the technology sources for the global supply chain technology vary and most companies use a combination of technology sources. In fact this study shows that more than half of respondents rely on in-house developed software, 48% use a best-of-breed license or on-demand application, 39% use their ERP system, and 38% use their freight forwarder's or third-party logistics provider's technology system.

However, most of existing solutions prove unable to support complex collaborations, offer only local order management based on the role in the supply chain which is not integrated with the systems of the other partners, require great effort for the integration with their internal systems or the migration of their current applications to the new ones, or require a huge investment from the companies' behalf – especially Small and Medium-sized Enterprises – to adopt them.

Cargo Transportation Logistics

As mentioned above, seaborne shipping comprises the major transportation mode of international trade. Over the past decades the world fleet has been continuously growing and nowadays includes more than 39,000 ships over 300 gross tons with a total capacity of almost 800 million deadweight tons as of mid-2001 (Christiansen, Fagerholt, & David, 2002). The world fleet consists of ships of various types with oil tankers and bulk carriers constituting almost 73% of the total deadweight capacity (ISL, 2001). A similar increase has taken place in the world's seaborne trade. In fact the world trade in 2002 was estimated to be 5.625 million tons representing comprising a 33% increase during the last decade (Fearnleys, 2002).

Transportation of large cargo volumes between continents is mainly supported by ship transportation. Globalisation trends of the world economy combined with the constantly increasing world population and the rising customer demands force the growth of complex collaborations among geographically dispersed companies. But even *short sea shipping* experiences growth due to great load on road networks and air corridors (Christiansen, Fagerholt, & David, 2002).

The investment required to own and operate a ship is tremendous. Thus the financial impact of improving fleet design and fleet utilization can be significant. It is hence obvious that the adoption of ship routing and scheduling decision support systems by shipping companies can be extremely beneficial. However, this requires combining a large set of data including different types of ships and cargos, their cost structures, demand for shipping services, representative routes for cargo transfer with their cost and time consumption among others. The problem becomes even more complicated when the route between each two ports must be also decided based, for example, on environmental conditions. And as collaborations among partners become more complex and wider the demand for a scalable and reliable

– and yet affordable – infrastructure that is able to support them and the resulting interactions becomes intense.

Business Analysis of the Collaborative Environments

Traditional on-premise applications prove to be unable to efficiently and effectively meet the strong collaboration requirements an SCM or a CTL environment poses and support the high number of daily transactions and orders processing or routing and scheduling requests respectively taking place. At this point Software as a Service (SaaS) model comes to fill in the gaps. Software as a Service (SaaS) solutions (Koenig, Guptill, McNee, & Cassell, 2006) offer an exciting alternative to the expensive and heavy applications of the past. SaaS is a rather recent model in software business which brings radical changes in accessing products. Users are able to combine services and software components from different providers and compose their own services based on their needs and budget. These services can be accessed remotely and they consume resources offered by the Grid Infrastructure based on their SLA agreements. SaaS solutions are easier and faster to deploy, less costly to acquire and maintain, whereas they offer additional functional capabilities that traditional in-house applications can often not provide. The most powerful facts to drive a company to a SaaS Solution include the comparably low cost, the potentially fast deployment and the lower monetary risk (Trumba Corporation, 2007). Therefore SaaS comprises the best way to rollout new technology for large organisations or SMEs.

Despite the above-mentioned advantages of SaaS solutions over traditional software delivery, still considerable disadvantages related to reliability, performance, security, and cost still exist (Kacin, 2006). To be more specific, a number of failure points able to create a service outage exist. In fact, the system may overload during rush

hours system or be down for application upgrades or hardware failure may occur. And what is more, SaaS on-demand applications offer non predictable performance and are not adjusted for the specific needs of the end-users. Moreover, the existence of internal threats (employees able to monitor, analyse and/or process data) and external threats (e.g., hackers) force many organisations to be reluctant in adopting a SaaS solution due to their fear for the cost of compromising their data privacy. Finally, although the pricing model of SaaS is on subscription basis and thus large up-front investment is not required, it proves to be a rather expensive solution in the long term.

However, by taking into advantage the capabilities of a well-defined Grid-based Solution most weaknesses can be eliminated. SaaS providers need to be able to maximise the use of resources in order to deliver an affordable, and yet profitable, solution. Grid Infrastructure can be the way out from this struggle SaaS providers give and still deliver a highly available, reliable and well performing, since it allows the software provider to build their IT architecture from the ground up with the provider being able to maximise the use of aggregated resources such as CPU, memory, storage, bandwidth. SaaS vendors are thus able to accelerate revenue, while at the same time the use of Grid Infrastructure provides an order of magnitude cost saving over owning the infrastructure and associated applications (Armijo, 2007). And what is more, by providing a common infrastructure for data access it allows for the interoperation and collaboration of organisations using different data schemes and platforms.

The business benefits of adopting a Grid-based solution in the SCM and the CTL sectors can be summarised in the following:

- Real(or 'near' real) time data integration and delivery across heterogeneous data sources.
- Ability to analyse real-time (business) data to accelerate decision making (inventory levels

in case of SCM; change in environmental conditions in the route followed by the ship between two ports in the case of CTL)

- Faster end-user access to key business data.
- A single, comprehensive view of the enterprise's information assets.
- Extension of the range of data warehouse querying for better decisions and combine data warehouses query on historic data with query on real-time business data to make better decisions (combining data from different customers within in a specified timeframe for order forecasting in SCM or cargo transportation demand in the case of CTL).
- Optimisation of investments through sharing computational and storage capabilities

Taking into account that a value chain analysis (Porter, 1985) gives the opportunity for better understanding the players/entities in the chain, a condensed view of the Grid value chain (Stanoevs-ka-Slabeva, Talamanca, Thanos, & Zsigri, 2007) for both of the presented scenarios is presented in Figure 4. The main roles identified include the *Resource Provider*, who offers resources (computational, network, data or expertise), the *Grid Middleware Provider*, who provides the Grid middleware, the *Application Provider*, who offers the application (e-Procurement, order forecasting, inventory monitoring etc in case of SCM, ship routing and scheduling in case of CTL), the *Grid Service Provider* who has the expertise to develop and maintain the Grid services for the specific application and integrate the application to the Grid. Figure 4 depicts two different views of the Grid value chain including the above roles. In Figure 4, the Application Provider does not have the resources or the expertise to offer their application as a service and thus the main initiator is the Grid Service Provider who is responsible for delivering the service to the end users, whereas the leading role is taken by the Grid Application

Provider who offers the Grid-enabled application to the end-user as a service.

One of the obvious particularities in the Collaborative Environments is the participation of numerous intermediate or *end-users* with different roles and interest in the provided services. In fact, in such environments the participating entities can also serve the role of the Resource Provider, either by offering part of their computational resources to the Grid Infrastructure or by providing data for the successful operation of the services, enabling and/or reinforcing this way the collaborations established. In the case of SCM, the end-users of the system can be the manufacturers, the suppliers, the distributors, the warehouses, the hospitals, the

Figure 4. Two examples of the Grid value chain in a collaborative environment (a,b)

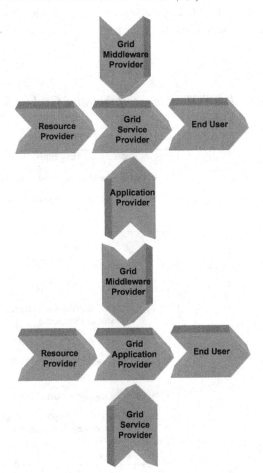

pharmacies, the importers, the exporters among others, whereas in the case of CTL they include the ship owners, and the cargo owners.

CONCERNS, CHALLENGES AND FUTURE TRENDS

Based on the business–technical analysis of the SCM and the CTL scenarios presented above this section will present the related concerns and challenges of these two collaborative environments within the Next Generation Grid environment as well the expected future trends. For this reason initially a common SWOT (Strengths, Weaknesses, Opportunities and Threats) analysis for these two scenarios is presented in Table 1. This table summarises the SWOT factors related to the above described scenarios.

In general, businesses are slow at adopting new IT solutions. In order for enterprises to pro-

ceed with adopting new technologies in general a widely accepted significant financial benefit is required. As it can be easily concluded from this table possibly the most deterring factors for businesses to adopt the new Grid solutions is the lack of successful grid business applications and the difficulty in quantifying the business benefits stemming from the use of the Grid technologies within the Collaborative Environments of SCM and CTL. Moreover, following the SaaS model comprises a considerable transformation for the companies and their customers and a period of adjustment is required. Data privacy is also another important concern since enterprises participating in the collaboration are really concerned about the exposure of their data to other parties over the network or their disclosure to other parties.

From the technological perspective, there are still open issues when it comes to Grid technologies supporting collaborations. Until recently the main focus of these technologies was on compu-

Table 1. SWOT table – collaborative Grid environment in SCM and CTL

Strengths	Weaknesses
Reduced operating expenses	Difficult to quantify the benefits
Operations performance improvement	Companies are unfamiliar with Grid technology
Reduced paperwork / eliminates manual entry	Unwillingness of customers to share their data externally
Opportunities	**Threats**
Increasing market maturity	Reluctance of SMEs to proceed with the adoption of new technology
First mover advantage	Vague presence of Grid application in the market
More efficient distribution increases customer satisfaction	Lack of awareness among possible users
Improved transaction efficiency	Security concerns for commercially
Near real-time analysis of critical business data	confidential data being exposed through an
Growing interest for Grid based	extended network.
applications beyond simply covering excessive computational demands	

tationally intensive applications – serving their initial aim – and thus Grid components offering and supporting job submission and monitoring to computational nodes in the Grid have been well studied and applied both for research and commercial applications. Collaborative environments however, as it has been presented through this chapter, pose new requirements related to efficient data management, user management, data privacy and security, dynamic SLA establishment among others, areas. In collaborative business environments – as the presented ones in this chapter – it is quite common that information comprises one of the most important – if not the most important – resource and thus efficient, reliable and cost-effective data management mechanisms addressing the dynamicity, heterogeneity and autonomy of resources are of great significance. Although feverish research – including numerous European projects such as EGEE (EGEE II, 2008) and OGSA-DAI (OGSA-DAI, 2008) – has taken and still takes place within this field, still many issues remain open. In fact, the main solutions for Grid data management and especially data replication are file-based, whereas they focus on data sharing and exchange for static Virtual Organisations with the new requirements of dynamic Virtual Organisations still not being met (Pacitti, Valduriez, & Mattoso, 2007). Furthermore, data security and privacy still require great improvements boosted by a multidisciplinary approach being the integrated effort of the legal, the business and the technical world before reaching a concrete solution satisfying the stricter business-oriented levels. NGGs – with their clear business orientation – aim at addressing these issues so that these solutions are adopted by businesses after they reach their maturity levels. More technical challenges have been presented in the Technical Analysis paragraph of the scenarios.

Concerning NGG solutions within the SCM field, future technical trends – based on the technical requirements described in the respective paragraph of this book chapter – move towards developing a *QoS-aware dynamic and automatic data replication management framework* able to support real-time operations. Given the fact that the most valuable resource within an SCM collaborative environment is information itself but also the reluctancy of enterprises to share their data for confidentiality reasons, *information security and privacy* issues also are on the top of the priority list for further improvement. In fact, in order to reach a solution able to meet the advanced need for information privacy posed by the business world, this solution must be the resultant of three components; business, legal and technical.

The above analysis of the CTL scenario has shown that *dynamic Service Level Agreement with the associated policies* being dynamically selected based on the combination of different factors/parameters and application *deployment "on the fly"* to specific resources following functional & non functional specifications comprise the two top NGG-related technical trends within this field. With mobility comprising a central aspect of CTL, the application of Mobile Grids into this field also comprises a great technical challenge. According to Litke et al. (2004), Mobile Grid comprises a full inheritor of Grid with its additional trait being its ability to support mobile resources (serving either as a service provider or a service consumer) in a seamless, transparent, secure and efficient way. In the case of CTL, automated services and sensors on the ships can be used in order to provide various kind of information (e.g. current weather conditions). These services and sensors will act as "mobile" nodes in a mobile Grid environment providing the information to the brokering mechanism of the CTL and therefore enabling decision making both to be based on valid information and to take into consideration any unexpected issues that may arise.

Extended work is expected on pricing strategies to be followed for these offered services based on the SaaS model taking into account the varying users of the system and the financial flows among partners within the Grid value chain. Moreover, business aspects of Grid, such as business models, extended value chains and detailed value networks comprise challenging research fields. Among the future trends is also the enrichment of these analyses with mobility issues as well as the development of a legal framework covering issues of informational privacy, identity management and trust within collaborative environments.

CONCLUSION

This book chapter presented two rapidly growing markets – Supply Chain Management and Cargo Transportation Logistics – the future viability and advancement of which strongly depends on the successful and efficient establishment and operation of the cooperation among companies serving similar or different roles within the collaboration but all sharing a common goal; profitability increase. Generic scenarios taken from these two business sectors have been presented emphasizing on the collaboration-related technical requirements and stressing the varying roles within the collaboration which underpin the need for affordable scalability, reliability and robustness; requirements that the Next Generation Grid (NGG) as presented in this book chapter will be able to fulfill. From the technological perspective the greatest challenges include efficient data management with availability, reliability and scalability being the of greatest interest and thus dynamic data replication comprising one of the most active areas and dynamic SLAs and policies, two NGG areas that have been presented within this book chapter.

The business analysis of these two scenarios showed the business need for the adoption of the NGG solutions described and presented the SaaS model as the most appropriate for the commercial exploitation of these applications with the driving forces for this proposal being solution affordability, profitability, fast deployment, low

monetary risk and expandability. The SWOT analysis performed stressed the reluctance of enterprises in adopting new technology as well as transforming their business operations and adopting new business models, whereas the main business and technical challenges and future trends were discussed.

REFERENCES

Anderson, D. L., & Lee, H. (1999). *Synchronized Supply Chains: The New Frontier.* Retrieved July 15, 2008, from http://www.ascet.com/ascet/wp/wpAnderson.html

Armijo, B. (2007). *How Utility Computing Benefits SaaS.* Software & Information Industry Association (SIIA).

Baraka, R. (May 2004). *A Foundation for a Mathematical Web Services Query Language: A Survey on Relevant Query Languages and Tools.* RISC Report Series. University of Linz, Austria.

BEinGRID Project. (2008). Available at: from http://www.beingrid.eu/

Christiansen, M., Fagerholt, K., & David, R. (2002). Ship Routing and Scheduling: Status and Perspectives. *Transportation Service, 38*(1), 1-18.

BEinGRID Consortium. (2008). *BEinGRID - Better Business Using Grid Solutions - Eighteen Successful Case Studies Using Grid.* Retrieved July 15, 2008, from http://www.beingrid.eu/fileadmin/beingrid/pr_folder/Case_Studies/BEinGRID_Case-Studies.pdf

EGEE II. (2008). *Enabling Grids for E-sciencE (EGEE).* Available at: http://www.eu-egee.org/

Epicor. (2005). *Managing Spend in a Distribution Environment: Supplier Relationship Management and the Distribution Enterprise.* Epicor.

Fearnleys. (2002). *Review 2001*. Oslo, Norway: Fearnsearch.

Foster, I., Kesselman, C., & Tuecke, S. (2001). The Anatomy of the Grid:Enabling Scalable Virtual Organizations. *International Journal Supercomputer Applications, 15*(3).

Grant, D. B., Lambert, D. M., Stock, J. R., & Ellram, L. M. (2006). *Fundamentals of Logistics Management: European Edition*. Maidenhead: UK: McGraw-Hill.

Group, A. A. (2007, Aug). *The Supply Chain Execution Market to Grow 10% Annually*. ARC Advisory Group. Retrieved July 15, 2008, from http://www.arcweb.com/AboutARC/Press/Lists/Posts/Post.aspx?List=fe0aa6f8%2D048a%2D418e%2D8197%2D2ed598e42370&ID=19

Group, A. (2006, Sept). *The Lean Supply Chain Report: Lean Concepts Transcend Manufacturing through the Supply Chain*. Aberdeen Group.

Guy, L., Kunszt, P., Laure, E., & Stock, H. (2002). *Replica Management in Data Grids*. Scotland: Global Grid Forum Informational Document, GGF5.

Hasselmeyer, P. (2006). Performance Evaluation of a WS Service Group based Registry. Paper presented at *7th IEEE/ACM International Conference on Grid Computing (Grid 2006)*. Barcelona.

i2. (2005). *i2 Next-Generation Supply Chain Management Overview*. Retrieved July 15, 2008, from i2: http://www.i2.com/assets/pdf/BRO_ng_scm_ovrvw_pds7310.pdf

ISL. (2001). *Shipping Statistics and Market Review*. Institute of Shipping Economics and Logistics.

Kacin, M. (2006). *Got The Enterprise Software Blues? Appliances Come to the Rescue*. KACE Networks.

Koenig, M., Guptill, B., McNee, B., & Cassell, J. (2006). *SaaS 2.0: Software-as-a-Service as Next-Gen Business Platform*. Saugatuck Technology.

Leinberger, W., & Kumar, V. (Oct-Dec 1999). Information Power Grid: The new frontier in parallel computing? *IEEE Concurrency, 7*(4), 75-84.

Litke, A., Skoutas, D., & Varvarigou, T. (2004). Mobile Grid Computing: Changes and Challenges of Resource Management in a Mobile Grid Environment. Paper presented at *Access to Knowledge through Grid in a Mobile World, PAKM 2004 Conference,* Vienna.

Ludwig, H., Keller, A., Dan, A., King, R. P., & Franck, R. (2003, January 28). *Service Level Agreement Language Specification*. Retrieved July 15, 2008, from http://www.research.ibm.com/wsla/WSLASpecV1-20030128.pdf

Next Generation GRIDs Expert Group, (2006). *Future for European Grids: GRIDs and Service Oriented Knowledge Utility*. Next Generation GRIDs Expert Group Report 3. Retrieved July 15, 2008, from ftp://ftp.cordis.europa.eu/pub/ist/docs/grids/ngg3_eg_final.pdf

OGSA-DAI (2008). *The OGSA-DAI Project*. Available at: http://www.ogsadai.org.uk/

Pacitti, E., Valduriez, P., & Mattoso, M. (2007). Grid Data Management: Open Problems and New Issues. *Journal of Grid Computing, 5*(3), 273–281.

Porter, M. E. (1985). *Competitive Advantage*. New York: The Free Press.

Ranganathan, K., & Foster, I. (2002). Decoupling Computation and Data Scheduling in Distributed Data-Intensive Applications. *Proceedings of the 11th IEEE Symposium on High Performance Distributed Computing (HPDC)*. Edinburgh, Scotland.

Ronen, D. (1993). Ship Scheduling: The last decade. *European Journal of Operational Research, 71*(3), 325-333.

Stanoevska-Slabeva, K., Talamanca, C. F., Thanos, G. A., & Zsigri, C. (2007). Development of a

Generic Value Chain for the Grid Industry. *Grid Economics and Business Models, 4th International Workshop, GECON 2007.* LNCS 4685/2007, 44-57. Rennes, France: Springer Berlin.

Takizawa, S., Takamiya, Y., Nakada, H., & Matsuoka, S. (2005). A Scalable Multi-Replication Framework for Data Grid. *Proceedings of the 2005 Symposium on Applications and the Internet Workshops (SAINT-W'05)*. IEEE.

Trumba, C. (2007). *Five Benefits of Software as a Service*. Trumba Corporation.

Tserpes, K., Kyriazis, D., Menychtas, A., & Varvarigou, T. (2008). A Novel Mechanism for Provisioning of High-Level Quality of Service Information in Grid Environments. *Special Issue on Performance Evaluation of QoS-aware Heterogeneous Systems, European Journal of Operational Research, 191*(3), 1113-1131.

Venugopal, S., Buyya, R., & Ramamohanarao, K. (2006). A Taxonomy of Data Grids for Distributed Data Sharing, Management, and Processing. *ACM Computing Surveys, 38*(1).

Wustenhoff, E. (2002). *Service Level Agreement in the Data Center*. Sun Professional Services. Sun BluePrints™ OnLine.

Chapter IV
Semantics–Based Process Support for Grid Applications

Gayathri Nadarajan
University of Edinburgh, UK

Areti Manataki
University of Edinburgh, UK

Yun-Heh Chen-Burger
University of Edinburgh, UK

ABSTRACT

The infrastructure of Grid is approaching maturity and can be used to enable the utilisation and sharing of large scale, remote data storages through distributed computational capabilities and support collaborations and co-operations between different organisations. Grid can therefore be suitably used to support the creation and running of a virtual organisation (VO). However, to assist the smooth operation of VOs, robust computational and storage facilities alone are not sufficient. There must also exist appropriate rich business infrastructure. In this chapter, the authors consider business process frameworks that utilise semantics-based business process modelling (BPM) technologies, and they illustrate the multidisciplinary nature of our approach by applying them to three different fields: Supply Chain Management, Business Intelligence and Knowledge Management, and Intelligent Video Analysis. They aim to show that these three application areas that incorporate semantics-based BPM methods could be used to support developing Grid applications, and to subsequently support VOs.

Copyright © 2009, IGI Global, distributing in print or electronic forms without written permission of IGI Global is prohibited.

INTRODUCTION

The Grid was envisioned to support collaboration between researchers who are not physically co-located. Thus, more sophisticated technologies and infrastructure are required to support flexible collaborations and computations between communicating e-Scientists. Current efforts which include the rapid development of Grid applications, however, lack to provide a high degree of easy-to-use and seamless automation that would allow such effective collaborations on a global scale (De Roure, Jennings & Shadbolt, 2005). Key requirements and technologies have been identified with respect to the pertaining gaps in existing Grid efforts. These include, among others, process description and enactment (e.g. workflows), information integration (e.g. Semantic Web technologies) and the use of ontologies and reasoning mechanisms. We attempt to address these key areas by incorporating traditional Business Process Modelling (BPM) methods which are rich in modelling aspects and in infrastructure.

We aim to show that BPM methods provide a suitable foundation to capture the process dynamics of an organisation, and when these methods are enhanced with semantics they could be used for the effective development of Grid applications that subsequently support VOs. The rest of the chapter is organised as follows. The *Background* section provides an overview of VO and Grid, enterprise and business process modelling and the different existing paradigms for activity modelling; the *Case Studies* section provides the context for the intelligent support in the fields of Supply Chain Management, Business Intelligence and Knowledge Management, and Automatic Video Processing with Grid Workflows using our proposed approach; the *Discussion* section discusses the relevance of our work to Grid applications and the last section concludes the chapter.

BACKGROUND

In this section, we present an overview of Virtual Organisation and Grid, Enterprise and Business Process Modelling and the paradigms for activity modelling. This will provide a background and motivation for the work before the case studies are presented in the next section.

Virtual Organisation and Grid

A Virtual Organisation (VO) is defined as a set of individuals or institutions that wish to share resources in a controlled and coordinated way (Foster & Kesselman, 2004). The sharing not only involves files and data, but also software, equipment and human skills. In this way closer collaboration is enabled for the achievement of shared common goals. It has been argued that the VO paradigm will undoubtedly come to play a major role in the theory and practice of management (Mowshowitz, 2002, p. 25). In fact, business experts state that currently competition is not between different enterprises but between different enterprise networks. Similarly, collaboration among different scientific groups and governmental organisations is crucial, thus signifying the era of VOs.

Issues in VO-related research include: i) trust and security, ii) the computing infrastructure, and iii) the capturing of the highly dynamic processes involved. Trust and cultural problems within the VO are studied mostly by business and information systems researchers. The Grid is suggested as the most suitable infrastructure for the emerging VOs; in fact, Foster and Kesselman adapt their first, computing-oriented definition of the Grid (Foster & Kesselman, 1998) to the era of VOs, as they consider relevant social and policy issues (Foster & Kesselman, 2004). Lately there is an increasing interest in a more encompassing view of VOs, including engineering management aspects such as knowledge management (Katzy & Löh, 2003). In this, the capturing of highly dynamic VO processes, the so-called "virtual operations", is considered to be crucial. We regard semantics-based BPM methods as a useful means for capturing these processes while allowing their use in the Semantic Web.

Enterprise and Business Process Modelling

The aim of applying an Enterprise Modelling (EM) method is to seek ways to improve an organisation's effectiveness, efficiency and profitability. EM methods are typically informal or semi-formal. They provide notations that enable entrepreneurs to describe aspects of their business operations. The notation is normally complemented with semi-formal or natural language descriptions which allow details of the business operations to be described.

Many EM methods have emerged to describe and redesign businesses, namely business process modelling, business system modelling and organisational context modelling methods. BPM methods are able to formally express informally practised procedures. More importantly, actions and effects of these processes can be demonstrated using simulation techniques. Some examples of BPM method representations include Process Specification Language (PSL) (Schlenoff et al., 1997), Integration DEFinition Language (IDEF3) (Mayer et al., 1995), extended UML's Activity Diagram (Rumbaugh et al., 2004) and Petri-Nets (Reisig, 1985). In the course of half a decade ago, new process languages and models have been developed to promote the understanding and interoperability of process semantics over the Web, with the extensibility of operating over the Semantic Web. They are characterised by XML and XML-based languages, such as the Resource Description Framework (RDF) (Klyne & Carroll, 2004) and the Web Ontology Language (OWL) (McGuiness & van Harmelen, 2004). Some of these languages include Business Process Execution Language for Web Services

(BPEL4WS, 2003), BPML (Arkin, 2002), Web Service Ontology (OWL-S) (Martin, 2006), and more recently, Web Service Modeling Ontology (WSMO) (Roman et al., 2005).

BPM technologies are established enterprise modelling methods that can be used to describe complex, informal domains. Their role within an organisation is to seek ways to improve its effectiveness, efficiency and profitability. BPM methods provide notations which enable entrepreneurs to describe aspects of their business operations. The notation is normally complemented with semi-formal or natural language descriptions which allow details of the business operations to be described. More importantly, actions and effects of these processes can be demonstrated using simulation techniques. Utilising BPM methods within emerging fields such as the Grid would prove useful as they could assist in providing a more mature framework incorporating both business- and semantics-specific technologies. This will be demonstrated by the application of semantics-based BPM methods in three fields that will be introduced in the next section.

One example BPM language is Fundamental Business Process Modelling Language (FBPML) (Chen-Burger & Stader, 2003) which is an inherited, specialised and combined version of several standard modelling languages. FBPML has two sections to provide theories and formal representations for describing processes and data: the Data Language (FBPML-DL) and the Process Language (FBPML-PL). FBPML-DL is first-ordered and describes the data model or ontology in Prolog-like predicate syntax. FBPML-PL is both formal and visual. Its constructs are composed using FBPML-DL plus its specific vocabularies for describing processes, events, actions, conditions, life cycle status and communication facilities. Thus, although FBPML contains separate means to describe data and process, the data model may be used as a construct in the process language; as such it is a fully integrated BPM language.

The main aim of FBPML is to provide support

for virtual organisations which are becoming more and more pervasive with the advancement of Web and Grid technologies. It ultimately seeks to provide distributed knowledge and semantics-based manipulation and collaboration. Most importantly, people with different responsibilities and capabilities could work together to accomplish tasks and goals without technological or communication barriers caused by the differences in their roles.

As Semantic Web-based languages such as OWL-S and BPEL4WS are procedural-based and cannot be directly used for logical reasoning, we wish to provide a neutral ground for such capability. One way of achieving this is by incorporating the more mature and established BPM methods in these emerging technologies. FBPML is goal-directed and exportable to Semantic Web-based languages, e.g. BPEL4WS (Guo et al., 2004) and OWL-S (Nadarajan & Chen-Burger, 2007). Hence, integrating FBPML with technologies such as ontologies would provide for rich semantics that is suitable to be used in a Grid context to support reasoning, analysis and flexibility of virtual organisations.

To this end, several efforts have been made to bridge the gap between EM methods and Semantic Web services. The notion of Semantic Business Process Management (SBPM) (Hepp et al., 2005) was proposed to utilise semantic capabilities within business process technologies in one consolidated technology. This is motivated by the limited degree of mechanisation within BPM methods which could be supplemented by Semantic Web service frameworks. The problem is understood at ontological level and a technology for querying and manipulating the process space is suggested. SBPM includes Semantics-Based Business Process Modelling, thus semantically annotated process models, which may facilitate semantics-based discovery of process fragments and auto-completion of process models (Wetzstein et al., 2007, p. 10). A different approach is adopted by Betz et al. (2006), who introduce a semantic description of Petri Nets with OWL DL. Finally,

Tripathi and Hinkelmann (2007) introduce a change management system that, among others, will translate the OWL-S specification of business processes to BPEL4WS.

We now turn our attention to the different paradigms taken to model activities and show how the one that we have adopted is relevant for the provision of semantics-based support for Grid applications.

Overview of the Paradigms for Activity Modelling

The different types of activity modelling paradigms are often distinguished based on their modelling objectives in capturing and emphasising the different types of domain objects during their modelling procedure. The most popular ones are: process-, data- and agent-centric. A process-centric approach treats the process (how things are done) as the first class modelling primitive over other modelling objects. It describes processes and their relationships as their main focus and often in great detail. A data-centric approach treats data (information on what is being manipulated by processes) as the first class primitive over processing. In this approach, data items and their relationships are explicitly represented as main modelling objects. Similarly, an agent-centric model treats agents as the main modelling objects.

This is analogous to the imperative versus declarative approaches. The data-centric approach allows large collections of data to be processed and passed between different components of a system and is primarily concerned with optimising the data flow between these components, e.g. functions within a scientific workflow. The process-centric approach is more concerned with the low-level achievement of the functions or tasks within an activity. Both these approaches capture the mechanistic components of an activity. On the other hand, an agent-centric approach captures specific aspects of the human component or software agent within the system, thus focuses on understanding an agent's roles, involvements, competence and collaboration with other agents in their tasks. This approach is useful in a distributed environment where the aim is to achieve a flexible mechanism to allow collaborative decision-making or task-achievements. In the following sub-section, we provide an example to discuss the applicability of the first two paradigms in relation to our work.

A Discussion: Process- vs. Data-Centric Modelling Approaches

When considering the approach taken by our framework, it is appropriate to discuss process- and data-oriented paradigms for modelling the activities in our applications, specifically in workflow systems. As mentioned before, the former treats processing (how things are done) as the first class primitive over data; while the latter treats data (what is being manipulated) as the first class primitive over processing. One may argue that scientific workflows are specialised for data-intensive applications where the flow of data takes precedence over the way the processes are manipulated. This implies that the sequence of steps taken to achieve the goal of the workflow execution is fixed. Figure 1 illustrates this.

Suppose the goal is to transform Data 1 to Data 4 (shown in Figure 1(a)). Figure 1(b) shows how this data transfer is achieved via two fixed processes, Process 2 and Process 3. If the workflow is fixed as such, then the main concern would be to optimise the data transfer between the two processes. Many data-intensive workflows op-

erate in this manner, for instance workflows for Bioinformatics applications. Figure 1(c) shows how the goal is achieved via a combination of a variable number of processes. In this case, the workflow is not fixed.

Our approach has focused on this aspect of workflow construction due to the nature of the problem we are trying to solve, e.g. a video processing task may be achieved using several different combinations of steps. When the workflow is not fixed, the concern would be to optimise the sequence of processes involved, which is to select the set that minimises the cost of achieving the overall goal. Thus by manipulating the way things are done, even for a large dataset, one could also optimise the way the data transfer takes place. Prioritising processing over data does not imply that the data is not of concern. By focusing on the techniques applied to the data, one is also implicitly giving importance to the data because the methods extract useful information from the videos. Thus the process-oriented approach complements the data-oriented approach. Similarly, process-centric approaches may also be used to help optimise processes in a Virtual Organisation to enhance performance of internal and external organisational collaborations, or to provide additional information to help knowledge consolidation and extraction in a complex distributed organisational context. In our example, we demonstrate how traditional BPM methods may be used to enact scientific workflows, workflow automation and optimisation and knowledge management in a distributed environment such as the Internet or Grid.

In the next section we demonstrate how semantics-based BPM technologies could be used

Figure 1. Data-centric (b) versus process-centric (c) approaches

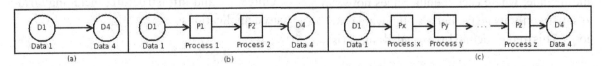

to provide intelligent support for Grid applications and VOs by presenting our work in three application areas.

CASE STUDIES

We now present three case studies where semantics-based BPM technologies are utilised. For each case study, the introduction and motivations are first presented, followed by the content of the work done.

Case Study 1: SCM and VO: The Need for a Knowledge-Based Approach

Supply Chain Management (SCM) is perceived as both an emergent field of practice and an emerging academic domain (Storey et al., 2006), and its role has growing importance in today's business world. From a purely operational approach of the 1960s we can now detect a more strategic one, where alignment, integration, collaboration and agility are seen as desirable characteristics of a supply chain (Storey et al., 2006; Chandra & Kumar, 2000; Tan, 2001). Hence, SCM is defined today as "the integration of key business processes from end user through original suppliers that provides products, services and information that add value for customers and other stakeholders" (Lambert & Cooper, 2000, p. 65).

In the knowledge and globalisation era, enterprises are expected to collaborate in order to gain competitive advantage; it has been argued that companies today are competing not only through their product range but also through their supply chains (Harrison & van Hoek, 2008; Lambert & Cooper, 2000; Tan, 2001). Thus enterprises form supply chains (SC) that are tightly connected and flexible, where each member does not wish to satisfy only its goals, but also the whole SC's goals. This trend is defined as extended enterprise,

which is "a kind of enterprise represented by all organisations or parts of organisations, customers, suppliers and sub-contractors, engaged collaboratively in the design development, production and delivery of a product to the end customer" (Browne & Zhang, 1999, p. 31).

One can clearly see that SCM and extended enterprises are closely related to virtual organisations and virtual enterprises specifically. As Storey et al. (2006) state, there is a shift of SCM to a collaborative model and virtuality, two basic characteristics of virtual organisations. Furthermore, Kangilaski (2005) views VOs as a SC strategy, while Browne and Zhang (1999) illustrate the similarities and differences of extended and virtual enterprises.

Our work on knowledge-based analysis of supply chain strategies is motivated by the increasing importance of SCM, and it intends to serve as a vehicle for insight into and comparison of different supply chain strategies. While most of the literature covers supply chain strategies and practices in a theoretical way, we suggest analysis at a lower level. We thus view semantics-based Business Process Modelling as a useful methodology for capturing SC strategies, and we suggest the use of a declarative workflow engine for the simulation of such business process models. The simulation results can be used when comparing different SC strategies, thus assisting further SCM analysis.

In our work we argue that knowledge-based techniques can be useful for the analysis of SC strategies. Given the strong relation between SCM and VO, we believe that the suggested framework presented in the section *Knowledge-Based Analysis for SCM* can also be applied in the case of a virtual organisation. Hence, BPM and simulation can assist in the decision-making procedure on the development of VO-related architecture and infrastructure, including Grid-based applications.

Knowledge-Based Analysis for SCM

Processes are perceived as the prevailing unit of organisational analysis (Adamides & Karacapilidis, 2006); similarly, business process models provide an abstraction of business strategies, and hence supply chain strategies. We recognise FBPML as a useful modelling language within our framework, as it has rich visual modelling methods and formal semantics, and it supports workflow system development. We also suggest a *cyclic modelling framework* for the development of a BPM that captures a firm's supply chain strategies. The framework is initiated with the identification of existing models and data from the organisational environment that are relevant to business and SC strategies. The second step involves the evaluation of the existing model and the detection of gaps. If no gaps are found, then the existing model is satisfactory and it constitutes the final BPM. Otherwise the modeller needs to deal with the gaps found and then to improve the existing BPM to create a new version, which is provided as input for the next cycle of the modelling procedure. The modelling framework is ended when no gaps are identified during the evaluation procedure. The relevant decision is made on the following four *evaluation criteria*: soundness, completeness, realism and level of detail of the model. Hence, the respective four questions are asked when evaluating a BPM: 1) Is it correct according to the modelling specification and does it behave correctly? 2) Does it cover all important SC strategies of the firm? 3) Does it correspond to correct business and SC strategies of the firm? 4) Is it abstract enough to provide an overview of the firm's SC strategies and detailed enough to provide interesting information?

After the development of a BPM that provides insight into a firm's SC strategies, we suggest its simulation with an appropriate *workflow engine*. We have designed and implemented such a meta-interpreter adopting a declarative approach. The workflow engine is business context sensitive, calculating the total duration and cost of a BPM execution (in the user defined time and cost units). Its architecture is described by three main components: a process model specification, a world state description and the workflow engine algorithm, all specified using logics. When the workflow engine is fed with a BPM and an initial world state description, the algorithm is activated and execution begins; throughout execution the workflow and world states are updated, and a relevant record is kept, while real-time feedback is provided to the user. An example for a process model specification is provided at the end of this section for the case study of Dell, while the predicates describing the entities and data of the world state are the following:

```
entity_occ(EntityName, EntityId, EntityAttribute).
data(SubjectID, Subject, Attributes).
```

The algorithm of the workflow engine has been implemented in Prolog, and an abstraction is provided below in pseudo code. We should briefly mention that time is treated explicitly, and in each time point the following sub-steps take place: actions scheduled for that time point are applied, junctions are checked for execution and are processed, and processes are checked for and are executed. The BPM stops execution at the time point when the finish junction has been reached, and no process is in execution, and no event is scheduled to fire the execution of some process at some later time point. The ActionsAgenda is a list with pairs of actions and time points at which they are scheduled, while the ProcessedList is a repository of junctions and processes that have been executed, thus keeping track of the internal workflow state.

1. Read the process model and initial world state.
2. Initialize the internal state of the workflow engine:
   ➢ Set T=0.
   ➢ Instantiate the **ActionsAgenda** to an empty list.

> Instantiate the **ProcessedList** to an empty list.

3. Execute scheduled actions:
   > Search **ActionsAgenda** for actions with firetime=T.
   > Execute them.

4. Check the process model for junctions to execute:
   > Search the process model for junctions whose execution semantics are satisfied.
   > Execute them at once and move them to the **ProcessedList**.

5. Check the process model for processes to execute:
   > Search the process model for processes whose triggers and preconditions are satisfied.
   > Calculate their completion time and move them to the **ProcessedList**.
   > Move their actions to the **ActionsAgenda** and schedule them to be fired at their completion time.

6. Check for completion of the process model execution:
   > If the finish-junction is in the **ProcessedList** and there is no process in the **ProcessedList** with completion time bigger than T and no event is expected in the future to trigger some process instance, then return T and the total cost of the processes in the **ProcessedList** and halt.
   > Else go to 7.

7. Set T=T+1. Go to 3.

The simulation of a firm's BPM that provides an insight into its SC strategies could serve the further analysis of its SCM practices. We suggest two types of experiments. The first involves the optimisation of the BPM by parallelising two or more sequenced processes, thus decreasing the duration of the BPM execution. The second deals with the comparison of the detected SC strategies with alternative ones. This can be done by creating a BPM for the alternative SC strategies, by simulating it and comparing the simulation results to the ones of the investigated firm. The advantage of this framework is that the difference between alternative SC strategies can be made clearer when comparing BPMs rather than when comparing theoretical issues.

We have applied the suggested framework for knowledge-based analysis and modelling of SC strategies on the *case study of Dell*, a PC company that owes a big part of its success to its supply chain strategies. The two most important points of its strategies are the direct model (i.e. direct sales to all customer segments) and the build-to-order strategy, which means that a computer is built only after a relevant order has been placed. In fact, Dell places high importance in its relation with its key suppliers and customers and aims to virtually integrate with the most important ones through ValueChain.Dell.com, Premier Pages and Platinum Councils (Dell & Fredman, 2006). So Dell adopts, to some extent, the VO approach, a fact that makes this successful case very interesting to investigate.

While most of the literature covers Dell's SC strategies from a theoretical viewpoint, we have applied the suggested modelling and analysis framework, satisfying the need for an analysis at a lower level. Hence, following the cyclic modelling framework we have developed a BPM for Dell that provides an insight into its SC strategies, and which is strategic, business-goal-oriented and executable (Manataki, 2007). The initial input for the cyclic modelling framework was the MIT Process Handbook (MIT, n.d.) entry on the decomposition of the process "Dell-Create Computers to Order" (MIT Process Handbook), as well as SCM-related literature that covers the successful case of Dell. The cyclic modelling framework has led to a three-phased modelling procedure for Dell: The first BPM was the one implied by the MIT Process Handbook; this was enriched with sequence details about the processes, providing us with the second BPM version, which was later enhanced by incorporating SCM-related infor-

Figure 2. Decomposition of "sell directly to large business and public sector customers"

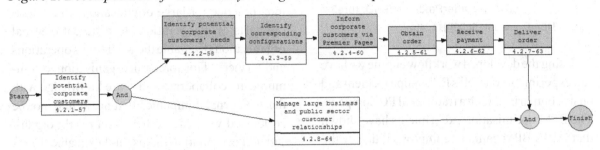

Figure 3. Decomposition of "buy standard item to order"

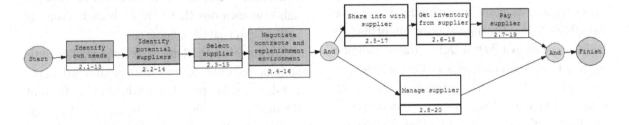

mation, leading to the final BPM for Dell. Two example processes of the final BPM that provide an insight into Dell's SC strategies can be seen in Figures 2 and 3.

Let us now explain the rationale and the logical specification of Figure 2. The presented process decomposition illustrates Dell's direct sales strategy adapted to the corporate customer segment. As mentioned previously, it is strategic, thus it aims to provide us with structured information about Dell's direct sales strategy, rather than focus on operational details. We should mention that the first process 4.2.1 is further decomposed into two sequential processes, "Identify key personnel" and "Identify employee groups", and process 4.2.8 is decomposed into the parallel processes "Support large business and public sector customers" and "Get feedback from large business and public sector customers". The further decomposition of the latter two makes clear the use of Premier Pages, Account Teams and Platinum Councils for the desired virtual integration (Manataki, 2007). The logical specification of the examined process model as seen in Figures 2 and 3 consists of the

junctions' and processes' description. A formal representation that describes the control structure of the process model in Figure 2 is provided below using the junction/3 predicate (where process IDs are used instead of their full names). The predicate process/7 is used to give process descriptions as included in Figure 2.

junction(JunctionType, PreProcesses, PostProcesses).

junction(start, [], [p4_2_1]).
junction(and_split, [p4_2_1], [p4_2_2, p4_2_8]).
junction(link, [p4_2_2], [p4_2_3]).
junction(link, [p4_2_3], [p4_2_4]).
junction(link, [p4_2_4], [p4_2_5]).
junction(link, [p4_2_5], [p4_2_6]).
junction(link, [p4_2_6], [p4_2_7]).
junction(finish_and, [p4_2_7, p4_2_8], []).

process(ProcessID, ProcessName, Trigger, Precond, Action, Duration, Cost).

process(p4_2_6, receivePayment,
[exist(event_occ(customerOrder)), exist(event_occ(customerPayment))],

[exist(entity_occ(customerPremierPage))],
[create_data(customerOrderPaid, [orderID_tbre34,
ccID_c3154a, amount_5000])], 1, 40).

Using the developed workflow engine we have run experiments on Dell's BPM improvement and on its comparison with a traditional PC company. The BPM optimisation experiments have shown that Dell's BPM cannot be improved, unless the semantics of the processes are changed. The SC strategies' comparison of Dell with a traditional PC company involved the creation of a BPM for the latter, and its simulation with the declarative workflow engine. The simulation results of the two BPMs have shown that: i) Dell's strategic choice of direct sales guarantees a faster and cheaper sales procedure ii) Dell's choice of buying to order and virtually integrating with its suppliers results in higher cost and time values in the case of a new supplier, but it leads to shorter duration than that of a traditional PC company on the long run (Manataki, 2007).

The main lesson learnt from the use of BPM and simulation on Dell's case is the fact that knowledge-based techniques can help extract essence of SCM's operations and assist the analysis and comparison of different supply chain strategies therefore constructing arguments to support or criticise certain SCM strategies. The presented BPM provides a logically structured view on Dell's SC strategies, and the conducted experiments with the use of the developed workflow engine allow us to structurally compare different SC strategies. Since VOs can be regarded as a specific case of SCM, we believe that the suggested framework for SCM could also be useful when analysing a VO constitution or when developing or improving Grid technologies for supporting VOs.

Case Study 2: Business Intelligence and Knowledge Management

Large enterprises today are virtual organisations that their sub-organisations are distributed across different parts of the world. In addition, it is common practice for large organisations to contract out parts of its operations to different external organisations to enable the whole of its operations and services. This forces an organisation to communicate, collaborate and share knowledge with these external companies that again may not be co-located with each other. As a result, organisational information that is vital to enable the efficient and effective running of an organisation's operations and to sustain its continuous growth is inevitably distributed in all of the cooperated sub-organisations that may be both internal as well as external to the company.

To make the problem worse, important organisational information may be tacit knowledge, i.e. not described explicitly anywhere in the form of documentation, and it may only be known locally, making it difficult to be gathered accurately and in a timely fashion. This means that it will not be a trivial task to gain an accurate overview of an organisation when it is needed to support important decision-making processes. To overcome this problem, personal knowledge and past experiences, educational guess and ad-hoc approaches are often employed that may be error-prone and deployed in an inconsistent manner.

Such difficulties stem from the problem of not being able to gain quality information and turn them into appropriate knowledge when needed. To address these important issues, Knowledge Management (KM) methodologies suggest to use a set of conceptual models to help capture relevant information; while offering a structural process whose aim is to help turn relevant information into usable knowledge and provide it to the end user *at the right time, presented in the right form and provided to the right people,* therefore helping them in doing their tasks and achieving overall organisational goals (Schreiber et al., 2000).

Moreover, business intelligence (BI) techniques may be used in conjunction with KM by utilising a holistic reasoning framework that allows one to carry out business motivated analysis based on knowledge already stored in those models, by leveraging knowledge technologies. In this approach, important aspects of an organisation are identified and described in individual models using appropriate modelling methods. These models can also be modified over time as the organisation evolves. Information described in those models is often used together to create a coherent overview of the organisation and to support business-goal oriented enquiries.

In this chapter, we describe a modelling framework that records three important aspects of an organisation: the Actor, Data and Process (ADP) aspects. These are the three corner stones of the domain knowledge of any (virtual) organisation. In this approach, each aspect is captured in a model using an appropriate modelling method and objects described in those models are formally defined in an underlying (formal) ontology. Because common concepts of different models are defined in the same ontology, relevant knowledge stored in different models can be related to each other, thus promotes knowledge sharing between these models. It also enables the derivation of new knowledge through cross-examination of different models.

This modelling framework therefore allows us to answer several types of business and knowledge management related questions that are frequently asked in an organisation, e.g. who created the data, who maintains the information, who authorised the operation, what is the impact of an operation, how critical is a dataset or an operation, etc. This line of work is therefore relevant to anyone who wishes to build a VO over the Grid or (a controlled) Internet, as it provides simple access to critical knowledge and an overview over the different components of a complex VO.

An Integrated Actor, Data and Process-Oriented (ADP) Approach

To support today's knowledge economy, an appropriately designed Organisational Memory must closely support organisational operations and its business aims. To address these needs, we combine the use of the ONA (Ontology Network Analysis) method that provides an analytical framework for data analysis together with two other modelling methods (Role, Activity and Communication Diagram (RACD) modelling and a semantics-based BPM method – FBPML) to capture and analyse the three important aspects of an organisation – data, human and operational aspects. The closely combined use of these three methods allows us to create an integrated ADP modelling and reasoning framework.

The ONA approach deals mostly with the data aspects of the domain – it systematically works out the relationships and builds structure between domain concepts based on their attributes. The RACD is a role modelling method that captures the human aspect of a (virtual) organisation, including the hierarchical and functional relationships between them. A rich semantics-based BPM method using FBPML is also presented that captures the operational aspect of an organisation that is linked with the data and actor aspects. In this approach, an underlying ontology is utilised to allow data exchange and knowledge integration between the different aspects of an organisation, thus allowing its user to ask complex questions that needs knowledge existing in different parts of a VO (Chen-Burger & Kalfoglou, 2007).

Figure 4 gives example models that may be created and used as a part of modelling initiatives using the ADP framework. Figure 4(a) gives a part of the domain ontology created for the US Air Operations where concepts, terminologies and the relationships between them are defined. Common concepts and terminologies used in different models are defined in the ontology, so that different models may communicate with each other (knowledge sharing) through this ontology. To enable automated knowledge sharing and derivation, a common formal language is used to represent this ontology. User queries may also make use of terminologies defined in the ontology

Figure 4. Example models used in the ADP framework – these are models developed for the domain of US Air Operations

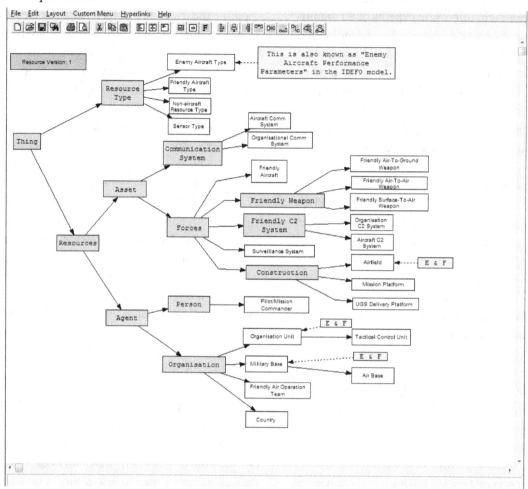

(a) Resource Ontology

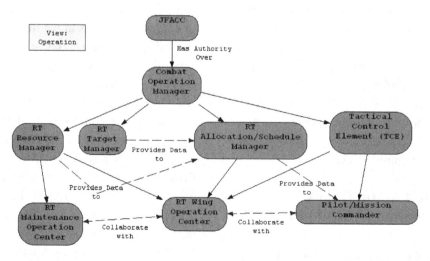

(b) RACD Role Model

continued on following page

Figure 4. continued

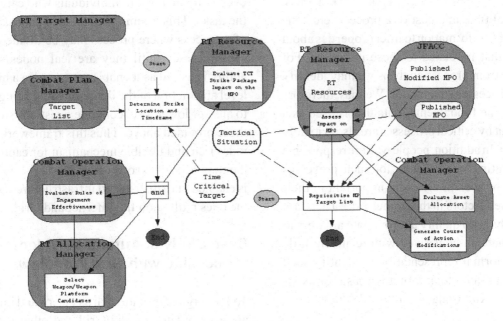

(c) Activity Model

for communicating with the system; and answers to those queries may also be provided based on those concepts and vocabularies, although they may have been derived from a combined examination of several diagrams from different models.

Figure 4(b) is a diagram that is a part of the RACD Role Model where roles of personnel involved in the air operations as well as the relationships between these roles are defined. In this diagram, formal and informal "Influences" over roles are presented as links within the VO and the information flow between them are also defined. Note that those roles may be decomposed into more detailed roles, when appropriate. Roles that are used in RACD are also being used (consistently) in other models, so that different models overlap with each other, thus enable knowledge sharing and integration between them.

Figure 4(c) gives an activity model where personnel and data information are included in the context of organisational operations. This combined description includes information that already exists in other models, i.e. the ontology and RACD role model, enables one to draw more comprehensive conclusions regarding an organisation's operations: such as who carries out what operations, how they interact with each other and what information is used as a part of their activities. As data is included as a part of activity descriptions, new relationships between data can be derived via relationships between activities. At the same time, new relationships between processes may also be discovered via the relationships between data that are defined elsewhere (e.g. in an ontology). One can use these new linkages between data and activities to derive dependencies, relationships and detect inconsistencies between different data items, between activities and between data and activities - even where related data and processes may be originally defined in remote parts of different models (Chen-Burger & Robertson, 2005).

When adding typical business process analysis information to the model, such as the frequency of a process execution (as normally carried out in an organisation), the criticality of a process, the typical time and cost of a process, etc., one may use this information to infer properties about the data that is related to those processes. For example, from process analysis we may identify critical processes in a model. We may therefore infer that the fundamental data that is used as a main input by critical processes are also critically important. In addition, people who are responsible for generating main results for such processes may also be seen as critically important in their roles (called Actors in the framework). These are reasonably good quality approximate answers to queries that can be derived with relatively little effort. A formal representation to identify such critical data and actor information based on existing process knowledge is provided below:

$$\forall P, D. \; criticalProcess(P) \wedge mainInput(D, P) \rightarrow criticalData(D).$$

$$\forall P, A. \; criticalProcess(P) \wedge mainActor(A, P) \rightarrow criticalActor(A).$$

Other example queries that the ADP framework may help answer are: "Who created these data items?", "What process(es) created them?", "How are they being used?" and "Who uses them?", "Where are they being stored", "How are they being stored" and "What are the frequencies that those data items are being used and in what operational context", "How critical are those data items?" and ultimately "What are the impacts of those data and processes to the enterprise?". A carefully combined ADP approach can provide good approximate answers to most of these questions.

What is also interesting is that since a VO may include several sub- and external organisations, the roles and activities described in the models may therefore be cross-organisational. It may therefore be necessary to give a higher level view of the functions in the (virtual) organisation. In RACD,

roles may be decomposed into sub-roles which are eventually mapped to individuals who carry out the tasks. This is similar to the decomposability of a process where process may be divided into sub-processes until they are leaf nodes. Such ability is useful as it enables one to give a higher level abstraction of the domain; while being able to answer lower level concrete questions such as those provided above. Thus this framework provides rich and flexible mechanism for capturing the complex context of a Virtual Organisation that is enabled via a distributed infrastructure such as the ones built upon the Internet and Grid.

Case Study 3: Automatic Video Processing with Grid Workflows

Today, large scale data such as videos and images are accumulated on the Grid and other similar storages, but not analysed in an efficient manner. Manual processing would prove to be impractical, thus effective automated mechanisms should be in place to allow such analyses to be conducted more efficiently. With Grid technology, there should be provisions to allow image processing applications or programs across distributed locations to access these data via a Grid middleware. Grid workflows could provide automation to tackle this problem, with a centralised management system that could coordinate the execution of the applications. This would mean that a user in one location can invoke applications from remote machines in different locations. However, the user may not have enough expertise to determine which application this is, e.g. a marine biologist wishing to analyse videos of underwater marine life is not able to determine the image processing function calls to do so.

Automatic workflow composition would be ideal for this purpose, i.e. one that doesn't require the end-user to know which image processing application to invoke but that does it automatically for them. This would support collaboration between different e-Scientists, such as domain experts, computer scientists and non-technical users. This is challenging because it is inherently difficult to capture the functionality of the workflow components and their data types based on user input alone. Existing Grid workflows such as Pegasus (Deelman et al., 2005), Kepler (Ludäscher et al., 2006), Taverna (Oinn et al., 2005) and Triana (Taylor et al., 2003) play a major force in realising Grid applications. However, they are still largely composed manually, that is the user will need to describe the components of the workflow either graphically or by other means. Triana is a visual workflow system that allows the user to create workflows by the use of drag-and-drop. Taverna is another system that helps biologists and bioinformaticians to compose workflows manually in a graphical manner. Kepler is a highly reliable system that is particularly useful for workflows with complex tasks, however it does not do this automatically. Pegasus is a configurable system that can map and execute complex workflows on the Grid, used in a range of applications. It has the capability of composing workflows automatically from a user- or automatically-generated abstract workflow. However, this provision is still limited because Pegasus does not support all the modelling primitives required for vision tasks (e.g. loops) and does not manipulate the extensive use of semantics-based technologies. Lack of automated workflow composition is an obstacle that needs to be addressed. We propose a semantics-based workflow enactment framework to support naive users who need to use specialised or technically-difficult-to-understand tools.

BPM and Intelligent Video Analysis

Semantics-based BPM workflow enactment could provide a suitable support to overcome some of the gaps pertaining to Grid-based applications. In this scenario, we investigate its application in providing intelligent video analysis. Data originating from a Grid source are often huge in quantity and will need to be processed in an efficient manner by applications distributed across the Grid. In

the Taiwanese EcoGrid project (EcoGrid, 2006), videos of underwater marine life have been acquired using wireless sensor nets and stored for analysis. One minute of video clip typically takes 1829 frames and is stored in 3.72 MB. That translates into 223.2 MB per hour, 5356.8 MB per day and 1.86 Terabytes per year for one operational camera. Due to the unpredictability of nature, one may not easily skip frames as they may contain vital information. Based on our own experience, one minute's clip will on average cost manual processing time of 15 minutes. This means that one year's recording of a camera would cost human experts 15 years' effort just to perform basic analysing tasks. Currently there are three under water cameras in operation and this will cost a human expert 45 years just to do basic processing task. This is clearly an impractical situation and more appropriate automation methods must be deployed.

In order to provide an intelligent BPM-based image processing (IP) system to tackle this problem, we have proposed a solution enriched with planning, process and case libraries and ontologies within a three-layered framework (Nadarajan, Chen-Burger & Malone, 2006). The system is grounded by ontologies that provide an agreed vocabulary between the Grid resources. The ontologies are contained within the design layer of the framework. We have provided three ontologies to describe the goals (IP tasks), domain description and capabilities (IP tools). A workflow system with full ontological integration has several advantages. It allows for cross-checking between ontologies, addition of new concepts into the workflow system and discovery of new knowledge within the system.

Initial work in the development of an image processing ontology was conducted through the Hermès project[1], whereby an extensive vocabulary was developed to describe user-friendly terminologies for image processing problems. The user ontology was built based on the fact that non-image processing experts are able to provide a priori information based on their domain expertise. The image processing ontology is used to formulate the image processing task and constraints. Extending this approach, we modularised these ontologies by separating the relevant components into goals, domain descriptions and capabilities. In particular, the capabilities were added as a new component of the ontology development process. This would contribute towards the use of ontologies within the *problem-solving* aspect as well, whereby a performance-based planning approach is adopted.

The goal ontology contains concepts related to the high-level IP task and the constraints on these tasks; it captures the user requirements in as much detail as possible. As a first step, the user interacts with the system by providing input values for the goal and constraints. The goal can be one of those specified in the ontology, e.g. Compression, Detection, etc. The constraints are additional parameters to specify rules or restrictions that apply to the goal. These include qualifiers e.g. Acceptable Errors, Optimisation Criteria, Detail

Level and Quality Criteria contained within the goal ontology. For instance, the user may have a high level goal *"Detect all fish in video."* This is interpreted as having the following meaning in the Goal ontology.

(Goal: Detection) [Occurrence = all occurrences] [Performance Criteria: Processing Time = real time]

Due to space limitation, only the relevant parts of the ontology are illustrated and highlighted in Figure 5. A more detailed version of the ontology is described in Nadarajan and Renouf (2007).

We have used FBPML to provide a basis for the data and process models. For a given video processing task such as 'Detection', a planning mechanism is used to obtain the sequence of sub-tasks involved to perform it. This is achieved by viewing it as a process modelling task using rich BPM constructs, where complex image processing tasks can be represented. Furthermore, the user can provide domain description such as the brightness level of the video and constraints that

Figure 5. Goal ontology containing concepts related to the user goal "detect all fish in video"

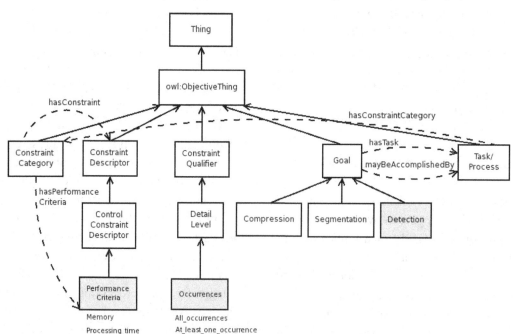

would restrict the task. Thus using the domain information and constraints, the system is assisted to provide a more accurate solution based on the user requirements as these details provide a basis for the preconditions and effects of the actions in the plan. For the detection task above, the high-level breakdown is given by *Pre-processing, Segmentation* and *Recognition*. For the sub-task *Segmentation*, it can be hierarchically decomposed as shown in Figure 6.

We can model this using FBPML process model constructs. One of the methods to perform segmentation is 'Background Subtraction'. In this method, first a background model is constructed by averaging a series of consecutive images. Once this is done, the difference between the current

frame and the background model is obtained. This would result in non-background objects, i.e. the fish. Then the background model is updated accordingly, that is by taking into account the new frame. This process is repeated until the last frame in the video sequence is obtained. The process model is described in Figure 7. Note that this process model includes a looping construct represented by the 'OR' control construct and arrow looping back.

Each of the processes may be decomposed into other sub-processes, for example one way of performing *Background Model Construction* is *Frame Extraction* which involves 3 steps: (1) Conversion of the original image to a suitable format for the proceeding computation, (2)

Figure 6. Hierarchical decomposition for sub-task Segmentation within overall task Detection

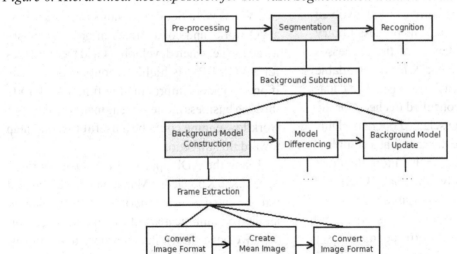

Figure 7. An FBPML representation of the method 'Background Subtraction'

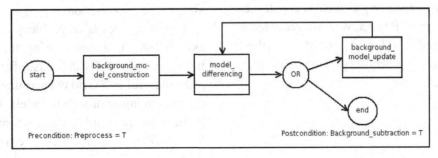

Creation of the mean image and (3) Conversion of the image to its original format again. All these processes are primitive, that is they are not decomposable and correspond to a function call in a vision library. These process model representations can be encoded as methods in the planning component of the workflow engine. A walkthrough of the mechanism of the workflow engine is provided below.

Walkthrough

The goal and constraints for the 'Detection' task above is fed by the user and read by the workflow. The planner interacts with the goal and domain ontologies to obtain the implementation-specific values for the user input via an extension of FBPML-DL. The goal, constraints and initial domain state are determined and fed to the Planner. Then the decomposition is performed to obtain a sequence of sub-tasks (primitive tasks) involved to perform the overall goal. The process library which contains the instances of the processes available is consulted to check for the available operator(s) to perform each sub-task. The capability ontology is then consulted to check for the performance level of the selected operator. During this phase, it may be the case that a complete sequence is not obtained, or that more than one sequence is found to solve the goal. When this happens, the case library is consulted to retrieve the most *similar* solution based on past solutions. This adapted solution that corresponds to a set of function calls in an IP library is obtained and finally deployed for execution.

By grounding the workflow system with ontologies and incorporating rich BPM constructs to model complex IP tasks, we have provided a semantics-based workflow composition method that would enable e-Scientists to perform complex video analyses.

RELEVANCE TO GRID APPLICATIONS AND VO

We have demonstrated how semantics-based BPM technologies are used in three application areas; Supply Chain Management, Business Intelligence and Knowledge Management, and Intelligent Video Analysis. We have used FBPML as our formal representation for process modelling and ontologies for modelling the data. Such a representation is ideal for information sharing and exchange across the Grid.

In Dell's SCM, we have shown that BPM can give a good insight into supply chain strategies, and, with the use of an appropriate workflow engine, we can simulate and check on different such strategies. Since VOs can be regarded as an extension of specific supply chain strategies, the framework that we have suggested in our work can be useful for the analysis and improvement of a VO as well. So, if one wants to capture how a VO works and collaborates in order to satisfy its goals (i.e. when developing Grid technologies for a VO), BPM is highly recommended. Also, if one considers improving the function of a VO through business process reengineering, then our workflow engine could be a useful tool and help toward this direction.

Using the ADP approach for Business Intelligence and Knowledge Management, each aspect is represented by an appropriate process modelling method communicated with an underlying ontology. We have shown that appropriate diagnosis, analysis and inference could be performed within an organisation. This approach is ideal for any VO as it captures the human, business and operational aims of the organisation.

For more pervasive problem domains such as distributed image processing, the approach of incorporating BPM with the use of ontologies has proved useful in a Grid context due to the complexities of image processing itself. The EcoGrid is one of such examples where automatic support for non-IP users is essential. The framework we have proposed is designed to be used in the Grid as we have data originating from one source (Taiwan), while the image processing algorithms are developed in Italy and the workflow management is controlled in Edinburgh. This is a typical Grid scenario and much work is under way to realise this framework. Once the whole system is in place, it would operate as a VO.

CONCLUSION

Semantics-based BPM could be used effectively to support Grid applications which provide a basis for the creation and running of a VO. BPM methods such as FBPML introduce an established formal representation to Grid applications that lack mature formalisms at present. This chapter gives three relevant applications where different semantics- and process-based techniques have been applied. In this chapter, knowledge-based techniques have been demonstrated to assist the analysis of Supply Chain strategies, and the simulation of corresponding semantics-based business process models can provide us with tangible numerical results to help gauge SCM (Supply Chain Management) performance.

The ADP approach uses and extends existing knowledge based modelling approaches to provide a useful framework to help answer queries that are frequently asked within a virtual organisation. It combines standard practices already existing in the different domains of knowledge management, ontology and business process modelling to provide a rich semantics-based support for organisational memory management. It is suitable for storing and presenting data and process information that is cross-organisational and can present organisational information at different levels of abstraction to suit different viewing and analytical needs. Based on information stored in these models, one is able to derive good quality approximate answers using logical inference techniques with relatively little effort.

In the field of Intelligent Video Analysis, BPMs provide a foundation for encoding methods and a language of communication between the workflow layer and other components. This provides a rich context-sensitive framework to allow e-Scientists to perform complex video processing tasks without possessing any technical expertise. Communicating the process models with underlying ontologies further enhances the support as ontologies are also formal, which enable machine processability. More importantly, they promote sharing and reuse of data, resources and applications across the Grid. To summarise, the benefits of utilising semantics-based BPM within Grid applications include support for reasoning, analysis and flexibility.

REFERENCES

Adamides, E., & Karacapilidis, N. (2006). A Knowledge Centred Framework for Collaborative Business Process Modelling. *Business Process Management Journal, 12*(5), 557-575.

Arkin, A., (2002). *Business Process Modeling Language (BPML), Version 1.0.* BPMI.org.

Betz, S., Klink, S., Koschmider, A., & Oberweis, A. (2006). Automatic User Support for Business Process Modeling. In K. Hinkelmann, D. Karagiannis, N. Stojanovic, & G. Wagner (Eds.), *Proceedings of the Workshop on Semantics for Business Process Management at the 3rd European Semantic Web Conference 2006.* Budva, Montenegro (pp. 1-12).

BPEL4WS (2003). *Business Process Execution Language for Web Services Version 1.1.* IBM, BEA Systems, Microsoft, SAP AG, Siebel Systems. Available at: http://www128.ibm.com/developerworks/library/specification/ws-bpel/

Browne, J., & Zhang, J. (1999). Extended and virtual enterprises - similarities and differences.

International Journal of Agile Management Systems, *1*(1), 30-36.

Chandra, C., & Kumar, S. (2000). Supply chain management in theory and practice: a passing fad or a fundamental change? *Industrial Management & Data Systems*, *100*(3), 100-113.

Chen-Burger, Y.-H., & Robertson, D. (2005). *Automating Business Modelling: A Guide to Using Logic to Represent Informal Methods and Support Reasoning*. Book Series of Advanced Information and Knowledge Processing, Springer-Verlag.

Chen-Burger, Y.-H., & Stader J. (2003). Formal Support for Adaptive Workflow Systems in a Distributed Environment. In L. Fischer (Ed.), *Workflow Handbook* (pp. 93-118). Florida, USA: Future Strategies Inc.

Chen-Burger, Y.-H., & Kalfoglou, Y. (2007). Knowledge Management Support for Enterprise Distributed Systems. In P. Rittgen (Ed.), *Handbook of Ontologies for Business Interactions* (pp. 294-310). IGI Global (formerly Idea Group Inc.).

De Roure, D., Jennings, N. R, & Shadbolt, N. R. (2005). The Semantic Grid: Past, Present, and Future. *Proceedings of the IEEE*, *93*(3), 669-681.

Deelman, E., Singh, G., Su, M.-H., Blythe, J., Gil, Y., Kesselman, C., Mehta, G., Vahi, K., Berriman, G. B., Good, J., Laity, A., Jacob, J. C., & Katz, D. S. (2005). Pegasus: A Framework for Mapping Complex Scientific Workflows onto Distributed Systems. *Scientific Programming Journal*, *13*(3), 219-237.

Dell, M., & Fredman, C. (2006). *Direct from Dell: Strategies that Revolutionized an Industry*. New York, NY: Harper-Collins Publishers.

EcoGrid. (2006). National Center for High Performance Computing, Taiwan. Available at: http://ecogrid.nchc.org.tw/.

Foster, I., & Kesselman, C. (1998). *The Grid: Blueprint for a New Computing Infrastructure*.

San Francisco, CA: Morgan Kaufmann Publishers Inc.

Foster, I., & Kesselman, C. (2004). *The Grid 2: Blueprint for a New Computing Infrastructure*. San Francisco, CA: Morgan Kaufmann Publishers Inc.

Guo, L., Chen-Burger, Y.-H., & Robertson, D. (2004). Mapping a Business Process Model to a Semantic Web Service Model. Paper presented at *3rd IEEE International Conference on Web Services (ICWS'04)*.

Harrison, A., & van Hoek, R. (2008). *Logistics Management and Strategy: Competing Through the Supply Chain*. FT: Prentice Hall.

Hepp, M., Leymann, F., Domingue, J., Wahler, A., & Fensel, D. (2005). Semantic Business Process Management: A Vision Towards Using Semantic Web Services for Business Process Management. In *Proceedings of the IEEE International Conference on e-Business Engineering*. IEEE Computer Society.

Kangilaski, T. (2005). Virtual organization and supply chain management. In *10th IEEE International Conference on Emerging Technologies and Factory Automation, 1*,705-712. IEEE.

Katzy, B., & Löh, H. (2003). Virtual Enterprise Research State of the Art and Ways Forward, In *9th International Conference on Concurrent Enterprising*. Centre for Concurrent Engineering, University of Nottingham, UK.

Klyne, G., & Carroll, J. (Eds.) (2004). *Resource Description Framework (RDF): Concepts and Abstract Syntax*. W3C Recommendation. Available at: http://www.w3.org/TR/rdf-concepts/

Kraemer, K., & Deddrick, J. (2001). *Dell Computer: Using E-commerce to Support the Virtual Company*. Paper 236, Center for Research on Information Technology and Organizations, Globalization of I.T.

Lambert, D. M., & Cooper, M. C. (2000). Issues in Supply Chain Management, *Industrial Marketing Management, 29*(1), 65-83.

Ludäscher, B., Altintas, I., Berkley, C., Higgins, D., Jaeger-Frank, E., Jones, M., Lee, E., Tao, J., & Zhao, Y. (2006). Scientific Workflow Management and the Kepler System. *Concurrency and Computation: Practice & Experience, 18*(10), 1039-1065.

Manataki, A. (2007). *A Knowledge-Based Analysis and Modelling of Dell's Supply Chain Strategies.* Unpublished masters dissertation, School of Informatics, University of Edinburgh, UK.

McGuinness, D., & van Harmelen, F. (2004). *OWL Web Ontology Language.* World Wide Web Consortium (W3C). Available at: http://www.w3.org/TR/owl-features/

Martin, D. (Ed.) (2006). *OWL-S Semantic Markup for Web Services, Pre-Release 1.2.* World Wide Web Consortium (W3C). Available at: http://www.ai.sri.com/daml/services/owl-s/1.2/ (Temporary location at SRI).

Mayer, R., Menzel, C., Painter, M., Witte, P., Blinn, T., & Perakath, B. (1995). *Information Integration for Concurrent Engineering (IICE) IDEF3 Process Description Capture Method Report.* Knowledge Based Systems Inc.

MIT (n.d.). *MIT Process Handbook*, Phios Repository, Case Examples, Dell. Retrieved June 12, 2008, from http://process.mit.edu/Info/CaseLinks.asp

Mowshowitz, A. (2002) *Virtual Organization: Toward a Theory of Societal Transformation Stimulated by Information Technology.* Westport, CT, USA: Greenwood Press.

Nadarajan, G., Chen-Burger, Y.-H., Malone, J. (2006). Semantic-Based Workflow Composition for Video Processing in the Grid. *IEEE/WIC/ACM International Conference on Web Intelligence (WI-2006)* (pp. 161-165). IEEE.

Nadarajan, G., & Chen-Burger, Y.-H. (2007). Translating a Typical Business Process Modelling Language to a Web Services Ontology through Lightweight Mapping. *IET Software* (Formerly IEE Proceedings Software), *1*(1), 1-17.

Nadarajan, G., & Renouf, A. (2007). A Modular Approach for Automating Video Analysis. In *Proceedings of the 12th International Conference on Computer Analysis of Images and Patterns (CAIP '07)* (pp. 133-140). Springer-Verlag.

Oinn, T., Greenwood, M., Addis, M., Alpdemir, M. N., Ferris, J., Glover, K., Goble, C., Goderis, A., Hull, D., Marvin, D., Li, P., Lord, P., Pocock, M. R., Senger, M., Stevens, R., Wipat, A., & Wroe, C. (2005). Taverna: Lessons in creating a workflow environment for the life sciences. *Concurrency and Computation: Practice and Experience, 18*(10), 1067-1100.

Reisig, W. (1985). Petri Nets, an Introduction. *Eatcs: Monographs on Theoretical Computer Science, 4.* Springer-Verlag.

Roman, D., Keller, U., Lausen, H., de Bruijn, J., Lara, R., Stollberg, M., Polleres, A., Feier, C., Bussler, C., & Fensel, D. (2005). Web Service Modeling Ontology. *Applied Ontology, 1*(1), 77-106.

Rumbaugh, J., Jacobson, I., & Booch, G. (2004). *The Unified Modeling Language Reference Manual, 2nd Edition.* Addison-Wesley.

Schlenoff, C., Knutila, A. & Ray, S. (Eds.) (1997). *1st Process Specification Language (PSL) Roundtable.* Sponsored by National Institute of Standards and Technology, Gaithersburg, MD. Available at: http://www.nist.gov/psl/

Schreiber, G., Akkermans, H., Anjewierden, A., de Hoog, R., Shadbolt, N., van de Velde, W., & Wielinga, B. (2000). *Knowledge Engineering and Management: The CommonKADS Methodology.* Cambridge, MA: The MIT Press.

Storey, J., Emberson, C., Godsell, J., & Harrison, A. (2006). Supply chain management: theory, practice and future challenges. *International Journal of Operations & Production Management, 26*(7), 754-774.

Tan, K. C. (2001). A framework of supply chain management literature. *European Journal of Purchasing & Supply Management, 7*(1), 39-48.

Taylor, I., Shields, M., Wang, I., & Rana, O. (2003). Triana Applications within Grid Computing and Peer to Peer Environments. *Journal of Grid Computing, 1*(2), 199-217.

Tripathi, U. K., & Hinkelmann, K. (2007). Change Management in Semantic Business Processes Modeling. In *Proceedings of the Eighth international Symposium on Autonomous Decentralized Systems* (pp. 155-162). IEEE Computer Society.

Wetzstein, B., Ma, Z., Filipowska, A., Kaczmarek, M., Bhiri, S., Losada, S., Lopez-Cobo, J. M., & Cicurel, L. (2007). Semantic Business Process Management: A Lifecycle Based Requirements Analysis. In M. Hepp, K. Hinkelmann, D. Karagiannis, R. Klein & N. Stojanovic (Eds.), *Semantic Business Process and Product Lifecycle Management. Proceedings of the Workshop SBPM 2007,* CEUR Workshop Proceedings.

ENDNOTE

[1] GREYC Laboratory, Image Team, Caen, France (http://www.greyc.ensicaen.fr/~arenouf/Hermes/index-en.html)

Chapter V
Placement and Scheduling over Grid Warehouses

Rogério Luís de Carvalho Costa
University of Coimbra, Portugal

Pedro Furtado
University of Coimbra, Portugal

ABSTRACT

The computational grid offers services for efficiently scheduling jobs on the grid, but for grid-enabled applications where data handling is a most relevant part, the data grid kicks in. It typically builds on the concept of files, sites and file transfers between sites. These use a data transfer service, plus a replica manager to keep track of where replicas are located. The authors consider a multi-site, grid-aware data warehouse, which is a large distributed repository sharing a schema and data concerning scientific or business domains. Differently from typical grid scenarios, the data warehouse is not simply a set of files and accesses to individual files. It is a single distributed schema and both localized and distributed computations must be managed over that schema. Given this difference, it is important to study approaches for placement and computation over the grid data warehouse and this is our contribution in this book chapter.

INTRODUCTION

The Grid is an infrastructure that coordinates and provides transparent access to distributed and heterogeneous resources for geographically distributed users. One of its main usages is to enable the implementation of *Virtual Organizations* (Foster, 2001).

Virtual Organizations (VO) are composed by (members of) distinct real organizations or institutions, which cooperatively participate in the Grid, sharing resources and using the shared resources in order to solve common problems or to achieve common objectives. In such multi-institutional grid it is somewhat frequent that individual domain administrators impose some kind

Copyright © 2009, IGI Global, distributing in print or electronic forms without written permission of IGI Global is prohibited.

of usage constraints on local domains' resources to remote users (Foster, 2001; Schopf & Nitzberg, 2002). Business historical information, molecular simulations and measurements of sensor data are examples of some current and future applications that run on VO and which can produce large amounts of distributed data.

In Data Grids (Chervenak et al., 2001; Krauter et al., 2002), the Grid software is used to manage data storage, transparent data access or the execution of data intensive jobs. Flat files are frequently used to store data. Grid-based services are used to execute efficient data movement (e.g. GridFTP (Allcock et al., 2005)) and to locate database replicas (e.g. Globus' Replica Location Service – RLS (Chervenak et al., 2004)).

On the other hand, Data Warehouses (DWs) are huge mostly read-only databases used primarily for decision support purposes. They are target of periodic data loads as part of ETL (Extraction Transform and Load) processes: data from several OLTP (Online Transaction Processing) systems' is transformed and loaded into the DW, which traditionally resides at a single site (Chaudhuri & Dayal, 1997) (parallel hardware is commonly used to improve performance).

Therefore, the Grid-based Data Warehouse can be used as a tool to support several processes in global Virtual Organizations, including decision making and knowledge discovery. It enables users from different geographical locations (and possibly from different real organizations), which are participating in the VO, to share and query shared data transparently and efficiently. Hence, given a data warehouse schema, grid-enabled DWs have queries, data mining analysis and computations of all kinds happening over large quantities of data. For instance, groups of scientific organizations may provide public multi-site data repositories and computing platforms for simulations and analysis, as it is already beginning to happen with biological data such as protein conformation studies.

Implementing efficient data placement and query scheduling strategies is one of the chal-

lenges in such environment. For instance, placing all the data at a single site may not be the most interesting choice. In Grids, distributed resources from multiple sites are available to be cooperatively used to perform tasks. Using such distributed resources to implement a Grid-based DW may lead to a high performance environment at a reduced monetary cost, when compared to placing all the DW at a single grid site (especially due to reduced requirements in hardware and network links at individual sites). Hence, data and query distribution across several sites should be considered in order to obtain a high performance grid-based DW.

Besides that, it is important to notice that warehouse users may query the database according to some kind of access pattern (Deshpande et al., 1998). For instance, users from distinct sites may be more interested in doing *drill-down* and *drill-up* operations in distinct geographically-related data (each user accessing data that is somewhat related to the region where the user is placed). As doing data movement across different grid sites may be time consuming, the existent users' interests must also be considered when doing placement across distinct sites. Furthermore, as workloads and resource characteristics may change over time, the system should also have some kind of dynamic data placement (or replication) strategy, which is also useful when users' access patterns are not known in advance (or change over time).

But the specialized data placement strategy and the abovementioned aspects lead to the need of a specialized query scheduling strategy, which may consider the existence of partitioned and replicated tables when scheduling query execution among distinct sites.

In this chapter we study data placement and query scheduling in the Grid-based DW. We present a distributed static placement strategy and propose an efficient dynamic placement policy which does replica management considering existent resource constraints. We also propose a query scheduling strategy that considers both local-domain query execution time estimations and data movement time estimations when scheduling query execution over the distributed DW. There is some related work on constructing warehouses over grids but the use of dynamic DW-oriented replica management and query scheduling over the distributed (not fully-replicated) database still remains open issues.

This chapter is organized as follows: in the next Section, we present some background on data grid-related aspects and on parallel and distributed data warehouses. Then, we discuss data placement and query scheduling on the grid-based DW. We present experimental results. Finally, we conclude by summarizing the main aspects of the chapter and presenting some issues that are still open for future research.

BACKGROUND

In this Section we review some important concepts and related work. First of all, we review DW-related concepts and the use of specialized techniques for parallel and distributed warehouses. Then, we discuss grid-related topics, including data placement and query scheduling.

Parallel and Distributed Data Warehouses

Data warehouses are repositories of large amounts of historical data, mainly used for decision sup-

port purposes. DWs are subject-oriented: a certain subject (e.g. sales) is analyzed considering several analysis measures (time period and region, for example). The domain of each analysis measure is called a *dimension*. Hence, a DW data can be viewed as a multi-dimensional database (Figure 1 represents a 3-dimensional data space).

In relational databases, DWs are usually organized as *star schemas* (Chaudhuri & Dayal, 1997) with a huge *fact table* that is related to several *dimension tables*, as represented in Figure 2. In such schema, the facts table stores data to be analyzed and pointers to dimensions, which are stored at dimension tables.

In order to improve complex query execution performance over huge DWs, several techniques have been studied, including the use of parallel and distributed environments. In the following discussion, we review some of those techniques.

The Multi-Dimensional Hierarchical Fragmentation strategy is proposed by Stöhr et al. (2000). It is oriented for shared-disk parallel machines and it partitions fact tables based on dimension attributes. The authors claim that the method has good performance even when queries are over attributes different from the ones used in table partitioning.

Furtado (2004a) proposes the Node-Partitioned Data Warehouse (NPDW) strategy. In NPDW, both fact table and large dimension tables are hash partitioned into disjoint fragments and distributed across the nodes of a shared-nothing machine. The other small dimension tables are

Figure 1. Cube representation of warehouse's data

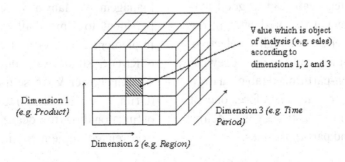

Figure 2. Sample Star Schema

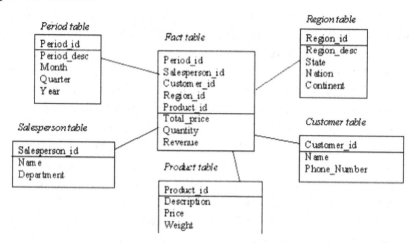

fully replicated into all nodes. In order to improve performance, partitions should be generated over the most frequently used equi-join attribute (reducing repartitioning costs) (Furtado, 2004b). Incoming queries that access partitioned tables are rewritten into several queries, each one accessing only one table fragment. This enables the parallel execution of such rewritten queries and increases the system speedup. Results from different nodes must be merged in order to generate the result of the original query.

In the Virtual Partitioning schema proposed by Akal et al. (2002), data is fully replicated in all the nodes of a shared-nothing machine and fact table's primary key index is partitioned considering one or more of its composing columns. The range used to partition the index is considered as the definition of the *virtual* partitions. Each incoming query is transformed into a set of queries that access different virtual partitions (the transformation occurs by appending a selection predicate). This strategy can lead to good performance improvement if the predicates in the new transformed queries are highly selective. On the other hand, if a great number of rewritten queries access non-partitioned tables, a drop in performance may occur. Therefore, one of the great challenges in such strategy is to define partitions' bounds and partitions sizes.

The Skalla system (Akinde et al., 2002) implements a distributed data warehouse about network trace data. A data warehouse is stored at Skalla Sites. Such sites are placed near data collection points (which collect data about IP flows). A coordinator node is responsible to construct distributed execution plans for all incoming queries. After each node executes its tasks in the plan, the coordinator node sends the final results back to the user.

In the next Section we present some concepts related to the implementation of Grid-based systems as underlying infra-structure to databases and data bound applications.

Grid-Based Databases

Grids should provide transparent access to distributed heterogeneous resources in multi-domain environments. In order to do that, several aspects must be considered, like security and remote job management. Many of those aspects are somewhat pertinent to almost all grid-based application implementations. Grid Resource Management (GRM) Systems were developed (e.g., Globus Toolkit (Foster & Kesselman, 1997) and Legion (Grimshaw et al., 1997)) to provide a wide range of functionalities that deal, mostly, with such *basic* grid-related implementation aspects.

The Globus Toolkit (GT) is a tools set: GT version 4 (Foster, 2005) provides services for remote job execution (GRAM), efficient data transfer over the Grid (GridFTP), replica location (RLS) and credential and security management (GSI), among others.

On the other hand, Legion aims at providing grid users an abstraction similar to a virtual machine, which would make them feel like using a single very powerful machine. Legion is like a framework that enables the use of several strategies: every grid participant, resource and job is modeled as an object and core components' functionalities are specified, but the user may decide how to implement most of them.

Grid-based applications are usually deployed on top of some GRM System. Grid-based systems that have particular objectives usually implement some kind of specialized policy that runs over the basic services provided by the GRM System. For instance, an application may implement a special job scheduling strategy but still uses Globus' services to start and monitor remote job execution or to do data transfer between sites.

Generic Job Scheduling and Schedulers

Different Grid implementations may have some special characteristics (like the number of shared resources and their heterogeneity degree) which lead to the use of different job scheduler architectures. Krauter et al. (2002) identifies three basic architectures for grid job scheduling:

- **Centralized:** In this model, only a single *Central Scheduler* is used (similar to single-domain centralized schedulers). The Scheduler is responsible to schedule the execution of all the incoming jobs, assigning them directly to the existent resources. Such architecture may lead to good scheduling decisions, as the scheduler may consider the characteristics and loads of all available resources. On the other hand, the centralized

scheduling model suffers from a scalability problem: if a wide variety of distributed heterogeneous resources is available, considering all the resources' individual characteristics may become time consuming. Besides that, in such architecture it is somewhat more difficult to accommodate the use of several domain-specific resource usage policies.

- **Hierarchical:** In the hierarchical model, each site has its own job scheduler (*Local Scheduler*) which is responsible to schedule job execution by the sites' resources. Besides that, there exists a *Community Scheduler* (or *Resource Broker*), which is responsible to assign jobs to sites. The Community Scheduler may interact with the Local Scheduler when planning a job assignment in order to establish some kind of Service Level Agreements (SLA). When compared to the Centralized model, the Hierarchical architecture has a greater scalability level and turns it easier to implement domain-specific scheduling strategies.

- **Decentralized:** In such architectural alternative, each site has its own *Local Scheduler*, just like in the Hierarchical Model, but there is no CS. Each scheduler is responsible for scheduling job execution at its site and must negotiate with other schedulers about remote job execution. This model is totally decentralized and each scheduler knows the current state of only a part of the system, which may lead to not so good scheduling decisions when compared with the other two models. In order to increase its knowledge about the system's state, schedulers may exchange messages with each other. But if the number of messages becomes too high, the system's performance may also be impacted.

Besides the architectural aspects, distinct schedulers may also have some special objectives.

In fact, several grid-based application level job schedulers consider some kind of user specified or job related requirement. Examples of such schedulers are Condor-G (Frey et al., 2001) and Nimrod-G (Buyya et al., 2000).

In Condor-G, Classified Advertisements (ClassAd) are used to advertise each site's characteristics and users' requirements for each job. A matchmaking process scans jobs' and sites' ClassAds. Each job is scheduled to a site whose advertised characteristics are compatible with the job's requirements.

Nimrod-G deals with two kinds of user specified requirements: job deadline and available budget. Each job is scheduled to be executed by the site with the lowest execution cost among those that can finish job execution by its deadline. In order to do that, it uses several economic inspired mechanisms, like auctions.

The abovementioned schedulers and strategies were developed for *general purpose* grids. Although some of them are widely used, they are neither database nor query oriented, which may lead to some low service levels when they are employed to do grid-based database query scheduling. Next, we review some works on database query scheduling in data grids.

Query and Job Scheduling in Data Grids

Several query scheduling strategies for grid-based data-centric jobs were studied by Ranganathan & Foster (2004). Some of the evaluated scheduling strategies were *Random*, *Least Loaded* (where the node with the least number of waiting jobs is select to execute the new job) and *Data Present* (where the job is assigned to a node that already has the necessary data to execute it). In the *Random* and *Least Loaded* strategies, if the chosen node does not have the necessary data to execute the query, then such data is fetched from a remote site. The authors claim that in most situations jobs should be scheduled to nodes which may execute them with local data (instead of scheduling to idle nodes that would have to fetch remote data to execute).

The use of local or remote data to execute data centric jobs is also discussed by Park & Kim (2003). The authors present a cost model which considers several parameters (like network bandwidth and the size of job's input and output data) to estimate the necessary time to execute a data centric job in several configurations: (i) executing a job in the site in which it was submitted but accessing data from other sites, (ii) executing a job in a different site from which it was submitted but accessing data from the local site, (iii) using both data from the local site and also execute the job locally, and (iv) execute the job and use data at a site different from the one that has submitted the job. The scheduler chooses the configuration with the lowest predicted execution time.

To implement an efficient and highly available grid-based DW is the major objective of Costa & Furtado (2006). At each grid site, the warehouse is partitioned according to the NPDW strategy. Inter-site replication of database fragments is done. An on-demand query scheduling strategy is used: whenever a site has an idle resource, it asks a Central Scheduler for a new query to execute. Although such query scheduling strategy maximizes resource utilization, the proposed model leads to a high consume of storage space. In Costa & Furtado (2007), the authors propose the use of the hierarchical scheduling model in order to achieve user-specified deadlines in query execution over grid-based DWs. A comparison on the use of centralized on-demand scheduling model with hierarchical scheduling model in terms of performance and Service Level Objectives (SLO) achievement is presented at Costa & Furtado (2008a). The authors argue that good efficiency levels and SLO-achievement rates can be obtained even in the hierarchical model (where the central scheduler does not have full control of the environment).

A two-tiered grid-based data warehouse is considered by Lawrence & Rau-Chaplin (2006) and Dehne et al. (2007). The first tier is composed by local domain (cached) data which is shared among local users. Remote database servers are in the second tier. Each submitted query is evaluated in order to verify if it can be answered with data from the local site. Then, if it cannot be entirely answered locally, the query is rewritten into a set of queries. Some of those are executed locally (with the existent data) and the others, which access the data that is missing at the first tier, are executed at the second tier (database servers).

Wehrle et al. (2007) use the Globus Toolkit together with a set of specialized services for grid based DWs. Fact table data is partitioned and distributed across participant nodes. Dimension tables data is replicated. A *local data index service* provides local information about data stored at each node. A *communication service* uses the *local data index* service from the participant grid's nodes to enable that remote data is accessed. The first step in query execution is to search for data at the local node (using the local index service). Missing data is located by the use of the communication service and accessed remotely.

As presented, most of the scheduling works consider that queries and data centric jobs must be answered mainly with the use of local data. Such strategy is used in order to reduce data movement over the inter-site grid network (WAN), which may have low bandwidths and high latencies when compared with the use of LAN networks. In order to reduce such data movement during query execution, a good data placement policy must be used. Data replicas should also be considered.

Replica Placement in Data Grids

Data replicas can be used in distributed database systems in order to improve query execution performance and data availability, but their use lead to several challenges, like selecting which data should be replicated and placing the data replica at the most suitable site. Next, we review some works on such issues.

Ranganathan & Foster (2001) proposed several file replication strategies, including *Best Client* and *Cascading Replication*. In such models, whenever the number of access to a certain data file is greater than a threshold value, a file replica is created. In Best Client, the replica is placed at the site that has requested the data more times. In *Cascading Replication*, the file replica is placed at the first neighbor node on the path from the data source to the best client site. In *Cascading Replication*, this mechanism is repeated until the file is replicated at the client node.

A hierarchical (tree-like) data grid is considered by Lin et al. (2006) and Liu & Wu (2006). In Lin et al. (2006), the database is placed at the central node (tree root). The scheduler tries to locate the required data at the node where the query is submitted. If it cannot be found, then it asks for the data to the node's parent node. If the parent node also fails to have the requested data, it asks for the data to its parent node, and so on (until the request reaches the root node). A *range limit* is defined as the number of steps towards the root that can be executed in order to find some data. The proposed replica placement strategy tries to determine the minimum necessary number of replicas and the correspondent placement which makes that every request can be answered by the range limit. Liu & Wu (2006) consider that the user of a site that is a leaf on the tree, first tries to access the database at its current site, then, if the database is not found, it is searched at the parent node (just like in Lin et al., 2006). Replicas are placed in order to balance workload across nodes.

Siva Sathya et al. (2006) present three data replication strategies: *Best Replica Site*, *Cost Effective Replication* and *Topology Based Replication*. The first strategy is inspired in the Best Client strategy (the number of access indicates that a replica should be created). But replica location is chosen by a combination of (1) the number of each site's access to the data set, (2) the replica's expected utility value for each site and (3) the distance between sites. In the *Cost Effective Replication* strategy, a cost function is used to compute the cost to a site of accessing remote data. When such cost is greater than a specified threshold value, a data replica is created at the site. In *Topology Based Replication* a database replica is created at the node that has the greatest number of direct connections to other nodes.

The economic grid environment is considered by Haddad & Slimani (2007). In such work, each node that wants to use a certain data fragment performs a reverse auction in order to decide which replica to use (each data provider offers access to a data set for a certain price). The data consumer node uses a function to predict the future value of each fragment. Then, it chooses which data fragments should be locally replicated in order to maximize the value of the available storage space.

DATA PLACEMENT AND QUERY SCHEDULING IN THE GRID DATA WAREHOUSE

The Grid-based data warehouse is an important tool for both real and virtual global organizations. It can be used in a variety of commercial and scientific domains. We consider that the Grid-based DW is composed by a set of sites connected by a wide-area network. Each site may provide several shared resources to the grid, including supercomputers, workstation clusters and storage systems. DW users are distributed across the sites.

DW data may come from geographically distributed sites and is organized in a star schema. We consider that all the warehouse data can be queried by all the grid participants and can be stored at any participant site (i.e. private or protected data is not loaded into the global data warehouse).

The database may be represented in three levels of abstraction:

- **Logical model:** It contains the logical representation of the DW's tables, independently of where they are physically stored or if they are partitioned or not. Such model is considered by users when submitting queries.
- **Global physical model:** Contains physical representations of tables at different sites. For instance, it contains information about the table replicas and the globally defined table fragments that are stored at each site. When using the Hierarchical Scheduling (discussed in the previous section), the Global Physical Model is considered by the Community Scheduler when assigning tasks to sites.
- **Local physical model:** Each site has its own Local Physical Model which contains information about the objects that are stored at the site. Such model may be an exact subset of the Global Physical Model or not, depending if the local domain administrator uses a specialized data placement policy. Anyway, it contains the correlation between the local objects and the objects that are represented at the Global Physical Model.

In the following, we present a static method for inter-site data partitioning and placement. Then, we discuss query scheduling strategy in the distributed DW. After that, we address the problem of dynamic replica selection and placement in the Grid-based DW.

Inter-Site Static Data Placement

One of the most common objectives of efficient methods for data placement in grid-based applications is to reduce inter-site data movement. Therefore, one straightforward approach to achieve such goal is to replicate the entire database across all sites. But such alternative is not feasible in most real grid-based DWs. Hence, it is necessary to choose a way of placing data across sites, considering that it can be partially replicated.

In our approach, DW data is organized into a star schema. Besides that, fact tables' data may be loaded to the DW from several sites. We call *Primary Data Source Site* (PDDS) to sites that do data loading and sharing at the grid-based DW. Therefore, each piece of shared data has one PDDS.

Query workload may follow some kind of access pattern, like geographically related ones, in which users from a PDDS may have more interest in the data that is loaded at the site than in data loaded at other sites. Therefore, in an initial static placement, each piece of loaded data is primarily stored at its PDDS. Such strategy leads to a partitioned fact table, which uses the data source location as the partition attribute (if such attribute does not exist in the facts table, then it must be created).

As a fact table is usually accessed together with dimension tables, we choose to replicate such dimension tables at every site. This solution is normally feasible, as dimension tables are usually small. It is also an efficient strategy, as it reduces data movement across grid sites when performing join operations between the facts table and dimension tables (which are very common operations in DW).

Besides that, creating several facts table's partitions increases the performance of join operations, even when all the partitions are placed in the same machine (Lima et al., 2004). But in such case, the data source attribute should not be the only partitioning criteria. We propose it should be used together with the attribute which is most commonly used in equi-join operations (as in Furtado, 2004b). Hence, each site stores several fragments of the facts table.

All the fragments that are created according to the proposed strategy have a unique identifier and are represented in the database's Global Physical Model. The proposed initial data allocation scheme is represented in Figure 3.

Such placement can lead to some degree of parallelism when executing queries and also provides good performance when users query data that is stored at (or near) the sites they belong to. But such strategy can be improved with the use of dynamic replica selection and placement, as we present later in this Section.

Scheduling Architecture and Intra-Site Data Placement

We use the hierarchical scheduling model described in an earlier section. A Community

Figure 3. Static data placement for the Grid-based data warehouse

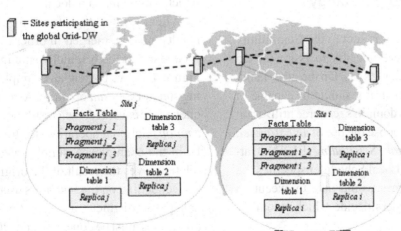

91

Scheduler is responsible to create tasks that have to be executed for each incoming query and to assign such tasks to sites. In each site, a Local Scheduler is responsible to manage the local execution of the site's tasks. Such local execution is highly dependent on the used intra-site data placement strategy.

The intra-site data allocation depends on the number and type of available resources. For instance, if a single server machine and storage system are available, all the fragments of the facts table and all the local replicas of dimension tables should be stored in the storage system and accessed by the server machine. But if a shared-nothing parallel machine is available, the use of specialized strategies (e.g. NPDW) can lead to high performance.

Hence, in order to better use the available resources at each site, each local domain administrator may choose to use its own intra-site data placement strategy. In such case, the used placement strategy must be transparent to the Community Scheduler. That is, the scheduler assigns tasks to local sites using the objects that are represented at the Global Physical Model (with global fact tables' fragment identifiers) and the Local Scheduler must transform the tasks it receives into other ones that are executed over the locally stored data. In order to do that, the Local Scheduler uses the Local Physical Model.

Query Scheduling Strategy

Each submitted query is sent to the Community Scheduler, which is responsible to assign the execution among available sites. On the other hand, each domain administrator should be capable of implementing local domain's resource utilization rules. Hence, we propose the use of an *Estimated Execution Time-Aware Scheduling* (EETA) strategy, in which each Local Scheduler specifies the time its site resources would take to execute a task (Local Schedulers decide which resources

to use and when to use them, according to local domain resource usage constraints).

As data is partitioned, the first step in the EETA is task generation. Such phase is mainly comprised by query transformation. Then, queries are assigned to sites and executed. Finally, results from distinct rewritten queries must be merged in order to generate the result of the original user-submitted query. Next, we detail each of such phases.

Task Generation and Results Merging

Users submit queries considering the Global Logical Schema. The Community Scheduler must transform the incoming query into other queries over the physically defined tables.

Data warehouses are usually target of queries with aggregate operators, like *sum*, *count* and *average*. Such operators may be somewhat changed during query rewritten. Figure 4 presents an example of queries transformations for the *sum* operator over a fragmented table (*sales*). The initial query (see Figure 4 (a)) is transformed into several others ones, each one over a fragment of the *sales* table (see Figure 4 (b)). The query in Figure 4 (a) references the object *sales* by its logical name. The transformed queries (Figure 4 (b)) access the physical fragments of such table (defined in the Global Physical Model). Such transformed queries are sent for Local Schedulers which should manage local execution.

After the rewritten queries are executed, their results must be merged in order to generate the final result of the originally submitted query. In Figure 4 (c), we present an example of the merging step for the *sum* operator. After the rewritten queries are executed, their results are combined by a *union* relational operation (forming the relation U, in the example). A simple *select* over the U relation gives the result of the original query.

Depending on the operators used at the original query, distinct transformations and merge operations must be done. Furtado (2005) presents

Figure 4. Query transformations between logical model and global physical model

(a) Initial query	(b) Rewritten query that access fragment i	(c) Generating final result
Select regionId, sum(sales) from JOIN$_{pkey}$ sales, product where <row conditions> group by regionId;	R(i):= Select regionId, sum(sales) from JOIN$_{pkey}$ salesFragment_i, product where <row conditions> group by regionId;	U = Union (R(i)), i = 1 to *fragmentNumber* Result:= Select regionId, sum(sales) from U group by regionId;

several examples on query transformations and results merging operations.

In order to obtain high efficiency in results merging, each site should do the results merging of all the tasks it executes. This generates intermediary merged results and reduces the amount of data that is transferred through the network. But in order to do not make the task allocation algorithm too complex, we assume that the final results' merging is always done at the site where the query was submitted.

Assigning Tasks to Sites

Our scheduling strategy aims at achieving high performance, but also maintains a certain degree of site independence, which is very important in VO. Such independence is provided by enabling that each Local Scheduler specifies the time its site would take to finish query execution: besides considering the locally available resources, each scheduler may incorporate local domain resource usage constraints (e.g. resource usage time windows or resource limits usage) when forecasting the necessary time to execute a query.

This way, after generating the tasks that should be executed, the Community Scheduler demands to Local Schedulers that they inform a forecast on how much time they would take to execute such tasks. Then, the Community Scheduler estimates the necessary time to transfer the required data to each site and the results back to the site that submitted the query, thus obtaining the total estimated execution time of each task. Finally, the

Community Scheduler assigns the tasks to sites according to the configuration that leads to the smallest total time to execute the job.

We now detail the main steps of the proposed scheduling model.

I. Generate Tasks

This phase is the one described earlier in this Section in which the incoming query that references the logical tables' name are rewritten into queries that access the existent database tables' replica and fragments.

II. Demand the Necessary Time to Execute

In the second phase of task scheduling model, the Community Scheduler sends the tasks to Local Schedulers in order to be evaluated. Broadcasting messages with all tasks to all sites may be resource consuming. Hence, the Community Scheduler should choose only a subset of the available sites for each task.

In our strategy, the Community Scheduler finds out what are the sites that store the required data for each task (data replicas at distinct sites may be available, with the use of the dynamic data placement strategy which is discussed later in this Section). This is done by the use of a replica catalog (e.g., Globus RLS). Such sites are selected as *candidates* for executing the task and its Local Schedulers should inform the forecasted time to execute each task.

The Community Scheduler also selects other sites to inform about their forecast. The site that submits the query is also a *candidate* to execute it (data may be shipped to such site in order to do task computation there). While the Grid may be highly heterogeneous and some sites might have idle resources, the Community Scheduler also selects as candidates sites that are neighbors of the ones that store the required data. Such neighbors are selected, as moving the required data to them may not be too expensive.

III. Forecast the Necessary Time to Execute the Task at Each Local Site

The Local Scheduler of nominee sites should forecast the necessary time to execute the task (ET). Each Local Scheduler may use its own forecasting method, which should consider both the local domain resource usage constraints and the type of available resources. Some sites may not have the data accessed by the query stored locally. Such sites should use a set of statistics about the database (which are propagated when data is loaded into the DW) in order to do query execution time forecasting. Such statistics must also be used to estimate the size of the task's output data.

Local Scheduler may use some specialized component or algorithm (e.g. Costa & Furtado (2008b); Tomov et al. (2004)) to forecast query execution time in specific hardware or software configurations.

IV. Estimate the Total Execution Time of Each Task

The estimated time to execute a task at a site (ET) should be combined with the estimated necessary time to move the input data to such site (MDI) and with the estimated necessary time to move the output data set from the execution site to its final destination (MDO).

Hence, the total execution time (TTE) of a task k at a site i may be estimated by Equation 1:

$$TTE_{(k,i)} = MDI_{(k,i)} + ET_{(k,i)} + MDO_{(k,i)} \quad (1)$$

The ET time component is estimated by each Local Scheduler, as discussed earlier. The Community Scheduler must estimate the MDI and the MDO components. In order to do that, it uses some forecasts about the network, which should be provided by a network monitoring service (e.g. the Network Weather Service (Wolski, 1997)). The used forecasted information about the network includes network latency (L) and data transfer throughput (DTT) between each data source site (s) and target site (t). Besides network information, the Community Scheduler also uses information about table's fragments sizes (Z) and about tasks result set's size (O). Hence, the MDI and the MDO time components may be computed by Equation 2 and 3 respectively:

$$MDI_{(k,i)} = L + (Z_{(k,i)} / DTT_{(s,t)}) \quad (2)$$

$$MDO_{(k,i)} = L + (O_{(k,i)} / DTT_{(s,t)}) \quad (3)$$

V. Assigning Task Execution to Sites

After evaluating the MDI and MDO time components and having received the information of forecasted execution time at each site (ET), the Community Scheduler computes the TTE value. In such model, the time to execute a query is close to the highest forecasted TTE value of its tasks (TTEh). Therefore, the task allocation configuration with the smallest forecasted value for TTEh is chosen by the Community Scheduler.

Dynamic Replica Selection and Placement

A dynamic replica selection and placement strategy is necessary to complement the initial static placement strategy. Such dynamic policy should consider the creation of inter-site replicas of the fact table fragments. We use a *Benefits-Aware* (BA) strategy, which is implemented by a *Replication Manager* (RM).

RM implements data replication asynchronously with query scheduling and execution, which means that when RM detects that some data should be replicated, it creates the replica without interrupting query scheduling and execution. RM updates the replica catalog with the information about the new replica and uses the underlying data movement infra-structure (e.g. GridFTP) to do efficient data copying between sites. RM decisions are based on information provided by the Community Scheduler: some scheduling decisions are stored at a historical database and are used in order to implement the dynamic replica selection and placement strategy.

In BA, for each executed task, RM verifies if locally stored data is used in query execution or not. RM also verifies if alternative replica placement would bring some benefit for the system. Hypothetical benefits of inexistent data replicas are computed. When the benefit of a certain replica is greater than a threshold value, a replica is created.

Computing Benefits when Executing in Sites that do not Store Required Data

A query is executed at a site that does not store replicas of the necessary data when the Community Scheduler considers that transferring the data to the site and executing the query at such site is faster than executing the query at the site that already stores the data. In such situation, creating a data replica at the site which executed the query would clearly bring some benefit for the system.

But even when a site is not chosen to execute a query, it may be selected to store new data replicas. For instance, let's consider that a site A would be the fastest one to execute a given query Q if it stores the required data, but A does not store such data and transferring it to A during query execution would be too costly. Hence, the Community Scheduler does not assign Q to A. But, in this situation, creating data replicas in A can benefit future execution of queries that access the same data that Q accesses.

The Benefits-Aware strategy deals with the abovementioned situation. Consider that at a certain time t, one site A is selected by the Community Scheduler to execute a task. Let MDI_A, TTE_A and MDO_A be the data transfer time of input data, the local task execution time and the data transfer time of task results in site A. The *foreseen hypothetical benefit value* (FBV) of creating new data replicas in such situation is computed by the algorithm presented in Figure 5.

The first step in the proposed algorithm is to find out which is the site among the candidates that would be the fastest (site B in Figure 5) to execute the task if it stores data replicas of tasks' input data. The sum of ET and MDO for the fastest site among the candidates that were not selected to execute the query is compared to the one of the site to which the query execution was assigned (A in Figure 5). If the computed sum for site B is higher than the one for A, then there is no benefit in creating a data replica in B. In fact, creating a replica at site A would benefit the system by reducing the query execution time on A by the MDI_A value. On the other hand, if the sum of ET and MDO for site B is lower than for site A, creating a data replica at B would reduce the execution time from the current TTE_A to the total time of task execution and result data transfer at site B (line 6 in Figure 5).

The historical values of FBV are managed by RM. Every time the total benefit (TFBV) of having a data set replication at a certain loca-

Figure 5. Decision on assigning hypothetical benefits to a site

```
1.  A := Site to which the query execution was scheduled
2.  B := Site with the best (ET + MDO) value among the
        candidates that do not executed the query (i.e. B <> A)
3.  if (MDO_B + ET_B >= ET_A + MDO_A) then
4.      FBV(t,A) := MDI_A;
5.  else
6.      FBV(t,B) := TTE_A - (MDO_B + ET_B);
7.  end if.
```

tion is greater than a threshold value, the replica creation should be evaluated (as we discuss later in this Section).

But the TFBV is not a simple sum of the historical FBV values. Data that was necessary for queries that were executed long time ago may be less relevant than data that is required for current queries (changes in data access patters may also occur). Considering that the FBV value of creating a data set at a certain site has been measured i times, the TFBV is computed according to Equation 4. In such equation w is a time discount function that is used to provide importance differentiation between older and newer information about benefits.

$$TFBV = \frac{\sum_i (w_i FBV_i)}{\sum_i w_i} \qquad (4)$$

Computing Benefits when Executing in Sites that Store Required Data

Existent replicas of table fragments also have their benefits computed (except for the original fragments created at the Primary Data Source sites). Such benefit values are used to support the decision on data replacement at a site.

When a query is executed at a site that already stores a data replica, the existence of such data replica causes a benefit to the system, to which we call *data replica benefit value* (DRBV). The DBRV is computed by the time difference between the TTE value with the data replica (TTE_R) and the foreseen TTE value that would be obtained without the data replica (TTE_{NR}). In order to discover the TTE_{NR} value, the observed ET and MDO values for the site that executed the query should be compared to the ones of the fastest site among the "not elected" candidates. Besides that, the system should also estimate the hypothetical (MDIh) value that MDI_A would have if the data replicas at site A did not exist.

Consider that a task was executed at a site A, which stored data replicas of the required data

($TTE_R = TTE_A$). Lines 1 to 7 in the algorithm presented in Figure 6 are used to compute the value of DRBV, as described above.

The algorithm in Figure 6 assigns a DRBV to site A (which is the one that was selected to execute the query), but may also assign a foreseen hypothetical benefit value (FBV) to the creation of a data replica at B. This is done only when such replica would reduce the task execution time (line 9 in Figure 6). The benefit value assigned for the replica creation at B is the difference of current total execution time and the one that would be obtained if such replica is created (line 10 in Figure 6).

The total estimated benefit value of the existence of a data replica (TDRBV) at a certain site considers the individual benefits of such data replica to executed tasks. Older values are considered less relevant than newer ones (like when computing TFBV). Therefore, the time discount factor w is also used when computing TDRBV.

TDRBV is computed by Equation 5, where i represents the number of times the replica was used to execute a task.

$$TDRBV = \frac{\sum_i (w_i DRBV_i)}{\sum_i w_i} \qquad (5)$$

Figure 6. Computing the benefits of a data replica

```
1.   A:= Site to which the query execution was scheduled
2.   B:= Site with the best (ET + MDO) value among the
          candidates that do not executed the query (i.e. B <> A)
3.   if (TTE_B) < (MDIh_A + ET_A + MDO_A) then
4.        TTE_NR := TTE_B;
5.   else
6.        TTE_NR := MDIh_A + ET_A + MDO_A;
7.   end if.
8.   DRBV_(t,A):= TTE_A - TTE_NR;
9.   if (MDO_B + ET_B < ET_A + MDO_A) then
10.       FBV(t,B) := TTE_A - (MDO_B + ET_B);
11.  end if;
```

Deciding on Creating or Destroying a Data Replica

The creation of a data replica depends on the foreseen value of its benefits. The TFBV should be compared to a threshold value β.

Whenever TFBV of having a data replica of fragment z at site A is greater than the value of β for A and there exists available space to create the replica, it should be created. On the other hand, if the benefits value is greater than β but there is not available space for creating the new replica, then the system must decide if an existent data replica of another fragment should be replaced or not.

In order to decide that, RM compares the values of TDRBV for the existent fragments with the one for the new fragment (z). When finding a replica fragment whose existence benefit is smaller than the benefit of creating a replica of z, the existent one is replaced. If no replica at the site has a TDRBV value smaller than TFBV(z), then the system should maintain the currently created data replicas, as their existence is more beneficial for the DW's performance than the creation of a replica of z.

EXPERIMENTAL EVALUATION

In order to evaluate our proposals, we made several experiments in a simulation environment, which is described in the following. Then, we present some results that were obtained in the first group of tests we made, in which we used a static data placement policy and compared query scheduling strategies in terms of response time and throughput. Afterward, we present results from the second test set in which the EETA scheduling strategy is used together with several dynamic data placement strategies.

Experimental Setup

Our experimental setup is composed by 11 sites, which have most of their characteristics similar to the ones used in (Sulistio et al., 2007) (in such work, the authors present the correspondence among the used values and the real sites of the LHCGrid testbed). The main characteristics of the considered sites are described in Table 1.

A star schema organized database is considered. The fact's table is partitioned into 121 fragments. Fragment sizes are generated considering Pareto's power-law distribution which is a good distribution to model file sizes in data grids (Sulistio et al., 2007). The mean fragment size is 1Gb. Each site stores 11 fragments of the facts table.

We use three distinct network topologies in our tests. Two of them are hierarchical (as the one used at the LHC Computing Grid Project (Bird et al., 2005)). In the first one (called *binary tree*), sites are organized in a binary tree which is built according their ids. The second topology (called *generic tree*) is inspired in the ones used by Siva Sathya et al. (2006). The third considered environment is a *nonhierarchical* dual ring topology. In such topology, each site is connected by links to two other sites. Data moves in opposite directions around the rings. The considered topologies are represented in Figure 7. In all the used topologies, we use a latency of 10 milliseconds and a data transfer rate of 50Mbps.

We have modeled a query workload which is composed of 1,000 tasks (re-written queries). Tasks' sizes vary about 2,000 kMIPS±30%, which means that a task execution would take about 40 seconds in the most powerful site and 30 minutes in the least powerful one. Queries are randomly submitted by users at different sites but the probability of a query being submitted by a certain site is proportional to the number of users at the site (the number of submitted queries at each site is also presented in Table 1). To model the users access patterns, we consider that half of the tasks access table fragments stored at user's site.

Table 1. Experimental setup description

Site Id	Number of Grid-DW Users at the Site	CPU Rating (MIPS) x 10^3	Storage Space (GB)	Number of Submitted Queries
1	24	49.0	2,750	118
2	32	62.0	1,800	150
3	8	20.0	1,000	43
4	16	21.0	500	80
5	24	14.0	1,350	137
6	48	70.0	2,500	246
7	8	7.0	350	34
8	4	3.0	100	24
9	8	6.0	250	33
10	4	1.0	80	22
11	24	80.0	5,000	113

Figure 7. Used topologies: Inter-site connections

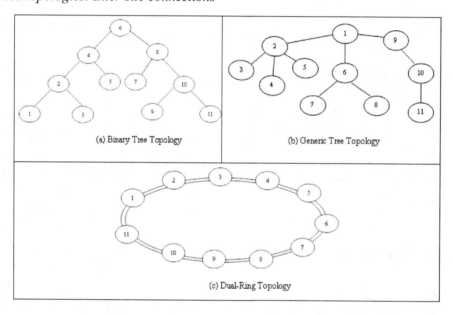

(a) Binary Tree Topology

(b) Generic Tree Topology

(c) Dual-Ring Topology

Evaluating the Query Scheduling Strategy

First of all, we intend to evaluate the effectiveness of our task scheduling strategy. Facts table fragments are distributed across sites as described in the previous subsection. Then, we created a replica of each data fragment and distributed such replicas across sites according to a round-robin policy. Hence, each facts table partition is stored at two distinct sites over the grid. During this set of tests, we do not use any dynamic replica creation mechanism.

We compare our Estimated Execution Time-Aware (EETA) scheduling strategy with two other policies: *Least Working Remaining* (LWR) and *Data Present* (DP). LWR is used for task scheduling in several distributed systems (e.g., it is the default scheduling policy of the Sun Grid Engine (Sun, 2002)) and sometimes referred to as *Least Loaded* scheduling policy (as in Ranganathan & Foster (2002)). In LWR, each task is assigned to the site that has the least work remaining for

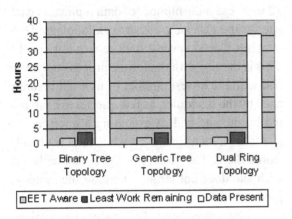

Figure 8. Workload execution time – Several scheduling algorithms and network topologies

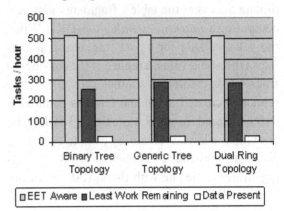

Figure 9. Measured throughput during workload execution – Several scheduling algorithms and network topologies

execution. If the site does not have the necessary data to execute the task, such data is moved during query execution and discarded when the execution finishes. In the DP scheduling strategy (Ranganathan & Foster, 2004), the scheduler assigns each task for a site that already stores a replica of the task's input data.

In Figure 8, we present the workload execution time (i.e. real or *wall* time) for the considered network topologies and scheduling algorithms. The measured throughput of each configuration is presented in Figure 9.

DP lead to the worst performance (LWR's throughput was ten times higher than the one of DP). DP aims at reducing data movement across grid's sites, while LWR aims at maximizing resource utilization. But the considered testbed environment is composed by very heterogeneous resources (where one site may be 80 times more powerful than another) and relatively small data fragments (where the typical table fragment may be transferred between neighbor sites in about 20 seconds). In such situation, the impact of resource heterogeneity in the system's performance is much higher than the impact of data movement operations. This explains the bad performance obtained by the DP strategy when compared to the other strategies. Nevertheless, data movement

operations still impact the system performance and the proposed EETA strategy is the only one that considers both resource heterogeneity and data placement. For such reason, the mean measured throughput of EETA was twice the one of LWR.

Hence, the obtained results show not only the effectiveness of our scheduling strategy, but also the importance of considering both resource heterogeneity and data placement while scheduling. Next we evaluate the use of dynamic replica selection and placement strategies in addition to the proposed scheduling mechanism.

Evaluating the Dynamic Data Placement Strategy

After evaluating the effectiveness of our scheduling strategy, we made several tests to verify the benefits of the proposed dynamic replica creation and placement strategy. In tests set, we use the EETA scheduling strategy together with some different replica creation and placement strategies.

We compare our *Benefits-Aware* (BA) replica creation and placement strategy with two other strategies: *Best Client* (BC) and *Data Least Loaded* (DLL). Variations of the BC strategy are used by Ranganathan & Foster (2001) and Siva Sathya et al. (2006). The DLL is used by Ranganathan & Foster (2004). Both in the BC strategy as in the DLL strategy, each site monitors the number of data access at the table's fragments it stores, computing a *data request indicator* (DRI). When the value of DRI for a data fragment is higher than a threshold value, a replica of the considered fragment is created at another site. In BC, the replica is created at the site that has demanded the considered fragment more times. In DLL, the site with the lowest remaining work to execute is chosen to store the new replica (in LWR scheduling strategy, the site with the lowest remaining work is chosen to execute a job but in the DLL placement strategy, such site is chosen to store a data replica).

The obtained results for workload execution time and measured throughput for the tested data placement strategies and network topologies are presented in Figures 10 and 11, respectively. The performance of the strategies BC and DLL was almost the same. The proposed Benefits-Aware replica creation and placement strategy achieved the best results, reducing the total execution time in almost 10% when compared to the static data placement execution presented in the previous subsection.

By creating data replicas at the site with less remaining work, the DLL strategy may create replicas in sites where they are useless. In Figure 12 we present the number of data replicas at each site for the *generic tree* network topology. DLL strategy placed several data replicas at site 10. This is the site with the lowest processing power and with the lowest number of users. It is rarely used by the scheduler, as few queries are submitted by the site and as executing a query at the site takes a long time even when data is already stored there. Therefore, placing a data replica at such site does not largely increase the system's performance.

On the other hand, BC places data replicas at the site that has requested for it more times. Hence, replicas are placed in sites where they have some probability of being useful. For instance, it placed a large number of fragments at sites 2 and 6, which are the sites with the highest number of users (and submitted queries). But the scheduler may choose not to execute tasks at the sites that have submitted them, even though such sites store the required data. This happens when such sites are not so powerful or when they are already under a great workload. In such situations, placing a replica in sites' neighbors may lead to

Figure 10. Workload execution time: Several data placement strategies and network topologies

Figure 11. Measured throughput during workload execution: Several data placement strategies and network topologies

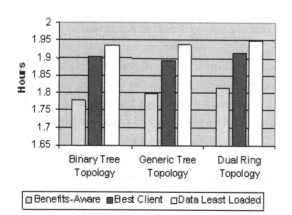

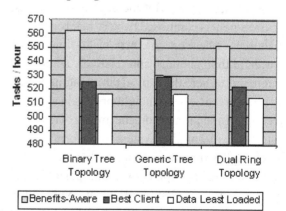

some performance improvement, especially if such neighbors have great processing power or are underutilized.

The proposed placement strategy deals with the abovementioned points. For instance, during query execution, both the BA and the BC placed a large number of replicas at site 2 and 6. But as the experiments goes on, the BA policy choose to place a large number of fragments at site 1 (Figure 12). Such site is neighbor of sites 2 and 6, which are sites with a great number of incoming queries. By doing that, it increased the available options for the scheduler, allowing that the scheduler assigns task execution for site 1 when sites 2 and 6 are overloaded. BA also placed a high number of data replicas at sites 3 and 4 (neighbors of site 2), which enabled the scheduler to use such sites to efficiently execute some of the queries submitted at site 2.

Another important aspect that should be considered is the number of replicas created for each fragment. In Figure 13, we present the number of replicas per facts table fragment in the generic tree topology. DLL created a small number of replicas that were almost evenly distributed across all sites, except for site 10, which received almost twice as many as any of the others sites (Figure 12). The proposed BA policy created just

little more data replicas than BC, but leaded to a higher performance especially because of its better replica location strategy.

CONCLUSION

In Virtual Organizations distinct real entities (or individuals from distinct organizations) cooperate in order to achieve a common goal. In such organizations, the Grid is used as an underlying infrastructure to enable resource and data sharing. On the other hand, the Data Warehouse is an environment specially designed to support business decision taking and knowledge discovery processes.

In such context, the *Grid-Based Data Warehouse* is an important tool for Virtual Organizations, as it enables users from different domains to access shared data efficiently and transparently, especially improving the quality of data analysis process. But there exist several challenging aspects that must be faced during the implementation of a grid-based DW, like data placement and query scheduling models. In this chapter, we discuss such aspects.

We consider a grid-based data warehouse that stores data in a distributed way, which may lead to better performance at a lower cost than

Figure 12. Number of facts table fragments at each site in Generic Tree Topology

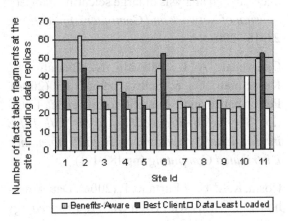

Figure 13. Number of replicas per facts table fragment: Generic Tree Topology

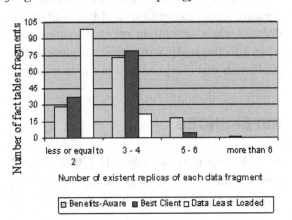

using a centralized DW. We present a static data placement model, which is used to implement the distributed DW. Then, we propose a query scheduling strategy that does efficient scheduling but also maintains some degree of local domain independence, which is especially important in Virtual Organizations as domain administrators may impose some restrictions on the usage of local resources by remote users. We also propose a dynamic replica creation and placement policy, which aims at creating and placing data replicas in order to benefit the whole system and not only a single site or node.

We experimentally evaluated the proposed strategies. The obtained results show the importance of using dynamic scheduling and data placement strategies that consider the system's heterogeneity, the current workload and the network characteristics.

Therefore, the main contributions of this work are: (1) the proposal of a static distributed data placement policy for grid-based data warehouses; (2) the proposal and evaluation of an efficient query scheduling strategy to be used in such environment; and (3) the proposal and evaluation of a dynamic replica selection and placement strategy and its use in the considered grid-based DW environment.

The proposed strategies are both applicable in multi-site global real and virtual organizations, since all the data stored at the warehouse can be queried by all the participants and can be stored at any participant site.

The ability to consider user-specified requirements (e.g. queries deadlines and data availability degree) when scheduling query execution and when selecting and placing replicas are among the challenges that must be faced in future work.

REFERENCES

Akal, F., Böhm, K., & Schek, H. (2002). OLAP Query Evaluation in a Database Cluster: A Performance Study on Intra-Query Parallelism. In *Proceedings of the 6th East European Conference.* LNCS, *2435*, 181-184.

Akinde, M. O., Böhlen, M. H., Johnson, T., Lakshmanan, L. V., & Srivastava, D. (2002). Efficient OLAP Query Processing in Distributed Data Warehouses. In *Proceedings of the 8th international Conference on Extending Database Technology: Advances in Database Technology.* LNCS, *2287*, 336-353.

Allcock, W., Bresnahan, J., Kettimuthu, R., & Link, M. (2005). The Globus Striped GridFTP Framework and Server. In *Proceedings of the 2005 ACM/IEEE Conference on Supercomputing* (pp. 54-65).

Bird, I., & The LCG Editorial Board (2005). *LHC Computing Grid Technical Design Report.* LCG-TDR-001, CERN-LHCC-2005-024.

Buyya, R., Abramson, D., & Giddy, J. (2000) Nimrod/g: An architecture of a resource management and scheduling system in a global computational grid. In *Proceedings Fourth International Conference on High Performance Computing in the Asia-Pacific Region, 1* (pp. 283-289).

Chaudhuri, S., & Dayal, U. (1997). An overview of data warehousing and OLAP technology. *SIGMOD Rec. 26, 1*, 65-74.

Chervenak, A., Foster, I., Kesselman, C., Salisbury, C., & Tuecke, S. (2001). The data grid: Towards an architecture for the distributed management and analysis of large scientific datasets. *Journal of Network and Computer Applications, 23*, 187-200.

Chervenak, A. L., Palavalli, N., Bharathi, S., Kesselman, C., & Schwartzkopf, R. (2004). Performance and Scalability of a Replica Location Service. In *Proceedings of the 13th IEEE international Symposium on High Performance Distributed Computing* (pp.182-191).

Costa, R. L., C. & Furtado, P. (2006). Data Warehouses in Grids with High QoS. In *Proceedings of the 8th International Conference on Data Warehousing and Knowledge Discovery*, LNCS, *4081*, 207-217.

Costa, R. L. C., & Furtado, P. (2007). An SLA-Enabled Grid DataWarehouse. In *Proceedings of the 11th international Database Engineering and Applications Symposium* (pp. 285-289). IEEE Computer Society.

Costa, R. L. C., & Furtado, P. (2008a). Scheduling in Grid Databases. In *22nd International Conference on Advanced Information Networking and Applications Workshops Proceedings* (pp. 696-701). IEEE Computer Society.

Costa, R. L. C., & Furtado, P. (2008b). A QoS-oriented external scheduler. In *Proceedings of the 2008 ACM Symposium on Applied Computing. SAC'08* (pp. 1029-1033).

Dehne, F., Lawrence, M., & Rau-Chaplin, A. (2007). Cooperative Caching for Grid Based Data Warehouses. In *Proceedings of the Seventh IEEE International Symposium on Cluster Computing and the Grid* (pp. 31-38). IEEE Computer Society.

Deshpande, P. M., Ramasamy, K., Shukla, A., & Naughton, J. F. (1998). Caching multidimensional queries using chunks. In *Proceedings of the 1998 ACM SIGMOD international Conference on Management of Data. SIGMOD '98* (pp. 259-270).

Frey, J., Tannenbaum, T., Livny, M., Foster, I., & Tuecke, S. (2001). Condor-G: A Computation Management Agent for Multi-Institutional Grids. In *Proceedings of the 10th IEEE international Symposium on High Performance Distributed Computing* (p. 55).

Foster, I. T. (2001). The Anatomy of the Grid: Enabling Scalable Virtual Organizations. *In Proceedings of the 7th international Euro-Par Conference on Parallel Processing.* LNCS, *2150*, 1-4.

Foster, I. (2005). Globus Toolkit Version 4: Software for Service-Oriented Systems *IFIP International Conference on Network and Parallel Computing*, LNCS *3779*, 2-13.

Foster, I., & Kesselman, C. (1997). Globus: A Metacomputing Infrastructure Toolkit. *Intl J. Supercomputer Applications*, 11(*2*), 115-128.

Furtado, P. (2004a). Workload-Based Placement and Join Processing in Node-Partitioned Data Warehouses. In *Proceedings of the 6th International Conference on Data Warehousing and Knowledge Discovery.* LNCS, *3181*, 38-47.

Furtado, P. (2004b). Experimental evidence on partitioning in parallel data warehouses. In *Proceedings of the 7th ACM international Workshop on Data Warehousing and OLAP* (pp. 23-30).

Furtado, P. (2005). Hierarchical Aggregation in Networked Data Management. *In Proceedings of the International Euro-Par Conference on Parallel Processing.* LNCS, *3648*, 360-369.

Grimshaw, A. S., Wulf, W. A., & The Legion Team, C. (1997). The Legion vision of a worldwide virtual computer. *Communications of the ACM, 40*(1), 39-45.

Haddad, C., & Slimani, Y. (2007). Economic Model for Replicated Database Placement in Grid. In *Proceedings of the Seventh IEEE international Symposium on Cluster Computing and the Grid* (pp. 283-292). IEEE Computer Society.

Krauter, K., Buyya, R., & Maheswaran M. (2002) A taxonomy and survey of grid resource management systems for distributed computing. *Softw. Pract. Exper., 32*(2),135-164.

Lawrence, M., & Rau-Chaplin, A. (2006). The OLAP-Enabled Grid: Model and Query Processing Algorithms. In *Proceedings of the 20th international Symposium on High-Performance Computing in An Advanced Collaborative Environment* (pp. 4).

Lima, A., Mattoso, M., & Valduriez., P. (2004). Adaptive Virtual Partitioning for OLAP Query Processing in a Database Cluster, In *Proceedings of the Brazilian Symposium on Databases* (pp. 92-105).

Lin, Y., Liu, P., & Wu, J. (2006). Optimal Placement of Replicas in Data Grid Environments with Locality Assurance. In *Proceedings of the 12th international Conference on Parallel and Distributed Systems* (pp. 465-474). IEEE Computer Society.

Liu, P., & Wu, J. (2006). Optimal Replica Placement Strategy for Hierarchical Data Grid Systems. In *Proceedings of the Sixth IEEE international Symposium on Cluster Computing and the Grid* (pp. 417-420). IEEE Computer Society.

Park, S., & Kim, J. (2003). Chameleon: A Resource Scheduler in A Data Grid Environment. In *Proceedings of the 3st international Symposium on Cluster Computing and the Grid* (p. 258). IEEE Computer Society.

Ranganathan, K., & Foster, I. T. (2001). Identifying Dynamic Replication Strategies for a High-Performance Data Grid. In *Proceedings of the Second international Workshop on Grid Computing* LNCS, *2242*, 75-86.

Ranganathan, K., & Foster, I. (2002). Decoupling Computation and Data Scheduling in Distributed Data-Intensive Applications. In *Proceedings of the 11th IEEE international Symposium on High Performance Distributed Computing* (pp. 352). IEEE Computer Society.

Ranganathan, K., & Foster, I. (2004). Computation scheduling and data replication algorithms for data Grids. In *Grid Resource Management: State of the Art and Future Trends* (pp. 359-373). Kluwer Academic Publishers.

Roy, A., & Sander, V. (2004) GARA: a uniform quality of service architecture. In *Grid Resource Management: State of the Art and Future Trends* (pp. 377-394). Kluwer Academic Publishers.

Schopf, J. M., & Nitzberg, B. (2002) Grids: The top ten questions. *Scientific Programming, 10*(2) 103-111.

Siva Sathya, S., & Kuppuswami, S., and Ragupathi, R. (2006). Replication Strategies for Data Grids. In *International Conference on Advanced Computing and Communications* (pp 123-128).

Stöhr, T., Märtens, H., & Rahm, E. (2000). Multi-Dimensional Database Allocation for Parallel Data Warehouses. In *Proceedings of the 26th international Conference on Very Large Data Bases* (pp. 273-284).

Sulistio, A., Cibej, U., Venugopal, S., Robic, B., and Buyya, R. (2007). *A Toolkit for Modelling and Simulating Data Grids: An Extension to GridSim.* Retrieved March 2008, from http://www.gridbus.org/gridsim/

Sun Microsystems, Inc. (2002). *Sun™ ONE Grid Engine Administration and User's Guide.* Santa Clara, California, U.S.A.

Tomov, N., Dempster, E., Williams, M. H., Burger, A., Taylor, H., King, P. J., & Broughton, P. (2004). Analytical response time estimation in parallel relational database systems. *Parallel Comput. 30*(2), 249-283.

Wehrle, P., Miquel, M., & Tchounikine, A. (2007). A Grid Services-Oriented Architecture for Efficient Operation of Distributed Data Warehouses on Globus. In *Proceedings of the 21st international Conference on Advanced Networking and Applications* (pp. 994-999). IEEE Computer Society.

Wolski, R. (1997). Forecasting network performance to support dynamic scheduling using the network weather service. In *Proceedings of the 6th IEEE international Symposium on High Performance Distributed Computing* (pp. 316). IEEE Computer Society.

Chapter VI
Leveraging Simulation Practice in Industry through Use of Desktop Grid Middleware

Navonil Mustafee
University of Warwick, UK

Simon J. E. Taylor
Brunel University, UK

ABSTRACT

This chapter focuses on the collaborative use of computing resources to support decision making in industry. Through the use of middleware for desktop grid computing, the idle CPU cycles available on existing computing resources can be harvested and used for speeding-up the execution of applications that have "non-trivial" processing requirements. This chapter focuses on the desktop grid middleware BOINC and Condor, and discusses the integration of commercial simulation software together with free-to-download grid middleware so as to offer competitive advantage to organizations that opt for this technology. It is expected that the low-intervention integration approach presented in this chapter (meaning no changes to source code required) will appeal to both simulation practitioners (as simulations can be executed faster, which in turn would mean that more replications and optimization are possible in the same amount of time) and management (as it can potentially increase the return on investment on existing resources).

INTRODUCTION AND MOTIVATION

Grid computing has the potential to provide users "on-demand" access to large amounts of comput-ing power, just as power grids provide users with consistent, pervasive, dependable and transparent access to electricity, irrespective of its source (Baker et al., 2002). Simulation in industry can

Copyright © 2009, IGI Global, distributing in print or electronic forms without written permission of IGI Global is prohibited.

potentially benefit from this as computing power can be an issue in the time taken to get results from a simulation (Robinson, 2005a). This is further supported by the observation that the use of grid computing in scientific simulation has certainly proved beneficial in disciplines such as particle physics, climatology, astrophysics and medicine, among others. Thus, our first motivation is to inform simulation users in industry as to how the practice of simulation can benefit from grid computing.

Another motivation is the low adoption rate of grid computing outside of academic and research domains. At present a major proportion of grid users comprise of researchers (physicists, biologists, climatologists, etc. who are the primary stakeholder of the applications running on the grid) and computer specialists with programming skills (the providers of IT support to the stakeholders). This is not unexpected as the majority of applications using grid computing are research applications. The adoption of grid computing technologies by

employees in industry has so far been relatively modest. One important reason for this is, although the employees are experts in their own discipline they generally do not have the necessary technical skills that are required to work with present generation grid technologies. A possible means to increase adoption is to incorporate grid support in software applications that require non-trivial amounts of computation power and which are used by the end-users to perform their day-to-day jobs. The *commercial, off-the-shelf (COTS) Simulation Packages (CSPs)* used in industry to model simulations are an ideal candidate for such type of integration. This chapter, thus, focuses on leveraging the practice of CSP-based simulation in industry through use of grid computing. Figure 1 shows the motivations of this research.

The remainder of this chapter is organised as follows. The second section gives an overview of the practice of simulation in industry and the CSPs used to model such simulations. The following two sections are devoted to grid computing and

Figure 1. Chapter motivations

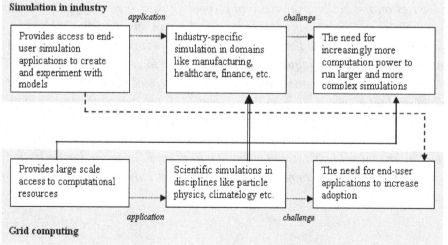

desktop grid computing respectively. The CSP-grid integration approaches are proposed in the subsequent section, followed by two CSP-grid integration case studies. The last section presents a summary of this research and brings the chapter to a close.

SIMULATION PRACTICE IN INDUSTRY

Defining Computer Simulation

A computer simulation uses the power of computers to conduct experiments with models that represent systems of interest (Pidd, 2004). Experimenting with the computer model enables us to know more about the system under scrutiny and to evaluate various strategies for the operation of the system (Shannon, 1998). Computer simulations are generally used for experimentation as they are cheaper than building (and discarding) real systems; they assist in the identification of problems in the underlying system and allow testing of different scenarios in an attempt to resolve them; allow faster than real-time experimentation; provide a means to depict the behaviour of systems under development; involve lower costs compared to experimenting with real systems; facilitate the replication of experiments; and provide a safe environment for studying dangerous situations like combat scenarios, natural disasters and evacuation strategies (Brooks et al., 2001; Pidd, 2004).

Application of Simulation in Industry

Various simulation techniques are applied to a wide range of application domains for a variety of purposes. For example, *System Dynamics (SD)* is used in industry for strategy development and supply chain management; *Discrete Event Simulation (DES)* is used to estimate availability of weapons systems in the military, in the manufacturing industry DES is used for inven-

tory management, scheduling and optimization; *Parallel and Distributed Simulation (PADS)* is used in the military for conducting large-scale simulation-based training; *Agent-Based Simulation (ABS)* has been used in defence to examine dynamic teaming and task allocation problems, in industry the possible applications of ABS include supply chain management, organizational design and process improvement (Eldabi et al., 2008). In healthcare, *Monte-Carlo Simulation (MCS)* has been used to evaluate the cost-effectiveness of competing technologies, SD has assisted in designing healthcare policies, ABS has been used to study problems such as the spread of epidemics, DES has been used to forecast the impact of changes in patient flow, to examine resource needs, to manage patient scheduling and admissions, etc.

This chapter focuses on DES and MCS performed for the purposes of (1) optimization of resources in the manufacturing industry and (2) risk analysis in the banking, insurance and finance sector. Simulations associated with both optimization and risk analysis can usually benefit from more computing power, since optimization generally involves conducting several sets of DES experiments with varying resource parameters and MCS involves executing thousands of Monte Carlo iterations. Although manufacturing and finance remain the focus of this chapter, the reader should note that the case study exemplars presented in this chapter could easily be generalized to other areas of use. The grid computing technologies that are subsequently proposed are ideally suited to SMEs who have a requirement for additional computing power to run optimization and credit risk simulations, but may not be willing to invest in additional computer hardware (like Beowulf clusters, computers with multi-core processors, etc.) or commercial "black-box" software (like Digipede Network, MathLab Parallel Computing Toolbox, etc.), but would instead be interested in increasing their Return on Investment (ROI) on existing hardware, software and technical resources. The proposed grid solutions are suitable for SMEs because they can be downloaded free of cost; they present an opportunity to harness idle CPU cycles from computing resources that already exist in an organization; they have the potential to increase the ROI on simulation software through their integration with the grid solutions; and finally, these grid solutions could increase the utilization of technical resources like IT staff and subscription to specialized online IT helpdesks, references and forums.

DES and MCS

DES and MCS are two simulation techniques that are widely used in industry. In DES the behaviour of a model, and hence the system state, changes at an instant of time (Brooks et al., 2001). DES is arguably the most frequently used classical Operational Research (OR) technique that is applied across a range of industries like manufacturing, travel, healthcare, among others (Hollocks, 2006).

MCS is yet another OR technique that is extensively used in application areas like finance and insurance (Herzog & Lord, 2002). MCS uses a sequence of random numbers according to probabilities assumed to be associated with a source of uncertainty, for example, stock prices, interest rates, exchange rates or commodity prices (Chance, 2004).

In the context of simulation practice in industry, although programming languages may be used to build simulations in certain circumstances, models are generally created using commercially available simulation packages (Robinson, 2005b). In this chapter the term *Commercial Off-The-Shelf (COTS) Simulation Packages (CSPs)* are used to refer to software used for modelling both DES and MCS. CSPs are described next.

COTS Simulation Packages

Visual interactive modelling systems usually refer to DES software that enable users to create models in a graphical environment through an interactive "click-and-drag" selection of pre-defined simulation objects (entry points, queues, workstations, resources, etc.) and linking them together to represent the underlying logical interactions between the entities they represent (Pidd, 2004). Examples of such software include DES packages like Witness (Lanner group) and Simul8 (Simul8 corporation). Similarly, MCS may be modelled in a visual environment using spreadsheet software like Excel (Microsoft), Lotus 1-2-3 (IBM, formerly Lotus Software); spreadsheet add-ins, for example @Risk (Palisade Corporation), Crystal Ball (Decisioneering); or through MC-specific simulation packages such as Analytica (Lumina Decision Systems) and Analytics (SunGard).

Swain (2005) has made a comprehensive survey of commercially available simulation tools based on the information provided by vendors in response to a questionnaire requesting product information. This list presently consists of 56 tools and features the most well known CSP vendors and their products (Swain, 2007). All the 45 CSPs (12 MCS CSPs and 33 DES CSPs) that have been identified from Swain's survey are supported in the Windows platform, 15.56% (approx.) are supported in UNIX and Linux platforms, and only 13.33% (approx.) are supported on Apple Macintosh Operating System (Mustafee, 2007). As will be discussed later in this chapter, platform support for CSPs is important when considering different grid technologies that can be potentially be used with existing CSPs. A discussion on grid computing is presented in the next section.

GRID COMPUTING

Defining Grid Computing

Grid computing (or Grids) was first defined by Ian Foster and Carl Kesselman in their book *"The Grid: The Blueprint for a New Computing Infrastructure"* as a hardware and software infrastructure that provides access to high-end computational resources (Foster & Kesselman, 1998). This definition has since then been modified twice by the grid veterans over a period of nearly 5 years. However, all the three definitions are consistent in terms of their focus on large-scale computing. Thus, Foster and Kesselman (1998) mention "access to high-end computational resources", Foster et al. (2001) refer to "large-scale resource sharing" and, finally, Foster and Kesselman (2004) highlight "delivery of nontrivial QoS". This definition of grid computing, referred to in this chapter as *cluster-based grid computing*, is generally geared towards dedicated high performance clusters and super computers running on UNIX and Linux flavour operating systems. However, as will be discussed in the subsequent section on desktop grid computing, cluster-based grid computing can be contrasted with *desktop-based grid computing* which refers to the aggregation of non-dedicated, de-centralized, commodity PCs connected through a network and running (mostly) the Microsoft Windows operating system. The following two sub-sections pertain only to *cluster-based grid computing.*

Grid Middleware

A grid middleware is a distributed computing software that integrates network-connected computing resources (computer clusters, data servers, standalone PCs, sensor networks, etc.), that may span multiple administrative domains, with the objective of making the combined resource pool available to user applications for number crunching, remote data access, remote application access, among others (Mustafee & Taylor, 2008). A grid middleware is what makes grid computing possible. Table 1 presents an overview of grid middleware that are commonly installed on distributed computing resources to create an underlying infrastructure for grid computing. The operating system support for each middleware is also highlighted.

Table 1. Examples of middleware for grid computing

Middleware	Description	Operating System support
Globus (GT 4)	Globus middleware is an open architecture and an open source set of services and software libraries which supports grids and grid applications (Foster et al., 2002).	UNIX, Linux and Windows. However, the WSRF- GRAM; the non-web services implementations for GRAM, MyProxy, etc. can only be run on UNIX and Linux platforms (Globus Alliance, 2005).
Condor	Condor is a job scheduling system that maximizes the utilization of collections of networked PCs through identification of idle resources and scheduling background user jobs on them (Litzkow et al., 1988).	UNIX, Linux and Windows platforms. However, several Condor execution environments like standard universe, PVM universe, etc. are not supported on Windows (Condor Version 6.9.1 Manual, 2007).
Virtual Data Toolkit (VDT)	It is a combined package of various grid middleware components, including Globus and Condor, and other utilities. The goal of VDT is to provide users with a middleware that is thoroughly tested, simple to install and maintain, and easy to use.	VDT (version 1.6.1) supports only Linux-based platforms like *Debian Linux, Fedora Core Linux, RedHat Enterprise Linux, Rocks Linux, Scientific Linux* and *SUSE Linux* (Virtual Data Toolkit, 2007).
GLite	gLite uses components developed from several other grid projects like Globus and Condor. gLite is primarily being developed for the LHC Computation Grid (LCG) and the EGEE grids (see section 3.3).	GLite-3 middleware is presently supported only on the *Scientific Linux* operating system (Burke et al., 2007).

Production Grids

Production grids can be defined as grid computing infrastructures that have transitioned from being "research and development" test beds to being fully-functional grid environments, offering users round-the-clock availability at sustained throughput levels. Production grids are usually supported by a team that is responsible for the day-to-day maintenance of the grid, solving technical problems associated with the grid, helping users through help-desk support, creating user documents, conducting training courses for knowledge dissemination purposes, among others. Table 2 lists some of the large production grids and the grid middleware running on them.

As can be seen from Table 2, most of these production grids have a resource base spanning multiple virtual organizations (VOs). These production grids are mainly being used for e-Science projects. There are very few examples of multiple VO-based grid computing being used in industry. However, it is also true that grid computing middleware like Globus is gradually being introduced within enterprises for processing enterprise-related applications. In this scheme the organizations seek to leverage their existing computing resources using grid middleware. Collaborations, if any, are limited to intra-organizational resource sharing and problem solving. Organizations that use grid computing middleware for their day-to-day operations or integrate these middleware within their own applications include SAP (Foster, 2005), GlobeXplorer (Gentzsch, 2004) and Planet Earth (Levine & Wirt, 2004).

It has to be said here that there is little agreement over what the term grid computing actually means and there is not one, all-accepted, defini-

Table 2. Examples of production grids

Grid Name	Purpose	Infrastructure	Grid MW	Reference
LCG (LHC Computing Grid), Europe	The purpose of LCG is to provide computation and storage resources for four LHC particle physics experiments at CERN, Geneva.	At present the LCG grid spans over 200 sites around the world and has access to more than 30,000 CPUs and 20 PB of data storage capacity.	LCG-2 /gLite	(Lamanna, 2004), and (Burke et al., 2007)
EGEE (Enabling Grids for E-sciencE) Grid, Europe	EGEE Grid infrastructure is ideal for any scientific research.	The EGEE project involves over 90 partner institutions across Europe, Asia and the United States and provides access to over 20,000 CPU and 5 Petabytes of storage.	LCG-2 /gLite	(EGEE, 2007)
NGS (National Grid Service), UK	Production use of computational and data grid resources in all branches of academic research.	NGS provides access to over 2,000 processors and over 36 TB storage capacities. These resources are provided by the Universities of Manchester, Leeds, Oxford and RAL, among others.	Globus	(Yang et al., 2005)
TeraGrid, USA	Research in genomics, earthquake studies, cosmology, climate and atmospheric simulations, biology, etc.	As of 2003, the TeraGrid infrastructure consists of the NCSA, SDSC, ANL, among others.	Globus	(Reed, 2003)

tion of grid computing. For example, Baker et al. (2002, p. 1437) mention that the "cooperative use of geographically distributed resources unified to act as a single powerful computer" is known by several names such as "meta-computing, scalable computing, global computing, Internet computing, and more recently peer-to-peer or Grid computing" and Luther et al. (2005) refer to enterprise desktop grid computing, public distributed computing and peer-to-peer computing as different names for Internet computing. However, as will be seen from the discussion presented in the next sub-section, grid computing, enterprise desktop grid computing and Internet / peer-to-peer / public resource computing generally have a different set of objectives that determine the design architecture of their underlying middleware technologies.

Different Forms of Grid Computing

The discussion on grid computing, until this point, has shown that grid infrastructures and middleware applications have traditionally been geared towards dedicated, centralized, high performance clusters and super-computers running on UNIX and Linux operating systems. This form of grid computing will henceforth be referred to as *cluster-based grid computing*. It can be contrasted with *desktop-based grid computing* which refers to the aggregation of non-dedicated, de-centralized, commodity PCs connected through a network and running (mostly) the Microsoft Windows operating system. Studies have shown that desktop PCs can be under utilized by as much as 75% of the time (Mutka, 1992). This coupled with the widespread availability of desktop computers and the fact that the power of network, storage and computing resources is projected to double every 9, 12, and 18 months respectively (Casanova, 2002), represents an enormous computing resource.

In this chapter the use of a desktop grid within the enterprise is termed as *Enterprise-wide Desktop Grid Computing (EDGC)*. Thus, EDGC refers

to a grid infrastructure that is confined to an institutional boundary, where the spare processing capacities of an enterprise's desktop PCs are used to support the execution of the enterprise's applications (Chien et al., 2003). User participation in such a grid is not usually voluntary and is governed by enterprise policy. Applications like Condor, Entropia DCGrid, and Digipede Network are all examples of EDGC.

Like EDGC, Internet computing seeks to provide resource virtualization through the aggregation of idle CPU cycles of desktop PCs. But unlike EDGC, where the desktop resources are generally connected to the corporate LAN and used to process enterprise applications, Internet computing infrastructure consists of volunteer resources connected over the Internet and is used either for scientific computation or for the execution of applications from which the user can derive some benefit (for example, sharing music files). This research distinguishes between two forms of Internet computing - *Public Resource Computing (PRC)* and *Peer-to-Peer Computing (P2P)* - based on whether the underlying desktop grid infrastructure is used for solving scientific problems or for deriving some user benefit respectively. The different forms of grid computing are shown in Figure 2.

Grid Middleware and CSPs

Discussions presented earlier in the chapter have highlighted that all CSPs are supported on the Windows platform, 15.56% on both UNIX and Linux operating systems and only 13.33% CSPs are supported on Macintosh. This shows the prevalence of Windows-based CSPs in industry. It is therefore arguable that for this research to be widely relevant to the practice of CSP-based simulation in industry, it should, first and foremost, focus on Windows-based grid computing solutions. Discussion on cluster-based UNIX and Linux grid solutions for CSP-based simulation modelling is thus outside the scope of this chapter.

Figure 2. Forms of grid computing

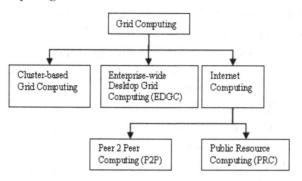

P2P computing is also not investigated further because it generally supports only file sharing and as such P2P networks cannot be used to execute programs (like CSPs) on the peer resources. Thus, the next section focuses only on PRC and EDGC forms of grid computing.

DESKTOP GRID COMPUTING

BOINC is an open source PRC middleware that allows users to create new BOINC-based projects to cater to their computational needs. Condor is an EDGC middleware that is used for both e-Science research and for enterprise application processing. Both BOINC and Condor are cycle stealing systems that can run on non-dedicated Windows PCs.

The rationale for choosing BOINC as a representative form of PRC middleware is as follows:

- It is arguably the most popular PRC middleware. "BOINC is currently used by about 20 projects, to which over 600,000 volunteers and 1,000,000 computers supply 350 TeraFLOPS of processing power" (Anderson et al., 2006, p. 33).
- It is presently the only PRC middleware that allows users to create their own projects.
- It is available free of cost.

The rationale for choosing Condor as a representative form of EDGC middleware is as follows:

- It has the largest EDGC deployment base. More than 80,000 Condor hosts around the world make up approximately 160 production-level Condor pools (see <http://www.cs.wisc.edu/condor/map/> for updated Condor statistics).
- It is available free of cost.

PRC Middleware BOINC

The BOINC system (see Figure 3) contains several server-side components, which may execute on separate machines if required. Most of the server side components can only be installed over a UNIX or Linux flavour operating system. The database holds all the metadata associated with the project and lifecycle information for each work unit. A client's command channel operates via the scheduling server, using an XML-based protocol. Results are transferred using HTTP via the data servers. In addition to work units and results, other files may be transferred between server and client, including application executables and any other interim data the application may require during the operation. The database also has a web-based front-end that is used for displaying project information specific to volunteers, for example, how many computers have been contributed by the user, the number of work units processed, etc. On the client side, the *BOINC core client* manages interaction with the server, while optional components (like screensaver and manager) provide graphical control and display elements for the benefit of the user. The core client can be installed in the Windows operating system. The BOINC client API provides the interface between the user-created *application client* and the BOINC core client. The API is a set of C++ functions and the application client is compiled with it. All communication between the BOINC core client and the BOINC project servers take place through HTTP on port 80. The BOINC core client can therefore operate behind firewalls and proxies.

The widespread availability of desktop PCs in organizations makes the deployment of an enterprise-wide BOINC infrastructure an attractive option. Thus, it may be possible to implement and deploy BOINC-based projects for use exclusively

Figure 3. The BOINC system. (©2007 IEEE. Used with permission.)

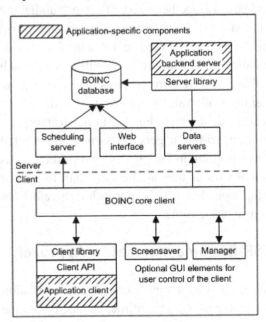

within an enterprise, such that it is geared up to support the execution of the enterprises' applications. The participants of such an enterprise-wide BOINC setup can be the employees of the organization who contribute their work PCs. The participation in such projects may not be voluntary and can be governed by the policy of the organization. The computations being performed by the BOINC clients will be in line with the needs of the enterprise, and unlike PRC where volunteers are encouraged to contribute their resources, only employees and other trusted sources will be allowed to participate in the enterprise-wide BOINC projects. BOINC features that are necessary in the PRC context but may not be required in an enterprise grid (for e.g., user rewards system, anti-cheating measures, mechanisms to deal with client failure or extended network non-connectivity, etc.) can be disabled.

EDGC Middleware Condor

Condor is an opportunistic job scheduling system that is designed to maximize the utilization of workstations through identification of idle resources and scheduling background jobs on them (Litzkow et al., 1988). A collection of such workstations is referred to as a Condor pool. Two fundamental concepts of Condor middleware, which are also important in our discussions on CSPs, are (a) Condor matchmaking and (b) Condor universe. These are described next:

a. Condor architecture defines resource providers and resource consumers. The resource providers make their resources available to Condor for the processing of jobs that originate from the resource consumers. Condor allows both resource consumers and providers to advertise these requirements, conditions and preferences by providing a language called *classified advertisements (ClassAds)* (Thain et al., 2004). The ClassAds are scanned by a Condor *matchmaker*

Figure 4. Condor resource management architecture - adapted from Basney and Livney (1999)

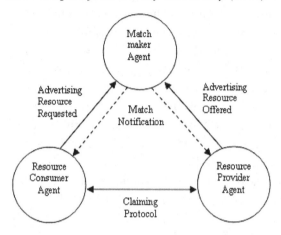

agent, running on only one computer in a Condor Pool, to find a match between the requirements advertised by the *resource consumer agents* and the resources advertised by the *resource provider agents*. Once a match has been found by the matchmaker agent, it notifies both the resource consumer and the resource provider agents. Upon receiving this notification, the resource consumer agent claims the resource advertised by the resource provider agent through a claiming protocol. The job is executed by the resource provider agent and the results of the computation are returned back to the resource consumer agent. The matchmaking process is illustrated in Figure 4. The figure has been adapted from Basney and Livney (1999).

Thus, in order to execute CSP-based simulations using Condor, PCs acting as resource provider agents will have to be installed with CSPs (Simul8, Excel, etc.) and will need to advertise this using ClassAds mechanism. The resource consumer agents will also be required to advertise their requirement (for example, 10 PCs required) with the condition that the resource providers will have the appropriate CSPs installed on them.

b. *Condor universe* is an execution environment for jobs that are submitted by the users. Depending upon the type of job to be executed and its requirements, the user needs to select an appropriate Condor universe. *Java universe* supports the execution of java programs and is appropriate for executing CSP-based simulations over Condor.

Three different approaches to integrating CSPs with grid computing middleware are discussed next.

CSP-GRID INTEGRATION APPROACHES

Three possible approaches for using desktop grids with CSPs are the *CSP-middleware integration approach*, the *CSP-runtime installation approach* and the *CSP-preinstalled approach* (Mustafee & Taylor, 2008).

CSP-Grid Middleware Integration Approach

One possible approach to using desktop grid middleware together with CSPs is to "bundle" the latter along with the former. When a desktop grid middleware is installed on a PC, the CSP is also installed on it. The problem with this approach is that it will require changes to the enterprise desktop grid middleware as a CSP will have to be integrated with it. Furthermore, an enterprise desktop grid is a general purpose distributed computing environment that allows the execution of various user applications (not limited to simulation alone). This approach is therefore not considered feasible.

CSP-Runtime Installation Approach

The second approach involves the installation of a CSP package at runtime, i.e. just before the simulation experiment is conducted. In this case the CSP itself is transferred to the desktop grid nodes, along with the data files associated with the simulation and the trigger code (executable code which starts the CSP-based simulation on a grid node). This approach may not be feasible for a number of reasons. (1) the size of CSPs frequently exceed 100s of MBs and it may not be feasible to transfer such large amounts of data to multiple clients over the network, (2) the CSP will first need to be installed on the desktop grid node before the simulation can start, (3) such an installation is normally an interactive process requiring human intervention, (4) an installation normally requires administrative privileges on the client computers, (5) transferring CSPs may lead to a violation of the software licence agreement that may be in place between the CSP vendor and the organization (if the number of desktop grid nodes executing simulations exceed the number of licences purchased).

CSP-Preinstalled Approach

The third CSP-grid integration approach is to install the CSP in the desktop grid resource, just like any other application is installed on a PC. The drawback with this approach is that the sandbox security mechanism implemented by most enterprise desktop grids may have to be forfeited. However, as simulations are created by trusted employees running trusted software within the bounds of a fire-walled network, security in this open access scheme could be argued as being irrelevant (i.e. if it were an issue then it is an issue with the wider security system and not the desktop grid).

Of the three CSP-grid integration approaches discussed in this section, the CSP-preinstalled approach is considered the most appropriate because (1) it does not require any modification to the CSPs – thus, CSPs that expose package functionality can be grid-enabled, (2) it does not require any modification to the grid middleware

– thus, existing Windows-supported grid middleware like BOINC and Condor can be used, and (3) CSPs that are installed on the user PCs can be utilized for running simulation experiments from other users.

The procedure to execute CSP-based simulation experiments over desktop grids following the CSP-preinstalled approach is as follows (see Figure 5):

1. The simulation user writes an executable "trigger" code in C++, Java, Visual Basic (VB), etc. that accesses the CSP functionality through exposed interfaces. The trigger code should generally invoke the CSP, load the model file, transfer experiment parameters into the model, execute the model, etc. Mustafee (2007) provides a list of CSPs that expose package functionality using well-defined interfaces.

2. The simulation user makes available the data files associated with the simulation (simulation model files, experiment parameter files,

Figure 5. Executing CSP-based simulation over grid resources using CSP-preinstalled approach

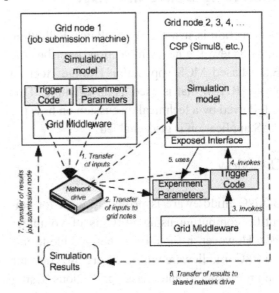

etc.) and the executable file containing the trigger code to the desktop grid nodes where the experiment will be executed. Two possible ways of accomplishing this are (1) by providing a shared grid access to a network drive, or (2) by transferring the required files using the desktop grid middleware.

3. The desktop grid middleware invokes the executable trigger code on a remote desktop node. The simulation starts and results are saved into a file. The user retrieves the results by (1) accessing them from the shared network drive, or (2) the result files are transferred back to the user through the grid middleware.

The next section of this chapter uses Microsoft Excel together with BOINC and Condor middleware to execute Monte Carlo simulations over the grid. Although Excel has been used here as an example, the CSP-preinstalled approach can generally be used with other DES and MCS CSPs that expose package functionality.

INTERFACING BOINC AND CONDOR WITH CSPs

Interfacing BOINC with Excel

This section is structured as follows. Following an overview, the next sub-section describes the Excel-based MCS application (Range Accrual Swap [RAS]) that is used as an example. This is followed by a technical discussion on how the RAS application is grid-enabled.

Overview

BOINC middleware is primarily used for scientific computing using millions of volunteer PCs. However, it should also be possible to use the PRC middleware within an organization for the processing of enterprise applications. Using the Excel-based RAS application, this research now investigates how BOINC can be used in a desktop grid environment to provide task farming service to the CSPs. Arguably, this is the first attempt to use a PRC middleware in an enterprise environment. There are no existing examples of enterprise application processing using BOINC in literature.

Range Accrual Swap (RAS) Application

The application that is used to implement task farming using BOINC is a Microsoft Excel-based spreadsheet application used for financial modelling by a leading European financial institution. The financial model calculates the risk of a *Range Accrual Swap* at various points in time until the maturity of the transactions. Range Accrual Swap is a type of financial derivative instrument in which certain fixed cash flows are exchanged for an uncertain stream of cash flows based on the movement of interest rates in the future. A screenshot of the RAS application is shown in Figure 6.

The successful and accurate calculation of risk using the RAS application requires a large number of MCS and takes a significant amount of time. Each simulation run (iteration) is independent of previous runs and is characterized by the generation of random values for various defined variables and by solving equations containing these variables. The conventional approach of using only one instance of Excel is not feasible in situations where the business desires a quick turnaround (answer). One solution to this is to distribute the processing of the MCS model over a grid and utilize the spare processing power of the grid nodes and the Excel software installed on them. This grid-facilitated execution of the RAS model has the potential of speeding up the simulation of the financial models manifold, depending on the number of grid nodes available and whether they are dedicated or non-dedicated resources.

Figure 6. Range Accrual Swap (RAS) application (created by the credit risk division of a leading European investment bank)

Range Accrual Swap PFE model	Simulate Fixed Rate		Results				

Inputs/Termsheet

Number of Monte-Carlo Simulation Iterations				10	
				Iteration #	10
Currency	USD				
Notional Amount	10,000,000				
Start Date	31-Jul-06				
Tenor (yrs)	13				
Reset/Payment freq	3	months			
Fixed Rate	6.7%				
Pay/Receive Fixed	Pay				
Underlying Libor	6	months			

N = total number of calender days in the interest period
n = the number of calender days in the interest period that the 12 month
USD LIBOR rate is within the following ranges at Fixing (inclusive)

Day Count	Act	/	365

Year	Range			Coupon
1	0%	-	7.00%	7.0%
2	0%	-	7.00%	7.0%
3	0%	-	7.00%	7.0%
4	0%	-	7.00%	7.0%
5	0%	-	7.00%	7.0%
6	0%	-	7.00%	7.0%
7	0%	-	7.00%	7.0%
8	0%	-	7.00%	7.0%
9	0%	-	7.00%	7.0%
10	0%	-	7.00%	7.0%
11	0%	-	7.00%	7.0%
12	0%	-	7.00%	7.0%
13	0%	-	7.00%	7.0%
14				
15				

Term Structure		HW parameters	
Tenor	df	alpha	
0.00	1.000	0.0650	
0.08	0.998	sigma	
0.25	0.995	1.00%	

Simulated df curve

Time step (yrs)	0	1	2	3	4	5	6	7
Y(t)		-0.692	-2.551	-0.483	0.907	1.194	-0.245	-1.188

		0	1	2	3	4	5	6	7
0	0.000	1.0000	1.0000	1.0000	1.0000	1.0000	1.0000	1.0000	1.0000
1	0.003	0.9999	1.0000	1.0000	0.9999	0.9999	0.9999	0.9999	0.9999
2	0.005	0.9999	0.9999	1.0000	0.9998	0.9997	0.9997	0.9998	0.9998
3	0.008	0.9998	0.9998	0.9999	0.9998	0.9996	0.9996	0.9997	0.9997
4	0.011	0.9998	0.9998	0.9999	0.9997	0.9995	0.9994	0.9995	0.9996
5	0.014	0.9997	0.9997	0.9999	0.9996	0.9994	0.9993	0.9994	0.9995
6	0.016	0.9997	0.9997	0.9999	0.9995	0.9992	0.9991	0.9993	0.9994
7	0.019	0.9996	0.9996	0.9999	0.9994	0.9991	0.9990	0.9992	0.9994
8	0.022	0.9996	0.9996	0.9998	0.9993	0.9990	0.9988	0.9991	0.9993
9	0.025	0.9995	0.9995	0.9998	0.9992	0.9988	0.9987	0.9990	0.9992
10	0.027	0.9995	0.9994	0.9998	0.9992	0.9987	0.9985	0.9989	0.9991
11	0.030	0.9994	0.9994	0.9998	0.9991	0.9986	0.9984	0.9988	0.9990
12	0.033	0.9993	0.9993	0.9997	0.9990	0.9984	0.9983	0.9986	0.9989
13	0.036	0.9993	0.9993	0.9997	0.9989	0.9983	0.9981	0.9985	0.9988
14	0.038	0.9992	0.9992	0.9997	0.9988	0.9982	0.9980	0.9984	0.9987
15	0.041	0.9992	0.9992	0.9997	0.9987	0.9980	0.9978	0.9983	0.9986
16	0.044	0.9991	0.9991	0.9997	0.9986	0.9979	0.9977	0.9982	0.9985
17	0.047	0.9991	0.9990	0.9996	0.9986	0.9978	0.9975	0.9981	0.9984
18	0.049	0.9990	0.9990	0.9996	0.9985	0.9977	0.9974	0.9980	0.9983
19	0.052	0.9990	0.9989	0.9996	0.9984	0.9975	0.9972	0.9978	0.9983
20	0.055	0.9989	0.9989	0.9996	0.9983	0.9974	0.9971	0.9977	0.9982
21	0.058	0.9989	0.9988	0.9995	0.9982	0.9973	0.9970	0.9976	0.9981
22	0.060	0.9988	0.9988	0.9995	0.9981	0.9971	0.9968	0.9975	0.9980
23	0.063	0.9988	0.9987	0.9995	0.9980	0.9970	0.9967	0.9974	0.9979
24	0.066	0.9987	0.9987	0.9995	0.9980	0.9969	0.9965	0.9973	0.9978
25	0.068	0.9986	0.9986	0.9995	0.9979	0.9967	0.9964	0.9972	0.9977
26	0.071	0.9986	0.9985	0.9994	0.9978	0.9966	0.9962	0.9970	0.9976
27	0.074	0.9985	0.9985	0.9994	0.9977	0.9965	0.9961	0.9969	0.9975
28	0.077	0.9985	0.9984	0.9994	0.9976	0.9963	0.9959	0.9968	0.9974
29	0.079	0.9984	0.9984	0.9994	0.9975	0.9962	0.9958	0.9967	0.9973
30	0.082	0.9984	0.9983	0.9993	0.9974	0.9961	0.9956	0.9966	0.9972
31	0.085	0.9983	0.9983	0.9993	0.9974	0.9960	0.9955	0.9965	0.9972
32	0.088	0.9983	0.9982	0.9993	0.9973	0.9958	0.9954	0.9964	0.9971
33	0.090	0.9982	0.9981	0.9993	0.9972	0.9957	0.9952	0.9963	0.9970

Input / Data / Simulation Results / RESULTS /

Grid-Enabling RAS Application

A BOINC-based project requires application specific implementation on both the client side and the server side. The client side implementation usually consists of writing a C++ application client that uses BOINC client library and APIs to integrate with the BOINC core client. The core client is downloaded from the BOINC website, installed on individual PCs and is attached to a BOINC project. Once successfully attached the core client downloads the project specific application client and work units for processing. The core client, which is in effect the manager of a compute resource, makes available CPU cycles to the attached project based on the user's preferences. These preferences can be set using either

Figure 7. Setting user preference using menu provided by BOINC core client

Open BOINC Manager...
Run always
● Run based on preferences
Suspend
Network activity always available
● Network activity based on preferences
Network activity suspended
About BOINC Manager...
Exit

the menu provided by the core client (Figure 7) or through a web interface (Figure 8). The latter offers the user more flexibility in specifying CPU, memory, disk and network usage. The core client can support multiple BOINC-based projects, but

Figure 8. Setting user preference using web interface

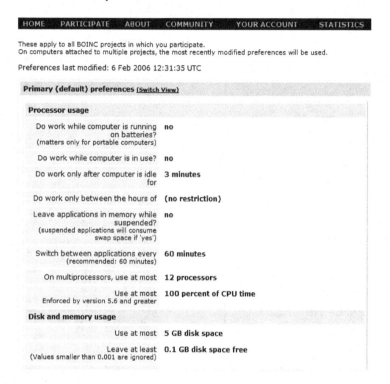

Figure 9. BOINC core client attached to multiple projects

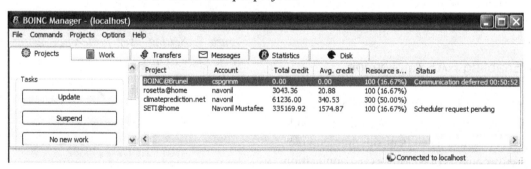

at any one time only one project can be executed. This is illustrated in Figure 9 where four different BOINC projects, viz, BOINC@Brunel, Rosetta@ Home, ClimatePrediction.net and SETI@home, are attached but only one project (SETI@home) is communicating with the BOINC server side scheduler.

In this chapter the software that has been developed to integrate BOINC with Excel is referred

to as *BOINC Proxy Application Client* or *BOINC-PAC* for short. It assumes that Microsoft Excel is installed on all the BOINC client computers.

BOINC-PAC is implemented in Visual C++. The VC++ code invokes CSP-specific operations (through interfaces exposed by the CSPs) defined by a Visual Basic DLL adapter. BOINC-PAC uses the BOINC client library and APIs to interface with the BOINC core client. It interacts with the

Figure 10. Execution of RAS application using BOINC

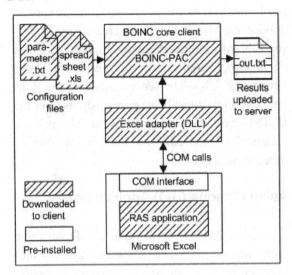

Excel adapter to execute operations on the RAS Excel-based spreadsheet. The Excel adapter, in turn, uses the COM interface of Excel to perform basic operations like opening and closing the simulation file, setting the number of iterations, executing the simulation and writing the results of the simulation to a text file (*out.txt*). The text file is subsequently uploaded to the BOINC server. The number of Monte Carlo iterations to be performed by the RAS application is not hard-coded and is read by BOINC-PAC from a parameter file (*parameter.txt* in Figure 10). The interaction of the different program components is shown in Figure 10. Once the BOINC-PAC is downloaded by the core client onto a PC it triggers the execution of the RAS MCS by utilizing the Excel software installed on the local resource.

The discussion that follows mainly concerns the BOINC server side implementation for the RAS application. When the BOINC core client first attaches itself with the RAS project it downloads the BOINC-PAC from the BOINC server. This application consists of a VC++ executable and a client initialization file called init_data.xml. Subsequently, the core client downloads the project workunits. In BOINC one unit of computation is represented as a workunit. These workunits are created using the BOINC *create_work* command and then placed in the download directory of the BOINC server. The arguments supplied to the *create_work* command include, among others, (1) the workunit template filename, (2) the result template filename and (3) the *command_line* parameter. The template files are XML files that describe the workunit (*work_unit_template.xml*) and its corresponding results (*result_template. xml*). The workunits are created by running a program that invokes the *create_work* command in a loop to generate the required number of workunits. The arguments to the *create_work* command are described next:

- The "workunit template file" lists the input files that are packed together as a workunit. In the RAS BOINC project the input files are the RAS Excel-based spreadsheet, the Excel adapter, and the parameter file. The workunit template file also mentions the quorum (XML tag *<min_quorum>*) and the maximum total results (XML tag *<max_total_results>*). However, since BOINC is being used in an enterprise grid environment that assumes some form of centralized control over the computing resources, the value for both *<min_quorum>* and *<max_total_results>* are set to one. In other words, it is expected that all the results that are returned are valid and therefore the same workunit will not be sent to more than one BOINC node.

- The "result template file" lists the files that will be uploaded to the BOINC server after the results have been computed by the BOINC-PAC. In the RAS application, the file that is uploaded from each BOINC client is called out.txt. As has been said earlier, this file contains the results of the RAS simulation.

- The optional *command_line* argument in the *create_work* command is used to pass a position value to the BOINC-PAC application. This position value represents an experiment number and BOINC-PAC reads the parameter file *parameter.txt* to extract the value at this position. This value, in our case, represents the number of Monte Carlo iterations that have to be performed on a simulation experiment being run on the client. The use of the *command_line* argument is specific to the BOINC-PAC application being developed.

200 MCS experiments (each with 300 iterations) were conducted in this study. A Java program was used to iteratively create these 200 work units by invoking *create_work* with *command_line* argument. These work units were downloaded by different BOINC nodes and the RAS application executed using the locally installed MCS CSP Excel. The results of the simulation were then automatically uploaded to the BOINC project server.

Interfacing Condor with CSPs

In this section EDGC middleware Condor is used to execute two different Excel-based Monte Carlo simulations simultaneously on different grid nodes. An overview of the case study is presented. The two applications being grid-enabled with the objective of executing them concurrently using Condor middleware are – the Asian Option application and the Range Accrual Swap application. The last section then discusses the technology used to grid-enable these applications.

Overview

Having the capability to run two or more simulation applications concurrently has the potential to execute different CSP models, which may belong to different simulation users, simultaneously over the grid. Furthermore, these models may be created and executed using different CSPs. However,

in this hypothetical case study, models created using the same MCS CSP (Microsoft Excel) are used. The first model is called the Asian Option application which has been created by Professor Eduardo Saliby (Federal University of Rio de Janeiro, Brazil; visiting professor at Brunel University, UK). The second model is the RAS application that has been previously used in the BOINC case study. The RAS model has been created by the credit risk division of a major investment bank.

Asian Options (AO) Application

The Asian Options Application uses Descriptive Sampling, which can be seen as a variance reduction technique, to calculate options whose payoffs are path-dependent on the underlying asset prices during the life of the option (Marins et al., 2004). The AO application estimates the value of the Asian options by simulating the model a number of times and then calculating the average of the results of the individual iterations. On a single PC, executing multiple iterations of the AO application takes a significant amount of time. CSP-specific task farming service has the potential to reduce the time taken to process the AO application by distributing its processing over multiple grid nodes. An average of the results returned from each node can then be calculated to determine the value of the options. Figure 11 shows the Microsoft Excel-based AO application.

Range Accrual Swap (RAS) Application

The RAS application has already been described in the preceding pages. The application is the same but the technologies used for interfacing RAS with BOINC and RAS with Condor are different. The integration of RAS with BOINC has been discussed earlier. The section that follows describes how both RAS and AO are used with the Condor Java universe execution environment.

Figure 11. Asian Options (AO) application (created by Professor Eduardo Saliby, Federal University of Rio de Janeiro, Brazil)

							H	I	J	K	L	M	N	O	P	Q	R	S
																		Arit_M
	Asian Call Option						2.75364	20%	30%	40%		0.48779	20%	30%	40%		K	2.500
							40	15.0937	14.9877	14.8939		40	1.0000	0.9949	0.9695		40	15.36
	Inputs			Black-Scholes			45	10.1754	10.1730	10.3141		45	0.9936	0.9461	0.8754		45	10.47
	S_0	55.00		d_1	0.0919		50	5.4615	5.8785	6.4179		50	0.8845	0.7726	0.6940		50	6.248
	K	55.00		d_2	-0.0306		52	3.8297	4.4592	5.1372		52	0.7635	0.6654	0.6052		52	4.323
	Sigma	30%		N(d_1)	0.5366		54	2.4809	3.2635	4.0344		54	0.6008	0.5474	0.5143		54	3.22€
	T	126		N(d_2)	0.4878		55	1.9325	2.7536	3.5499		55	0.5122	0.4878	0.4695		55	3.30
	R_f	3%		C(S,T)	2.7536		56	1.4714	2.3020	3.1090		56	0.4246	0.4295	0.4259		56	2.861
	a	0.0075					58	0.7947	1.5647	2.3520		58	0.2677	0.3212	0.3439		58	1.564
	sig_a	0.1732					60	0.3902	1.0254	1.7478		60	0.1503	0.2293	0.2711		60	1.184
							62	0.1742	0.6485	1.2766		62	0.0754	0.1565	0.2089		62	0.67
				Run			64	0.0710	0.3963	0.9174		64	0.0340	0.1024	0.1575		64	0.681
							66	0.0265	0.2344	0.6491		66	0.0138	0.0643	0.1164		66	0.377
							68	0.0091	0.1344	0.4526		68	0.0051	0.0389	0.0844		68	0.22C
							70	0.0029	0.0749	0.3113		70	0.0017	0.0228	0.0602		70	0.054

Trial	0	1	2	3	4	5	6	7	8	9	10	11	12	13	14	15	16	17
1	1	-0.3719	-0.9346	0.1383	0.2404	0.8239	-1.0152	0.4261	0.4538	-2.1701	0.1383	-1.9600	0.5388	-1.1031	-0.1383	-0.4538	-0.9741	-0.511
2	2	0.6588	0.0125	-0.1891	0.8965	0.0125	1.0152	1.0152	-1.9600	0.6588	-0.6280	-0.7554	0.3186	0.2924	0.2924	0.6280	-0.2663	0.48
3	3	0.1891	0.7554	-0.4261	-0.2404	-1.4395	0.7554	-0.0627	-0.4538	-0.5388	1.4395	0.2404	0.3451	-1.5141	-0.0376	0.2924	-0.5978	0.85
4	4	0.0878	0.3186	-0.6903	0.1891	-0.4817	-0.0125	-0.6903	-0.6903	-0.1130	1.2536	0.2663	1.6954	0.6903	0.5388	-0.9741	0.0125	1.10
5	5	-0.5101	-0.6588	0.3186	-0.3719	-0.5388	0.1637	0.6280	1.4395	0.5388	0.1891	-0.8596	-0.8239	0.3989	-1.8119	2.1701	-0.4261	-0.53
6	6	0.8239	1.0152	-0.2147	0.0627	1.2536	0.9741	-1.9600	0.5978	0.5978	-0.6588	1.6954	1.1503	-1.2004	1.3106	-1.8119	-0.8596	0.13
7	7	-0.8965	0.2663	0.2663	-0.7225	-0.0878	-0.1383	0.0376	-0.0878	0.1383	0.3451	0.0125	0.8965	-1.3722	-1.1503	-1.0152	-0.3186	0.510
8	8	0.5101	-0.1383	0.9346	1.3106	-0.3989	1.5141	-0.4261	0.1383	0.4261	-0.5101	0.9346	1.2536	0.7225	-0.3451	-0.5681	-0.7554	0.51
9	9	0.3719	0.2924	-0.1637	0.2663	-0.5978	-2.5758	-1.4395	-0.1891	-1.5141	-0.2663	1.3106	-0.9346	1.2004	2.5758	-1.3106	-0.7892	-1.05
10	10	0.1130	-0.4817	-0.1383	-0.1130	0.0627	1.8119	0.6903	1.1031	1.1031	0.9741	1.9600	-0.2404	-0.6903	0.7892	2.5758	-0.0627	1.05
11	11	-0.9741	-0.9741	-0.5978	-0.7554	0.3186	-0.2924	-0.9741	1.9600	1.3106	-2.5758	-1.0152	0.9741	-1.0581	1.9600	1.9600	0.6280	1.43
12	12	0.8965	1.1503	-0.2924	1.4395	0.9346	0.6588	0.2663	1.5982	-2.5758	-0.0125	1.4395	-1.2536	-0.3186	0.3451	-0.8239	1.3106	-0.45
13	13	-0.7225	1.3722	1.1031	1.9600	1.8119	-0.7225	0.9346	-0.6588	0.1891	0.0376	0.2147	-0.3719	-2.1701	-0.7554	-0.0376	1.8119	0.16
14	14	-0.2404	-0.7225	0.0125	0.7225	-0.1130	-0.1891	-0.9346	0.3719	-0.8596	-2.1701	-0.2404	0.5101	0.9346	-1.4395	1.8119	-1.5982	-0.24
15	15	-1.1503	0.0376	1.8119	-0.6280	0.1891	0.0376	-0.2404	-0.7554	-0.2147	0.5388	1.1503	-1.8119	-1.9600	1.5982	-1.1031	0.7554	-2.57
16	16	-0.0376	0.4261	1.4395	-1.3722	-1.2536	1.4395	-0.2663	0.3451	0.3451	0.3989	1.5982	0.6903	1.1031	-0.3186	-0.7554	-0.3719	0.18
17	17	-1.5141	0.5681	-0.0878	1.3722	0.5388	-1.3722	0.3451	0.9346	-0.0627	-0.5681	-0.9741	1.4395	-1.0152	-0.5978	-0.4817	2.5758	1.150

Grid-Enabling AO and RAS Applications

The Condor Java universe execution environment is designed for the execution of Java programs. Different Java programs (AO.class and RAS.class) and adapters (AO adapter and RAS adapter) have been developed for AO and RAS applications respectively. As shown in Figure 12, the AO.class/RAS.class communicates with the AO/RAS adapter to control the Excel-based AO/RAS application. The results of the simulation are written back to their respective out.txt files, which are then transferred back to the Condor node from which the jobs were originally submitted. The figure also shows the files that have been transferred to the remote Condor nodes from the job submission node. Both the AO and RAS applications are executed concurrently over the Condor pool.

The discussion now focuses on the Condor mechanism that allows the submission of multiple jobs. There are two applications in this case study.

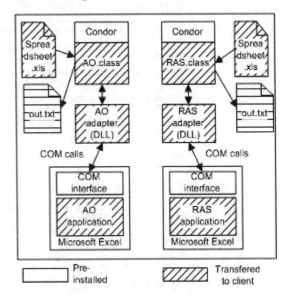

Figure 12. Execution of RAS and AO applications on a Condor pool

For supporting multiple applications it is generally required that it should be possible to submit multiple instances of each application over the Condor pool. The job submission file is used to achieve this. Every Condor job has a corresponding job submit file (.*sub* file) that defines variables that control different aspects of job submission. The most important of these Condor-defined variables, for the purpose of task farming, is the *queue* variable. The integer value assigned to this variable determines the number of replications of the same job that are to be executed over the Condor pool. Figures 13 and 14 show the .sub file for the AO and the RAS applications respectively. The value "50" assigned to the *queue* variable (the last variable in the screenshots) suggests that both the AO and the RAS applications will be executed for a total of 50 times over different grid nodes. Some of the other job submission variables shown in the .sub file are discussed next.

The *universe* variable is assigned a value "Java" because the Condor Java execution en-

vironment is being used to run the simulations. The *executable* variable defines the name of the Java class file that has the *main()* method. The *argument* variable is used to pass a command line argument to the Java program. For this hypothetical case study, the number of iterations for each simulation model has been set to a modest value of "10" through the use of this *argument* variable. The reader is however reminded that both AO and RAS applications will be executed 50 times over, and therefore the total number of simulation iterations for each application, taken as a whole, will be 500 (50*10).

Each simulation experiment will have a unique working directory associated with it. These directories should be present on the Condor node from which jobs are submitted, or on a network drive that can be accessed by the job submission

Figure 13. Job submit file for AO application

```
####################################################
# Asion Stock Option Monte Carlo Simulation
# Submit 10 Monte Carlo simulation jobs to CONDOR.
# Author: Navonil Mustafee
# Date  : 25th February' 2007
####################################################

# Submit jobs to CONDOR java universe
universe = java

# The java class class file which will be executed by the JVM
executable = ..\AsianStockOption.class

# The number of Monte Carlo iterations
arguments = AsianStockOption 10

# Setup so each job has its own working directory. The first will have
# a initial working directory of dir.0, the second dir.1, etc.
initialdir = dir1.$(Process)

# The JAVA-COM bridge
jar_files = ..\jacob.jar

# The files that have to be transfered to execution directory of remote syste
transfer_input_files = ..\AsianStockOption.class, ..\jacob.jar, ..\Asian Call

# The output has to be transfered from local execution directory to shared di
when_to_transfer_output = ON_EXIT

# The files will have to be transfered
should_transfer_file = yes

# The console output file name
output = ExcelMonteCarloConsoleOutput_ASO.out.txt

# The error file name
error = ExcelMonteCarloErrorOutput_ASO.err.txt

# The log file name
log = ExcelMonteCarloLogOutput_ASO.log.txt

# Say we Never want to receive email about this job...
notification = Never

# copy the user environment into the job's environment
getenv = True

# Submit 50 instances of this job!
queue 50
```

node. The working directories are represented by the variable *initialdir*. In the case of the AO and the RAS applications the values assigned to this variable are "dir1.$(process)" and "dir.$(process)" respectively. *$process* is a Condor-defined integer variable that is incremented automatically depending on the number of instances of a particular job that have been submitted. Thus, if *queue*=50 then the value of the *$process* variable will start from 1 and will end at 50. This in turn suggests that the working directory for the first job will be "dir1.1" and for the last job it will be "dir1.50" (in case of AO application). These working directories are important because they will contain the results of the individual experiments and the log files that are output by Condor during execution of each experiment (Figure 15). The variables that define the names of the three different Condor

log files for console output, error information and Condor-specific messages are *output, error* and *log* respectively. It has to be added, however, that a Condor job is in-effect executed under a temporary directory that it created by Condor on the grid node that is assigned the task of processing the job (Figure 16 shows a temporary directory called "dir_3768" that has been created for executing one instance of a simulation). Once the simulation is complete, the results from the temporary directory are transferred to the individual working directories and the temporary directory deleted.

The files to be transferred to the execution host are indicated by the *transfer_input_files* variable. These files are transferred to the temporary execution directory created by the job executing node. The variable *when_to_transfer_output* and its

Figure 14. Job submit file for RAS application

```
###################################################
# Range Accrual Swap Monte Carlo Simulation
# Submit 10 Monte Carlo simulation jobs to CONDOR.
# Author: Navonil Mustafee
# Date   : 24th February' 2007
###################################################

# Submit jobs to CONDOR java universe
universe = java

# The java class class file which will be executed by the JVM
executable = ..\RangeAccrualSwap_ExcelMonteCarloSimulation.class

# The number of Monte Carlo iterations
arguments = RangeAccrualSwap_ExcelMonteCarloSimulation 10

# Setup so each job has its own working directory. The first will have
# a initial working directory of dir.0, the second dir.1, etc.
initialdir = dir.$(Process)

# The JAVA-COM bridge
jar_files = ..\jacob.jar

# The files that have to be transfered to execution directory of remote system
transfer_input_files = ..\RangeAccrualSwap_ExcelMonteCarloSimulation.class, ..\jacob.jar,

# The output has to be transfered from local execution directory to shared dir.
when_to_transfer_output = ON_EXIT

# The files will have to be transfered
should_transfer_file = yes

# The console output file name
output = ExcelMonteCarloConsoleOutput.out.txt

# The error file name
error = ExcelMonteCarloErrorOutput.err.txt

# The log file name
log = ExcelMonteCarloLogOutput.log.txt

# Say we Never want to receive email about this job...
notification = Never

# copy the user environment into the job's environment
getenv = True

# Submit 50 instances of this job!
queue 50
```

Figure 15. Results from the simulation experiments

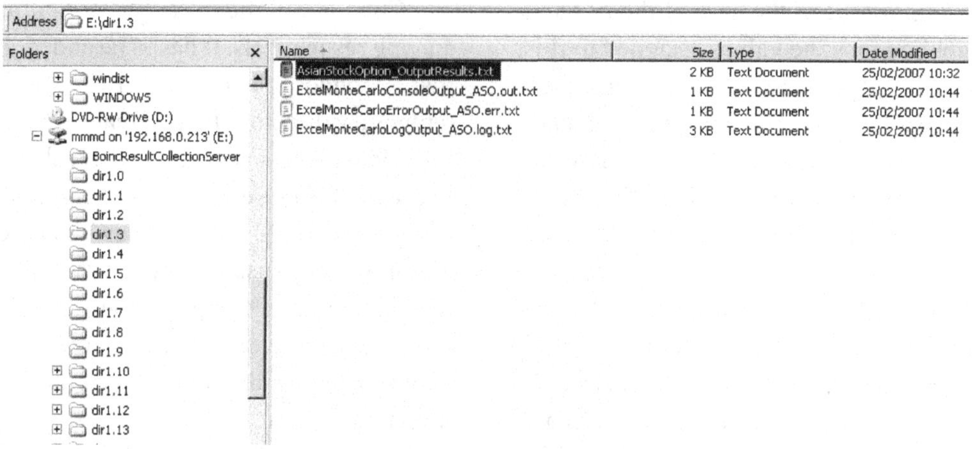

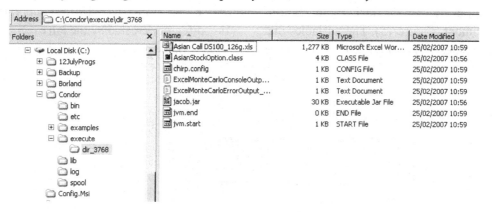

Figure 16. Condor jobs getting executed in temporary execution directory

corresponding value "ON_EXIT" suggest that the simulation results (and the Condor log files) are transferred back from the temporary execution directory to their respective working directories. This concludes the discussion on the variables defined in the Condor submit files.

Jobs are submitted for execution using the Condor command *condor_submit*. The argument to this command is the job description file associated with each job. Figure 17 shows that .sub files for both the AO application (aso.sub) and the RAS application (ras.sub) are submitted using this command, and that 50 instances of each application are created automatically by Condor (see message: "50 jobs(s) submitted to cluster 109/110"). Once the jobs have been submitted the

status of the Condor pool can be determined using the command *condor_status*. Figure 17 shows that at present three grid nodes (computers with names 210-A, 214-E and 215-F) are executing the jobs that have been submitted (Activity="Busy"), while the remaining are "Idle". However, all the nodes have been claimed by Condor (State="Claimed") and it is expected that these will soon start executing the simulations.

The status of jobs that have been submitted can be found using the command *condor_q*. However, only jobs that are yet to be completed or are presently running are displayed by this command (Figure 18). The jobs that have been completed are not shown.

Figure 17. AO and RAS applications execution over Condor pool

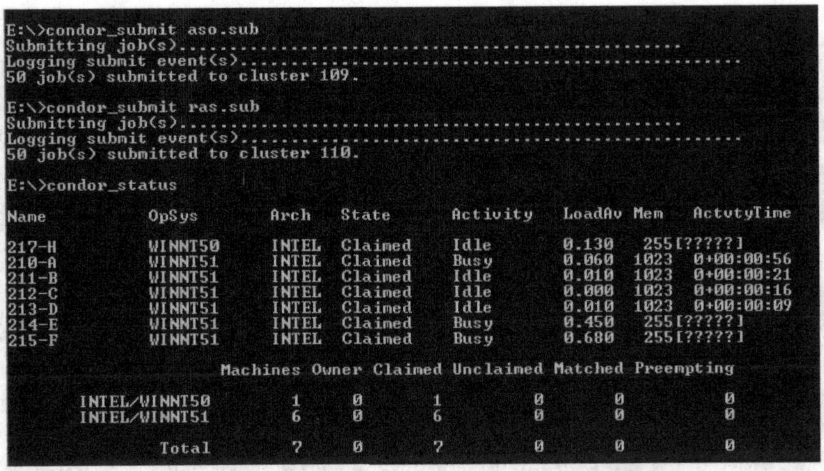

```
E:\>condor_submit aso.sub
Submitting job(s)............................................
Logging submit event(s)......................................
50 job(s) submitted to cluster 109.

E:\>condor_submit ras.sub
Submitting job(s)............................................
Logging submit event(s)......................................
50 job(s) submitted to cluster 110.

E:\>condor_status

Name          OpSys      Arch    State      Activity   LoadAv Mem   ActvtyTime

217-H         WINNT50    INTEL   Claimed    Idle       0.130  255[?????]
210-A         WINNT51    INTEL   Claimed    Busy       0.060  1023  0+00:00:56
211-B         WINNT51    INTEL   Claimed    Idle       0.010  1023  0+00:00:21
212-C         WINNT51    INTEL   Claimed    Idle       0.000  1023  0+00:00:16
213-D         WINNT51    INTEL   Claimed    Idle       0.010  1023  0+00:00:09
214-E         WINNT51    INTEL   Claimed    Busy       0.450  255[?????]
215-F         WINNT51    INTEL   Claimed    Busy       0.680  255[?????]

             Machines Owner Claimed Unclaimed Matched Preempting

INTEL/WINNT50       1     0       1         0       0          0
INTEL/WINNT51       6     0       6         0       0          0

       Total        7     0       7         0       0          0
```

Figure 18. Status of job queue displayed using Condor command "condor_q"

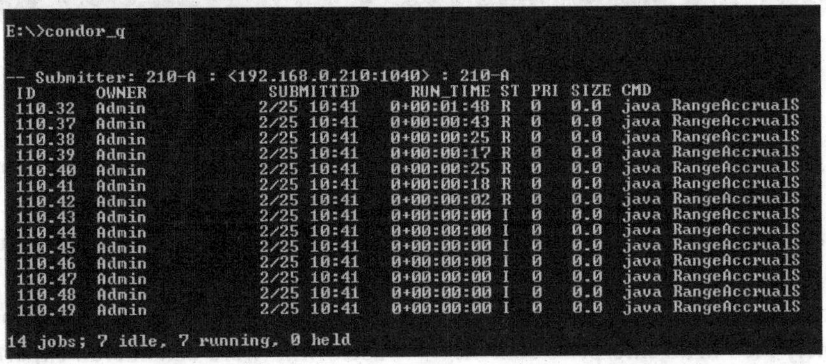

```
E:\>condor_q

-- Submitter: 210-A : <192.168.0.210:1040> : 210-A
ID       OWNER          SUBMITTED     RUN_TIME ST PRI SIZE CMD
110.32   Admin          2/25 10:41  0+00:01:48 R  0   0.0  java RangeAccrualS
110.37   Admin          2/25 10:41  0+00:00:43 R  0   0.0  java RangeAccrualS
110.38   Admin          2/25 10:41  0+00:00:25 R  0   0.0  java RangeAccrualS
110.39   Admin          2/25 10:41  0+00:00:17 R  0   0.0  java RangeAccrualS
110.40   Admin          2/25 10:41  0+00:00:25 R  0   0.0  java RangeAccrualS
110.41   Admin          2/25 10:41  0+00:00:18 R  0   0.0  java RangeAccrualS
110.42   Admin          2/25 10:41  0+00:00:02 R  0   0.0  java RangeAccrualS
110.43   Admin          2/25 10:41  0+00:00:00 I  0   0.0  java RangeAccrualS
110.44   Admin          2/25 10:41  0+00:00:00 I  0   0.0  java RangeAccrualS
110.45   Admin          2/25 10:41  0+00:00:00 I  0   0.0  java RangeAccrualS
110.46   Admin          2/25 10:41  0+00:00:00 I  0   0.0  java RangeAccrualS
110.47   Admin          2/25 10:41  0+00:00:00 I  0   0.0  java RangeAccrualS
110.48   Admin          2/25 10:41  0+00:00:00 I  0   0.0  java RangeAccrualS
110.49   Admin          2/25 10:41  0+00:00:00 I  0   0.0  java RangeAccrualS

14 jobs; 7 idle, 7 running, 0 held
```

Finally, it is possible to mark submitted jobs for removal from the job queue. This is done using the command *condor_rm*. The job number that represents the job to be deleted has to be provided as an argument to this command. The job number can be determined from the output of the command *condor_q* (field ID). The output of *condor_rm* command is shown in Figure 19.

The concluding section discusses the contribution of the research presented in this book chapter and identifies future research that can be conducted in this area.

DISCUSSION

The research presented in this chapter has been motivated by the advances being made in the field of grid computing and the realization that simulation in industry could potentially benefit through the use of grid computing technologies. This research recognises that end-user adoption of grids could be facilitated by focusing on software tools that are commonly used by employees at their workplace. In the context of simulation in industry, the end-users are the simulation practitioners and the tools that are generally used to model simulations are the CSPs. Thus, this re-

Figure 19. Jobs removed from the queue using Condor command "condor_rm"

search has investigated how grid computing can further the field of CSP-based simulation practice and, thereby, offer some benefits to simulation end-users.

This research has identified the form of grid computing, namely PRC in an enterprise context and EDGC, that can be used to grid-enable existing CSPs. This research has shown that cluster-based grid computing is generally unsuitable for integration with Windows-based end-user applications like the CSPs. Using PRC and EDGC forms of grid computing for CSP-based simulation in industry can not only speed up simulation experimentation, replication, optimization, etc., but it can also maximize the utilization of hardware, software and technical resources within an organization.

Yet another contribution of the research is the identification of specific grid computing middleware, namely BOINC and Condor, which can be used to interface with CSPs. BOINC and Condor are also considered appropriate for use by simulation users since they are available for download free of charge, include installation manuals and

user guides, and are supported by user forums and training programs (for example, *Condor Week* is an annual training program conducted by the University of Wisconsin, Madison).

Although this research had focused on end-users who were considered experts in modeling and simulation but were not expected to be IT specialists, the CSP-grid integration technology that has been proposed in this work requires some knowledge of Java and Visual Basic programming. Furthermore, the end-users will also need to know the middleware-specific mechanisms to create jobs, submit jobs, retrieve results, etc. Some of this knowledge could be acquired through self-study and imparted through training. However, for the wider adoption of grid technology for CSP-based simulation, it may be necessary to develop higher-level tools that would hide the complexity of the CSP-grid integration technology and middleware specific mechanisms, and provide end users with easy to use graphical interfaces through which they could possibly integrate CSPs with grid middleware. This is an area for future research.

ACKNOWLEDGMENT

In the course of this study we have collaborated with fellow researchers and people in industry, and we would like to express our gratitude to Prof. Eduardo Saliby, Jingri Zhang, Jonathan Berryman, Jon Saville, Rahul Talwalkar and Robert Watson.

REFERENCES

Anderson, D. P. (2004). BOINC: a system for public-resource computing and storage. *5th International Workshop on Grid Computing* (pp. 4-10). Washington, DC, USA: IEEE Computer Society.

Anderson, D. P., Christensen, C., & Allen, B. (2006). Designing a runtime system for volunteer computing. In *International Conference on High Performance Computing, Networking, Storage, and Analysis (Supercomputing, 2006)*. Article No. 126. New York, NY, USA: ACM Press.

Baker, M., Buyya, R., & Laforenza, D. (2002). Grids and grid technologies for wide-area distributed computing. *Software - Practice and Experience, 32*(15), 1437-1466.

Basney, J., & Livny, M. (1999). Deploying a high throughput computing cluster. In R. Buyya (Ed.), *High Performance Cluster Computing, Volume 1* (chapter 5). NJ, USA: Prentice Hall PTR.

Brooks, R., Robinson, S., & Lewis, C. (2001). *Simulation and inventory control (Operational Research Series)*. Hampshire, UK: Palgrave.

Burke, S., Campana, S., Peris, A. D., Donno, F., Lorenzo, P. M., Santinelli, R., & Sciaba, A. (2007). *gLite 3 user guide, manuals series*. Document identifier CERN-LCG-GDEIS-722398. Retrieved June 28, 2008, from https://edms.cern.ch/file/722398//gLite-3-UserGuide.pdf

Casanova, H. (2002). Distributed computing research issues in grid computing. *ACM SIGACT News, 33*(3), 50-70.

Chance, D. M. (2004). *Monte Carlo simulation, teaching note 96-03*. Retrieved June 28, 2008, from http://www.bus.lsu.edu/academics/finance/faculty/dchance/Instructional/TN96-03.pdf

Chien, A., Calder, B., Elbert, S., & Bhatia, K. (2003). Entropia: architecture and performance of an enterprise desktop grid system. *Journal of Parallel and Distributed Computing, 63*(5), 597-610.

Condor Version 6.9.1 Manual. (2007). *Platform-specific information on Microsoft Windows, Condor 6.9.2 manual*. Retrieved June 28, 2008, from http://www.cs.wisc.edu/condor/manual/v6.9/6_2Microsoft_Windows.html

EGEE. (2007). *Enabling grids for e-science project*. Retrieved June 28, 2008, from http://www.eu-egee.org/

Eldabi, T, Jahangirian, M, Mustafee, N, Naseer, A., & Stergioulas, L. (2008). Applications of simulation techniques in commerce and defence: A systematic survey. A paper presented at *4th Simulation Workshop (SWO8)* (pp. 275-284). OR Society, UK.

Foster, I. (2005). *A globus primer (draft version)*. Retrieved June 2008, from http://www.globus.org/toolkit/docs/4.0/key/

Foster, I., & Kesselman, C. (1998). *The grid: blueprint for a new computing infrastructure*. San Francisco, CA: Morgan Kaufmann.

Foster, I., & Kesselman, C. (2004). Concepts and architecture. In I. Foster, & C. Kesselman (Eds.), *The Grid: Blueprint for a New Computing Infrastructure (2nd Edition)*, chapter 4. San Francisco, CA: Morgan Kaufmann.

Foster, I, Kesselman, C., & Tuecke, S. (2001). The anatomy of the grid: enabling scalable virtual organizations. *International Journal of High Performance Computing Applications, 15*(3), 200-222.

Foster, I., Kesselman, C., Nick, J. M., & Tuecke, S. (2002). Grid services for distributed system integration. *IEEE Computer, 35*(6), 37-46.

Gentzsch, W. (2004). Enterprise resource management: applications in research and industry. In I. Foster, & C. Kesselman (Eds.), *The Grid: Blueprint for a New Computing Infrastructure (2nd Edition)*, chapter 12. San Francisco, CA: Morgan Kaufmann.

Globus Alliance. (2005). *GT4 administration guide*. Retrieved June 28, 2008, from http://www. globus.org/toolkit/docs/4.0/admin/docbook/index.html

Herzog, T. N., & Lord, G. (2002). *Applications of Monte Carlo methods to finance and insurance*. Winstead, Conn: ACTEX Publications. Retrieved June 28, 2008, from http://books.google.com/

Hollocks, B. W. (2006). Forty years of discrete-event simulation - a personal reflection. *Journal of the Operational Research Society, 57*(12), 1383-1399.

Lamanna, M. (2004).The LHC computing grid project at CERN. *Nuclear Instruments and Methods in Physics Research (Section A: Accelerators, Spectrometers, Detectors and Associated Equipment), 534*(1-2), 1-6.

Levine, D., & Wirt, M. (2004). Interactivity with scalability: infrastructure for multiplayer games. In I. Foster, & C. Kesselman (Eds.), *The Grid: Blueprint for a New Computing Infrastructure (2nd Edition)*, chapter 13. San Francisco, CA: Morgan Kaufmann.

Litzkow, M., Livny, M., & Mutka, M. (1988). Condor - a hunter of idle workstations. *8th International Conference of Distributed Computing Systems* (pp. 104-111). IEEE Computer Society, Washington, DC, USA.

Luther, A., Buyya, R., Ranjan, R., & Venugopal, S. (2005). Alchemi: a .NET-based enterprise grid computing system. *6th International Conference on Internet Computing (ICOMP '05)* (pp. 269-278). CSREA Press, USA.

Marins, J. T. M., Santos J. F., & Saliby, E. (2004). Variance reduction techniques applied to Monte Carlo simulation of Asian calls. *2004 Business Association of Latin American Studies (BALAS) Conference*. Business Association of Latin American Studies.

Mustafee, N. (2007). *A grid computing framework for commercial simulation packages*. Unpublished doctoral dissertation. School of Information Systems, Computing and Mathematics, Brunel University, UK.

Mustafee, N., & Taylor, S. J. E. (2008). Investigating grid computing technologies for use with commercial simulation packages. Paper presented at *2008 Operational Research Society Simulation Workshop (SW08)* (pp. 297-307). OR Society, UK.

Mutka, M. W. (1992). Estimating capacity for sharing in a privately owned workstation environment. *IEEE Transactions on Software Engineering, 18*(4), 319-328.

Pidd, M. (2004). *Computer simulation in management science (5th edition)*. Chichester, UK: John Wiley & Sons.

Reed, D. A. (2003). Grids, the teragrid and beyond. *IEEE Computer, 36*(1), 62-68.

Robinson, S. (2005a). Discrete-event simulation: from the pioneers to the present, what next? *Journal of the Operational Research Society, 56* (6), 619-629.

Robinson, S. (2005b). Distributed simulation and simulation practice. *Simulation, 81*(5), 5-13.

Shannon, R. E. (1998). Introduction to the art and science of simulation. *30th Winter Simulation*

Conference (pp. 7-14). Los Alamitos, CA: IEEE Computer Society Press.

Swain J. J. (2005). Gaming reality: biennial survey of discrete-event simulation software tools. *OR/MS Today (December 2005)*. Institute for Operations Research and the Management Sciences (INFORMS), USA. Retrieved June 28, 2008, from http://www.lionhrtpub.com/orms/orms-12-05/frsurvey.html

Swain J. J. (2007). INFORMS simulation software survey. *OR/MS Today*. Institute for Operations Research and the Management Sciences (IN-FORMS), USA. Retrieved June 28, 2008, from http://www.lionhrtpub.com/orms/surveys/Simulation/Simulation.html

Thain, D., Tannenbaum, T., & Livny, M. (2004). Distributed computing in practice: the Condor experience. *Concurrency and Computation: Practice and Experience, 17*(2-4), 323-356.

Virtual Data Toolkit. (2007). *What is in VDT 1.6.1 (supporting platforms)?* Retrieved June 28, 2008, from http://vdt.cs.wisc.edu/releases/1.6.1/contents.html

Yang, X., Chohan, D., Wang, X. D., & Allan, R. (2005). A web portal for the national grid service. *2005 UK e-Science All Hands Meeting*, (pp. 1156-1162). Retrieved June 28, 2008, from http://epubs.cclrc.ac.uk/bitstream/1084/paper05C.pdf

Zhang, J., Mustafee, N., Saville, J., & Taylor, S. J. E. (2007). Integrating BOINC with Microsoft Excel: a case study. *29th Information Technology Interfaces Conference* (pp. 733-738). Washington, DC, USA: IEEE Computer Society.

Section II
Social Aspects in Grid Environments

Chapter VII
Trust, Virtual Teams, and Grid Technology

Genoveffa (Jeni) Giambona
University of Reading, UK

Nicholas L. J. Silburn
Henley Business School, UK

David W. Birchall
Henley Business School, UK

ABSTRACT

Flexible and remote working is becoming more and more widespread. In particular, virtual team working is growing rapidly. Although virtual teams have attracted the attention of many researchers, until recently little investigation had been carried out specifically on what impact trust – a key element in favouring cooperation among team members – has on the performance of such teams. In the authors' opinion Grid computing, through the collaborative nature of the technologies employed, provides an opportunity to build trust through the sharing of common resources and the enabling of rich communications.

INTRODUCTION

The rapid development of new technologies has made flexible and remote working more and more widespread. In particular, virtual team working is growing rapidly throughout many types of organization. Although virtual teams have at-tracted the attention of many researchers (see for example, Lipnack & Stamps, 2000; Lurey & Raisinghani, 2001; Powell et al., 2004; Townsend et al., 2000) until recently (see for example, Zolin & Hinds, 2004) little investigation had been carried out specifically on what impact trust has on the performance of such teams.

Copyright © 2009, IGI Global, distributing in print or electronic forms without written permission of IGI Global is prohibited.

Undoubtedly, trust is a key element in favouring cooperation among team members as it avoids suspicions of opportunism and avoids the occurrence of egotistic behaviour. However, an analysis of the role of trust in the specific field of setting up and maintaining virtual teams would be of great benefit in an age where global working is becoming the norm.

Recent research has looked at trust in virtual teams (Birchall & Giambona, 2007; Birchall et al., 2008), information assurance, (Birchall et al., 2003; Birchall et al., 2004), and a variety of issues around the individual's interaction with information resources (Stewart et al., 2007). All three of these research areas give useful insights into the creation, use, and sharing of information through the lenses of trust and virtual teams – do I trust someone that I am not co-located with enough to share "my" information resources with them and to commit to working jointly with them and sharing responsibility for the outcomes?

Grids, through the collaborative nature of the technologies employed, provide an opportunity to build trust through the sharing of common resources and the enabling of rich communications. But is this enough for effective team working? And how can Grid technology help encourage trust overcome these issues linked to trust development? This is the question that this chapter seeks to answer.

In this chapter firstly we will cover some of the relevant aspects of the development of Grid computing and its application to modern organizations. We then go on to examine the nature of collaboration and virtual teams in business and organizations, including aspects of trust and its importance. The role that the Grid and Grid concepts can have in supporting virtual teamwork and facilitating trust in virtual organizations is then explored. The final part of the chapter draws out the conclusions of the material presented and closes with an examination of the implications.

BACKGROUND

Grid Technology

Grid technology, or Grid computing, is rooted in scientific research ranging from seismology to medicine and pharmaceuticals, to climate modelling (Smith, 2005). It was originally considered as a means of using under-utilised large scale computing resources to solve complex numerical problems (Foster & Kesselman, 1998).

Unsurprisingly, today Grid technology is a mix of computer technologies, softwares and protocols which, among other aspects, are concerned with "coordinated resource sharing and problem solving in dynamic, multi-institutional virtual organizations." (Foster et al., 2001, p. 2). Foster (2002) reinforces the concepts of resource sharing and the "multi-institutional virtual organization" when he suggests that a Grid "integrates and coordinates resources and users that live within different control domains" which can include "different administrative units of the same company; or different companies" (2002, p. 1). Foster goes on to suggest two further central elements of a Grid: the use of "standard, open, general-purpose protocols and interfaces"; and the delivery of "nontrivial qualities of service." (2002, pp. 1-2). This idea of quality of services is particularly relevant to trust as it covers such issues as resource availability, reliability, and security – issues which will be discussed more later on in this chapter.

The Grid in Organizations

In the context of business and organizations there are two main uses for Grid technology which are particularly relevant to organizations and team working. The first finds Grid technology being used in its more conventional sense – the more efficient use of existing organizational computer resources. This use is increasingly finding a place within business as a means of sharing "computing resources more effectively, internally at first but increasingly with partners and even through public grids. This sharing of resources will allow companies to boost their computational power while cutting costs." (Smith & Konsynski, 2004, p. 7). Alkadi and Alkadi (2006) cite a number of examples where Grid technology is being used in the oil exploration and financial services industries: in both cases under-utilised computing resources are being used to process data faster. This is particularly relevant to virtual teams as it gives them greater processing power and less reliance on any one system's reliability of service. The second use of Grid technology is more sophisticated and has the potential to provide opportunities for people and organizations to collaborate with each other on an unprecedented scale. Here the Grid provides "virtualization, of both information and workload" (Kourpas, 2006, p. 4) where the "Workload is spread across servers and data can be seamlessly retrieved." (Kourpas, 2006, p. 4). When Grid technology is used in this way, a single user interface can enable the sharing of data, information, knowledge and ideas utilising new media. In the context of business it can facilitate collaboration on new products and services as well as the delivery of the resulting output to consumers and other businesses and organizations. Grid technologies can facilitate resource sharing, such as data, information and codified knowledge, through access to corporate databases and content management systems. It can facilitate the exchange of uncodified knowledge through people-to-people communication utilising new media. It enables collaboration on documentation. In all of these instances, many of these activities can take place within a single organization dispersed across a number of sites. It can also occur across organizations (Alkadi & Alkadi, 2006; Jacob et al., 2005). Hence, in both cases, it can enhance virtual team working, although in its application in either mode, it raises issues around how these resources are shared, controlled and made secure. To overcome

this, Meliksetian et al. (2004, p. 646) suggest that "resource providers and consumers [should define] clearly and carefully just what is shared, who is allowed to share, and the conditions under which sharing occurs" for this sharing not to trespass into exploitation.

Virtual Teams: What are They?

As Torrington et al. (2002) point out, team working is not a new concept: self-managed working groups were already quite common in the 1960s and 1970s (Birchall, 1975). Moreover, in the 1990s team working was offered as a means of empowering employees, improving work-life balance and increasing their responsibility for a more fulfilling work experience (Torrington et al., 2002). However, Kirkman et al. (2002, p. 67) also state that "while work teams were used in the U.S. as early as the 1960s, the widespread use of teams... began in the Total Quality Management of the 1980s. In the late 1980s and early 1990s, many companies implemented self-managed or empowered work teams. To cut bureaucracy, reduce cycle time and improve service, line-level employees took on decision-making and problem-solving responsibilities traditionally reserved for management."

On the other hand, Torrington et al. (2002) go on to warn that generating openness and trust, essential factors for a team to work, is difficult. Indeed, teams lacking in trust and commitment lead to lower productivity and higher dissatisfaction.

As already mentioned, virtual team working is a phenomenon which has emerged as a consequence of rapidly developing technologies: information and communication technologies have played a particularly important role in the development of novel organizational work structures and virtual team working (Zakaria et al., 2004). Computerised information systems have led to lower unit costs and higher productivity. Sheer size is no longer sufficient for large companies to dominate in a world of fast-moving, flexible smaller organizations. Rapidly changing technology has made the concept of the experience curve obsolete as a strategic competitive tool, and the customer and consumer are both smarter and more demanding (Christopher, 2005). In addition, emerging around the trends identified above is the whole new information economy in which the fundamental sources of wealth are knowledge and communication, rather than natural resources and labour. As a consequence, the notion of new organizational forms began to gain momentum around fifteen years ago (Foss, 2002) and it was related to an increase in firms "adopting new ways of structuring their boundaries and their internal organization" (Foss, 2002, p. 1). Management scholars and practitioners all over the world began to promote concepts such as "knowledge economy" and "new information economy" (Halal, 1998). Nowadays it is accepted that there are several names for these new organizational forms, among others "flexible firms" (Kalleberg, 2003), "shamrock organizations" (Bridge et al., 2003; Handy, 1995; Harris, 2001), "network firms" (Chetty & Blankenburg, 2000; Dyer & Nobeoka, 2000), "boundaryless organizations" (Baruch, 2004). All of them are based around virtual team working.

As it might be expected, there is no agreement on a single definition of what virtual teams are. According to some researchers, virtual teams are groups of people working interdependently across space, time and organization boundaries to achieve a common goal and who use technology to communicate and collaborate (see for example, Lipnack & Stamps, 2000). Virtual team members may be located in the same country or across the world, they rarely meet face-to-face and often come from different countries (Maznevski & Chudoba, 2000).

Jarvenpaa and Shaw (1998) offer a slightly different definition of virtual teams: they see them as an often self-managed knowledge work team with distributed expertise. They can be formed

and/or dismantled to respond to the organization's specific goals. However, according to Alper et al. (2000) those who propose self-management and those who instead see socio-technical characteristics as the main distinctive feature of virtual teams at least agree on a minimum critical specification, that is to say the assumption that employees work better in a team when they can control their own internal mechanisms and coordination with minimal external supervision. Ultimately, peer control within the team ensures the application of an internal control system. Indeed, team members are expected to respect the team's norms and rules as their violation would result in sanctioning by the other members of the team (Wright & Barker, 2000). All this means that teams can have various degrees of autonomy when it comes to the different aspects of decision-making and various organizational forms.

Gibson and Manuel (2003) see virtual teams as having the following three main attributes:

1. They must be functioning teams, i.e. members must be interdependent in task management and must have shared responsibility with regard to outcomes.
2. Team members must be geographically dispersed.
3. Team members must rely on technology-mediated communication to carry out their tasks.

However, the mere use of technology to communicate does not make a team "virtual" as even collocated teams rely on technology to work together. Hence, we do agree with Zakaria et al. (2004, p. 16) when they say that "what is paramount is the degree of reliance on electronic communication… as virtual teams have no option as to whether or not to use it, since they depend on virtuality." Indeed, more often than not, virtual team members never meet face-to-face.

Global teams are seen as a special category within virtual team working (Massey et al.,

2003; Maznevski & Chudoba, 2000). According to Maznevski and Chudoba (2000) these teams work on projects which usually have international components and repercussions. Also, there is a good chance that these teams will never have face-to-face meetings and they just rely on technology to cement their relationships. But as noted by Zakaria et al. (2004, p. 19) an "area of potential conflict in information technology-mediated communication is the language itself." For example, in the case of global virtual teams who communicate in English, research has demonstrated that native and non-native English speakers have culture-based differences (Ulijn et al., 2000). However, these same language and cultural barriers can be, for example, one of the reasons why global virtual teams are set up, i.e. to work on how best to solve them. In these cases more than ever an atmosphere of trust is vital. Moreover, as these teams usually deal with complex issues lacking clearly defined processes and procedures, trust between virtual team members is vital to achieve effective knowledge generation and transfer.

What we have been discussing so far clearly demonstrates that, as already mentioned, there is no single definition of what a virtual team is or can be. However, the temporary lifespan of virtual groups seems to be recognised by most investigators as being a basic characteristic of these teams (Jarvenpaa et al., 2004; Torrington et al., 2002). Other researchers (see for example, Duarte & Tennant-Snyder, 1999; Hoyt, 2000) see the development of technology as the main factor contributing to the rise of virtual team working. We can say though that due to both globalisation and the fast-improving technological tools we have now virtual teams working across boundaries, with time and place no longer being obstacles. Thanks to virtual teams, organizational flexibility, knowledge transfer and sharing among geographically dispersed members in order to increase the organization's knowledge base, and working together while being apart are becoming a reality.

It is worth pointing out that for the purposes of this chapter we will adopt the already mentioned Cohen and Gibson's (2003) definition of virtual teams, with a stress on their reliance on technology-mediated communication to carry out tasks as the most defining characteristic.

VIRTUAL TEAMS AND THE IMPORTANCE OF TRUST

What we have been discussing shows that trust appears vital to team working, especially when virtual, so an understanding of it for those involved seems quite important.

However, what is trust? And what is the nature of trust in virtual communities? Undoubtedly, trust allows teams to organize their work more quickly, manage themselves better, work more creatively and with more belief (Handy, 1995; Lipnack & Stamps, 2000). Trust facilitates problem solving by encouraging information exchange and aids team members in the absorption of new knowledge and in the formulation of a sense of self-identity (Misztal, 1996). Trust is also a key determinant of co-operation among team members as it protects team members from opportunism and egotistic behaviour: if trust mechanisms are understood, then we will be better equipped to recognise and solve co-operation problems (Eggert, 2001).

Much has been written about the nature of trust and many definitions have been offered. Trust is at the basis of human relationships (Barber, 1983; Mayer et al., 1995; Rempel et al., 1985) and in the management world, in particular, trust seems to be an important factor in successful leadership (Mayer et al., 1995), innovation (Clegg et al., 2002; Ruppel & Harrington, 2000) and effective decision-making processes (Driscoll, 1978; Spreitzer & Mishra, 1999). Although authors like Lewis and Weigert (1985) comment that most empirical studies fail to agree on a common working definition of trust, recently a more commonly agreed concept seems to be emerging in the literature. However, it should be borne in mind that context is critical to the creation of trust and that such a specific field as virtual relationships requires a somewhat higher level of trust (Jarvenpaa et al., 2004).

As people are mainly used to building work relationships based around face-to-face encounters and informal chats over a coffee, the physical barriers which come with a virtual environment, the lack of human contact and media richness, and the asynchronous nature of much of the communication within the virtual community are likely to generate uncertainty and ambiguity which, in turn, can easily jeopardise interactions and task achievement (Birchall & Giambona, 2007). Trust, by its own nature, erodes these barriers. Hence, understanding how trust is engendered and maintained in virtual communities is paramount in order to better design virtual teams and ensure they work effectively.

Although, as already mentioned, there is no universally accepted definition of trust, a number of key elements stand at its basis:

1. **Risk:** Trust always involves an element of risk and doubt (Lewis & Weigert, 1985);
2. **Expectation:** Trust implies that one party expects another one to be honest, reliable, competent and, based on such expectations, is willing to become "vulnerable" (Ishaya & Macaulay, 1999).
3. **Inability to monitor another party and need to act despite uncertainties:** If trust exists, the lack of constant monitoring will be accepted, even when the other party's actions have a bearing on one own's choices (McEvily et al., 2003).

There is no doubt that trust is a mental and emotional state. It has been pointed out (McKnight et al., 1998) that trustworthiness often comes before trust and that the latter can be seen as the voluntary acceptance to depend on somebody else.

Of course, a certain degree of predictability of the other's behaviour and actions play a major role in this process. However, in practical terms, as far as virtual teams are concerned, we are inclined to agree with Saunders and Thornhill (2004, p. 499) in believing that trust may be seen as "the likelihood of suspending disbelief and a corresponding willingness to become vulnerable."

A culture of trust and openness is needed to allow meaningful knowledge to be exchanged (van Winkelen, 2003). Indeed, if we do not trust other people, we will not open up and work with them. Consequently, some level of trust is both an initial condition for the formation of the relationships as well as a result of positive interactions over time (Sheppard & Sherman, 1998). Ishaya and Macaulay (1999) purport that trust can be systematically developed and is built incrementally in line with Tuckman's (1965) team development theory which suggests four sequential stages: *Forming; Storming; Norming;* and *Performing.* *Forming* centres on team members working out their roles and responsibilities. *Storming* is where members express strongly held views, implying conflict, competition and power play. At this stage some members will push forward, others withdraw. *Norming* is the stage characterised by organization, listening, more openness and problems being seen as belonging to the group. *Performing* is where all contribute, openness and trust exist and group loyalty has developed. Although having a degree of face validity and of practical use in observing groups at work, the major criticism of Tuckman's theory is its assumption that development takes place in a linear fashion. Trust development is unlikely to progress in such a neat way as pointed out by Abdul-Rahman and Hailes (2000). The determinants of trust are past history, predictability and repeated interactions. Some prior experience is a necessary condition for establishing the cognitive element of trust and familiarity is the precondition of trust. Trust is strengthened by factors and activities such as collective identity, co-location in the same office, joint goals and commonly shared values. Clearly many of these conditions are not present if strangers are brought together into a virtual team. Jarvenpaa and Leidner (1999) suggest that trust is difficult in virtual environments due the potential lack of social interaction. They also indicate that trust development is impaired if an "e-communication only" environment exists as there is an elimination of team roles. Additionally, according to Tyler and Degoey (1996), trust is difficult to build in the short-term so the time span of many virtual teams would seem to preclude this.

Many researchers assert that embedded predisposition to trust or "propensity to trust" can be added to the process of trust production (Becerra & Gupta, 2003; Duarte & Tennant-Snyder, 1999; Jarvenpaa et al., 1998; Mayer et al., 1995). Moreover, Creed & Miles (1996) lend further support to the proposition that trust builds incrementally.

Abdul-Rahman and Hailes (2000) point out that whatever role trust plays in physical communities it also applies to virtual communities, as, ultimately, all virtual interactions are human bound.

Hence, from the more general research, we can draw pointers that are particularly relevant to virtual communities. The selection process for community membership could play a key role. If those forming the virtual team have the respect of other members, if members believe that the selection process will result in members with similar competence levels as well as credible and trustworthy participants there is likely to be a stronger predisposition to trust. Actions taken at the early stages of community building should include dialogue to share personal goals, as well as measures both to reduce cognitive distance and to achieve a sufficiency in alignment of mental frames to foster understanding. Particularly important is the strategy adopted to engage members in deep dialogue and for this to be seen as a legitimate modus operandi by participants.

The research by Lewis and Weigert (1985) is particularly useful in understanding the nature of trust emerging through interaction in teams. They reported the work of Anderson, who studied relationships and identified four parameters:

1. The greater the homogeneity of the group the higher the trust level.
2. The greater the connectedness of a social network the greater the trust level.
3. The greater the size and complexity of a community the lower the level of trust.
4. The greater the social change the lower the trust.

They also found that trust declines in the context of rapid change, when there is an increase in heterogeneity, a decrease in interaction frequency and an increase in the number of outsiders. This suggests that teams within one organization are likely to develop trust in a different way and in different forms to teams comprising people from different organizations, particularly where there is a contractual relationship governing interactions such as buyer-supplier contracts. Individual pre-disposition to trust may be higher within the organization than with unknown people from outside.

In his research Larson (1992) suggested that the process by which significant relationships are built between entrepreneurial firms is based on reciprocity, trust and mutual respect. However, according to Fuller and Lewis (2002) most inter-firm relations are not densely collaborative ties. Trust and reciprocity are seen as processes of governance in inter-firm networks. The very act of personal social actions such as exchanging knowledge and problem solving convert intermittent relationships into ongoing relationships which form the basis for inter-firm business (Boissevain & Mitchell, 1973, quoted in Fuller & Lewis, 2002). After studying 36 independent small businesses, Fuller and Lewis (2002) identified five categories of relationship strategy:

network, contract, personal, personal service and strategic development. The descriptions of trust varied between each category but were present in all five. The network relationship strategy put the business at the centre of information flows enabling the trading of information and then being able to act proactively on emergent opportunities. The personalised relationship strategy includes adapting relationships as appropriate and the tasks involved in doing business appear to be the medium for the personal relationships rather than vice versa. This indicates the different ways in which individuals will approach relationship building and the centrality, or otherwise, of trust in this process.

Although they are not determinants of trust in themselves, time and leadership/facilitation appear to be moderating variables, influencing the relationships between the other factors, e.g. the elapsed time and environment available for interaction and dialogue between team members. Effective leadership behaviour is linked to trust development. Kayworth and Leidner's (2000) research suggests that a crucial role of the leader is to provide a setting for group socialisation and cohesiveness building as an aid to developing trust. There is some evidence that facilitation can support the development of relationships and hence trust. The building of relationships between team members is a fundamental concern of facilitators (McFadzean & McKenzie, 2001). Pauleen and Yoong (2001) see effective communication as key in building relationships which then influence team effectiveness. In turn they report research which has demonstrated the impact of strong relational links in enhancing creativity and motivation, increasing morale, improving decisions and reducing process losses. Their research focussed particularly on boundary-crossing virtual teams and they emphasised the role of the facilitator in blending the team members' individual cultures into a single team culture. Building on the work of Nonaka and Takeuchi (1995), they conclude that, in order to build mutual trust, individual emotions, feelings, and mental models must be shared.

As already mentioned, communication is a key factor in trust building. Hence, in relation to information and communications technology, important aspects of trust development include availability, reliability, capacity and user-friendliness, all of which are important in the process of communicating trustworthiness (Kasper-Fuehrer & Ashkanasy, 2000) and network security (Aldridge et al., 1997).

The selection and utilisation of communications methods to initiate and develop meaningful dialogue is the first step in building trust and collaboration (Holton, 2001). Face-to-face communication has been found to be the most efficient means for co-ordinating individual co-operative behaviour (trust) to achieve maximum outcome (Eggert, 2001; Lipnack & Stamps, 1999). Nevertheless, the researchers acknowledged the constraint of time and it was noted that trust decays in large groups when confronted with co-operation problems.

Many virtual teams are programmed to have only short lives. Hence they may differ from other groups in ways which preclude the long-term development of trust. According to Duarte and Tennant-Snyder (1999) trust should be built as quickly as possible; models of trust which focus on building long-term relationships may not apply to many virtual teams due to their short life. The concept of *Swift Trust* may instead apply. Swift trust is less about relating than it is about doing. Inferences are driven by generic features of the setting rather than by personalities or interpersonal relations (Meyerson et al., 1996). It is therefore likely to be rooted in the rational perspective. Jarvenpaa et al. (1998) found that swift trust was evident in high trust teams: it enabled members to take action, making them less likely to be distracted from the task. Meyerson et al.'s view (1996) is that in temporary teams not enough time is available for things to go wrong and interactivity reduces ambiguity, uncertainty and strengthens trust. They posit that people in these circumstances deal with each other primarily in terms of the professional roles each individual performs, making clear what specific value each member brings into the virtual team, not in terms of developing social relationships. Whilst swift trust might apply in virtual teams, it seems less relevant to learning communities which exhibit some different features such as lack of focus on a common task, lack of time pressure, no established working processes, voluntary membership and the importance attached by participants to networking, in part to open up new business opportunities.

In summary, the emergent view is that communication, interaction, leadership and contextual factors can all combine in the development of trust amongst team members. But it is clear that some of the features supporting trust development in face-to-face working are less likely to be found in virtual team working. This is mainly due to physical barriers, the lack of human contact and media richness, and the asynchronous nature of much of the communication within the virtual community.

FACILITATING TRUST IN VIRTUAL TEAMS: THE ROLE OF THE GRID

Earlier in this chapter nine key elements of interpersonal trust were identified:

1. Risk expectation
2. Inability to monitor another party and need to act despite uncertainties
3. Past history
4. Predictability
5. Repeated interactions
6. Level of connectedness
7. Size and complexity of a community
8. Communication
9. Group homogeneity

Whilst all of these trust elements are dependent upon some degree of human behaviour or human relationships, some are also open to support and encouragement by technology. So how can Grid technology facilitate some of these trust elements? Firstly, through the multiplicity of resources within the Grid appearing seamless to the user it can help to mitigate the virtual organization's size and complexity. Secondly, Grid technology can provide versatile tools of communication: asynchronously through data and information repositories and synchronously through rich media systems such as audio and video. Thirdly, by ensuring that everyone in the virtual organization has access to the technology, the level of connectedness between members can be maximised. Fourthly, by ensuring Grid content is up to date (which may require continuous, or very frequent, synchronisation of Grid components), the risk of accessing out of date data will be minimised. Lastly, allowing users access to authorship meta-data associated with data and documents held in such Grids will enable consumers of the data/document to form a view on the quality, reliability and trustworthiness of the document based on their level of interpersonal trust of the author.

However, there are issues around the use of Grid technologies and the technology itself that need to be addressed if such technology is going to gain wider acceptance in the business community.

In whatever way Grid technology is used within an organization or across organizations, it can only act as a facilitator of typical group tasks such as generating ideas, planning activities, problem solving, decision making, resolving conflict, and executing agreed activities (McGrath & Hollingshead, 1994). Grid technology can encourage teams to undertake these tasks in a virtual environment, by being seamless, easy to use and reliable, but it cannot force the kind of sharing and collaboration required by these tasks on its own. Ultimately "People will use it only because they want to communicate with resources or people that they care about and need to do their work." (Smarr, 2003, p. 8). There are two categories of issues to be considered here – trust in other members of the team, and trust in the technology supporting the virtual team.

The important area of interpersonal trust amongst members of the team has been discussed at length in earlier parts of this chapter, however it is worth noting at this point that a lack of trust between individuals (whether that be within the same organization they work for or some other organization) can have serious consequences for the usefulness of the Grid. If interpersonal or organizational trust is compromised in some way then the desire by an individual or organization to share resources with another individual or organization will be reduced. A contributor to the Grid can therefore be reluctant to deposit content because they do not trust other individuals, or organizations, which might have access to it.

A second issue is a Grid user's trust in the Grid itself – does the user have confidence that the Grid will provide them with what they want when they want it? Will the Grid also keep the data or information they are sharing secure as well?

This idea of the Grid providing what people want when they want it is nothing new. Indeed it is one of the key issues with more established client/server based systems in common use within organizations today – for example content management systems. However, research by Davis through his technology acceptance model (TAM) (Davis 1989; Davis et al., 1989) suggests that the main influences on whether a user will use technology or not is down to the perception of its "usefulness" and "ease of use". The former is based on whether the user sees the technology as useful – in this case is the Grid useful? Does it provide users with the information they need, when they want it, in a form they can use and to a standard of quality that is required? If not, trust in the technology is likely to be compromised. Some of Davis's concepts were developed further by the research of, amongst others, DeLone and McLean (1992, 2003). They have shown that

there are a number of key criteria which need to be met in order for an information system to deliver the benefits sought. These criteria include system quality, information quality and service quality. System quality centres on system security, reliability and availability, ease of use and functionality. Information quality includes such elements as information accuracy, timeliness, relevance and completeness. The third concept of system quality encompasses the user's perception of the level of support provided by the information system providers. The DeLone and McLean model suggests that failure to deliver appropriate levels of quality in any of these three areas will have a negative impact on user satisfaction and the user's intention to use the system thereby compromising the net benefits of implementing the system. Research by Ashleigh and Nandhakumar (2007) provides an interesting discussion of some of the research that has been carried out into trust in computer-based systems suggesting that system experience, meaningful system feedback, and technology reliability are key to developing trust in technology. This reinforces DeLone and McLean's message on system quality and Davis's message on system "usefulness" and "ease of use".

Whilst it is possible to use literature and models from the wider information systems research field, the technologically complex nature of the Grid would suggest a more appropriate review of Grid specific literature on security and reliability to explore further these issues and the impact they might have on Gird usage.

For instance Rana and Hilton (2006a) suggest that Grid security "remains one of the most significant barriers for the wider adoption of Grid computing even within the same company," (2006a, p. 8). Cody et al. (2007) suggest that currently, the emphasis in distributed computing is on performance above security. Obviously an appropriate balance needs to be drawn between the two but compromising security will only raise the barrier to Grid adoption in business. It is worth bearing in mind though that Grid security is not just a technical issue of whether the most appropriate protocols and security technology systems are in place, there are also human behavioural issues as well. Because much of the information that will be within the Grid's databases will have been generated by humans, the quality of the information, its availability and reliability are attributable to human endeavour suggesting a lower level of trust between information consumer and information contributor. At a technology level though, the concept of Grid security is complex with a range of possible means of attacking the Grid resources and networks that connect them (Rana & Hilton, 2006a). There are however a variety of means of securing Grids. Using the example of a construction engineering project comprising a virtual organization of designers, suppliers and product manufacturers, Rana and Hilton (2006b) describe the security services in place to prevent unauthorised access to the supporting Grid. Foster et al. (2001) describe a similar set of underlying security technologies but suggest that these technologies be flexible enough to appear seamless to the user, and accommodate the individual security setups of the resources being shared in the Grid.

Picking up on Grid reliability, Huedo et al. (2006) state that it is focused on two areas: Grid failure or a loss of quality of service. Either of these can be triggered by the failure of a Grid component or resource, an interconnecting network issue or the failure of a system job. Their paper goes on to discuss the results of empirical research into how fault tolerance can be improved using two different approaches – the GridWay metaschedular and Globus services, concluding that the GridWay metaschedular is the better of the two.

Clearly, from information systems literature, the usefulness of the Grid to a virtual organization will be dependent upon the resources available, and the reliability and security of the Grid. Whilst resource availability is down to a willingness, by both organizations and users, to share technology and content, Grid reliability and security is very much down to the appropriate use of technology. It is worth noting though that such technologies are continuously evolving and this needs to be taken into account when setting up a Grid. Failure to respond to the ever changing threats to Grids, particular when it comes to security, will have a detrimental effect on trust in the virtual organization's Grid.

CONCLUSION

As we have seen, Grid technology has the ability to enhance virtual team working by providing a common system, a common language and the possibility of sharing common resources. Moreover, it provides an instantaneous way of accessing resources and communicating, something which certainly improves the quality of decision-making. The Grid can provide team members with a common language which can facilitate interdependence, a key feature of virtual teams. Indeed, we have seen that the Grid could provide team members with easier data-sharing and real-communication tools which, as discussed, could aid the development of trust within a team environment, especially in dispersed teams.

However, Grid technology can also disrupt trust within virtual teams through:

- Having inappropriate security settings which restricts access from one organization to another for data required.
- Leaders and team members having to commit to sharing and making use of resources.

In any case, we cannot assume that all this will happen automatically; on the contrary, for virtual teams to work as expected, with the aid of the Grid, a number of steps should be taken.

Hence, for it to work properly, management need to make sure that:

- A suitable communication infrastructure is provided. This should meet not just the task demands but also, as far as possible, the team members' personal preferences.
- A team charter which guides behaviours within the team is set up.
- Coaching of team members in order to avoid long delays in responding, unilateral priority shifts and failure to follow-up on commitments is in place.

Moreover, managers should make every effort in order to create a supportive climate where ideas can be exchanged freely, where conflict resolution is open and fair and where solutions to problems are well understood and widely accepted (Gibson & Manuel, 2003).

In other words, grid technology's great potential for business is here and ready to be exploited. It is now up to businesses and their managers to make the best use possible of it.

REFERENCES

Abdul-Rahman, A., & Hailes, S. (2000). Supporting Trust in Virtual Communities. Paper presented at *Hawaii International Conference on System Sciences*, *33*, Maui, Hawaii.

Aldridge, A., White, M., & Forcht, K. (1997). Security considerations of doing business via the Internet: cautions to be considered. *Internet Research: Electronic Networking Applications and Policy*, *7*(1), 9-15.

Alkadi, I., & Alkadi, G. (2006). Grid Computing: The past, now, and future. *Human Systems Management*, *25*(3), 161-166.

Alper, S., Tjosvold, D., & Law, K. S. (2000). Conflict management, efficacy, and performance in organisational teams. *Personnel Psychology*, *53*(5), 625-642.

Ashleigh, M. J., & Nandhakumar, J. (2007). Trust and technologies: Implications for organizational work practices. *Decision Support Systems*, *43*(2), 607-617.

Barber, B. (1983). *The Logic and Limits of Trust*. New Brunswick: Rutgers University Press.

Baruch, Y. (2004). Transforming careers: from linear to multidirectional career paths: Organizational and individual perspectives. *Career Development International*, *9*(1), 58-73.

Becerra, M., & Gupta, A. (2003). Perceived trustworthiness within the organization: The moderating impact of communication frequency on trustor and trustee effects. *Organization Science*, *14*(1), 32-45.

Birchall, D. W. (1975). *Job Design*. Epping: Gower Press.

Birchall, D. W., Ezingeard, J-N., & McFadzean, E. (2003) *Information Security - Setting the Boardroom Agenda*. London: Grist Ltd.

Birchall, D. W., Ezingeard, J.-N., McFadzean, E., Howlin, N., & Yoxall, D. (2004). *Information Assurance: Strategic Alignment and Competitive Advantage*. London: Grist Ltd.

Birchall, D. W., Giambona, G., & Gill, J. (2008). Who is on the other side of the screen? The role of trust in virtual teams. In T. Kautonen, & H. Karjaluoto (Eds.), *Trust and New Technologies: Marketing and Management on the Internet and Mobile Media*. London: Edward Elgar Publishing.

Birchall, D. W., & Giambona, G. (2007). SME manager development in virtual learning communities and the role of trust: A conceptual study. *Human Resource Development International*, *10*(2), 187-202.

Boissevain, J., & Mitchell, J. C. (1973). *Network Analysis Studies in Human Interaction*. The Hague: Monkton.

Bridge, S., O'Neill, K., & Cromie, S. (2003). *Understanding Enterprise, Entrepreneurship and Small Business*. London: Palgrave Mcmillan.

Chetty, S., & Blankenburg, H. D. (2000). Internationalisation of small to medium-sized manufacturing firms: A network approach. *International Business Review, 9*(1), 77-93.

Christopher, M. (2005). *Logistics and Supply-Chain Management: Creating Value-Adding Networks*. London: Pearson Education.

Clegg, C. W., Unsworth, K. L., Epitropaki, O., & Parker, G. (2002). Implicating trust in the innovation process. *Journal of Occupational and Organizational Psychology 75*(4), 409-422.

Cody, R., Sharman, R., Rao, R. H., & Upadhyaya, S. (2008). Security in Grid Computing: A Review and Synthesis. *Decision Support Systems, 44*(4), 749-764.

Cohen, S. G., & Gibson, C. B. (Eds.) (2003). Introduction to *Virtual Teams That Work: Creating Conditions for Virtual Team Effectiveness*. San Francisco: Jossey Bassey.

Creed, W. E. D., & Miles, R. E. (1996). A Conceptual Framework Linking Organizational Forms, Managerial Philosophies, and the Opportunity Costs of Controls. In R. Kramer, & T. Tyler (Eds.), *Trust in Organizations: Frontiers of Theory and Research*, Thousand Oaks: Sage.

Davis, F. D. (1989). Perceived Usefulness, Perceived Ease of Use, and User Acceptance of Information Technology. *MIS Quarterly, 13*(3), 318-340.

Davis, F. D., Bagozzi, R. P., & Warshaw, P. R. (1989). User Acceptance of Computer Technology: A Comparison of Two Theoretical Models. *Management Science, 35*(8), 982-1003.

DeLone, W. H., & McLean, E. R. (1992). Information Systems Success: The Quest for the Independent Variable. *Information Systems Research, 3*(1), 60-95.

DeLone, W. H., & McLean, E. R. (2003). The DeLone and McLean Model of Information Systems Success: A Ten-Year Update. *Journal of Management Information Systems, 19*(4), 9-30.

Driscoll, J. W. (1978). Trust and Participation in Organizational Decision Making as Predictors of Satisfaction. *The Academy of Management Journal, 21*(1), 44-56.

Duarte, D., & Tennant-Snyder, N. (1999). *Mastering Virtual Teams: Strategies, Tools and Techniques that Succeed*. San Francisco: Jossey-Bass Publishers.

Dyer, J. H., & Nobeoka, K. (2000). Creating and managing a high-performance knowledge-sharing network: The Toyota case. *Strategic Management Journal, 21*(3), 345-367.

Eggert, A. (2001). The Role of Communication in Virtual Teams. *Electronic Journal of Organizational Virtualness, 3*(2).

Foss, N. J. (2002). Introduction: New organisational forms – Critical perspectives. *International Journal of the Economics of Business, 9*(1), 1-8.

Foster, I. (2002). *What is the Grid?* Retrieved Feb 13, 2008, from http://www-fp.mcs.anl.gov/~foster/Articles/WhatIsTheGrid.pdf

Foster, I., & Kesselman, C. (1998). Computational Grids. In I. Foster, & C. Kesselman (Eds.), *The Grid: Blueprint for a Future Computing Infrastructure*. Morgan Kaufmann.

Foster, I., Kesselman, C., & Tuecke, S. (2001). The Anatomy of the Grid: Enabling Scalable Virtual Organizations, *International Journal of High Performance Computing Applications, 15*(3), 200-222.

Fuller, T., & Lewis, J. (2002). Relationships Mean Everything: A typology of Small Business Relationship Strategies in a Reflexive Context. *British Journal of Management, 4*, 9-23.

Gibson, C. B., & Manuel, J. A. (2003). Building Trust: Effective Multicultural Communication Processes in Virtual Teams. In S. G. Cohen, & C. B. Gibson (Eds.)*Virtual Teams That Work: Creating Conditions for Virtual Team Effectiveness.* San Francisco: Jossey-Bassey.

Halal, W. E. (1998). *The New Management: Bringing Democracy and Markets Inside Organisations.* San Francisco: Berrett-Koehler Publishers.

Handy, C. (1995). Trust and the virtual organisation. *Harvard Business Review, 73*, 40-50.

Harris, R. (2001). From fiefdom to service: The evolution of flexible occupation. *Journal of Corporate Real Estate, 3*(1), 7-16.

Holton, J. A. (2001). Building Trust and Collaboration in a Virtual Team. *Team Performance Management, 7*(4), 15-26.

Hoyt, B. (2000). Techniques to manage participation and contribution of team members in virtual teams. *WebNet Journal, 2*(4), 16-20.

Huedo, E., Montero, R. S., & Llorente, I. M. (2006). Evaluating the reliability of computational grids from the end user's point of view. *Journal of Systems Architecture, 52*, 727-736.

Ishaya, T., & Macaulay, L. (1999). The role of trust in virtual teams. In P. Sieber, J. & Griese (Eds.), *Organizational Virtualness & Electronic Commerce, Proceedings of the 2nd International VoNet* - Workshop, September 23-24, Bern, Switzerland (pp. 135-152).

Jacob, B., Brown, M., Fukui, K., & Trivedi, N. (2005). *Introduction to Grid Computing.* IBM International Technical Support Organization. Retrieved 15 Feb, 2008, from http://www.redbooks.ibm.com/redbooks/pdfs/sg246778.pdf

Jarvenpaa, S. L., Knoll, K., & Leidner, D. (1998). Is Anybody Out There? Antecedents of Trust in Global Virtual Teams. *Journal of Management Information Systems, 14*(4), 37-53.

Jarvenpaa, S. L., & Leidner, D. E. (1999). *The Development and Maintenance of Trust in Global Virtual Teams.* Fontainebleau: INSEAD.

Jarvenpaa, S. L., & Shaw, T. R. (1998). Global virtual teams: Integrating models of trust. Iin P. Sieber, & J. Griese, (Eds.), *Organizational Virtualness Proceedings of the 1st VO Net - Workshop,* April, Bern, Switzerland (pp. 35-51).

Jarvenpaa, S. L., Shaw, T. R., & Staples, D. S. (2004). The role of trust in global virtual teams. *Information Systems Research, 15*(3), 250–267.

Kalleberg, A. L. (2003). Flexible firms and labour market segmentation. *Work and Occupations, 30*(2), 154-175.

Kasper-Fuehrer, E. C. & Ashkanasy, N. M. (2000). Communicating Trustworthiness and Building trust in inter-organizational virtual organizations. *Journal of Management, 27*(3), 235-254.

Kayworth, T. R. & Leidner, D. (2000). The Global Virtual Manager: a prescription for success. *European Management Journal, 18*(2), 67-79.

Kirkman, B. L., Rosen, B., Gibson, G. B., Tesluk, P. E., & McPherson, S. O. (2002). Five challenges to virtual team success: Lessons from Sabre, Inc. *Academy of Management Executive, 16*(3), 67-79.

Kourpas, E. (2006). *Grid Computing: Past, Present and Future - An Innovation Perspective.* Retrieved 13 Feb, 2008, from http://www-03.ibm.com/grid/pdf/innovperspective.pdf?S_TACT=105AGX52&S_CMP=cn-a-gr.

Larson, A. (1992). Network dyads in entrepreneurial settings: a study of the governance of exchange relationships. *Administrative Science Quarterly, 37*(1), 79-93.

Lewis, D., & Weigert, A. (1985). Trust as a Social Reality, *Social Forces, 63*(4), 967-976.

Lipnack, J., & Stamps, J. (1999). Virtual teams. *Executive Excellence, 16*(5), 14-16.

Lipnack, J., & Stamps, J. (2000). *Virtual Teams. People Working Across Boundaries with Technology.* New York: John Wiley.

Lurey, J. S., & Raisinghani, M. S. (2001). An empirical study of best practices in virtual teams. *Information and Management, 38*(8), 523-544.

Massey, A. P., Montoya-Weiss, M. M., & Hung, Y. T. (2003). Because time matters: Temporal coordination in global virtual project teams. *Journal of Management Information Systems, 19*(4), 129-155.

Mayer, R. C., Davis, J. H., & Schoorman, F. D. (1995). An integrative model of organizational trust. *Academy of Management Review, 20*(3), 709-734.

Maznevski, M. L., & Chudoba, K. M. (2000). Bridging space over time: Global virtual team dynamics and effectiveness. *Organization Science, 11*(2), 473-493.

McEvily, B., Perrone, V., & Zaheer, A. (2003). Trust as an organising principle. *Organisation Science, 14*(1), 91-103.

McFadzean, E., & McKenzie, J., (2001). Facilitating Virtual Learning Groups. A Practical Approach. *Journal of Management Development,* 20 (6), 37-49.

McGrath, J. E., & Hollingshead, A. B. (1994). *Groups Interacting with Technology: Ideas, Evidence, Issues and an Agenda.* Thousand Oaks, Sage Publications Inc.

McKnight, D. H., Cummings, L. L., & Chervany, N. L. (1998). Initial trust formation in new organisational relationships. *The Academy Management Review, 23*(3), 473-490.

Meliksetian, D. S., Prost, J-P., Bahl, A. S., Boutboul, I., Currier, D. P., Fibra, S., Girard, J-Y., Kassab, K. M., Lepesant, J-L., Malone, C., & Manesco, P. (2004). Design and implementation of an enterprise grid. *IBM Systems Journal, 43*(4), 646-664.

Meyerson, D., Weick, K., & Kramer, R. (1996). Swift Trust and Temporary Groups. In T. Tyler (Ed.), *Trust in Organizations: Frontiers of Theory and Research.* Thousand Oaks: Sage.

Misztal, B. (1996). *Trust in Modern Societies.* Cambridge, MA: Polity Press.

Nonaka, I., & Takeuchi, H. (1995). *The Knowledge-Creating Company.* New York: Oxford University Press.

Pauleen, D. J., & Yoong, P. (2001). Relationship Building and the use of ICT in boundary-crossing virtual teams: a facilitator's perspective. *Journal of Information Technology, 16*(4), 45-62.

Powell, A., Piccoli, G., & Ives, B. (2004). Virtual teams: a review of current literature and directions for future research. *ACM SIGMIS Database, 35*(1), 6-36.

Rana, O., & Hilton, J. (2006a). Securing the Virtual Organization – Part 1: Requirements from Grid Computing. *Network Security, 2006*(4), 7-10.

Rana, O., & Hilton, J. (2006b). Securing the Virtual Organization – Part 2: Grid Computing in Action. *Network Security, 2006*(5), 6-10.

Rempel, J. K, Holmes, J. G., & Zanna, M. P. (1985). Trust in close relationships. *Journal of Personality and Social Psychology, 69*(1), 95-112.

Ruppel, C. P., & Harrington, S. J. (2000). The relationship of communication, ethical work climate, and trust to commitment and innovation. *Journal of Business Ethics, 25*(4), 313-328.

Saunders, M. N. K., & Thornhill, A. (2004). Trust and mistrust in organisations: An exploration using an organisational justice framework.

European Journal of Work and Organisational Psychology, 13 (4), 492-515.

Sheppard, B. H., & Sherman, D. M. (1998). The grammars of trust: a model and general implications. *Academy of Management Review, 23*(3), 33-45.

Smarr, L. (2003). Grids in Context. In I. Foster, & C. Kesselman, (Eds.) *The Grid 2 Blueprint for a New Computing Infrastructure.* 2nd ed.. Morgan Kaufmann.

Smith, R. (2005). *Grid Computing: A Brief Technology Analysis.* Retrieved Feb 14, 2008, from http://www.ctonet.org/documents/GridComputing_analysis.pdf

Smith, H., & Konsynski, B. (2004). Grid Computing. *MIT Sloan Management Review, 46*(1), 7-9.

Spreitzer, G. M., & Mishra, A. K. (1999). Giving Up Control without Losing Control: Trust and its Substitutes' Effects on Managers' Involving Employees in Decision Making. *Group & Organization Management, 24*(2), 155-187.

Stewart, J.-A., Silburn, N. L. J., & Birchall, D. W. (2007). *Survey into the Finding, Use and Sharing of Information Within Organizations.* Henley-on-Thames: Henley Management College.

Torrington, D., Hall, L., & Taylor, S. (2002). *Human Resource Management.* Essex: Pearson Education.

Townsend, A. M., Demarie, S. M., & Hendrickson, A. R. (2000). Virtual teams: Technology and the workplace of the future. *IEEE Engineering Management Review, 28*(2), 69-80.

Tuckman, B.W. (1965). Development Sequence in Small Groups, *Psychological Bulletin*, *63*(6), 12-24.

Tyler, T., & Degoey, P. (1996). Trust in Organizational Authorities: Frontiers of Theory and Research. In T. Tyler (Ed.) *Trust in Organizations.* Thousand Oaks: Sage.

Ulijn, J., O'Hair, D., Weggeman, M., Ledlow, G., & Hall, H. T. (2000). Innovation, corporate strategy and cultural context: What is the mission for international business communication?. *The Journal of Business Communication, 37*, 293-316.

van Winkelen, C. (2003). *Inter-organizational Communities of Practice.* ESeN EU funded E-Action project. Henley-on-Thames: Henley Management College.

Wright, B. M., & Barker, J. R. (2000). Asserting concerting control in the team environment. *Journal of Occupational and Organisational Psychology, 73*(3), 345-361.

Zakaria, N., Amelinckx, A., & Wilemon, D. (2004). Working together apart? Building a knowledge-sharing culture for global virtual teams. *Creativity and Innovation Management, 13*(1), 15-29.

Zolin, R., & Hinds, P. J. (2004). Trust in context: The development of interpersonal trust in geographically distributed work. In R. M. Kramer, & K. Cook (Eds.), *Trust and Distrust in Organizations.* New York: Sage.

Chapter VIII
The Socio–Technical Virtual Organisation

Rob Smith
Newcastle University, UK

Rob Wilson
Newcastle University, UK

ABSTRACT

A Virtual Organisation (VO) or Virtual Enterprise is a loosely-coupled group of collaborating organisations, acting to some extent as though they were part of a single organisation. This implies that they exhibit some properties of a conventional organisation without actually being one. In practice, this involves overcoming organisational boundaries, which tend to make collaborative working difficult. The authors of this chapter propose that this is a socio-technical problem, requiring both a technical (software) infrastructure and a sociological approach to building, deploying and operating the VOs supported by it. This joint approach can help to overcome some of the problems associated with collaborative working, ranging from poorly coordinated activity, to ineffective problem solving and decision-making. The authors describe a socio-technical approach to building and operating VOs in highly dynamic environments and present two factual scenarios from the chemical and health industries. They describe a platform supporting such VOs, which was developed as part of the EPSRC E-Science Pilot Project GOLD.

INTRODUCTION

We propose that the building and operation of virtual organisations (VOs) is a socio-technical problem, requiring both a suitable technical infrastructure and a sociological method for building and evolving VOs supported by it. Such an approach is necessary because of the complexity and dynamism inherent in many VOs, particularly those involving novel aggregations of knowledge,

Copyright © 2009, IGI Global, distributing in print or electronic forms without written permission of IGI Global is prohibited.

skills and expertise or which exist in uncertain or highly-dynamic environments. Because of these traits, meaningful integration of diverse organisations to realize some coherent enterprise can be difficult (Ludwig & Wittingham, 1999). Organisational boundaries, including technical, cultural, procedural, managerial structural and others limit the potential for interaction. In particular, they can reduce an enterprise's ability to solve problems and make decisions in response to changing circumstances (Jarratt & Fayed, 2001).

Organisational boundaries can be overcome with large amounts of shared infrastructure, but at high financial cost and to the detriment of agility, autonomy and time to market. If an enterprise is to achieve coherence whilst retaining such traits as agility and flexibility, it must rely on a service-based, federated infrastructure which can be rapidly co-configured and reconfigured by participant organisations. This requires a deep understanding of the nature of the enterprise, the roles and relationships of its participants and the impacts of events or changes on other participants and on the subsequent activities of the enterprise. For this reason we present an approach that brings together research from sociology and computer science. The result is a software architecture that is flexible and agile enough to support the almost infinite number of deployment scenarios required by actual VO protagonists plus methodology, supported by tooling, which enables the rapid development of connected rich pictures (Checkland & Scholes, 1990) describing the enterprise to be undertaken. These rich pictures can be used to configure the deployment scenarios and can become part of the VO's instrumentation, so that the primary means of understanding and communicating information about the enterprise also becomes the primary means of interacting with it.

This chapter will explain some of the problems and issues relating to the crossing of organisational boundaries, particularly among complex, dynamic and 'knowledge-oriented' VOs. It will describe some important non-functional requirements that are desirable in this type of VO. It will then outline our socio-technical approach to building VOs, illustrating it with two factual scenarios from the chemical R&D and multi-agency health care industries. The chapter concludes with a description of a socio-technical platform developed in collaboration between the EPSRC e-Science Pilot Project GOLD and Newcastle University's Centre for Knowledge, Innovation, Technology and Enterprise (KITE).

BACKGROUND

It has been remarked that there are as many definitions of "Virtual Organisation" as there are researchers in the field (Metselaar & Van Dael, 1999). In practice, these definitions tend to fall roughly onto a spectrum with an emphasis on the sharing of physical resources such as storage and processing power at one end and an emphasis on exploiting novel aggregations of knowledge, skills and capacity at the other. At the more 'resource-oriented' end of the spectrum, VOs are often characterised by relative stability; well-defined central or hierarchical management; well-defined access to resources across simple interfaces; easily-defined tasks; and a set of well-understood, well-communicated common goals (Foster, 2001). An example is an outsourced data processing facility, where data is securely shipped off-site for manipulation by third-party algorithms using grid technology because the client does not possess either appropriate algorithms or required processing power in-house. The problems and issues associated with these types of VO are largely *technical*, including:

- How to overcome local technical restrictions such as firewalls; details of internal networks etc.
- How to provide secure, governable access control to shared resources.

- How to coordinate resource use across organisational boundaries
- How to protect information security
- How to generate evidence of activity in the event of disputes
- How to federate different technologies, processes and standards
- How to provision and deploy services, tools and applications

Many of these problems have received recent attention from the Grid community and have technical solutions. For example, semantic firewall approaches have been used to dynamically mediate access to web services (Jacyno et al., 2007); distributed workflow solutions have been developed to coordinate access to grid services in the presence of organisational boundaries (Shrivastava & Wheater, 1998); dynamic deployment of services (Chrysoulas et al., 2007; Watson et al., 2006); as well as mainstream grid infrastructure components such as the Globus Toolkit (http://www.globus.org/). For this reason, the majority of technical approaches to VOs have used amalgamations of various grid technology components.

Conversely, VOs positioned more towards the 'knowledge-oriented' end of the spectrum tend to be characterised by dynamism; uncertainly; poorly-defined tasks, interfaces, technology and requirements; highly distributed or frequently changing management and composition; conflicting goals, tasks and priorities; a greater reliance on human relationships and skills, problem-solving, coordinated expertise and novel aggregations of knowledge (Goh, 2005). Examples of this type of VO are R&D projects with numerous partners providing specialist expertise contributing to an ill-defined whole and the provisioning of individualised services in multi-agency environments. The problems and issues associated with this type of VO tend to be more complex, including (Wright & Smith, 2007):

- How to identify what activity is occurring within a given organisation and whether that is in accordance with the VO's overall objectives.
- How to detect, diagnose and solve problems that may occur within other organisations or due to interactions between several organisations.
- How to overcome the use of diverse and possibly incompatible technologies, processes, standards, policies, etc. by different partners.
- How to coordinate effectively, maintain control and make decisions given the existence of different organisational and ethnic cultures, motivations, priorities, management styles, ethics, etc, which can otherwise lead to conflicts and misunderstanding.
- How to reach a mutual understanding of *language and technical terms* across organisational and cultural boundaries. This is often more problematic than might be expected: different types of practitioner in a common field might use identical terms slightly differently. This might not be detected at the outset and lead to unexpected downstream consequences.
- How to reach a mutual understanding of *intent* across organisational and cultural boundaries. It is not uncommon for every participant of a meeting to leave with an entirely different understanding of whatever was agreed. This tends to be exacerbated in multi-organisational contexts because communication is likely to be more sparse and lateral feedback more difficult.
- How to mitigate the problems of rapid magnification of problems due to the lack of feedback and transparency, difficulty of communication, changing environment and great potential for misunderstanding in multi-organisational contexts. Small errors in communication of intent can be inflated in an organisation due to sparse commu-

nication, leading to rapidly diverging (and expensive to reconcile) activities.

Issues of this type cannot always be solved by purely technical means because they are largely concerned with the amalgamation of *knowledge, skills and expertise* rather than of *resources*. Characteristically, for example, knowledge of how to solve a problem might exist *in potentia* within a VO but may be inaccessible in practice due to organisational boundaries. This is covered in detail in the case studies, but a brief example is given here:

Social care in the UK is roughly divided into care for children and care for adults. Problems that do not fall neatly within one category might go entirely undetected. If detected, the solution may not be clear: diagnosis might require information and expertise that is widely distributed across organisational boundaries and not apparent to a single observer. Solutions might require coordinated mobilisation of resources administered by different groups with different priorities, motivations and funding.

Problems of this type cannot be entirely solved with technology alone, largely because each problem or scenario is likely to be different, so different resources must be mobilised in unexpected ways to overcome them (Wognum & Faber, 2002). As described in the scenarios, it is common for such an enterprise to be only vaguely definable at the outset and to change significantly throughout its lifetime. Specific technology solutions can therefore not be anticipated. In this example, the main problem is that the agencies do not know enough about each other to jointly solve problems: they do not understand each other's capabilities, resources and expertise or the roles they play in their relationships with users. It is therefore very difficult for them to coordinate their activities in solving a problem that crosses the divide. There are also important issues of security and transi-

tive trust, which are sufficiently complex that they must often be addressed on a case by case basis (Dimitrakos et al., 2004). Some form of infrastructure would be required to help bridge the gap. This might include:

- Some means of federating or otherwise connecting different technologies and processes
- Processes for requesting information and resources, and protocols for tracking them.
- A shared, secure information repository
- A deep understanding of the roles, responsibilities, structure, capabilities etc of each service.
- Some means of coordinating unanticipated activity.
- An understanding of how changes in an organisation or its environment might impact partners and their activity.
- Mechanisms for escalating problem reports for action within virtual organisations
- A means for making decisions jointly as circumstances change
- An ontology framework for translating terms, concepts and ideas

In realistic commercial environments, technology can support many of these infrastructure components but not automate them entirely. For this reason, such an infrastructure will require two principal layers:

- A technical infrastructure, providing fundamental services that allow VOs to be built and operated. This will need to be provisioned, deployed and managed by a host organisation.
- A sociological method for building, operating and evolving VOs, which allows rapid development of a shared, deep understanding of the enterprise to be conducted, the roles and responsibilities of the participants and the relationships those entail. This under-

standing should take the form of connected *rich pictures* (Checkland & Scholes, 1990; Monk & Howard, 1998) which illustrate various *projections* of the enterprise (Martin, 2004) (see 'Social infrastructure'). These rich pictures can subsequently become part of the *instrumentation* of the resulting VO, so that the shared understanding, co-developed by participants, becomes the primary means of interacting with it.

When appropriately deployed, these components can better equip participants to manage novel aggregations of skills, knowledge and expertise in solving problems across organisational boundaries. In order to realise this goal, the architecture must be carefully designed, taking into account a number of non-functional requirements, as described below.

Non-Functional VO Requirements

Loosely-Coupled Tight Integration

Tight integration of business units has conventionally been achieved through shared infrastructure. For example, ERM systems integrate functions within an enterprise by providing a mapping between those functions (Esteves & Pastor, 2001). In general, this is *tightly-coupled* and often dominated by a lead organisation, which is able to exert pressure on partners to adopt common technology, standards, processes and platforms. It is most appropriate in conventional supply-chains, such as those found in traditional manufacturing industries. It has the advantage of rich, powerful, highly transparent and governable resource sharing, but the disadvantage of poor flexibility/agility and very high initial and maintenance costs.

Tightly-coupled solutions are likely to be inappropriate where an enterprise is highly dynamic, consists of numerous diverse organisations and is knowledge-oriented (Al-Mashari, 2001). Although ERM helps resources to be shared between organisations, it does not assist with the bringing to bear of unanticipated aggregations of knowledge and expertise to address unexpected situations. In these scenarios, a more *loosely-coupled* approach may be more appropriate. These systems place less reliance on shared infrastructure, resulting in greater autonomy for partners, greater agility for the resulting enterprise and lower cost for all concerned. However, they also tend to be more poorly integrated, severely limiting ability to solve problems.

In a given situation, an appropriate balance between loose coupling and tight integration is required. This is achievable given the right kind of technical architecture, deployment infrastructure and a means of rapidly building and modifying application functionality.

Dynamism

Many environments are characterised by dynamic behaviour where change is the norm and may occur widely throughout an enterprise, including frequent and unpredictable changes. These are shown in Table 1.

Co-Building a Solution

One of the most critical aspects of building and managing VOs is for all stakeholders to become actively involved in the process (Ornetzeder & Rohracher, 2006). This is because:

- Each stakeholder's view of a solution is likely to differ greatly in terms of goals, priorities, approaches, processes, management styles, decision-making styles etc. These organisational boundaries will make integration difficult unless they are understood and compensated for. For example, misunderstood priorities can result in wasted effort and missed deadlines. Conflicting goals can result in poorly-integrated products and counter-productive behaviour.

Table 1. Dynamic Behaviour including Frequent and Unpredictable Changes to the following. Dealing with highly dynamic scenarios requires an agile technical infrastructure.

Partners	The number, identity and character of partners may change frequently throughout a project, particularly in tasks such as R&D, where the expected outcome is not fully known at the outset.
Structure	There may be shifts in relationships between organisations as an enterprise moves through its lifecycle. This may have far-reaching consequences such as shifts in the balance of power within a consortium or dramatic changes in ability to communicate and cooperate.
Products	It is not unusual for an enterprise engaged in R&D to deliver an entirely different product to that envisioned at the outset. Lessons learned along the way close off some avenues and foster innovation in others, creating new opportunities. New aggregations of knowledge and expertise may result in new products, new types of product or even new market sectors.
Processes	The way activities are carried out, success is measured and communication managed is often subject to change over time. An example of this is the different phases of a project, which may move from R&D to development, to operations, changing how activities are perceived by stakeholders.
Problem-solving and decision-making style	The approach to problem-solving and decision-making may change depending on current balance of power, distribution of expertise, individual charisma etc. and as a result of an enterprise's learning.
Priorities	Priorities change according to availability of resources, changes in organisational structure, changes in environment and in risks (such as likelihood of hitting a window of opportunity)
Ownership	Ownership of partners, processes or tasks may change, with corresponding effects on how things are done. For example, a new owner of a task might have a different set of priorities, different decision-making style, different types of communication, reporting etc.

- Managing processes and solving problems requires a clear understanding of roles and responsibilities as circumstances change. A complex VO might be neither highly centralised nor fully distributed: some decisions can be made locally, whereas others require expertise from a variety of sources. Effective management requires that the most qualified resources be brought to bear on any task.
- It might not be clear in advance how actions taken within a VO will impact others. For example, a hardware upgrade in one organisation may require another to upgrade its software, which will divert engineers from their main task, which may lead to a missed deadline.

By co-building the VO, participants learn about each other, about the joint activity to be undertaken about their role in this activity and about how to express their intentions, requirements and capabilities in a way that is understood by the other participants. This facilitates rapid building and re-configuration of effectively-managed VOs in dynamic, uncertain environments.

A SOCIO-TECHNICAL APPROACH

The problems illustrated above are the result of poor integration across organisational boundaries. They are caused by discontinuities in technical and

Figure 1. Three-layered technical architecture

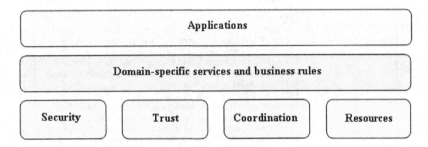

information systems, management or particularly in *understanding*. In predictable, well-understood, static environments, this can be addressed by technological means such as ERM, but this generally inappropriate when the environment is dynamic or uncertain. To ensure effective management in such environments, it is necessary that all parties understand their roles and the tasks at hand and that a technical infrastructure is put in place to deploy it.

Participants must understand how their activities relate to those of others and how changes or delays on their part might impact the VO's overall objectives. It is also necessary to understand the priorities and motivations of other partners, and about other partners' cultures and processes, since this will affect trust, risk and how problems are solved and decisions made.

The goal of the socio-technical approach is to facilitate the co-construction of VOs that constitute new aggregations of skills, knowledge and resources and which are capable of true collaborative action and collective decision-making. There are two major aspects to this socio-technical system:

- **A technical infrastructure:** This is a middleware platform providing fundamental services for resource sharing, coordination, security and trust, plus lightweight business logic/application layer that configures services towards application domains.

- **A social infrastructure:** This is a tool-supported method of creating rich pictures representing a consortium's shared understanding of its enterprise and environment. These rich pictures can be connected to the technical infrastructure, becoming part of the VO's instrumentation

Technical Infrastructure

The technical infrastructure should consist of service-based middleware, which provides key VO functionality. We propose a three-layered architecture to maximise flexibility and deployment options (see Figure 1).

Three-Layered Architecture

At the lowest level are services fundamental to the operation of VOs. These are grouped into four categories as shown in Table 2.

At the middle level are domain-specific services and business logic. These will configure the low-level services towards a specific application domain and might include standard workflows, resource federation interfaces, simulation and model resources etc. It is conceivable that packages of middle-layer services will be assembled by industry bodies or third parties.

At the top level are applications and portals providing a specific VO's functionality.

Table 2. Lower-level services

Security	Security is vital in most VO applications. This category should contain generic security services providing authorisation and authentication. At a minimum, this should include a Role-Based Access Control scheme, but research indicates [Oh & Park 2000] that in many cases this is insufficient, since roles will typically change with context. A hybrid Role- and Task-Based scheme is therefore recommended. Other services, such as encryption, should also be included in this category.
Trust	Trust is a difficult issue in VOs, particularly in dynamic environments. It is likely that organisations will be required to work together without prior experience of each other [La Porta 1997]. Because of this, some means for establishing, managing and mitigating issues of trust is required. At minimum, this should include a non-repudiable audit trail, which records activity occurring within the VO to provide evidence in the event of a dispute. This can be coupled with electronic contracts, which specify the *rights* and *obligations* of each party within a relationship. The result can be used to configure access control as well as police activity and anticipate problems. Other facilities might include some means of rating the trust of other parties, recording good vs bad behaviour etc, but facilities of this type must be used with care. In general, trust is complex and non-transitive, being highly dependent on circumstance.
Resource management	Managing resources is fundamental to most VOs. It may range from integrating physical resources such as disk space and processing power to running a query across several widely different databases. To address this problem, we propose a *Process Service Bus*, which provides facilities for communication between resources and for rapid development of federation interfaces to aid integration. The Process Service Bus is a generalisation of conventional grid technologies and its task is to orchestrate federation between different types of grid technology. In addition, a distributed information repository will usually be required. This will record information *about* the VO and may be used as a secure shared space for placing shared information.
Coordination	Coordinated activity is an important measure of success for a VO. Numerous schemes have been proposed, the most prevalent being workflow. However, workflow is appropriate only in relatively well-understood and static situations. Additionally, it may be unfeasible to force companies to adopt a particular workflow scheme and difficult in practice to federate between different workflow engines. We therefore propose that the basis of coordination should be a low-level primitive such as an event model, governed by a notification service. This will provide facilities allowing users (subject to access control) to register to receive events generated by activity within the VO. This can be used as the entire coordination scheme, or could be used to drive a distributed workflow [Shrivastava & Wheater 1998] or other higher-level coordination technology.

Deployment Issues

It is important to consider the deployment and hosting of such architecture. We anticipate that instances of the technical architecture (hubs) will be hosted by industry bodies, consultants and other interested parties, who will configure them towards the specific needs of their customers. By these means, hub operators will facilitate the formation and operation of VOs between their customers.

Federation will allow customers of different hubs to form VOs, sharing resources, knowledge etc. and coordinating their activities despite their use of different technologies, processes and third party facilitators (see Figure 2).

This configuration allows hub operators to provide value-added services specifically for their customers. This might include domain-specific services, applications and resources, but also federation services and protocols to increase the scope of interaction. Federation services are likely

Figure 2. Federated hubs allow universal and scalable VO membership

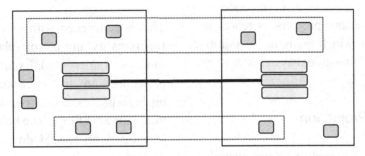

to include the translation of low-level protocols such as security tokens, coordination primitives etc, perhaps supported by ontologies, generalised access to multiple resources etc. This facilitates a scalable approach to local service provisioning.

Social Infrastructure

The proposed technical infrastructure provides building blocks for implementing highly diverse and dynamic VOs. However, it does not provide guidelines about how those facilities are to be used in practice. As discussed above, this can limit the ability of VOs to solve real-world problems. We therefore need a structured means for participants to co-build a shared understanding of an enterprise and their place in it and to capture this understanding in a form that is meaningful, is communicable to others, and can be used as a means of interacting with the resulting VO. Stakeholders need a context in which they can discuss, negotiate and agree the ways in which they will work together and share information. This is a continuing need because the process is a continuous one associated with governance of shared information and joint activity as systems and their environments change. They also require a vehicle through which their collective interests can be represented in the process of procuring, commissioning and managing shared services.

A recognised difficulty of formal and diagrammatic approaches is their tendency towards reduction. Expressive power is sacrificed for gains in generalisation, predictive ability, mathematical formalism and perspicuity of representation. Herbert et al., (ANSA, 1989) propose the use of *projections* to improve the expressive power and scope of systematic representations. Using this approach, an enterprise and its environment may be described in a number of different ways, each involving a particular set of concerns. A major value of this approach is that it allows us to construct links between projections, showing how objects and activity in one projection are related to objects and activity in another. In the context of VOs, this allows us to construct links between different views of an enterprise by different participants, thus defining a set of *mirrors,* in which participants can see their view of a system illustrated, and *windows,* which allow them to see other participants' views of the same system.

Our method proposes a series of facilitated workshops through which the stakeholders in a proposed VO rapidly co-build a series of connected projections describing the enterprise and its environment from the point of view of each participant.

Many different types of projection are possible. However, best practice (ISO, 1993; Martin, 2004; Sowa & Zachman, 1992) suggests the specific projections of *enterprise, information, computation, engineering* and *technology.* A more general formulation of these five projections has since evolved, relabeling and refining the projections as in the following sections.

Each projection represents a frame of discourse and analysis which addresses a set of concerns. Together, the five generic projections represent a framework within which many or all significant aspects of socio-technical systems may be articulated.

The Enterprise Projection

This is concerned with structuring responsibilities, rights and obligations. It supports the consideration of what responsibilities exist and how they are related, separately from how we combine and allocate them. It therefore underpins the exploration of issues such as the internalisation or externalisation of relationships (setting the boundaries of an enterprise) and the conflicts or synergies of interest arising when different roles are combined and allocated. More generally, the enterprise projection can be considered to describe the structure of a potential VO and what it and its constituents intend to achieve.

The Instrumental Projection

This is concerned with the means by which agents interact. The exchanges or *conversations* are defined in terms of sequences of acts. An instrument corresponds to a physical resource, which serves to link intended acts with performed actions. The term has many connotations. For example, its legal use implies an association with the physical embodiment and record of a contract or other legal device, whereas in the scientific sense it implies the use of a tool to acquire and present information. In the musical sense, an instrument is associated with performance. Instruments may take the form of documents or records, or may be embodied in the use of associations between objects or situations. For example, we may commit to a course of action verbally or by signing a contract. In each case, the corresponding resource *instrumentalises* the activity.

The Behavioural Projection

This is concerned with specification of a VO's functionality and its role-players (users, operators, maintainers etc.). Examples of behavioural projections are an object model coupled with a business process or a software system in conjunction with workflows. The behavioural projection specifies who should do what to achieve the desired goals.

The Design Projection

This is concerned with the mobilisation of resources to orchestrate the activities defined in the behavioural projection. The design projection can also be considered as a deployment model. It concerns the usual trade-offs inherent in the design process, such as division of functionality between technical and human resources, between different layers of a systems architecture etc. The design projection may also describe the allocation of domains of ownership and governance of resources and activities.

The Physical Projection

This provides the inventory of solution capabilities, the rules controlling their deployment and any constraints they place on the design process. This might include technical or physical capabilities or concepts of human performance, expertise, knowledge etc. Functionality implies capability and the physical projection defines the set of available capabilities and the rules of their combination and disposition.

Other Projections

The majority of complex systems will require these projections at a minimum, although some may be quite sparsely populated. In addition, many systems will require additional and less formal projections. For example, a projection might model a user interface or record a system's state in some easily-understood way (consistent with a view of the system familiar to the participants. Alternatively, two or more views might show a piece of behaviour from the perspective of an individual's or group's point of view. Such a view may contain elements from other projections, packaged in a way that makes sense to the people observing it and so aid in explanation of what is occurring within the system.

Co-Construction Revisited

The method requires that projections of these types – along with any sub-projections that might be useful – are co-constructed by participants to create a context in which they can discuss their roles, relationships, capabilities etc. This is achieved through a series of facilitated meetings supported by the use of tools. A tool developed for this purpose is described in 'GOLD: Towards a Socio-Technical VO Platform'. By using this tool, participants iteratively create a series of connected animations embodying the various aspects of the system, showing how it functions from multiple points of view and incorporating UI elements or other explanatory views where necessary. In other words, through facilitated meetings, the various overlapping understandings of different aspects of the system have been combined into a description of what the proposed VO needs to do and how this is to be achieved. Such a solution can be deployed very rapidly given a sufficiently flexible technical infrastructure and appropriate tooling.

Summary of the Socio-Technical Approach

The essence of the socio-technical approach is the co-construction of a joint understanding of the enterprise to be carried out, based on the five projections of enterprise, instrument, behaviour, design and physical (and others where helpful). Each of these projections is realised as one or more diagrams containing objects that depict real world or conceptual objects and animations that denote behaviour. These projections are linked by *events*: an event that triggers some behaviour in one projection might also trigger behaviour in others.

For example, a relationship denoted in the enterprise projection might oblige two organisations to share some specific information. This might be denoted by an animation showing a representation of the information moving between icons representing these two parties. However, it should be remembered that this conversation must be *instrumented* in order to occur in the real world. Assuming the information is contained in a document of some kind, that document can be considered as the instrument of that conversation. Therefore, the instrumental projection will depict a document exchange. Let's assume, however, that the document is commercially sensitive and permission must be obtained from a manager before it can be released. This should be depicted in the behavioural projection through the activation of appropriate roles. To achieve secure exchange, resources must be deployed to store the document in a managed space. This should be shown in the physical projection as the creation of a logical space connected to and instrumented by various physical resources. From the user's perspective, this might be viewed as a simple document upload, so this could be shown in a UI projection.

All this activity is triggered by a single event (the sharing of some information), but this event triggers activity in several different projections or views of the system. The set of connected projections therefore collectively shows the effects of that event from a variety of different points of view.

A Commercial Manager might be concerned with delivering results and less so with how this is achieved. A Human Resources Manager is likely to be more concerned with how individuals become qualified to share documents. An IT manager will care more about how and where the document leaves the company's infrastructure and ensuring that no other information is inadvertently exchanged.

The various projections describe these different points of view but – more importantly – the event-based links between the projections explain to these various managers how their view relates to others'.

Through an iterative series of facilitated meetings, using software tools, roleplaying, game playing etc, a consortium can rapidly develop a connected set of projections that illustrate the proposed enterprise. Each member will learn more about the enterprise and how it is to be deployed and managed than would otherwise be the case without extensive study and experience. In the process, it is likely that tacit and latent needs will be uncovered, which will prevent problems later in the process.

These projections will be captured as a series of animated rich pictures, which will be used to configure services at the various levels of the technical architecture and to provide requirements for any applications development needed. Once initial development is complete, the pictures will become part of the instrumentation of the resulting VO, so that the joint understanding of the enterprise becomes the primary means of interacting with it.

SCENARIOS

This section presents two real-world scenarios that illustrate the need for a socio-technical approach to supporting virtual organisations. They describe problems that can occur due to the complexity, dynamism and uncertainty of consortium working and suggest ways in which a socio-technical approach could improve matters.

Chemicals Industry Scenario

The UK Fine Chemical industries have a $9 - $12 billion share of the $250 billion global markets.

Manufacturers focus on new product development as a means of growth with time to market as the primary driver. Because of increasing competition it is now recognised that more structured mechanisms for managing the innovation process must emerge if companies are to extract maximum profitability. An increasing trend to outsource services creates a supply network of specialist companies interacting with manufacturers. Different specialist companies may be involved at all stages in the R&D lifecycle, providing services ranging from basic research or safety testing to commercial or legal services.

Coalitions of this type are examples of VOs. A large chemical company may operate hundreds of R&D projects, each with a VO of unique composition. Each project is a highly dynamic entity in which members, roles, relationships and even goals, directions, success criteria etc. may change frequently and rapidly in response to decisions made throughout the its lifecycle and unexpected external events.

This case study is based on an actual chemical process development (CPD) project which was conducted by a consortium of partners including the School of Chemical Engineering and Advanced Materials at Newcastle University. Names of other partners have been changed.

Scenario Background

Eau de Chem owns and operates a batch processing plant producing a widely-used chemical. This plant is approaching the end of its serviceable life and needs to be updated. The company must therefore decide whether to:

- Initiate a major refit to bring the plant up to date.
- Phase out the plant and build another to replace it.

Eau de Chem decided on the latter and at the same time to convert the process that produces this chemical from *batch* to *continuous*. In making this decision it was recognised that new technology would have to be developed and that the outcome was far from certain: such a conversion can be highly complex and may turn out to be unfeasible or impractical. A VO approach for the project was adopted at the outset because the range of skills required is not available in either Eau de Chem or any single contractor. In addition the VO approach offers substantial cost savings, as will become clear.

In the following discussions, the role undertaken by the chemical engineer from Newcastle University is that of the Reaction Engineering Consultant (RE), providing amongst other things a laboratory service analysing the details of the chemical reactions involved in the process; assessing the reaction kinetics; and reactor simulation and design. In addition to Eau de Chem and RE, there are a number of other VO members providing a range of different specialist knowledge and skills when required. These participants include Pilot Plant Designers (PPD); Equipment Vendors (EV); Equipment Manufacturers (EM); and a Term Contractor providing engineering, procurement and construction services (TC). Figure 3 shows the VO configuration that had been established at the end of Phase 1, with solid arrows indicating relatively fixed relationships and dashed arrows representing more uncertain ones.

Figure 3. The structure of the Chemical Development Project at the end of Phase 1

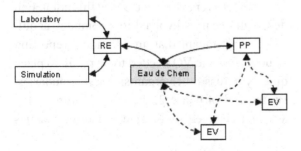

Dynamic Nature of CPD

The chemical R&D lifecycle is highly dynamic. Unanticipated changes in direction may occur at any time. The entire plan for developing a given product is not generally known at the outset. It is not just that the details haven't been worked out yet: it is that even apparently unimportant details might have a significant effect on high-level project plans. For example, a need for different or additional outsourcing of specialist services may become apparent as project knowledge increases. Similarly, the operational, technical and legal basis of how a company accesses another's resources or the goals and criteria for the project's success may evolve as the result of environmental changes. Everything about a CPD project can change in unexpected directions at any time. It is crucial that the VO remain agile and flexible in order to respond to changes of this type and ensure that efficiency increases and time to market is minimised.

Table 3 shows the initial project plan for the CPD project that was based on 4 phases.

Although this plan seems superficially straightforward, it is virtually certain that even small change in the project technology or the business environment may change even this high-level view, with further ramifications at every level of detail. Table 4 illustrates what the risk analysis revealed at the beginning of the project.

Dynamic Changes Occurring During the Course of Phase 1 and Phase 2 of the Project

During Phase 1 the chemistry required for continuous operation was found to work well. However, downstream separation of the catalyst proved problematic using filtration technology. Trials using alternative continuous centrifuge technology were therefore initiated with a different equipment supplier. This constituted a significant change to the consortium: introducing a new

Table 3. Initial project plan for the CPD project

Phase 1	Preliminary laboratory / modelling investigations to determine whether the conversion from batch to continuous operation is feasible. Preliminary trials of downstream processing separation methods.
Phase 2	Design of a pilot plant using information collected in Phase 1.
Phase 3	Build and operation of the pilot plant to identify suitable modes of operation, potential problems with start-up/shut-down etc.
Phase 4	Design and build of the full production plant

Table 4. Risk analysis results

Conversion not feasible	Conversion of the process to continuous operation may not be feasible for variety of reasons. For example, the chemical reactions may not be compatible with continuous operation. In which case upgrading existing batch plant may be the only option.
Downstream processing problems	The new operating conditions might unexpectedly affect the downstream recovery of the catalyst and a new separation method must be found. This may require modification to the VO membership through the introduction of a new specialist partner.

partner required renegotiation of contracts, shifting priorities and shifting deadlines. Since Eau de Chem had no prior experience of continuous centrifuge technology, it was necessary to invoke expertise from throughout the entire consortium in order to properly evaluate the technology and its provider.

Following the success of the chemistry a decision was made to move to Phase 2 and the project transferred from an R&D budget to a capital budget. A new set of managers in a different country became responsible for the project. This resulted in changes in priority, direction, motivation and management style. It also resulted in widespread uncertainty and concern throughout the project as changes were poorly communicated and the future direction became unclear.

Towards the end of Phase 2, a completely unexpected external event occurred: the supplier of the catalyst ceased to operate without warning. It was therefore necessary to find a new supplier, but this was complicated by the fact that the catalyst is a naturally occurring substance and its properties vary considerably with the geographical region supplying it. A new catalyst source joined the VO

and Phase 1 Chemistry had to be restarted to ensure that its product was an adequate replacement. The catalyst worked well with the old batch plant but not in continuous operation laboratory trials. Many more catalysts had to be investigated and potential suppliers became temporary members of the VO. This also meant that the separation trials had also to be restarted.

The managers associated with the capital budget now required rapid communication of progress across all aspects the project including the now continuously changing pilot plant design and suppliers of catalysts. Project coordination and communication became increasingly important as the capital budget had been set and the decision to move to Phase 3 had to be made before the end of the financial year. This restriction had ramifications across the entire the project.

Another event also occurred at this point, Eau de Chem became involved in a company acquisition. This meant that an additional reporting structure for the VO needed to be put in to place quickly across other organisational boundaries. By the end of phase 2, the whole nature of the VO had changed, with many more companies

Figure 4. Complexity increases as unexpected events occur

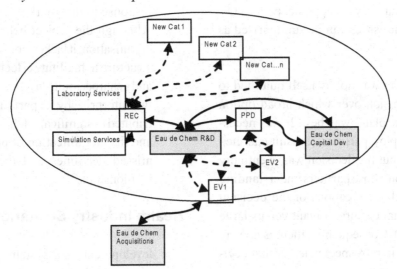

and management groups being involved and the expectations of those companies differing from the expectations at the outset. In particular, the rate of expected progress of the project had been significantly increased due to the pressures of the financial year end.

Figure 4 depicts the implications of dynamic events in the CPD environment on the project, showing the more complex structure of the VO and the additional tasks required to complete the project during Phase 2.

The CPD as a Virtual Organisation

When unexpected events occurred, the CPD VO members collaborated to find a solution. This contrasts with a more conventional outsourcing model, where projects tend to be tree structured, with communication taking place more or less entirely up and down the branches.

Effective VOs are more network-like in structure and therefore able to bring the full range of skills and resources belonging to their member organisations to bear on problems to solve them more efficiently. The CPD project was able to respond in an agile fashion, dynamically recon-

figuring itself to address the new environment. Naturally, this agility is not without resource implications. In this case, the principle cost is the management effort required to coordinate the various partners and force effective communication. Urgency was also a factor, since from Phase 2 onwards, the project was operating on capital budget and so had to be completed by the financial year end. The potential cost of missed opportunity was therefore very great.

If this were the only project Eau de Chem participated in, the management costs might be tolerable. However, this is not the case: the same companies and the same managers were simultaneously involved in several other development projects of similar complexity, but comprising different team membership and at different life-cycle stages. The resources needed to maintain all CPD projects as agile as the above are not realistically available.

Lessons Learned from the Chemical R&D Scenario

Although the scenario describes a perfectly ordinary chemicals R&D project, it is an order of magnitude more complex than scenarios considered by the majority of approaches to VOs. The problems and issues can be summarised as follows:

- Eau de Chem was not by itself qualified to make a decision over which broad option (refit or new plant) was best. It was necessary to employ partners (consultants etc.) for advice, but the decision was eventually made without those partners understanding the political ramifications of the decision (e.g. potential closure of plant versus large investment). Consequently, there is no way to measure in retrospect whether that decision was correct.

- The initial VO configuration was somewhat hierarchical, with Eau de Chem dominating the value chain, management activities and decision-making. This reduced the VO's effective agility, since local expertise could not easily be brought to bear on local problems.

- The decision to move to Phase 2 of the project was inappropriate: if the expertise available to the consortium had been fully exploited, it is likely that this decision would have been delayed. This would probably have resulted in a wider range of options being available at an earlier stage.

- Testing of the new catalyst was unnecessarily delayed because it was not immediately recognised that the new source would cause difficulties. Had the full range of expertise within the consortium been brought to bear on this issue, it is likely that large savings in time and money could have been achieved.

- The acquisition of Eau de Chem had enormous repercussions throughout the enterprise, changing the priorities, expectations, management styles and even the goals of partner organisations. It may even have changed some aspects of the market itself and consequently the member companies' response to that market.

- Although the project behaved as a virtual organisation, it lacked both a technical infrastructure to facilitate effective coordination and a shared, multi-layered understanding of the enterprise by its participants. This contributed to significant delays, poor decisions and the magnification of problems, delays, missed deadlines and damaged working relationships.

Health Industry Scenario

The development of a system of e-prescribing policy in England is closely related to key strands of UK Government policy in the National Health Service (NHS), described in *Delivering 21st Century IT Support for the NHS* and *Pharmacy in the Future*, which are being supported by under a range of services and applications being offered in England through the Connecting for Health, NHS National Programme for IT (NPfIT) including the Electronic Prescribing Service (EPS). The current UK government has been keen to re-shape pharmacy services, including the development of prescribing, dispensing and reimbursement processes, and setting drug prices, within the broader agenda of the National Health Service (NHS) modernisation outlined in *The NHS Plan*. The policy document *Pharmacy in the Future* (DH 2000) set out the intentions and plans across a wide range of policy areas, affecting all the organisations that currently provide these services, with the aim being to improve the service to patients. A range of initiatives have sprung from the modernisation agenda including repeat dispensing, medicines management, independent pharmacist prescribing and local pharmacy services (LPS) agreements. A key part of the supporting infrastructure to support the pharmacy modernisation in terms of prescription services was the mobilisation of information using computer technology.

More recent developments have seen a report on the regulation of retail pharmacy services in the UK by the Office of Fair Trading (OFT, 2003). The DH responded by setting up an Advisory Committee (DH, 2004) which as part of its remit delivered a set of outline proposals (for the purposes of consultation) for the reform of retail pharmacy services from the DH (DH, 2004). The outline proposals include the introduction of new criteria of 'competition and choice' to the current regulatory test, as well as exemption for four types of application including pharmacies described as 'wholly internet or mail-order based' (DH, 2004). In contrast to the three other types of applications where decisions are made by PCTs discussions about applications for Internet Pharmacies will be made at the national level between the DH and the NHS perhaps reflecting the significant impacts internet pharmacy service provision might be thought to have.

Our experiences from a range of work in the area of e-prescribing R&D developments including CDSS for prescribing, repeat prescribing and messaging around prescribing reveal a range of issues to consider in the context of prescribing policy and practice development. E-prescribing

in many ways can be seen as a no-brainer. Evidence from the literature suggests a number of advantages including improvements safety by reducing prescription errors and providing better information at the point of prescribing and reductions in administration overhead. Advocates for e-prescribing claim improvements in patient satisfaction that it will also ensure that prescription information should be a core part of a future electronic health record. Although the roll-out of current arrangements in the UK requires information to be keyed in on three occasions: by the prescriber, the pharmacist, and the Prescription Pricing Authority (PPA). With ETP in place, information will only need to be entered into the system once. With over 624 million prescription items issued in 2002-3 and volumes growing by around four to five and a half per cent annually, ETP is seen as essential to meet increased demand whilst saving staff time and costs. The overall objective is to implement a National Electronic Prescriptions Service by 2005 for 50 per cent of transactions, with full implementation by 2007.

Figure 5 demonstrates the complex organizational context of e-prescribing policy development in the context of ETP, distinguishing between

Figure 5. Policy context: solid lines show formal reporting or working relationships between DH Prescribing Branch; dotted lines indicate membership of groups; not all links or relationships are shown

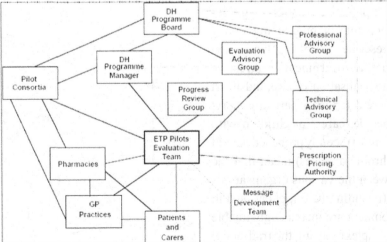

ultimate customers, influencers, intermediaries and advisers, other organizations with an interest in the conduct of e-prescribing and its outcome, and specific organizations and types of user directly involved as pilot participants. It was this latter group, comprising GP practices, pharmacies, and patients, from which information gathering took place for this evaluation. Pharmacies that participated in the three pilots included a mix of independent pharmacies, and small and large multiple pharmacy sites, operating in urban, suburban and rural areas, in order to provide opportunities for observation of differences in attitude and outcome between different types of pharmacy.

Understanding of the role of administrators and the social context (colleagues conferring with each other and sharing intelligence about patients) of prescribing is a key part of the 'prescribing system' of which e-prescribing is a part. Even in this single enterprise example the implementation of a 'technology fix' caused significant practical and prescribing safety issues to potentially arise.

We conclude by suggesting the potential service models of e-prescribing in the UK are likely to be particularly appropriate for some cohorts of patients receiving particular types of services. Given the ongoing complexity of local relationships (with the establishment of internet pharmacies issuing prescriptions), development in case law around certain medications (in the context of post-code prescribing and NICE guidelines), the developments in prescribing policy including new prescriber roles for Nurses and Pharmacists, and the governments aggressive agenda around 'personalisation' of care, and direct care budgets (where a range of patient cohorts including older people, carers of children with disabilities and the most recently proposed patient with particular chronic diseases) mean that the relationships between the various organisations and legacy tools (including ICT applications) in the service environment are increasingly unable to deal with the complexity using the traditional

structures (e.g. PCT Prescribing and Joint Formulary committees using Memos (see Jenkings ref), Prescribing Advisors etc), existing and National Agencies such as Connecting for Health offering 'shrink-wrapped' product sets without the governance tools to support local policy development and implementation and responses to national development (e.g. safety concerns and new guidance). Therefore a much more dynamic

Figure 6. Pre- and Post-ETP: The current and new prescribing processes

Pre-ETP - Current Prescribing Process

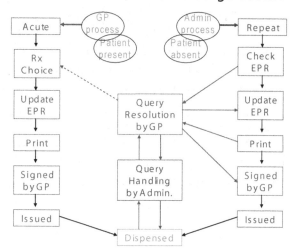

Post ETP – New Prescribing Process

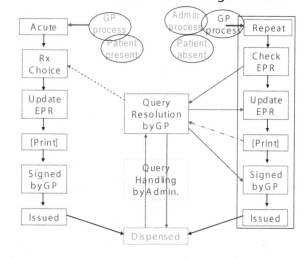

set of tools are required which can provide service environments including catalogues of devices, equipment, pharmaceutical technologies, one to one consultations with a range of professionals and services from physiotherapy to counselling to dance classes. These need to be built on a safe and secure environment where the patients' personal details are accessible with appropriate safeguards and appropriate contexts.

Lessons Learned from the Health Industry Scenario

- The prescribing of drugs is an exceedingly complex scenario involving many partners.
- Security and privacy concerns are paramount, especially when they relate either to patient safety or patient confidentiality.
- These concerns are highly complex and apparently small changes can have very large and unexpected downstream consequences that may compromise patient safety.
- Shrink-wrapped product sets are inappropriate due to the government's aggressive agenda for personalized health care, the need for specialist care to be provided in specialist centres, but the inability of such services to address problems and concerns that fall between the gaps between specialised clinical and managerial services.
- For this reason, a co-constructed approach is needed, where doctors, patients, administrators, policy-makers etc. configure services according to personal need.
- A technical system is required to achieve the move from current prescription services to e-prescription. It is clear from the above lessons that an infrastructural approach, such as the one described in this chapter, is appropriate, since the various services must be highly integrated to ensure safety and confidentiality and yet the services are frequently subject to policy change, are

characterised by different management styles, budgeting requirements, priorities, motivations etc.

- Understanding the prescription process at a number of different levels is vital, since small changes can have large and unexpected consequences that could compromise patient safety or confidentiality. A socio-technical approach, such as the one described, is therefore appropriate.

GOLD: Toward a Socio-Technical VO Platform

GOLD is a service-based middleware infrastructure platform developed as part of the DTI/EPSRC e-Science Programme Pilot Project of the same name. It provides fundamental services to support highly dynamic virtual organisations plus some tooling and demonstrator applications.

GOLD has also adopted and further developed work by the Centre for Knowledge, Innovation, Technology and Enterprise (KITE) at Newcastle University. In particular, it incorporated a tool called *The Demonstrator*, developed by KITE for the purposes of creating connected rich pictures of VO projections. It facilitates the connection of these pictures across a network to each other and to the VO they describe through the capture of events. In this way, the model can become part of the instrumentation of the VO, as illustrated in Figure 7.

GOLD Architecture

GOLD is a set of web services providing functionality in four major areas:

1. **Security:** In every collaborative enterprise, security is paramount. Collaborators in one project may be competitors in others, so it is vital that secure spaces can be constructed, within which access to shared resources can be strictly controlled. GOLD employs

a Role-Based Access Control system, augmented by tasks to provide context. XACML polices are used to configure this security system. Since policies might be developed by multiple parties, there is opportunity for conflict, potentially resulting in deadlock or livelock conditions. For this reason, we have developed a mathematical scheme for formally validating policies. GOLD is agnostic about the implementation of authentication and credentials may be federated between hubs operating different schemes.

2. **Trust:** Some of the greatest barriers preventing organisations from working closely together are matters of trust. This is especially true in dynamic situations, where there is little time for the formation of lasting, trusting relationships. Trust often has to be assumed and a reliance on policing of relationships fostered. For this reason, GOLD provides a non-repudiable audit trail, configured according to electronic contracts, which specify the rights and obligations of parties engaging in a relationship. For example, a project might require that a document is made available to the consortium by one of the partners by a particular date. That partner is trusted to do this and the economic results of failure might be severe. For this reason, disputes may arise within the consortium over whether the information was in fact made available as required. In this case, the e-contract would specify the obligations of the provider to make the data available and the rights of other partners to read it. This would be used to generate security policies and configure access control. This is used in conjunction with the audit trail and notification to ensure that evidence can be generated when interactions occur and then examined in the light of e-contracts should disputes occur.

3. **Coordination:** The performance of coordinated activity within a VO must be facilitated by a description of the activity to be carried out and the associated dynamic changes in access control required to carry out individual tasks. Participating organisations might employ a variety of technologies to implement coordination. It is important that companies are able to coordinate their activity despite these differences. For this reason, it is inappropriate to impose a particular workflow engine or other high-level coordination scheme. GOLD provides a publish/subscribe notification service, whereby organisations can publish the types of event they are able to generate with tags for context. Other organisations may subscribe to receive notifications when certain types of event occur and may thereby construct a coordination scheme despite differences in technology, granularity, interest and motivation. It is also possible to build high-level coordination schemes such as workflow on top of this infrastructure. GOLD has implemented DECS, which is a distributed workflow engine allowing multiple parties at diverse locations to participate in a workflow.

4. **Resource management:** One of the most important aspects of collaborative working is the sharing of resources between partners. Resources might include information, knowledge, expertise (in the form of services) or of physical resources such as computing power, storage or laboratory equipment. In GOLD, resource management is mediated by access control, but use any common grid technology may be used for this. In this way, GOLD federates access to resources without imposing any particular scheme.

This service infrastructure has been developed to place as few demands on participants as possible, while nevertheless providing high levels of integration. It is expected that in practice, GOLD

Figure 7. The Demonstrator provides instrumentation for VOs created by the GOLD technical infrastructure

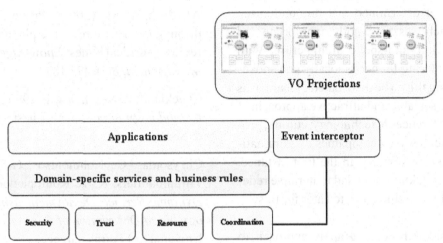

will be deployed as a series of 'hubs', each catering to the demand of a specific group of users or community. Hubs will be federated so that members of different hubs can form VOs together and/or use services provided by different hubs.

Lessons Learned

The GOLD middleware was developed alongside work conducted by the University of Lancaster Management School, conducting ethnographic studies with a variety of chemicals companies to determine requirements (particularly tacit and latent requirements), in addition to the case studies detailed above. This study resulted in some changes of direction in middleware development. The most significant of these were:

1. It was originally expected that GOLD participants would wish to engage in a marketplace of services, which would be specified using a high-level description. Users would choose services based on their properties and in doing so would bring the organisation offering that service into the VO. This was found to be unrealistic. Companies are more concerned with the identity, reputation and track record of organisations providing services than they are with the specification of the services themselves.

2. It was thought that some scheme for tracking reputation and assigning quantitative trust values would be required, with appropriate mechanisms for reward or punishment. This would aid decision-making with regard to which companies to use for particular purposes. However, we found that trust was a much more complex issue and tended to be based on relationships between individuals and personal experience.

3. It was at first assumed that a GOLD instance would be deployed and managed by each company wishing to participate on a GOLD-type VO. However, it was discovered that many organisations do not possess the technical resource to manage such a solution and furthermore that most companies require a complete solution to their individual problems, rather than a toolkit to help them solve those problems.

4. It was expected that clusters of organisations with similar needs would form spontaneously and that communities of practice would emerge to cater for them. This led to an em-

phasis on support for building and deploying services within individual organisations. It was later determined that this bottom-up approach was not wholly appropriate and that a hub-and-spoke architecture, with hubs catering for needs locally and spokes allowing this to be distributed globally was a more scalable and attractive approach.

5. The differences in technology, culture, process etc. between companies was dramatically underestimated in the first instance. Increasing knowledge led to iterative redesign of the architecture to cater for this.

We consider the ethnographic approach to requirements capture to be a major strength of the project, contributing greatly to the GOLD platform and resulting in an infrastructure that more closely matches industry requirements.

CONCLUSION

Building and managing VOs is a socio-technical problem, requiring an appropriately designed and deployed technical infrastructure and a sociologically-based means of building, managing and evolving an enterprise. The GOLD infrastructure, appropriately deployed, in conjunction with The Demonstrator, can bridge the gap between those types of problem, resulting in agile yet governable distributed enterprises capable of widespread rapid evolution and innovation and can provide an environment where integrated problem-solving and decision-making can take place. Without a socio-technical approach, dynamic and knowledge-oriented VOs cannot easily achieve high levels of integration and are likely to fail when collective decision-making or problem-solving is required. We have developed a structured methodology which can turn a rash of ideas about what some shared activity should entail into a deployed, operational, governable virtual organisation.

REFERENCES

Al-Mashari, M. (2001). Process orientation through enterprise resource planning (ERP): A review of critical issues. *Knowledge and Process Management, 8*(3), 175-185.

Checkland, P., & Scholes, J. (1990). *Soft systems methodology in action.* Chichester: John Wiley & Sons.

Chrysoulas, C., Koumoutsos, G., Denazis, S., Thramboulidis, K., & Koufopavlou, O. (2007). *Dynamic Service Deployment using an Ontology based Description of Devices and Services.* University of Patras, Greece.

Dimitrakos, T., Golby, D., & Kearney, P. (2004). Towards a Trust and Contract Management Framework for Dynamic Virtual Organisations. *Proceedings of the eChallenges Conference, 2004.*

Esteves, J., & Pastor, J. (2001). Enterprise Resource Planning Systems Research: An Annotated Bibliography. *Communications of the Association for Information Systems, 7*(8).

Foster, I. (2001). The anatomy of the grid: enabling scalable virtual organizations. *International Journal of High Performance Computing Applications, 15*(3) (August 2001), 200-222.

Goh, A. L. S. (2005). Harnessing knowledge for innovation: an integrated management framework. *Journal of Knowledge Management 2005, 9*(4), 6-18.

ISO (1993). *Open Systems Interconnection, Data Management and Open Distributed Processing.* Draft ODP Trading Function. Report No. ISO/IEC JTC 1/SC21/WG7/N880, International Organization for Standardization.

Jacyno, M., Payne, T. R., Watkins, E. R., Taylor, S. J., & Surridge, M. (2007). Mediating Semantic Web Service Access using the Semantic Firewall.

Paper presented at *UK E-Science Programme All Hands Meeting 2007 (AHM2007)*, 10th-13th September 2007, Nottingham, UK.

Jarratt, D., & Fayed, R. (2001). The Impact of Market and Organisational Challenges on Marketing Strategy Decision-Making: A Qualitative investigation of the Business-to-Business Sector. *Journal of Business Research, 51*(1) (January 2001), 61-72.

La Porta, R. (1997). Trust in Large Organizations. *The American Economic Review, 87*(2), 333-338. Papers and Proceedings of the Hundred and Fourth Annual Meeting of the American Economic Association (May, 1997).

Ludwig, H., & Whittingham, K. (1999). Virtual Enterprise Co-Ordinator – Agreement-driven Gateways for Cross-Organisational Workflow Management. *Engineering Notes, 24*(2) (March 1999), 19-38.

Martin, M. J. (2004). Diagrams and Big Pictures: The problems of representing large, complex socio-technical systems. Paper presented at *Diagrams 2004: Third International Conference on the Theory and Application of Diagrams* (March 2004).

Metselaar, C., & van Dael, R. (1999). Organisations Going Virtual. *AI & Society, 13*(1-2) (December 1999) Special issue on science, technology and society, 200-209. London, UK: Springer-Verlag.

Monk, A., & Howard, S. (1998). Methods & Tools: the rich picture: a tool for reasoning about work context. *Interactions 5*(2), March/April 1998, 21-30.

Oh, S., & Park, S. (2000). Task-Role Based Access Control (T-RBAC): An Improved Access Control Model for Enterprise Environment. *Lecture Notes in Computer Science, 1873/2000*, 264-273.

Ornetzeder, M., & Rohracher, H. (2006). User-led innovations and participation processes: lessons from sustainable energy technologies. *Energy Policy, 34*(2) (January 2006), 138-150, Reshaping Markets for the Benefit of Energy Saving.

Shrivastava, S. K., & Wheater, S. M. (1998). Architectural Support for Dynamic Reconfiguration of Distributed Workflow Applications. *IEE Proceedings – Software, 145*(5), 155-162. Institution of Electrical Engineers (IEE).

Shrivastava, S. K., & Wheater, S. M. (1998). Architectural Support for Dynamic Reconfiguration of Distributed Workflow Applications. *IEE Proceedings - Software 145*(5), 155-162. Institution of Electrical Engineers (IEE).

Sowa, J. F., & Zachman, J. A. (1992). Extending and formalising the framework for information systems architecture. *IBM Systems Journal, 31*(3), 590-616.

Watson, P., Fowler, C. P., Kubicek, C., et al. (2006). Dynamically Deploying Web Services on a Grid using Dynasoar. In S. Lee, U. Brinkschulte, B. Thuraisingham, et al. (Eds), *Proceedings of the Ninth IEEE International Symposium on Object and Component-Oriented Real-Time Distributed Computing (ISORC 2006)*. Gyeongju, Korea, April 24-26 2006 (pp. 151-158). IEEE Computer Society Press.

Wognum, P. M., & Faber, E. C. C. (2002). Infrastructures for collaboration in virtual organisations. *International Journal of Networking and Virtual Organisations, 2002, 1*(1), 32-54.

Wright, A. R., & Smith, R. (2007). *Virtual Organisation Design and Application: A Chemicals Industry Case Study.* Paper presented at UK e-Science All-Hands Meeting, Nottingham, 2007.

Chapter IX
Modelling Trust–Control Dynamics for Grid–Based Communities:
A Shared Psychological Ownership Perspective

Marina Burakova-Lorgnier
University of Bordeaux 4, INSEEC Business Schools, France

ABSTRACT

The aim of this chapter is to appreciate the need for and propose some thoughts on modelling trust–control dynamics for communities that use grid technology. It takes the viewpoint that members within a grid-based community require a trust framework that brings together and takes into account both social and technological approaches to trust. It also emphasises the importance of the simultaneous analysis of trust and control in their co-development. In line with the duality perspective that considers trust and control as independent yet interrelated dimensions, trust is explored in its relation to control. Control is examined as a multi-dimensional phenomenon that includes personal, formal, and social scopes. The analysis of trust appeals to its cognitive and affective dimensions. The model introduced also takes into account the mediating role of psychological ownership in the trust–control dynamics. Specifically, shared psychological ownership is singled out as a new explanatory variable of this dynamic.

INTRODUCTION

The main trend in the organisational behaviour research puts forward the importance of a mini- mum level of trust for the success of any form of collaboration (Bijlsma-Frankema & Costa, 2005). Numerous empirical studies (Clases et al., 2003; Das & Teng, 1998; McKnight et al., 2004)

Copyright © 2009, IGI Global, distributing in print or electronic forms without written permission of IGI Global is prohibited.

have defined trust as a primary determinant of collaborative success. At the same time, Köller (1988) and McLain & Hackman (1999) have demonstrated that control reduces trust. This effect is due to certain social attribution mechanisms. First, mere presence of a control system causes the perception of partners as less trustworthy. Second, cooperation in the presence of a control system is attributed to the constraints imposed by the control system rather than trustworthiness, which inhibits the development of trust (Coletti et al., 2005). Some researchers (Das & Teng, 2001; Şengün & Wasti, 2007), who reject the negative influence of control on trust development, believe that the negative effects of control systems are due to certain limitations of the previous studies. Coletti et al. (2005) even posit that control may enhance the level of trust between the partners.

It is clear that a collaborative environment, such as a grid-based community (GC), represents a challenge in terms of control. Attempts both to identify optimal levels of control mechanisms and to consider the impact of such mechanisms on interpersonal trust are undertaken (Coletti et al., 2005). The specificity of the GC stems from the following characteristics. First, a GC does not provide fixed paths towards the resources needed. Second, the resources per se are not constantly available, which results in the absence of the prescribed interaction patterns. Third, there is a high need for formal control mechanisms to maintain an efficient functioning of the community. Those mechanisms assure that all the processes within a GC run smoothly. Fourth, the resources exploited may be of a high level of confidence. Hence, resource sharing (an expression of trust and shared psychological ownership) and resource protection (an expression of personal control and individual psychological ownership) of resources may come to conflict. Any interaction contains an element of risk due to the fact that an interaction partner might not reciprocate (Stewart, 2003). Mediated interaction that characterises the GC context has a significantly higher level of risk as compared

to face-to-face interaction (Ratnasingam, 2005). This inevitably brings up the questions of the routes of the risk reduction. Depending upon a conceptual position, both control and trust may be considered risk reducing mechanisms.

According to a few though rigorous empirical studies (Bijlsma-Frankema & Costa, 2005; Khodyakov, 2007; Şengün & Wasti, 2007), trust does not develop without control. The relationship between trust and control is understood in the perspective of duality (Figure 1). In particular, *trust is defined as a positive expectation about the outcome of an interaction based on the benevolence of the other party involved* (Möllering, 2005). Trust is conceptualised through cognitive and affective dimensions (Mayer et al., 1995). *Control is defined as a positive expectation about the outcome of an interaction based on the structural influences of the social system on the other party involved* (Möllering, 2005). Control is conceptualised through internal and external dimensions (Berrenberg, 1987). The latter is, in turn subdivided into formal and social control (Khodyakov, 2007). There is empirical evidence that trust and control mutually influence each other. Thanks to the verification of the partner's reputation, competencies and other capacities, formal control provides a basis for the cognitive trust development, which is nurtured by knowledge of the partner's reliability (Coletti et al., 2005). Informal control influences both cognitive and affective trust (Şengün & Wasti, 2007). Trust, in turn, makes possible the use of new policies and standards (measures of formal control), etc. (idem).

Control is known to be a route of psychological ownership (Pierce et al., 2001) (Figure 1). *Psychological ownership as a feeling of possession over an object (which is "mine")* may cause unwillingness to share this same object with others in order to keep this feeling of possession and preserve self-identity (Van Dyne & Pierce, 2004). In the collaboration context, psychological ownership as it is primarily conceptualised

Figure 1. Psychological ownership as a mediator of trust–control relationship

(Pierce et al., 2001) may be an obstacle towards resource sharing. This refers to the individual form of the felt ownership. Although when experienced as co-ownership, it changes the perception of resource sharing, which is considered an equal and fair access to the collective property. Thus, the shift from the personal to the shared form of psychological ownership will define how and what type of control would be exerted.

Inkpen and Currall (2004) claim that over time as a result of collaboration, the level of trust changes, which means that trust should be viewed as an evolving rather than static concept. The present chapter attempts to envision a dynamic model of control–trust development in the perspective of psychological ownership. The logic of structural relationships between three principal variables discussed in the chapter that consists in the moderating effect of psychological ownership on the relationship between trust and control (Figure 1) helps to develop a dynamic model presented at the end of the chapter (Figure 2). The former (Figure 1) considers that psychological ownership may modify the impact control and trust may have on each other. Depending upon its form (either personal or shared), psychological ownership may reduce or enhance the positive influence control may have on trust, and vice versa. The latter (Figure 2) offers three different opportunities of trust building within a GC that comprise different sequences of the control and trust phases.

In spite of its conceptual character, the chapter aims at developing long-term practical impact on the understanding and, thus, effective manipulation of the evolution of individual, interpersonal, and social-system variables responsible for the overall success of GCs. It classifies well-known assurance mechanisms in terms of different forms of external formal control (input, output and behavioural), It stresses the importance of developing effective and explicit social control mechanisms. It also contrasts between the routes towards cognitive and affective trust. Finally, it speculates that developing the sense of shared psychological ownership has a positive mediating effect on trust development, and thus, reduces the costs due to the setting of control mechanisms. American psychologist Kurt Lewin once said, there is nothing more practical than a good theory (1951). The chapter follows this logic and, hence, intends such conceptual prediction of the trust - control causality and dynamics that facilitates understanding of the GC social structure functionality. Such systemic vision, which reveals "back" social processes, complements more practical technical solutions increasing the efficiency of GCs.

TRUST–CONTROL CONCERNS IN GRID-BASED COMMUNITIES

The grid concept has emerged as an important research area differentiated from traditional Information and Communication Technologies (ICT). Several views exploring their differences are described in Bessis et al. (2007). In brief, the added value that grid provides as compared to conventional distributed technologies lies in the inherent ability of the grid to dynamically orchestrate large scale distributed computational resources across grid members, so as to leverage maximal computational power towards the solution of a particular problem.

A number of advanced features that are integral to grid-based solutions facilitating relevant communities are rarely found in other large scale conventional distributed networks, particularly those that need to co-operate and co-ordinate dynamically across organizational and geographical boundaries. Hence, it is the ability of such grid-based solutions supporting distributed communities to orchestrate their activities autonomously and dynamically that make them primarily differ from other non-grid based computer-mediated communities. To keep autonomy and flexibility heightened, formal control is not a sufficient remedy; moreover, it risks impeding constant structural fluctuations. A grid-based community has to seek for other methods that enhance cooperation and effective use of resources. Communities using grid-based technology for their works encompass resource sharing, including ICT resources, as well as, non-ICT resources like ideas, interests, goals, skills and knowledge. Thus, such 'grid-based communities' are burdened with resource ownership (Garrity et al., 2006). Together with objective ownership, which is regulated by technical norms and policies, psychological ownership for resources and a GC determines the way and the extent to which resources are shared.

Mechanisms of psychological ownership may differ in its collective and individual forms. For example, someone may suppose that ICT resources are easily perceived as a collective property, while tacit knowledge and competencies are objects of individual possession. Then, the sense of collective ownership would promote resource sharing which is considered as the access to the shared resources. At the same time, perceived ownership for one's own expertise would result in its protection. Hence, the sharing of such vague resources needs a high level of trust both at a GC level and between its members involved in the process. Trust does not play the role of control substitute, but rather adds missing elements to the grid puzzle. Grid research has developed

a comprehensive repertory of instruments and techniques that provide a "control side" of the trust–development process. Although, the latest trends (Clapses et al., 2003; Nooteboom, 2007) in the trust–control area consider control an incontrovertible element of trust, and thus, warn of applying the logic of substitute for trust. Given that a GC is particularly flexible and unstable in terms of resource flow (their availability and transferability), psychological ownership, at least, for a GC member's own resources, might be an obstacle toward their sharing.

Grid security issues are currently being addressed mainly from the perspective of existing tangible security mediators and methods such as: Secure Sockets Layer certificates for Grid Security Infrastructure user authentication, a set of technologies that are designed to ensure that grid services are invoked in a secure manner. Those methods are means of formal control since they fulfil the criteria of predictability of outcomes that stem from formal standards and rules. On this basis, trust is seen by many to be simply an extension of "hard", tangible security issues in the context of service based architectures (French et al., 2007).

Thus, the view is that trust development must be a far more elusive and subtle process than implied by existing ICT models and initiatives or trust architectures. Wider organisational factors influence trust formation within a GC, not merely local contextual cues. Organisational, social, and psychological factors pre-determine trust development within a GC that combines both strict technological norms and social interactions. Furthermore, if analysed as a social phenomenon, trust is not merely a rational construct but has a strong emotional component. Therefore, the view is that the current trust related models and mechanisms should ideally aim to go well beyond "hard" tangible security aspects of grid technology. In the proposed model, formal and informal control and cognitive and affective trust are distinguished. Psychological ownership is examined as a mediator of control–trust dynamics. The proposed model introduces a new form of psychological owner-ship – a shared one – that explains why resource sharing does occur. The scenarios represent the possible ways of control–trust evolution in a GC: (1) linear control–trust development; (2) reputation shift; and (3) leap towards trust.

APPROACHES TO THE RELATIONSHIP BETWEEN TRUST AND CONTROL

For a long time control had been the central concept in management sciences (Coletti et al., 2005). As a reaction to such a taken-for-granted approach, a new wave of studies has shifted the usual focus from control to trust. This shift has resulted in putting trust forward as a mechanism invoked to compensate or to substitute for the lack of coercive means of management (Das & Teng, 1998). Identified with risk-taking intentions and behaviours, trust has become a sort of panacea for many organisational dysfunctions (Rousseau et al., 1998). Control, in turn, has appeared a nega-tive symptom associated with poor organisational culture and uncomfortable organisational climate. The present chapter addresses four principal ap-proaches to Trust in relation to Control. These conceptualise trust either as an opposite ($T \neq C$), close to control ($T \approx C$), independent ($T \parallel C$) or interrelated dimension ($T \leftrightarrow C$).

The first approach is based on the *social-psy-chological interpretations* of trust. In this perspec-tive, trust and control are seen as inter-excluding phenomena, substitutes or poles of the very same dimension. Numerous researchers (Mayer, 1995; McLain & Hackman, 1999; Rousseau et al., 1998) have conceptualised trust through risk taking, vulnerability and positive expectations about the other party that meant a low level or absence of control. Psychologically-oriented approaches tend to put trust to the "risk pole" of the "risk–control" dimension. They define trust as the willingness to rely on another, the confident and positive expectations about the intentions or behaviour of another and the willingness to be vulnerable and take risk (Mayer et al., 1995; Rousseau et al., 1998). According to this viewpoint, risk, as a likelihood of negative outcomes (McLain & Hackman, 1999), is an essential condition of trust emergence, when none or almost none of assurance mechanisms are

Table 1. Summary of the approaches to the trust–control relationship

	1. Psychological Approaches ($T \neq C$)	2. ICT Approaches ($T \approx C$)	3. Dualism Approach ($T \parallel C$)	4. Duality Approach ($T \leftrightarrow C$)
Trust	Vulnerability Benevolence Risk taking Reliance	Security measure System reliability	Vulnerability Reliance	Positive expectation based on benevolence of partner
Control	Certainty Zero-risk Assurance Knowledge of incentive structure	Governance mechanisms Technical standards	Certainty Constraint imposed by partner	Positive expectation based on structural influences of the social system
Trust–Control Relationship	Opposite poles of the same dimension Reverse dependence	No clear distinction between trust and control mechanisms	Independent dimensions with no influence on each other	Independent yet interrelated dimensions Mutual influence

available to build an interaction between partners. As a kind of vicious circle trust, in turn, entails a willingness to take risks based on the sense of confidence that others will respond as expected and will act in mutually supportive ways, or at least, that others do not intend harm (McKnight et al., 2004). Hence, the relationship between trust and control has a reverse dependence: the stronger trust is, the weaker control is, and vice versa (e.g., Mayer et al., 1995). In this approach control represents assurance, which comes from knowledge of an incentive structure that encourages benign behaviour. Trust, identified with the inferences about a partner's personal traits and intentions, has no chance to develop in the context of the assurance structures, because there is little opportunity to learn about the partner and the partner's dispositions and intentions (Molm et al., 2000). The degree of risk affects the degree of trust toward an interaction partner: an individual concludes that s/he trusts the interaction partner, if s/he finds that s/he interacted with his/her partner in risky situation (Köller, 1988). McLain and Hackman (1999) demonstrated that in the context of lack of information about an interaction partner, trust emerges in a high risk, insecure environment, and at the same time, plays the role of a risk-reducing mechanism. The weakness of the present approach consists in the attention to only one of the concepts, either trust or control, and the conceptualisation of trust and control as opposite poles (Möllering, 2005).

The second approach is the *technology-oriented one*. Since it is mainly focused on the issues of security and shared norms, trust is associated with external control. This is evident as ICT users are mostly required to authenticate and verify their identity credentials using various traditional security mechanisms like Public Key Infrastructure (PKI) or X.509 digital certificates. These mechanisms establish who has the privilege rights to access relevant ICT based resources. Therefore, trust, when using ICT, is often seen as a security measure, a guarantor,

and thus, as a control-based phenomenon. Indeed, understandings of the relationship between trust and control and control-related phenomena in this area considerably differ from the psychological interpretations of trust as a risk-taking phenomenon. Ratnasingam (2005) defines technology trust as "the subjective probability by which organisations believe that the underlying technology infrastructure ... is capable of facilitating transactions according to their confident expectations". Sydow and Windeller (2003) single out trust in technical systems that represent equipment or expert systems and are used by a social system. Technology trust is based on technical safeguards, protective measures, and control governance mechanisms (Ratnasingam, 2005). In order to guarantee high trust standards, security services examine confidentiality, integrity, authentication, non-repudiation, access controls, availability of requested systems and operations (idem). In terms of social systems, this conceptualisation rather corresponds to the notion of formal structural control that aims at increasing the predictability of outcomes (Khodyakov, 2007).

In order to reconcile "trust ≠ control" and "trust ≈ control" approaches, several attempts have been made. First of all, trust has been defined as a fluctuating phenomenon. This has opened up further room in the relationship between control and trust. On the one hand, they complement each other and, thus, may be substitutes (Nooteboom, 2007). On the other one, trust cannot be identified or reduced either to complete control or to uncertainty (Clapses et al., 2003). As Clapses et al. (2003) put it, "an individual aware of all relevant facts does not need to trust, while an individual not knowing anything about the issue in question is unable to trust, but only to hope or believe". Nooteboom (2007) proposes to introduce the notion that reconciles the "purist" approach to trust and that "technological" by introducing the idea of reliance. Reliance can involve both benevolence and control, or one of them, while trust proper is based only on benevolence and goes beyond control, deterrence and self-interest (idem). If trust–vulnerability is based on intrinsic mechanisms, trust–reliance is based rather on extrinsic ones.

The third approach examined here is referred to as the *dualism approach* (Möllering, 2005). It suggests breaking with the one-dimensional approach to trust and control and instead defining them as two independent scopes. This gives room for the coexistence of both high trust and high control. Trust is viewed as an enhancer of control mechanism effectiveness (Vryza & Fryxel, 1997) or as a control prerequisite (Das & Teng, 1998). Costa & Bijlsma-Frankema (2007) argue that a minimum level of trust is needed for the success of any form of collaboration. Besides, the absence of one of them may be harmful for another. In this sense, trust and control reinforce each other. They are interrelated yet not static phenomena. They co-exist and evolve through time in a dynamic manner. Interaction partners may build their relationship on different combinations of trust and control depending upon the current situation. Thus, in the beginning, users may observe a high level of control with a sudden leap of trust as soon as they decide to engage in collaboration. Also, control–trust dynamics may develop slower and include all the phases of cognitive and affective trust building. The critique of the dualism approach focuses on the idea that trust and control are two independent scopes, where trust is defined as a positive expectation toward the interaction partner and control is defined as a constraint imposed by the interaction partner (Möllering, 2005).

Finally, as an alternative to the dualism approach, Möllering (2005) introduces the *duality perspective* that has much in common with Gidden's (1986) thesis of the duality of structure. Möllering (2005) argues that in spite of the fact that it has been extensively investigated, trust still remains quite elusive. The duality perspective aims at converting this dilemma into an explicit and clear relationship, where trust and control

"refer to each other and create each other, but remain irreducible to each other" (Möllering, 2005, p. 284). The author builds his arguments on the basis of the idea of embedded agency and identifies both control and trust with positive expectations. The distinction between the concepts lies in the source of those positive expectations. As regards control, they stem from the "structural influences on the embedded other" (Möllering, 2005, p. 287), while for trust they stem from the "assumption of benevolent agency on the part of the other" (idem). From this point of view, cognitive trust includes a somewhat high level of control, because it refers to the knowledge provided by the social system. Category-, role-, or rule-based trust (Kramer, 1999) refer to the structural influences the trustee may undergo from the social structure s/he belongs to. The knowledge of someone's membership, status, position, or previous behaviour reveals the extent to which s/he is controllable (or has been controlled) by the system. Hence, this knowledge is a kind of prediction about his/her fair behaviour in the future. At the same time, this knowledge does not guarantee 100% control over the partner, which gives room for benevolence. This illustrates the rationale of the duality approach, which is based on the ideas of 1) the co-existence of high levels of both trust and control, and 2) their mutual influence on each other. In accordance with this logic, trust dynamics cannot be scrutinised in isolation. Since both trust and control are defined as routes of risk reduction and interrelated phenomena, technological and social scopes of a GC can legitimately be brought together in a single conceptual model. The next two paragraphs reveal the way trust and control are to be examined. The attention paid to their structures is determined by the willingness to find out the very subtle relationships between different components/ types of trust and control. This aims at understanding of what type of control enhances trust in a GC and/or between GC members of a particular type (cognitive or affective) and vice versa.

DIMENSIONS OF TRUST

Trust is a part of many social occurrences either as a cause or an antecedent. It has been extensively investigated and described in terms of its components (expectations, intentions, and behaviours), types (affective and cognitive), and dynamics (emerging, stable and declining trust). In different approaches trust is identified with a type of cooperative behaviour, a general disposition, an affect-based evaluation about another person, a characteristic of social systems (Rousseau et al., 1998), etc. Even though there is no single view on the nature of trust, at present, the majority of researchers agree that its structure refers to the cognitive and affective scopes (McAllister et al., 2006; Nooteboom, 2007; etc.).

Cognitive trust is based on rational choice and entails exchange relations. Positive intentions in cognitive trust derive from the credible information about the intentions or competence of another that is based either on reputation (provided by others) or certification (provided by an institution) (Rousseau et al., 1998). Cognitive trust originates from the reliability of trustee and the interdependability of trustor and trustee (McAllister, 1995). Cognitive trust is also defined as "critical" trust, which brings together reliance and healthy scepticism (Poortinga & Pidgeon, 2003).

In the situation, when face-to-face interaction cannot take place or cannot generate trusting intentions (e.g., mediated interactions), cognitive trust develops in a depersonalised manner as category-based, role-based or rule-based trust (Kramer, 1999). Category-based trust derives from information about a trustee's membership. Role-based trust is predicated on knowledge about a particular role an individual occupies (idem). This form of trust is based on expertise and corresponds to competence-based trust introduced by Abrahams and colleagues (2003). Rule-based trust is predicated on shared understanding regarding the system of rules of appropriate behaviour (Kramer, 1999). In spite of such expanded knowledge, the concept of cognitive trust cannot avoid some critical remarks. It is not considered exhaustive due to the fact that it relies on the empirical indefensibility of rational choice models and has little consideration of emotional and social influences on trust decisions.

The critique mentioned above together with the analysis of trust dynamics (e.g., McAllister, 1995) indicated the necessity of bringing in another component of trust, having less rational mechanisms. *Affective trust* is rather conceptualised as a social orientation toward other people (Kramer, 1999). It develops thanks to the repeated interactions between trustor and trustee, where positive expectations arise from reliability and dependability formed in previous interactions (Rousseau et al., 1998). As a consequence of frequent and long-term interactions, emotions become relations and attachment develops. Affective trust involves care about the partner's welfare, belief in the intrinsic value and reciprocity of the relationship (McAllister, 1995). McAllister et al. (2006, G6) stress the crucial and unique role of emotional component in the trust development process: "clearly affective bonds become more salient as trust relationships mature, and these effects merit consideration". Cognitive and affective forms of trust rely on different mechanisms.

In GCs, cognitive trust is close to informal structural control and it may arise as a consequence of formal structural control. Contrary to that, affective trust, which is not determined by knowledge of the partner's reliability, emerges partly on the basis of the former positive experience, partly thanks to the willingness to take risks and to be vulnerable in face of the future outcomes.

DIMENSIONS OF CONTROL

Giddens (1984) defines control in terms of influencing and steering actions and events in a reflexive way that fits the interest of those who control. More detailed interpretations of control distinguish between internal and external forms of control (Berrenberg, 1987). Control is viewed as a phenomenon, where either the self or some force outside the self is perceived as the primary causal agent of outcomes (idem).

Personal, or internal, control is defined as the individual's beliefs in his/her ability to effect a change, in a desired direction, on the environment (Ashforth & Saks, 2000). It is identified with bargaining power, referent power, formal authority, informal leadership, job autonomy, knowledge utilisation, participation, and access to resources (idem) and effectance (Berrenberg, 1987). Personal control brings the controlled object into a citadel of the self and, thus, serves as a basis of the distinction between the self and the non-self (Pierce et al., 2004). In a GC, personal control may embrace such domains as control over the technological system, control over the community's norms, control over one's personal resources, etc. It reflects the belief that outcomes are the direct results of one's own actions, abilities, efforts, etc. (idem).

External control represents any phenomenon leading to conformity and/or obedience (Milgram, 1974). It is also identified with coercive social power that defines and sanctions deviant behaviours/outcomes (French & Raven, 1959). External control reflects the belief that outcomes are the direct result of some external causal agent (Berrenberg, 1987). From the point of view of Giddens' theory of social structure (Giddens, 1984), external control is not only a constraint, but also an enabler of behaviours.

Although researchers are not agreed upon the types of external control, they share the vision of control as a two-fold phenomenon including formal and informal aspects. Formal control aims at increasing the predictability of outcomes by means of formal standards and rules that regulate the goal-achievement process (Khodyakov, 2007). Informal control focuses on the development of shared values, beliefs and goals among members

(Şengűn & Wasti, 2007). Formal control is, in turn, multidimensional and comprises behavioural, input and output forms (Das & Teng, 2001; Khodyakov, 2007). Behavioural control is a structural control that monitors employees' behaviours via defined rules and procedures (Khodyakov, 2007). Input control refers to the manipulation of resources in order to improve organisational performance (Khodyakov, 2007). Output control occurs when the results of organisational activities aimed at goal achievement are regulated (Khodyakov, 2007). In terms of organisational effectiveness, formal control has a two-fold impact. Exploited in isolation from trust, formal control mechanisms may become too expensive and, thus, reduce returns on investment. At the same time, formal control may relieve problems due to increased distrust.

Informal external, or social, control is a form of influence on people's behaviour through the creation of shared goals and norms (Das & Teng, 1998; Khodyakov, 2007). Thanks to the norms and values that constitute organisational culture, social control fosters organisational socialisation and, hence, the internalisation of organisational principles. Şengűn and Wasti (2007) observe that reputation is one of the most powerful facets of social control. It creates implicit moral obligations between interaction partners. Thus, social control becomes a dominant control mechanism in the relationship where the reputation for non-opportunistic behaviour and informal contacts are of high probability (Şengűn & Wast, 2007).

Within a GC, formal control is a sine qua non requirement of the membership accreditation and withdrawal (Table 2). Input control refers to ranking and reputation scores. It is a prerequisite of the emergence of cognitive trust. Output control refers to the evaluation of performance. Output control contributes to the adjustment of formal structural control procedures. Behavioural control provides operational norms and, thus, speeds up routine operations (Khodyakov, 2007). Informal control embraces norms and values of interactions between GC members. Informal control may enhance the development of affective trust. Both forms of external control provide an optimal course of events within a GC. Along with external control (formal and informal), the GC's reality may be characterised by personal control. At initial stages of partners' interactions, personal control consists in the protection of one's own resources, such as expertise, competencies and skills. Further, it refers to the control over the GC as a social system and takes forms of participation in decision making, social norms definitions, etc. It is difficult to discuss personal control in terms of the "formal – informal" dimension. It is in an individual's power to decide whether s/he wants to weaken or strengthen his/her personal control. The leap from personal control to trust may happen suddenly such that the intermediate phase between personal control and trust remains a "black box" (Möllering, 2005). The path towards trust and, in particular, this missing element in trust–control dynamics may be understood through the phenomenon of psychological ownership. Why does an individual, who feels ownership over his/her resources and, thus, exerts control over them, move towards trust and resources sharing?

PSYCHOLOGICAL OWNERSHIP: FROM INDIVIDUAL TO SHARED PERSPECTIVE

Psychological ownership is defined as a feeling of possession that one or all parts of the object of possession are "mine" (Pierce et al., 2001; Van Dyne & Pierce, 2004). In contrast with objective ownership, psychological ownership transmits the idea of perceived and/or felt possession (Pierce et al., 2004). The former is closely tied up with the rights to share the value of, to have information about, and to exercise control over the target of ownership (Pierce et al., 1991). The latter is identified with the principal scopes of psyche:

attitudes, motivation, and behaviour (Van Dyne & Pierce, 2004).

Primarily, psychological ownership is conceptualised as an attitude with both affective and cognitive components (Pierce et al., 2001). The affective aspect of psychological ownership refers to a positive feeling about tangible or intangible targets of ownership (Van Dyne & Pierce, 2004) that has a self-enhancing character. It means that people evaluate more favourably those ideas and objects for which they feel a sense of ownership (idem). The cognitive aspect of psychological ownership relates to the process of self-categorisation that results in the perception of the targets of possession as the extended self (idem). As a consequence, the sense of ownership triggers the willingness to protect one's own property. This willingness implies high control over the resources. In a motivational perspective, psychological ownership relates to the satisfaction of three basic needs: belongingness (or sense of home), self-identity, and efficacy and effectance (Pierce et al., 2001). Belongingness is a sense of place that provides a feeling of comfort, pleasure and security. Due to the sense of belongingness people are more attached to the things that they feel they possess than to similar things that they do not feel they possess (Van Dyne & Pierce, 2004). Efficacy concerns the need to feel capable in specific areas (idem). Together with effectance motivation, it facilitates feelings of control and influence over objects and people. Self-identity is a need to have a clear sense of self (idem). In this regard, possessions express the core values of one's being and symbolically represent one's identity.

Pierce et al. (2001) define the routes an individual experiences ownership through as follows: (a) control over the target, (b) intimate knowledge of the target, and (c) investment of oneself into the target. Being able to control an object gives rise to feelings of ownership towards that object, which further becomes a part of one's self. Intimate knowledge of the target refers to the quality and the quantity of knowledge about an object. Investment of oneself into the target relates to the investment of one's energy, time, effort, and attention. Repetitive and intensive investment produces a sort of fusion with the target of possession such that one's self becomes one with the object. Thus, the feeling of psychological ownership toward that object rises (idem).

In spite of the fact that the concept of psychological ownership provides a new explanatory framework of how the work environment links up with employees' attitudes and behaviours (O'driscoll et al., 2006), it has not been extensively applied and tested in empirical research. The few studies (O'driscoll et al., 2006; Pierce et al., 2004; Van Dyne & Pierce, 2004) that have been conducted in this area provide homogenous findings about the positive influence of psychological ownership on certain organisational variables. Thus, it positively affects employees' commitment, satisfaction, and organisational citizenship (Van Dyne & Pierce, 2004).

The strength of the feeling of possession varies upon the level of psychological ownership. Overall, psychological ownership of the job is more significant than psychological ownership of the organisation (O'driscoll et al., 2006). The mediating effect of psychological ownership also depends upon its levels. O'driscoll and colleagues (2006) demonstrated that organisational ownership has a more significant mediating effect, while job ownership has a more significant direct effect on such variables as organisational commitment and satisfaction. Van Dyne and Pierce (2004), who have principally focused on the organisational form of psychological ownership, emphasise the necessity of refining the conceptualisation of the target of ownership. They propose to extend the targets of psychological ownership up to work groups, work equipment, products, services, etc. Obviously, more thorough conceptualisation of psychological ownership would bring about a more subtle picture of the causal relationship it may have with different organisational phenomena.

Although psychological ownership has been differentiated in terms of the object of possession, there was no distinction made about the subject of possession. It is evident that the individual feeling of possession for the organisation (it is mine and not yours) differs from the collective feeling of possession for the organisation (it is ours). In the first case, psychological ownership may result in heightened personal control over the organisation, while in the second, psychological ownership is perceived as an equal access to the object of possession. In this chapter, it is posited that the distinction between personal and shared psychological ownership offers the explanation of how personal control over resources grows into trust and, subsequently, into resource sharing. The feeling that resources are mine leads to their protection. The feeling that resources (even my personal expertise and competencies) are ours results in their sharing. The leap from personal to shared psychological ownership is accompanied by the leap from personal control to trust, regardless of all the external control mechanisms applied in a GC.

The findings of the psychological ownership research (O'driscoll et al., 2006; Pierce et al., 2004; Van Dyne & Pierce, 2004) are not only limited by its focus on the individual's experience, but also by the fact they concern habitual forms of organisation having well marked boundaries, and explicit in terms of their material and geographical existence. Specifically, a GC should be seen as a sub-set of entities when it is compared to other forms of communities. In addition to the difficulties in pinpointing its boundaries, a GC per se is a constantly fluctuating social system with no fixed roles, patterns of interactions and needs. In this sense, every member who possesses any knowledge/resource would strive to preserve it in such an unstable environment. Nevertheless, the main purpose of this community is as opposite as it could be. Relevant questions raised include: 1) what is the relationship between the willingness to protect one's own resources and the necessity to share them; 2) what is the role of this relationship with respect to formal and informal control mechanisms and cognitive and affective trust formation within a GC; and 3) what is the relationship between personal and external forms of control?

PSYCHOLOGICAL OWNERSHIP, TRUST AND CONTROL IN THE CONTEXT OF RESOURCE SHARING

The main purpose of a GC is the effective collaboration around resource sharing that may include tangible (equipment, hardware) and intangible (individual and community knowledge) resources. As mentioned at the beginning of the chapter, the process of resource sharing in a GC possesses several distinctive characteristics. 1. There is no fixed path towards the resources needed. 2. Resources per se are not constantly available. This results in the absence of predetermined interaction patterns between GC members. 3. There is a high need for formal control mechanisms to maintain an efficient functioning of the community. According to the conceptualisation of formal control in this chapter, those mechanisms include input, behavioural, and output forms of control. Input control implies building a repertory of reputations of the current and future GC members. Behavioural control assures that all the GC members follow the same operational routine and, thus, processes within a GC run smoothly. Output control aims at maintaining or withdrawing a GC membership on the basis of the performance indicators and the perceived quality of services. 4. Resources in use may have a high level of confidence. Hence, resource sharing (an expression of trust and collective psychological ownership) and resource protection (an expression of personal control and individual psychological ownership) of resources may come into conflict.

The overall idea of psychological ownership is the conceptualisation of the self through the perceived/imaginary possession. In this sense, Pierce, Kostova and Dirks (2001) emphasise the role of control over the target either in a direct or mediated modality. Intimate knowledge over and investment into the target are other forms of social control. Psychological ownership is more inclined towards the control dimension (O'driscoll et al., 2006). Hence, it produces the conflict between the control over of resources possessed and their sharing. The importance of this issue grows even more in the context of a GC, given the eventual confidentiality of resources discussed in regard to the specificity of the GC. How should different forms of control (personal, formal and social) and of psychological ownership (personal and shared) affect the development of trust (cognitive and affective)?

First, the relationship between personal control and psychological ownership is addressed. According to Pierce et al. (2004), control is one of the primary determinants of the experienced state of ownership. Yet, it mediates the relationship between an organisation and an individual (Pierce et al., 2004). O'driscoll et al. (2006) argue that a routine technology characterised by the system control and mass production has an alienation effect on employees, while a non-routine technology results in employees' satisfaction and better supervisory ratings. A lower level of structure is associated with a higher level of felt ownership for the job and the organisation. Each of the variables that measure work environment structure – job design autonomy, participative decision making and non-routine technology – has a significant relationship with psychological ownership. In addition to the direct effects, psychological ownership is reported to be a mediating variable in the relationship between work environment structure and organisational citizenship behaviour and organisational commitment (idem). A particularly strong effect has been observed in relation to affective organisational commitment.

Insofar as we are talking about "personal possession", there is little chance that resources will be shared within a GC. In terms of trust and control, psychological ownership is more inclined toward the control dimension, since it implies control over the target (O'driscoll et al., 2006). As soon as we shift the focus from the individual form of psychological ownership ("mine") and enable psychological co-ownership ("ours"), knowledge/resource sharing is no more perceived in terms of loss, but rather in terms of equal access to the shared property. This effect relates to the needs for self-identity and for belongingness singled out by Pierce et al. (2001). In accordance with social identity paradigm (Haslam, 2004) and previously mentioned empirical evidence (Van Dyne & Pierce, 2004), organisational psychological ownership heightens organisational commitment. Organisational commitment, in turn, implies a high level of trust (either cognitive or affective) towards an organisation. Shared psychological ownership for the GC rises in a work environment that is structured such that it allows its members to exercise control over, know and invest themselves into the community. This occurs if GC members participate in the policies elaboration/modification, performance standards adjustment, technical norms definition, etc.

The second axis of the analysis of the relationship between psychological ownership, control and trust addresses the combined dynamics of control and trust. In collaborative settings, control induces cooperation, which, in turn, positively affects trust. Cooperative behaviour allows partners to build trust in one another. This trust reinforces the positive effect of formal control on the future cooperation. Thus, the effect of control on cooperation is reinforced by the trust that it engenders: the percentage of collaborators grows in the presence of formal control mechanisms (Coletti et al., 2005). Contrary to the previous study, Inkpen and Currall (2004) view trust as an independent variable in the causal relationship of trust and control. They believe that trust creates the initial climate that shapes partners' interactions. These interactions lead to the decision about the nature of control: either formal or informal.

The influence of each form of trust and control should be specified as well. In relatively stable cooperation, partners rely more on output control than behavioural control (Das & Teng, 2001). According to Şengűn and Wasti (2007), output control is an important type of monitoring mechanism since it provides the measurability of outcomes. It underlies both cognitive and affective forms of trust (idem). Social control is most appropriate in high-trust situations and is called for to resolve problems. Social control enhances both types of trust. In turn, affective and cognitive trust both render social control mechanisms more effective (idem). According to Das & Teng (2001), in a non-equity alliance cognitive trust (originally defined as competence trust) is more important than affective trust (originally defined as goodwill trust). In the viewpoint of Şengűn and Wasti (2007), cognitive and affective trusts can substitute for each other.

In this chapter, it is posited that the distinction between personal and shared psychological ownership offers the explanation of how personal control over resources grows into trust and, subsequently, into resource sharing. The feeling that resources are mine leads to their protection. The feeling that resources (even my personal expertise and competencies) are ours results in their sharing. The leap from personal to shared psychological ownership is accompanied by the leap from personal control to trust, regardless of all the external control mechanisms applied in a GC.

A MODEL OF TRUST–CONTROL DYNAMICS WITHIN A GRID-BASED COMMUNITY FROM A PSYCHOLOGICAL OWNERSHIP PERSPECTIVE

The analysis of the relevant literature enables bringing together both social and technological contexts, including the one of trust development within a GC. First, the elements that constitute different forms of control and trust are identified (Table 2). Second, the sequence of the control and trust phases is described (Figure 2).

Table 2 depicts the forms in which control and trust occur within a GC. This vision includes three levels of relationships a (future or actual) member may have in a GC. The micro level refers to the interpersonal interactions between individuals who represent organisational members of the GC. The meso level concerns the inter-members (or inter-group from a social-psychological perspective) interactions. In regard to the individual, it supposes the way an individual perceives a GC member from an organisation other than his/her own. Finally, the macro level is associated with the perception of the GC as an institution, as an objective reality. The distinction between the three levels is intended to convey the movement from perceived subjectivity to perceived objectivity that may determine the route of psychological ownership of resources. It also helps to separate control mechanisms appropriate at each single level and trust in the partner or in the community.

The first phase is defined as the personal control phase. In the case when an organisation is not yet accepted as a GC member, this is a pre-community stage. Individuals, who belong to the candidate organisation, experience the need to protect their resources. Personal control

may also take place within a GC as participatory decision-making and collective norms definitions, that is through the processes that endow a GC member with control over the GC and its formal and informal norms.

External control is divided into formal and social dimensions. Formal control includes behavioural, input and output control. Within a GC, input control principally refers to the macro level and includes such procedures as members' ranking on the basis of their reputation and capacity assessment. Output control concerns all the levels and takes the form of performance assessment, quantified quality of service and technological reliability of the system at the macro level. All the same parameters are applicable to the assessment of the GC members and, thus, to the meso level. At the micro level, output control measures individual performances. Behavioural control is assured by written GC technical norms at the macro level, by routine norms at the meso level, and by operational norms at the micro level.

Informal control is based on the GC policies and organisational culture. Yet, this issue is quite complex given the absolutely virtual character of interactions with a GC. However, some shared norms and values may emerge as a result of intense and frequent interactions between certain GC remembers.

Table 2. Dimensions of control and trust in a Grid-based community

Level	Internal Control	External Control				Trust		
	Personal Control	Formal Control			Informal Control	Cognitive Trust	Affective Trust
		Input	Output	Behavioural			
Macro	Control over the GC, shared resources	Ranking weighting	GC performance Quality of service System reliability	Technical norms	GC policies GC culture	Rule-based trust Perceived reliability	Identification with a GC
Meso	Control over the partner	Measured reputation	GC member's productivity & performance Satisfaction	Routine norms	Shared social norms and values	Category-based trust Role-based trust Reputation	Interdependence
Micro	Control over own resources	Specification of what is of satisfaction for the weighting (Benchmark)	Individual performance	Operational norms	Personal attitudes	Role-based trust Individual competence & expertise	Reciprocity Moral obligations Empathy & friendship

Trust is analysed in accordance with the cognitive and affective dimensions. Kramer's (1999) typology of cognitive trust is adopted to describe the development of cognitive trust at the macro, meso and micro levels of a GC. At the micro level, cognitive trust develops as a role-based trust, in other words, thanks to the perceived expertise and competencies of the partner. At the meso level, cognitive trust refers to the category-based trust, which mechanism is similar to the social categorisation process. In practice, category-based trust arises from the knowledge that the partner belongs to the trusted social category, in the case of a GC, to the trusted GC member. At the macro level, cognitive trust takes form of the rule-based trust that refers to the acceptance of social norms and policies (social control). Affective trust that is not based on reliance, but on the acceptance of vulnerability and, thus, risks, may result in shortening psychological distance between the partners. At the micro level, it gives rise to mutual moral obligations and reciprocity, friendship and empathy. At the meso level, the GC partners become interdependent. At the macro level, affective trust brings about identification with a GC.

As mentioned earlier, a GC is burdened by extremely complex technological requirements. Interactions between its partners become possible when all parties meet the system's criteria.

Therefore, the proposed model of control–trust development incorporates the phases of control that permit the assessment of relational and technology risks and technical capacities. The model proposed here supports the idea that control does not systematically decrease, but can, in particular settings, increase the level of trust. Control–trust dynamics may follow three scenarios (Figure 2).

1. *Linear control → trust development.* This scenario implies the passage through all five phases displayed in the diagram (Figure 2), including personal, formal, and social control, and cognitive and affective trust. Psychological ownership moderates this dynamics in two ways. Personal psychological ownership of resources (mediator A) has a positive relationship with personal control (O'driscoll et al., 2006) and a negative relationship with formal output control (Pierce et al., 2004). Thus, personal psychological ownership for resources would impede external control dynamics and, thus, the emergence of cognitive trust. In turn, the shift from the personal to the shared form of psychological ownership (mediators A to B) should have positive impact on trust dynamics. Shared psychological ownership for the resources, which is felt as a shared access to the target of possession (Pierce et al., 2001), is predicted to have a positive influence on

Figure 2. Trust–control dynamics in a Grid-based community: Moderating effect of psychological ownership

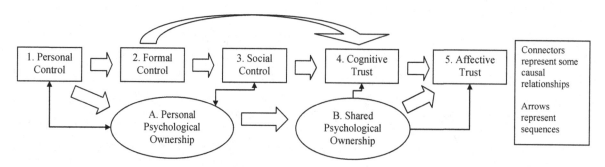

the external control mechanisms (phases 2 and 3) and cognitive trust (phase 4). Input control that aims at the verification of the candidate's capacities and reputation contributes to the building of cognitive trust. They both relate to reputation, either measured or perceived. For instance, at the macro level of the GC, this corresponds to the rational assessment of the partner's membership and reputation, which in other words is defined as category-based trust. Given the context of mediated interaction, at this level, trust mainly emerges thanks to the transfer of knowledge either from the third party or from the source. Output control also enhances cognitive trust, but by means of various performance indicators. Thus, an indicator of the speed of service availability (at the meso level) may affect the development of cognitive trust (as a role-based trust and reputation). Behavioural control is interdependent with both cognitive and affective forms of trust and the only form of the external control that may influence affective trust development (Şengűn & Wasti, 2007).

As far as cognitive trust is built on the basis of numerous ranking, performance and satisfaction measures, and operational norms and social policies, reliance of cognitive trust may leave room for benevolence. The established interdependence between partners leads to the increase of the emotional component, the basis of mutual moral obligations (such as the impossibility of free-riding behaviour). The need to deepen knowledge about institutionalised norms and protocols permits GC members to establish cognitive trust towards a GC. According to Sydow and Windeler (2003), cognitive trust in institutions relates to the confidence in abstract principles and procedures of system regulation. Subsequent to the cognitive trust phase, and if being a part of a GC goes beyond self-interest and successful transactions, a GC member may identify with the whole system. It brings an affective attachment, thus, it takes form of affective trust (phase 5).

2. *Reputation shift (phase 2 → phase 4)*. This scenario occurs when formal control measures (phase 2) are perceived as sufficient to guarantee a low risk of free-riding behaviour. Especially powerful are input and output controls. The former gives a report of the GC member's reputation based on the partners' feedback. The latter directly refers to its technical parameters that ensure correct functioning and satisfactory performance. Exclusively on the basis of those indicators, a GC member may develop cognitive trust towards its partner (phase 4).

3. *Leap towards trust (phase 1 → phase 5)*. This scenario consists in such trust development that by-passes the phases of external control and shifts directly from personal control to trust, either cognitive or affective. This happens thanks to the moderating influence of psychological ownership that develops from the personal into the shared form. This scenario is similar to the decision to take risks without any previous assessments. Such a leap may be due to the extremely complex and unstable environment of the GC, addressed previously in the chapter. Instead of involving a long assessment process, one (an individual or an organisation) may decide to take an adventure.

CONCLUSION

Trust aspects within a grid based community (GC) are being increasingly seen as "hard" issues. The chapter reinforced the rationale that trust must be seen as a far more elusive and subtle process than implied by existing ICT models and initiatives or trust architectures. That is to say, organisational, social, and even psychological factors pre-determine trust development within a GC that combines both strict technological norms and social interactions. The proposed model introduces and distinguishes between personal, formal and social control, and cognitive and affective trust. Psychological ownership is conceptualised through a new dimension – shared psychological ownership – and is examined as a mediator of control–trust dynamics.

The proposed model offers a more explicit vision of how and what types of trust may develop within a GC. It attempts to discern the interrelationships between different parameters of trust development stages and, thus, predict the possibility of trust modelling. Being a both very complex and flexible social system, a GC is difficult to examine as a whole. Moreover, characteristics of each level of trust need further refinement. In order to ascertain the model's applicability it will be necessary, to construct a simulation using a realistic scenario. This will enable assessment of the applicability of a GC (future or present) member by an appropriate set of social structure-related constraints in respect to trusted service invocation and trusted resource provision operating within a variety of simulated settings involving different kinds of bi-lateral and multi-lateral simulated GC members.

ACKNOWLEDGMENT

The author would like to express her gratitude to Prof. Jon Pierce for his attention and exchanges about individual versus shared psychological ownership; Prof. Jean-Pierre Neveu for his advice and help in structuring the author's ideas; and three anonymous reviewers for their critical remarks and valuable comments.

REFERENCES

Ashforth, B. E., & Saks, A. M. (2000). Personal Control in Organisations: A Longitudinal Investigation with Newcomers. *Human Relations*, *53*(3), 311-339.

Berrenberg, J. L. (1987). The Belief in Personal Control Scale: A measure of God-Mediated and Exaggerated Control. *Journal of Personality Assessment, 51*(2), 194-206.

Bessis, N., French, T., Burakova-Lorgnier, M., & Huang, W. (2007). Using Grid Technology for Data Sharing to Support Intelligence in Decision Making. In M. Xu (Ed.), *Managing Strategic Intelligence: Techniques and Technologies* (pp. 179-201). IGI.

Bijlsma-Frankema, K. M., & Costa, A. C. (2005). Understanding the Trust-Control Nexus. *International Sociology. 20*(3), 259-282.

Clases, C., Bachman, R., & Wehner, T. (2003). Studying Trust in Virtual Organizations. *International Studies of Management and Organization, 33* (3), 7–27.

Coletti, A. L., Sedatole, K. L., & Towry, K. L. (2005). The Effect of Control Systems on Trust and Cooperation in Collaborative Environments. *The Accounting Review, 80*(2), 477-500.

Das, T. K., & Teng, B. (1998). Between Trust and Control: Developing Confidence in Partner Cooperation in Alliances. *Academy of Management Review, 23*, 491-512.

Das, T. K., & Teng, B. S. (2001). Trust, Control, and Risk in Strategic Alliances: An Integrated Framework. *Organization Studies, 22*, 251-283.

Foster, I. (2002). What is the Grid? A Three Point Checklist. *Grid Today, 1*(6), July 22, 2002. Available at: http://www.gridtoday.com/02/0722/100136.html

French, J. R. P., & Raven, B. (1959). The Bases of Social Power. In D. Cartwright (Ed.), *Studies in Social Power* (pp. 150-167). Ann Arbour, MI: Institute for Social Research, University of Michigan.

French, T., Bessis, N., & Huang, W. (2007). Grid Enabled Computing: A Semiotic Approach to Virtual Organisational Trust, 21st century IS: do organisations matter? *UKAIS 2007 10th In-*

ternational Conference in Information Systems, 11th-12th April, Manchester.

Garrity, E. J., Moon, J., & Sanders, J. L. (2006). Achieving Implementation Success in Ubiquitous Computer Environment: Understanding the Role of Psychological Ownership. In M. Khosrow-Pour (Ed.), *Emerging Trends and Challenges in Information Technology Management* (pp. 34-38). 2006 IRMA International Conference. Idea Group Inc.

Giddens, A. (1984). *The Constitution of Society.* Cambridge: Polity.

Inkpen, A. C., & Curall, S. C. (2004). The Co-evolution of Trust, Control, and Learning in Joint Ventures. *Organization Science, 15*(5), 586-599.

Khodyakov, D. M. (2007). The Complexity of Trust-Control Relationships in Creative Organizations: Insights from a Qualitative Analysis of a Conductorless Orchestra. *Social Forces, 86*(1), 1-22.

Köller, M. (1988). Risk as a Determinant of Trust. *Journal of Basic and Applied Social Psychology, 9*(4), 265-276.

Kramer, R. M. (1999). Trust and Distrust in Organizations: Emerging Perspectives, Enduring Questions. *Annual Review of Psychology, 50,* 569-598.

Lewin, K. (1951). *Field Theory in Social Science.* NY: Harper & Row.

Mayer, R. C., Davis, J. H., & Schoorman, F. D. (1995). An Integrated Model of Organizational Trust. *Academy of Management Review, 20*(3), 709-734.

McAllister, D. J. (1995). Affect- and Cognition-Based Trust as Foundations for Interpersonal Cooperation in Organizations. *Academy of Management Journal, 38*(1), 24-59.

McAllister, D. J., Lewicki, R. J., & Chaturvedi, S. (2006). Trust in Developing Relationships: From Theory to Measurement. *Academy of Management Best Conference Paper,* G1-G6.

McKnight, D. H., Kacmar, C. J., & Choudhury, V. (2004). Dispositional Trust and Distrust Distinction in Predicting High- and Low-Risk Internet Expert Advice Site Perceptions. *E-Service Journal, 3*(2), 35-58.

McLain, D. L., & Hackman, K. (1999). Trust, Risk, and Decision-Making in Organizational Change. *Public Administration Quarterly, 23*(2), 152-176.

Milgram, S. (1974). *Obedience to Authority: An Experimental View.* New York: Harper & Row.

Molm, L. D., Takahashi, N., & Peterson, G. (2000). Risk and Trust in Social Exchange: An Experimental Test of a Classical Proposition. *American Journal of Sociology, 105*(5), 1396-1427.

Möllering, G. (2005). The Trust/Control Duality: An Integrative Perspective on Positive Expectations of Others. *International Sociology, 20*(3) 283-305.

Nooteboom, B. (2007). Social Capital, Institutions and Trust. *Review of Social Economy, LXV*(1), 29-53.

O'Driscoll, M. P., Pierce, J. L., & Coghlan, A.-M. (2006). The Psychology of Ownership: Work Environment Structure, Organizational Commitment, and Citizenship Behaviors. *Group & Organization Management, 31,* 388-416.

Pierce, J. L., Kostova, T., & Dirks, K. (2001). Toward a Theory of Psychological Ownership in Organizations. *Academy of Management Review, 26,* 298-310.

Pierce, J. L., O'driscoll, M. P., & Coghman, A.-M. (2004). Work Environment Structure and Psychological Ownership: The Mediating Effect of Control. *The Journal of Social Psychology, 144*(5), 507-534.

Poortinga, W., & Pidgeon, N. F. (2003). Exploring the Dimensionality of Trust in Risk Regulations. *Risk Analysis, 23*(5), 961-972.

Ratnasingam, P. (2005). E-commerce Relationships: The Impact of Trust on Relationship Continuity. *International Journal of Commerce and Management, 15*(1), 1-16.

Rousseau, D. M., Sitkin, S. B., Burt, R. S., & Camerer, C. (1998). Not So Different after All: A Cross-discipline View of Trust. *Academy of Management Review, 23*, 393-404.

Sydow, J., & Windeler, A. (2003). Knowledge, Trust, and Control. *International Studies of Management and Organisation, 33*(2), 69-99.

Şengün, A. E., & Wasti, S. N. (2007). Trust, Control, and Risk: A Test of Das and Teng's Conceptual Framework for Pharmaceutical Buyer-Supplier Relationships. *Group & Organization Management, 32*(4), 430-464.

Van Dyne, L., & Pierce, J. L. (2004). Psychological Ownership and Feelings of Possession: Three Field Studies Predicting Employee Attitudes and Organizational Citizenship Behavior. *Journal of Organizational Behavior, 25*, 439-459.

Vlaar, P. W. L., Van den Bosch, F. A. J., & Volberda, H. W. (2007). On the Evolution of Trust, Distrust, and Formal Coordination and Control in Interorganizational Relationships: Toward an Integrative Framework. *Group & Organization Management, 32*(4), 407-429.

Xu, M., Hu, Z., Long, W. & Liu, W. (2004). Service Virtualisation: Infrastructure and Applications. In I. Foster, & C. Kesselman (Eds.), *The Grid 2, Blueprint for a New Computing Infrastructure*. CA, USA: Elsevier.

Section III
Grid Services for Advancing Virtual Organizations

Chapter X
Small World Architecture for Building Effective Virtual Organisations

Lu Liu
University of Leeds, UK

Nick Antonopoulos
University of Surrey, UK

ABSTRACT

A Virtual Organisation in large-scale distributed systems is a set of individuals and/or institutions with some common purposes or interests that need to share their resources to further their objectives, which is similar to a human community in social networks that consists of people have common interests or goals. Due to the similarity between social networks and Grids, the concepts in social science (e.g. small world phenomenon) can be adopted for the design of new generation Grid systems. This chapter presents a Small World Architecture for Effective Virtual Organisations (SWEVO) for Grid resource discovery in Virtual Organisations, which enables Virtual Organisations working in a more collaborative manner to support decision makers. In SWEVO, Virtual Organisations are connected by a small number of inter-organisational links. Not every local network node needs to be connected to remote Virtual Organisations, but every network node can efficiently find connections to specific Virtual Organisations.

INTRODUCTION

Grids are large-scale distributed computing systems providing mechanisms for sharing and integrating computing resources, data and services.

The rapid growth of distributed resources in Grids makes resource discovery far more challenging than traditional computer systems. In order to provide information that is actually useful and essential for decision makers, we need new mod-

Copyright © 2009, IGI Global, distributing in print or electronic forms without written permission of IGI Global is prohibited.

els for resource discovery from multiple service providers in the large-scale Grid systems.

The new concept, Virtual Organisation, is emerging in the recent distributed system design (Foster, Kesselman, & Tuecke, 2001). Dynamic and distributed resources in large-scale distributed systems, such as Grids and peer-to-peer (P2P) networks, can be organised as Virtual Organisations for coordinated resource sharing and problem solving (Foster et al., 2001; Walker, 2001).

Many properties need to be considered in design of effective Virtual Organisations, such as availability, affordability, security, dependability, flexibility and scalability. In effective VOs, users should be able to communicate with each other easily and securely, and share and discover desirable resources for specific purposes. In the last decade, many studies have been made to address the problem of communication and resource sharing in dynamic, multi-institutional Virtual Organisations, while the study of resource discovery in Virtual Organisations was paid little attention to. However, we will not reap all the benefits of utilising these shared resources in Virtual Organisations unless we have an efficient way to discover them. Owing to the dynamic and distributed nature of Virtual Organisations, efficient resource discovery remains a challenge for designing effective Virtual Organisations, which will be addressed here.

A Virtual Organisation in large-scale distributed systems is a set of individuals and/or institutions with some common purposes or interests that need to share their resources to further their objectives (Walker, 2001), which is similar to a human community in social networks that consists of people having common interests or goals (Khambatti, Ryu, & Dasgupta, 2002). Due to the similarity between social networks and Grids, where Grid nodes can be regarded as people and connections can be regarded as relationships, the concepts and theories in social science (e.g. small world phenomenon (Watts &

Strogatz, 1998)) can be adopted for the design of new generation Grid systems.

In this chapter, we present a Small World architecture for Effective Virtual Organisations (SWEVO) focusing on the issue of resource discovery for building effective Virtual Organisations, which is based on the previous research on resource discovery in P2P networks and Grids (Antonopoulos & Salter, 2004; Liu, Antonopoulos, & Mackin, 2007a, 2007b, 2008). In SWEVO, a semi-structured P2P search algorithm is utilized for efficient resource discovery in Grid network, which enables Virtual Organisations working in a more collaborative manner to support decision makers.

BACKGROUND

Resource Discovery in Virtual Organisations

In many existing VOs, a centralised resource index provides the functionalities to publish and discover resources (Foster, Kesselman, & Tuecke, 2001; Winton, 2005). Using a centralised resource index, a resource can be quickly found and consumed. However, the centralisation of the resource index service raises the issues of scalability caused by the limitation of resources at the index node, such as network bandwidth, CPU capability and storage space. Moreover, the centralisation of the resource index also introduces a single-point-of-failure to the system. The index node centralises all responsibilities for publishing and handling enquiries about resources. Once the resource index fails, all the information about accessible resources will be unavailable.

To reduce the problem of single-point-of-failure, each network node should have the capability to efficiently discover desirable resources by interacting with connected nodes. In SWEVO, each Grid node does not rely on a centralised index to provide resource discovery service, which can support and co-operate with each other in a P2P manner to quickly discover accessible resources to support real-time decision making.

P2P Search

Since large-scale resource sharing is one goal of Grids, P2P networks and Grid systems are starting to converge to a common structure, leading to application of P2P techniques to Grid systems (Marzolla, Mordacchini, & Orlando, 2007). Since resource and service discovery in Grids involves a lot of elements in common with resource discovery in P2P networks, P2P search approaches are applicable for service discovery in large-scale Grid systems, which could help to ensure Grid scalability (Mastroianni, Talia, & Verta, 2005). In this section, existing P2P search systems will be investigated by classifying them into two broad categories: structured and unstructured P2P systems.

Structured P2P systems have a dedicated network structure on the overlay network which establishes a link between the stored content and the IP address of a node. DHTs are widely used for resource discovery in the structured P2P systems like Chord (Stoica, Morris, Karger, Kaashoek, & Balakrishnan, 2001), ROME (Salter & Antonopoulos, 2005), Pastry (Rowstron & Druschel, 2001), CAN (Ratnasamy, Francis, Handley, Karp, & Shenker, 2001) and Kademlia (Maymounkov & Mazières, 2002). In DHT-based P2P systems, each file is associated with a key generated by hashing the file name or content. Each peer node in these systems is responsible for storing a certain range of keys. Network structure is sorted by routing tables (or finger tables) stored on individual peer nodes. Each peer node only needs a small amount of "routing" information about other nodes (e.g., nodes' addresses and the range of keys the node is responsible for). With routing tables and uniform hash functions, peer nodes can conveniently put and get files to and from other peer nodes according to the keys of files. However,

some recent studies (e.g., Rhea, Geels, Roscoe, & Kubiatowicz (2004), Vuong & Li (2003), Yang & Garcia-Molina (2002)) argue that the cost of maintaining a consistent distributed index is very high in the dynamic and unpredictable Internet. Some structured P2P systems (e.g., Kademlia (Maymounkov & Mazières, 2002)) are beginning to seek ways to save the cost of maintaining a consistent index. Moreover, structured P2P cannot afford to strictly control data placement and the topology of the network, especially when system users come from non-cooperating organisations (Vuong & Li, 2003). Another problem observed in structured P2P systems is that these systems can only support search-by-identifiers and lack the flexibility of keyword searching (Li & Vuong, 2004). In a frequently changing network, DHTs require frequent redistribution of content which could lead to significant network traffic.

In contrast to structured P2P systems, unstructured P2P systems do not maintain network structure, and therefore the address and content stored on a given peer node are unrelated. Unstructured P2P systems do not control data placement in dynamic environments. Various approaches, like random walkers (Adamic, Lukose, Puniyani, & Huberman, 2001; Lv, Cao, Cohen, Li, & Shenker, 2002), Iterative Deepening (Yang & Garcia-Molina, 2002), Adaptive Probabilistic Search (Tsoumakos & Roussopoulos, 2003) and Routing Indices (Crespo & Garcia-Molina, 2002), have been proposed to improve performance of content lookup in the Gnutella network. But these search methods in unstructured P2P systems tend to either require high storage overhead or generate massive network traffic to search networks. Despite the fact that unstructured P2P approaches are more resilient in dynamic environments, the efficiency of these unstructured P2P approaches is still far lower than DHTs.

In contrast, SWEVO uses a semi-structured P2P search method combining the techniques of both structured and unstructured search methods. SWEVO does not strictly rely on DHTs, which can find the requested data inside and outside of Virtual Organisations efficiently with small world effect, even though hash functions can not provide accurate information of data locations.

Small World Phenomenon

The small world phenomenon, first proposed by the social psychologist Stanley Milgram, is an important hypothesis in social science that everyone in the world can be reached through a short chain of social acquaintances (Milgram, 1967). In 1960s, Milgram conducted a famous small-world experiment (Milgram, 1967). He sent 60 letters to various recruits in Omaha, Nebraska who were asked to forward the letters to a stockbroker living at Massachusetts. The participants were only allowed to pass the letter by hand to friends who they thought might be able to reach the destination, no matter if directly or via a "friend of a friend". The most famous result of his experiment is that the average length of the resulting acquaintance chain is about six, which leads to the well-known phase "six degrees of separation".

Working much more recently, Duncan Watts proposed a mathematical model (Watts & Strogatz, 1998) to analyze the small world phenomenon in highly clustered sub-networks consisting of local nodes and random long-range shortcuts that help produce short paths to remote nodes. Watts demonstrated that the path-length between any two nodes of his model graph is surprisingly small. Following Watts's study, Kleinberg (2000) discussed the navigation issue in small-world networks and analysed small world networks by adding the long-range connections to a two-dimensional lattice (Kleinberg, 2000). Fraigniaud et al. (2007, 2008) extended the Kleinberg's model by modelling greedy routing in augmented networks.

A characteristic feature of small-world networks is the short diameter of network, which means there is always a very short path between any nodes in the network. However, neither Watts's model nor Kleinberg's model shows how

to use a local search algorithm to discover the local neighbouring Grid nodes that have specific external connections. Current search algorithms have difficulty in distinguishing among these random long-range shortcuts and efficiently finding a set of proper long-range links located in its Virtual Organisation for a specific resource lookup. For this reason, Iamnitchi, Ripeanu and Foster (2002) raised the open question of how to form and maintain inter-cluster connections and how to let nodes know which nodes have external connections (Iamnitchi, Ripeanu, & Foster, 2002), which will be discussed in this chapter.

In SWEVO, Grid nodes are organised in multiple Virtual Organisations. A semi-structured P2P algorithm of SWEVO is used to create and discover long-range shortcuts between different Virtual Organisations, which can satisfy the following requirements of design:

1. Not every node needs to connect to other Virtual Organisations.
2. Each node needs to know or can easily find which nodes have external connections to which Virtual Organisations.
3. External links to other Virtual Organisations need to be distributed within the Virtual Organisation and cannot be centralized in one or a few nodes.

MODEL DESCRIPTION

SWEVO is designed to enable distributed information sharing and discovery among different companies and organisations which are organised in Virtual Organisations. Different from some other VOs which utilise the centralised resource index service to publish and discover resources (Winton, 2005), SWEAO uses a distributed P2P mechanism for efficient resource discovery inside or outside of Virtual Organisations. For example, a global company needs to make a decision of the placement of a new branch. The decision makers can gather internal information from different divisions and partners located in different countries, but also desirable information about investment environment in potential branch locations form external organisations located in different VOs with SWEVO. Data and information collected from different resources are processed locally to help decision makers find the best location of a new branch. Organisations or companies can work and collaborate with each other in a P2P manner on a non-hierarchical structure which can generate high flexibility and adaptability in responding to new needs of future business (Sculley & Woods 2000).

SWEVO is built upon a generic group structure (Kleinberg, 2001). Studies like (Cuenca-Acuna & Nguyen, 2002; Khambatti, Ryu, & Dasgupta, 2003; Vassileva, 2002) have presented the methodologies of building an information sharing system by grouping nodes into different Virtual Organisations with similar interests. In SWEVO, the resource registration service in the previous system (Salter & Antonopoulos, 2007) is utilised in SWEVO. Machines of new resource providers register with the bootstrap server which stores the details of each machine's resources and capabilities. Then a machine will be assigned to a Virtual Organisation according to the context of its shared resources.

In this section, a new information publishing and retrieval algorithm of SWEVO is presented for resource advertising and discovery inside and outside of Virtual Organisations. By using a compact representation mechanism (e.g. Bloom Filters (Bloom, 1970)), each node maintains an inconsistent list about members in the same Virtual Organisation and regards other members as "acquaintances". Nodes in each Virtual Organisation keep a small number of long links to distant nodes. A semi-structured P2P search approach is presented to create long-range links between Virtual Organisations, as well as to discover the local nodes that have specific external connections. The algorithms of SWEVO will

be described from three aspects in this section: intra-organisational content searching, inter-organisational content searching, and Virtual Organisation maintenance.

Intra-Organisational Content Searching

Each shared file in SWEVO is published by an associated content advertisement. A content advertisement is an XML file that provides the relevant meta-information on the file (e.g. file name, file size, file description, address of the host node). The content advertisement is pushed to a target node according to the hash value of the name of the file, as well as the internal neighbours of the target node in the member list within a specific distance d to increase the probability of discovery of the advertisement. The advertisement lookup procedure involves two steps: a structured P2P search followed by an unstructured P2P search. The query originator first searches the target nodes generated from the same hash function (structured P2P search). If the requested advertisement cannot be found in the target node (e.g. the target node is offline at the moment), the query originator will continue to search the neighbours of the target node in the member list within a distance d (unstructured P2P search), and can find the requested files with a high probability.

Figure 1 illustrates an example of content advertisement publishing and retrieving. *P1* shares a file with the name *K1*. The publication service on node *P1* pushes the associated advertisement of *K1* to *P4* according to the hash value of *K1* and the neighbours of *P4* (*P3* and *P5*) within the distance $d = 1$. Then other nodes in the same Virtual Organisation can easily find the advertisement with a high probability. In this case, *P6* looks for the advertisement by generating the same hash value pointing to *P4* with the same hash function, sends a query to *P4* and finds the advertisement with *K1* in *P4*. However, if the requested advertisement cannot be found in *P4*,

Figure 1. Advertisement publishing and searching

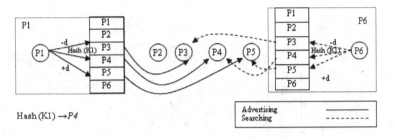

Hash (K1) → P4

Figure 2. Algorithm for generating the searching successor

Algorithm: Next_Node (p_id, s_id, d)

1. $d' = |\ p\_id - s\_id\ |$
2.   IF $d' \geq d$ THEN
3.   IF $p\_id \geq s\_id$ THEN
4.   RETURN
5.   ELSE
6. $n' = |\ p\_id - d\ |$
7.   RETURN n'
8.   END IF
9.   ELSE
10.   IF $p\_id \geq s\_id$ THEN
11. $n' = |\ p\_id + d' + 1\ |$
12.   RETURN n'
13.   ELSE
14. $n' = |\ p\_id - d'\ |$
15.   RETURN n'
16.   END IF
17.   END IF

the query originator will continue to search *P3* and *P5*, which are the neighbours of *P4* within the distance $d = 1$.

The algorithm illustrated in Figure 2 shows the node selection procedure for getting the next node to search, where *p_id* is the node ID generated from the hash function (e.g. *4* of *P4*), and *s_id* is the ID of the current node that is selected from the member list. The algorithm returns the index ID of the node we are going to search next. If the return value is null, the selection procedure is completed. The publication and searching parameter *d* is a system-wide parameter, which is defined based on network churns. Generally, a bigger *d* is required in a dynamic network with a higher network churn rate to achieve the same success rate.

Inter-Organisational Content Searching

In SWEVO, a new Virtual Organisation is advertised by an XML-based advertisement of Virtual Organisation that provides the meta-information about the Virtual Organisation (e.g. ID of the Virtual Organisation, name of the Virtual Organisation, addresses of contact points, and description of the Virtual Organisation). The Virtual Organisation advertisement will be multicast through the network. Not all the nodes in the network will receive the advertisement, but many of them will.

When a node receives a Virtual Organisation advertisement, it will push the advertisement to a target node in the Virtual Organisation according to the hash value of the name of the Virtual Organisation as well as the neighbours of the target node within a specific distance *d* to increase the probability of discovery of the advertisement. Similarly to the intra-organisational content searching, if the query originator cannot find the requested advertisement in the structured P2P search procedure due to network churns, the requested advertisement can still be found

Figure 3. Inter-organisational link formation

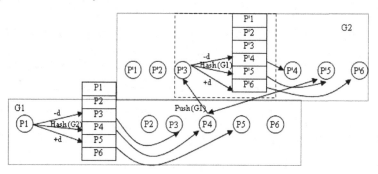

Figure 4. Example of lookup in dynamic environments

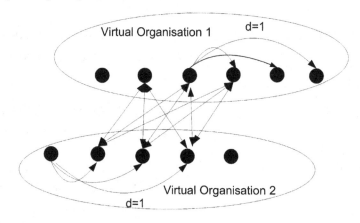

in the neighbours of the target node. Therefore, even though only one node is informed, all the nodes in the same Virtual Organisation potentially can find and pull the Virtual Organisation advertisement.

Figure 3 illustrates the process of inter-organisational link formation. When *P1* receives a advertisement about Virtual Organisation *G2* with contact point *P'3*, it will push the advertisement to the target node *P4* according to the hash function as well as its neighbours (*P3* and *P5*) within the distance *d* = 1. Then *P4* will inform the contact point of Virtual Organisation *G2*: *P'3* with the advertisement of its Virtual Organisation *G1*. When *P'3* gets the advertisement of *G1*, *P'3* will do the same as *P1* in forwarding the advertisement of *G1* toward the target node *P'5* according to the

hash function, as well as its neighbours within the distance *d*. When *P'5* receives the advertisement, *P'5* will do the same as *P4*, sending the advertisement of its Virtual Organisation *G2* back to *P4*. When *P4* receives it and sends an acknowledgement of the inter-organisational link back to *P'5*, an inter-organisational link will have been built between *G1* and *G2*, which is maintained by *P4* and *P'5*.

In the same way, more inter-organisational links will be created and maintained between *P3*, *P4*, *P5*, and *P'4*, *P'5*, *P'6*, in case of *d* = 1. Each of them normally keeps 2*d* + 1 inter-organisational links as illustrated in Figure 4, which makes Virtual Organisations connected even in highly dynamic environments. Inter-organisational search queries can be propagated toward the requested Virtual Organisation efficiently via the inter-organisational links, and relevant shared files can be found. Context-keyword queries (Salter & Antonopoulos, 2007) are utilised in SWEVO which are composed of one or more sets of context-keyword pairs. A single pair could be "colour = orange", where "colour" is the name of Virtual Organisation and "orange" is the keyword for the requested content.

Maintenance

Different from the currently used strategies of maintaining membership information of Virtual Organisations, the member list is only required to be loosely maintained in the case of infrequent node joining and leaving of a Virtual Organisation due to its high fault-tolerant capability. Based on the studies from prior Internet applications (e.g., Bhagwan, Savage, & Voelker (2003)), the network churns caused by computers going online or offline temporarily is much higher than the network churns caused by nodes joining and leaving a Virtual Organisation permanently. In SWEVO, no overhead is required for other members of the Virtual Organisation to update their member list in the same Virtual Organisation if a node becomes offline temporarily. Therefore, a great deal of communication overhead for nodes arriving and departing can be eliminated in SWEVO, which is a significant problem for most structured P2P networks where each node needs to maintain a consistent distributed hash index in a highly dynamic environment.

Because the content advertisements are distributed not only to the target node but also to its neighbours within a specific distance d in the member list, the neighbouring nodes are always keeping similar lists of content advertisements. Therefore, each node can synchronise the Virtual Organisation status with its neighbours and obtain the information that it missed during its offline period when representing the network. When a node reconnects to the network, it will multicast

notifications to its neighbours with a time stamp marking the time it last left the network. The neighbours will select and send back the content advertisement(s) with the publishing dates later than the time of the time stamp, and the hash values of the names of advertisements pointing to the node (all nodes use the synchronised network time).

When a node intends to join a new Virtual Organisation, it can utilise the Virtual Organisation search protocol to find the relevant Virtual Organisation advertisement and initialise connections to the Virtual Organisation. In order to keep the member list up to date, each node periodically and probabilistically selects a given number of nodes and reconciles the member list of the Virtual Organisation. The study in Byers, Considine, Mitzenmacher and Rost (2002) addresses the reconciliation problems of set differences using Bloom Filters (Bloom, 1970). A Bloom filter is a summary technique that aims to encode the entries of a data set into several positions in a bit vector through the use of hash functions. The theory is extended to synchronise the status of member lists in SWEVO as follows: suppose node P_A has a list of nodes, L_A, with a time stamp of the last update T_A and P_B has a list of nodes, L_B, with a time stamp T_B. If T_A is newer than T_B, P_B will send P_A a Bloom Filter about L_B. P_A will then check each node on L_A against the Bloom Filter, and send a list of nodes that do not lie in L_B together with a Bloom Filter about L_A. P_B will add the new nodes into its list and remove nodes that do not lie in L_A. Because of false positives, not all the information about nodes in $L_B - L_A$ will be sent, but most of them will.

CHARACTERISTICS OF SMALL WORLD

In the Watts's model (Watts & Strogatz, 1998), small world networks are distinguished by high clustering coefficients and short average path lengths. These two characteristics of small world will be mathematically analysed in this section.

The clustering coefficient of a node is the proportion of the links between nodes within its neighbourhood divided by the maximum number of links that could possibly exist between them (Watts, 2005).

Similarly to Watts's model (Watts & Strogatz, 1998), the clustering coefficient of SWEVO is analysed in an n-node "graph" as shown in Figure 5, where each node has k internal neighbours and i external neighbours ($n >> (k+i) >> 1$), and non-overlapping Virtual Organisations are connected by inter-organisational links.

The clustering coefficient of the node with i inter-organisational links (Appendix A) is:

$$\gamma_i \approx \frac{2}{(k+i)(k+i-1)}\left(\frac{k(k-1)}{2}\right) = \frac{k(k-1)}{(k+i)(k+i-1)}$$

The weighted average is:

$$\overline{\gamma} = \sum_{i=0}^{l} p_i\gamma_i = \sum_{i=0}^{l} p_i\frac{k(k-1)}{(k+i)(k+i-1)}$$

where p_i is the probability that a node keeps i external links and l is the maximum of the inter-organisational links of a node. The inter-organisational links are randomly distributed with a hash function. The distribution of inter-organisational links can be regarded as a Poisson distribution:

$$p_i \approx \frac{\lambda^i \cdot e^{-\lambda}}{i!}$$

where $\lambda = \frac{g-1}{k+1}$ and $g = \frac{n}{k+1}$

So:

$$\overline{\gamma} = \sum_{i=0}^{l} p_i\frac{k(k-1)}{(k+i)(k+i-1)}$$

$$\approx \sum_{i=0}^{l} \frac{\left(\frac{n-k-1}{(k+1)^2}\right)^i}{i!} \cdot e^{-\frac{n-k-1}{(k+1)^2}} \cdot \frac{k(k-1)}{(k+i)(k+i-1)} \quad (1)$$

The average path length between all pairs of nodes (Appendix B) is:

$$L = \frac{1}{N}\left(N_{local} \cdot d_{local} + N_{global} \cdot d_{global}\right)$$

$$= \frac{3k+1}{k+1} - \frac{2k-1}{n-1} - \frac{1}{(k+1)(n-1)} \quad (2)$$

The clustering coefficient of a small world graph is much larger than the random graph with the same number of nodes and connections, but the average path length is close to level of the random graph (Watts & Strogatz, 1998). Figure 6 shows the clustering coefficient and average path length of SWEVO to that of a random network with the same number of nodes and connections, where x-axis indicates the number of nodes in the network. The clustering coefficients and average path lengths of SWEVO are given by the equation (1) and (2) where $k = 99$. As shown in Figure 6, the clustering coefficient of SWEVO is much greater than but the average path length of SWEVO is in the order of that of the random network with the same number of nodes and connections. From the results in Figure 6, we can see that the small world phenomenon appears in the SWEVO network with a high clustering coefficient and a low average path length.

In a static environment, consistent DHTs can achieve good performance. Chord is a well-known

Figure 5. Topology example

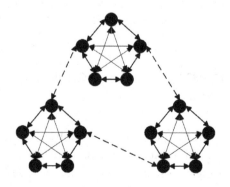

Figure 6. Comparison between SWEVO and a random network (a) clustering coefficient (b) average path length

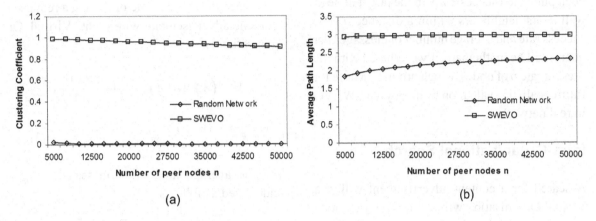

(a)   (b)

Figure 7. Average path length of SWEVO and Chord

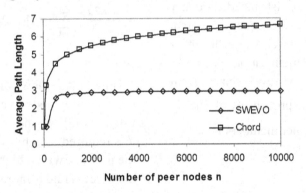

DHT method using one-dimensional routing table like SWEVO. The average path lengths of SWEVO and Chord are compared in this section. In an *n*-node Chord network, only $O(\log n)$ nodes need to be visited to resolve a query. The average path length of *n*-node Chord network is only $(1/2)\log_2 n$ (Stoica et al., 2001). Generally, Chord only needs to keep a shorter hash table with less information than SWEVO. However, the shorter table is required to be rigidly maintained whenever changes occur in the network. In contrast, the member list in SWEVO is loosely maintained to fit the dynamic nature of Internet. Figure 7 shows the average path length of the Chord network and the SWEVO network (*k* = 99), where x-axis indicates the number of nodes in the network and

y-axis shows the average path length. In Figure 7, we observe that SWEVO needs fewer hops to target an object than Chord in this case. SWEVO achieves better performance in query processing due to its higher connectivity and the small world effect.

MATHEMATIC PERFORMANCE EVALUATION

The performance of SWEVO is evaluated in dynamic P2P environments with frequent nodes temporarily online and offline. A number of nodes ($p \cdot n$) are randomly selected to be offline according to the present rate of nodes *p*. In this section, performance is evaluated under the assumption that the requested advertisements have been published successfully to the target node as well as its neighbours within a distance d. The success rate and average number of messages per query will be mathematically evaluated with the present rate p of nodes, which provides a base for future realistic evaluation by deploying SWEVO in real networks.

Intra-Organisational Search

A search for a content advertisement within a Virtual Organisation will fail if the target node and its neighbours within distance d are all offline. Because advertisements are distributed, the query originator can possibly find the requested content advertisement from itself as well as from the other members in the Virtual Organisation. The probability of finding a requested advertisement from itself is $P(A) = \dfrac{2d+1}{k+1}$. The probability of finding an advertisement from other members is:

$$P(B \mid \overline{A}) = \sum_{i=1}^{2d+1} p \cdot (1-p)^{i-1}$$

and it requires i messages. The probability of failing to find an advertisement on other members is $P(\overline{B} \mid \overline{A}) = (1-p)^{2d+1}$ and it generates $2d + 1$ messages.

Hence the success rate of finding a requested content advertisement within the Virtual Organisation is:

$$P_{intra} = 1 - P(\overline{A})P(\overline{B} \mid \overline{A}) = 1 - \left(1 - \frac{2d+1}{k+1}\right) \cdot (1-p)^{2d+1}$$

$$= 1 - \frac{k-2d}{k+1} \cdot (1-p)^{2d+1} \tag{3}$$

The average number of messages N_{intra} is calculated as follows:

$$N_{intra} = P(A) \cdot 0 + P(\overline{A}) \cdot [P(B \mid \overline{A}) \cdot i + P(\overline{B} \mid \overline{A}) \cdot (2d+1)]$$

$$= \left(\frac{k-2d}{k+1}\right) \left\{ \sum_{i=1}^{2d+1} \left[p \cdot (1-p)^{i-1} \cdot i \right] + (1-p)^{2d+1} \cdot (2d+1) \right\} \tag{4}$$

Figure 8(a) shows the success rate versus the present rate of nodes with $k = 100$ generated from Equation (3). As the present rate falls, a bigger d is required to achieve a good success rate. In the network with a high present rate ($p > 60\%$), the success rate is more than 93% by setting $d = 1$ only. In the network with a low present rate of nodes ($p = 10\%$), we can still achieve a 91% success rate by setting $d = 10$. Figure 8(b) shows the number of messages for different present rates of

Figure 8. Performance parameters in the intra-organisational searches (a) success rate (b) average number of messages

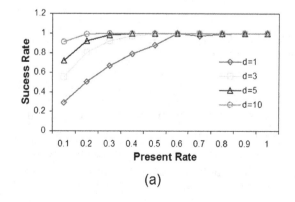

(a)

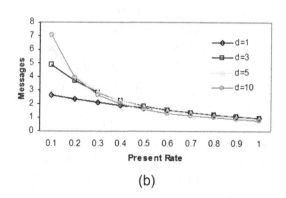

(b)

nodes in the network with $k = 100$ generated from Equation (4). In the network with a high present rate $p > 50\%$, the average number of messages per query is less than two in all observed results. In the network with a low present rate of nodes with $p = 10\%$, only about seven messages are generated on average by setting $d = 10$.

Figure 9 shows that the minimal value of d is needed to achieve the required success rate in the networks with different present rates of nodes, where x-axis indicates the minimal value of d required and y-axis shows the corresponding present rate. If $d \geq 3$, all observed success rates are more than 50%. Moreover, success rates can reach 90% by setting $d = 10$ in the network with a 10% present rate of nodes.

Inter-Organisational Search

In SWEVO, three conditions must be satisfied to find an advertisement in a different Virtual Organisation as shown in Figure 4:

C = "Succeed in finding an advertisement about the requested Virtual Organisation"

D = "Succeed in contacting the requested Virtual Organisation"

E = "Succeed in finding a requested content advertisement in the requested Virtual Organisation".

Figure 9. The minimal publishing distances for different required success rates in the intra-organisational searches

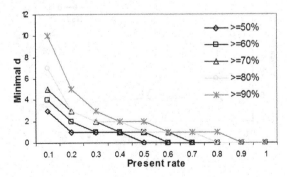

The success rate of finding a content advertisement in the requested Virtual Organisation (Appendix C) is:

$$P_s = P(EDC) = P(E|DC) \cdot P(D|C) \cdot P(C)$$
$$= \left[1 - \frac{k-2d}{k+1} \cdot (1-p)^{2d+1}\right]^2 \left[1 - (1-p)^{2d+1}\right]$$
$$(5)$$

The expected number of messages per query (Appendix C) is shown in Equation (6).

Figure 10(a) and (b) show the success rate and the average number of messages generated by inter-organisational searches in the networks with different node present rates generated from Equation (5) and (6), respectively (in case of $k = 100$). In the network with a high present rate $p = 70\%$, SWEVO achieves a 92% success rate by defining a small $d = 1$. If $d = 10$, the success rate is more than 70% for the network with a low present rate $p = 10\%$, and the success rate will soar to 97% when the present rate p increases to 20%. In the network with a low present rate $p = 10\%$, only about 21 messages on average are generated per query, and a 70% success rate is achieved by setting $d = 10$. In Figure 10(b), the number of messages rises due to increasing success in the network with a low present rate (when $p < 40\%$) and a short publication distance d (e.g. $d = 1$). From the results shown in Figure 10, SWEVO achieves good performance in most situations by achieving high success rates with low traffic cost.

However, if d is defined as a small value, the success rate is also very low in the network with a low node present rate; this is the situation needs to be avoided in practice. As shown in Figure 10(a), the success rates of the samples with $d = 1$, 3, 5, are all below 40% with a 10% present rate. Therefore, defining a proper value of d is essential for SWEVO to achieve a satisfactory success rate. Figure 11 shows the minimal values of d required to achieve different satisfactory success rates with different node present rates. Networks with

$d \geq 15$ can get more than 90% success rates of finding a required advertisement in the network with no less than 10% present rate. Moreover, if the node's present rate reaches 70%, we only need to set $d = 1$ to achieve more than 90% success rate in all testing cases.

SIMULATION-BASED PERFORMANCE EVALUATION

The performance of SWEVO is further evaluated by simulations in dynamic environments. The simulator of SWEVO for this purpose is programmed in the Java language. In the simulation, we follow the same assumption that the requested advertisements are published successfully to the target node as well as to its neighbours within a distance d. Thus, a search will succeed if either the target node or one of its neighbours within distance d is visited successfully.

In the simulations, 1000 nodes are initialised as online in the network. Two Virtual Organisations are generated, and each keeps 500 nodes. At the beginning of each search, a set of nodes ($p \cdot n$) is randomly selected and set as offline according to

Equation (6).

$$
\begin{aligned}
\mathrm{E}[N] &= E\left[N\left(ADE\right)\right] + E\left[N\left(AD\overline{E}\right)\right] + E\left[N\left(A\overline{D}\right)\right] + E\left[N\left(\overline{A}BDE\right)\right] + E\left[N\left(\overline{A}BD\overline{E}\right)\right] + E\left[N\left(\overline{A}B\overline{D}\right)\right] + E\left[N\left(\overline{A}\overline{B}\right)\right] \\
&= \left(1 - \frac{2d+1}{k+1}\right)\left\{ \sum_{i=1}^{2d+1}\left\{ p \cdot (1-p)^{i-1} \cdot \sum_{j=1}^{2d+1}\left[p \cdot (1-p)^{j-1}\left(\frac{2d+1}{k+1}\cdot(j+i) + \left(1 - \frac{2d+1}{k+1}\right)\sum_{m=1}^{2d+1} p \cdot (1-p)^{m-1}\cdot(m+j+i)\right)\right] \right\} \right. \\
&\quad + \sum_{i=1}^{2d+1}\left[p \cdot (1-p)^{i-1}\sum_{j=1}^{2d+1} p \cdot (1-p)^{j-1}\cdot\left(1 - \frac{2d+1}{k+1}\right)\cdot(1-p)^{2d+1}\cdot(2d+1+j+i)\right] \\
&\quad \left. + \sum_{i=1}^{2d+1} p \cdot (1-p)^{i-1}(1-p)^{2d+1}\cdot(2d+1+i) + (1-p)^{2d+1}\cdot(2d+1)\right\} \\
&\quad + \frac{2d+1}{k+1}\left\{ \sum_{j=1}^{2d+1} p \cdot (1-p)^{j-1}\left[\frac{2d+1}{k+1}\cdot j + \left(1 - \frac{2d+1}{k+1}\right)\cdot\sum_{m=1}^{2d+1} p \cdot (1-p)^{m-1}\cdot(m+j)\right] \right. \\
&\quad \left. + \sum_{j=1}^{2d+1} p \cdot (1-p)^{j-1}\cdot\left(1 - \frac{2d+1}{k+1}\right)\cdot(1-p)^{2d+1}\cdot(2d+1+j) + (1-p)^{2d+1}\cdot(2d+1)\right\}
\end{aligned}
$$

Figure 10. Performance parameters in the inter-organisational searches (a) success rate (b) average number of messages

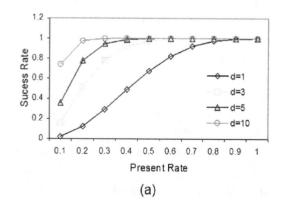

(a)

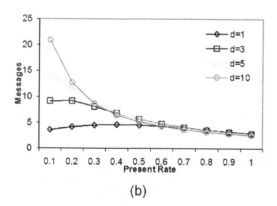

(b)

Figure 11. The minimal publishing distance for different required success rates in the inter-organisational searches

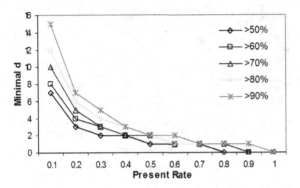

the parameter of present rate; the query originator is randomly selected from the set of online nodes, and the target node with its neighbours are randomly selected from the set of nodes regardless of their online situation. In each data search, the query originator initialises a query that will be passed with the SWEVO protocols.

In the simulations of intra-organisational searches, the query originator and the target node are allocated in the same Virtual Organisation. On the contrary, the query originator and the target node are separated into different Virtual Organisations in the simulations of inter-organisational searches. Figure 12(a)–(d) show the results of the success rate and the average number of messages per query in the intra-organisational searches and inter-organisational searches, respectively (for 1000 queries), in which the theoretical results are generated from Equations (3)–(6).

As shown in Figure 12(a)–(d), the results of success rates from our simulation results are very close to the theoretical results. Actually, the simulation results could be slightly smaller than the theoretical results, due to the method of generating present rate. In order to generate a dynamic environment, we randomly mark $(p \cdot (k+1))$ nodes from $(k+1)$ nodes as offline. Because an online node has already been selected as the query originator, $p * (k+1)-1$ online nodes

are available to search in the network with a total of $(k + 1)$ node. The present rate of remaining nodes have been actually decreased from p to $\frac{p*(k+1)-1}{k} \leq p$ in the view of the query originator, which could lead that simulation results are marginally smaller than the theoretical results.

FUTURE TRENDS

SWEVO is based on the concept of clustering Grid nodes intentionally into Virtual Organisations. Communication overhead is still required to compensate for the server for organisation management and resource discovery. In contrast, in social networks, communities are formed naturally by daily intercommunications between people. No additional overhead is required for maintenance of social communities. If Grid nodes can self-organise themselves like social networks, a large communication cost for organisation construction, maintenance and discovery can be saved, which will significantly improve overall performance of Grids. Some attempts have been proposed in the studies (Liu, Antonopoulos, & Mackin, 2007c; Liu et al., 2008), which will be investigated and evaluated further via modelling and simulations in the future. Some human behaviours in social networks (Haythornthwaite, 1996; McCarty, 2002; Watts, 2002) will be mimicked in unstructured P2P environment in order to build efficient Virtual Organisations in a social-like P2P network.

Moreover, the new design methodology of using social network concepts to improve the resource discovery in VOs will, in turn, affect the structure of existing social and business networks. Social and business consequence will be further analysed and evaluated in the next step.

CONCLUSION

The small world phenomenon is a well known hypothesis that greatly influences the social sci-

Figure 12. Performance Evaluation. Success rate: (a) intra-organisational searches (b) inter-organisational searches. Messages: (c) intra-organisational searches (d) inter-organisational searches

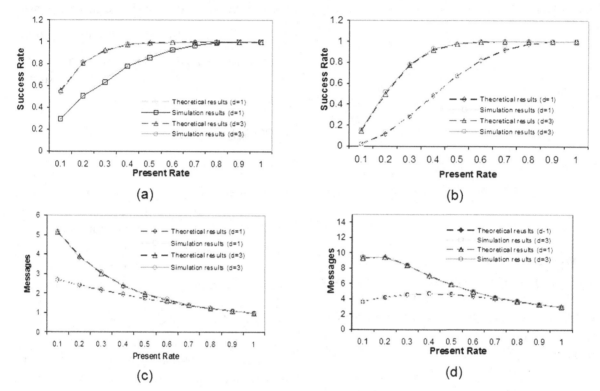

ences. With respect to the similarity between social networks and Grids, we believe and confirm that the small-world phenomenon is useful for improving resource discovery in Grids by building a small-world environment.

In this chapter, we present the SWEVO model which enables Virtual Organisations working in a more collaborative manner to support decision makers. In SWEVO, each Grid node keeps a list of neighbouring nodes in the same Virtual Organisation and Virtual Organisations are connected by a small number of inter-organisational links that can also be seen as long links to distant nodes in the network. Not every node needs to be connected to remote Virtual Organisations, but every node can easily find which nodes have external connections to a specific Virtual Organisation in the network. A semi-structured P2P search

method is presented in this chapter combining the techniques of both structured and unstructured search methods. This search algorithm is fault-tolerant and able to discover the requested resource inside and outside of Virtual Organisations, even though hash functions cannot provide accurate information about data locations. From our analysis and simulations, the proposed model achieves better performance in both static and dynamic environments when compared to other existing systems.

REFERENCES

Adamic, L. A., Lukose, R. M., Puniyani, A. R., & Huberman, B. A. (2001). Search in Power Law Networks. *Physical Review, 64*, 1-8.

Antonopoulos, N., & Salter, J. (2004). Efficient Resource Discovery in Grids and P2P Networks. *Internet Research, 14*, 339-346.

Bhagwan, R., Savage, S., & Voelker, G. M. (2003). *Understanding Availability.* Paper presented at the International Workshop on Peer-to-Peer Systems, Berkeley, CA.

Bloom, B. (1970). Space/time Tradeoffs in Hash Coding with Allowable Errors. *Communications of the ACM, 13*(7), 422-426.

Byers, J., Considine, J., Mitzenmacher, M., & Rost, S. (2002). Informed Content Delivery Across Adaptive Overlay Networks. *ACM SIGCOMM Computer Communication Review, 32*, 47-60.

Crespo, A., & Garcia-Molina, H. (2002). *Routing Indices for Peer-to-Peer Systems.* Paper presented at the International Conference on Distributed Computing Systems, Vienna, Austria.

Cuenca-Acuna, F. M., & Nguyen, T. D. (2002). *Text-based Content Search and Retrieval in ad hoc P2P Communities.* Paper presented at the International Workshop on Peer-to-Peer Computing, Cambridge, MA.

Foster, I., Kesselman, C., & Tuecke, S. (2001). The Anatomy of the Grid: Enabling Scalable Virtual Organizations. *International Journal of Supercomputer Applications, 15*.

Fraigniaud, P., Lebhar, E., & Lotker, Z. (2008). *Recovering the Long-Range Links in Augmented Graphs.* Paper presented at 15th International Colloquium on Structural Information and Communication Complexity (SIROCCO), Villars-sur-Ollon, Switzerland.

Fraigniaud, P. (2007). *Small Worlds as Navigable Augmented Networks: Model, Analysis, and Validation.* Invited talk at the 15th Annual European Symposium on Algorithms (ESA), Eilat, Israel.

Haythornthwaite, C. (1996). Social Network Analysis: An Approach and Technique for the Study of Information Exchange. *Library & Information Science Research, 18*, 323-342.

Iamnitchi, A., Ripeanu, M., & Foster, I. (2002). *Locating Data in Peer-to-Peer Scientific Collaborations.* Paper presented at the International Workshop on Peer-to-Peer Systems, Cambridge, USA.

Khambatti, M., Ryu, K., & Dasgupta, P. (2002). Efficient Discovery of Implicitly Formed Peer-to-Peer Communities. *International Journal of Parallel and Distributed Systems and Networks, 5*, 155-164.

Khambatti, M., Ryu, K. D., & Dasgupta, P. (2003). *Structuring Peer-to-Peer Networks using Interest-Based Communities.* Paper presented at the International Workshop on Databases, Information Systems, and Peer-to-Peer Computing, Berlin, Germany.

Kleinberg, J. (2000). Navigation in a Small World. *Nature, 406*, 845.

Kleinberg, J. (2001). Small-World Phenomena and the Dynamics of Information. *Advances in Neural Information Processing Systems (NIPS), 14*.

Li, J., & Vuong, S. (2004). *An Efficient Clustered Architecture for P2P Networks.* Paper presented at the 18th International Conference on Advanced Information Networking and Application, Fukuoka, Japan.

Liu, L., Antonopoulos, N., & Mackin, S. (2007a). Fault-tolerant Peer-to-Peer Search on Small-World Networks. *Journal of Future Generation Computer Systems, 23*(8), 921-931.

Liu, L., Antonopoulos, N., & Mackin, S. (2007b). *Small World Peer-to-peer for Resource Discovery.* Paper presented at the International Conference on Information Networking, Lecture Notes in Computer Science, Estoril, Portugal.

Liu, L., Antonopoulos, N., & Mackin, S. (2007c). *Social Peer-to-Peer for Resource Discovery.* Paper presented at the 15th Euromicro International Conference on Parallel, Distributed and Network-based Processing, Naples, Italy.

Liu, L., Antonopoulos, N., & Mackin, S. (2008). Managing Peer-to-Peer Networks with Human Tactics in Social Interactions. *Journal of Super-computing, 44*(3), 217-236.

Lv, Q., Cao, P., Cohen, E., Li, K., & Shenker, S. (2002). *Search and Replication in Unstructured Peer-to-Peer Networks.* Paper presented at the ACM SIGMETRICS, Marina Del Rey, CA.

Marzolla, M., Mordacchini, M., & Orlando, S. (2007). Peer-to-peer systems for discovering resources in a dynamic gridstar, open. *Parallel Computing, 33*(4-5), 339-358.

Mastroianni, C., Talia, D., & Verta, O. (2005). *A P2P Approach for Membership Management and Resource Discovery in Grids.* Paper presented at the 2005 International Symposium on Information Technology: Coding and Computing, Las Vegas, NV.

Maymounkov, P., & Mazières, D. (2002). *Kademlia: A Peer to Peer Information System Based on the XOR Metric.* Paper presented at the International Workshop on Peer-to-Peer Systems, Cambridge MA.

McCarty, C. (2002). Structure in Personal Networks. *Journal of Social Structure, 3*, 1-19.

Milgram, S. (1967). The Small World Problem. *Psychology Today, 2*, 60-67.

Ratnasamy, S., Francis, P., Handley, M., Karp, R., & Shenker, S. (2001). *A Scalable Content-Addressable Network.* Paper presented at the ACM SIGCOMM, San Diego, CA.

Rhea, S., Geels, D., Roscoe, T., & Kubiatowicz, J. (2004). *Handling Churn in a DHT.* Paper presented at the USENIX Annual Technical Conference, Boston, MA.

Rowstron, A., & Druschel, P. (2001). *Pastry: Scalable, Distributed Object Location and Routing for Large-scale Peer-to-Peer Systems.* Paper presented at the IFIP/ACM International Conference on Distributed Systems Platforms, Heidelberg, Germany.

Salter, J., & Antonopoulos, N. (2005). *ROME: Optimising DHT-based Peer-to-Peer Networks.* Paper presented at the 5th International Network Conference, Samos, Greece.

Salter, J., & Antonopoulos, N. (2007). An Optimised 2-Tier P2P Architecture for Contextualised Keyword Searches. *Journal of Future Generation Computer Systems, 23*, 241-251.

Sculley, A. & Woods, W. (2000). *B2B Exchanges: The Killer Application in the Business-to-Business Internet Revolution.* ISI Publications.

Stoica, I., Morris, R., Karger, D., Kaashoek, M. F., & Balakrishnan, H. (2001). *Chord: A Scalable Peer-to-Peer Lookup Service for Internet Applications.* Paper presented at the ACM SIGCOMM, San Diego, CA.

Tsoumakos, D., & Roussopoulos, N. (2003). *Adaptive Probabilistic Search for Peer-to-Peer Networks.* Paper presented at the Third International Conference on Peer-to-Peer Computing, Linköping, Sweden.

Vassileva, J. (2002). *Motivating Participation in Peer-to-Peer Communities.* Paper presented at the Workshop on Engineering Societies in the Agent World, Madrid, Spain.

Vuong, S., & Li, J. (2003). *Efa: an Efficient Content Routing Algorithm in Large Peer-to-Peer Overlay Networks.* Paper presented at the International Conference on Peer-to-Peer Computing, Linköping, Sweden.

Walker, D. W. (2001). *The Grid, Virtual Organizations, and Problem-Solving Environments.* Paper presented at the International Conference on Cluster Computing, Brisbane, Australia.

Watts, D. (2005). *The Dynamic of Networks Between Order and Randomness*. Princeton: University Press.

Watts, D. J., Dodds, P. S., & Newman, M. E. J. (2002). Identity and Search in Social Networks. *Science, 296*, 1302-1205.

Watts, D., & Strogatz, S. H. (1998). Collective Dynamics of Small-World Networks. *Nature 393*, 440-442.

Winton, L. J. (2005). *A Simple Virtual Organisation Model and Practical Implementation*. Paper presented at the Australasian workshop on Grid computing and e-research, Newcastle, Australia, 2005.

Yang, B., & Garcia-Molina, H. (2002). *Efficient Search in Peer-to-Peer Networks*. Paper presented at the International Conference on Distributed Computing Systems, Vienna, Austria.

APPENDIX A: CLUSTERING COEFFICIENT

The clustering coefficient of SWEVO is analysed in an n-node "graph", where each node has k internal neighbours and i external neighbours ($n \gg (k+i) \gg 1$), and Virtual Organisations do not overlap which are connected by inter-organisational links. Therefore, there are a total of $k+1$ nodes in each Virtual Organisation and a total of g $= \dfrac{n}{k+1}$ Virtual Organisations in the network. The publication and searching parameter $d = 0$ in the static environment with the present rate of nodes $p = 100\%$.

A node has i inter-organisational links. Therefore, it has $k+i$ "neighbours" in the network (k internal neighbours and i external neighbours), as shown in Figure 13. The possible links between its neighbours are $\dfrac{(k+i)(k+i-1)}{2}$. But in a static environment with $d = 0$, i external neighbours do not keep inter-organisational links to k internal neighbours. There are approximately $\dfrac{(\langle i \rangle \cdot n)}{2}$ inter-organisational links out of a total $\dfrac{n(n-1)-n \cdot k}{2}$ possible links, where $\langle i \rangle$ is the average number of inter-organisational links. The probability that two external neighbours are connected to each other by an inter-organisational link is $\dfrac{\langle i \rangle}{n-k-1}$, which will be very low because $n \gg (k+i) \gg 1$. Therefore, the actual links in the neighbourhood of a node are the links among its k internal neighbours: $\dfrac{k(k-1)}{2}$. Thus, the clustering coefficient of the node with i external neighbours is:

$$\gamma_i \approx \frac{2}{(k+i)(k+i-1)}\left(\frac{k(k-1)}{2}\right) = \frac{k(k-1)}{(k+i)(k+i-1)}$$

APPENDIX B: AVERAGE PATH LENGTH

The average path length, L, is evaluated here. d_{local} is defined as the average distance between the nodes in the same Virtual Organisation and d_{global} is defined as the average distance for the nodes from different Virtual Organisations. Each node needs one step to reach the other nodes in the same Virtual Organisation except for itself, so $d_{local} = \dfrac{k}{k+1}$. The average distance d_{global} for nodes in different Virtual Organisations can be divided into three average sub-distances:

Figure 13. Neighbourhood of a node

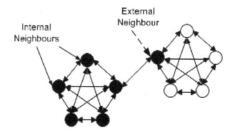

Figure 14. Path length in SWEVO

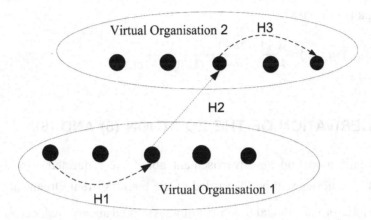

1. The average distance to get out of the starting Virtual Organisation: H_1.
2. The average distance to move between Virtual Organisations: H_2.
3. The average distance to get into the requested Virtual Organisation: H_3.

Therefore, $d_{global} = H_1 + H_2 + H_3$ as illustrated in Figure 14.

To get out of a Virtual Organisation toward a specific remote Virtual Organisation, k nodes need one hop to find a specific node that keeps the specific inter-organisational link, except for the specific node itself. Therefore, the average distance to get out of a Virtual Organisation is:

$$H_1 = 1 \cdot \frac{k}{k+1} + 0 \cdot \frac{1}{k+1} = \frac{k}{k+1}$$

In the same way, we can also acquire the same average distance to get into the requested Virtual Organisation: $H_3 = H_1 = \frac{k}{k+1}$. Virtual Organisations are connected to each other via inter-organisational links, and thus $H_2 = 1$.

$$d_{global} = H_1 + H_2 + H_3 = \frac{k}{k+1} + 1 + \frac{k}{k+1} = 1 + \frac{2k}{k+1}$$

The number of the pairs of nodes in a Virtual Organisation is $C_{k+1}^2 = \frac{((k+1)-1)(k+1)}{2}$ and there are a total of g Virtual Organisations, hence the sum of pairs of nodes in the same Virtual Organisation is:

$$N_{local} = \frac{((k+1)-1)(k+1)}{2} \cdot g = \frac{k(k+1)}{2} \cdot \frac{n}{k+1} = \frac{n \cdot k}{2}$$

The sum of the pairs between nodes inside and outside of Virtual Organisations in the whole network is:

$$N_{global} = C_n^2 - N_{local} = \frac{n(n-k-1)}{2}$$

The sum of the pairs of nodes in the whole network is: $N = C_n^2 = \frac{n(n-1)}{2}$. Hence, the average path length between all pairs of nodes is:

$$L = \frac{1}{N}\left(N_{local} \cdot d_{local} + N_{global} \cdot d_{global}\right) = \frac{3k+1}{k+1} - \frac{2k-1}{n-1} - \frac{1}{(k+1)(n-1)}$$

APPENDIX C: DERIVATION OF THE EQUATION (5) AND (6)

The probability of failing to find an advertisement about the requested Virtual Organisation is: $P(\overline{C}) = \frac{k-2d}{k+1}(1-p)^{2d+1}$. Queries will be forwarded to the target Virtual Organisation if the nodes on the both ends of the inter-organisational link are online. As noted above, the local Virtual Organisation keeps inter-organisational links toward $2d + 1$ nodes in a remote Virtual Organisation. We will fail to contact the requested Virtual Organisation, if all $2d + 1$ nodes are all offline. Therefore, the probability of failing in contacting the requested Virtual Organisation is: $P(\overline{D}|C) = (1-p)^{2d+1}$. The probability of finding an advertisement about the requested Virtual Organisation is $P(E|DC) = P(C)$. The success rate of finding a content advertisement in the requested Virtual Organisation is:

$$P_s = P(EDC) = P(E|DC) \cdot P(D|C) \cdot P(C) = \left[1 - \frac{k-2d}{k+1} \cdot (1-p)^{2d+1}\right]^2 \left[1 - (1-p)^{2d+1}\right] \tag{5}$$

The expected number of messages per query is calculated to judge the traffic cost per query in each of the following cases:

Case 1: Succeed in finding an advertisement of the requested Virtual Organisation in the node itself, succeed in contacting the requested Virtual Organisation, and succeed in finding a requested content advertisement in the requested Virtual Organisation.

$$E[N(ADE)] = \frac{2d+1}{k+1}\left\{\sum_{j=1}^{2d+1} p \cdot (1-p)^{j-1}\left[\frac{2d+1}{k+1} \cdot j + \left(1 - \frac{2d+1}{k+1}\right) \cdot \sum_{m=1}^{2d+1} p \cdot (1-p)^{m-1}(m+j)\right]\right\}$$

Case 2: Succeed in finding an advertisement of the requested Virtual Organisation in the node itself, succeed in contacting the requested Virtual Organisation, but fail in finding a requested content advertisement in the requested Virtual Organisation.

$$E[N(AD\overline{E})] = \frac{2d+1}{k+1}\sum_{j=1}^{2d+1} p \cdot (1-p)^{j-1} \cdot \left(1 - \frac{2d+1}{k+1}\right) \cdot (1-p)^{2d+1} \cdot (2d+1+j)$$

Case 3: Succeed in finding an advertisement of the requested Virtual Organisation in the node itself, but fail in contacting the requested Virtual Organisation.

$$E[N(A\overline{D})] = \frac{2d+1}{k+1}(1-p)^{2d+1}(2d+1)$$

Case 4: Fail in finding an advertisement of the requested Virtual Organisation in the node itself, but succeed in finding an advertisement of the requested Virtual Organisation in the other members, succeed in contacting the requested Virtual Organisation, and succeed in finding a requested content advertisement in the requested Virtual Organisation.

$$\mathrm{E}\left[N\left(\overline{A}BDE\right)\right]=\left(1-\frac{2d+1}{k+1}\right)\sum_{i=1}^{2d+1}\left\{p\cdot(1-p)^{i-1}\cdot\sum_{j=1}^{2d+1}\left[p\cdot(1-p)^{j-1}\cdot\left(\frac{2d+1}{k+1}\cdot(j+i)+\left(1-\frac{2d+1}{k+1}\right)\cdot\sum_{m=1}^{2d+1}p\cdot(1-p)^{m-1}\cdot(m+j+i)\right)\right]\right\}$$

Case 5: Fail in finding an advertisement of the requested Virtual Organisation in the node itself, but succeed in finding an advertisement of the requested Virtual Organisation from the other members, succeed in contacting the requested Virtual Organisation, and fail in finding a requested content advertisement in the requested Virtual Organisation.

$$E\left[N\left(\overline{A}BD\overline{E}\right)\right]=\left(1-\frac{2d+1}{k+1}\right)\sum_{i=1}^{2d+1}\left[p\cdot(1-p)^{i-1}\cdot\sum_{j=1}^{2d+1}p\cdot(1-p)^{j-1}\cdot\left(1-\frac{2d+1}{k+1}\right)\cdot(1-p)^{2d+1}\cdot(2d+1+j+i)\right]$$

Case 6: Fail in finding an advertisement of the requested Virtual Organisation in the node itself, succeed in finding an advertisement of the requested Virtual Organisation from the other members, but fail in contacting the requested Virtual Organisation.

$$E\left[N\left(\overline{A}B\overline{D}\right)\right]=\left(1-\frac{2d+1}{k+1}\right)\sum_{i=1}^{2d+1}p\cdot(1-p)^{i-1}\cdot(1-p)^{2d+1}\cdot(2d+1+i)$$

Case 7: Fail in finding an advertisement of the requested Virtual Organisation either in the node itself or the other members.

$$E\left[N\left(\overline{A}\overline{B}\right)\right]=\left(1-\frac{2d+1}{k+1}\right)\cdot(1-p)^{2d+1}\cdot(2d+1)$$

Hence the expected number of messages is:

$$\mathrm{E}[N]=E\left[N\left(ADE\right)\right]+E\left[N\left(AD\overline{E}\right)\right]+E\left[N\left(A\overline{D}\right)\right]+E\left[N\left(\overline{A}BDE\right)\right]+E\left[N\left(\overline{A}BD\overline{E}\right)\right]+E\left[N\left(\overline{A}B\overline{D}\right)\right]+E\left[N\left(\overline{A}\overline{B}\right)\right]$$

$$=\left(1-\frac{2d+1}{k+1}\right)\left\{\sum_{i=1}^{2d+1}\left\{p\cdot(1-p)^{i-1}\cdot\sum_{j=1}^{2d+1}\left[p\cdot(1-p)^{j-1}\left(\frac{2d+1}{k+1}\cdot(j+i)+\left(1-\frac{2d+1}{k+1}\right)\sum_{m=1}^{2d+1}p\cdot(1-p)^{m-1}\cdot(m+j+i)\right)\right]\right\}\right.$$

$$+\sum_{i=1}^{2d+1}\left[p\cdot(1-p)^{i-1}\sum_{j=1}^{2d+1}p\cdot(1-p)^{j-1}\cdot\left(1-\frac{2d+1}{k+1}\right)\cdot(1-p)^{2d+1}\cdot(2d+1+j+i)\right]$$

$$+\sum_{i=1}^{2d+1}p\cdot(1-p)^{i-1}(1-p)^{2d+1}\cdot(2d+1+i)+(1-p)^{2d+1}\cdot(2d+1)\Big\}$$

$$+\frac{2d+1}{k+1}\left\{\sum_{j=1}^{2d+1}p\cdot(1-p)^{j-1}\left[\frac{2d+1}{k+1}\cdot j+\left(1-\frac{2d+1}{k+1}\right)\cdot\sum_{m=1}^{2d+1}p\cdot(1-p)^{m-1}\cdot(m+j)\right]\right.$$

$$+\sum_{j=1}^{2d+1}p\cdot(1-p)^{j-1}\cdot\left(1-\frac{2d+1}{k+1}\right)\cdot(1-p)^{2d+1}\cdot(2d+1+j)+(1-p)^{2d+1}\cdot(2d+1)\Big\} \qquad (6)$$

Chapter XI
Runtime Service Discovery for Grid Applications

James Dooley
City University, UK

Andrea Zisman
City University, UK

George Spanoudakis
City University, UK

ABSTRACT

This chapter describes a framework to support runtime service discovery for Grid applications based on service discovery queries in both push and pull modes of query execution. The framework supports six different types of trigger conditions that may prompt service replacement during run-time of grid business application, and evaluates the relevance of a set of candidate services against service discovery queries. The chapter also describes the language used to express service discovery queries and the three types of fitness measurement used to evaluate the candidate services against these queries. Both synchronous (pull) and asynchronous (push) mechanisms for service discovery are presented and shown to be complimentary in dealing with all six service discovery trigger conditions. The chapter is illustrated through examples.

INTRODUCTION

Traditionally, grid computing has been a form of distributed computing that is concerned with resource sharing across communications networks.

In this model, individual computers are called nodes and virtualize certain resources such as processor, memory and storage. Other nodes can then access these virtual resources over a network connection. These nodes are physically distributed

Copyright © 2009, IGI Global, distributing in print or electronic forms without written permission of IGI Global is prohibited.

and are usually under the control and ownership of different entities. Examples of controlling entities are: governments, universities, corporations, and businesses. Grids implement models of virtualisation and rely on standard protocols for communication, both of which are captured in a software layer known as middleware.

More recently, Service Oriented Architecture (SOA) has emerged from the IT world in the form of web-services. SOA is an approach to enable a set of loosely coupled functional components to exist and be remotely usable. As opposed to grid computing, the emphasis of SOA is more on how to exchange information which is well defined whilst still being of open standard (as opposed to grid computing that places emphasise on the infrastructure). Foster and Tuecke (2005) capture the description of a service as *"A service is a self-contained implementation of some function(s) with a well defined interface specifying the message exchange patterns used to interact with the function(s)."*

The web-services incarnation, allows a service to exist as a Uniform Resource Locator (URL) to which requests can be sent and responses solicited in both synchronous and asynchronous modes. Over the following four paragraphs we account for some approaches that have been recently proposed to support different areas of SOA. The approaches discussed are concerned with (a) languages to describe services, (b) service discovery, (c) service composition, and (d) service monitoring, validation, verification, and evolution.

Various XML-based languages have been proposed to support descriptions of service components and choreography. Web Services Description Language - WSDL (Christensen et al., 2001) is currently the most used language for service description and supports interface-based definition in terms of input/output signatures. The semantic markup for Web Services - OWL-S (Martin et al., 2004) is an ontology that exists within the web ontology language (OWL) and extends input/output signatures by allowing the

description of pre- and post-conditions to represent value-based restrictions, while Web Services Modelling Ontology - WSMO (Bruijn et al., 2005) provides a language for describing semantic aspects of services. The Business Process Execution Language for Web Services - BPEL4WS (Andrews et al., 2003) is a language that describes observable behaviour of web services by message-flow oriented interface. The Web Service Conversation Language - WSCL, (Banerji et al., 2002) goes beyond description of input/output messages, and defines transitions with associated conditions. More recently, OpenModel Modelling Language - OMML (Hall & Zisman, 2004b) has been proposed to support full behaviour specification of computer-based services.

Different approaches have been proposed to support service discovery. Some semantic match-making approaches have been suggested to support service discovery based on logic reasoning of terminological concept relations represented as ontology's. METEOR-S (Aggarwal et al., 2004) adopts a constraint driven discovery approach in which queries are integrated into a system composition process. In (Horrocks et al., 2003) the discovery of services is addressed by matching queries specified as a variant of description logic with services specified in OWL-S. The work in (Klusch, 2006) extends existing approaches by supporting explicit and implicit semantic by using logic based, approximate matching, and information retrieval techniques. The discovery mechanism in (Hausmann et al., 2004) is based on the use of Resource Description Framework Data Query Language (RDQL) by testing sub-graph relations and establishing whether specification matching relation holds between the query and the service description. The approach in (Horrocks et al., 2003) identifies services that satisfy task requirement properties expressed in temporal logic by using a lightweight reasoning tool. A flexible and modular Web Service Discovery Architecture (WSDA) was introduced in (Hoschek, 2002) where interface queries are checked based on string matching and cannot account for changes in the order of the parameters. In addition, the service selection problem has been proposed as multi-dimensional (Wang et al., 2006) or multi-ontology (Oundhakar et al., 2005) based where matching is performed against more than one service quality. Such qualities include functional, non-functional and quality of service information. In order to increase the precision of the discovery process, some approaches based on the use of behavioural signatures (Shen & Su, 2005) and full behavioural models (Hall & Zisman, 2004a) have been proposed. Similarly, business process matchmaking (Wombacher et al., 2005) has also been proposed that considers the behaviour of a service. A framework that supports run-time service discovery for services that become malfunctioning or unavailable has been proposed in (Spanoudakis et al., 2005). This approach is part of a larger technique for discovery in service-centric system engineering (Jones et al., 2005) that involves requirements-based (Zachos et al., 2006), architecture-time (Kozlenkov et al., 2006), and run-time (Spanoudakis et al., 2005) service discovery.

Work in service composition and orchestration has been proposed in (Albert et al., 2005; Chafle et al., 2005; Courbis & Finkelstein, 2005; Di Penta et al., 2006; Pistore et al., 2005). In (Albert et al., 2005) the authors present a configuration technique for automatic workflow composition. The work in (Pistore et al., 2005) describes a technique for automated synthesis from BPEL4WS processes based on planning and symbolic model checking. The work in (Chafle et al., 2005) and (Courbis & Finkelstein, 2005) are concerned with the orchestration of composite web services. The approach in (Chafle et al., 2005) uses decentralized orchestration based on data flow constraints represented as XML, rule filtering mechanism for topology filtering, and deployment mechanisms to enforce constraints at run time. In (Courbis & Finkelstein, 2005), the authors propose an aspect-based weaving approach to allow service

orchestration evolution. A framework for allowing dynamic binding and re-binding of service composition based on functional and quality constraints is proposed in (Di Penta et al., 2006).

Service monitoring is an important activity for service oriented systems which requires time accurate information about web-services. This proves a problem in the traditional use of web-services which are pull based. This is discussed in (Brenna & Johansen, 2005), where push based communication is used to tackle the problems associated with using a pull based mechanism. The work in monitoring can be classified in three different groups: (a) approaches for event generation and monitoring (Mahbub & Spanoudakis, 2005; Robinson, 2003), (b) formalisms for specifying and verifying requirements to be monitored (Hall & Zisman, 2004c; Robinson, 2003), and (c) mechanisms for adapting systems to avoid further deviations from requirements at run-time (Feather et al., 1998). The generation of events can be executed by using special instrumentation mechanism (Robinson, 2003), or reflective middleware (Capra et al., 2001). There are different ways of representing the requirement to be monitored ranging from the use of proprietary event pattern specification language (Robinson, 2003), linear temporal logic (Hall & Zisman, 2004c), or event calculus (Mahbub & Spanoudakis, 2005). Regarding service validation and verification, in (Baresi et al., 2003), the authors propose run-time validation of consistency of web service composition based on assertion checking of pre-/post-conditions. The work in (Fu et al., 2004) proposes a top down approach for designing and verifying web service compositions with respect to system goals. In (Foster et al., 2004), the authors apply a Labelled Transition System Analyzer (LTSA) tool to check the models of web service compositions based on advanced knowledge of complete static configuration.

Both grid computing and SOA have the same high level property of creating applications that segment and distribute the use of their resources across a number of network peers. Whilst they work to the same high level goal, they have distinct focus on achieving this property. Grid computing is a more integrated framework in which implementations operate in some overlay network. Examples are found in the peer-to-peer form of grid computing such as Napster (Fox, 2001) and Bit-Torrent (Cohen, 2008). These grid implementations have well defined and specific data exchange formats, and focus on dynamic infrastructure. SOA web-services however operate in the more ad-hoc environment of the world-wide-web. In this case, the infrastructure is more rigid and already defined. Moreover, the focus in SOA is on message exchange interfaces. These two techniques are rapidly converging and are currently at a point where the boundaries between them are blurred. (Foster & Tuecke, 2005) argue that people describing either grid computing or SOA are in fact describing the same thing from a different perspective. Both the Open Grid Services Architecture (OGSA) and the Open Grid Gateway initiative (OSGi) have established standards and implementations where grid computing uses services to expose the resources/functionality of the grid node. In fact, the popular international grid organisation ("The Globus Alliance") implements its standards (developed at the open grid forum) in an open source framework called the "Globus Toolkit". This toolkit is a service-oriented grid computing environment that uses SOA standards to achieve service functionality.

Grid and SOA convergence produces an interesting mix where applications can be created as a composition (at least partial if not complete) of distributed functional components. While SOA can achieve this alone (Andrews et al., 2003), the grid can be used to bring different services together. This is analogous to the notion of shops and towns in which shops permit people to enter, browse and buy at will. They can offer these facilities wherever they are situated, but it is not until they are brought together into towns/villages

that they gain the advantages of infrastructure, co-operation, and competition.

It is useful to note that while there is convergence of grid and SOA, they originated from opposite ends of the same model. Grid computing was mainly a product of research, whose goal was to create virtual computers of greater power and reliability than any single computer (bottom-up). In contrast, SOA has emerged from the business world where its primary goal is to streamline business logic to reduce cost and become more agile (top-down). Mary Shacklett (2007) captures the promise of SOA as *"... an effective means of modularizing pieces of business logic that were common to many different business processes so that this logic could be pluggable and reusable...."*

The above promise encapsulates the very strength of SOA, modules can be dynamically included or excluded from applications as and when the functionality is required. The promise is however not as easily realised as early protagonists had hoped. This is because any application that uses a service has an unavoidable dependency for that service. Unfortunately, this dependency on service availability and performance also affects application availability and performance. Obviously this has consequences in business applications, particularly those which require guarantees about their IT systems reliability (such as safety critical systems, or government departments/agencies). Consider for example the situation in which an application retrieves an employee list and then filters the results for all employees that have a certain qualification. The application could be created using an employee service (offered by the human resources department of the company) to retrieve the list. If however that service is performing poorly (due to high use at the time), or even worse is unavailable, we can see that the application will in turn suffer (and may not function at all).

Increasing reliability and performance of SOA systems is thus a major subject for research and development. One such thread of research is into that of dynamic service binding, where an application can change the exact service that is being used in its composition during runtime. The application still gets the same functionality, but a change in source can increase efficiency and reliability. To illustrate this, consider the example in which a sales department of a business wishes to revaluate the credit rating of its customers as part of a six monthly cycle in which it offers credit packages to some selected customers. Clearly, for a large number of customers this process will take a long time. Thus, if a credit rating service on which this grid application relies is not performing very well, or if it fails all-together, then the application will suffer. Dynamic service binding would permit an alternative credit rating service, which performs better, to be located and bound to the grid application that performs customer's evaluation. The subsequent performance and stability of the application would improve, allowing the application to complete in a shorter space of time. More specifically, if the under-performing service is taking 10 minutes to complete a single credit rating and there are 180 customers, the entire set of calculations would take 30 hours. If an alternative service can be found offering even a slightly better performance of 8 minutes per calculation, this application would complete in only 24 hours. Obviously, the larger the difference in performance, the more valuable the change is in terms of application efficiency. From this example it is easy to see how dynamic service binding can increase application performance and reliability. Any application hoping to take advantage of this needs the dynamic ability to:

1. Recognise the conditions that require a change
2. Find appropriate services
3. Compare services to select the *"best"* for an application
4. Perform steps 1,2 and 3 above in an efficient manner so that disruption to application execution is minimised

The above requirements have also been advocated by industrial partners in the areas of telecommunications, automotive software, media and banking in European framework 6 projects focusing on service centric systems engineering (project SeCSE: http://secse.eng.it/) and grid infrastructures (project GREDIA: http://www.gredia.eu/).

In this chapter we present a grid run-time service discovery (GRSD) framework that encapsulates all of the above requirements for enabling dynamic service binding of web-services into applications. The framework to be presented is part of a large programme of research in the area of service oriented computing.

The remainder of this chapter is structured as follows. We start by examining the conditions under which service replacement is necessary for both dependency satisfaction and optimisation. We present runtime service discovery modes of execution and compare them with specific reference to the conditions of service replacement that they satisfy. We continue the chapter by presenting a language to express service discovery requests. These requests are the entry point for the runtime service discovery framework. We also present the main components of the GRSD framework and the technique used to compare candidate services against service requests (fitness matching) We finalise the chapter with a conclusion of the material discussed and some directions for future work.

CONDITIONS FOR SERVICE REPLACEMENT

Services offer different types of functionality to their networked environment. Applications are created based on the composition of these services. Each service is included in an application to fulfil some functional requirement of an application that requires specific services to be bound to the application. This binding of services into applications can happen when one of the following abstract service replacement conditions occurs:

- **SRC-1. Initialisation:** A certain service functionality is required by an application, but no service has been previously bound,
- **SRC-2. Replacement:** A currently bound service being used by an applications fails or becomes malfunctioning,
- **SRC-3. Optimisation:** A currently bound service being used by an application can be replaced by a service that better fits the application requirements.

It should be noted that when SRC-3 occurs, the new "better" service SHOULD replace the currently bound service in the application. This is to ensure the application will run in an optimal way. When SRC-1 or SRC-2 occur, however, a service MUST be found and bound to an application in order for the application to be able to function correctly and continue its execution.

The exact trigger conditions which prompt run-time service discovery are discussed below. Each condition is assigned a unique reference label (of the form "TCX", where X is the trigger condition number) and has a brief description. These conditions are:

- **TC1. Application initialisation:** A component service that implements a certain required functionality of an application must be found and bound to the application for the first time (i.e. there is no bound service to replace). This is typically at application initialisation time, but can also occur at any time in the application life-cycle (for example when a previously disabled function becomes enabled or when an application evolves to support other functionalities). This can especially occur if the application uses a *"bind on-demand"* policy where the component is not bound until it is needed.

- **TC2. Service failure/malfunction:** The currently bound service being used by an application fails or malfunctions. This requires a new service to be found and bound to ensure correct application execution. This condition is an unfortunate property of distributed computing models such as SOA/Grid where services and communications with these services are outside the control of the application.
- **TC3. Unspecified application event:** Any application event that leads to a service discovery. For example, the event in which a user selects an item from a menu of options such as "change service").
- **TC4. New candidate service:** A new service becomes available in service registries, which could be a better match to the applications requirements than a currently bound service.
- **TC5. Application context change:** The context in which an application is running changes. This change of an application context can either cause a currently bound service not to be relevant to the application any more (e.g., services that are specific to a certain location), or to cause the application not to be executed in its optimal efficiency (there is another service that better matches the application requirements).
- **TC6. Candidate service characteristic change:** The characteristics of a service change. This may change which service

Table 1. Relationships between service replacement conditions and trigger conditions

Mode	Trigger Condition					
	TC1	TC2	TC3	TC4	TC5	TC6
SRC-1	X	--	X	--	--	--
SRC-2	--	X	--	--	--	--
SRC-3	--	--	X	X	X	X

best satisfies the application requirements, in turn prompting the application to change the service it is using. These characteristics of the services that may change are:

1. **Structural:** The operation signatures (names, parameters and return data) that a service exposes.
2. **Behavioural:** The functional characteristics of a service in terms of the order in which service operations are executed.
3. **Non-Functional:** Quality characteristics of a service.
4. **Context changes:** Quality characteristics of a service that change dynamically.

Table 1 summarises the relationships between the service replacement conditions above (SRC-1, SRC-2, SRC-3) and the trigger conditions (TC1 to TC6). A failure to account for **TC1** or **TC2** will compromise application reliability (i.e., at best, a function will not be available; at worst, the application will fail totally). Whilst failing to account for **TC3-6** will compromise application performance (i.e., although performance may still be within acceptable levels, it will not be optimal).

In order to illustrate, consider the example in Figure 1 about a service-based application that allows users to watch videos on hand-set PDAs. This example examines an application from start time and references the conditions by label where necessary. You will notice that this example deliberately avoids exact mechanisms (they are discussed later in this chapter) and only provides an overview of the desired runtime service discovery behaviour.

Figure 1. An example scenario

Fred is travelling from London to Paris and doesn't want to miss an important football match in which his team is playing. Fortunately he has a PDA (we assume that his internet access is constant by some mechanism) equipped with a service-based application for watching video and listening to commentary from different web-service sources. When he starts the application, an initial commentary service needs to be found (**TC1**), the application contacts the pre-set RSD framework which responds with an appropriate service. After some time of enjoying the game, the commentary service fails (**TC2**). In this case, the application reacts by automatically using the RSD framework to acquire a replacement service. Soon after the replacement service is identified and starts to provide commentary to Fred, he realises that this commentary is being given by an individual that Fred dislikes. Fred decides to manually request (**TC3**) a replacement commentary service. The replacement is found and bound to the application, allowing Fred to settle and s into enjoying his game with adequate commentary again.

A few minutes later, a new service becomes available (**TC4**) which the RSD framework recognises and evaluates it as "better" according to Fred's criteria (the commentator is Fred's all time favourite player). The commentary service in the application is switched to this new one and Fred smiles with agreement on the commentary. Fred is now crossing into France (**TC5**), where he is now being charged for the service he is using. The RSD framework matches his new context (location=France) to a commentary that is cheaper (and is still in English) for him to use.

Whilst waiting to start the next leg of his journey, a competing service slashes its prices and offers the service for free (**TC6**). The RSD framework recognises this service context change and calculates that this service is better for Fred to use (it is free!). Fred's application binds this service to the application and Fred uses it which he enjoys until the end of the game (his team wins 5-0!).

SERVICE DISCOVERY MODES

As illustrated in Figure 1, the trigger conditions described above require the GRSD framework to identify services for the application. In some situations, the replacement services can be identified in *pull* mode of execution, in which the application requests the GRSD framework to discovery services in a synchronous way. In other situations, the replacement services need to be identified in *push* mode of execution, in which asynchronous notifications are sent to the application from the GRSD framework.

More specifically, trigger conditions **TC1**, **TC2** and **TC3** (and sometimes **TC5**) lie within the scope of an application and can be recognised by the application. These trigger conditions require an immediate response (i.e., identified services) in order for the application to resume execution. In the case of trigger conditions **TC3** and **TC5**, a new service is required to support optimisation of application execution. These conditions are performed in *pull* mode of execution, as shown in Figure 2.

Conversely, trigger conditions **TC4**, **TC6** (and sometimes **TC5**) can not be recognised from within the application and are recognised by some external entity. Therefore, the run-time service discovery process must also be initiated externally with respect to the application. In this case, an application subscribes service requests to the GRSD framework . When these trigger conditions occur, the subscribed requests are examined and relevant results are *pushed* to the application in an asynchronous manner, as shown in Figure 3.

In general, the pull mode of execution is largely concerned with guaranteeing that an application can run by satisfying service dependencies and in turn fulfilling the functional requirements of that application. In contrast, the push mode of execution is mainly concerned with providing a better alternative to a currently bound service; therefore it is an optimisation mechanism for the application. This is reflected by the fact that a pull mode is a single-response mechanism (after the response is sent, no further messages are exchanged with respect to a query), while a push mode is a repetitive multi-response mechanism (after a notification is sent, another may be sent to reflect new trigger conditions).

Table 2 summarises the relationships between trigger conditions **TC1-TC6** and the push and pull modes of service discovery execution together with the number of response mechanisms (response count). As shown in Table 2, both pull and push modes of execution are necessary to cope with all the six trigger conditions. In addition, neither pull nor push modes can cope with all trigger conditions on their own. The push mode

Figure 2. Pull mode of service discovery execution

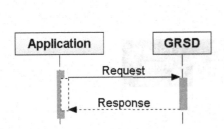

Figure 3. Push mode of service discovery execution

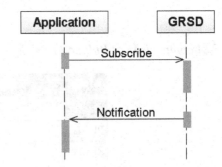

of execution has higher complexity and requires the use of monitors to provide notifications to the framework about the trigger conditions **TC4**, **TC5** and **TC6**. In order to support this situation, it is necessary to have mechanisms of managing subscriptions (including removing dead subscriptions and updating subscriptions on lease expiry) and keeping track of which subscriptions apply to which queries. In the framework, we use the WS-Eventing model (Box et al., 2006) to support these subscriptions and notifications.

SERVICE REQUEST LANGUAGE

For either of the two modes of service discovery execution, it is necessary to submit a service discovery request to the GRSD framework. In the case of pull mode of execution, the request is answered immediately. In the case of push mode of execution, the requests are subscribed, and the results are asynchronous. These asynchronous results may occur at any time until the application cancels the request or it expires.

The service discovery requests are matched against different types of service specifications represented as facets. These facets specify different aspects of the services such as (1) structural describing the operations of a services with their data types using WSDL, (2) behavioural, describing behavioural models of services in BPEL, (3) quality of service, represented in XML-based schema, (4) context information for a service and its location represented in XML-based ontologies, as well as (5) general information about a service.

A service discovery request is composed of several items of information necessary for the framework to find appropriate services for the application based on structural, behavioural, quality, and contextual characteristics of the applications and services to be replaced. More specifically, the items that are required in both pull and push modes are:

- **SDR-1. Mode.** The mode of runtime service discovery being requested (either PULL or PUSH).
- **SDR-2. Structural requirements.** A description of the required service in terms of its operations and the data types involved in calling those operations. In the framework these are expressed using WSDL (Christensen et al., 2001).
- **SDR-3. Behavioural requirements.** A description of the application behaviour to which a service must be able to conform representing the order in which the service operations are executed. In the framework these are expressed using BPEL (Andrews et al., 2003) workflows.
- **SDR-4. Hard constraints.** A description of extra structural, behavioural, or quality characteristics of a service that must be satisfied for a service to be considered as a candidate for the respective application. These are expressed using a proprietary constraint service query language C-SQL.

Table 2. A comparison of Pull and Push RSD modes

Mode	Trigger Condition						Response Count
	TC1	TC2	TC3	TC4	TC5	TC6	
PULL	X	X	X	--	X	--	1
PUSH	--	--	--	X	X	X	1..N

- **SDR-5. Soft constraints.** A description of extra structural, behavioural, or quality characteristics of a service that are used to rank candidate services. These constraints support the framework's ability to compare candidate services against each other and rank them as better or worse for a specific application. These are expressed using a proprietary constraint service query language C-SQL.

- **SDR-6. Context constraints.** A description of contextual characteristics of a service or application environment to which a service needs to conform. These are expressed using a proprietary context-aware service query language CA-SQL (Spanoudakis et al., 2007).

In addition, the push mode of execution also requires:

- **SDR-7. Push endpoint.** The URL of the application to which the framework can send asynchronous notifications. These notifica-

tions are sent to indicate that the application should change the service it is using.

In order to support the description of constraints (soft, hard, and contextual) we have developed two XML-based languages, namely C-SQL and CA-SQL, respectively, as mentioned above. We describe these two languages below.

The C-SQL (constraint service query language), which is used for specifying hard and soft constraints, relies on the ability to examine information held about a service in the service registry. This information is captured as named 'facets' and covers high level areas such as signature, behaviour, quality of service, provider, and context. Each facet is XML formatted and validated against an XML schema.

Figure 4 shows part of the XML schema for C-SQL. As shown in the figure, a constraint query is defined as a single logical expression or a sequence of logical expressions combined by logical operators. Each logical expression is evaluated to TRUE or FALSE, and can be additionally negated. The supported logical opera-

Figure 4. The C-SQL Constraint query

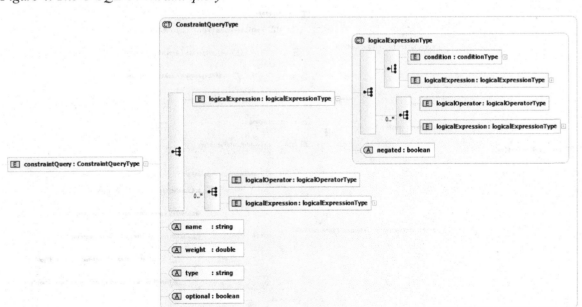

tors are AND and OR, to reflect conjunction and disjunction respectively. Furthermore a logical expression can either be an atomic condition, or a composition of sub-conditions, this support allows an unambiguous specification for the order of evaluation. For example the logical combination "(C1 AND C2) OR C3", is described as a disjunction of the conditions "C1 AND C2" and "C3". Each atomic condition consists of two operands (O1 and O2) with a relation between them. The supported relations are:

- **Equal-To:** This is TRUE when O1 and O2 have the same value.
- **Not-Equal-To:** This is TRUE when O1 and O2 do not have the same value.
- **Less-Than:** This is TRUE when the value of O1 is less than the value of O2.
- **Greater-Than:** This is TRUE when the value of O1 is greater than the value of O2.
- **Less-Than-Equal-To:** This is TRUE when the value of O1 is less than or equal to the value of O2.

- **Greater-Than-Equal-To:** This is TRUE when the value of O1 is greater than or equal to the value of O2.

As shown in Figure 5, the operands O1 and O2 can be either:

- **Arithmetic expressions:** These are used to express computations over values of service facet elements. These consist of two operands with an arithmetic operator between them, the supported operators are plus, minus, multiply and divide. The source values are embedded and derived from service facets using query operands (discussed below). Furthermore, arithmetic expressions can be atomic, or a composition of other arithmetic expressions.
- **Constants:** These are fixed values which can be used to evaluate against.
- **Query operands:** These specify the source of the value for comparison. This is given as an XPath expression (Berglund et al., 2007;

Figure 5. C-SQL operand types

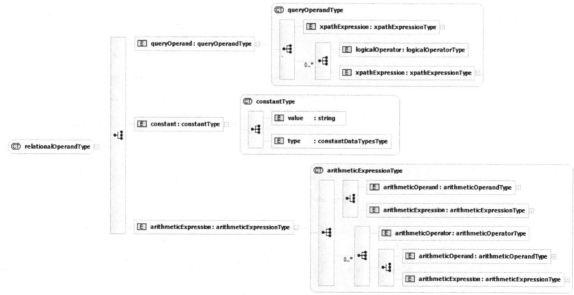

Clark & DeRose, 1999) to directly reference certain XML elements of a service facet.

An example of a hard constraint is given in Figure 6. This example is concerned with the identification of services that offer football commentary in English and costs a pound or less. The service information regarding these two properties

are represented in facets called *Provision* and *Commerce* respectively. The query is structured as a conjunction of two logical expressions, the first examines service cost and the second examines the language of the commentator that the service delivers. The first expression compares a query operand against a constant in a "less than or equal to" evaluation, where operand1 retrieves

Figure 6. An example hard constraint

```xml
<normalQuery name=" £1 Football commentary" weight="1.0" type="hard" optional="false">
  <logicalExpression>
    <condition negated="false">
      <lessThanEqualTo>
        <operand1>
          <queryOperand>
            <xpathExpression>
              <facet>
                <name>Commerce</name>
                <type>Commerce</type>
              </facet>
              <xpath>
                //SportsCostings/GameCost/[GameTypeCostName = "Single Usage Cost"]/CostValue
              </xpath>
            </xpathExpression>
          </queryOperand>
        </operand1>
        <operand2>
          <constant>
            <value>1</value>
            <type>NUMERICAL</type>
          </constant>
        </operand2>
      </lessThanEqualTo>
    </condition>
  </logicalExpression>
  <logicalOperator>and</logicalOperator>
  <logicalExpression>
    <condition negated="false">
      <equalTo>
        <operand1>
          <queryOperand>
            <xpathExpression>
              <facet>
                <name>Provision</name>
                <type>Provision</type>
              </facet>
              <xpath>
                //Provision/Commentator/Language
              </xpath>
            </xpathExpression>
          </queryOperand>
        </operand1>
        <operand2>
          <constant>
            <value>English</value>
            <type>STRING</type>
          </constant>
        </operand2>
      </equalTo>
    </condition>
  </logicalExpression>
</normalQuery>
```

the service information located at the given XPath in its commerce facet. If the value in the facet was for example 0.50 (50 pence), the condition would evaluate to true as 0.50 is less than the constant specified which is 1. The second expression compares a query operand against a constant in an "equal-to" evaluation. Operand1 retrieves the service information located at the given XPath in its provision facet, this is known to be the language of the commentator. This value is compared against the string constant in Operand2, only if the two match will the condition pass.

It should be noted that in the root element of this XML snippet, there are attributes for name, weight, type and optional. The name allows this query to be described/named while weighting can take a value [0..1] and is used in the fitness matching algorithm to determine how important this query is. The type attribute allows the constraint to be classed as hard or soft. The optional flag is a Boolean (TRUE or FALSE) and is used to cope for situations where a service does not have facets of a required type. Any service that does not have a required facet when the optional flag is set to TRUE will be ignored, while when the flag is FALSE the service will still be checked.

The CA-SQL (context aware service query language), is used to specify contextual constraints. This language is similar to C-SQL with two main differences. The first difference is concerned with the use of weight and type attributes, in CA-SQL neither of these exist. The second difference is

concerned with the use of context operands (see Figure 7) instead of query operands. A context operand represents operations that will provide context information at runtime. More specifically, a context operand describes the *semantic category* of context operations instead of the signature of the operation. This is due to the fact that context operations may have different signatures across different services. The context operands are composed of:

- The service identity (within the registry)
- The name of the operation that should be called to get the precise values at that time.
- The context category conditions that are captured using XPath to refer to either the service facet document or the ontology that is used to describe the context service operations.

The XPath expressions that make up these operands are comparable in the same way as the logical operands that make up the query. This is done using the same logical operators equal-to, not-equal-to, less-than, greater-than, less-than-equal-to, greater-than-equal-to. In addition, the operands of these logical operations can also be constants for comparing service context data against. An example context query is shown in Figure 8, in this example the service location is compared against a constant. This is achieved

Figure 7. The Context Operand

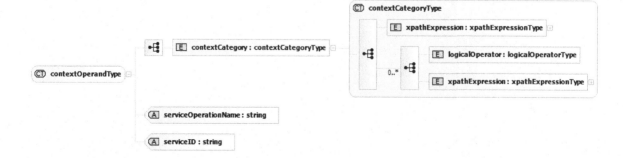

by the operation "sendSMS" of service "SMS-Service-1" in operand1 being invoked and the return data interpreted according to the referenced ontology data type. The ontology in question is an extended CoDAMoS (http://www.cs.kuleuven.be/cwis/research/distrinet/projects/CoDAMoS/) ontology, and the data type from that ontology is "SECSELocation". For this condition to pass, the value retrieved from the service operation must equal the content of operand2 which is a longitude-latitude geographic location.

RUN-TIME SERVICE DISCOVERY FRAMEWORK

Web service technology is based on the *"publish-find-bind"* model shown in Figure 9 (adapted from Booth et al., 2004; Cervantes & Hall, 2003; Dustdar & Schreiner, 2005; Pilioura et al., 2003; Ran, 2003). In this model, service providers publish service location and descriptions into a registry, a client application finds services in the registry and binds these service into it.

Our GRSD framework builds on this model and permits a client application to use the grid run-time service discovery framework to handle the "find" functionality of the model. Our framework also extends the model by the use of both push and pull modes of execution.

The grid run-time service discovery framework is composed of five main components as described below and shown in Figure 10.

- **Service Requestor:** This component orchestrates the discovery process and maintains necessary information to execute push service discovery modes (e.g., subscribed service requests). It interacts with the matchmaker and controls matchmaker invocation based on the various trigger conditions.

Figure 8. An example Context Query

```
<contextQuery name="ContextQuery1" optional="true">
  <logicalExpression negated="false">
    <condition negated="false">
      <equalTo>
        <operand1>
          <contextOperand serviceID="SMS-Service-1" serviceOperationName="sendSMS">
            <contextCategory>
              <xpathExpression>
                <equalTo>
                  <qualifiedXpath>
                    <ontology>
                      http://localhost:8082/ontology/CoDAMoS_Extended.xml
                    </ontology>
                    <xpath>string(/owl:Class/@rdf:ID)</xpath>
                  </qualifiedXpath>

                  <constant>SECSELocation</constant>
                </equalTo>
              </xpathExpression>
            </contextCategory>
          </contextOperand>
        </operand1>

        <operand2>
          <constant dataType="STRING">LOC-LONG-100:LOC-LATIT-200</constant>
        </operand2>
      </equalTo>
    </condition>
  </logicalExpression>
</contextQuery>
```

- **Monitors:** These components provide asynchronous notifications to the service requestor about context changes (Application and Service Context monitor components) or service characteristic changes (Service characteristic monitor component).

- **Matchmaker:** This component is responsible for the identification of services against requests. It accepts a query from the service requestor and evaluates the query against the search space. Upon completion of this evaluation, it returns an ordered set of candidate services that fulfil the query. The ordering of the set is determined by the fitness measure (discussed in the "Fitness Matching" section of this chapter) and is largely determined by the presence of soft constraints in the query. The ordering is necessary to cope with the situations in which there are more than one compatible candidate service as illustrated below:

  > Let the set of candidate services returned by the matchmaker be CS, where CS = {S1, S2, S3, S4}
  >
  > All members of CS are functionally compatible with the requirements and hard constraints of the query against

which they were selected. The requesting application APP1 only requires one service. If CS is unordered, the selection would need to be random and no guarantee that this is the best for the job. As CS is ordered (i.e. for any member X, any member Y preceding it is "better" according to the soft constraints), the service that APP1 SHOULD select for binding is S1, there is however no way of enforcing that this MUST be the binding that APP1 makes (indeed, every application should be free to choose using its own mechanisms that its implementers see fit).

- **Service Registry Intermediary:** This component supports parallel searches of multiple service registries. It is basically a multiplexor which frees the matchmaker from maintaining multiple registry associations. It also provides logical segmentation for possible future work.

- **Service Registry:** This component stores information of services. It is essentially a database (the back-end of our project registries are actually XML databases) which has a specific interface for the storage and

Figure 9. The publish-find-bind model

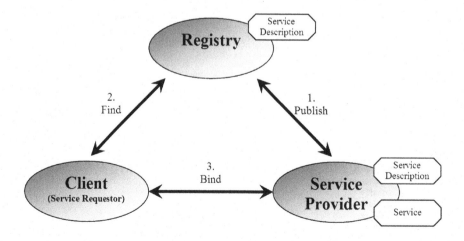

Figure 10. The main components of RSD

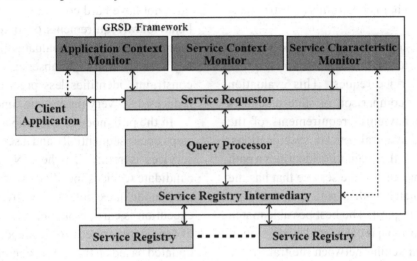

retrieval of certain service specifications. It is the responsibility of service providers to populate these registries with information about their services.

FITNESS MATCHING

The grid run-time service discovery framework needs to compare service discovery requests against specifications of candidate services within service registries. We call this process *"Fitness Matching"* as it evaluates how fit an individual candidate service is for inclusion in the requesting application (based on the service discovery request). The process is handled exclusively by the matchmaker component, which identifies a set of services held in known service registries. Fitness matching is a multi-step process, with each step providing a logical reduction in the search space for the next step. In this section, we discuss fitness matching for all five criteria that can be used in a service request, namely structural, behavioural, hard constraints, soft constraints, and context constraints). In our framework, the fitness matching between service requests and service speci-

fications is based on the computation of distance measures between the requests and services. The exact algorithms for the calculation of the fitness matching and the computation of the distance measures is beyond the scope of this chapter and is described in (Zisman et al., 2008).

In the first step of the fitness matching process, services in the registries are evaluated against hard constraints in a request, where each service can either pass or fail. This requires the matchmaker to request the registry intermediary component to get the services from the known registries. The services that comply with the hard constraints form a set of candidate services (CS) that will be used in the second step of the process.

In the second step of the process, the services in set CS are evaluated against structural requirements of the service request. This is done using an extension of the graph comparison VF2 (Cordella et al., 2004) algorithm that compares the signatures of the service operations with the signatures of the operations in the service discovery request. Furthermore, the operation names and parameters undergo lexical analysis, the results of which are combined with the results of the modified VF2 algorithm. The services in CS that fail the match are removed from the set leaving only services that have passed both hard constraints and structural requirements.

In the third step of the process, the services in CS are evaluated against behavioural requirements of the service request. This evaluation is based on the comparison of state machines representing behavioural requirements of the request and behavioural service specifications. More specifically, the evaluation identifies a path p in the state machine of the service that has the best possible match with a path q in the state machine of the request. The best possible match between paths p and q is calculated by the sum of the structural matching between the transitions in p and q. The transitions in p and q represent the operations in the service and request. Like structural matching, the services that fail the behavioural matching are removed from CS. After this stage, CS has candidate services that match the hard constraints, structural requirements, and behavioural requirements of a request.

In the fourth stage of the process, the services in CS are evaluated against the soft constraints of a request. The soft constraints are used to rank the candidate services, depending on the weights of the constraints in a request. At the end of this stage, the CS set is ordered according to the soft constraints and contains only the services that have passed hard constraints, structural requirements and behavioural requirements.

In the fifth stage of the process, the services in CS are evaluated against context constraints of the service request. This evaluation is based on information obtained as a result of invoking context service operations. The services in the set that match the context constraints of the request are added to a final set of candidate services (US). At the end of this stage the US set contains only services that have passed hard constraints, structural requirements, behavioural requirements and context constraints. The US set preserves the soft constraint ordering that exists in the CS set.

It should be noted that if the service request does not have hard constraints, soft constraints, behavioural requirements, or context constraints, the respective step that evaluates these constraints are not executed. The absence of any of these constraints identifies less precise services, but reduces discovery processing time.

In the pull mode of execution, the above five steps occur sequentially and a set of N candidate services is returned (where N is a number of candidate services specified in the request). In the push mode of execution, initially, a pull mode of execution is carried out and the sets CS and US of candidate services are retained. These sets are updated based on the trigger conditions related to the push mode of execution, as described below. This is necessary to avoid a complete fitness matching process every time a trigger condition is prompted.

- **TC4: New service availability.** The new service is evaluated against hard constraints, structural requirements, behavioural requirements, and soft constraints of a request. If the service matches these constraints, it is inserted into CS in the correct order and evaluated against context constraints. If the service matches the context constraints, it is also inserted into US. If this service is the first element in set US, this new service fits the request better than the current service being used by the application and it is pushed to the application.
- **TC5: Application context change.** In this case, all candidate services in set CS are evaluated against context constraints, and a new set US is generated. The first element in this set is pushed to the application.
- **TC6: Candidate service characteristic change.** If the service to which the change refers is a member of CS, it has its context recalculated against the query. If it fails and was previously a member of US as well, it is

removed from US. If it passes it is inserted into US at the correct rank (or moved to that rank if it was previously a member of US). If the top position in the ordered set US is changed (added or removed), the new top ranking candidate is pushed to the requesting application.

FUTURE TRENDS

Runtime service discovery (RSD) is a flexible mechanism that relies on correctly expressed queries. This is intended to automate the task of human decision making to select the services which an application uses. These queries do not currently take into account business level policies or the change thereof. Such policies are required to guide both service selection and the conditions under which service replacement should be initiated (for example, should a "prefer one I used before" policy, or a "use a different one every month" policy be used). The alignment between these policies and the services which are selected for business applications is a subject of future work. This is further reinforced by work of service level agreements (SLA) such as (Czjkowski et al., 2002; Jin & Wu, 2005; Lamanna et al., 2003) where service producers and consumers agree on what a service is contractually committed to do.

Both grid and SOA are set to continue deployment in the business place where applications will be composed to solve specific problems. This is reflected in the *"internet of services"* vision that the *"Web 2.0"* (O'Reilly, 2005) concept is aiming to enable. With an increase in the number of web services available due to both business and web deployments, the need for and ability of dynamic binding is also set to increase. This places a heavy requirement on the decision processes involved in selecting and engaging services, RSD is set to play a leading role in this decision making process. Furthermore, RSD should be scalable from corporate intranets to mobile devices whose

applications require service selection. This is primarily the focus of making RSD "embeddable" within applications.

While current RSD is performed against atomic services and the application assumes that all operations are registered to a single service, future work is required to bring the concept of run-time composition to reality. This is where the RSD framework could take a query and find component services that can be bound together into a composite service which satisfies the query requirements (something that any of the components can not do alone). Although the problem is easy to define in terms of required functionality, performing evaluation against all possible combinations in an efficient manor is complex and considered a combinatorial optimisation problem.

The recently (March 2008) formed S-Cube project (http://www.s-cube-network.eu/) which is part of the European Unions Seventh Framework Programme, is tasked with establishing a multi-disciplinary research community for future work in service computing. This is aimed at both research and industry, including the education and training in relevant technologies.

CONCLUSION

The computing world is beginning to see real implementations of grid software outside the research labs. These implementations are fulfilling the promises of previous models such as utility computing (envisioned by John McCarthy), which were made over half a century ago.

Grid applications that wish to exploit these distributed services must however be prepared to cope with the circumstances under which optimisation and indeed availability are threatened. By optimisation here, we refer to the reduction in application cost that can be obtained by using a less costly component. In this context, cost can be measured using one of many metrics that has priority for that application, for example some applications may make it a priority to reduce monetary cost, while others may make it a priority to reduce execution-time or resource use. These problems are partially reduced through the use of *"Dynamic Binding"*, but still manifest. We have accounted for six such circumstances and formalised them into *"trigger conditions" (TC1-6)* which must be observed and dealt with autonomously within computing software. This is achieved through the use of *"Runtime Service Discovery"* (RSD) as a mechanism for selecting services for applications where those services match the application requirements.

This chapter has accounted for the general architecture required, interaction of the main components and the modes of RSD necessary to cope with all six trigger conditions. We have explored the RSD process as client initiated with a detailed query including all information (structural, behavioural, context and constraint) necessary to make a correct service selection. We have followed this query into the framework where it undergoes a multi-stage execution and returns the result or holds on to the query for externally recognised trigger conditions. The search space S, the compatible service set CS and the usable service set US are accounted for through the RSD process where they play a critical role in calculating *"fitness measure"*.

The whole process of RSD (both in PULL and PUSH modes) allow client applications to select component services from those currently available in the applications scope of execution. It promotes service redundancy (more services available than are in actual use at any one time) to provide a search space of candidate services. But most importantly, it takes advantage of service redundancy to select the best services for an applications purpose, thus optimising that application at (and throughout) runtime.

Our group promotes the use of RSD in grid applications as a key method of service selection and application optimisation. An application, its users and its creators can take advantage of RSD to enforce preferences, policies and legal requirements against both functional and non-functional properties of candidate services.

The described RSD framework extends the traditional publish-find-bind model used in grid computing and permits more precise and persistent (in the case of PUSH) find operations to be conducted. The framework described here reflects the current state of our research, possible future extensions to which are focused around expressiveness and efficiency. In terms of expressiveness, we are examining the use of a behavioural language which will permit more precise descriptions of operations. From the perspective of efficiency, there are a wide number of optimisations which could be implemented. We however see research into efficient context monitoring a priority if context aware service discovery of the type required for mobile applications is to be realised.

ACKNOWLEDGMENT

The work reported in this chapter has been funded by the European Commission under the Information Society Technologies Programme as part of the project and GREDIA (contract FP6-34363).

REFERENCES

Aggarwal, R., Verma, K., Miller, J., & Milnor, W. (2004). Constraint Driven Web Service Composition in METEOR-S. *International Conference on Services Computing (SCC 2004)* (pp. 23-30).

Albert, P., Henocque, L., & Kleiner, M. (2005). Configuration-Based Workflow Composition. In *Proceedings of the IEEE International Conference on Web Services (ICWS 2005)*, USA. (pp. 285-292).

Andrews, T., Curbera, F., Dholakia, H., Goland, Y., Klein, J., Leymann, F., Liu, K., Roller, D., Smith,

D., Thatte, S., Trickovic, I., & Weerawarana, S. (2003). *Business process Execution language for Web Services (BPEL4WS) 1.1*. IBM DeveloperWorks. Retrieved on March 25, 2008, from http://download.boulder.ibm.com/ibmdl/pub/software/dw/specs/ws-bpel/ws-bpel.pdf

Banerji, A., Bartolini, C., Beringer, D., Chopella, V., Govindarajan, K., Karp, A., Kuno, H., Lemon, M., Pogossiants, G., Sharma, S., & Williams, S. (2002). *Web Services Conversation Language (WSCL) 1.0*. W3C Technical Reports and Publications. Retrieved on March 25, 2008, from http://www.w3.org/TR/wscl10/

Baresi, L., DiNitto, E., & Ghezzi, C. (2003). Inconsistency and Ephemerality in a World of e-Services. In *Proceedings of the 2003 Workshop on Requirements Engineering for Open Systems*, in conjunction with the *11th IEEE International Requirements Engineering Conference*, 2003.

Booth, D., Haas, H., McCabe, F., Newcomer, E., Champion, M., Ferris, C., & Orchard, D. (2004). *Web Services Architecture*. W3 Technical Reports and Publications. Retrieved March 4, 2008, from http://www.w3.org/TR/ws-arch/

Box, D., Cabrera, L. F., Critchley, C., Curbera, F., Ferguson, D., Graham, S., Hull, D., Kakivaya, G., Lewis, A., Lovering, B., Niblett, P., Orchard, D., Samdarshi, S., Schlimmer, J., Sedukhin, I., Shewchuk, J., Weerawarana, S., & Wortendyke, D. (2006). *Web Services*

Eventing (WS-Eventing). W3C Member Submissions. Retrieved on March 25, 2008, from http://www.w3.org/Submission/WS-Eventing/

Brenna, L., & Johansen, D. (2005). Engineering Push-based Web Services. *International Journal of Web Services Practices, 1*(1-2). (pp. 89-100).

Bruijn, J., Bussler, C., Domingue, J., Fensel, D., Hepp, M., Keller, U., Kifer, M., Konig-Ries, B., Kopecky, J., Lara, R., Lausen, H., Oren, E., Polleres, A., Roman, D., Scicluna, J., & Stollberg, M.

(2005). *Web Service Modeling Ontology (WSMO)*. W3C Member Submissions. Retrieved on March 25, 2008, from http://www.w3.org/Submission/WSMO/

Berglund, A., Boag, S., Chamberlin, D., Fernández, M. F., Kay M., Robie J., & Siméon, J. (2007). *XML Path Language (XPath) 2.0*. W3C Technical Reports and Publications. Retrieved on March 25, 2008, from http://www.w3.org/TR/xpath20/

Capra, L., et al. (2001). Reflective Middleware Solutions for Context-Aware Applications. In *Lecture Notes in Computer Science 2192, Proceedings of the Third International Conference on Metalevel Architectures and Separation of Crosscutting Concerns* (pp. 126-133).

Cervantes, H., & Hall, R. S. (2003). *Automating Service Dependency Management in a Service-Oriented Component Model*. Paper presented at 6th International Conference on Software Engineering (ICSE) Workshop on Component-Based Software Engineering: Automated Reasoning and Prediction (ICSE CBSE6), May 2003, Portland, USA.

Chafle, G., Chandra, S., Mann, V., & Nanda, M. G. (2005). Orchestrating Composite Web Services Under Data Flow Constraints. In *Proceedings of the IEEE International Conference on Web Services (ICWS 2005)*, USA (pp. 211-218).

Christensen, E., Curbera, F., Meredith, G., & Weerawarana, S. (2001). *Web Services Description Language (WSDL) 1.1*. W3C Technical Reports and Publications. Retrieved on March 25, 2008, from http://www.w3.org/TR/wsdl/

Czajkowski, K., Foster, I., Kesselman, C., Sander, V., & Tuecke, S. (2002). SNAP: A Protocol for Negotiating Service Level Agreements and Coordinating Resource Management in Distributed Systems. In *8th Workshop on Job Scheduling Strategies for Parallel Processing* (pp. 153-183).

Clark, J., & DeRose, S. (1999). *XML Path Language (XPath)*. W3C Technical Reports and Publications. Retrieved on March 25, 2008, from http://www.w3.org/TR/xpath/

Cohen, B. (2008). *The BitTorrent Protocol Specification*. Online specification. Retrieved on June 25, 2008, from http://www.bittorrent.org/beps/bep_0003.html

Cordella, L. P., Foggia, P., Sansone, C., Vento, M. (2004). A (Sub)Graph Isomorphism Algorithm for Matching Large Graphs. *IEEE Transactions on Pattern Analysis and Machine Intelligence, 26*(10), 1367-1372.

Courbis, C., & Finkelstein, A. (2005). Weaving Aspects into Web Service Orchestration. In *Proceedings of the IEEE International Conference on Web Services (ICWS 2005)*, USA (pp. 219-226).

Di Penta, M., Esposito, R., Villani, M. L., Codato, R., Colombo, M., & Di Nitto, E. (2006). WS Binder: a Framework to enable Dynamic Binding of Composite Web Services. In *International Workshop of Service Oriented Software Engineering (IW-SOSE 2006), Shanghai* (pp. 74-80).

Dustdar, S., & Schreiner, W. (2005). A survey on web services compositions. *International Journal Web and Grid Services, 1*(1), 1-30.

Feather, M. S., et al. (1998). Reconciling System Requirements and Runtime Behaviour. *Proceedings of Ninth International Workshop on Software Specification & Design* (pp. 50-59).

Foster, H., Uchitel, S., Magee, J., & Kramer, J. (2004). Compatibility Verification for Web Service Choreography. In *Proceedings of the IEEE International Conference on Web Services (ICWS 2004)* (pp. 738-741).

Foster, I., & Tuecke, S. (2005). Describing the elephant: The different faces of IT as service. *Queue, ACM Enterprise Distributed Computing 3*(6) (July/August 2005), 30.

Fox, G. (2001). Peer-to-Peer Networks. *Computing in science and engineering, 3*(3), 75-77.

Fu, X., Bultan, T., & Su, J. (2004). Conversation Protocols: A Formalism for Specification and Verification of Reactive Electronic Services. *Theoretical Computer Science (TCS), 328*(1-2), 19-37.

Hall, R. J., & Zisman, A. (2004a). Behavioral Models as Service Descriptions. In *Proceedings of the 2nd International Conference on Service oriented computing, (ICSOC 2004)*, New York (pp. 163-172).

Hall, R. J., & Zisman, A. (2004b). OMML: A Behavioural Model Interchange Format. In *International Conference in Requirements Engineering*, Japan (pp. 272-282).

Hall, R. J., & Zisman, A. (2004c). Validating Personal Requirements by Assisted Symbolic Behavior Browsing. In *Proceedings of the 19th IEEE International Conference on Automated software engineering (ASE 2004)*, Austria (pp 56-66).

Hausmann, J. H., Heckel, R., & Lohman, M. (2004). Model-based Discovery of Web Services. In *Proceedings of the IEEE International Conference on Web Services (ICWS 2004)* (pp. 324-331).

Horrocks, I., Patel-Schneider, P. F., & Harmelen, F. (2003). From SHIQ and RDF to OWL: The making of a Web ontology language. *Journal of Web Semantics, 1*(1), 7-26.

Hoschek, W. (2002). The Web Service Discovery Architecture. In *Proceedings of the IEEE/ACM Supercomputing Conference, Baltimore*, USA (pp. 1-15).

Jin, H., & Wu, H. (2005). Semantic-enabled Specification for Web Services Agreement. *International Journal of Web Services Practices, 1*(1-2), 13-20.

Jones, S., Kozlenkov, A., Mahbub, K., Maiden, N., Spanoudakis, G., Zachos, K., Zhu, X., & Zisman, A. (2005). Service Discovery for Service Centric Systems. Paper presented at *eChallenges Conference 2005*, Slovenia.

Klusch, M., Fries, B., & Sycara, K. (2006). Automated Semantic Web Service Discovery with OWLS-MX. *Proceedings of the fifth international joint conference on Autonomous agents and multiagent systems* (pp. 915-922).

Kozlenkov, A., Fasoulas, V., Sanchez, F., Spanoudakis, G., & Zisman, A. (2006). A Framework for Architecture-driven Service Discovery. In *Proceedings of the 2006 International Workshop on Service-Oriented Software Engineering (IW-SOSE'06)*, China (pp. 67-73).

Lamanna, D. D., Skene, J., & Emmerich, W. (2003). SLAng: A Language for Defining Service Level Agreements. In *Proceedings of the 9th IEEE Workshop on Future Trends in Distributed Computing Systems (FTDCS 2003.* (pp. 100).

Mahbub, K., & Spanoudakis, G. (2005). Run-time Monitoring of Requirements for Systems Composed of Web-Services: Initial Implementation and Evaluation Experience. In *Proceedings of the IEEE International Conference on Web Services (ICWS 2005)* (pp. 257-265).

Martin, D., Burstein, D., Hobbs, J., Lassila, O., McDermott, D., McIlraith, S., Narayanan, S., Paolucci, M., Parsia, B., Payne, T., Sirin, E., Srinivasan, N., & Sycara, K. (2004). *OWL-S: Semantic Markup for Web Services*. Retrieved on March 25, 2008, from http://www.w3.org/Submission/2004/SUBM-OWL-S-20041122/

O'Reilly, T. (2005). What Is Web 2.0. Oreillynet.com. Retrieved on June 25, 2008, from http://www.oreillynet.com/pub/a/oreilly/tim/news/2005/09/30/what-is-web-20.html

Oundhakar, S., Verma, K., Sivashanmugam, K., Sheth, A., & Miller, J. (2005). Discovery of Web Services in a Multi-Ontology and Federated Registry Environment. *International Journal of Web Services Research, 2*(3) (pp. 8-39).

Pilioura, T., Tsalgatidou, A., & Batsakis, A. (2003). *Using WSDL/UDDI and DAML-S in Web Service Discovery*. Paper presented at WWW 2003 Workshop on E-Services and the Semantic Web (ESSW 2003), Budapest, Hungary.

Pistore, M., Traverso, P., Bertoli, P., & Marconi, A. (2005). Automated Synthesis of Composite BPEL4WS Web Services. *Proceedings of the IEEE International Conference on Web Services (ICWS 2005)*, USA (pp. 293-301).

Ran, S. (2003). A model for web services discovery with QoS. *ACM SIGecom Exchanges, 4*(1),1-10.

Robinson, W. N. (2003). Monitoring Web Service Requirements. In *Proceedings of 11th IEEE International Requirements Engineering Conference* (pp. 65-74).

Shacklett, M. (2007). *The SOA business Process Revolution*. Network and Systems Professional Association. Retrieved on March 25, 2008, from http://www.naspa.com/soa-business-process-revolution

Shen, Z., & Su, J. (2005). Web Service Discovery based on behavior Signatures. In *Proceedings of the 2005 IEEE International Conference on Services Computing* (SCC 2005), USA (pp. 279-286).

Spanoudakis, G., Mahbub, K., & Zisman, A. (2007). A Platform for Context-Aware Run-time Web Service Discovery. *Proceedings of the 2007 IEEE International Conference on Web Services (ICWS 2007)*, USA (pp. 233-240).

Spanoudakis, G., Zisman, A., & Kozlenkov, A. (2005). A Service Discovery Framework for Service Centric Systems. *Proceedings of the 2005 IEEE International Conference on Services Computing,* (SCC 2005), USA (pp. 251-259).

Wombacher, A., Fankhauser, P., Mahleko, B., & Neuhold, E. (2005). Matchmaking for Business Processes based on Conjunctive Finite State Automata. *International Journal of Business Process Integration and Management, 1*(1), 3-11.

Zachos, K., Zhu, X., Maiden, N., & Jones, S. (2006). Seamlessly Integrating Service Discovery into UML Requirements Processes. In *International Workshop of Service Oriented Software Engineering (IW-SOSE 2006)*, Shanghai (pp. 60-66).

Zisman, A., Spanoudakis, G., & Dooley, J. (in press, 2008). A Framework for Dynamic Service Discovery. To appear in the *23rd IEEE International Conference on Automated software engineering (ASE 2008)*.

Chapter XII
Model Architecture for a User Tailored Data Push Service in Data Grids

Nik Bessis
University of Bedfordshire, UK

ABSTRACT

Much work is under way within the Grid technology community on issues associated with the development of services to foster collaboration via the integration and exploitation of multiple autonomous, distributed data sources through a seamless and flexible virtualized interface. However, several obstacles arise in the design and implementation of such services. A notable obstacle, namely how clients within a data Grid environment can be kept automatically informed of the latest and relevant changes about data entered/committed in single or multiple autonomous distributed datasets is identified. The view is that keeping interested users informed of relevant changes occurring across their domain of interest will enlarge their decision-making space which in turn will increase the opportunities for a more informed decision to be encountered. With this in mind, the chapter goes on to describe in detail the model architecture and its implementation to keep interested users informed automatically about relevant up-to-date data.

INTRODUCTION

The ability to achieve competitive advantage is regarded as a significant factor in determining a firm's success (Pratali, 2003). Research relating to SMEs and strategy by Duhan et al. (2001) argued that there is a need to view competitive advantage from the perspective of resources, particularly information systems resources. Information systems and business software integration has long

Copyright © 2009, IGI Global, distributing in print or electronic forms without written permission of IGI Global is prohibited.

been discussed in other literature reviews. Many concerns have been encountered, as most of the datasets addressed by individual applications are very often heterogeneous and geographically distributed. These are used by communities of users, which are also geographically distributed. Hence, the ability to make data stores interoperable remains a crucial factor for the development of these types of systems (Wohrer et al., 2004). Clearly, one of the challenges for such facilitation is that of data integration, which aims to provide seamless and flexible access to information from multiple autonomous, distributed and heterogeneous data sources through a query interface (Calvanese, 1998; Levy, 2000; Reinoso Castillo et al., 2004; Ulman, 1997). Moreover, the combination of large dataset size, geographic distribution of users and resources, and computationally intensive analysis results in complex and stringent performance demands that, until recently, have not been satisfied by any existing computational and data management infrastructure (Foster et al., 2001).

On the other hand, working with obsolete data yields to an information gap that in turn may well compromise decision-making. It is a value creation for individuals and/or collaborators to automatically stay informed of data that may change over time (Asimakopoulou, 2006; Bessis, 2003). Repeatedly searching data sources for the latest relevant information on a specific topic of interest can be both time-consuming and frustrating. In response, a set of technologies collectively referred to as 'Push', 'NetCasting' or 'WebCasting' was introduced in late 90s. This set of technologies allowed the automation of search and retrieval functions. Ten years on, Web Services have overtaken most of Push technology functionality and become a standard supporting recent developments in Grid computing with state-of-the-art technology for data and resource integration.

Grid computing addresses the issue of collaboration, data and resource sharing (Kodeboyina,

2004). It has been described as the infrastructure and set of protocols to enable the integrated, collaborative use of distributed heterogeneous resources including high-end computers, networks, databases, and scientific instruments owned and managed by multiple organizations, referred to as Virtual Organizations (Foster, 2002). A Virtual Organization (VO) is formed when different organizations come together to share resources and collaborate in order to achieve a common goal (Foster et al., 2002). The most important standard that has emerged within the Grid community is the Open Grid Services Architecture (OGSA), an informational specification that aims to define a common, standard and open architecture for Grid-based applications. The need to integrate databases into the Grid has also been recognized (Nieto-Santisteban, 2004) in order to support science and business database applications (Antonioletti et al., 2005). Significant effort has gone into defining requirements, protocols and implementing the OGSA-DAI (Data Access and Integration) specification as the means for users to develop relevant data Grids to conveniently control the sharing, accessing and management of large amounts of distributed data in Grid environments (Antonioletti et al., 2005; Atkinson et al., 2003). Ideally, OGSA-DAI as a data integration specification aims to allow users to specify 'what' information is needed without having to provide detailed instructions on 'how' or 'from where' to obtain the information (Reinoso Castillo et al., 2004).

If a Grid is a system to enable flexible, secure, coordinated resource sharing among dynamic collections of individuals, institutions and resources (Foster, 2002) then it should be all about designing a dynamic service that is inherent in a VO (Weishaupl & Schikuta, 2004). That is to say, updates within a distributed data environment are much more frequent and can happen from within any data source in the network. Hence, there is a need for updates to be migrated to other sites in the network so that all the copies of the latest, relevant and up-to-date data are synchronized and communicated to maintain a consistency and homogeneity across the VO. Several authors have highlighted the need from different viewpoints, including Foster (2002), Bessis (2003), Magowan (2003), Raman (2003), Watson (2003), and Venugopal et al. (2005). On this basis, OGSA-DAI as a data integration specification should ideally address the ability to allow users to specify 'what' information is needed without having to provide detailed instructions on 'how' or 'from where' to obtain the information, as well as to automatically 'keep' users 'informed' of latest, relevant, specific changes about data in a single or multiple autonomous distributed database(s) and/or data source(s) that are registered within the VO. That is to say, an OGSA-DAI notification service requires extending its current function by keeping all interested VO users informed of the latest, relevant and up-to-date data changes committed within the VO environment. The requirement is widely regarded as a highly important service for individual and collaborative decision-making, as it will sustain competitive advantage and maintain consistency and homogeneity across an organizational setting.

Within this chapter, the main intention is to describe in detail the model architecture and its real-world implementation for such a Data Push service in OGSA-DAI. Hence, the chapter's main goals are multi-fold: firstly, to provide an overview of related technologies including Grid technology, OGSA-DAI services, and re-visit the Pull-Push models; secondly, to present the benefits of a Data Push service for decision-making in VOs and therefore, to discuss the theoretical underpinnings of the development approach describing a relevant model and its architecture; and thirdly, to describe in detail the implementation of such a user tailored Data Push service in OGSA-DAI.

AN OVERVIEW OF RELATED TECHNOLOGIES

The Concept of Grid Technology

The concept of Grid technology has emerged as an important research area differentiated from open systems, clusters and distributed computing (Bessis et al., 2007). Specifically, open systems such as Unix, Windows or Linux servers, remove dependencies on proprietary hardware and operating systems, but in most instances are used in isolation. Unlike conventional distributed systems, which are focused on communication between devices and resources, Grid technology takes advantage of computers connected to a network, making it possible to compute and to share data resources. Unlike clusters, which have a single administration and are generally geographically localized, Grids have multiple administrators and are usually dispersed over a wide area. But most importantly, clusters have a static architecture, whilst Grids are fluid and dynamic with resources entering and leaving.

In terms of standards, Grids share the same protocols with Web Services (XML: Extensible Mark-up Language, WSDL: Web Services Definition Language, SOAP: Simple Object Access Protocol, UDDI: Universal Description, Discovery and Integration). This often serves to confuse as to exactly what the differences between the two actually are. The aim of Web Services is to provide a service-oriented approach to distributed computing issues, whereas Grid arises from an object-oriented approach. That is to say, Web Services typically provide stateless, persistent services whereas Grids provide state-full, transient instances of objects.

In fact, the most important standard that has emerged recently is the OGSA, which was developed by the Global Grid Forum (GGF). OGSA is an informational specification that aims to define a common, standard and open architecture for Grid-based applications. Its goal is to specify a

Service-Oriented Architecture for the Grid that realizes a model of a computing system as a set of distributed computing patterns realized using Web Services as the underlying technology. An important merit of this model is that all components of the environment can be virtualized. It is the virtualization of Grid services that underpins the ability to map common service semantic behaviour seamlessly on to native platform facilities. These particular characteristics extend the functionality offered by Web Services and other conventional open systems. In turn, the OGSA standard defines service interfaces and identifies the protocols for invoking these services. The potential range of OGSA services is vast and currently includes data and information services, resource and service management, and core services such as name resolution and discovery, service domains, security, policy, messaging, queuing, logging, events, metering and accounting.

Data Grids

OGSA-DAI services provide a means for users to Grid-enable their data resources. It is a middleware that allows data resources to be accessed via Web Services. OGSA-DAI is compliant with Web Services Inter-operability (WS-I) and the Web Services Resource Framework (WSRF). OGSA-DAI as a middleware supports the integration and virtualization of data resources, such as relational databases, XML databases, file systems or indexed files. Various interfaces are provided and many popular database management systems are supported, including but not limited to MySQL, Oracle and DB2. Data within each of these resource types can be queried, updated, transformed, compressed and/or decompressed. Data can also be delivered to clients or other OGSA-DAI Web Services, URLs, FTP servers, or files. OGSA-DAI is designed to be extensible, so users can add their own additional functionality. DAI service is intended to provide a basis for higher-level services to be constructed, for

example, to provide federation across heterogeneous databases. Applications can either use the core OGSA-DAI components directly to access individual data stores or a distributed query processor (DQP), OGSA-DQP, to co-ordinate access to multiple database services (Baker, 2002).

Data Push Technology and OGSA-DAI's Notification Service

In general, there are two models, namely the Pull and Push models, for a client to retrieve data from a data source. The distinction between the Pull and the Push models is shown in Figure 1. In the Pull model, a web client (W-C) needs to initiate a search by specifying search parameters. The web server (W-S) receives the client's request and it performs a data query to the database server (DB-S). If there are any retrieved data, these are made available to the web client via the web server. In this model, web clients are always required to initiate the search function in order to retrieve data.

In the Push model, a web client (W-C) needs to subscribe by specifying a set of parameters and the period in which they wish to keep informed of any new and/or data updates occurring at the data source level, as relevant to the specified parameters. These parameters are stored as a new record in the subscriber's table (S-T) that is located in the web server (W-S). The Push approach as discussed in Bessis (2003) suggests that every time a data provider commits a new data entry in the database server (DB-S), a data description record (with reference to the new data entry) is generated and stored in a Data Description Table (DD-T). Once a record is stored in the DD-T, a trigger will cause an automatic search between the records stored in the DD-T and subscriber's table (S-T) to identify relevant matches. If there are any retrieved data, these are pushed to the client via the web server. In this model, web clients are required to subscribe once and are not required to

Figure 1. Sequence diagrams of Pull and Push models

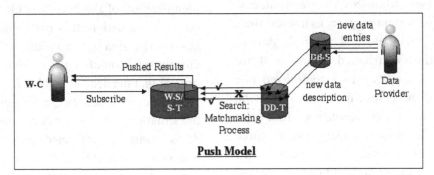

initiate the search function every time new data are committed within a data source.

Overall, Push can streamline the delivery of user tailored, specific information to a variety of users via Internet or a web browser. There are various technologies including Web 2.0, AJAX, WS-Notification and/or WS-Eventing supporting the development of pure or feel a-like push mechanisms. For example, RSS (Really Simple Syndication) feed technology is mainly a push feel a-like mechanism that is used to publish frequently updated content containing either a summary of content from an associated web site or the full text in an automated manner. The user subscribes to a feed by entering the feed's link into the reader or by clicking an RSS icon in a browser, which in turn it initiates the subscription request. The main difference is that Push transactions can be based on a user's specific information preferences. Whenever such new content matching a user's specific preference(s) is made available on one of those sites, the server would automatically push that information to the subscriber. Technically

speaking, RSS are pulled by the user. That is to say, it is the users who request the server periodically for new content; the server itself does not send information to the client without their request. These continual requests have many disadvantages and again technically speaking they are bandwidth inefficient. In contrast, a Push service residing at the server side would automatically inform subscribers as soon as only relevant – with regard to the user's tailored, specific request – content has been updated.

For example, a decision maker may request to be automatically kept informed on one or more specific conditions ('and' Boolean logic), let's say when – the intended to buy – stock X price range is 'x_i' that is less than others' stock 'y_i', 'z_i', etc. price ranges. The decision maker may also wish to use a Push agent to automatically take action on their behalf based on their predefined set of conditions, i.e. automatically sell stock Z in order to buy stock X when the aforementioned predefined conditions are met. It is also well known that decisions are not merely single actions but they are dependant on parts or results of other decisions. In brief, user tailored Push technology enables a decision maker to specify a set of parameters into a subscriber form and as those conditions match specific parts of the newly updated and/or created content, such information are 'pushed' to the subscribed decision maker.

It is therefore the viewpoint that user tailored Push technology addresses data consistency, which it is an important property as it determines how 'relevant', 'accurate' and 'fresh' the data is. Updates within a distributed environment are more frequent compared to a centralized one and therefore, these specific updates must be also checked about their consistency first prior to a potential further action like a two or a three commit protocol when they have to be migrated to other sites in the network. It must be stressed that a two or a three commit protocol may not be an appropriate action since synchronization over a data Grid refers to the data synchronization in the virtualized table layer and not in the actual data source layer. If however, it is required this will then enable all the copies of the data to be consistently synchronized and provide the homogeneous status that may be critically required by a VO and its individual members.

Within a Grid environment, virtualization services can use the Grid notification service to know about various changes occurring at the data sources. These include schema related changes (important for federated query processing) and state related changes (important for identifying failures of data source, which may have an impact on the processing of many virtualization services). However, it is evident that the Grid notification service is limited and overall, there is a feeling that data Grids and P2P networks generally do not provide strong consistency guarantees because of the overhead of maintaining locks on huge volumes of data and the ad hoc nature of the network respectively (Venugopal et al., 2005).

ADVANCING VIRTUAL ORGANIZATIONS' DECISION MAKING USING USER TAILORED DATA PUSH IN OGSA-DAI AND DATA GRIDS

Decision-making is either a normative or prescriptive process, which is always concerned with the identification of the best possible decision in a particular situation. It is particularly important that the decision maker is fully informed of the current situation of concern. That is to say, it is critical that the decision maker has access to the most 'relevant', 'accurate' and 'fresh' data about the situation prior to any decisions so that their decisions are fully informed decisions. The reader is directed to other relevant sources (Anand, 2002; Arthur, 1991; Clemen, 1996) whose primary goal is to leverage the options available.

Decision-Making in Virtual Organizations

With this in mind, the section presents the theoretical underpinnings for the model architecture that will be used for the implementation of a user tailored Data Push service in OGSA-DAI and data Grids. Although direct references to – the easy to follow – Simon's decision-making model along with the concept theory of bounded rationality are used, there is no reason to restrict the VO conceptualization and its implementation in other theoretical settings.

Simon's (1977) systematic decision-making process includes the three phases of "intelligence-design-choice". In the first phase of intelligence, someone must clearly define the problem – like providing a more accurate prediction service to customers as part of the organizational goal or objective – by identifying symptoms and examining the reality. Once these have been defined, the organization must move to the design phase, the second phase of Simon's model. This phase involves finding or developing and analyzing possible courses of action towards the identification of possible solutions against the identified "problem space". A problem space represents a boundary of the identified problem and contains all possible solutions to that problem: optimal, excellent, very good, acceptable, bad solutions, and so on. At this stage, the organization must move to the choice, the last phase of Simon's model. In other words, the organization needs to make a decision based on the alternatives derived from the previous phase.

The rational model of decision-making suggests that the decision maker would seek out and test each of the solutions found in the domain of the problem space until all solutions are tested and compared. At that point, the best solution will be known and identified. However, what really happens is that the decision maker actually simplifies reality since reality is too large to be handled within human cognitive limitations. This narrows the problem space and clearly leads a decision-maker to attempt to search within the actual problem space, which is far smaller than the reality.

It is the viewpoint here that decision makers working with obsolete data or scenarios will disadvantage their decision since their decision space will be compromised. The approach will lead the decision maker to settle for a satisfactory rather a potentially better solution. If however, the organization had access to a Grid integration service (Bessis et al., 2007) which allowed them to make decisions based on the most up-to-date data – from multiple dispersed sources – with regard to their domain of interest, decision makers will most likely enlarge their decision-making space which in turn will increase the possibility that a better solution will be encountered. The approach is shown in the Figure 2.

THE ARCHITECTURE FOR A USER TAILORED DATA PUSH IN OGSA-DAI AND DATA GRIDS

The following example illustrates the importance of a Data Push service in OGSA-DAI. ICONS (Bessis & Asimakopoulou, 2008) is a fictional brand name and a typical international construction services company that has offices across the world. The company is usually involved in planning, managing and delivering large-scale construction projects worldwide. ICONS – through

Figure 2. Search space (extended version of Simon's bounded rationality theory, 1977)

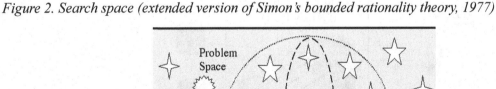

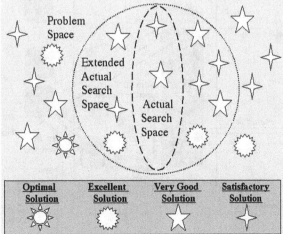

their supply chain instruments – is constantly seeking to make informed decisions about 'with whom to collaborate' including identification and selection of engineers, architects, 3-D modellers and animators, lawyers, builders, plumbers, painters, project managers and material suppliers. It is anticipated that this resource collaboration will form a VO towards the completion of the construction project. Each of the partners will have to offer their time, expertise and resource for the time period required to accomplish their task(s). It is also anticipated that the VO is a transient service and its individual VO members have to co-operate under each other's policies, hierarchical structures and as a whole within the regulations set by the local planning department.

ICONS as an evolving VO is also constantly seeking to make informed decisions about 'when to buy' and 'where to buy from' services and resources, such as partners or construction materials. To achieve this, they – as a VO – need to continuously monitor pricing and availability in a real-time worldwide basis over a specified period

of time. There is also a need to constantly monitor currency movements on real-time in order to match their budget constraints, as well as to make their order at the right time in order to maximize their profits and/or compensate for prior or future compromised decisions.

The view here is that ICONS' VO members repeatedly querying for updates from available data sources may compromise their decision space. The aforementioned highly simplified scenario clearly demonstrates that if a Data Push service were made available to the ICONS' VO members, they would have been kept informed of data updates more efficiently and effortlessly.

Based on earlier discussion, Figure 3 illustrates the low detail sequence diagram of the proposed push architecture for OGSA-DAI. The client as a data service seeker needs to subscribe by specifying a set of parameters and the period in which they wish to keep informed of any new and/or data updates, which are relevant to the specified parameters. These parameters are stored as a new record in the subscriber's table (S-T) that

Figure 3. Low detailed sequence diagram of the proposed data push service

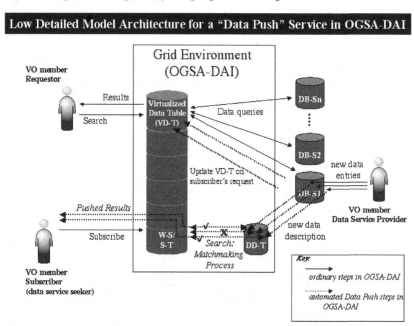

is located in the web server (W-S). Every time a data service provider commits a new data entry in a database server (DB-S1), a data description record (with reference to the new data entry) is generated and stored in a Data Description Table (DD-T) that is also located in the web server (W-S). Once a record is stored in the DD-T, a trigger will cause an automatic search (matchmaking process) between the records stored in the DD-T and subscriber's table (S-T) to identify relevant matches. If there are any retrieved data, these are pushed to the data service seeker (subscriber) and are made available through the VO's Virtualized Data Table (VD-T) on request.

Consider <ogsa> to be the database for the Glasgow based ICONS' VO member called A, which contains the summary of sales information of their office. It uses a MySQL database to store information. Another office B – based in Athens – is also an ICONS' VO member that holds its sales information in a database called <ogsa2>. It also uses a MySQL database that is of a different schema – compared to the <ogsa> database – to store their data.

The envisaged Grid environment comprises of five simple hosting environments: two that run ICONS's data analysts' user applications (A and B) and three that encapsulate dispersed computing and storage resources (C, D, E) belonging to other partners of the same VO. In particular, the <ogsa> database is stored in C and the <ogsa2> in D. C also encapsulates accounting models made available from A; while D encapsulates data mining tools made available from B. Finally, hosting environment E remains idle but could take over computing related tasks and/or host data moved from a partner environment (C and/or D). To complicate the scenario, we assume also that the hosting environment E provides advanced cutting-edge modelling tools on an on-demand basis. The detailed process model's architecture is shown in Figure 4.

Let's assume that both partners (A and B) act as "Service Providers" via the provision of their databases and accounting models. To achieve this, both partners have to register their <ogsa> and <ogsa2> data sources with the Grid Data Services Factory (GDSF) so that they can be found. Similarly, it is anticipated that partners' accounting models and any other data mining tools have been registered as a service so they can be found too. Now let's assume that a data analyst (Service Requestor) as a decision maker needs to obtain 'X' information on the domain of their interest. At this stage, it is important to note that the data analyst does not need to know which database(s) are able to provide this data and where these are located. It might be the case that information is stored in more that one data set (DS). The following – as shown also in Figure 4 – lists the steps required for "Service Requestor A" to interact with appropriate data services:

- **Action 1:** The data analyst from A as "Service Requestor A" has to request the Data Access and Integration Service Grid Register (DAISGR) for a source of data about X.

- **Action 2:** Register returns a handle to "Service Requestor A".

- **Action 3:** "Service Requestor A" sends a request to the Factory (GDSF) to access the relevant data sets that are registered with it.

- **Action 4:** Factory creates a Grid Data Service (GDS) to manage access to relevant data sets.

- **Action 5:** Factory returns a handle of the GDS to "Service Requestor A".

- **Action 6a:** "Service Requestor A" performs the query to the respective GDS using a database language.

- **Action 7:** The GDS interacts with the dataset(s).

- **Action 8a:** The GDS returns query results in a XML format to "Service Requestor A".

In the event that GDSF has identified more than one of the data sets (DS_1, DS_2) that contain the relevant information, "Service Requestor A" has a choice to either select a particular GDS (for example, GDS_1) based on his preference(s) or request for data to be integrated into a sink GDS (6b). That is to say, a sink GDS handles the communications (6c) between "Service Requestor A" and the multiple GDSs (GDS_1 and GDS_2), which further interacts (7) with their respective data sets (DS_1 and DS_2) so as to return query's results in a XML format (8b) to "Service Requestor A". Similarly, "Service Requestor A" can submit a request for a particular advanced modelling tool that is either a service of B or registered with another Grid partner (i.e. E). In general, "Service Requestor A" can be either a data analyst from A or a partner advisor from B who is available to offer advice or to assist "Service Requestor A" in applying a special type of advanced modelling tool on an on-demand basis. Once data and models have been collected via the GDS, "Service Requestor A" or the partner advisor B could then for example run their simulation tests. In the event that a service fails another registered resource (E as "Service Provider") will take over the outstanding task(s). For example, if during perform computations, one resource (D) becomes unavailable, another idle "Service Provider N" (E) will carry on the computation. This is due to the Grid fault tolerance service that allows a task to carry over to a different registered and available resource.

Finally assume that new (specific) data – that is of critical interest for "Service Requestor A" – committed in <ogsa2> database from "Service Provider B". Pulling data using the traditional method requires "Service Requestor A" to repeatedly querying available data sources for information on a particular topic of their interest. Our view is that repeatedly querying for new data or updates from available data sources will shift away Service Requestors from their primary goal, which is other than performing repeated queries.

On the other hand, working on an obsolete set of data can be critical. Pushing 'fresh and relevant' data is a very important service. With this in mind, let's assume that "Service Requestor A" subscribes his interest to a user tailored Data Push service so they can be informed automatically of forthcoming – and only relevant– entries. Let's assume that at a later stage, "Service Provider B" updates data stored in the <ogsa2> database. Our approach suggests that if such entries are of interest to the subscriber, the user tailored Data Push service should automatically inform "Service Requestor A" of them. In brief, the view is that keeping "Service Requestor A" – without repeatedly searching for it – informed of changes occurring across their domain of particular interest (like in <ogsa2>) will be of value as it will enlarge their decision-making space which in turn will increase the opportunities for an advantage to be encountered. The following, also shown in Figure 4, lists the steps required for "Service Requestor A" to keep informed automatically of specific changes committed in dispersed heterogeneous databases:

- **Action 9:** "Service Requestor A" as a "Service Request Subscriber" has to request subscription to the Subscribe_Data Access and Integration Service Grid Register (S_DAISGR) – a service that is a subset of the Data Access and Integration Service Grid Register (DAISGR) – for a source of specific new/updated data about X where xi = x1

- **Action 10:** S_DAISGR returns a handle to "Service Request Subscriber A".

- **Action 11:** S_DAISGR sends a request to the Factory (GDSF) to access the relevant data sets that are registered with it.

- **Action 12:** "Service Provider B" commits new data and (metadata) descriptions about new data entries are automatically generated.

- **Action 13:** When new data has been committed within any dataset registered to the GDSF, a trigger will cause an automatic search between the records storing new data description and subscribers' parameters (also stored in the GDSF) to identify relevant matches (check whether $x_i = x_1$ or else):
  - If no matches (i.e. $x_i \neq x_1$) found GDSF does nothing (i.e. not return a handle).
- **Action 14:** If matches found (i.e. $x_i = x_1$) GDSF creates a Subscriber_Grid Notification Data Service (S_GNDS) to manage access to relevant data sets.
- **Action 15:** The S_GNDS interacts with the dataset(s) to pull out matches.
- **Action 16:** The S_GNDS creates a temporary table <Temp> to store pulled matches.
- **Action 17:** The trigger attached to the <Temp> automatically runs a search facility

to select any differences with previous GDS including the GDS Sink:
  - If no differences found GDSF does not return a handle to the "Subscriber A" and deletes S_GNDS' <Temp> contents automatically.
- **Action 18:** If differences found GDSF returns a handle of the S_GNDS to the "Subscriber A".
- **Action 19:** "Service Request Subscriber A" performs the query to the <Temp> using a database language.
- **Action 20:** The <Temp> returns query results in a XML format to the "Subscriber A".

The process model's algorithm is discussed in greater detail during the service implementation section. Overall, the availability of computing resources alongside the ability of accessing a larger selection of datasets, and the ability to keep

Figure 4. Process model architecture for a user tailored "Data Push" in a Data Grid

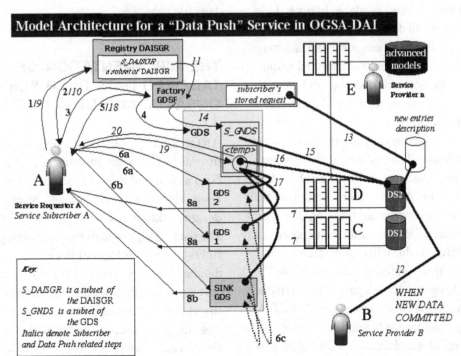

informed automatically of new entries/updates – using the built-in OGSA-DAI based user tailored Data Push service – that can be data mined using additional tools and advice from other partners on an –on-demand basis will most likely assist in "Service Request Subscriber A's" decision-making process.

The Data Push service assumes that someone subscribes for a certain period of time, which cannot exceed his or her time as a VO member or the time of the VO lifespan as a whole, whichever is shorter. The notification is sent to the subscriber once the automated search results in match(es) between the subscriber's parameters and data updates committed at the data source level. Obviously, notifications will only be sent if relevant updated data are found. The notification method could vary – depending the implementation method – including an email message and prompting automatically every time the subscriber logs in to the web virtualized interface, unless the subscriber disables the prompting feature or acts upon the prompt notification (i.e., opens the message). Email notifications will remain at the subscriber's email box, but it does not necessarily imply that data updates will be valid and available in time. This is due to the nature of data changing over time or because the VO is a transient service. Data may not be available anymore or VO membership may have expired for some reason (i.e. VO closure after task accomplishment). It can be arranged – through the notification service – to register for the Data Push service to include all data updates (last and previously data updates) which are currently valid and available unless the subscriber has actioned them. A subscriber's action refers to query, view, and download, transfer, delete or store data updates. Downloading data updates at the virtualized data table will immediately update existing data. Finally, subscribers are necessarily involved in delegacy. To delegate is to entrust a representative to act on someone else's behalf. A key delegacy challenge is the ability to interface with secure, reliable and scalable VOs, which can

operate in an open, dynamic and competitive environment. To achieve this, a number of existing 'hard' security and authentication mechanisms have to be seamlessly integrated within the Grid environment. Suggestions include the use of IBC (Identity-based Cryptography), PKI (Public Key Infrastructure) and X.509 Digital Certificates.

The technical architecture, shown in Figure 5, suggests the automatic creation of an XML file consisting of parameters taken from "Service Request Subscriber A's" form. The XML file is stored at a proxy database (UDDI) level so it can be found from the GDSF. Similarly, when new data are committed – by "Service Provider B" at the local data source level – an XML file consisting of the URL and relevant searchable values is automatically created and stored at the local level UDDI. Once the latter XML file is created and stored, a Java file is automatically run to identify whether there are matches between the XML files. If there are matches, another automatic service informs relevant subscribers via a notification method. Regardless of whether there are matches or not, all XML files related to the new data committed at the local level shall be deleted once the Java file runs.

THE IMPLEMENTATION OF A USER TAILORED DATA PUSH SERVICE IN OGSA-DAI AND DATA GRIDS

An OGSA-DAI web based service was produced in order to provide an interface to allow Data Grid authorized clients to share and exploit data from these two distributed and heterogeneously designed databases. Now consider <P_OGSA> as a data service, which manages, integrates and filters customer information via a virtualized join database. The purpose of this <P_OGSA> data service is to allow authorized clients to query, insert and update data stored in <ogsa> and/or <ogsa2> database(s). The main idea was then to create a layer that provides a set of basic functions

Figure 5. Technical model architecture for a user tailored "Data Push" in a data Grid

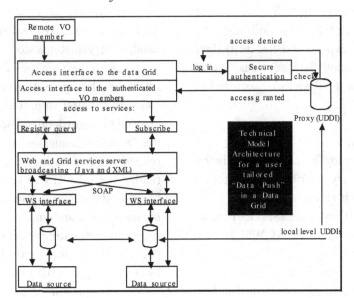

to support the user tailored 'Push' technology service in a Data Grid environment. This is by specifying 'what' information (in the form of a set of parameters) is needed without having to provide detailed instructions on 'how' or 'from where' to obtain the information (<ogsa> and/or <ogsa2>), but most importantly, to keep these clients automatically informed of the latest, relevant, specific changes of data entered/committed from any authorized client(s) in a single (<ogsa> or <ogsa2>) or multiple autonomous distributed datasets (<ogsa> and <ogsa2>). This scenario aims to prove that the data distribution with OGSA-DAI technology in which real-time and user tailored 'Data Push' coming from multiple databases, i.e. from <ogsa> and <ogsa2> databases, is the result of these multiple databases joined into the one dataset by using OGSA-DAI join query functionality. In fact, the most important function of join queries within the OGSA-DAI environment is based upon a predefined set of request parameters outlined by the client in the system database.

The development of the <P_OGSA> as a web-based graphical user interface service (Bessis & Chauhan, 2008) incorporated the combination of open source software including MySQL, Apache, AXIS, OGSA-DAI, OGSA-DAI-WSI, HTML, DHTML and JSP on Windows XP Home Edition PC. In particular, the versions installed included JAVA 1.5.0._06, JACARTA TOMCAT 1.6.5, Apache ANT 1.6.5, MySQL 4.0, MySQL Control Centre 0.9.4-beta, Apache AXIS 1.1 in TOMCAT, OGSA-DAI 2.1 and OGSA-DAI WSI 2.1.

OGSA-DAI Data Push Service Development

Initially, two databases namely <ogsa> and <ogsa2> have been created using MySQL. The two databases have been created with a different schema. That is to say, the customer purchase summary information in the warehouse A_1 is stored in the database <ogsa> as <CustID, CreditCardNumber, P_Date> and <P_Amount>, whereas the customer purchase summary information in the warehouse B_2 is stored in the database <ogsa2> as <Cust_ID, Credit_Card_Number, Purchase_ and_Date and Purchase_Amount>.

Once all installations were finished, OGSA-DAI WSI New Data Services Resource for both databases were deployed using the List function. The deployment included the OGSA-DAI WSI End-to-End Client and WSI Multi-join tests. To install, deploy, add, expose and list (test) data services (including new data services) using OGSA-DAI WSI via a <P_OGSA> web based graphical interface:

- Shutdown Tomcat
- Run $ ant guiDeployTomcat from within the OGSA-DAI binary distribution directory.
- Ensure Tomcat is running.
- Run $ ant guiDeployDataServiceTomcat from within the OGSA-DAI WSI binary distribution directory.
- Enter the URL of the data service.
- Select the dynamically configurable box to request that the data service supports dynamic service configuration.
- Run $ ant guiCreateResourceTomcat from within the OGSA-DAI WSI binary distribution directory.
- Configure data service resource by selecting the JARs if they are not installed on server.
- Run $ ant guiAddResourceTomcat from within the OGSA-DAI WSI binary distribution directory.
- Enter the URL of the data service.
- Shutdown and then Restart Tomcat.
- Run $ ant listResourcesClient from within the OGSA-DAI WSI binary distribution directory.
- Run $ ant databrowser from within the OGSA-DAI WSI binary distribution directory.
- Construct and run an SQL statement of preference.

To exemplify the service produced, let's assume that a <Customer> (Customer1, Customer 2 or Customer n) as a "Service Requestor" wants to find information that is stored in <ogsa> and/or <ogsa2> databases. Firstly, all "Service Providers" are required to register their data sources to the Factory and make them available. On the other hand, a "Service Requestor" is also required to register their request via the <P_OGSA> web-based interface. The registration process consists of two steps. In the first step, the "Service Requestor" enters their login details. The second step requires the "Service Requestor" to specify information related to the data they are looking for. In particular, the <P_OGSA> service will prompt the "Service Requestor" to enter their personal details including name and email address via the customer registration <custreg> form. It also prompts the "Service Requestor" to construct SQL statements by specifying join parameters. To help assist the "Service Requestor" in constructing queries, the right part of the screen shows a diagram with all schema related information about the <ogsa> and <ogsa2> databases.

For example, to store and run an SQL statement related to the <ogsa>, "Service Requestor A" needs to construct a select statement like the one below:

<SELECT 'ogsa' as Organization, a.CustID as CustID, b.CreditCardNumber as CreditCard-Number, a.FName as First_Name, a.MName as Middle_Name, a.LName as Last_Name,b. P_Date as Date_Of_Purchase, b.P_Amount as Purchased_Amount from custreg a, cust_purchase b where a.CustID = b.CustID >

Next to this, "Service Requestor A" needs to virtualize results from <ogsa> database by creating a 'TMPA' table like the one below:

<CREATE TABLE TMPA (CustID varchar(15), First_Name varchar(30), Middle_Name varchar(30), Last_Name varchar(30), Date_Of_Purchase datetime, Purchased_Amount int(11), CreditCardNumber varchar(19), Organisation varchar(19))>

Similar 'select' and 'create table' statements are required if "Service Requestor A" needs to retrieve and store virtualized results to a 'TMPB' produced from the <ogsa2> database. The following statement could be used when "Service Requestor A" constructs a join query to retrieve data from both databases (via the use of the 'TMPA' and 'TMPB' virtualized results) that are available from the <P_OGSA> virtualized table:

<SELECT Organisation, CustID, First_Name, Middle_Name, Last_Name, Date_Of_Purchase, Purchased_Amount, CreditCardNumber from TMPA where CustID = '001' UNION

SELECT Organisation, CustID, First_Name, Middle_Name, Last_Name, Date_Of_Purchase, Purchased_Amount, CreditCardNumber from TMPB where CustID = '001'>

The results of the above query are shown in Figure 6. Pulling new data using the aforementioned method requires a "Service Requestor" to repeatedly query available sources for data on a particular topic of their interest, which can be both time-consuming and frustrating. But most importantly, this will shift away a "Service Requestor" from their primary goal, which is other than performing repeated queries. So pushing new/updated data from these heterogeneous sources by using a join query to 'keep' Service Requestor(s) automatically 'informed' of latest, relevant, specific changes committed about data entered from any authorized Service Provider(s) in a single (<ogsa> or <ogsa2>) or multiple autonomous distributed datasets (<ogsa> and <ogsa2>) is the focus of the following task.

Let's assume that "Service Provider B" wants to update "customer_purchase" data stored in the <ogsa2> dataset. The following SQL statement could achieve this:

<UPDATE 'Customer_Purchase' set Purchase_Amount= 200 where Cust_ID = '001' and Credit_Card_Number = '9999 9999 9999 9999' and Purchase_Date = '2006-06-23'>

The result of the above query in the MySQL Control Centre is shown in Figure 7. Clearly, the last row (9) highlighted column name <Purchace_Amount> value has been updated from <400> to <200>. The proposed approach results in an additional <Temp> virtualized table, which stores new data only. This is to inform "Service Requestor(s)" of these changes and allow them to decide whether these changes should replace respective parts from the original virtualized dataset. To achieve this, "Service Requestor A" must subscribe using a <cust_subscriber> form that is similar to the <custreg> form. In this form, "Service Requestor A" as a subscriber specifies using a set of parameters the information they

Figure 6. Results returned from the <P_OGSA> virtualized database

Organisation	Credit Card Number	Date of Purchase	Purchased Amount
Ogsa	1234 5678 9899 2344	2006-05-21	100
Ogsa	1234 5678 9899 2344	2006-06-24	50
Ogsa	9999 9999 9999 9999	2006-06-24	333
Ogsa2	1234 5678 9899 2344	2006-05-10	100
Ogsa2	9999 8888 7777 6666	2006-05-11	100
Ogsa2	1234 5678 9899 2344	2006-05-23	90
Ogsa2	9999 8888 7777 6666	2006-05-25	175
Ogsa2	1234 5678 9899 2344	2006-06-03	102
Ogsa2	9999 8888 7777 6666	2006-06-05	222
Ogsa2	1234 5678 9899 2344	2006-06-13	82
Ogsa2	9999 8888 7777 6666	2006-06-15	250
Ogsa2	9999 9999 9999 9999	2006-06-23	400

Figure 7. Results shown after "Service Provider B" updates the <ogsa2> dataset

	Cust_ID	Credit_Card_Number	Purchase_Date	Purchase_Amour
1	001	1234 5678 9899 2344	2006-05-10 00:00:00	100
2	001	9999 8888 7777 6666	2006-05-11 00:00:00	100
3	001	1234 5678 9899 2344	2006-05-23 00:00:00	90
4	001	9999 8888 7777 6666	2006-05-25 00:00:00	175
5	001	1234 5678 9899 2344	2006-06-03 00:00:00	102
6	001	9999 8888 7777 6666	2006-06-05 00:00:00	222
7	001	1234 5678 9899 2344	2006-06-13 00:00:00	82
8	001	9999 8888 7777 6666	2006-06-15 00:00:00	250
9	001	9999 9999 9999 9999	2006-06-23 00:00:00	200

interested in being informed of over a period of time. Finally, the user specified 'pushed data' service from these two heterogeneous data sources is achieved using the Windows XP Schedule Check facility. In particular, the functionality for the JAVA class file follows:

- Connect to databases <P_OGSA>, <ogsa> <ogsa2> and <factory>.
- Loop only 'Service_Request_Subscriber' in the <cust_subscriber> table.
- Based on the select statement stored in the subscriber <factory> table, perform join database query.
- Store join query result in the <temp> table.
- Empty subscriber <latest> table.
- If executed first time, then copy all data from <temp> to subscriber <master> table and subscriber <latest> data table.
- If it is executed a subsequent time, then check <temp> table result with subscriber's <master> table for any new or update data available.
- If any data is found in the above step, then update corresponding data in subscriber <master> table and subscriber <latest> tables.

The functionality of the JAVA class file in form of an algorithm expressed in pseudo code can be seen in Figure 8.

A Batch file called <RunOGSAJoinQuery. bat> was created for invoking the JAVA class file from the DOS prompt automatically once "Service Requestor A" logs in to the <P_OGSA> web interface. When the Batch file is executed, it executes the JAVA class, which in turn calls the function <Push Data>. This <Push Data> function performs join query functionality and is based upon the predefined set of request parameters outlined by the "Service Requestor" in the system database, it sends only <update> and/or <new> data from the <custreg> latest table to the corresponding "Service Requestor". The results returned after the execution of the application are shown in Figure 9.

Data Push Service Testing and Limitations

The <P_OGSA> functionality was tested with three users who were generally satisfied with the service interface. In particular, testing comprised of the following activities:

- A number of queries were executed through the MySQL command line client editor and the results were compared with those produced through the database shown in the web interface.
- All normal pathways of execution were tried to ensure the system functioned as expected.

Figure 8. The algorithm of the data push Java file expressed in pseudo code

```
Algorithm 1 – Trigger Update

1        Function Update (P_OGSA, OGSA, OGSA2, FACTORY) return Boolean;
2        If NOT Available(P_OGSA, OGSA, OGSA2, FACTORY) then
3                Return FALSE ;
4        End If
5        Try
6                For Each Customer C in FACTORY. <custreg>
7                        <temp>[C]:=OGSA + OGSA2 where C.Keywords applies;
8                        Empty(C.<latest>);
9                        If IsEmpty(C.<master>) then
10                       Begin
11                               C.<master>=<temp>[C];
12                               C.<latest>=<temp>[C];
13                       End
14                       Else
15                       Begin
16                               Records <R>=Compare(C.<master>, <temp>[C]);
17                               If (NOT IsEmpty(R)) then
18                               Begin
19                                       C.<master>+=<R>;
20                                       C.<latest>+=<R>;
21                               End;
22                       End;
23               End For
24               Return TRUE;
25       Catch (Any Exceptions)
26               Return FALSE ;
27       End;
28 End Function
```

Figure 9. Results shown after the execution of the data push service in OGSA-DAI

Organisation	Credit Card Number	Date of Purchase	Purchased Amount
Ogsa2	9999 9999 9999 9999	2006-06-23	200

- Changes were made to the parameters in the user registration data, the application run and results checked against the database.
- Logout and re-login to check that the Windows scheduler has executed the batch file and run the application as expected.

Based on the model architecture presented in Figures 4 and 5, the creation of XML files consisting of values taken from a "Service Requestor" subscriber form to perform search on new data committed at local level would have been a more open source friendly and sustainable approach.

Similarly, we suggest the creation of another XML file consisting of the URL and relevant parameters of the new entries at local level. The suggestion is that these files should reside on different tiers as to separate them from the business logic (OGSA-DAI) and database application servers (MySQL). Once the latter XML file is created the Java file should run and if there are matches another service should inform subscribers via email or other notification method. Regardless of whether there are matches or not, all XML files related to the new data entered/committed at the local level are deleted once the script runs. Another suggestion would be that the Java file could run after certain specified time intervals or every time new data is entered. Finally, it is worth noting that the current implementation has not been tested for its scalability performance.

In distributed heterogeneous systems, it is often necessary to use virtualizing data sources from different database providers, which was not the case in the aforementioned implementation. This is not considered a limitation – as there are many organizations working on the same platform, with the same software but with different data and data types – but as an item for future development. It is also worth noting that there will always be organizations working on various local infrastructures and incompatible technologies in which it is not always the case that their local manifestations always comply to all standards. It is therefore important to emphasize that these – want-to-be – VO members should not be limited due to limitations of the resources they own; otherwise it will contradict the concept of the democratization of Grid technology.

IMPLICATIONS AND CHALLENGES IN DEPLOYING USER TAILORED DATA PUSH SERVICES IN OGSA-DAI AND DATA GRIDS

One of the major implications for decision makers in using OGSA-DAI is their ability to conveniently access and manage large amounts of data, which are made available via the integration and exploitation from multiple autonomous, distributed data sources. In turn, this will help to enlarge the actual search space boundaries within the term of "problem space", as described by Simon (1977).

Working with dynamically generated fresh data yields, decision makers can fully exploit and challenge their decision-making, which in turn will dynamically generate new situations requiring further and even more efficient and effective decisions. This will be particularly important in parallel and dynamic supply-chain environments where opportunistic and extreme types of critical decisions are required.

Clearly the combination of multiple co-working data push services like multi-agents potentially vastly increases the size and complexity of the problem spaces that can realistically be addressed not only by SMEs but by all types of organization.

Within the business community large companies have been amongst the first to exploit the power of the Grid to leverage extra value from vast legacy systems. Now, businesses are most likely able to dynamically observe and act upon previously intractable opportunities and complex problems and to leverage competitive advantage from the proposed enhanced power of user tailored data push services within multiple Grid environments. It is expected that the deployment of multiple co-working user tailored data push services dynamically scanning multiple data Grids (representing various business sectors) as a combinational technology will allow individual and group-based decision makers to be able to address or re-address complex multi-dimensional problems and/or opportunities, which are dynamically generated and reside outside their businesses' boundaries.

The deployment of the data push services will have cost implications. That is to say, data may be pushed at different rates depending on the frequency and the volume of data pushed, the complexity and the policies attached to the resources required to support multiple co-working of data push agents, the impact value of pushed data and the competitive advantage to the work of a number of subscribers. For example, a stock market will cause many simultaneous updates which in turn, will cause different implications for different subscribers.

Technically speaking, the combinational power of multi-data user-specified push agents scanning multiple data Grids will challenge the current form of accessing the hidden web and use of next generation technologies. In particular, it is envisaged that it could lead to the evolution of RSS technology as a more personalized service via scanning distributed businesses data in a customer based preference, which in turn will assist business decision makers to cluster and target customers in a much more meaningful manner (Bessis & Asimakopoulou, 2008).

Finally, like all enabling technologies, investment needs to be made in properly harnessing the combinational power of the Grid and multi-data push agents without exposing the business to potential risks including security, trust and policy fee making. These challenges also remain to be solved if such an emerging technology is indeed to become a normative tool of the business community.

CONCLUSION

The chapter has endorsed the logic that data and resource integration using concepts and practices associated with Data Grid technology could support managers in making informed decisions within a VO. The extended view of keeping interested decision makers informed of changes occurring across their domain of particular interest will enlarge their decision-making space which in turn will increase and/or unfold new opportunities. Overall, it will facilitate methods towards normative thinking as required for a better quality of service.

On this basis, the chapter presented and illustrated the model architecture and its real-world implementation for extending current functionality offered by the OGSA-DAI specification to keep interested decision makers informed automatically about relevant up-to-date data. The testing has demonstrated that the user tailored 'Data Push' service functionality in a Data Grid is working well.

A number of limitations with the current implementation have been also highlighted, including

the use of XML and Java files, which would have been led to a more open source friendly and sustainable approach. In distributed heterogeneous systems, it is often necessary to use virtualizing data sources from different database providers. Even if this is not considered as a limitation, current developments towards the implementation of a data push service in Data Grids to automatically keep interested clients informed about relevant up-to-date data that are stored in distributed environments by different database vendors and data source providers is sought.

Finally, the Data Push model in OGSA-DAI should not be seen as a mere mechanism for use in Data Grids only but also as a mechanism for other types of resources. Therefore work needs to be undertaken to investigate its potential to serve as a Service Push Model in various Grid environments.

REFERENCES

Anand, P. (2002). *Foundations of Rational Choice Under Risk*. Oxford: Oxford University Press.

Antonioletti, M., Atkinson, M. P., Baxter, R., Borley, A., Chue Hong, N., P., Collins, B., Hardman, N., Hume, A., Knox, A., Jackson, M., Krause, A., Laws, S., Magowan, J., Paton, N., Pearson, D., Sugden, T., Watson, P., & Westhead, M. (2005). The design and implementation of grid database services in OGSA-DAI. *Concurrency and Computation: Practice and Experience*, 7(2-4), 357-376.

Arthur, W. B. (1991). Designing Economic Agents that Act like Human Agents: A Behavioral Approach to Bounded Rationality. *American Economic Review, 81*(2), 353-359.

Asimakopoulou, E., Anumba, C. J., Bouchlaghem, D., & Sagun, A. (2006, August). *Use of ICT during the response phase in emergency management in Greece and the United Kingdom*. Paper presented at the International Disaster Reduction Conference (IDRC), Davos, Switzerland.

Atkinson, M., Dialani, V., Guy, L., Narang, I., Paton, N., Pearson, P., Storey, T., & Watson P. (2003). *Grid database access and integration: requirements and functionalities*. Report. Retrieved August 17, 2008, from http://www.ggf.org/documents/GFD.13.pdf

Baker, M., Buyya, R., & Laforenza, D. (2002). *Grids and grid technologies for wide-area distributed computing*. New York: John Wiley & Sons, Inc.

Bessis, N. (2003). Towards a homogeneous status of communicated research. In *Sixth International Conference on the Next Steps: Electronic Theses and Dissertations Worldwide*, Berlin. Retrieved August 17, 2008, from http://edoc.hu-berlin.de/conferences/etd2003/bessis-nik/PDF/index.pdf

Bessis, N., French, T., Burakova-Lorgnier, M., & Huang, W. (2007). Using grid technology for data sharing to support intelligence in decision making. In M. Xu (Ed.), *Managing Strategic Intelligence: Techniques and Technologies* (pp. 179-202). Hershey, PA: Information Science Publishing.

Bessis, N., & Chauhan, J. (2008, April). *The design and implementation of a grid database consistency service in OGSA-DAI*. Paper presented at the IADIS International Conference on Information Systems, Algarve, Portugal.

Bessis, N., & Asimakopoulou, E., (2008, July). *The development of a personalized and dynamic driven RSS specification for the built environment*. Paper presented at the IADIS International Conference on Web Based Communities, Amsterdam, The Netherlands.

Calvanese, D., Giacomo, G., & Lenzerini, M. (1998, August). *Information integration: conceptual modelling and reasoning support*. Paper presented at the third Conference on Cooperative Information Systems, New York, USA.

Clemen, R. (1996). *Making Hard Decisions: An Introduction to Decision Analysis*. (2nd ed.). Belmont, CA: Duxbury Press.

Duhan, S., Levy, M., & Powell, P. (2001). Information systems strategies in knowledge-based SMEs: the role of core competencies. *European Journal of Information Systems, 1(*10), 25-40.

Foster, I., Kesselman, C., & Tuecke, S. (2001). The anatomy of the grid: enabling scalable virtual organisations. *International Journal of Supercomputer Applications, 15*(3), 200-222.

Foster, I. (2002). What is the grid? a three point checklist. *Grid Today, 1*(6). Retrieved August 17, 2008, from http://www.gridtoday.com/02/0722/100136.html

Foster, I., Kesselman, C., Nick, N. M., & Tuecke, S. (2002). *The physiology of the grid: an open grid services architecture for distributed systems integration*. Globus. Retrieved August 17, 2008, from http://www.globus.org/alliance/publications/papers/ogsa.pdf

Kodeboyina, D., & Plale, B. (2004). *Experiences with OGSA-DAI: portlet access and benchmark*. Report. Retrieved August 17, 2008, from http://www-unix.mcs.anl.gov/~keahey/DBGS/DBGS_files/dbgs_papers/kodeboyina.pdf

Levy, A. (2002). Logic-based techniques in data integration. In J. Minker (Ed.), *Logic Based Artificial Intelligence* (pp. 575-595). Norwell: Kluwer Academic Publishers.

Magowan, J. (2003, April). *A view on relational data on the grid*. Paper presented at the International Parallel and Distributed Processing Symposium, Nice, France.

Nieto-Santisteban, M. A., Gray, J., Szalay, A. S., Annis, J., Thakar, A. R., & O'Mullane, W. J. (2004). *When database systems meet the grid*. Technical Report. Microsoft Research, Microsoft Corporation.

Raman, V., Narang, I., Crone, C., Haas, L., Malaika, S., Mukai, T., Wolfson, D., & Baru, C. (2003). *Data access and management services on grid. Global Grid Forum.* Retrieved August 17, 2008, from http://61.136.61.58:81/gate/big5/www. cs.man.ac.uk/grid-db/papers/dams.pdf

Reinoso Castillo, J. A., Silvescu, A., Caragea, D., Pathak, J., & Honavar, V. G. (2004). *Information extraction and integration from heterogeneous, distributed, autonomous information sources – a federated ontology – driven query-centric approach.* Paper presented at IEEE International Conference on Information Integration and Reuse. Retrieved August 17, 2008, from http://www. cs.iastate.edu/~honavar/Papers/indusfinal.pdf

Pratali, P. (2003). The strategic management of technological innovations in the small to medium enterprise. *European Journal of Innovation Management, 6*(1), 18-31.

Simon, H. (1977). *The new science of management decision.* Englewood Cliffs, New Jersey: Prentice Hall.

Watson, P. (2002). *Databases and the grid.* Technical Report. Retrieved August 17, 2008, from http://www.cs.ncl.ac.uk/research/pubs/books/ papers/185.pdf

Ullman, J. (1997, January). *Information integration using logical views.* Paper presented at the Sixth International Conference on Database Theory, Delphi, USA.

Venugopal, S., Buyya, R., & Ramamohanarao, K. (2005). *A taxonomy of data grids for distributed data sharing management and processing.* Retrieved August 17, 2008, from http://arxiv. org/abs/cs.DC/0506034

Weishaupl, T., & Schikuta, E. (2004). *Dynamic service evolution for open languages in the grid and service oriented architecture.* Paper presented at the Fifth International Workshop on Grid Computing, Pittsburgh, USA.

Wohrer, A., Brezany, P., & Janciak, I. (2004). *Virtalisation of heterogeneous data sources for grid information systems.* Retrieved August 17, 2008, from http://www.par.univie.ac.at/publications/other/inst_rep_2002-2004.pdf

Chapter XIII
Using Grid Technology for Maximizing Collaborative Emergency Response Decision Making

Eleana Asimakopoulou
Loughborough University, UK

Chimay J. Anumba
Pennsylvania State University, USA

Dino Bouchlaghem
Loughborough University, UK

ABSTRACT

This chapter demonstrates how Grid technology can be used to support intelligence in emergency response management decision-making processes. It discusses how the open Grid service architecture and data access integration (OGSA-DAI) specification services can facilitate the discovery of and controlled access to data, resources, and other instrumentation to improve the effectiveness and efficiency of emergency response tasks. A core element of this chapter is to discuss the major limitations with information and communication technology (ICT) in use when a natural disaster occurs. Moreover, it describes emergency response stakeholders' requirements and their need to seamlessly integrate all their ICT resources in a collaborative and timely manner. With this in mind, it goes on to describe in detail a Grid-aware emergency response model as the practice to maximize potential and make the best of functionality offered by current ICT to support intelligence in emergency response decision-making.

Copyright © 2009, IGI Global, distributing in print or electronic forms without written permission of IGI Global is prohibited.

INTRODUCTION

In general, natural phenomena are considered as normal, unavoidable and necessary planetary actions, which may cause disastrous results to the human environment if they occur in extreme forms (Asimakopoulou et al., 2006). In turn, the emergency management discipline has been formed to organize, analyze, plan, make decisions, and finally assign available resources to mitigate, prepare for, respond to, and recover from all effects of disasters (Nalls, 2003; Trim, 2003; Shaw et al., 2003). In managing disasters, it is apparent that a number of teams and individuals from multiple, geographically distributed organizations are required to communicate, co-operate and collaborate in order to take appropriate decisions and actions (Graves, 2004; Otten et al., 2004). 'The need for information exchange during an emergency situation is present; however it can be very diverse and complex' (Carle et al., 2004). Carle et al. (2004) also report that 'there are frequent quotes regarding the lack and inconsistent views of information shared in emergency operations'. There are communities that 'do not have the resources, personnel and expertise to develop a set of requirements to assist them in managing their activities as they pertain to emergency response' (Bui & Lee, 1999).

Moreover, recent emergency management approaches are characterized inefficient because of their unstructured poor resource management and centralized nature with fixed hierarchical instructions. Many scholars in the field point out that for the management of emergency response operations, a number of information and communication technologies (ICT) and relevant collaborative computer-based systems have been developed to assist the requirements of many segmented organizations to bring together their intellectual resources and the sharing of accurate information in a timely manner (Graves, 2004; Howard et al., 2002). However, findings as presented by National Research Council (NRS)

(2006) suggest that sustained efforts should be made with respect to data and resource archiving, sharing and dissemination. It refers to it as the hazards and disaster research informatics problem that is not unique to this research specialty, but it demands immediate attention and resolution. That is to say there is inefficiency in emergency managers' ICT infrastructure.

To tackle these limitations the authors proposed a Grid-Aware Emergency Response Model (G-AERM). This demonstrates the applicability of Grid technology to emergency response by supporting stakeholders in monitoring, planning, controlling and managing actions within emergency situations caused by natural disasters in a far more informed way in terms of effectiveness and efficiency. The G-AERM for natural disasters stands as an attempt to support the collaborative and dynamic provision of all available resources and instrumentation towards the accomplishment of emergency response tasks. This has been achieved by making provision for collecting, storing and integrating data from multiple distributed and heterogeneous ICT sources in a seamless and dynamic way. The approach adopted in the G-AERM architecture allows stakeholders to be part of a wider Virtual Organization (VO) to identify and select choices from the far wider range of resources available. Clearly, this may increase the possibilities for decision makers to take and issue more informed decisions of a collaborative nature towards the accomplishment of issued tasks in a far more effective and efficient way.

Finally, the chapter concludes by presenting the implications of a real-world implementation of the G-AERM. They may uncover scenarios of a cross-disciplinary nature that have been previously regarded as intractable because of organizations' interaction, size and complexity. For example, there will be a requirement for organizations to share their data with others across the technical infrastructure. It may lead to digitization of paper-based data and manual processes in order to enhance the availability of resources via the G-AERM infrastructure. It will lead to the need for user training in order to take advantage of G-AERM's full potential. Last but not least, the implementation phase may prove a challenging experience for stakeholders and computer scientists because of G-AERM's complexity and scale.

BACKGROUND

This section is concerned with the current state of emergency response managers' requirements with particular reference to ICT when natural disasters occur. It discusses the limitations with regard to ICT resource and data integration methods and provides an overview of where emergency management is and where it has been with particular reference to emergency response.

Naturally-occurring physical phenomena caused either by rapid or slow onset events and they have atmospheric, geologic and hydrologic origins on solar, global, regional, national and local scales as supported by UNESCO (2006). However, there are various natural phenomena which when they occur in 'extreme forms may cause large-scale changes into the shape and anatomy of the planet and can even be catastrophic and cause disastrous results on human life, property and the environment' (Asimakopoulou, 2008). This is evident as natural phenomena have periodically decimated the population of the planet (Mitra, 2001). The level of the disaster mainly depends on the scale, time and area of occurrence of the phenomenon. It is therefore clear that extreme natural phenomena may be characterized as catastrophic and disastrous by the scope of people in relation to the effects caused to their societies. The consequences of extreme natural phenomena depend on the existence or not in the area of affect of human societies and on the general level of civilization and technological advantages. However, over the last quarter of the twentieth century the number of reported natural disasters

and their impact on human and economic development worldwide has been increasing yearly (United Nations (UN), 2004). This is related to the frequency, complexity, scope and destructive capacity of natural disasters. Relevant bodies, such as UNESCO (2006) support that during the past two decades, earthquakes, windstorms, tsunamis, floods, landslides, volcanic eruptions and wildfires have killed millions of people, adversely affected the life of at least one billion more people and resulted in enormous economic damages. However, history is proving that natural disasters always occur and people need to find ways to overcome their consequences. Therefore, there is the need for integrated approaches in policies development and planning, able to take into account disaster reduction and response goals to the overall benefit of the socio-economic development process (Asimakopoulou, 2008).

Thus, a professional discipline – called emergency or disaster management – has been established and it is responsible for dealing with natural disasters. Emergency Management Australia (2002) and other relevant bodies describe the aim of disaster management as a range of measures to manage potential risks related to natural catastrophic phenomena to communities and the environment. This discipline is divided into four phases; mitigation, preparedness, response – which is the focus of this chapter – and recovery. These phases cover the full life cycle of the disaster, by being the body of policy, administrative decisions and operational activities, which pertain to the various stages of a disaster at all levels of vulnerability (UN, 2004) and by being in place all the time.

The four phases that the generic plan is divided into allow emergency managers to be able to organize, analyze, plan, make decisions, control, co-ordinate and finally assign available resources to mitigate, prepare for, respond to, and recover from all the effects of all catastrophic events (Shaw et al., 2003; Trim, 2003). The whole process is controlled by disaster legislation, which is the bodies

Figure 1. The four phases of disaster management

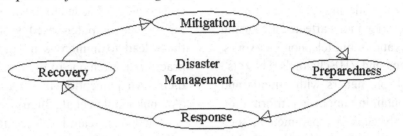

of law that govern and designate responsibility for disaster management concerning the various phases of disaster vulnerability (UN, 2004).

Specific bodies have been funded at international, national, regional and local level to cope with natural disasters by applying the theories of emergency management to practice and by acting in line with the discipline and under the relevant legislation. In particular, several international bodies, such as the North Atlantic Treaty Organization (NATO), the UN and the European Union (EU) have recognized the great problem related to the losses to humanity caused by natural disasters and they have funded relevant departments responsible for the application of emergency management, as well as for the improvement of relevant processes through research into the area of natural catastrophic phenomena and investigation of the current and future needs of humanity. Further to these bodies, each country is responsible to fund and maintain its own disaster management bodies at governmental level, which according to the administrative organization of the country cover all administrative levels with relevant departments. The bodies mentioned above are responsible to ensure – among others – an effective and efficient response to complex emergencies and disasters. Their actions include assessment, co-ordinated appeals, field co-ordination arrangements and the development of humanitarian polices, through an inter-agency decision making process. Disaster management requires flexibility in decision support and ability

to respond to varying situations because the scale of the residual effects varies according to the type and scale of the disaster. Bringing in expertise from different parties is essential as 'emergency response involves multiple organizations and teams, geographically distributed operations and a high need for co-ordinated control and decision making' (Graves, 2004). This will assist in managing disasters in a more informed and holistic approach. It is therefore clear that each one of the involved bodies has its own administrative organization, policies, expertise, personnel and equipment. However, they all need to work collaboratively and to communicate information, findings, decisions and actions in order to respond effectively and efficiently to a disaster.

Communication takes place via the use of ICT. In particular, the equipment which the emergency management bodies use during the response consists of computing and telecommunication facilities. These may include local area networks (LANs), wide area networks (WANs) and geographical information systems (GIS), integrated services digital network (ISDN) telephone lines, VHF and high frequency (HF) radio systems, global system for mobile communication (GSM), international mobile satellite communication (INMARSAT) telephones and fax machines. In addition to these, mobile units, which play the role of the "on-site eye" of the operation center, may be equipped with satellite communication tools, GSM communication tools, videoconferencing, TV receiver and transmitter, video and equipment for collection of meteorological data and detection of toxic gases. The mobile units provide information about the situation in the affected area using existing landlines and mobile telephone networks, satellite telephones, and VHF channels. They also provide the decision makers with e-mails and text messages containing important information about continuously changing parameters, such as the level of toxic gases, where applicable. Collected information is stored and assessed in the computerized systems of the local emergency management unit, running over LANs and WANs. Based on this information, authorities' leaders make decisions and give directions of action to the operational units. It is therefore clear that in the particular field of emergency response information exchange can be very diverse and complex (Carle et al., 2004). Moreover, people must take life and death decisions and act based – sometimes – upon incomplete information (Alles et al., 2004) which is static or dynamic in nature. According to UNESCO (2006), modern technologies have been developed in order to reduce the exposure of the physical and built environment and the other elements of socio-economic life to extreme natural phenomena and disasters. However, emergency management stakeholders seem to face many problems in practice, which are directly related to the limitations of ICT. These limitations may lead to major breakdowns, which in this field could lead to important losses, such as human lives.

In practice, the different parties are not always aware of each other which results in a lack of communication, co-ordination and collaboration and consequently, in a less effective crisis response organization (Oomes, 2004). Further to this, team members often hardly know each other and frequently have to work co-located. Therefore, the way professionals and specialists contribute their knowledge and experience has to be structured carefully. However, even the best-structured technique can be unsuccessful if it is not communicated effectively. In general, the need to bring together the intellectual resources of the

parties involved and to communicate effectively and efficiently has led to the development of collaborative computer-based systems. However, these lead to numerous misunderstandings in practice, as each one of the involved parties has their own perception in a particular situation (Asimakopoulou et al., 2006).

A response team has to perform many tasks partly in parallel, partly in succession during fighting a disaster (Rijk & Berlo, 2004). It is important for all stakeholders to have a common understanding about the current situation as this ensures a quick response to contain the consequences. However, many departments and organizations cannot share data based on current technologies. The authorities involved in response operations use a range of ICT to assess the disastrous situation and to respond to it; however, they often face problems. In particular, they find the current process of physical meetings at the office of the leader of the operation inefficient. The gathering of stakeholders is time-consuming and at the same time decision makers do not have access to their own data. Emergency management stakeholders believe that if the decision-making process was conducted with the contribution of all relevant participants, but from their own physical bases and with the opportunity to have access – at any time – to any important information required, then the whole process would be more informed and therefore more effective and efficient. In addition to this, during an emergency people revert to establish rules of behavior and the essential creativity and improvizations, and therefore emergency response is compromised. This is also occurred when critical information is present but hidden in the "noise" due to information overload – a phenomenon which is quite common in computer-based communication systems and likely to be exacerbated in emergency situations (Alles et al., 2004; Hiltz & Turoff, 1985; Turoff 2002; Turoff et al., 1993).

Another very important factor that makes the decision-making process even more difficult is that the exact information about the phenomenon reaches the operation center in no less than 20-25 minutes after its occurrence. During this time, the responsible scientific laboratory collects all the relevant information about the phenomenon, processes it and the exact details are forwarded to the operation center. Stakeholders believe that this time span is long and it may be prove vital for the victims of the disaster. It has been observed that the landline networks, by which the fax machines operate, have been destroyed by the impact of the phenomenon and sometimes they have been overloaded by people trying to communicate with each other. A further important parameter is the continuous flow of information between decision makers and operational units. In particular, the decision makers assess the situation and make decisions based on the information provided by the operational units, feeding them back with the orders resulting from the decision making process. Therefore, the accuracy of both information channels is important for the successful completion of the operation. This information is usually transferred between the two parties by mobile phones and VHF radios.

During an operation it is difficult for the leader of each authority to know at any given time what is available in terms of resources, where each one of the resources is located and if the task assigned

to it is completed or not. The lack of availability of this piece of information in time may result in delays, or prevent resource availability to be taken into consideration for another task. It is therefore clear that in such instances decision makers will most likely not choose a better solution because the narrowed search of the actual problem search space makes it improbable that the better solution will ever be encountered. Another important problem during emergency response is that ICT continue to break down during crises. On these bases, recent emergency management approaches are inefficient because of their unstructured poor resource management and centralized nature with fixed hierarchical instructions (Scalem et al., 2004) which are not easy to be communicated. Overall, the limitations of current ICT in use by emergency management stakeholders during response operations are summarized in Table 1.

These limitations clearly suggest that there is a need for a computerized method that will allow emergency management decision makers to make more informed decisions. This ICT method should fulfil the set of requirements of Table 2.

Concluding this section, some may argue that a real time system where each one of the resources could report the completion of the task, its availability, any problems and in general, its status at any time would prove beneficial for the whole

Table 1. Current ICT limitations during the emergency response operations

Current ICT Limitations during Emergency Response Operations
Gathering of stakeholders to a centralized place is time consuming
Centralized store of important information
Gathering of stakeholders to a centralized place limits access to individuals' centralized resources/data
Non-timely exact information about the phenomenon
Not exact information about available resources
No real-time pictures
Failing of telephone networks
Overloaded telephone networks
Possible computer network failure
Incompatibility of computerized means of communication

emergency response operation. This is because emergency managers would have access to more up-to-date information about the situation, which would enable them to assess the situation in a more informed way. Therefore, this approach would lead them to identify the best possible available solution.

The following section examines the provision of concepts and practices of VOs, Grid technology and Open Grid Services Architecture Data Access and Integration (OGSA-DAI) into the real world and how these may maximize decision-making during response operations. Further to these, the role of collaborative resource sharing is analyzed in order to highlight its association with making the best possible decision.

MAXIMIZING COLLABORATIVE DECISION-MAKING IN EMERGENCY RESPONSE

In general, advances in computer networking technologies have been predominant in our society and have caused the need for people to work electronically (Gentzsch, 2001). Networks are used to allow users to share their resources towards the achievement of a goal. Advances in science and other disciplines have been made it possible through the collaborative efforts of many researchers in a particular domain. In turn, collaborative work using computing technologies enabled people in dispersed environments to work together towards the achievement of common goals. Deelman et al. (2004) and other researchers point out that, currently there are collaborations of hundreds of scientists in areas, such as gravitational-wave and high energy physics, astronomy and many others coming together and sharing a variety of resources within a collaborative manner in pursuit of common goals. In this context, resources located in dispersed environments are called distributed resources (Connolly & Begg, 2002; Joseph et al., 2004; Rob & Corronel, 2004) while technologies supporting distributed resource exchange are known as distributed technologies (Wulf, 2003). Further to this, a distributed system containing different hardware and software working together in a co-operative manner to solve a problem is called

Table 2. Set of requirements for the emergency response model

SET OF REQUIREMENTS for the EMERGENCY RESPONSE MODEL
1. Emergency management authorities' stakeholders to work remotely and collaboretively in order to plan, control, coordinate and communicate relevant actions in a more effective and efficient way
2. Stakeholders to receive dynamically the most up-to-date information about the current situation (upon request)
3. Stakeholders to receive dynamically the most up-to-date information in relation to what resource is available to use (upon request)
4. Stakeholders to work in an environment that is free of any ICT compatibility problems
5. ICT resources to dynamically collect and store the most up-to-date information about the current situation
6. ICT resources to dynamically assess and allocate incomplete jobs to other available resources if the becomeunavailable
7. ICT resources to interoperate in a compatible way
8. All resources to dynamically and collaboratively work in an environment as defined by the set of policies

heterogeneous (Burback, 1998). Distributed collaborative work utilising ICT requires and caused continuous developments in computing technologies. Among others, references to that have been made by Anumba et al. (2003), Antonioletti et al. (2003), Brezany et al. (2003), Foster and Kesselman, (2004), Foster et al. (2001), Mann (2003), and Waters et al. (2004). Many scientific communities require the analysis of large datasets for solving scientific problems (Brezany et al., 2003; Mann, 2003). The datasets addressed by individual applications are very often heterogeneous and geographically distributed and used for collaboration by the communities of users, which are often large and/or geographically distributed.

Hence, the ability to make data stores interoperable remains a crucial factor for the development of collaborative systems (Wohrer et al., 2004). One of the remaining challenges for such facilitation is that of data integration, which aims to provide seamless and flexible access to information from multiple, autonomous, distributed and heterogeneous data sources through a query interface (Calvanese et al., 1998; Castillo et al., 2003; Levy, 2000; Ullman, 1997). However, the combination of large dataset size, geographic distribution of users and resources, and computationally intensive analysis results in complex and stringent performance demands that, until recently, have not been satisfied by any existing computational and data management infrastructure (Foster & Kesselman, 2004).

In tackling these problems, the latest developments in relation to networking and resource integration have resulted in the new concept of Grid technology. It refers to an emerging infrastructure designed to enable flexible, secure, co-ordinated sharing of processing power, data or other types of resources to be used for large-scale and/or intensive problem solving purposes among a dynamic collection of resources including individuals or teams. Moreover, Grid technology is described as the infrastructure and a set of protocols to enable the integrated, collaborative use of distributed

heterogeneous resources including high-end computers, networks, databases, and scientific instruments owned and managed by multiple organizations, referred to as VOs (Foster, 2002). A VO is formed when different organizations come together to share resources and collaborate in order to achieve common goals (Foster et al., 2001). In this context, resource sharing is highly controlled, with resource providers and consumers defining clearly and carefully what is shared, who is allowed to share, and the conditions under which sharing occurs.

The added value that Grid computing provides, as compared to conventional distributed systems, lies in its ability to allocate and re-schedule resources dynamically in real-time according to the availability or non-availability of optimal solution paths and computational resources. Should a resource become compromised, untrustworthy or simply prove to be unreliable, then 'dynamic re-routing and re-scheduling capabilities can be used to ensure that the quality of service is not compromised' (French et al., 2007). Finally, the Grid is a type of a parallel and distributed system that enables the sharing, selection, and aggregation of resources distributed across multiple administrative domains based on their availability, capability, performance, cost, and users' quality of service requirements.

Based on the above, Grid technology is the appropriate technology to support decision makers and operational units during the emergency response operations (Asimakopoulou, 2008). In fact, the notion of Grid has emerged as a thoroughly viable method to support the co-ordination of electronically and dynamically available shared resources over a distributed heterogeneous environment to assist distributed and heterogeneous virtual teams to solve common problems. The deployment of a Grid infrastructure on top of the existing resources that relief bodies currently have could assist in solving ICT related limitations. This is due to the fact that Grid technology emerged as the computer-based method to allow multiple distributed owners to form a VO via sharing, integrating and vitalising their numerous heterogeneous resources and expertise in a dynamic fashion that are governed by differing policies. This will offer stakeholders with numerous opportunities in response to the limitations presented in Table 1. In particular, these limitations adversely affect the effective and efficient accomplishment of tasks in relation to the set of requirements identified by emergency management stakeholders (Table 2) (Asimakopoulou, 2008). However, Grid technology experts indicate that there are a number of Grid related methods, which can be employed to assist in addressing the limitations of current ICT in use. These will enable more effective and efficient accomplishment of tasks in relation to the identified set of requirements.

In particular, videoconferencing could be used to address the ICT limitation of gathering stakeholders to a centralized place that is time consuming and evidently limits access to individuals' centralized resources/data. The use of "Data and Quality of Service register mechanisms via the methods of OGSA-DAI, Web Services and the Semantic Web" and "remote resource management via Web Services" could offer the ability to manage centralized stores of information in a distributed manner. On the same basis, "Data discovery mechanisms via the use of OGSA-DAI, Web Services, Semantic Web and Decision Support Systems", "Mechanisms that can intelligently and transparently identify, select and allocate computer-based resources capable of running user's request; via the use of Intelligent Agents and Job Schedulers", as well as "Integration and virtualization of multiple distributed, heterogeneous, and independently managed instrumentation based sources via OGSI, OGSA-DAI and Advanced Visualization Systems" could be employed to assist emergency response stakeholders receiving timely and exact information about resource availability, phenomenon status and access to real-time information, including real time images. Moreover,

ICT limitations related to failures of computer or telephone networks caused from overloads or other physical reasons could be overcome by using "wireless communications", "Backup/restore mechanisms and policies necessary to prevent data loss and minimize unplanned downtime across the Grid" or via embedded "Failure detection and fail-over mechanisms" which would allow "Dynamic job re-scheduling, re-routing and re-allocation once resource becomes unavailable". This can be achieved via the OGSA/OGSI Fault Tolerance services. Finally, "Integration and virtualization of multiple distributed, heterogeneous, and independently managed data, resource and instrumentation based sources via OGSI and OGSA-DAI" could be utilized to address various ICT incompatibility issues.

The next section introduces the G-AERM that has been developed by the authors based on the emergency management stakeholders' requirements and describes the functionalities of various Grid services that support these requirements. In particular, it describes how the G-AERM architecture supports the collaborative and dynamic provision and use of all currently available resources/instrumentation in order to dynamically integrate and seamlessly support intelligence in emergency response decision-making.

THE GRID-AWARE EMERGENCY RESPONSE MODEL (G-AERM)

Apparently, the most important underlying opportunity in using Grid technology in emergency response is that it will foster collaboration between decision makers and enable them to take more informed decisions. In particular, the deployment of Grid technology will facilitate seamless integration of what is availably known and therefore, enable the emergence of relevant VOs consisting of dispersed resources, operational units, ICT, instrumentation, experts and decision makers. In turn, the VO will foster better communication, co-ordination and collaboration between its members. That is to say, decision makers as VO members will be able to utilize other VO member resources, request, access, assess and make use of more available resources at a given time in order to run complex and intensive what-if scenarios collaboratively and in parallel. Stakeholders will also be able to search for resources or information about the emergency from a wider search space, which will increase the opportunities for a better solution to be encountered.

Therefore, the above mentioned facts, along with the emergency management stakeholders' requirements are addressed in a Grid-aware model that is owned, managed and operated by a VO that is dynamically formed by emergency management and other directly involved authorities when a natural disaster occurs. The VO will improve the effectiveness and the efficiency of emergency response operations in terms of controlling, co-ordinating and communicating the emergency management procedures and the relevant resources, by:

- Allowing utilization of parallel distributed power processing to run complex tasks.
- Providing seamless integrated access to assess what is currently available, known and relevant to the emergency from multiple dispersed resources.
- Assisting the collaborative nature of the emergency response and rescue operations.

The following statement outlines the G-AERM:

- A Grid-Aware Emergency Response Model in the form of a VO to support the collaborative and dynamic provision and use of all currently available resources and instrumentation in order to dynamically integrate and seamlessly collect and store all data relevant to the emergency. In turn, the VO should allow the collaborative and collective assessment of this data, and if required to dynamically alert relevant registered and authorized resources and instrumentation including emergency management stakeholders about the emergency. Individual and/or collaborative resources, such as decision makers (as members of the VO) should be able to collectively access as much as possible integrated data from various relevant resources in order to collaboratively and collectively assess data and make an informed decision. This should then be forwarded and allocated dynamically to an appropriate and available collaborative operational unit(s) and/or other collaborative resource(s) as specified in the produced emergency response job plan. Following this, the operational unit(s) and/or other resource(s) have to take collaborative action(s) and run the allocated job(s) and finally, to dynamically report job(s) completion, failure or the need for additional resource(s). In the event of the need for external resource(s), the VO should dynamically alert relevant decision maker(s) to allow external resource(s) to collaboratively join the VO. Finally, for all these functions to run smoothly and according to the bodies of law, the codes of practice, the quality of service, the ethicality and other issues including environmental and humanitarian concerns, a set of pre-defined and/or dynamically generated policies as required appropriately should be embedded within the VO.

Figure 2 illustrates how the proposed Grid layer embraces all conventional ICT resources made available by participating authorities in order to respond to the disruption caused by the occurrence of a disaster. As time passes, the disruption reaches a number of peak levels required for it to progressively cease. The use of

Figure 2. Outline graphical representation of the G-AERM

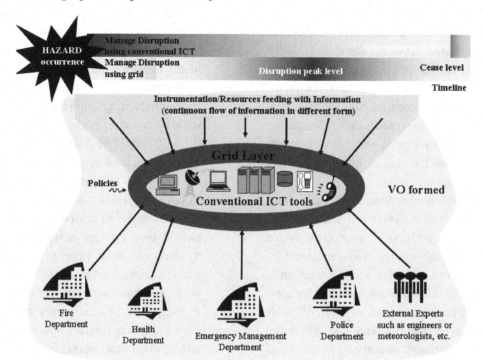

the proposed G-AERM will speed up the time required to manage the situation by shortening the disruption time compared to a situation where various conventional non-Grid tools have been used. This is due to the fact that VO members will benefit from taking remote decisions and actions dynamically and collaboratively from a far larger range of Grid-enabled resources (provided by the other VO members) that are free of ICT compatibility problems.

Clearly, a number of distributed resources and instrumentation generate a continuous flow of information in various forms. The proposed Grid layer enables the emergency response management team to make real-time intelligent decisions and act accordingly by assessing these multiple dispersed resources. The G-AERM enables the utilization of these distributed and heterogeneous resources by feeding (manually or by pushing dynamically to) the VO members with relevant information in a more integrated form, as it may

be required by an emergency management stakeholder. This will serve as a combined method of an oral and/or text messaging report, received by a member of an operational unit using a mobile phone. The Grid layer may also convert and save information, such as combined reports and associated images in a format that can be used (retrieved) for future reference if required. Further to these, the proposed G-AERM alerts stakeholders of situations requiring urgent attention. It also fosters team working and collaboration between dispersed decision makers as VO members whose decisions may be dependent on each other's interactions. Resource integration at that level supports decision makers since it allows them to view satellite images of the affected area, observe seismic activity, forecast, simulate and run what-if scenarios using other members' data modeling and mining tools, collaborate with (internal and external) experts and other authorities. Overall, the G-AERM approach as a whole assists VO members to request and access as much information as required and possible to acquire about a particular instance from different sources, and therefore to allow them to have a holistic view of the current situation. In turn, these assist decision makers to prioritize and ultimately make more informed decisions, which will be disseminated to available operational units who will then take care of the operational tasks. The latter are able to receive better-described emergency response (ER) job plans, push more meaningful reports and request resources if required. Similarly, VO members would benefit from the use of each others' spare computational capacity to run highly intensive operations.

However, for the VO to operate within the G-AERM environment, involved emergency management authorities need to set a number

of policies. To achieve this, stakeholders will be required to register their services using the "set of policies" activity. These policies will identify the quality of service to which each VO member will operate. Such quality of service will also include information related to authorization levels. Authorities wishing to utilize expertise from external parties will also be required to seek and set up an agreed policy with the invited party. External resources may include, but not be limited to, structural and mechanical engineers, meteorologists, geologists, military or other, non-human resources. Figure 3 illustrates the aforementioned types of interactions between VO members when using the G-AERM, along with the main interactions between emergency response managers, operational unit leaders, external experts, data

Figure 3. VO members' interactions when using the G-AERM

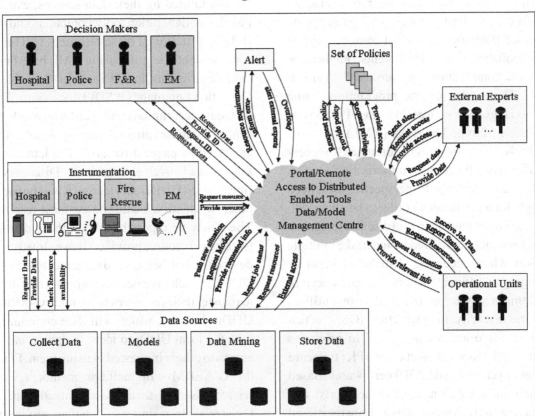

sources, model sources, data mining, computers and other instrumentation.

A real world application based on the G-AERM will facilitate access to either individuals or members of VOs. These members are required to gain access to the G-AERM via a secure authentication mechanism, which will check the user's credentials. Checking will be performed using the user's credentials across a proxy database, which will hold the user's log-in details. It is expected that users will have registered their log-in details prior to their first attempt to use the system. They should be able to register their details and log-in via the Grid Services Portal Interface (GSPI). This should be accessible via a Web browser, which supports a Graphical User Interface (GUI). The GSPI, located in the Grid Customised Applications Layer and its underlying specification relies on the OGSI, OGSA and the DAIS specification framework. In particular, a number of Application Programming Interfaces (APIs) have to be in place in order to provide access to the required services, such as access to dispersed data sources, model sources, mining tools, collaborative environments, application software, computational power and instrumentation. These APIs can be programmed using various languages, such as C++, Java, Python and Extensible Markup Language (XML).

Firstly, VO members will be required to access the GSPI using the Secure Authorisation service. To gain access to the GSPI, perspective users need to apply for a certificate in order to be allowed to sign-on. This allows them to utilise single sign-on so they will not be required to undertake multiple sign-on when accessing distributed services belonging to different owners. As can be seen in the Connectivity Layer, the Grid system utilises the Grid Security Infrastructure (GSI), which allows reliable and secure access to resources using Public Key Infrastructure (PKI), Secure Socket Layer (SSL) and X509 certificates. Based on their authentication, the VO member(s) will have access only to services, which are registered

to their account. These services are located in the Grid Customised Applications Layer and are described in the Grid Services database system, which recalls resource authentication via the "set of policies" service. For example, an emergency manager decision maker has the right to "access" a number of resources in order to "assess" them and "decide a relevant ER job plan", which is accessible by the operational units. When external expertise is required, the relevant leader is provided with the ability to amend or set up a policy at an appropriate level as required, in order for the invited external resource to join the VO environment. Similarly, leaders can amend or set up policies following the organisation hierarchy.

Once emergency management stakeholders are authenticated to the GSPI, they will have access to a number of services – as detailed in the G-AERM – via the embedded Grid functionality. That is to say, authenticated members will be able to register their owned resources including, but not limited to, their data sources, expertise profiles, collaboration tools, computers and other ICT. Registration of these resources will require some semantic tagging using XML based metadata descriptions in the form of Web Service Definition Language (WSDL) documents. These metadata descriptions will then be forwarded to a central database (proxy database), which will act as a "yellow pages directory". The latter is also known as a Universal Description Discovery and Integration (UDDI) service and it will be used by others to identify, locate and use these resources. There may be a possibility that those members (service or resource providers) have already made descriptions of their owned resources to their local UDDI. In such instances, members will still have to register their resources to the main G-AERM's UDDI directory, which will then communicate with the local UDDI to identify, locate and give access to others interested in using them. Finally, the G-AERM will facilitate members with a wizard assisting them to semantically tag and register their resources. Another service that will be available to the G-AERM members is the ability to request the availability of resources including data, models, mining and collaborative tools, computational power, etc. Identification of requested resources will be based on the XML metadata descriptions that have been provided by resource owners during the registration phase. Again, a wizard assisting members as service and/or resource requestors (service or resource seeker) should be made available for their disposal. It is important to note that services and resources registered with the G-AERM are external entities and therefore, it is expected that the respective owners autonomously manage them. Figure 4 outlines the G-AERM architecture.

Upon a member's request, a Web Server broadcasting multiple Web and Grid Services

compatible messages will be required. The Grid and Web Services Broadcaster (GWSB) will enable multiple requests for services and resources based on the XML metadata descriptions submitted by a VO member when registering or requesting them. For example, requesting a particular data service will require the searching of all data sources that are listed in the main UDDI service, which will then be able to identify and locate the listed service in local UDDIs, if there are multiple results. Assuming that the member, as a requestor, is authenticated to access the requested data items, access will be provided via means of a virtualized data source. Request for and delivery of, services and resources will be achieved via the communication between the GSPI, GWSB and registered services/resources.

Figure 4. The outline architecture of the G-AERM

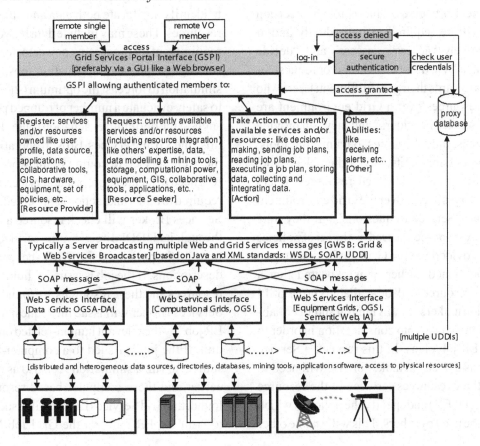

That is to say, a VO member requesting an XML metadata description based data service will be received by the GWSB. The latter will distribute the request identification (via the UDDI services) of registered services/resources via multiple XML based Simple Object Access Protocol (SOAP) messages. Identified registered services or resources that are available will then become accessible via an XML based Web Services Interface. A similar functionality for computational and equipment Grid service providers and seekers will be offered. This will enable GSPI members to register and request computation power to run what-if scenarios and for others to view real-time images from a satellite.

The expectation is that the VO will consist of single or multiple VO users, who will access the collaborative environment either as decision makers, invited external experts or operational unit leaders. It is also expected that decision makers will broadly follow current emergency management processes. That is to say, decision makers will be required to individually and/or collaboratively "access", "assess" and "decide ER job plans" via the provision and/or request for resources towards their goal fulfilment. Users who provide resources over a Grid environment are termed "Service Providers" and they can provide data sources, model sources, data mining tools, power processing units, and other electronic, mechanical or human-related resources. Users who request resources over the Grid environment are termed "Service Requestors" and they may request any resource covered by the set of policies that are provided via the Grid environment.

As mentioned earlier, it is expected that a number of resources will be available via the GSPI for decision makers to individually and/or collaboratively take them into consideration in order to produce ER job plans. In this respect, a Service Provider as a decision maker or else will need to register their resources/services to the resource directory (UDDI) and specify the policy in which they will be used by others. This will enable other parties to locate registered resources/services. In particular, to register resources/services, the Service Providers will be required to describe them using the Web Services Description Language (WSDL) in order to define how the service is to be used by others. Registered services/resources can be found using the Grid Services Broker, which includes registered services/resources metadata services (XML), which are connected to a Service Requestor using the SOAP. The Grid Services Broker is located in the Collective Layer. On the other hand, an individual or a group of decision makers as Service Requestors will need to "access" a number of appropriate and relevant resources/services including data sources, model sources, data mining, decision support applications, processing power and other physical resources in order to "assess" the current situation and "decide the best possible ER job plan".

The Grid Services Broker enables the Semantic Web functionality via the use of Intelligent Agents to identify and locate both data and other types of resources. These may include data harvesting or a requirement for processing power to, for example, run highly intensive application jobs, such as a simulation to forecast the optimum (shortest) time to safely evacuate a number of trapped people and suggest the optimum evacuation route. To achieve this, the Grid Services Broker operating under the Web Service Resource Framework (WSRF) will need to locate appropriate services/resources required to undertake action as specified. The Grid Services Broker will check resource availability through its UDDI directory, the service description and the policies, using XML-based metadata descriptions. If the job is issued to human-related resources and these resources are found, the Grid Services Broker will issue the request to "run the ER job" by the relevant human-related operational unit. If the job is issued to a computer-based resource, to run a simulation scenario as described earlier and these computer based resources are found, the Grid Services Broker will issue a request to "run the ER job" via the Grid Job Manager, which will act as a non-human operational unit leader. The Grid Job Manager is located in the Grid Middleware Resource Layer and it takes responsibility of controlling, managing, monitoring and scheduling (computationally related) issued jobs. If resources are not found to satisfy the policy requirements or not found at all through the UDDI directory, the Grid Services Broker will "alert" decision makers to take appropriate action, such as to negotiate policy requirements and/or seek alternative resources.

Once a computational related job is issued to the Grid Job Manager via the "take action/run ER job" and the Grid Services Broker, the Grid Job Manager will need to check its scheduler and its job queues in order to discover the resource (for example, a cluster) and ultimately submit the ER job via the Grid Resource Allocator. Once the resource is found, the Grid Resource Allocator will send the job to the resource in order to execute the job. Initially, the job will be sent to the Master node, which will co-ordinate and spread sub-job tasks (as defined in the job plan) to the co-operating slave nodes. If a sub-job is interrupted for any reason, the Grid Manager will order it to retry job completion for a predefined number of times. The Grid Monitor Services will alert the Grid Manager in the event that the retry has been unsuccessful. In such a case, the embedded Grid Services fault tolerance will request the Grid Manager to firstly save the partially completed work to a secondary storage and secondly, alongside the Grid Resource Allocator, to identify and issue an alternate path to execute the remaining sub-jobs. Once the job is completed, the Monitoring Services, which are located at the Grid Job Manager, will inform the Job Status Services, which will further notify the "Report" system activity, which will be stored to the data sources of the "Collect" activity. The Job Status Services will concurrently inform the Grid Job Manager that resources are available for future use via the Monitoring and Discovery Services. If a job has not been completed, or has failed because no resources have been found

available at the specified time, the Grid Controller will keep the job in the Monitor Queues and will attempt to identify alternate solutions for a predefined number of times. In the case that the process is unsuccessful because of the expiration of the numbers of attempts or because of policies specified in the job plan, the Job Status Services will raise an "alert".

Finally, the fabric layer consists of the currently available, distributed and potentially incompatible instrumentation/resources owned by involved authorities. It is expected that human-related resources, such as operational units and external experts will be notified about their duties via the appropriate ICT equipment as mentioned above. These instrumentation/resources – depending on their physical nature – will be registered in the G-AERM's Data Grids, Computational Grids or Equipment Grids so they can be accessed accordingly. These will then feed the "collect data" activity with appropriate information about the natural phenomenon and the current situation. These types of information are then stored in database or model-base management systems via the "store collected data" activity. This activity functions as the gateway for the OGSI, OGSA-DAI Services Specification and the Grid Services Broker to locate and make instrumentation/resources available to the decision makers via the "access/assess data" in order to "decide ER job plan".

IMPLICATIONS AND BENEFITS OF THE GRID-BASES DECISION SUPPORT SYSTEMS (GBDSS) APPROACH

Clearly the use of Grid technology vastly increases the size and complexity of the problem spaces that can realistically be addressed not only by emergency management bodies but also by all types of organizations. Problems that have hitherto been regarded as being intractable either because of the size of the data-sets needed, their distributed nature or the sheer complexity of the multi dimensional analysis required.

One of the major implications in using Grid technologies as a vehicle to assist emergency management decision makers is the ability to enlarge the actual search space boundaries. By searching in a narrow space, where decision makers do not have full access of the current situation will most likely lead them not to choose an optimal solution. The following lists the ability that incorporation of the activities of the emergency response management process with Grid will offer:

- Various individuals and/or collective resources to make a more that currently informed decision by increasing the opportunities for a better solution to be encountered as, it will allow them to know more about the concerned situation by:
  o Running complex and intensive what if scenarios and/or other problem-solving scenarios in parallel.
  o Providing them with seamless integrated access to assess what is currently available and relevant from multiple dispersed resources.
  o Allowing them to work in a collaborative manner.

Another very important implication of embedding the G-AERM in the real world is that there is the need for some of the ICT methods currently used by emergency management stakeholders to be able to work in a Grid environment. Apparently, the G-AERM requires the use of electronic based resources to take full advantage of the proposed method. Therefore, it is expected that emergency management stakeholders will have databases holding information about their physical resources, and that they are willing to share them with others across the Grid infrastructure. It is important to note that the G-AERM assumes that the involved authorities have access to a number of instruments and that any related data needed to be accessed and assessed shall be stored in electronic form. Currently there is data that is paper based, such as maps, materials specifications, building, engineering and town plans; however, there is much activity in developing relevant middleware. Therefore, authorities involved will be able to utilize existing resources and infrastructure towards the creation of the G-AERM.

However, this implementation will create the need for users' training in order to be able to use the real world application in its full potential. Emergency managers, authorities' leaders and operational units need to be trained using simulation exercises to be familiar and feel confident to operate in using the G-AERM. At the same time, the G-AERM has the ability to keep a record of its functions, during both training and real world operations. This function therefore offers emergency management stakeholders the opportunity to identify good and bad practices after the completion of the operation, to use them for further training purposes and to amend emergency plans, laws and other relevant documentation in governmental level. Finally, the G-AERM needs to be compatible with the legal framework of the country of its implementation. That is to say, during the creation of real world applications emergency management authorities need to work together with the central government of the country to address and resolve any legal conflicts.

CONCLUSION

Overall, this chapter has investigated the areas emergency response to natural disasters with particular interest to the conflicts and ICT limitations, which emergency management stakeholders face during response operations. To overcome such problems, it has proposed the integration of Grid technology in the field of emergency response management, as the most appropriate way to address the set of problems, requirements and issues that emergency management stakeholders face. This has been done via the development of the G-AERM for natural disasters. The produced G-AERM supports the collaborative and dynamic provision of all available resources and instrumentation towards the accomplishment of emergency response tasks. This achieved by collecting, storing and integrating data from multiple distributed and heterogeneous ICT sources in a seamless and dynamic way. The approach adopted in the G-AERM architecture allowed stakeholders to identify and select choices from a far larger range of available resources. In turn, this increases the possibilities for emergency management decision makers to take and issue more informed decisions of a collaborative nature towards the accomplishment of issued tasks in a far more effective and efficient way.

REFERENCES

Alles, M., Kogan, A., Vasarhelyi, M., Hiltz, R., & Turoff, M. (2004, May). *Assuring Homeland Security: Continuous Monitoring, Control and Assurance of Emergency Preparedness.* Paper presented at the International Community on Information Systems for Crisis Response Management (ISCRAM) 2004 Conference, Brussels, Belgium.

Antonioletti, M., Atkinson, M., Borley, A., Chue Hong, N. P., Collins, B., Davies, J., Hardman, N., Hume, A., Jackson, M., Krause, A., Laws, S., Paton, N. W., Qi, K., Sugden, T., Vyvyan, D., Watson, P., & Westhead, M. (2003). OGSA-DAI Usage Scenarios and Behavior: Determining good practice. *UK e-Science All Hands Meeting 2004*, August 2004. Retrieved Sept 20, 2006, http://www.ogsadai.org.uk

Anumba, C. J., Aziz, Z., & Ruikar, D. (2003, February). *Enabling technologies for next-generation collaboration systems.* Paper presented at the International Conference on Construction Information Technology (INCITE2004), Langkawi, Malaysia.

Asimakopoulou, E. (2008). *A Grid-Aware Emergency Response Model for Natural Disasters,* Unpublished doctoral dissertation. Loughborough University, UK.

Asimakopoulou, E., Sagun, A., Anumba, C. J., & Bouchlaghem, N. M. (2006, August). *Use of ICT during the Response Phase in Emergency Management in Greece and the United Kingdom.* Paper presented at the International Disaster Reduction Conference (IDRC), Davos, Switzerland.

Brezany, P., Hofer, J., & Wohrer, A. (2003, September). *Towards an Open Service Architecture for Data Mining on the Grid.* Paper presented at the 14th International Workshop on Database and Expert Systems Applications (DEXA '03), Prague, Czech Republic.

Bui, T., & Lee, J., (1999). An Agent-Based Framework for Building Decision Support Systems, *The International Journal Decision Support Systems, 25*(3).

Burback, R. (1998*). Software Engineering Methodology: The Watersluice* (PhD Thesis). USA, Stanford University.

Calvanese, D., Lenzerini, M., & Nardi, D. (1998). *Description logics for conceptual data modeling, Logics for databases and information systems,* USA: Kluwer Academic Publishers.

Castillo-R. J. A., Silvescu, A., Caragea, D., Pathak, J., & Honavar, V. G. (2003, October). *Information Extraction and Integration from Heterogeneous, Distributed, Autonomous Information Sources–A Federated Ontology–Driven Query-Centric Approach.* Paper presented at the IEEE International Conference on Information Reuse and Integration, Las Vegas, USA.

Carle, B., Vermeersch, F., & Palma, C. R. (2004, May). *Systems Improving Communication in Case of a Nuclear Emergency.* Paper presented at the International Community on Information Systems for Crisis Response Management (ISCRAM2004) Conference, Brussels, Belgium.

Connolly, T., & Begg, C. (2002). *Database Systems,* 3rd ed. UK: Addison Wesley.

Deelman, E., Singh, G., Atkinson, M. P., Chervenak, A., Chue Hong, N. P., Kesselman, C., Patil, S., Pearlman, L., & Su, M. H. (2004, June). *Grid-Based Metadata Services,* Paper presented at the IEEE 16th International Conference on Scientific and Statistical Database Management, Santorini Island, Greece.

Foster, I. (2002) *What is the Grid? A Three Point Checklist.* Retrieved August, 10, 2008, from http://www-fp.mcs.anl.gov/~foster/Articles/WhatIsTheGrid.pdf

Foster, I., & Kesselman, C. (2004). *The Grid 2: Blueprint for a new computing infrastructure.* USA: Morgan Kaufmann Publishers, Elsevier.

Foster, I., Kesselman, C., & Tuecke, S. (2001). The Anatomy of the Grid: Enabling Scalable Virtual Organizations. *International Journal of Supercomputing Applications.* 15(3) Retrieved October 10, 2003, from http://www.globus.org/alliance/publications/papers/anatomy.pdf

French, T., Bessis, N., & Huang, W. (2007, April). *Grid Enabled Computing: A Semiotic Approach to Virtual Organizational Trus, 21st century IS: do organizations matter?* Paper presented at the UKAIS 2007: 10th International Conference in Information Systems, Manchester, UK.

Gentzsch, W. (2001) *Grid Computing: A New Technology for the Advanced Web.* Sun Microsystems. Retrieved March 20, 2004, from http://www.sun.com/products-n-solutions/edu/whitepapers/whitepaper_gridcomp.html

Graves, R. J. (2004, May). *Key Technologies for Emergency Response.* Paper presented at the International Community on Information Systems

for Crisis Response (ICSCRAM2004) conference, Brussels, Belgium.

Hiltz, S. R., & Turoff, M. (1985). Structuring Computer Mediated Communication Systems to Avoid Information Overload. *Communications of the ACM, 7*(28).

Howard, R., Kiviniemi, A., & Samuelson, O. (2002, June). *The Latest Developments in Communications and e-commerce – IT Barometer in 3 Nordic Countries.* Paper presented at the CIB w87 conference, Aarhus School of Architecture. International Council for Research and Innovation in Building and Construction.

Joseph, J., Ernest, M., & Fellenstein, C. (2004). Evolution of Grid Computing Architecture and Grid Adoption Models. *IBM Systems Journal, 4*(43). Retrieved June 15, 2004, from http://www.informatik.uni-trier.de/~ley/db/journals/ibmsj/ibmsj43.html

Levy, A. (2000). Logic-based Techniques in Data Integration. In J. Minker (Ed.), *Logic Based Artificial Intelligence.* USA: Kluwer Publishers.

Mann, B. (2003). *The Virtual Observatory as a Data Grid.* Edinburgh, UK: e-Science Institute. Retrieved August, 08, 2008 from http://www.nesc.ac.uk/technical_papers/UKeS-2003-03.pdf

Mitra, B. S. (2001). *Dealing with Natural Disaster: Role of the Market.* USA: Hoover Press.

Oomes, A. H. J. (2004, May). *Organization Awareness in Crisis Management.* Paper presented at the International Community on Information Systems for Crisis Response (ISCRAM2004) Conference, Brussels, Belgium.

Otten, J., Heijningen, B., & Lafortune, J. F. (2004, May). *The Virtual Crisis Management Centre. An ICT Implementation to Canalise Information.* Paper presented at the International Community on Information Systems for Crisis Response Management (ISCRAM2004), Brussels, Belgium.

National Research Council (2006). *Facing Hazards and Disasters: Understanding Human Dimensions.* USA: National Academy Press.

Rijk, R., & Berlo, M. (2004, May). *Using Crisiskit and Moped to Improve Emergency Management Team Training.* Paper presented at the International Community on Information Systems for Crisis Response (ISCRAM2004) Conference, Brussels, Belgium.

Rob, P., & Corronel, C. (2004). *Database Systems Design, Implementation & Maintenance*, USA: Thomson Learning.

Scalem, M., Bandyopadhyay, S., & Sircar, A. K. (2004, October). *An approach towards a decentralized disaster management information network.* Paper presented at the Second Asian Applied Computing Conference, Kathmandu, Nepal.

Shaw, R., Manu, G., & Sarma, A. (2003). Community Recovery and its Sustainability: Lessons from Gujarat earthquake of India. *The Australian Journal of Emergency Management, 2*(18).

Trim, P. R. F. (2003). Disaster Management and the Role of the Intelligence and Security Services. *Disaster Prevention and Management, 1*(12).

Turoff, M. (2002). Past and Future Emergency Response Information Systems. *Communications of the ACM, 4*(45).

Turoff, M., Hiltz, S. R., Bahgat, A. N. F., & Rana, A. (1993). Distributed Group Support Systems, MIS Quarterly, *17*(4), USA: Carlson School of Management, University of Minnesota, Minneapolis.

Ullman, J. (1997). Information Integration Using Logical Views. In *Procs. 6th International Conference Database Theory (ICDT '97)*, Delphi, Greece. LNCS, *1186*, 19-40.

United Nations Educational Scientific and Cultural Organization (UNESCO) (2006). Retrieved July, 05, 2008 from http://portal.unesco.org/en/ev.php-URL_ID=29008&URL_DO=DO_TOPIC&URL_SECTION=201.html

United Nations (2004, January). *Hyogo Framework for Action 2005-2015: Building the Resilience of Nations and Communities to Disasters.* Paper presented at the World Conference on Disaster Reduction, Kobe, Hyogo, Japan.

Waters, G., Crawford, J., & Lim, S. G. (2004). Optimising Multicast Structures for Grid Computing. *Computer Communications, 27*.

Wohrer, A., Brezany, P., & Janciak, I. (2004). Visualization of Heterogeneous Data Sources for Grid Information Systems. Retrieved June 12, 2005, from http://66.102.9.104/search?q=cache:oejheA3mPFkJ:www.gridminer.org/publications/woehrer_mipro04.pdf+Wohrer+A+Brezany+P+and+Janciak+I+(2004)&hl=en&ct=cln&cd=5&gl=uk

Wulf, W. (1989). SIPP ACCESS, an Information System for Complex Data: a Case Study creating a Collaboratory for Social Sciences. *Internet Research: Electronic Networking Applications and Policy, 5*(2).

Chapter XIV
Unified Data Access/Query over Integrated Data-Views for Decision Making in Geographic Information Systems

Ahmet Sayar
Indiana University, USA

Geoffrey C. Fox
Indiana University, USA

Marlon E. Pierce
Indiana University, USA

ABSTRACT

Geographic information is critical for building disaster planning, crisis management, and early-warning systems. Decision making in geographic information systems (GIS) increasingly relies on analyses of spatial data in map-based formats. Maps are complex structures composed of layers created from distributed heterogeneous data belonging to the separate organizations. This chapter presents a distributed service architecture for managing the production of knowledge from distributed collections of observations and simulation data through integrated data-views. Integrated views are defined by a federation service ("federator") located on top of the standard service components. Common GIS standards enable the construction of this system. However, compliance requirements for interoperability, such as XML-encoded data and domain specific data characteristics, have costs and performance overhead. The authors investigate issues of combining standard compliance with performance. Although their framework is designed for GIS, they extend the principles and requirements to general science domains and discuss how these may be applied.

Copyright © 2009, IGI Global, distributing in print or electronic forms without written permission of IGI Global is prohibited.

INTRODUCTION

The World Wide Web and its associated Web programming models have revolutionized accessibility to data/information sources. At the same time, numerous incompatible data formats, data heterogeneity (both the data types and storage formats), and machine un-readability of this data have limited data integration and federation. The seamless integration and sharing of data from distributed heterogeneous data sources have been the major challenges of information system communities and decision support systems. In order to be able to integrate and share data/information, data sources need to be in interoperable formats and provide standard service interfaces that interact with standard message formats and transport protocols. The interoperability issues have been studied by many public/private organizations over the last two decades at the data and service levels. Among these are the Web Service standards (WS-I) for cross-language, platform and operating systems, and International Virtual Observatory Alliance (IVOA) and Open Geospatial Consortium (OGC) for defining domain specific data model and online service definitions in Astronomy and Geographic Information Systems, respectively. We are now at the point that we can put this work into practice. Moreover, the merging of GIS standards with Web Service standards enables us to investigate the integration of geophysical application services with geographic data services.

Geographic information is critical to effective and collaborative decision making for building disaster planning, crisis management and early-warning systems. Decision making in Geographic Information Systems (GIS) increasingly relies on analyses of spatial data in map-based formats. Maps are complex structures composed of layers created from distributed heterogeneous data and computation resources belonging to separate virtual organizations from various expert skill levels.

Map-based services are both a crucial application for decision making and an interesting area for researching problems in distributed service architectures. Our proposed federated service-oriented information system framework supports collaborative decision making over integrated data views, described in layer-structured hierarchical data. The users access the system as though all data and functions come from one site. The data distribution and connection paths stay hidden and formulated as hierarchical data defined in federator's capability metadata. The users access the system through integrated data-views (maps) with the event-based interactive mapping display tools. Tools create abstract queries from users' actions through action listeners and communicate with the system through federator.

Our framework is based on standard GIS Web Service components that provide standard service interfaces defined by Open GIS standards and are developed in accordance with the Web Service Interoperability Organization's standards (WS-I, 2002). The federation service ("federator") combines standard GIS data services through aggregating their standard capability metadata and enables unified data access/query. Moreover, although the proposed framework is designed for GIS, our experiences with GIS have shown that it can be generalized to many application areas. We provide the overview architecture in Section 3. We give blueprint for this general architecture in terms of principles and requirements, with example applications for chemistry and astronomy.

GIS is particularly useful in emergency early-warning, preparedness, and response systems with applications in homeland security and natural disasters (earthquake, flood, etc). Such applications demand good performance. However, because of the distributed system's nature, interoperability requirements (compliance costs), characteristics of geo-data (large and variable-sized), and time-consuming rendering processes, performance and responsiveness stand as the toughest challenges in distributed modern GIS applications. Thus, despite the advantages of Web Service federation, we have to go beyond naïve implementations to address problems in scalability and performance. This has led us to investigate novel strategies including performance enhancing client-based caching, load balancing, and parallel processing techniques through attribute based query decomposition.

BACKGROUND

Geographic Information Systems (GIS) (Peng & Tsou, 2003) are systems for creating, storing, sharing, analyzing, manipulating and displaying geospatial data and the associated attributes. GIS introduce methods and environments to visualize, manipulate, and analyze geospatial data. The nature of the geographical applications requires seamless integration and sharing of spatial data from a variety of providers.

The general purpose of GIS is modeling, accessing, extracting and representing information and knowledge from the raw geo-data. The raw data is collected from sources ranging from sensors to satellites and stored in databases or file systems. The data goes through the filtering and rendering services and is ultimately presented to the end-users in human recognizable formats such as images, graphs, charts, etc. GIS is used in a wide variety of tasks such as urban planning, resource management, emergency response planning in case of disasters, crisis management and rapid response.

Over the past two decades, GIS has evolved from traditional centralized mainframe and desktop systems to collaborative distributed systems. Centralized systems provide an environment for stand-alone applications in which data sources, rendering and processing services are all tightly coupled and application specific. Therefore, they are not capable of allowing seamless interaction with the other data or processing/rendering services. On the other hand, the distributed systems are composed of autonomous hosts (or geographically distributed virtual organizations) that are connected through a computer network. They aim to share data and computation resources collaborating on large scale applications.

Modern GIS requires data and computation resources from distributed virtual organizations to be composed based on application requirements, and queried from a single uniform access point over the refined data with interactive display tools. This requires seamless integration and interaction of data and computation resources. The resources span organizational disciplinary and technical boundaries and use different client-server models, data archiving systems and heterogeneous message transfer protocols.

The primary function of a GIS is to link multiple sets of geospatial data and graphically display that information as maps with potentially many different layers of information (see Figure 1). Each layer of a GIS map represents a particular "theme" or feature, and one layer could be derived from a data source completely different from the other layers (Koontz, 2003). As long as standard processes and formats have been arranged to facilitate integration, each of these themes could be based on data originally collected and maintained by a separate organization. Analyzing this layered information as an integrated entity (map) can significantly help decision makers in considering complex choices.

Open GIS Standards and GIS Web Services

In order to achieve such a layered display (see Figure 1) whose layers come from autonomous, heterogeneous data resources provided by various virtual organizations, the domain-specific common data models, standard service functionalities and interfaces need to be described and widely adopted. There are two well-known and accepted standards bodies in the GIS domain aiming at these goals. These are Open Geospatial Consortium

Figure 1. Layered display – a map is composed of distributed multiple set of layers (Adapted from Koontz, 2003)

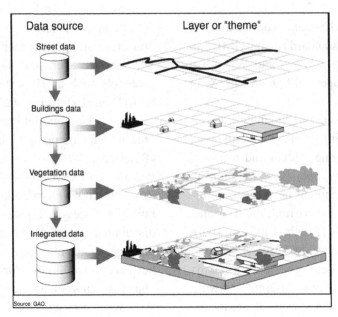

(OGC, 1994) and the Technical Committee tasked by the International Standards Organization (ISO/TC211). The standards bodies' aims are to make the geographic information and services neutral and available across any network, application, or platform by defining common data models and online service descriptions.

The standards bodies specify methods, tools and services for data management, accessing, processing, analyzing, presenting and transferring such data in digital/electronic form between different users and systems. ISO/TC211 defines a high-level data model for public sectors, such as governments, federal agencies, and professional organizations (Peng & Tsou, 2003). On the other hand, OGC is interested in developing both abstract definitions of Open GIS frameworks and technical implementation details of data models and to a lesser extent services. They are compatible with each other (JAG, 1999).

OGC's standards definition for data model (Geographic Markup Language -GML) (Cox, Daisey, Lake, Portele, & Whiteside, 2003) and

online data services are well-known and widely adopted. As more GIS vendors are releasing compatible products and more academic institutions use OGC standards in their research and implementations, OGC specifications are becoming de facto standards in GIS community, and GML is rapidly emerging as the standard XML encoding for geographic information.

The Web Map Service (WMS) (Beaujardiere, 2004; Kolodziej, 2004) and the Web Feature Service (WFS) (Vretanos, 2002) are two major services defined by OGC for creating a basic GIS framework enabling information rendering of heterogeneous data sources as map images. WMS is the key service to the information rendering/visualization in GIS domain. WMS produces maps from the geographic data in GML provided by WFS. It also enables attribute/feature based data querying over data display by its standard service interfaces. OGC's WFS implementation specification defines interfaces for data access and manipulation operations on geographic features. Via its standard service interfaces, a web user/client can combine, use and manage geo-data from different sources by invoking several standard operations (Vretanos, 2002). By creating an interoperable standard GIS framework as a result of adopting Open GIS standards (using GML and standard online services WMS and WFS), we open the door of interoperability to this growing community.

In addition to the domain-level interoperability and extensibility, information systems need cross-language, operating system and platform interoperability to enable data sharing/federating and analysis over autonomous heterogeneous resources provided by various virtual organizations. Web Service standards (Booth et al., 2004) are a common implementation of Service Oriented Architectures (SOA) ideas, giving us a means of interoperability between different software applications running on a variety of platforms. Grid computing (Foster & Kesselman; 2004; Fox, 2004) has a converging Web Service-based architecture. By implementing Web Service versions of GIS services, we can integrate them directly with scientific application Grids (Atkinson et al., 2005; Aydin et al., 2008).

A Web Service is an interface that describes a collection of operations that are network accessible through standardized XML messaging (Kreger, 2001). Web Services collectively are a software system designed to support interoperable machine-to-machine interaction over a network. A typical service has an interface described in a machine-processable format called the Web Service Description language (WSDL) (Christensen, Curbera, Meredith, & Weerawarana, 2001). Other systems interact with the Web Services in a manner prescribed by its description using SOAP-messages (Simple Object Access Protocol), typically conveyed using HTTP with an XML serialization in conjunction with other Web-related standards. Representational State Transfer (REST) (Fielding & Taylor, 2002; Khare & Taylor, 2004) is a variation of this architecture that replaces WSDL with standard HTTP operations (GET, POST, PUT,

DELETE). REST can be used to transmit SOAP messages as well as other formatted transmissions such as RSS, ATOM, or JSON.

The major difference between Web Services and other component technologies is that Web Services are accessed via the ubiquitous Web protocols such as Hypertext Transfer Protocol (HTTP) and Extensible Markup Language (XML) instead of object-model-specific protocols such as Distributed Component Object Model (DCOM) (Redmond, 1997) or Remote Method Invocation (RMI) (RMI, 2004) or Internet Inter-Orb Protocol (IIOP) (Kirtland, 2001). One typically builds services to be stateless and places the distributed system state in a single state machine that aggregates clients to services. This simplifies several well-known problems in distributed object systems (such as fault tolerance), enabling Web Service-based systems to have better scalability.

Adopting GIS Open Standards to Web Service standards and implanting Web Service versions of standard GIS services permit applications to span programming languages, platforms and operating systems. It also enables application developers to integrate the third party geospatial functionality and data into their custom applications easily.

FEDERATING GIS WEB SERVICE COMPONENTS: DISTRIBUTED SERVICE ARCHITECTURE

Our federator framework provides an infrastructure for understanding and managing the production of knowledge from distributed observation, simulation and analysis through integrated data-views in the form of multi-layered map images. Infrastructure is based on a common data model, OGC compatible standard GIS Web-Service components and a federator. The federator is actually an extended Web Map Server (WMS) federating GIS services and enabling unified data access/query and display over integrated data-views.

By federation, we mean providing one global view over several data sources that are processed as one source. There are three general issues here. The first is the data modeling (how to integrate different source schemas); the second is their querying (how to answer to the queries posed on the global schema); and the third is the common presentation model of data sources, i.e. mapping of common data model to a display model enabling integration/overlaying with other data sets (integrated data-view). The first two groups of research issues are related to lower level (database and files) data format/query/access heterogeneities summarized as semantic heterogeneity. In the proposed framework we take them as granted by applying Open Geographic Standards specifications for data models (GML) and online services (WMS and WFS).

Our extended standard GIS Web Service components are integrated into the system through a federator, which is actually a WMS that is extended with capability-aggregating and stateful service capabilities to enable high performance support for responsive GIS applications. This section presents view-level information presentation through federation of standard GIS Web Service components. The framework is designed for GIS domain; however we present the generalization architecture in terms of principles and requirements in Section 5.

Geo-Data and Integrated Data-View

Geo-data is provided by geographically distributed services from many different vendors in different formats, stored in various different storage systems and served through heterogeneous service API and transport protocols. The heterogeneity of geographic resources may arise for a number of reasons, including differences in projections, precision, data quality, data structures and indexing schemes, topological organization (or lack

of it), set of transformation and analysis services implemented in the source.

The OGC and ISO/TC-211 have tried to address these issues. The specifications for data models and online service descriptions define compliance requirements at data and service API level. In brief, according to the standard specifications there are three general groups of data services: Web Map Services, Web Feature Services, and Web Coverage Services (Evans, 2003). WMS provides rendered data in maps in MIME/image formats; WFS provides annotated feature-vector data in XML-encoded GML, and WCS provides coverage data as objects or images. Since they have standard service API and capability metadata about their services and data, they can be composed, or chained, by capability exchange and aggregation through their common service method called *getCapability*.

This idea has inspired us to develop an infrastructure for creating and managing the production of knowledge from distributed observation, simulation and analysis through integrated data-views in the form of multi-layered map images (see Figure 2) enabling unified data access/query/display from a single access point. As shown in the figure, the geo-data is accessed through a federator service, and data is always kept in its originating resources. They are integrated into the system with user's on-demand querying (just-in-time federation). This enables easy data maintenance and autonomy.

There is a three-level hierarchy of data. At the top layer, there is a federator service providing human comprehensible data display in multi-layered map images. The federators compose the data from the standard data services located at the middle level (WMS and WFS). The bottom levels are consisted of heterogeneous data sources integrated into the system through standard data services at the middle level. WMS are rendering and displaying services, and WFS are mediator/adaptor services providing heterogeneous data in common data model, and provide resource and data specific query/response conversions. They provide heterogeneous data in common data model with standard service interfaces as defined in Open GIS standards.

Heterogeneous data sources, which form the bottom layer of the hierarchy, are integrated into the system through mediators. Mediators provide an interface for the local data sources and play the roles of connectors between the local source and the global one. The principle of integration is to create non-materialized view in each mediator. These views are then used in the query evaluation. Mapping rules that express the correspondence between the global schema (GML) and the data source ones are essential. The problem of answering queries is another point of the mediation integration – a user poses a query in terms of a mediated schema (such as *getFeature* to WFS), and the data integration system needs to reformulate the query to refer to the sources. Therefore, an information integration architecture emerges based on a common intermediate data model (GML) providing an abstraction layer between legacy storage structures and exposed interfaces. In our system, we use OGC to enable these interfaces. GML provides a semantic abstraction layer for data files and is exposed through a higher level data delivery service called WFS.

There are several advantages in adopting the approach shown in Figure 2. The mediators not only enable data sources integrated into the system conform to the global data model, but also enable the data sources to maintain their internal structure. In the end, the whole mediator system provides a large degree of autonomy. The integration process does not affect the individual data sources' functionality. These data sources can continue working independently to satisfy the requests of their local users. Local administrators maintain control over their systems and yet provide access to their data by global users at the federation level.

The remainder of the chapter focuses on upper levels (view-level) of dataflow and query refinements illustrated in Figure 2. Since the OGC's standard services are developed as Web Service components, they can be chained/orchestrated with Web Service workflow tools, such as Kepler (Ludäscher et al., 2006) and Taverna (Turi, Missier, Goble, Roure, & Oinn, 2007), but we do not attempt to delve into those issues in this chapter. We instead focus on the definition of service compositions and integrated data views as presented in the following sections. Workflow execution abstraction is a higher-level abstraction than the capability metadata federation that we investigate.

Figure 2. Data life-cycle and integrated data-view creation

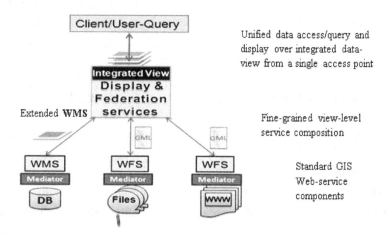

Hierarchical Data Definition as Multi-Layer Maps

Hierarchical data is defined as an integrated data-view in the federator's capability metadata. It actually defines a static workflow starting from the federator and ending at the original data sources (WFS serving GML or WMS serving map layer images). The services are linked through the reference-tags defined in their capability metadata. Decision makers' interactions with the system are carried over the integrated data views through event-based interactive map tools. Integrated data-views are defined in the hierarchical data format as explained below:

Map -> Layer -> Data {GML / binary images} -> Raw data (any type)

A map is an application-based, human-recognizable, integrated data display and is composed of layers. A layer is a data rendering of a single homogeneous data source. Layers are created from the structured XML-encoded common data model (GML) or binary map images (raster data). Heterogeneous data sources (*raw data*) are integrated into the system as GML or binary map

images through the resource specific mediators. The mediators have resource specific adaptors for request and response conversions and appropriate capability metadata describing the data and resources.

Different applications need different maps that are composed of different data layers in different numbers and combinations (see Figure 3). Maps are multi-layered, complex structures whose layers come from distributed heterogeneous resources and are rendered from any type of data. This type of multi-layered map image is defined and managed in the federator with utilization of its cascading WMS properties and inter-service communication between the components.

Federation Framework

Our federation framework is built over a service-oriented GIS framework and its components (WMS and WFS). Federation is based on federating capabilities metadata from the GIS Web Services components. Capabilities are aggregated through inter-service communication using standard service interfaces. We do not define common data models, online standard service components and their capability metadata definitions in GIS.

Figure 3. Federated GIS framework

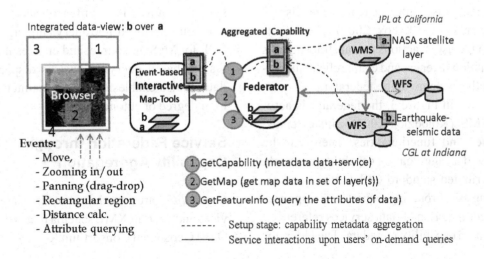

These are already defined by Open Geographic Standards (OGC). We instead have developed the components according to the open standard specifications, and applied them to our proposed information system framework by defining required extensions at implementation and application levels in compliance with WS-I Web Service standards (Sayar, Pierce, & Fox, 2005). They also serve as a test bed for implementing and testing general concepts in service architectures.

This section presents a federation framework based on common data models (GML), standard Web Service components, federator and event-based interactive decision making tools over integrated data views in the form of multi-layered map images. The general architecture is illustrated in Figure 3. This figure presents the proposed federation framework with a sample application using earthquake seismic data (from WFS) and NASA satellite map images (from WMS). WMS is the NASA OnEarth server located at the NASA Jet Propulsion Laboratory (JPL) (OnEarth, 2007) and WFS is located at Community Grids Labs (CGL) at Indiana University.

The framework enables users (i.e., decision-makers) to access the system as though all the data and functions come from one site. The data distribution and connection paths stay hidden and formulated as hierarchical data defined in federator's capability metadata. The users access the system through integrated data-views (maps) with the event-based interactive mapping display tools (Sayar, Pierce, & Fox, 2006). These tools transform the users' actions into abstract queries through action listeners and enable client interaction with the system via the federator.

As shown in Figure 3, the federator is actually a WMS (Kolodziej, 2004) with extended capabilities and functionalities. These can be summarized as aggregating capability metadata from distributed standard GIS services and orchestrating/synchronizing requests and responses over the composition of data services referenced in aggregated capability metadata. The federator

enables stateful service access over the stateless GIS Web Service components, and results in a better performance for responsive GIS systems. These issues are addressed later.

The federation framework is based on a two-stage process. The first stage is the setup (or initialization) stage. The second stage is the application run-time stage. In the setup stage, an integrated data-view (in the form of multi-layered map image) is defined in the federator's aggregated capability metadata. The federator searches for standard GIS Web Service components (WMS or WFS) providing required data layers and organize them into one aggregated capability file (see the following section). This is shown as dotted lines in the Figure 3. There is no client/user interaction with the system in this first stage. In the second stage (*run-time stage*), a user/client interacts with the system through a browser that provides event-based interactive display and query tools over the integrated data-view. The second stage is illustrated with solid arrows in the figure.

Interactive information visualization tools provide researchers with capabilities to support discovery. We developed these tools for interacting with standard WMS providing OGC compatible online services such as *getMap*, *getFeatureInfo* and *getCapabilities*. Since the federator is also a WMS, clients still use *getMap* service interface to display multi-layered map images and/or query it through *getFeatureInfo* service interface. The system removes the burden of accessing each data source with ad-hoc query languages such as SQL for MySQL source, and enables interactive feature based querying besides displaying the data. It also enables easy data-maintenance and high degree of autonomy.

Service Federation through Capability Aggregation

Capabilities are metadata about the data and services and have an XML schema that is defined by Open Geospatial Consortium (OGC). Capability descriptions include information about data and its corresponding operations with the attribute-based constraints and acceptable request/response formats. It supplements the Web Service Description Language (WSDL) (Christensen et al., 2001), which specifies key low-level message formats but does not define information or data architecture. These are left to domain specific capabilities metadata and data description languages (such as GML). Capabilities also provide machine and human readable information that enables integration and federation of data/information. It also aids the development of interactive, re-usable client tools for data access/query and display. We use the open standard specifications' definitions and present the required extensions for the federation through hierarchical data creation by service chaining.

The integrated data-view in multi-layered map images is defined in the federator's aggregated capability metadata. There are two major issues here: a) definition of aggregated capability metadata and b) definition of multi-layered map images.

As mentioned earlier, the federation framework is built over the standard GIS Web Service components, and the federator concept is inspired from OGC's cascading WMS definition (Beaujardiere, 2004). In this respect, the federator is actually a cascading WMS with extended capabilities. In the following sections, we describe how we apply OGC's ideas related to the service chaining and aggregation, and define multi-layered map images in the aggregated capability metadata.

Extending WMS as a Federator Service

The federator is actually a cascading Web Map Server. A cascading Web Map Server is a WMS that behaves like a client to other WMSs and like a WMS to other clients. It can receive input from other WMS (and WFS) and display layers from them. For example, a cascading Web Map Server can aggregate the contents of several distinct map servers into one service. Furthermore, it can even perform additional functions such as output format conversion or coordinate transformation on behalf of other servers.

There are two possible ways to chain the services to be able to create a federator framework and application specific hierarchical data in integrated data-view. One is extending the WMS capability file by giving the reference to the service access points providing the required layer (WMS) and/or feature data (WFS). Another way is using Web Map Context's standards defining chaining in a context document (described below). In any case, we utilize the cascading WMS definitions to develop a federator providing information/ knowledge in multi-layered map images.

Federating through Context Document

OGC's WMS and WFS services are inherently capable of being cascaded and chained in order to create more complex data/information. In order to standardize these issues, OGC has introduced the Web Map Context (WMC) (Sonnet, 2005) standard specifications. Before that, OGC recommended application developers to extend their services' capabilities for cascading. WMC is actually a companion specification to WMS.

The present context specification states how a particular grouping of one or more maps from one or more map servers can be described in a portable, platform-independent format for storage in a repository or for transmission between clients. This description is known as a "Web Map Context Document," or simply a "*context*." Presently, *context* documents are primarily designed for WMS bindings. However, extensibility is envisioned for binding to other services.

A *context* document is structured using XML, and its standard schema is defined in the WMC specifications (Sonnet, 2005). A *context* document includes information about the server(s) providing layer(s) in the overall map, the bounding box and map projection shared by all the maps, sufficient operational metadata for client software to reproduce the map, and additional metadata used to annotate or describe the maps and their provenance for the benefit of end-users.

There are several possible uses for *context* documents besides providing chaining and binding of services. The *context* document can provide default startup views for particular classes of users. For example specific applications require a specific list of layers. The context document can store not only the current settings but also additional information about each layer (e.g., available styles, formats, spatial reference system, etc.) to avoid having to query the map server again once the user has selected a layer. Finally, the *context* document could be saved from one client session and transferred to a different client application to start up with the same context. In this document, we just focus on its binding functionalities.

Federating through Aggregated WMS Capability

This is another alternative approach to extend the WMS as a federator. It is based on extending the standard WMS capabilities file.

Data providing in WMS is called "layer" and defined in layer tags in capability metadata with attributes and features according to the standard WMS capability schema (Beaujardiere, 2004). Service chaining is accomplished through the cascaded layer definition. A Layer is regarded to have been "cascaded" if it was obtained from an originating server and then included in the Capabilities XML of a different server. The second server may simply offer an additional access point for the layer, or may add value by offering additional output formats or spatial reference systems.

If a WMS cascades the content of another WMS, then it must increment the value of the cascaded attribute for the affected layers by 1. If that attribute is missing from the originating WMS's Capabilities XML (that is, the layer has not been cascaded before), then the Cascading WMS inserts the "cascade" attribute to the layer

tag and set it to 1. The default value of cascading is 0 (Kolodziej, 2004).

In order to illustrate service federation, we give a real geo-science application as an example. In the Pattern Informatics (PI) application (Tiampo, Rundle, Mcginnis, & Klein, 2002), decision makers need to see earthquake forecast values and seismic data records plotted on satellite map images. Satellite map images are provided by NASA OnEarth project's WMS at the NASA Jet Propulsions Laboratory, and earthquake seismic data records are provided from WFS at the Community Grids Labs (CGL) at Indiana University. The federator aggregates these services' standard capability metadata and creates an aggregated one as if those data sets are its own. The users access the system as though all the data and functions come from the federator. The data distribution and connection paths stay hidden and formulated in federator's aggregated capability metadata.

HIGH-PERFORMANCE SUPPORT IN DISTRIBUTED GEO-DATA RENDERING

General Performance Issues in Interoperable Service-Oriented Geographic Information Systems

Distributed GIS systems typically handle a large volume of datasets. Therefore the transmission, processing and visualization/rendering techniques need to be responsive to provide quick, interactive feedback. There are some characteristics of GIS services and data that make it difficult to design distributed GIS with satisfactory performance.

In order to provide interoperable and extensible framework, we have adopted domain-specific standard specifications for data model (GML) and online services from OGC, and Web Services specifications from WS-I (WS-I, 2002). However, these adoptions degrade the performance even more for large-scale applications because using

XML-encoded data models and Web Services' XML-based SOAP protocol introduces significant processing overhead. These issues and proposed enhancement approaches are presented in the following sections. The aim is to combine compliance requirements with competitiveness and to create a responsive information system framework providing map images for interactive decision making tools.

Distributed Nature of Data

The data ownership issues (that is, various data provided by geographically distributed various virtual public/private organizations) and large data volumes make it infeasible to put all geospatial data into one large data center. In addition, the computational resources associated with those data centers are naturally distributed. Furthermore, decision making requires these distributed heterogeneous data sources to be shared, and represented/rendered to extract useful knowledge giving sense to anybody joining the decision making process. Although we concentrate on the performance issues related to compliance requirements such as using XML-encoded data model GML and Open GIS compatible Web Service components, throughout the section we touch upon the general issues briefly mentioned above.

Using Semi-Structured Data Model

GML is the data modeling language for OGC specifications. GML carries content and the presentation tags together with the core data. This enables the data sources to be queried and displayed together (i.e., map images interactively query-able through interactive map tools). Querying and displaying data in the GML format requires parsing and rendering tools to extract requested tag elements such as geometry elements to draw map features or non-geometry elements to answer content-related queries.

Structured data representations enable adding some attributes and additional information (annotations) to the data. Those resulting XML representations of data tend to be significantly larger than binary representations of the same data. The larger document size means that the greater bandwidth is required to transfer the data, as compared to the equivalent binary representations.

In addition, due to the architectural features (integration of autonomous resources), the system spends a lot of time on query/response transformations for relational database-to-GML mappings. WFS enable mediation of autonomous databases and serving the data in common data model through the standard service interfaces and message formats. However, it is often time consuming because of the requirements for query and response conversions (getFeature to SQL and relational tables to GML). In summary, advantages of using structured/annotated data come with its costs.

Geo-Data Characteristics

Geo-data is described with its location on the earth. A location in a 2-dim surface is formulated as (x, y) coordinates. Based on the location attribute, geo-data is unevenly distributed (consider human populations, earthquakes, and temperature distributions) and variably sized. In addition, geo-data collected from sensors are dynamically changed and/or updated over time.

Because of these stringent characteristics of data, it is not easy to make load balancing and parallel processing over the unpredictable workload. Figure 4 illustrates this problem. The work is decomposed into independent work pieces, and the work pieces are of highly variable-sized. In the following two sections, we present our solution approaches.

Figure 4. Unbalanced load sharing. Server assigned R2: "((a+b)/2, (b+d)/2), (c, d) " gets the most of the work

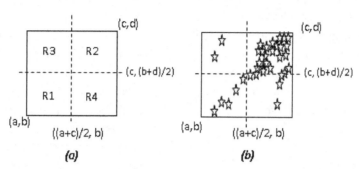

(a)   *(b)*

Extending Open GIS Standards with Streaming Data Transfer Capability

The OGC's initial standard WMS and WFS specifications were based on HTTP Get/Post methods, but this type of services have several limitations such as the amount of data that can be transported, the rate of the data transportation, and the difficulty of orchestrating multiple services for more complex tasks. Web Services help us overcome some of these problems by providing standard interfaces to the tools and applications we develop (Aydin, 2007).

Our experience shows that although we can easily integrate several GIS services into complex tasks by using Web Services, providing high-rate transportation capabilities for large amounts of data remains a problem because the pure Web Services implementations rely on SOAP (Gudgin et al., 2007) messages exchanged over HTTP. This conclusion has led us to an investigation of topic-based publish-subscribe messaging systems for exchanging SOAP messages and data payload between Web Services. We have used NaradaBrokering (Pallickara & Fox, 2003), which provides several useful features such as streaming data transport, reliable delivery, ability to choose alternate transport protocols, security and recovery from network failures. This allows us to provide higher level qualities of service in GIS services.

NaradaBrokering is a message oriented middleware (Tran, Greenfield, & Gorton, 2002) system that facilitates communications between entities through the exchange of messages. This also allows us to receive individual results and publish them to the messaging substrate instead of waiting for the whole result set to be returned. In case of using streaming, the standard Web Service interfaces are used for handshaking, and the actual data transfer is done between subscriber and publisher deployed in proposed GIS Web Service components respectively. Besides giving better performance in general, the streaming data transfer technique enables data rendering and processing even on partially returned data. It can even be applied to the real-time data rendering.

Federator-Oriented Design Approaches

The system supports fully distributed, decentralized, just-in-time, on-demand data fetching and rendering in which data sources are heterogeneous and autonomous. Autonomy in this context means keeping the data in their originating sources at all times. The originating sources are autonomous and control their own data definitions. Autonomy indirectly results in scalability and enables decentralized data maintenance. On the other hand, it has performance and reliability drawbacks coming from accessing and querying the heterogeneous data sources through WFS-based mediations. Mediators perform time-consuming query and response conversions to provide GML data in standard service interfaces.

In the following sections we present techniques to reduce the negative effects of time-consuming query and data response conversions and data transfer latencies. We focus on the issues at the upper level of data handling, which is view-level data handling at the federator.

The main idea behind the performance enhancement design is enabling stateful service capabilities by developing client-based caching, and parallel data fetching and processing for un-cached data queries. Since the data are kept only in their originating sources and not stored in intermediary places, this architecture provides consistency and strong autonomy.

Adaptive Client-Based Caching

OGC Open Standard's GIS services are inherently stateless and based on on-demand processing. They don't maintain the state information between message calls. Introducing a federator service over the OGC's WMS and WFS data services enable stateful service capabilities. The federator's stateful service capabilities also have inspired us to develop novel caching, load balancing and parallel processing approaches in distributed data access/query/display from a single access point. This is presented in the following section.

Client-based caching keeps records about the previously requested layer-data and corresponding query and data attributes, and stores them as session-class objects. The client's cache is kept up-to-date as in working window concept in operating systems. The server differentiates the clients based on their IDs defined in the request. Adaptive client-based caching helps make efficient load balancing over the unpredictable workload by utilizing the locality (Denning & Schwartz, 1972) and nearest neighborhood (Dasarathy, 1991) principles. By the "locality principle," we mean

that if a region has a high volume of data, then the regions in close neighborhood are also expected to have high volume of data. The human population data across the earth can be given as an example: Obviously urban areas have higher human population than the rural areas. Differentiating dense data regions from sparse regions enables us to find the most efficient number of partitions for parallel processing and reduces the overhead timings for handling an unnecessary number of partitions. Clustering techniques (Buyya, 1999; Pfister, 1998) provides a more precise way for determining this if one has access to data, but in our architecture we must treat the data servers as black boxes.

Processing from the cache gives better performance results over going to the remote data resources or even to the local disk. However, for large scale applications it might be impossible to cache whole data at intermediary servers because of the physical storage limitations. Client-based caching addresses this issue by proposing a way to get high performance with the limited storage capacities.

In Figure 3, cached data is shown as browser, which the user interacts with through the interactive map tools. The query-regions not overlapping with cached data (boxes numbered as 1, 3 and 4 in the figure) are processed from remote resources through novel distributed load-balancing and parallel processing techniques mentioned in the following section. On the other hand, the queries overlapping with cached data (such as box-2 in the figure and some parts of boxes numbered 1, 3 and 4) are processed from the federator's cache.

Load-Balancing and Parallel Processing through Query Decomposition

A federator inherently makes workload sharing by fetching the different data layers from separate resources to create multi-layered map image. We call this as vertical load balancing. This is a natural load balancing and parallel processing result from the architectural features.

In addition to the layer-based natural load-balancing, a layer (in the multi-layered map image) itself can be split into smaller bounding box tiles and each tile can be farmed out to a worker WFSs/WMSs. Layer-based partitioning is based on attribute-based query decomposition in which the attribute is the bounding box defining the requested data's range in a rectangular shape. This section focuses on individual layer partitioning and gives the architectural details in Figure 5.

In our federator framework, the load balancing and parallel processing techniques are applied over the un-cached regions of the main query. Queried regions overlapping with cache is met from the users' cached data.

The main idea is to decompose an un-cached region's bounding box (defined in the main query) and to create small sub-regions (defined again as smaller, constituent bounding boxes) (see Figure 5). After having partitions in small bounding boxes, each partition is assigned to a separate thread of work, and the results to partitions are merged to create a final response for the main query. The partitions are assigned to threads in a round-robin fashion.

Figure 5 shows a sample case in which there are 3 WFS worker nodes and 5 partitions. BBtotal is the main query's bounding box. Bb1, bb2, bb3, bb4 and bb5 are the partitions obtained from partitioning BBtotal.

Overall Evaluation of the System Performance

The overall performance results change considerably depending on the cached data available and queried region, and their positioning to each other. Here we analyze those affects on overall performance results. Figure 3 is the test setup. In Figure 3, "browser" shows the user the previous request's answer (cached data in federator) and boxes 1, 2, 3 and 4 illustrate the user's successive query region.

Figure 5. Architectural comparisons of parallel fetching (5-partition) with straightforward single thread fetching. BBtotal=bb1+bb2+bb3+bb4+bb5

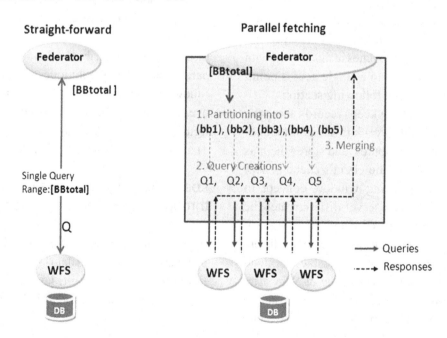

Here we analyze end-to-end response times based on all possible cases of query and cached data ranges positioning (see Figure 3). Overall performance changes depending on cached data and main query positioning. Queries and cached data can be positioned in three possible ways. These are:

1. Main query range falls outside of cached data ranges [worst case].
2. Main query range falls in cached data ranges [best case].
3. Query range partially overlaps cached data ranges [in between].

The first group of requests is typically first-time queries. The federator does not have prior state information about them. In such cases, federator fetches whole data falling in the requested ranges from remote databases through WFSs.

The second group of requests results typically from users zooming-in or panning (cutting a rectangular region over the display map) actions over the event-based interactive map tools. In such cases, the query falls in the cached data ranges and gives the best performance result. In this case the federator does not need to make successive queries to fetch the required data from the remote distributed databases through WFS-based mediators. The cache meets the whole requested ranges. Cached data is GML data kept in federator from the previous request. It is used to create the map image shown as "browser" in Figure 3.

The third group of requests comes primarily from moving (drag and drop) and zooming-out actions over the event-based interactive map tools displaying the previous map images. In such cases, cache cannot meet the whole requested range. This is called partial overlapping with cache. These three groups of requests are illustrated in Figure 3.

We now evaluate the performance of the system. The test setup is shown in Figure 3: The system is evaluated with a Geo-science application, Pattern Informatics (PI) (Nanjo, Holliday, Chen, Rundle, & Turcotte, 2006) at its core. Performance results are obtained with two-layer map images for simplicity. The bottom layer is from NASA's satellite map images provided by OnEarth project's WMS (OnEarth, 2007), and the top layer is earthquake seismic data provided by WFS for Geo-science application.

We run the test in Local Area Network (LAN). We have used machines having 2 Quad-core Intel Xeon processors running at 2.33 GHz with 8 GB of memory. For the partitioning process we have used 6 WFS workers to which partitions are assigned in a round-robin fashion.

The systematic uncertainty for our timer is in 10's of milliseconds.

Figure 6 shows that stateful access to OGC's stateless data services through the federator and

Table 1. Average response times and standard deviations for response times in different possible cases. The values are in seconds and the test setup was run 50 times to get each value in the table

Data MB	(No-Cache) (No-PRT) Single process	StdDev	(No-cache) (PRT) multi-process partition to 10 (1)	StdDev	(Cache) (No-PRT) Cache meets whole query (2)	StdDev
0.01	1.81	0.14	2.33	0.13	1.04	0.23
0.1	2.64	0.31	2.76	0.10	1.15	0.23
0.5	5.00	0.24	3.46	0.12	1.37	0.44
1	8.23	0.20	4.64	0.11	1.69	0.42

resulting parallel processing through query decomposition and caching techniques enhanced the system responsiveness to a great extent. The performance results are end-to-end response times in which one end is the database and the other end is the user.

Depending on how many partition of the main query is met from the cache, the performance changes in region-2 between the lines tagged as no-cache and full-cache. As the overlapped partition increases, the performance gain increases and gets close to the full-cache line. The full-cache line shows the performance results in case of that the queries are served fully from cache. The performance results also show that as the data size increases, the performance gain from the proposed techniques increases.

ABSTRACTION OF THE FRAMEWORK FOR THE GENERAL DOMAINS

Our experiences with GIS have shown that a federated, service-oriented, GIS-style information model can be generalized to many application ar-

eas and scientific domains. We call this generalized framework Application Specific Information System (ASIS), and provide a blueprint architecture in terms of principles and requirements. Developing such a framework requires first defining a core language (such as GML) expressing the primitives of the domain; second, key service components, service interfaces and message formats defining services interactions; and third, the capability file requirements (based on core-language) enabling inter-service communications to link the services for the federation (see Figure 7).

GIS is a mature domain in terms of information system studies and experiences. It has standards bodies defining interoperable online service interfaces and data models such as OGC ISO/TC211, but many other fields do not have this. In order to see the applicability of the GIS-style information model given in Figure 3, we have surveyed two science domains (Astronomy and Chemistry). Table 2 presents the results briefly in terms of service counterparts (ASIS vs. science domains).

Astronomy has a standards body, the International Virtual Observatory Alliance (IVOA), for defining data formats and online services that

Figure 6. End-to-end response times according to possible query cases. Figure 3 shows the test setup

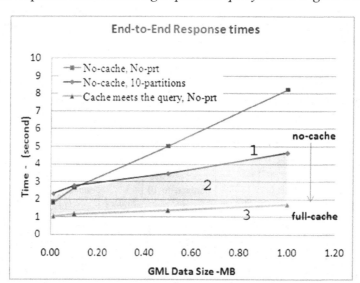

Figure 7. Application specific information system (ASIS)

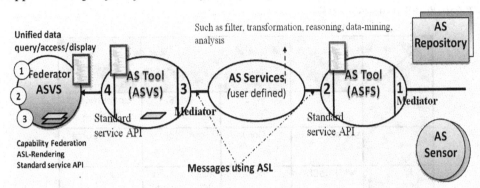

are somewhat analogous to the OGC standards. FITS (Flexible Image Transfer), Images and VOTable (Williams et al., 2002) are the data models. SkyNodes are database servers with an ADQL (Astronomy Distributed Query Language) based SOAP interfaces that return VOTable-encoded results. VOPlot and TopCat are two services to visualize the astronomy data in the format of VOTable, FITS and images. VOResource and UCD are the metadata definition and standards for the service descriptions (Yasuda et al., 2004).

Chemistry, although a vastly different field, does provide a common data model (CML (Holliday, Murray-Rust, & Rzepa, 2006)) that can be used to build up Web Services. Although many research groups have investigated service architectures for chemistry and chemical informatics, the field has (to our knowledge) no Web Service standards-defining body equivalent to the OGC or IVOA.

This chapter presents a high level architecture that consists of abstract components and explains their data flow and components interactions. In this section, we focus on the principles and requirements to generalize GIS-like architecture to any other information system domains. It should be noted that this abstract architecture is intended to be domain-specific. That is, it may be realized in chemistry or astronomy, for example, but we are not suggesting cross-domain interoperability.

ASIS is a proposed solution to heterogeneous data integration. This solution enables inter-service communication through well-defined service interfaces, message formats and capabilities metadata. Data and service integration is done through capability federation of these services, which are implemented in Web Services. In ASIS approach, there are two general groups of services. These are Application Specific Feature Service (ASFS) and Application Specific Visualization Service (ASVS), and each service is described by corresponding generic metadata descriptions that can be queried through Web Service invocations. In addition to allowing service discovery, this approach also enables at least three important qualities of services. First, services of the same type that provide a subset of the request can be combined into a "super-service" that spans the query space and has the aggregate functionality of its member services. Second, the capability metadata can be used to determine how to combine services into filter chains with interconnected input-output ports. Third (and building on the previous two), capabilities of super-services can be broken into smaller, self-contained capabilities that can be associated with specific services. This enables performance gains through load-balancing.

ASIS must consist of filter-like Web Services components (ASFS and ASVS) having common interfaces and communicating with each other

Table 2. Components and common data model matching for generalization of GIS to ASIS. Two selected domains are astronomy and chemistry

ASIS Science Domains	Common data Model ASL	Components		Metadata
		ASFS	ASVS	
GIS	GML	WFS	WMS	capability.xml schema
Astronomy	VOTable, FITS	SkyNode	VOPlot TopCat	VOResource
Chemistry	CML, PubChem	None	NO standard JChemPaint, JMOL	None

through a capability metadata exchange. Being a Web Service enables filter services to publish their interfaces, locate each other and chain together easily. Filters have inter-service capabilities and are chainable. If the filter is capable of communicating and obtaining data from other filters, and updates (or aggregates) its capability metadata with these data (after capability files exchange), then it can claim that it serves these data. Filter Services are information/data services that enable distributed data/information access, querying and transformation through their predictable input/output interfaces defined by capability document. Filter located in the same community network can update their capability metadata dynamically through "getCapabilities" service interface of the filters. Dynamically updating capabilities of filters enable removal of obsolete data or down filters.

Abstract Components and Matching to Sample Science Domains: Chemistry and Astronomy

In ASIS, there are two groups of filter services, ASVS and ASFS, which correspond to the OGC's WFS and WMS, respectively. Since they have different service APIs and provided data, they have different schema of capabilities. The capability metadata defines service and data attributes, and their constraints and limitations to enable clients to make valid queries and get expected results. Capabilities metadata and Application Specific Language (ASL) are closely related to each other. One defines the domain-specific data and other defines the query and response constraints over the service and data provided.

ASVS must visualize information and provides a way of navigating ASFS and their underlying database. ASVS must provide human readable information such as text and graphs (scalable vector graphic (SVG) or portable network graphic (PNG)) images. An ASFS is an annotation service providing heterogeneous data in common data model with an attribute-based query capability. ASFS serves data in ASL, which must be realized as a domain specific XML-encoded common data model containing content and representation tags. Heterogeneity in queries and data formats is handled through resource specific mediators.

User defined services in ASIS (see Figure 7) provide application specific data and services. These can include transformations, reasoning, event-detection, and data-mining tools for extraction knowledge from the feature data provided by ASFS in ASL format.

Inter-Service Communications

Inter-service communication is achieved through common service interfaces and capability meta-data exchange. The standard service interfaces can be grouped into three types: (a) capability metadata exchange: inter-service communication (set-up stage); (b) interactive data display: selecting layer composition and bounding box regions; and (c) querying of data itself over the display, getting further information about the data content and attributes.

As mentioned before, capability helps clients make valid requests for its successive queries. Capability basically provides information about the data sets and operations available on them with communication protocols, return types, attribute based constraints, etc. Each domain has different set of attributes for the data and it is defined in ASL common data model. For example, in GIS domain, attributes might be bounding box values (defining a range query for data sets falling in a rectangular region) and coordinate reference system.

Standard requests/query instances for the standard service interfaces are created according to the standard agreed-on request schemas. These are defined by open standards bodies in corresponding domains. The request instances contain format and attribute constraints related to the ASL common data model. For example in the GIS domain, *getMap* request defines a map images' return format (JPEG, PNG, SVG, etc.), height, width, bounding box values, and so on. Format, height and width are related to display, but bounding box values are related to the attributes of the data defined in its ASL representation provided by ASFS. In this specific example of the *getMap* request, ASVS must both visualize information through the *getMap* service interface and provide a way of navigating ASFS services and their underlying database. ASVS make successive queries to the related ASVSs to get the

ASL data and render it to create final display for its clients.

In ASIS, the task of mediators is to translate requests to the standard service interfaces to those of the information/data sources', and transform the results provided by the information source back to the ASIS's standard formats. For ASFS, the returned data is ASL, and for ASVS the returned results can be any kind of display format such as images.

The mediators-wrappers (in Figure 7) enable data sources integrated to the system conform to the global data model (ASL) but enable the data sources to maintain their internal structure. At the end, this whole mediator system provides a large degree of autonomy. Instead of actual physical data federation, system makes distributed querying and response composition on the fly.

CONCLUSION

We have presented a service-oriented architecture for understanding and managing the production of knowledge from the distributed observation, simulation and analysis data through integrated data-views in the form of multi-layered map images. The infrastructure is based on a common data model, standard GIS Web-Service components, and a federation service. The federator integrates GIS data service components and enables unified data access and query over integrated data-views through event-based interactive display tools. Integrated data-views are defined in the federator's capability metadata, which consists of composition of layers provided by standard GIS Web-Services. The framework applies just-in-time (late-binding) federation in which the data is kept in its originating sources all the time. This enables autonomy and easy data maintenance.

Creating a GIS in accordance with OGC and Web Services standards, and the compatibility nature of open standard GIS services and their capability definitions, inspired us to develop an information system enabling both a unified data access/query and a display from a single access point. Open standards and Web Service technologies also enable integrating the third party geospatial functionality and data into the custom applications easily.

We have developed a framework for federated service-oriented Geographic Information Systems and addressed interoperability issues by integrating Web Services with open geographic standards. This enables us to provide interoperability at data, service and application levels. We have enhanced the standard GIS Web Service components with the streaming data-transfer capability by using a publish/subscribe-based messaging middleware. We have investigated performance efficient designs for the federator, data transfer, and distributed rendering to support responsiveness in GIS requiring interactive response times.

Open standard GIS services are inherently stateless and based on on-demand processing. They do not maintain state information between message calls, and that causes poor performance. Our federator architecture enables stateful access to stateless GIS data services from a single access point through client-based caching technique.

The federator architecture inherently enables workload sharing by fetching the different data layers from separate resources to create a multi-layered map image. This is a natural load balancing and parallel processing resulting from the architectural features. However, we can take this general idea further. In addition to layer-based natural load-balancing, a layer (in the multi-layered map image) itself can be split into smaller bounding box tiles and each tile can be farmed out to a worker WFSs/WMSs. Layer-based partitioning is based on attribute-based query decomposition.

Although the framework is fine-grained for GIS, we have also defined the principles for generalizing federated service-oriented GIS to the general science domains. We have defined two

general service types (ASFS and ASVS) with limited number of service interfaces. Service interfaces enable metadata exchange and data querying. Data flows from databases to users through ASFS and then ASVS. Due to the domain specific data heterogeneity, each domain should define its own ASL and corresponding queries.

REFERENCES

Atkinson, M., DeRoure, D., Dunlop, A., Fox, G., Henderson, P., Hey, T., et al. (2005). Web Service Grids: An Evolutionary Approach *Concurrency & Computation: Practice&Experience, 17*(2-4), February/April 2005, 377-389.

Aydin, G. (2007). *Service Oriented Architecture for Geographic Information Systems Supporting Real Time Data Grid.* Unpublished doctoral dissertation, Indiana University, Bloomington.

Aydin, G., Sayar, A., Gadgil, H., Aktas, M. S., Fox, G. C., Ko, S., et al. (in press, 2008). Building and Applying Geographical Information Systems Grids. *Concurrency and Computation: Practice and Experience.*

Beaujardiere, J. d. l. (2004). *OGC Web Map Service Interface* (Report No. 03-109r1): Open GIS Consortium Inc. (OGC).

Booth, D., Haas, H., McCabe, F., Newcomer, E., Champion, M., Ferris, C., et al. (2004). *Web Services Architecture.* Electronic Version. Retrieved July 15, 2008 from http://www.w3.org/TR/ws-arch/

Buyya, R. (1999). *High Performance Cluster Computing: Architectures and Systems, 1.* NJ, USA: Prentice Hall PTR.

Christensen, E., Curbera, F., Meredith, G., & Weerawarana, S. (2001). *Web Services Description Language (WSDL).* No. NOTE-wsdl-20010315. World Wide Web Consortium (W3C).

Cox, S., Daisey, P., Lake, R., Portele, C., & Whiteside, A. (2003). *OpenGIS® Geography Markup Language (GML) Encoding Specification* (No. 02-023r4). Open Geospatial Consortium (OGC).

Dasarathy, B. V. (1991). *Nearest Neighbor (NN) Norms: NN Pattern Classification Techniques.* IEEE Computer Society Press.

Denning, P. J., & Schwartz, S. C. (1972). Properties of the working-set model. *Communications of the ACM, 15*(3), 130.

Evans, J. D. (2003). *Web Coverage Service (WCS), Version 1.0.0.* OpenGIS® Standard Specification No. 03-065r6.

Fielding, R. T., & Taylor, R. N. (2002). Principled design of the modern web architecture. *ACM Transactions on Internet Technology, 2*(2), 115-150.

Foster, I., & Kesselman, C. (2004). *The Grid 2: Blueprint for a new Computing Infrastructure.* San Francisco, USA: Elsevier.

Fox, G. C. (2004). Grids of Grids of Simple Services. *Computing in Science and Engineering, 6*(4), 84-87.

Gudgin, M., Hadley, M., Mendelsohn, N., Moreau, J.-J., Nielsen, H. F., Karmarkar, A., et al. (2007). *SOAP Version 1.2 Part 1: Messaging Framework* (Standard Specification). W3C. Available at: http://www.w3.org/TR/soap12-part1/

Holliday, G. L., Murray-Rust, P., & Rzepa, H. S. (2006). Chemical markup, XML, and the world wide web. 6. CMLReact, an XML vocabulary for chemical reactions. *Journal of chemical information and modeling, 46*, 145-157.

JAG. (1999). *Joint Advisory Group.* Retrieved March 27, 2008, from http://www.isotc211.org/organizn.htm#jag

Khare, B. R., & Taylor, R. N. (2004, May 2004). *Extending the Representational State Transfer (REST) Architectural Style for Decentralized Systems.* Paper presented at the 26th International Conference on Software Engineering (ICSE'04), Edinburgh, Scotland.

Kirtland, M. (2001). *A Platform for Web Services.* Technical Report. Microsoft.

Kolodziej, K. (2004). *OpenGIS Web Map Server Cookbook.* Implementation Specification No. 03-050r1. Open Geospatial Consortium Inc. (OGC).

Koontz, L. D. (2003). *Geographic Information Systems: Challenges to Effective Data Sharing.* Report No. GAO-03-874T. Washington, DC: United States General Accounting Office (GAO).

Kreger, H. (2001). *Web Services Conceptual Architecture (WSCA 1.0).* IBM.

Ludäscher, B., Altintas, I., Berkley, C., Higgins, D., Jaeger, E., Jones, M., et al. (2006). Scientific Workflow Management and the Kepler System. *Concurrency and Computation: Practice and Experience, 18*(10), 1039-1065.

Nanjo, K. Z., Holliday, J. R., Chen, C.-C., Rundle, J. B., & Turcotte, D. L. (2006). Application of a modified pattern informatics method to forecasting the locations of future large earthquakes in the central Japan. *Tectonophysics, 424*, 351-366.

OGC (1994, 06/12/2008). *The Open Geospatial Consortium, Inc.* Retrieved Feb 14, 2008, from http://www.opengeospatial.org/

OnEarth (2007, 12/08/2007). *OnEarth.* JPL WMS Server. Retrieved March 15, 2008, from http://onearth.jpl.nasa.gov/

Pallickara, S., & Fox, G. (2003). *NaradaBrokering: A Distributed Middleware Framework and Architecture for Enabling Durable Peer-to-Peer Grids.* Paper presented at the ACM/IFIP/USENIX. Retrieved July 15, 2008 from http://grids.ucs.indiana.edu/ptliupages/publications/NB-Framework.pdf

Peng, Z.-R., & Tsou, M.-H. (2003). *Internet GIS: Distributed Geographic Information Services for the Internet and Wireless Networks*. New Jersey, USA: John Wiley & Sons.

Pfister, G. F. (1998). *In Search of Clusters*. Upper Saddle River, NJ: Prentice-Hall, Inc.

Redmond, F. E. (1997). *DCOM: Microsoft Distributed Component Object Model with CDrom* (1st edition). Foster City, USA: IDG Books Worldwide, Inc.

RMI (2004). *Java Remote Method Invocation Specification*. Electronic Version. Retrieved June 2008, from http://java.sun.com/j2se/1.4.2/docs/guide/rmi/

Rundle, J. B., Turcotte, D. L., Shcherbakov, R., Klein, W., & Sammis, C. (2003). Statistical physics approach to understanding the multiscale dynamics of earthquake fault systems. *Geophysics, 41*(4).

Sayar, A., Pierce, M., & Fox, G. (2005). *OGC Compatible Geographical Information Services* (Technical Report No. TR610). Bloomington: Indiana University.

Sayar, A., Pierce, M., & Fox, G. (2006). *Integrating AJAX Approach into GIS Visualization Web Services*. Paper presented at the IEEE, International Conference on Internet and Web Applications and Services, ICIW'06.

Sonnet, J. (2005). *Web Map Context Documents (WMC)*. Standard specs No. 05-005. Open Geospatial Consortium Inc. (OGC).

Tiampo, K. F., Rundle, J. B., Mcginnis, S. A., & Klein, W. (2002). Pattern Dynamics and Forecast Methods in Seismically Active Regions. *Pure and Applied Geophysics, 159*(10), 2429-2467.

Tran, P., Greenfield, P., & Gorton, I. (2002). *Behavior and performance of message-oriented middleware systems*. Paper presented at the International Conference on Distributed Computing Systems Workshops, ICDCSW.

Turi, D., Missier, P., Goble, C., Roure, D. D., & Oinn, T. (2007). *Taverna Workflows: Syntax and Semantics*. Paper presented at the 3rd IEEE International Conference on e-Science and Grid Computing (e-Science'07), Bangalore, India.

Vretanos, P. A. (2002). *Web Feature Service Implementation Specification*. Reference Document No. 02-058). OGC.

Williams, R., Ochsenbein, F., Davenhall, C., Durand, D., Fernique, P., Giaretta, D., et al. (2002). *VOTable: A Proposed XML Format for Astronomical Tables* (Standard Specification). US National Virtual Observatory.

WS-I. (2002). *Web Service Interoperability*. Retrieved April 23, 2008, from http://www.ws-i.org/

Yasuda, N., Mizumoto, Y., Ohishi, M., O'Mullane, W., Budavári, T. A., Haridas, V., et al. (2004). *Astronomical Data Query Language: Simple Query Protocol for the Virtual Observatory*. Paper presented at the Astronomical Data Analysis Software and Systems XIII. ASP Conference Series. Retrieved July 15, 2008 from http://www.adass.org/adass/proceedings/adass03/reprints/P3-10.pdf

Compilation of References

Abdul-Rahman, A., & Hailes, S. (2000). Supporting Trust in Virtual Communities. Paper presented at *Hawaii International Conference on System Sciences, 33*, Maui, Hawaii.

Adamic, L. A., Lukose, R. M., Puniyani, A. R., & Huberman, B. A. (2001). Search in Power Law Networks. *Physical Review, 64*, 1-8.

Adamides, E., & Karacapilidis, N. (2006). A Knowledge Centred Framework for Collaborative Business Process Modelling. *Business Process Management Journal, 12*(5), 557-575.

Aggarwal, R., Verma, K., Miller, J., & Milnor, W. (2004). Constraint Driven Web Service Composition in METEOR-S. *International Conference on Services Computing (SCC 2004)* (pp. 23-30).

Akal, F., Böhm, K., & Schek, H. (2002). OLAP Query Evaluation in a Database Cluster: A Performance Study on Intra-Query Parallelism. In *Proceedings of the 6th East European Conference*. LNCS, *2435*, 181-184.

Akinde, M. O., Böhlen, M. H., Johnson, T., Lakshmanan, L. V., & Srivastava, D. (2002). Efficient OLAP Query Processing in Distributed Data Warehouses. In *Proceedings of the 8th international Conference on Extending Database Technology: Advances in Database Technology*. LNCS, *2287*, 336-353.

Albert, P., Henocque, L., & Kleiner, M. (2005). Configuration-Based Workflow Composition. In *Proceedings of the IEEE International Conference on Web Services (ICWS 2005)*, USA. (pp. 285-292).

Aldridge, A., White, M., & Forcht, K. (1997). Security considerations of doing business via the Internet: cautions to be considered. *Internet Research: Electronic Networking Applications and Policy, 7*(1), 9-15.

Alfieri, R., Cecchini, R., Ciaschini, V., Dell'Agnello, L., Frohnere, Á., Lőrentey, K., & Spataro, F. (2005). From gridmap-file to VOMS: managing authorization in a Grid environmen. *Future Generation Computer Systems 21*(4), 549-558. Elsevier.

Alkadi, I., & Alkadi, G. (2006). Grid Computing: The past, now, and future. *Human Systems Management, 25*(3), 161-166.

Allcock, W., Bresnahan, J., Kettimuthu, R., & Link, M. (2005). The Globus Striped GridFTP Framework and Server. In *Proceedings of the 2005 ACM/IEEE Conference on Supercomputing* (pp. 54-65).

Alles, M., Kogan, A., Vasarhelyi, M., Hiltz, R., & Turoff, M. (2004, May). *Assuring Homeland Security: Continuous Monitoring, Control and Assurance of Emergency Preparedness*. Paper presented at the International Community on Information Systems for Crisis Response Management (ISCRAM) 2004 Conference, Brussels, Belgium.

Al-Mashari, M. (2001). Process orientation through enterprise resource planning (ERP): A review of critical issues. *Knowledge and Process Management, 8*(3), 175-185.

Alper, S., Tjosvold, D., & Law, K. S. (2000). Conflict management, efficacy, and performance in organisational teams. *Personnel Psychology, 53*(5), 625-642.

Copyright © 2009, IGI Global, distributing in print or electronic forms without written permission of IGI Global is prohibited.

Anand, P. (2002). *Foundations of Rational Choice Under Risk*. Oxford: Oxford University Press.

Anderson, D. L., & Lee, H. (1999). *Synchronized Supply Chains: The New Frontier*. Retrieved July 15, 2008, from http://www.ascet.com/ascet/wp/wpAnderson.html

Anderson, D. P. (2004). BOINC: a system for public-resource computing and storage. *5th International Workshop on Grid Computing* (pp. 4-10). Washington, DC, USA: IEEE Computer Society.

Anderson, D. P., Christensen, C., & Allen, B. (2006). Designing a runtime system for volunteer computing. In *International Conference on High Performance Computing, Networking, Storage, and Analysis (Supercomputing, 2006)*. Article No. 126. New York, NY, USA: ACM Press.

Andreozzi, S., Burke, S., Field, L., et al. (2005). *GLUE Schema Specification version 1.2*. Technical report. Available at: http://infnforge.cnaf.infn.it/glueinfomodel

Andreozzi, S., Ferrari, T., Ronchieri, E., & Monforte, S. (2005). Agreement-Based Workload and Resource Management. In *Proceedings of the First International Conference on e-Science and Grid Computing* (pp.181-188). IEEE Computer Society.

Andrews, T., Curbera, F., Dholakia, H., Goland, Y., Klein, J., Leymann, F., Liu, K., Roller, D., Smith, D., Thatte, S., Trickovic, I., & Weerawarana, S. (2003). *Business process Execution language for Web Services (BPEL4WS) 1.1*. IBM DeveloperWorks. Retrieved on March 25, 2008, from http://download.boulder.ibm.com/ibmdl/pub/software/dw/specs/ws-bpel/ws-bpel.pdf

Antonioletti, M., Atkinson, M. P., Baxter, R., Borley, A., Chue Hong, N., P., Collins, B., Hardman, N., Hume, A., Knox, A., Jackson, M., Krause, A., Laws, S., Magowan, J., Paton, N., Pearson, D., Sugden, T., Watson, P., & Westhead, M. (2005). The design and implementation of grid database services in OGSA-DAI. *Concurrency and Computation: Practice and Experience, 7*(2-4), 357-376.

Antonioletti, M., Atkinson, M., Borley, A., Chue Hong, N. P., Collins, B., Davies, J., Hardman, N., Hume, A.,

Jackson, M., Krause, A., Laws, S., Paton, N. W., Qi, K., Sugden, T., Vyvyan, D., Watson, P., & Westhead, M. (2003). OGSA-DAI Usage Scenarios and Behavior: Determining good practice. *UK e-Science All Hands Meeting 2004*, August 2004. Retrieved Sept 20, 2006, http://www.ogsadai.org.uk

Antonopoulos, N., & Salter, J. (2004). Efficient Resource Discovery in Grids and P2P Networks. *Internet Research, 14*, 339-346.

Anumba, C. J., Aziz, Z., & Ruikar, D. (2003, February). *Enabling technologies for next-generation collaboration systems*. Paper presented at the International Conference on Construction Information Technology (INCITE2004), Langkawi, Malaysia.

Arkin, A., (2002). *Business Process Modeling Language (BPML), Version 1.0*. BPMI.org.

Armijo, B. (2007). *How Utility Computing Benefits SaaS*. Software & Information Industry Association (SIIA).

Arthur, W. B. (1991). Designing Economic Agents that Act like Human Agents: A Behavioral Approach to Bounded Rationality. *American Economic Review, 81*(2), 353-359.

Asadzadeh, P., Buyya, R., Kei, C. L., Nayar, D., & Venugopal, S. (2004). *Global grids and software toolkits: A study of four grid middleware technologies*. Technical report, University of Melbourne, Australia. Retrieved July 3, 2008, from http://arxiv.org/ftp/cs/papers/0407/0407001.pdf

Ashforth, B. E., & Saks, A. M. (2000). Personal Control in Organisations: A Longitudinal Investigation with Newcomers. *Human Relations, 53*(3), 311-339.

Ashleigh, M. J., & Nandhakumar, J. (2007). Trust and technologies: Implications for organizational work practices. *Decision Support Systems, 43*(2), 607-617.

Asimakopoulou, E. (2008). *A Grid-Aware Emergency Response Model for Natural Disasters*, Unpublished doctoral dissertation. Loughborough University, UK.

Asimakopoulou, E., Anumba, C. J., Bouchlaghem, D., & Sagun, A. (2006, August). *Use of ICT during the response phase in emergency management in Greece and the United Kingdom.* Paper presented at the International Disaster Reduction Conference (IDRC), Davos, Switzerland.

Atkinson, M., DeRoure, D., Dunlop, A., Fox, G., Henderson, P., Hey, T., et al. (2005). Web Service Grids: An Evolutionary Approach *Concurrency & Computation: Practice&Experience, 17*(2-4), February/April 2005, 377-389.

Atkinson, M., Dialani, V., Guy, L., Narang, I., Paton, N., Pearson, P., Storey, T., & Watson P. (2003). *Grid database access and integration: requirements and functionalities.* Report. Retrieved August 17, 2008, from http://www.ggf.org/documents/GFD.13.pdf

Aydin, G. (2007). *Service Oriented Architecture for Geographic Information Systems Supporting Real Time Data Grid.* Unpublished doctoral dissertation, Indiana University, Bloomington.

Aydin, G., Sayar, A., Gadgil, H., Aktas, M. S., Fox, G. C., Ko, S., et al. (in press, 2008). Building and Applying Geographical Information Systems Grids. *Concurrency and Computation: Practice and Experience.*

Baker, M., Buyya, R., & Laforenza, D. (2002). Grids and grid technologies for wide-area distributed computing. *Software - Practice and Experience, 32*(15), 1437-1466.

Banerji, A., Bartolini, C., Beringer, D., Chopella, V., Govindarajan, K., Karp, A., Kuno, H., Lemon, M., Pogossiants, G., Sharma, S., & Williams, S. (2002). *Web Services Conversation Language (WSCL) 1.0.* W3C Technical Reports and Publications. Retrieved on March 25, 2008, from http://www.w3.org/TR/wscl10/

Baraka, R. (May 2004). *A Foundation for a Mathematical Web Services Query Language: A Survey on Relevant Query Languages and Tools.* RISC Report Series. University of Linz, Austria.

Barber, B. (1983). *The Logic and Limits of Trust.* New Brunswick: Rutgers University Press.

Barbera, R., Fargetta, M., & Giorgio, E. (2007). Multiple Middleware Co-existence: Another Aspect of Grid Interoperation. In the *Third IEEE International Conference on e-Science and Grid Computing* (pp. 577-583). Bangalore, India.

Baresi, L., DiNitto, E., & Ghezzi, C. (2003). Inconsistency and Ephemerality in a World of e-Services. In *Proceedings of the 2003 Workshop on Requirements Engineering for Open Systems*, in conjunction with the *11th IEEE International Requirements Engineering Conference*, 2003.

Baruch, Y. (2004). Transforming careers: from linear to multidirectional career paths: Organizational and individual perspectives. *Career Development International, 9*(1), 58-73.

Basney, J., & Livny, M. (1999). Deploying a high throughput computing cluster. In R. Buyya (Ed.), *High Performance Cluster Computing, Volume 1* (chapter 5). NJ, USA: Prentice Hall PTR.

Beaujardiere, J. d. l. (2004). *OGC Web Map Service Interface* (Report No. 03-109r1): Open GIS Consortium Inc. (OGC).

Becerra, M., & Gupta, A. (2003). Perceived trustworthiness within the organization: The moderating impact of communication frequency on trustor and trustee effects. *Organization Science, 14*(1), 32-45.

BEinGRID Consortium. (2008). *BEinGRID - Better Business Using Grid Solutions - Eighteen Successful Case Studies Using Grid.* Retrieved July 15, 2008, from http://www.beingrid.eu/fileadmin/beingrid/pr_folder/Case_Studies/BEinGRID_Case-Studies.pdf

BEinGRID Project. (2008). Available at: from http://www.beingrid.eu/

Berglund, A., Boag, S., Chamberlin, D., Fernández, M. F., Kay M., Robie J., & Siméon, J. (2007). *XML Path Language (XPath) 2.0.* W3C Technical Reports and Publications. Retrieved on March 25, 2008, from http://www.w3.org/TR/xpath20/

Berrenberg, J. L. (1987). The Belief in Personal Control Scale: A measure of God-Mediated and Exaggerated Control. *Journal of Personality Assessment, 51*(2), 194-206.

Bessis, N. (2003). Towards a homogeneous status of communicated research. In *Sixth International Conference on the Next Steps: Electronic Theses and Dissertations Worldwide*, Berlin. Retrieved August 17, 2008, from http://edoc.hu-berlin.de/conferences/etd2003/bessis-nik/PDF/index.pdf

Bessis, N., & Asimakopoulou, E., (2008, July). *The development of a personalized and dynamic driven RSS specification for the built environment.* Paper presented at the IADIS International Conference on Web Based Communities, Amsterdam, The Netherlands.

Bessis, N., & Chauhan, J. (2008, April). *The design and implementation of a grid database consistency service in OGSA-DAI.* Paper presented at the IADIS International Conference on Information Systems, Algarve, Portugal.

Bessis, N., French, T., Burakova-Lorgnier, M., & Huang, W. (2007). Using grid technology for data sharing to support intelligence in decision making. In M. Xu (Ed.), *Managing Strategic Intelligence: Techniques and Technologies* (pp. 179-202). Hershey, PA: Information Science Publishing.

Betz, S., Klink, S., Koschmider, A., & Oberweis, A. (2006). Automatic User Support for Business Process Modeling. In K. Hinkelmann, D. Karagiannis, N. Stojanovic, & G. Wagner (Eds.), *Proceedings of the Workshop on Semantics for Business Process Management at the 3rd European Semantic Web Conference 2006*. Budva, Montenegro (pp. 1-12).

Bhagwan, R., Savage, S., & Voelker, G. M. (2003). *Understanding Availability.* Paper presented at the International Workshop on Peer-to-Peer Systems, Berkeley, CA.

Bijlsma-Frankema, K. M., & Costa, A. C. (2005). Understanding the Trust-Control Nexus. *International Sociology. 20*(3), 259-282.

Birchall, D. W. (1975). *Job Design.* Epping: Gower Press.

Birchall, D. W., & Giambona, G. (2007). SME manager development in virtual learning communities and the role of trust: A conceptual study. *Human Resource Development International, 10*(2), 187-202.

Birchall, D. W., Ezingeard, J.-N., McFadzean, E., Howlin, N., & Yoxall, D. (2004). *Information Assurance: Strategic Alignment and Competitive Advantage.* London: Grist Ltd.

Birchall, D. W., Ezingeard, J-N., & McFadzean, E. (2003) *Information Security - Setting the Boardroom Agenda.* London: Grist Ltd.

Birchall, D. W., Giambona, G., & Gill, J. (2008). Who is on the other side of the screen? The role of trust in virtual teams. In T. Kautonen, & H. Karjaluoto (Eds.), *Trust and New Technologies: Marketing and Management on the Internet and Mobile Media.* London: Edward Elgar Publishing.

Bird, I., & The LCG Editorial Board (2005). *LHC Computing Grid Technical Design Report.* LCG-TDR-001, CERN-LHCC-2005-024.

Bloom, B. (1970). Space/time Tradeoffs in Hash Coding with Allowable Errors. *Communications of the ACM, 13*(7), 422-426.

Boissevain, J., & Mitchell, J. C. (1973). *Network Analysis Studies in Human Interaction.* The Hague: Monkton.

Booth, D., Haas, H., McCabe, F., Newcomer, E., Champion, M., Ferris, C., & Orchard, D. (2004). *Web Services Architecture.* W3 Technical Reports and Publications. Retrieved March 4, 2008, from http://www.w3.org/TR/ws-arch/

Box, D., Cabrera, L. F., Critchley, C., Curbera, F., Ferguson, D., Graham, S., Hull, D., Kakivaya, G., Lewis, A., Lovering, B., Niblett, P., Orchard, D., Samdarshi, S., Schlimmer, J., Sedukhin, I., Shewchuk, J., Weerawarana, S., & Wortendyke, D. (2006). *Web Services*

BPEL4WS (2003). *Business Process Execution Language for Web Services Version 1.1.* IBM, BEA Systems, Microsoft, SAP AG, Siebel Systems. Available at: http://www128.ibm.com/developerworks/library/specification/ws-bpel/

Brenna, L., & Johansen, D. (2005). Engineering Push-based Web Services. *International Journal of Web Services Practices, 1*(1-2). (pp. 89-100).

Brezany, P., Hofer, J., & Wohrer, A. (2003, September). *Towards an Open Service Architecture for Data Mining on the Grid.* Paper presented at the 14th International Workshop on Database and Expert Systems Applications (DEXA '03), Prague, Czech Republic.

Bridge, S., O'Neill, K., & Cromie, S. (2003). *Understanding Enterprise, Entrepreneurship and Small Business.* London: Palgrave Mcmillan.

Brooks, R., Robinson, S., & Lewis, C. (2001). *Simulation and inventory control (Operational Research Series).* Hampshire, UK: Palgrave.

Browne, J., & Zhang, J. (1999). Extended and virtual enterprises - similarities and differences. *International Journal of Agile Management Systems, 1*(1), 30-36.

Bruijn, J., Bussler, C., Domingue, J., Fensel, D., Hepp, M., Keller, U., Kifer, M., Konig-Ries, B., Kopecky, J., Lara, R., Lausen, H., Oren, E., Polleres, A., Roman, D., Scicluna, J., & Stollberg, M. (2005). *Web Service Modeling Ontology (WSMO).* W3C Member Submissions. Retrieved on March 25, 2008, from http://www.w3.org/Submission/WSMO/

Bui, T., & Lee, J., (1999). An Agent-Based Framework for Building Decision Support Systems, *The International Journal Decision Support Systems, 25*(3).

Burback, R. (1998*). Software Engineering Methodology: The Watersluice* (PhD Thesis). USA, Stanford University.

Burke, S., Campana, S., Peris, A. D., Donno, F., Lorenzo, P. M., Santinelli, R., & Sciaba, A. (2007). *gLite 3 user guide, manuals series.* Document identifier CERN-LCG-GDEIS-722398. Retrieved June 28, 2008, from https://edms.cern.ch/file/722398//gLite-3-UserGuide.pdf

Buyya, R. (1999). *High Performance Cluster Computing: Architectures and Systems, 1.* NJ, USA: Prentice Hall PTR.

Buyya, R., Abramson, D., & Giddy, J. (2000) Nimrod/g: An architecture of a resource management and scheduling system in a global computational grid. In *Proceedings Fourth International Conference on High Performance Computing in the Asia-Pacific Region, 1* (pp. 283-289).

Byers, J., Considine, J., Mitzenmacher, M., & Rost, S. (2002). Informed Content Delivery Across Adaptive Overlay Networks. *ACM SIGCOMM Computer Communication Review, 32*, 47-60.

Calvanese, D., Giacomo, G., & Lenzerini, M. (1998, August). *Information integration: conceptual modelling and reasoning support.* Paper presented at the third Conference on Cooperative Information Systems, New York, USA.

Calvanese, D., Lenzerini, M., & Nardi, D. (1998). *Description logics for conceptual data modeling, Logics for databases and information systems,* USA: Kluwer Academic Publishers.

Capra, L., et al. (2001). Reflective Middleware Solutions for Context-Aware Applications. In *Lecture Notes in Computer Science 2192, Proceedings of the Third International Conference on Metalevel Architectures and Separation of Crosscutting Concerns* (pp. 126-133).

Carle, B., Vermeersch, F., & Palma, C. R. (2004, May). *Systems Improving Communication in Case of a Nuclear Emergency.* Paper presented at the International Community on Information Systems for Crisis Response Management (ISCRAM2004) Conference, Brussels, Belgium.

Casanova, H. (2002). Distributed computing research issues in grid computing. *ACM SIGACT News, 33*(3), 50-70.

Castillo-R. J. A., Silvescu, A., Caragea, D., Pathak, J., & Honavar, V. G. (2003, October). *Information Extraction and Integration from Heterogeneous, Distributed, Autonomous Information Sources–A Federated Ontol-*

ogy–Driven Query-Centric Approach. Paper presented at the IEEE International Conference on Information Reuse and Integration, Las Vegas, USA.

Cervantes, H., & Hall, R. S. (2003). *Automating Service Dependency Management in a Service-Oriented Component Model*. Paper presented at 6th International Conference on Software Engineering (ICSE) Workshop on Component-Based Software Engineering: Automated Reasoning and Prediction (ICSE CBSE6), May 2003, Portland, USA.

Chafle, G., Chandra, S., Mann, V., & Nanda, M. G. (2005). Orchestrating Composite Web Services Under Data Flow Constraints. In *Proceedings of the IEEE International Conference on Web Services (ICWS 2005)*, USA (pp. 211-218).

Chance, D. M. (2004). *Monte Carlo simulation, teaching note 96-03*. Retrieved June 28, 2008, from http://www.bus.lsu.edu/academics/finance/faculty/dchance/Instructional/TN96-03.pdf

Chandra, C., & Kumar, S. (2000). Supply chain management in theory and practice: a passing fad or a fundamental change? *Industrial Management & Data Systems*, *100*(3), 100-113.

Charters, S. M., Holliman, N. S., & Munro, M. (2004). *Visualisation on the grid: A web services approach*. Third UK eScience All-Hands Meeting, Nottingham, UK.

Chaudhuri, S., & Dayal, U. (1997). An overview of data warehousing and OLAP technology. *SIGMOD Rec. 26*, *1*, 65-74.

Checkland, P., & Scholes, J. (1990). *Soft systems methodology in action*. Chichester: John Wiley & Sons.

Chen-Burger, Y.-H., & Kalfoglou, Y. (2007). Knowledge Management Support for Enterprise Distributed Systems. In P. Rittgen (Ed.), *Handbook of Ontologies for Business Interactions* (pp. 294-310). IGI Global (formerly Idea Group Inc.).

Chen-Burger, Y.-H., & Robertson, D. (2005). *Automating Business Modelling: A Guide to Using Logic to Represent Informal Methods and Support Reasoning*. Book Series of Advanced Information and Knowledge Processing, Springer-Verlag.

Chen-Burger, Y.-H., & Stader J. (2003). Formal Support for Adaptive Workflow Systems in a Distributed Environment. In L. Fischer (Ed.), *Workflow Handbook* (pp. 93-118). Florida, USA: Future Strategies Inc.

Chervenak, A. L., Palavalli, N., Bharathi, S., Kesselman, C., & Schwartzkopf, R. (2004). Performance and Scalability of a Replica Location Service. In *Proceedings of the 13th IEEE international Symposium on High Performance Distributed Computing* (pp.182-191).

Chervenak, A., Foster, I., Kesselman, C., Salisbury, C., & Tuecke, S. (2001). The data grid: Towards an architecture for the distributed management and analysis of large scientific datasets. *Journal of Network and Computer Applications*, *23*, 187-200.

Chetty, S., & Blankenburg, H. D. (2000). Internationalisation of small to medium-sized manufacturing firms: A network approach. *International Business Review*, *9*(1), 77-93.

Chien, A., Calder, B., Elbert, S., & Bhatia, K. (2003). Entropia: architecture and performance of an enterprise desktop grid system. *Journal of Parallel and Distributed Computing*, *63*(5), 597-610.

Christensen, E., Curbera, F., Meredith, G., & Weerawarana, S. (2001). *Web Services Description Language (WSDL) 1.1*. W3C Technical Reports and Publications. Retrieved on March 25, 2008, from http://www.w3.org/TR/wsdl/

Christiansen, M., Fagerholt, K., & David, R. (2002). Ship Routing and Scheduling: Status and Perspectives. *Transportation Service, 38*(1), 1-18.

Christopher, M. (2005). *Logistics and Supply-Chain Management: Creating Value-Adding Networks*. London: Pearson Education.

Chrysoulas, C., Koumoutsos, G., Denazis, S., Thramboulidis, K., & Koufopavlou, O. (2007). *Dynamic Service Deployment using an Ontology based Description of Devices and Services*. University of Patras, Greece.

Clabby, J. (2004). *The Grid report, 2004 edition*. Clabby Analytics. Retrieved July 3, 2008, from http://www-03.ibm.com/grid/pdf/Clabby_Grid_Report_2004_Edition.pdf

Clark, J., & DeRose, S. (1999). *XML Path Language (XPath)*. W3C Technical Reports and Publications. Retrieved on March 25, 2008, from http://www.w3.org/TR/xpath/

Clases, C., Bachman, R., & Wehner, T. (2003). Studying Trust in Virtual Organizations. *International Studies of Management and Organization, 33* (3), 7–27.

Clegg, C. W., Unsworth, K. L., Epitropaki, O., & Parker, G. (2002). Implicating trust in the innovation process. *Journal of Occupational and Organizational Psychology 75*(4), 409-422.

Clemen, R. (1996). *Making Hard Decisions: An Introduction to Decision Analysis*. (2nd ed.). Belmont, CA: Duxbury Press.

Cody, R., Sharman, R., Rao, R. H., & Upadhyaya, S. (2008). Security in Grid Computing: A Review and Synthesis. *Decision Support Systems, 44*(4), 749-764.

Cohen, B. (2008). *The BitTorrent Protocol Specification*. Online specification. Retrieved on June 25, 2008, from http://www.bittorrent.org/beps/bep_0003.html

Cohen, S. G., & Gibson, C. B. (Eds.) (2003). Introduction to *Virtual Teams That Work: Creating Conditions for Virtual Team Effectiveness*. San Francisco: Jossey Bassey.

Coletti, A. L., Sedatole, K. L., & Towry, K. L. (2005). The Effect of Control Systems on Trust and Cooperation in Collaborative Environments. *The Accounting Review, 80*(2), 477-500.

Condor Version 6.9.1 Manual. (2007). *Platform-specific information on Microsoft Windows, Condor 6.9.2 manual*. Retrieved June 28, 2008, from http://www.cs.wisc.edu/condor/manual/v6.9/6_2Microsoft_Windows.html

Connolly, T., & Begg, C. (2002). *Database Systems,* 3rd ed. UK: Addison Wesley.

Cordella, L. P., Foggia, P., Sansone, C., Vento, M. (2004). A (Sub)Graph Isomorphism Algorithm for Matching Large Graphs. *IEEE Transactions on Pattern Analysis and Machine Intelligence, 26*(10), 1367-1372.

Costa, R. L. C., & Furtado, P. (2007). An SLA-Enabled Grid DataWarehouse. In *Proceedings of the 11th international Database Engineering and Applications Symposium* (pp. 285-289). IEEE Computer Society.

Costa, R. L. C., & Furtado, P. (2008). Scheduling in Grid Databases. In *22nd International Conference on Advanced Information Networking and Applications Workshops Proceedings* (pp. 696-701). IEEE Computer Society.

Costa, R. L. C., & Furtado, P. (2008). A QoS-oriented external scheduler. In *Proceedings of the 2008 ACM Symposium on Applied Computing. SAC'08* (pp. 1029-1033).

Costa, R. L., C. & Furtado, P. (2006). Data Warehouses in Grids with High QoS. In *Proceedings of the 8th International Conference on Data Warehousing and Knowledge Discovery*, LNCS, *4081*, 207-217.

Courbis, C., & Finkelstein, A. (2005). Weaving Aspects into Web Service Orchestration. In *Proceedings of the IEEE International Conference on Web Services (ICWS 2005)*, USA (pp. 219-226).

Cox, S., Daisey, P., Lake, R., Portele, C., & Whiteside, A. (2003). *OpenGIS® Geography Markup Language (GML) Encoding Specification* (No. 02-023r4). Open Geospatial Consortium (OGC).

Creed, W. E. D., & Miles, R. E. (1996). A Conceptual Framework Linking Organizational Forms, Managerial Philosophies, and the Opportunity Costs of Controls. In R. Kramer, & T. Tyler (Eds.), *Trust in Organizations: Frontiers of Theory and Research*, Thousand Oaks: Sage.

Crespo, A., & Garcia-Molina, H. (2002). *Routing Indices for Peer-to-Peer Systems*. Paper presented at the International Conference on Distributed Computing Systems, Vienna, Austria.

Cuenca-Acuna, F. M., & Nguyen, T. D. (2002). *Text-based Content Search and Retrieval in ad hoc P2P Communities.* Paper presented at the International Workshop on Peer-to-Peer Computing, Cambridge, MA.

Czajkowski, K., Foster, I., Kesselman, C., Sander, V., & Tuecke, S. (2002). SNAP: A Protocol for Negotiating Service Level Agreements and Coordinating Resource Management in Distributed Systems. In *8th Workshop on Job Scheduling Strategies for Parallel Processing* (pp. 153-183).

Das, T. K., & Teng, B. (1998). Between Trust and Control: Developing Confidence in Partner Cooperation in Alliances. *Academy of Management Review, 23*, 491-512.

Das, T. K., & Teng, B. S. (2001). Trust, Control, and Risk in Strategic Alliances: An Integrated Framework. *Organization Studies, 22*, 251-283.

Dasarathy, B. V. (1991). *Nearest Neighbor (NN) Norms: NN Pattern Classification Techniques.* IEEE Computer Society Press.

Davis, F. D. (1989). Perceived Usefulness, Perceived Ease of Use, and User Acceptance of Information Technology. *MIS Quarterly, 13*(3), 318-340.

Davis, F. D., Bagozzi, R. P., & Warshaw, P. R. (1989). User Acceptance of Computer Technology: A Comparison of Two Theoretical Models. *Management Science, 35*(8), 982-1003.

De Roure, D., & Surridge M. (2003). Interoperability Challenges in Grid for Industrial Applications. *Proceedings of Semantic Grid Workshop at GGF9.* Chicago, USA.

De Roure, D., Jennings, N. R, & Shadbolt, N. R. (2005). The Semantic Grid: Past, Present, and Future. *Proceedings of the IEEE, 93*(3), 669-681.

Deelman, E., Singh, G., Atkinson, M. P., Chervenak, A., Chue Hong, N. P., Kesselman, C., Patil, S., Pearlman, L., & Su, M. H. (2004, June). *Grid-Based Metadata Services,* Paper presented at the IEEE 16ᵗʰ International Conference on Scientific and Statistical Database Management, Santorini Island, Greece.

Deelman, E., Singh, G., Su, M.-H., Blythe, J., Gil, Y., Kesselman, C., Mehta, G., Vahi, K., Berriman, G. B., Good, J., Laity, A., Jacob, J. C., & Katz, D. S. (2005). Pegasus: A Framework for Mapping Complex Scientific Workflows onto Distributed Systems. *Scientific Programming Journal, 13*(3), 219-237.

Dehne, F., Lawrence, M., & Rau-Chaplin, A. (2007). Cooperative Caching for Grid Based Data Warehouses. In *Proceedings of the Seventh IEEE International Symposium on Cluster Computing and the Grid* (pp. 31-38). IEEE Computer Society.

Dell, M., & Fredman, C. (2006). *Direct from Dell: Strategies that Revolutionized an Industry.* New York, NY: Harper-Collins Publishers.

DeLone, W. H., & McLean, E. R. (1992). Information Systems Success: The Quest for the Independent Variable. *Information Systems Research, 3*(1), 60-95.

DeLone, W. H., & McLean, E. R. (2003). The DeLone and McLean Model of Information Systems Success: A Ten-Year Update. *Journal of Management Information Systems, 19*(4), 9-30.

Denning, P. J., & Schwartz, S. C. (1972). Properties of the working-set model. *Communications of the ACM, 15*(3), 130.

Deshpande, P. M., Ramasamy, K., Shukla, A., & Naughton, J. F. (1998). Caching multidimensional queries using chunks. In *Proceedings of the 1998 ACM SIGMOD international Conference on Management of Data.* SIGMOD '98 (pp. 259-270).

Di Penta, M., Esposito, R., Villani, M. L., Codato, R., Colombo, M., & Di Nitto, E. (2006). WS Binder: a Framework to enable Dynamic Binding of Composite Web Services. In *International Workshop of Service Oriented Software Engineering (IW-SOSE 2006), Shanghai* (pp. 74-80).

Dimitrakos, T., Golby, D., & Kearney, P. (2004). Towards a Trust and Contract Management Framework for Dynamic Virtual Organisations. *Proceedings of the eChallenges Conference, 2004.*

Driscoll, J. W. (1978). Trust and Participation in Organizational Decision Making as Predictors of Satisfaction. *The Academy of Management Journal, 21*(1), 44-56.

Duarte, D., & Tennant-Snyder, N. (1999). *Mastering Virtual Teams: Strategies, Tools and Techniques that Succeed.* San Francisco: Jossey-Bass Publishers.

Duhan, S., Levy, M., & Powell, P. (2001). Information systems strategies in knowledge-based SMEs: the role of core competencies. *European Journal of Information Systems, 1(*10), 25-40.

Dustdar, S., & Schreiner, W. (2005). A survey on web services compositions. *International Journal Web and Grid Services, 1*(1), 1-30.

Dyer, J. H., & Nobeoka, K. (2000). Creating and managing a high-performance knowledge-sharing network: The Toyota case. *Strategic Management Journal, 21*(3), 345-367.

EcoGrid. (2006). National Center for High Performance Computing, Taiwan. Available at: http://ecogrid.nchc.org.tw/.

EGEE II. (2008). *Enabling Grids for E-sciencE (EGEE).* Available at: http://www.eu-egee.org/

EGEE. (2007). *Enabling grids for e-science project.* Retrieved June 28, 2008, from http://www.eu-egee.org/

Eggert, A. (2001). The Role of Communication in Virtual Teams. *Electronic Journal of Organizational Virtualness, 3*(2).

Eldabi, T, Jahangirian, M, Mustafee, N, Naseer, A., & Stergioulas, L. (2008). Applications of simulation techniques in commerce and defence: A systematic survey. A paper presented at *4th Simulation Workshop (SWO8)* (pp. 275-284). OR Society, UK.

Elmroth, E., & Tordsson, J. (2005). An interoperable, standards-based grid resource broker and job submission service. Paper presented at *First IEEE International Conference on e-Science and Grid Computing.* Melbourne, Australia.

Epicor. (2005). *Managing Spend in a Distribution Environment: Supplier Relationship Management and the Distribution Enterprise.* Epicor.

Erl, T. (2005). *Service-Oriented Architecture: Concepts, Technology, and Design.* Crawfordsville, Indiana: Prentice Hall PTR.

Esteves, J., & Pastor, J. (2001). Enterprise Resource Planning Systems Research: An Annotated Bibliography. *Communications of the Association for Information Systems, 7*(8).

Evans, J. D. (2003). *Web Coverage Service (WCS), Version 1.0.0.* OpenGIS® Standard Specification No. 03-065r6.

Eventing (WS-Eventing). W3C Member Submissions. Retrieved on March 25, 2008, from http://www.w3.org/Submission/WS-Eventing/

Expert Group Report (2003). *Next generation grid(s), European Grid Research 2005-2010.* Retrieved July 3, 2008, from ftp://ftp.cordis.europa.eu/pub/ist/docs/ngg_eg_final.pdf

Fearnleys. (2002). *Review 2001.* Oslo, Norway: Fearnsearch.

Feather, M. S., et al. (1998). Reconciling System Requirements and Runtime Behaviour. *Proceedings of Ninth International Workshop on Software Specification & Design* (pp. 50-59).

Fielding, R. T. (2000). *Architecture styles and the design of network-based software architectures.* Unpublished doctoral dissertation, University of California, Irvine, USA.

Fielding, R. T., & Taylor, R. N. (2002). Principled design of the modern web architecture. *ACM Transactions on Internet Technology, 2*(2), 115-150.

Foss, N. J. (2002). Introduction: New organisational forms – Critical perspectives. *International Journal of the Economics of Business, 9*(1), 1-8.

Foster, H., Uchitel, S., Magee, J., & Kramer, J. (2004). Compatibility Verification for Web Service Choreography. In *Proceedings of the IEEE International Conference on Web Services (ICWS 2004)* (pp. 738-741).

Foster, I. (2001). The anatomy of the grid: enabling scalable virtual organizations. *International Journal of High Performance Computing Applications, 15*(3) (August 2001), 200-222.

Foster, I. (2002) *What is the Grid? A Three Point Checklist.* Retrieved August, 10, 2008, from http://www-fp.mcs.anl.gov/~foster/Articles/WhatIsTheGrid.pdf

Foster, I. (2002). What is the grid? A three point checklist. *Grid Today, 1*(6). Retrieved August 17, 2008, from http://www.gridtoday.com/ 02/0722/100136.html

Foster, I. (2005). *A globus primer (draft version).* Retrieved June 2008, from http://www.globus.org/toolkit/docs/4.0/key/

Foster, I. (2005). Globus Toolkit Version 4: Software for Service-Oriented Systems *IFIP International Conference on Network and Parallel Computing,* LNCS 3779, 2-13.

Foster, I., & Kesselman, C. (1997). Globus: A Metacomputing Infrastructure Toolkit. *Intl J. Supercomputer Applications,* 11(2), 115-128.

Foster, I., & Kesselman, C. (1998). Computational Grids. In I. Foster, & C. Kesselman (Eds.), *The Grid: Blueprint for a Future Computing Infrastructure.* Morgan Kaufmann.

Foster, I., & Kesselman, C. (1998). *The grid: Blueprint for a new computing infrastructure.* San Francisco, CA: Morgan Kaufmann.

Foster, I., & Kesselman, C. (2003). *The Grid 2: Blueprint for a New Computing Infrastructure.* San Francisco, CA, USA: Morgan Kaufmann Publishers Inc.

Foster, I., & Kesselman, C. (2004). Concepts and architecture. In I. Foster, & C. Kesselman (Eds.), *The Grid: Blueprint for a New Computing Infrastructure (2nd Edition),* chapter 4. San Francisco, CA: Morgan Kaufmann.

Foster, I., & Roy, A., & Sander, V. (2000). A Quality of Service Architecture that Combines Resource Reservation and Application Adaptation. In the *8th International Workshop on Quality of Service (IWQOS).* LNCS, Springer-Verlag.

Foster, I., & Tuecke, S. (2005). Describing the elephant: The different faces of IT as service. *Queue, ACM Enterprise Distributed Computing 3*(6) (July/August 2005), 30.

Foster, I., Kesselman, C., & Tuecke, S. (2001). The anatomy of the grid: enabling scalable virtual organisations. *International Journal of Supercomputer Applications, 15*(3), 200-222.

Foster, I., Kesselman, C., Nick, J. M., & Tuecke, S. (2002). Grid services for distributed system integration. *IEEE Computer, 35*(6), 37-46.

Foster, I., Kesselman, C., Nick, N. M., & Tuecke, S. (2002). *The physiology of the grid: an open grid services architecture for distributed systems integration.* Globus. Retrieved August 17, 2008, from http://www.globus.org/alliance/publications /papers/ogsa.pdf

Fox, G. (2001). Peer-to-Peer Networks. *Computing in science and engineering, 3*(3), 75-77.

Fox, G. C. (2004). Grids of Grids of Simple Services. *Computing in Science and Engineering, 6*(4), 84-87.

Fraigniaud, P. (2007). *Small Worlds as Navigable Augmented Networks: Model, Analysis, and Validation.* Invited talk at the 15th Annual European Symposium on Algorithms (ESA), Eilat, Israel.

Fraigniaud, P., Lebhar, E., & Lotker, Z. (2008). *Recovering the Long-Range Links in Augmented Graphs.* Paper presented at 15th International Colloquium on Structural Information and Communication Complexity (SIROCCO), Villars-sur-Ollon, Switzerland.

French, J. R. P., & Raven, B. (1959). The Bases of Social Power. In D. Cartwright (Ed.), *Studies in Social Power* (pp. 150-167). Ann Arbour, MI: Institute for Social Research, University of Michigan.

French, T., Bessis, N., & Huang, W. (2007, April*). Grid Enabled Computing: A Semiotic Approach to Virtual Organizational Trus, 21st century IS: do organizations matter?* Paper presented at the UKAIS 2007: 10th International Conference in Information Systems, Manchester, UK.

Frey, J., Tannenbaum, T., Livny, M., Foster, I., & Tuecke, S. (2001). Condor-G: A Computation Management Agent for Multi-Institutional Grids. In *Proceedings of the 10th IEEE international Symposium on High Performance Distributed Computing* (p. 55).

Fu, X., Bultan, T., & Su, J. (2004). Conversation Protocols: A Formalism for Specification and Verification of Reactive Electronic Services. *Theoretical Computer Science (TCS), 328*(1-2), 19-37.

Fuller, T., & Lewis, J. (2002). Relationships Mean Everything: A typology of Small Business Relationship Strategies in a Reflexive Context. *British Journal of Management, 4*, 9-23.

Furtado, P. (2004). Workload-Based Placement and Join Processing in Node-Partitioned Data Warehouses. In *Proceedings of the 6th International Conference on Data Warehousing and Knowledge Discovery.* LNCS, *3181*, 38-47.

Furtado, P. (2004). Experimental evidence on partitioning in parallel data warehouses. In *Proceedings of the 7th ACM international Workshop on Data Warehousing and OLAP* (pp. 23-30).

Furtado, P. (2005). Hierarchical Aggregation in Networked Data Management. *In Proceedings of the International Euro-Par Conference on Parallel Processing.* LNCS, *3648*, 360-369.

Garrity, E. J., Moon, J., & Sanders, J. L. (2006). Achieving Implementation Success in Ubiquitous Computer Environment: Understanding the Role of Psychological Ownership. In M. Khosrow-Pour (Ed.), *Emerging Trends and Challenges in Information Technology Management* (pp. 34-38). 2006 IRMA International Conference. Idea Group Inc.

Gentzsch, W. (2001) *Grid Computing: A New Technology for the Advanced Web.* Sun Microsystems. Retrieved March 20, 2004, from http://www.sun.com/products-n-solutions/edu/ whitepapers/whitepaper_gridcomp.html

Gentzsch, W. (2004). Enterprise resource management: applications in research and industry. In I. Foster, & C. Kesselman (Eds.), *The Grid: Blueprint for a New Computing Infrastructure (2nd Edition)*, chapter 12. San Francisco, CA: Morgan Kaufmann.

Gibson, C. B., & Manuel, J. A. (2003). Building Trust: Effective Multicultural Communication Processes in Virtual Teams. In S. G. Cohen, & C. B. Gibson (Eds.)*Virtual Teams That Work: Creating Conditions for Virtual Team Effectiveness.* San Francisco: Jossey-Bassey.

Giddens, A. (1984). *The Constitution of Society.* Cambridge: Polity.

Globus Alliance. (2005). *GT4 administration guide.* Retrieved June 28, 2008, from http://www.globus.org/toolkit/docs/4.0/admin/docbook/index.html

Goh, A. L. S. (2005). Harnessing knowledge for innovation: an integrated management framework. *Journal of Knowledge Management 2005, 9*(4), 6-18.

Grant, D. B., Lambert, D. M., Stock, J. R., & Ellram, L. M. (2006). *Fundamentals of Logistics Management: European Edition.* Maidenhead: UK: McGraw-Hill.

Graves, R. J. (2004, May). *Key Technologies for Emergency Response.* Paper presented at the International Community on Information Systems for Crisis Response (ICSCRAM2004) conference, Brussels, Belgium.

Grimshaw, A. S., Wulf, W. A., & The Legion Team, C. (1997). The Legion vision of a worldwide virtual computer. *Communications of the ACM, 40*(1), 39-45.

Group, A. (2006, Sept). *The Lean Supply Chain Report: Lean Concepts Transcend Manufacturing through the Supply Chain.* Aberdeen Group.

Group, A. A. (2007, Aug). *The Supply Chain Execution Market to Grow 10% Annually.* ARC Advisory Group. Retrieved July 15, 2008, from http://www.arcweb.com/AboutARC/Press/Lists/Posts/Post.aspx?List=fe0

aa6f8%2D048a%2D418e%2D8197%2D2ed598e4237
0&ID=19

Gudgin, M., Hadley, M., Mendelsohn, N., Moreau, J.-J., Nielsen, H. F., Karmarkar, A., et al. (2007). *SOAP Version 1.2 Part 1: Messaging Framework* (Standard Specification). W3C. Available at: http://www.w3.org/TR/soap12-part1/

Guo, L., Chen-Burger, Y.-H., & Robertson, D. (2004). Mapping a Business Process Model to a Semantic Web Service Model. Paper presented at *3rd IEEE International Conference on Web Services (ICWS '04)*.

Guy, L., Kunszt, P., Laure, E., & Stock, H. (2002). *Replica Management in Data Grids*. Scotland: Global Grid Forum Informational Document, GGF5.

Haddad, C., & Slimani, Y. (2007). Economic Model for Replicated Database Placement in Grid. In *Proceedings of the Seventh IEEE international Symposium on Cluster Computing and the Grid* (pp. 283-292). IEEE Computer Society.

Halal, W. E. (1998). *The New Management: Bringing Democracy and Markets Inside Organisations*. San Francisco: Berrett-Koehler Publishers.

Hall, R. J., & Zisman, A. (2004). Behavioral Models as Service Descriptions. In *Proceedings of the 2nd International Conference on Service oriented computing, (ICSOC 2004)*, New York (pp. 163-172).

Hall, R. J., & Zisman, A. (2004). OMML: A Behavioural Model Interchange Format. In *International Conference in Requirements Engineering*, Japan (pp. 272-282).

Hall, R. J., & Zisman, A. (2004). Validating Personal Requirements by Assisted Symbolic Behavior Browsing. In *Proceedings of the 19th IEEE International Conference on Automated software engineering (ASE 2004)*, Austria (pp 56-66).

Handy, C. (1995). Trust and the virtual organisation. *Harvard Business Review, 73*, 40-50.

Harris, R. (2001). From fiefdom to service: The evolution of flexible occupation. *Journal of Corporate Real Estate, 3*(1), 7-16.

Harrison, A., & van Hoek, R. (2008). *Logistics Management and Strategy: Competing Through the Supply Chain*. FT: Prentice Hall.

Hasselmeyer, P. (2006). Performance Evaluation of a WS Service Group based Registry. Paper presented at *7th IEEE/ACM International Conference on Grid Computing (Grid 2006)*. Barcelona.

Hausmann, J. H., Heckel, R., & Lohman, M. (2004). Model-based Discovery of Web Services. In *Proceedings of the IEEE International Conference on Web Services (ICWS 2004)* (pp. 324-331).

Haythornthwaite, C. (1996). Social Network Analysis: An Approach and Technique for the Study of Information Exchange. *Library & Information Science Research, 18*, 323-342.

Hepp, M., Leymann, F., Domingue, J., Wahler, A., & Fensel, D. (2005). Semantic Business Process Management: A Vision Towards Using Semantic Web Services for Business Process Management. In *Proceedings of the IEEE International Conference on e-Business Engineering*. IEEE Computer Society.

Herzog, T. N., & Lord, G. (2002). *Applications of Monte Carlo methods to finance and insurance*. Winstead, Conn: ACTEX Publications. Retrieved June 28, 2008, from http://books.google.com/

Hiltz, S. R., & Turoff, M. (1985). Structuring Computer Mediated Communication Systems to Avoid Information Overload. *Communications of the ACM, 7*(28).

Holliday, G. L., Murray-Rust, P., & Rzepa, H. S. (2006). Chemical markup, XML, and the world wide web. 6. CMLReact, an XML vocabulary for chemical reactions. *Journal of chemical information and modeling, 46*, 145-157.

Hollocks, B. W. (2006). Forty years of discrete-event simulation - a personal reflection. *Journal of the Operational Research Society, 57*(12), 1383-1399.

Holton, J. A. (2001). Building Trust and Collaboration in a Virtual Team. *Team Performance Management, 7*(4), 15-26.

Horrocks, I., Patel-Schneider, P. F., & Harmelen, F. (2003). From SHIQ and RDF to OWL: The making of a Web ontology language. *Journal of Web Semantics, 1*(1), 7-26.

Hoschek, W. (2002). The Web Service Discovery Architecture. In *Proceedings of the IEEE/ACM Supercomputing Conference, Baltimore*, USA (pp. 1-15).

Howard, R., Kiviniemi, A., & Samuelson, O. (2002, June). *The Latest Developments in Communications and e-commerce – IT Barometer in 3 Nordic Countries.* Paper presented at the CIB w87 conference, Aarhus School of Architecture. International Council for Research and Innovation in Building and Construction.

Hoyt, B. (2000). Techniques to manage participation and contribution of team members in virtual teams. *WebNet Journal, 2*(4), 16-20.

Huedo, E., Montero, R. S., & Llorente, I. M. (2006). Evaluating the reliability of computational grids from the end user's point of view. *Journal of Systems Architecture, 52*, 727-736.

i2. (2005*). i2 Next-Generation Supply Chain Management Overview.* Retrieved July 15, 2008, from i2: http://www. i2.com/assets/pdf/BRO_ng_scm_ovrvw_pds7310.pdf

Iamnitchi, A., Ripeanu, M., & Foster, I. (2002). *Locating Data in Peer-to-Peer Scientific Collaborations.* Paper presented at the International Workshop on Peer-to-Peer Systems, Cambridge, USA.

Inkpen, A. C., & Curall, S. C. (2004). The Coevolution of Trust, Control, and Learning in Joint Ventures. *Organization Science, 15*(5), 586-599.

Ishaya, T., & Macaulay, L. (1999). The role of trust in virtual teams. In P. Sieber, J. & Griese (Eds.), *Organizational Virtualness & Electronic Commerce, Proceedings of the 2nd International VoNet* - Workshop, September 23-24, Bern, Switzerland (pp. 135-152).

ISL. (2001). *Shipping Statistics and Market Review.* Institute of Shipping Economics and Logistics.

ISO (1993). *Open Systems Interconnection, Data Management and Open Distributed Processing.* Draft ODP

Trading Function. Report No. ISO/IEC JTC 1/SC21/WG7/N880, International Organization for Standardization.

Jacob, B., Brown, M., Fukui, K., & Trivedi, N. (2005). *Introduction to Grid Computing.* IBM International Technical Support Organization. Retrieved 15 Feb, 2008, from http://www.redbooks.ibm.com/redbooks/pdfs/sg246778.pdf

Jacyno, M., Payne, T. R., Watkins, E. R., Taylor, S. J., & Surridge, M. (2007). Mediating Semantic Web Service Access using the Semantic Firewall. Paper presented at *UK E-Science Programme All Hands Meeting 2007 (AHM2007)*, 10th-13th September 2007, Nottingham, UK.

JAG. (1999). *Joint Advisory Group.* Retrieved March 27, 2008, from http://www.isotc211.org/organizn.htm#jag

Jarratt, D., & Fayed, R. (2001). The Impact of Market and Organisational Challenges on Marketing Strategy Decision-Making: A Qualitative investigation of the Business-to-Business Sector. *Journal of Business Research, 51*(1) (January 2001), 61-72.

Jarvenpaa, S. L., & Leidner, D. E. (1999). *The Development and Maintenance of Trust in Global Virtual Teams.* Fontainebleau: INSEAD.

Jarvenpaa, S. L., & Shaw, T. R. (1998). Global virtual teams: Integrating models of trust. Iin P. Sieber, & J. Griese, (Eds.), *Organizational Virtualness Proceedings of the 1ˢᵗ VO Net - Workshop*, April, Bern, Switzerland (pp. 35-51).

Jarvenpaa, S. L., Knoll, K., & Leidner, D. (1998). Is Anybody Out There? Antecedents of Trust in Global Virtual Teams. *Journal of Management Information Systems, 14*(4), 37-53.

Jarvenpaa, S. L., Shaw, T. R., & Staples, D. S. (2004). The role of trust in global virtual teams. *Information Systems Research, 15*(3), 250–267.

Jin, H., & Wu, H. (2005). Semantic-enabled Specification for Web Services Agreement. *International Journal of Web Services Practices, 1*(1-2), 13-20.

Jones, S., Kozlenkov, A., Mahbub, K., Maiden, N., Spanoudakis, G., Zachos, K., Zhu, X., & Zisman, A. (2005). Service Discovery for Service Centric Systems. Paper presented at *eChallenges Conference 2005*, Slovenia.

Joseph, J., Ernest, M., & Fellenstein, C. (2004). Evolution of Grid Computing Architecture and Grid Adoption Models. *IBM Systems Journal, 4*(43). Retrieved June 15, 2004, from http://www.informatik.uni-trier.de/~ley/db/journals/ibmsj/ibmsj43.html

Kacin, M. (2006). *Got The Enterprise Software Blues? Appliances Come to the Rescue.* KACE Networks.

Kacsuk, P., & Sipos, G. (2005). Multi-Grid, multi-user workflows in the P-GRADE Grid Portal. *Journal of Grid Computing 3*(3-4), 221-238. The Netherlands: Springer

Kacsuk, P., Kiss, T., & Sipos, G. (2008). Solving the grid interoperability problem by P-GRADE portal at workflow level. *Future Generation Computer Systems, 24*, 744-751. Elsevier.

Kalleberg, A. L. (2003). Flexible firms and labour market segmentation. *Work and Occupations, 30*(2), 154-175.

Kangilaski, T. (2005). Virtual organization and supply chain management. In *10th IEEE International Conference on Emerging Technologies and Factory Automation, 1*, 705-712. IEEE.

Kasper-Fuehrer, E. C. & Ashkanasy, N. M. (2000). Communicating Trustworthiness and Building trust in inter-organizational virtual organizations. *Journal of Management, 27*(3), 235-254.

Katzy, B., & Löh, H. (2003). Virtual Enterprise Research State of the Art and Ways Forward, In *9th International Conference on Concurrent Enterprising.* Centre for Concurrent Engineering, University of Nottingham, UK.

Kayworth, T. R. & Leidner, D. (2000). The Global Virtual Manager: a prescription for success. *European Management Journal, 18*(2), 67-79.

Khambatti, M., Ryu, K. D., & Dasgupta, P. (2003). *Structuring Peer-to-Peer Networks using Interest-Based Communities.* Paper presented at the International Workshop on Databases, Information Systems, and Peer-to-Peer Computing, Berlin, Germany.

Khambatti, M., Ryu, K., & Dasgupta, P. (2002). Efficient Discovery of Implicitly Formed Peer-to-Peer Communities. *International Journal of Parallel and Distributed Systems and Networks, 5*, 155-164.

Khare, B. R., & Taylor, R. N. (2004, May 2004). *Extending the Representational State Transfer (REST) Architectural Style for Decentralized Systems.* Paper presented at the 26th International Conference on Software Engineering (ICSE'04), Edinburgh, Scotland.

Khodyakov, D. M. (2007). The Complexity of Trust-Control Relationships in Creative Organizations: Insights from a Qualitative Analysis of a Conductorless Orchestra. *Social Forces, 86*(1), 1-22.

Kirkman, B. L., Rosen, B., Gibson, G. B., Tesluk, P. E., & McPherson, S. O. (2002). Five challenges to virtual team success: Lessons from Sabre, Inc. *Academy of Management Executive, 16*(3), 67-79.

Kirtland, M. (2001). *A Platform for Web Services.* Technical Report. Microsoft.

Kleinberg, J. (2000). Navigation in a Small World. *Nature, 406*, 845.

Kleinberg, J. (2001). Small-World Phenomena and the Dynamics of Information. *Advances in Neural Information Processing Systems (NIPS), 14*.

Klusch, M., Fries, B., & Sycara, K. (2006). Automated Semantic Web Service Discovery with OWLS-MX. *Proceedings of the fifth international joint conference on Autonomous agents and multiagent systems* (pp. 915-922).

Klyne, G., & Carroll, J. (Eds.) (2004). *Resource Description Framework (RDF): Concepts and Abstract Syntax.* W3C Recommendation. Available at: http://www.w3.org/TR/rdf-concepts/

Kodeboyina, D., & Plale, B. (2004). *Experiences with OGSA-DAI: portlet access and benchmark.* Report. Retrieved August 17, 2008, from http://www-unix.mcs.anl.gov/~keahey/DBGS/DBGS_files/dbgs_papers/kodeboyina.pdf

Koenig, M., Guptill, B., McNee, B., & Cassell, J. (2006). *SaaS 2.0: Software-as-a-Service as Next-Gen Business Platform*. Saugatuck Technology.

Köller, M. (1988). Risk as a Determinant of Trust. *Journal of Basic and Applied Social Psychology, 9*(4), 265-276.

Kolodziej, K. (2004). *OpenGIS Web Map Server Cookbook*. Implementation Specification No. 03-050r1. Open Geospatial Consortium Inc. (OGC).

Koontz, L. D. (2003). *Geographic Information Systems: Challenges to Effective Data Sharing*. Report No. GAO-03-874T. Washington, DC: United States General Accounting Office (GAO).

Kourpas, E. (2006). *Grid Computing: Past, Present and Future - An Innovation Perspective*. Retrieved 13 Feb, 2008, from http://www-03.ibm.com/grid/pdf/innovperspective.pdf?S_TACT=105AGX52&S_CMP=cn-a-gr.

Kozlenkov, A., Fasoulas, V., Sanchez, F., Spanoudakis, G., & Zisman, A. (2006). A Framework for Architecture-driven Service Discovery. In *Proceedings of the 2006 International Workshop on Service-Oriented Software Engineering (IW-SOSE'06)*, China (pp. 67-73).

Kraemer, K., & Deddrick, J. (2001). *Dell Computer: Using E-commerce to Support the Virtual Company*. Paper 236, Center for Research on Information Technology and Organizations, Globalization of I.T.

Kramer, R. M. (1999). Trust and Distrust in Organizations: Emerging Perspectives, Enduring Questions. *Annual Review of Psychology, 50*, 569-598.

Krauter, K., Buyya, R., & Maheswaran M. (2002) A taxonomy and survey of grid resource management systems for distributed computing. *Softw. Pract. Exper., 32*(2),135-164.

Kreger, H. (2001). *Web Services Conceptual Architecture (WSCA 1.0)*. IBM.

La Porta, R. (1997). Trust in Large Organizations. *The American Economic Review, 87*(2), 333-338. Papers and Proceedings of the Hundred and Fourth Annual Meeting of the American Economic Association (May, 1997).

Lamanna, D. D., Skene, J., & Emmerich, W. (2003). SLAng: A Language for Defining Service Level Agreements. In *Proceedings of the 9th IEEE Workshop on Future Trends in Distributed Computing Systems (FTDCS 2003*. (pp. 100).

Lamanna, M. (2004).The LHC computing grid project at CERN. *Nuclear Instruments and Methods in Physics Research (Section A: Accelerators, Spectrometers, Detectors and Associated Equipment), 534*(1-2), 1-6.

Lambert, D. M., & Cooper, M. C. (2000). Issues in Supply Chain Management, *Industrial Marketing Management, 29*(1), 65-83.

Larson, A. (1992). Network dyads in entrepreneurial settings: a study of the governance of exchange relationships. *Administrative Science Quarterly, 37*(1), 79-93.

Lawrence, M., & Rau-Chaplin, A. (2006). The OLAP-Enabled Grid: Model and Query Processing Algorithms. In *Proceedings of the 20th international Symposium on High-Performance Computing in An Advanced Collaborative Environment* (pp. 4).

Leinberger, W., & Kumar, V. (Oct-Dec 1999). Information Power Grid: The new frontier in parallel computing? *IEEE Concurrency, 7*(4), 75-84.

Levine, D., & Wirt, M. (2004). Interactivity with scalability: infrastructure for multiplayer games. In I. Foster, & C. Kesselman (Eds.), *The Grid: Blueprint for a New Computing Infrastructure (2nd Edition)*, chapter 13. San Francisco, CA: Morgan Kaufmann.

Levy, A. (2000). Logic-based Techniques in Data Integration. In J. Minker (Ed.), *Logic Based Artificial Intelligence*. USA: Kluwer Publishers.

Levy, A. (2002). Logic-based techniques in data integration. In J. Minker (Ed.), *Logic Based Artificial Intelligence* (pp. 575-595). Norwell: Kluwer Academic Publishers.

Lewin, K. (1951). *Field Theory in Social Science*. NY: Harper & Row.

Lewis, D., & Weigert, A. (1985). Trust as a Social Reality, *Social Forces, 63*(4), 967-976.

Li, J., & Vuong, S. (2004). *An Efficient Clustered Architecture for P2P Networks.* Paper presented at the 18th International Conference on Advanced Information Networking and Application, Fukuoka, Japan.

Lima, A., Mattoso, M., & Valduriez., P. (2004). Adaptive Virtual Partitioning for OLAP Query Processing in a Database Cluster, In *Proceedings of the Brazilian Symposium on Databases* (pp. 92-105).

Lin, Y., Liu, P., & Wu, J. (2006). Optimal Placement of Replicas in Data Grid Environments with Locality Assurance. In *Proceedings of the 12th international Conference on Parallel and Distributed Systems* (pp. 465-474). IEEE Computer Society.

Lipnack, J., & Stamps, J. (1999). Virtual teams. *Executive Excellence, 16*(5), 14-16.

Lipnack, J., & Stamps, J. (2000). *Virtual Teams. People Working Across Boundaries with Technology.* New York: John Wiley.

Litke, A., Skoutas, D., & Varvarigou, T. (2004). Mobile Grid Computing: Changes and Challenges of Resource Management in a Mobile Grid Environment. Paper presented at *Access to Knowledge through Grid in a Mobile World, PAKM 2004 Conference,* Vienna.

Litzkow, M., Livny, M., & Mutka, M. (1988). Condor - a hunter of idle workstations. *8th International Conference of Distributed Computing Systems* (pp. 104-111). IEEE Computer Society, Washington, DC, USA.

Liu, L., Antonopoulos, N., & Mackin, S. (2007). Fault-tolerant Peer-to-Peer Search on Small-World Networks. *Journal of Future Generation Computer Systems, 23*(8), 921-931.

Liu, L., Antonopoulos, N., & Mackin, S. (2007). *Small World Peer-to-peer for Resource Discovery.* Paper presented at the International Conference on Information Networking, Lecture Notes in Computer Science, Estoril, Portugal.

Liu, L., Antonopoulos, N., & Mackin, S. (2007). *Social Peer-to-Peer for Resource Discovery.* Paper presented at the 15th Euromicro International Conference on

Parallel, Distributed and Network-based Processing, Naples, Italy.

Liu, L., Antonopoulos, N., & Mackin, S. (2008). Managing Peer-to-Peer Networks with Human Tactics in Social Interactions. *Journal of Supercomputing, 44*(3), 217-236.

Liu, P., & Wu, J. (2006). Optimal Replica Placement Strategy for Hierarchical Data Grid Systems. In *Proceedings of the Sixth IEEE international Symposium on Cluster Computing and the Grid* (pp. 417-420). IEEE Computer Society.

Loosely, C. (2006). *Rich Internet Applications: Design, measurement, and management challenges.* Keynote Systems. Retrieved July 3, 2008, from http://www.keynote.com/docs/whitepapers/RichInternet_5.pdf

Ludäscher, B., Altintas, I., Berkley, C., Higgins, D., Jaeger-Frank, E., Jones, M., Lee, E., Tao, J., & Zhao, Y. (2006). Scientific Workflow Management and the Kepler System. *Concurrency and Computation: Practice & Experience, 18*(10), 1039-1065.

Ludwig, H., & Whittingham, K. (1999). Virtual Enterprise Co-Ordinator – Agreement-driven Gateways for Cross-Organisational Workflow Management. *Engineering Notes, 24*(2) (March 1999), 19-38.

Ludwig, H., Keller, A., Dan, A., King, R. P., & Franck, R. (2003, January 28). *Service Level Agreement Language Specification.* Retrieved July 15, 2008, from http://www.research.ibm.com/wsla/WSLASpecV1-20030128.pdf

Lurey, J. S., & Raisinghani, M. S. (2001). An empirical study of best practices in virtual teams. *Information and Management, 38*(8), 523-544.

Luther, A., Buyya, R., Ranjan, R., & Venugopal, S. (2005). Alchemi: a .NET-based enterprise grid computing system. *6th International Conference on Internet Computing (ICOMP'05)* (pp. 269-278). CSREA Press, USA.

Lv, Q., Cao, P., Cohen, E., Li, K., & Shenker, S. (2002). *Search and Replication in Unstructured Peer-to-Peer Networks.* Paper presented at the ACM SIGMETRICS, Marina Del Rey, CA.

Magowan, J. (2003, April). *A view on relational data on the grid*. Paper presented at the International Parallel and Distributed Processing Symposium, Nice, France.

Mahbub, K., & Spanoudakis, G. (2005). Run-time Monitoring of Requirements for Systems Composed of Web-Services: Initial Implementation and Evaluation Experience. In *Proceedings of the IEEE International Conference on Web Services (ICWS 2005)* (pp. 257-265).

Manataki, A. (2007). *A Knowledge-Based Analysis and Modelling of Dell's Supply Chain Strategies*. Unpublished masters dissertation, School of Informatics, University of Edinburgh, UK.

Mann, B. (2003). *The Virtual Observatory as a Data Grid*. Edinburgh, UK: e-Science Institute. Retrieved August, 08, 2008 from http://www.nesc.ac.uk/technical_papers/UKeS-2003-03.pdf

Marins, J. T. M., Santos J. F., & Saliby, E. (2004). Variance reduction techniques applied to Monte Carlo simulation of Asian calls. *2004 Business Association of Latin American Studies (BALAS) Conference*. Business Association of Latin American Studies.

Martin, D. (Ed.) (2006). *OWL-S Semantic Markup for Web Services, Pre-Release 1.2*. World Wide Web Consortium (W3C). Available at: http://www.ai.sri.com/daml/services/owl-s/1.2/ (Temporary location at SRI).

Martin, D., Burstein, D., Hobbs, J., Lassila, O., McDermott, D., McIlraith, S., Narayanan, S., Paolucci, M., Parsia, B., Payne, T., Sirin, E., Srinivasan, N., & Sycara, K. (2004). *OWL-S: Semantic Markup for Web Services*. Retrieved on March 25, 2008, from http://www.w3.org/Submission/2004/SUBM-OWL-S-20041122/

Martin, M. J. (2004). Diagrams and Big Pictures: The problems of representing large, complex socio-technical systems. Paper presented at *Diagrams 2004: Third International Conference on the Theory and Application of Diagrams* (March 2004).

Marzolla, M., Mordacchini, M., & Orlando, S. (2007). Peer-to-peer systems for discovering resources in a dynamic gridstar, open. *Parallel Computing, 33*(4-5), 339-358.

Massey, A. P., Montoya-Weiss, M. M., & Hung, Y. T. (2003). Because time matters: Temporal coordination in global virtual project teams. *Journal of Management Information Systems, 19*(4), 129-155.

Mastroianni, C., Talia, D., & Verta, O. (2005). *A P2P Approach for Membership Management and Resource Discovery in Grids*. Paper presented at the 2005 International Symposium on Information Technology: Coding and Computing, Las Vegas, NV.

Mayer, R. C., Davis, J. H., & Schoorman, F. D. (1995). An integrative model of organizational trust. *Academy of Management Review, 20*(3), 709-734.

Mayer, R., Menzel, C., Painter, M., Witte, P., Blinn, T., & Perakath, B. (1995). *Information Integration for Concurrent Engineering (IICE) IDEF3 Process Description Capture Method Report*. Knowledge Based Systems Inc.

Maymounkov, P., & Mazières, D. (2002). *Kademlia: A Peer to Peer Information System Based on the XOR Metric*. Paper presented at the International Workshop on Peer-to-Peer Systems, Cambridge MA.

Maznevski, M. L., & Chudoba, K. M. (2000). Bridging space over time: Global virtual team dynamics and effectiveness. *Organization Science, 11*(2), 473-493.

McAllister, D. J. (1995). Affect- and Cognition-Based Trust as Foundations for Interpersonal Cooperation in Organizations. *Academy of Management Journal, 38*(1), 24-59.

McAllister, D. J., Lewicki, R. J., & Chaturvedi, S. (2006). Trust in Developing Relationships: From Theory to Measurement. *Academy of Management Best Conference Paper*, G1-G6.

McCarty, C. (2002). Structure in Personal Networks. *Journal of Social Structure, 3*, 1-19.

McEvily, B., Perrone, V., & Zaheer, A. (2003). Trust as an organising principle. *Organisation Science, 14*(1), 91-103.

McFadzean, E., & McKenzie, J., (2001). Facilitating Virtual Learning Groups. A Practical Approach. *Journal of Management Development*, 20 (6), 37-49.

McGrath, J. E., & Hollingshead, A. B. (1994). *Groups Interacting with Technology: Ideas, Evidence, Issues and an Agenda*. Thousand Oaks, Sage Publications Inc.

McGuinness, D., & van Harmelen, F. (2004). *OWL Web Ontology Language*. World Wide Web Consortium (W3C). Available at: http://www.w3.org/TR/owl-features/

McKnight, D. H., Cummings, L. L., & Chervany, N. L. (1998). Initial trust formation in new organisational relationships. *The Academy Management Review*, *23*(3), 473-490.

McKnight, D. H., Kacmar, C. J., & Choudhury, V. (2004). Dispositional Trust and Distrust Distinction in Predicting High- and Low-Risk Internet Expert Advice Site Perceptions. *E-Service Journal*, *3*(2), 35-58.

McLain, D. L., & Hackman, K. (1999). Trust, Risk, and Decision-Making in Organizational Change. *Public Administration Quarterly*, *23*(2), 152-176.

Meliksetian, D. S., Prost, J-P., Bahl, A. S., Boutboul, I., Currier, D. P., Fibra, S., Girard, J-Y., Kassab, K. M., Lepesant, J-L., Malone, C., & Manesco, P. (2004). Design and implementation of an enterprise grid. *IBM Systems Journal*, *43*(4), 646-664.

Metselaar, C., & van Dael, R. (1999). Organisations Going Virtual. *AI & Society, 13*(1-2) (December 1999) Special issue on science, technology and society, 200-209. London, UK: Springer-Verlag.

Meyerson, D., Weick, K., & Kramer, R. (1996). Swift Trust and Temporary Groups. In T. Tyler (Ed.), *Trust in Organizations: Frontiers of Theory and Research*. Thousand Oaks: Sage.

Milgram, S. (1967). The Small World Problem. *Psychology Today, 2*, 60-67.

Milgram, S. (1974). *Obedience to Authority: An Experimental View*. New York: Harper & Row.

Misztal, B. (1996). *Trust in Modern Societies*. Cambridge, MA: Polity Press.

MIT (n.d.). *MIT Process Handbook*, Phios Repository, Case Examples, Dell. Retrieved June 12, 2008, from http://process.mit.edu/Info/CaseLinks.asp

Mitra, B. S. (2001). *Dealing with Natural Disaster: Role of the Market*. USA: Hoover Press.

Möllering, G. (2005). The Trust/Control Duality: An Integrative Perspective on Positive Expectations of Others. *International Sociology, 20*(3) 283-305.

Molm, L. D., Takahashi, N., & Peterson, G. (2000). Risk and Trust in Social Exchange: An Experimental Test of a Classical Proposition. *American Journal of Sociology, 105*(5), 1396-1427.

Monk, A., & Howard, S. (1998). Methods & Tools: the rich picture: a tool for reasoning about work context. *Interactions 5*(2), March/April 1998, 21-30.

Moses, T., et al. (2005). *eXtensible Access Control Markup Language (XACML), Version 2.0*. OASIS Standard. Available at: http://www.oasisopen.org/committees/tc_home.php?wg_abbrev=xacml

Mowshowitz, A. (2002) *Virtual Organization: Toward a Theory of Societal Transformation Stimulated by Information Technology*. Westport, CT, USA: Greenwood Press.

Mustafee, N. (2007). *A grid computing framework for commercial simulation packages*. Unpublished doctoral dissertation. School of Information Systems, Computing and Mathematics, Brunel University, UK.

Mustafee, N., & Taylor, S. J. E. (2008). Investigating grid computing technologies for use with commercial simulation packages. Paper presented at *2008 Operational Research Society Simulation Workshop (SW08)* (pp. 297-307). OR Society, UK.

Mutka, M. W. (1992). Estimating capacity for sharing in a privately owned workstation environment. *IEEE Transactions on Software Engineering, 18*(4), 319-328.

Nadarajan, G., & Chen-Burger, Y.-H. (2007). Translating a Typical Business Process Modelling Language to a Web Services Ontology through Lightweight Mapping. *IET Software* (Formerly IEE Proceedings Software), *1*(1), 1-17.

Nadarajan, G., & Renouf, A. (2007). A Modular Approach for Automating Video Analysis. In *Proceedings of the 12th International Conference on Computer Analysis of Images and Patterns (CAIP'07)* (pp. 133-140). Springer-Verlag.

Nadarajan, G., Chen-Burger, Y.-H., Malone, J. (2006). Semantic-Based Workflow Composition for Video Processing in the Grid. *IEEE/WIC/ACM International Conference on Web Intelligence (WI-2006)* (pp. 161-165). IEEE.

Nanjo, K. Z., Holliday, J. R., Chen, C.-C., Rundle, J. B., & Turcotte, D. L. (2006). Application of a modified pattern informatics method to forecasting the locations of future large earthquakes in the central Japan. *Tectonophysics, 424*, 351-366.

National Research Council (2006). *Facing Hazards and Disasters: Understanding Human Dimensions.* USA: National Academy Press.

Next Generation GRIDs Expert Group, (2006). *Future for European Grids: GRIDs and Service Oriented Knowledge Utility.* Next Generation GRIDs Expert Group Report 3. Retrieved July 15, 2008, from ftp://ftp.cordis.europa.eu/pub/ist/docs/grids/ngg3_eg_final.pdf

Nieto-Santisteban, M. A., Gray, J., Szalay, A. S., Annis, J., Thakar, A. R., & O'Mullane, W. J. (2004). *When database systems meet the grid.* Technical Report. Microsoft Research, Microsoft Corporation.

Nonaka, I., & Takeuchi, H. (1995). *The Knowledge-Creating Company.* New York: Oxford University Press.

Nooteboom, B. (2007). Social Capital, Institutions and Trust. *Review of Social Economy, LXV*(1), 29-53.

O'Driscoll, M. P., Pierce, J. L., & Coghlan, A.-M. (2006). The Psychology of Ownership: Work Environment Structure, Organizational Commitment, and Citizenship Behaviors. *Group & Organization Management, 31*, 388-416.

O'Reilly, T. (2005). What Is Web 2.0. Oreillynet.com. Retrieved on June 25, 2008, from http://www.oreillynet.com/pub/a/oreilly/tim/news/2005/09/30/what-is-web-20.html

OGC (1994, 06/12/2008). *The Open Geospatial Consortium, Inc.* Retrieved Feb 14, 2008, from http://www.opengeospatial.org/

OGSA-DAI (2008). *The OGSA-DAI Project.* Available at: http://www.ogsadai.org.uk/

Oh, S., & Park, S. (2000). Task-Role Based Access Control (T-RBAC): An Improved Access Control Model for Enterprise Environment. *Lecture Notes in Computer Science, 1873/2000*, 264-273.

Oinn, T., Greenwood, M., Addis, M., Alpdemir, M. N., Ferris, J., Glover, K., Goble, C., Goderis, A., Hull, D., Marvin, D., Li, P., Lord, P., Pocock, M. R., Senger, M., Stevens, R., Wipat, A., & Wroe, C. (2005). Taverna: Lessons in creating a workflow environment for the life sciences. *Concurrency and Computation: Practice and Experience, 18*(10), 1067-1100.

OnEarth (2007, 12/08/2007). *OnEarth.* JPL WMS Server. Retrieved March 15, 2008, from http://onearth.jpl.nasa.gov/

Oomes, A. H. J. (2004, May). *Organization Awareness in Crisis Management.* Paper presented at the International Community on Information Systems for Crisis Response (ISCRAM2004) Conference, Brussels, Belgium.

Ornetzeder, M., & Rohracher, H. (2006). User-led innovations and participation processes: lessons from sustainable energy technologies. *Energy Policy, 34*(2) (January 2006), 138-150, Reshaping Markets for the Benefit of Energy Saving.

Otten, J., Heijningen, B., & Lafortune, J. F. (2004, May). *The Virtual Crisis Management Centre. An ICT Implementation to Canalise Information.* Paper presented at the International Community on Information Systems for Crisis Response Management (ISCRAM2004), Brussels, Belgium.

Oundhakar, S., Verma, K., Sivashanmugam, K., Sheth, A., & Miller, J. (2005). Discovery of Web Services in a Multi-Ontology and Federated Registry Environment. *International Journal of Web Services Research, 2*(3) (pp. 8-39).

Pacitti, E., Valduriez, P., & Mattoso, M. (2007). Grid Data Management: Open Problems and New Issues. *Journal of Grid Computing, 5*(3), 273–281.

Pallickara, S., & Fox, G. (2003). *NaradaBrokering: A Distributed Middleware Framework and Architecture for Enabling Durable Peer-to-Peer Grids*. Paper presented at the ACM/IFIP/USENIX. Retrieved July 15, 2008 from http://grids.ucs.indiana.edu/ptliupages/publications/NB-Framework.pdf

Park, S., & Kim, J. (2003). Chameleon: A Resource Scheduler in A Data Grid Environment. In *Proceedings of the 3st international Symposium on Cluster Computing and the Grid* (p. 258). IEEE Computer Society.

Pauleen, D. J., & Yoong, P. (2001). Relationship Building and the use of ICT in boundary -crossing virtual teams: a facilitator's perspective. *Journal of Information Technology, 16*(4), 45-62.

Peng, Z.-R., & Tsou, M.-H. (2003). *Internet GIS: Distributed Geographic Information Services for the Internet and Wireless Networks*. New Jersey, USA: John Wiley & Sons.

Pfister, G. F. (1998). *In Search of Clusters*. Upper Saddle River, NJ: Prentice-Hall, Inc.

Pidd, M. (2004). *Computer simulation in management science (5th edition)*. Chichester, UK: John Wiley & Sons.

Pierce, J. L., Kostova, T., & Dirks, K. (2001). Toward a Theory of Psychological Ownership in Organizations. *Academy of Management Review, 26*, 298-310.

Pierce, J. L., O'driscoll, M. P., & Coghman, A.-M. (2004). Work Environment Structure and Psychological Ownership: The Mediating Effect of Control. *The Journal of Social Psychology, 144*(5), 507-534.

Pilioura, T., Tsalgatidou, A., & Batsakis, A. (2003). *Using WSDL/UDDI and DAML-S in Web Service Discovery*. Paper presented at WWW 2003 Workshop on E-Services and the Semantic Web (ESSW 2003), Budapest, Hungary.

Piro, R. M., Guarise, A., & Werbrouck, A. (2003). An economy-based accounting infrastructure for the datagrid. In *Proceedings of Fourth International Workshop on Grid Computing*. IEEE.

Pistore, M., Traverso, P., Bertoli, P., & Marconi, A. (2005). Automated Synthesis of Composite BPEL4WS Web Services. *Proceedings of the IEEE International Conference on Web Services (ICWS 2005)*, USA (pp. 293-301).

Poortinga, W., & Pidgeon, N. F. (2003). Exploring the Dimensionality of Trust in Risk Regulations. *Risk Analysis, 23*(5), 961-972.

Porter, M. E. (1985). *Competitive Advantage*. New York: The Free Press.

Powell, A., Piccoli, G., & Ives, B. (2004). Virtual teams: a review of current literature and directions for future research. *ACM SIGMIS Database, 35*(1), 6-36.

Pratali, P. (2003). The strategic management of technological innovations in the small to medium enterprise. *European Journal of Innovation Management, 6*(1), 18-31.

Rajasekar, A., Wan, M., Moore, R., Schroeder, W., Kremenek, G., Jagatheesan, A., Cowart, C., Zhu, B., Chen S., & Olschanowsky, R. (2003). Storage Resource Broker – Managing distributed data in a Grid. *Computer Society of India Journal, Special Issue on SAN, 33*(4), 42-54.

Raman, V., Narang, I., Crone, C., Haas, L., Malaika, S., Mukai, T., Wolfson, D., & Baru, C. (2003). *Data access and management services on grid. Global Grid Forum*. Retrieved August 17, 2008, from http://61.136.61.58:81/gate/big5/www.cs.man.ac.uk/grid-db/papers/dams.pdf

Ran, S. (2003). A model for web services discovery with QoS. *ACM SIGecom Exchanges, 4*(1),1-10.

Rana, O., & Hilton, J. (2006). Securing the Virtual Organization – Part 1: Requirements from Grid Computing. *Network Security, 2006*(4), 7-10.

Rana, O., & Hilton, J. (2006). Securing the Virtual Organization – Part 2: Grid Computing in Action. *Network Security, 2006*(5), 6-10.

Ranganathan, K., & Foster, I. (2002). Decoupling Computation and Data Scheduling in Distributed Data-Intensive Applications. In *Proceedings of the 11th IEEE international Symposium on High Performance Distributed Computing* (pp. 352). IEEE Computer Society.

Ranganathan, K., & Foster, I. (2002). Decoupling Computation and Data Scheduling in Distributed Data-Intensive Applications. *Proceedings of the 11th IEEE Symposium on High Performance Distributed Computing (HPDC)*. Edinburgh, Scotland.

Ranganathan, K., & Foster, I. (2004). Computation scheduling and data replication algorithms for data Grids. In *Grid Resource Management: State of the Art and Future Trends* (pp. 359-373). Kluwer Academic Publishers.

Ranganathan, K., & Foster, I. T. (2001). Identifying Dynamic Replication Strategies for a High-Performance Data Grid. In *Proceedings of the Second international Workshop on Grid Computing* LNCS, *2242*, 75-86.

Ratnasamy, S., Francis, P., Handley, M., Karp, R., & Shenker, S. (2001). *A Scalable Content-Addressable Network.* Paper presented at the ACM SIGCOMM, San Diego, CA.

Ratnasingam, P. (2005). E-commerce Relationships: The Impact of Trust on Relationship Continuity. *International Journal of Commerce and Management, 15*(1), 1-16.

Redmond, F. E. (1997). *DCOM: Microsoft Distributed Component Object Model with CDrom* (1st edition). Foster City, USA: IDG Books Worldwide, Inc.

Reed, D. A. (2003). Grids, the teragrid and beyond. *IEEE Computer, 36*(1), 62-68.

Reinoso Castillo, J. A., Silvescu, A., Caragea, D., Pathak, J., & Honavar, V. G. (2004). *Information extraction and integration from heterogeneous, distributed, autonomous information sources – a federated ontology – driven query-centric approach.* Paper presented at IEEE International Conference on Information Integration and Reuse. Retrieved August 17, 2008, from http://www.cs.iastate.edu/~honavar/Papers/indusfinal.pdf

Reisig, W. (1985). Petri Nets, an Introduction. *Eatcs: Monographs on Theoretical Computer Science, 4.* Springer-Verlag.

Rempel, J. K, Holmes, J. G., & Zanna, M. P. (1985). Trust in close relationships. *Journal of Personality and Social Psychology, 69*(1), 95-112.

Rhea, S., Geels, D., Roscoe, T., & Kubiatowicz, J. (2004). *Handling Churn in a DHT.* Paper presented at the USENIX Annual Technical Conference, Boston, MA.

Rijk, R., & Berlo, M. (2004, May). *Using Crisiskit and Moped to Improve Emergency Management Team Training.* Paper presented at the International Community on Information Systems for Crisis Response (ISCRAM2004) Conference, Brussels, Belgium.

RMI (2004). *Java Remote Method Invocation Specification.* Electronic Version. Retrieved June 2008, from http://java.sun.com/j2se/1.4.2/docs/guide/rmi/

Rob, P., & Corronel, C. (2004). *Database Systems Design, Implementation & Maintenance*, USA: Thomson Learning.

Robinson, S. (2005). Discrete-event simulation: from the pioneers to the present, what next? *Journal of the Operational Research Society, 56* (6), 619-629.

Robinson, S. (2005). Distributed simulation and simulation practice. *Simulation, 81*(5), 5-13.

Robinson, W. N. (2003). Monitoring Web Service Requirements. In *Proceedings of 11th IEEE International Requirements Engineering Conference* (pp. 65-74).

Roman, D., Keller, U., Lausen, H., de Bruijn, J., Lara, R., Stollberg, M., Polleres, A., Feier, C., Bussler, C., & Fensel, D. (2005). Web Service Modeling Ontology. *Applied Ontology, 1*(1), 77-106.

Ronen, D. (1993). Ship Scheduling: The last decade. *European Journal of Operational Research, 71*(3), 325-333.

Rousseau, D. M., Sitkin, S. B., Burt, R. S., & Camerer, C. (1998). Not So Different after All: A Cross-discipline View of Trust. *Academy of Management Review, 23*, 393-404.

Rowstron, A., & Druschel, P. (2001). *Pastry: Scalable, Distributed Object Location and Routing for Large-scale Peer-to-Peer Systems.* Paper presented at the IFIP/ACM International Conference on Distributed Systems Platforms, Heidelberg, Germany.

Roy, A., & Sander, V. (2004) GARA: a uniform quality of service architecture. In *Grid Resource Management: State of the Art and Future Trends* (pp. 377-394). Kluwer Academic Publishers.

Rumbaugh, J., Jacobson, I., & Booch, G. (2004). *The Unified Modeling Language Reference Manual, 2nd Edition.* Addison-Wesley.

Rundle, J. B., Turcotte, D. L., Shcherbakov, R., Klein, W., & Sammis, C. (2003). Statistical physics approach to understanding the multiscale dynamics of earthquake fault systems. *Geophysics, 41*(4).

Ruppel, C. P., & Harrington, S. J. (2000). The relationship of communication, ethical work climate, and trust to commitment and innovation. *Journal of Business Ethics, 25*(4), 313-328.

Salter, J., & Antonopoulos, N. (2005). *ROME: Optimising DHT-based Peer-to-Peer Networks.* Paper presented at the 5th International Network Conference, Samos, Greece.

Salter, J., & Antonopoulos, N. (2007). An Optimised 2-Tier P2P Architecture for Contextualised Keyword Searches. *Journal of Future Generation Computer Systems, 23*, 241-251.

Saunders, M. N. K., & Thornhill, A. (2004). Trust and mistrust in organisations: An exploration using an organisational justice framework. *European Journal of Work and Organisational Psychology, 13* (4), 492-515.

Sayar, A., Pierce, M., & Fox, G. (2005). *OGC Compatible Geographical Information Services* (Technical Report No. TR610). Bloomington: Indiana University.

Sayar, A., Pierce, M., & Fox, G. (2006). *Integrating AJAX Approach into GIS Visualization Web Services.* Paper presented at the IEEE, International Conference on Internet and Web Applications and Services, ICIW'06.

Scalem, M., Bandyopadhyay, S., & Sircar, A. K. (2004, October). *An approach towards a decentralized disaster management information network.* Paper presented at the Second Asian Applied Computing Conference, Kathmandu, Nepal.

Scardaci, D., & Scuderi, G. (2007). A Secure Storage Service for the gLite Middleware. In the *Proceedings of third International Symposium on Information Assurance and Security* (pp. 261-266). Manchester, United Kingdom: IEEE Computer Society.

Schlenoff, C., Knutila, A. & Ray, S. (Eds.) (1997). *1st Process Specification Language (PSL) Roundtable.* Sponsored by National Institute of Standards and Technology, Gaithersburg, MD. Available at: http://www.nist.gov/psl/

Schopf, J. M., & Nitzberg, B. (2002) Grids: The top ten questions. *Scientific Programming, 10*(2) 103-111.

Schreiber, G., Akkermans, H., Anjewierden, A., de Hoog, R., Shadbolt, N., van de Velde, W., & Wielinga, B. (2000). *Knowledge Engineering and Management: The CommonKADS Methodology.* Cambridge, MA: The MIT Press.

Sculley, A. & Woods, W. (2000). *B2B Exchanges: The Killer Application in the Business-to-Business Internet Revolution.* ISI Publications.

Şengün, A. E., & Wasti, S. N. (2007). Trust, Control, and Risk: A Test of Das and Teng's Conceptual Framework for Pharmaceutical Buyer-Supplier Relationships. *Group & Organization Management, 32*(4), 430-464.

Shacklett, M. (2007). *The SOA business Process Revolution.* Network and Systems Professional Association. Retrieved on March 25, 2008, from http://www.naspa.com/soa-business-process-revolution

Shannon, R. E. (1998). Introduction to the art and science of simulation. *30th Winter Simulation Conference* (pp. 7-14). Los Alamitos, CA: IEEE Computer Society Press.

Shaw, R., Manu, G., & Sarma, A. (2003). Community Recovery and its Sustainability: Lessons from Gujarat earthquake of India. *The Australian Journal of Emergency Management, 2*(18).

Shen, Z., & Su, J. (2005). Web Service Discovery based on behavior Signatures. In *Proceedings of the 2005 IEEE International Conference on Services Computing* (SCC 2005), USA (pp. 279-286).

Sheppard, B. H., & Sherman, D. M. (1998). The grammars of trust: a model and general implications. *Academy of Management Review, 23*(3), 33-45.

Shoshani, A., Sim, A., & Gu, J. (2003). Storage Resource Managers – Essential Components for the Grid. In A. Shoshani, A Sim, & J. Gu (Eds.), *Grid Resource Management: state of the art and future trends.* Norwell, MA, USA: Kluwer Academic Publishers.

Shrivastava, S. K., & Wheater, S. M. (1998). Architectural Support for Dynamic Reconfiguration of Distributed Workflow Applications. *IEE Proceedings – Software, 145*(5), 155-162. Institution of Electrical Engineers (IEE).

Simon, H. (1977). *The new science of management decision.* Englewood Cliffs, New Jersey: Prentice Hall.

Siva Sathya, S., & Kuppuswami, S., and Ragupathi, R. (2006). Replication Strategies for Data Grids. In *International Conference on Advanced Computing and Communications* (pp 123-128).

Smarr, L. (2003). Grids in Context. In I. Foster, & C. Kesselman, (Eds.) *The Grid 2 Blueprint for a New Computing Infrastructure.* 2nd ed.. Morgan Kaufmann.

Smith, H., & Konsynski, B. (2004). Grid Computing. *MIT Sloan Management Review, 46*(1), 7-9.

Smith, R. (2005). *Grid Computing: A Brief Technology Analysis.* Retrieved Feb 14, 2008, from http://www.ctonet.org/documents/GridComputing_analysis.pdf

Sonnet, J. (2005). *Web Map Context Documents (WMC).* Standard specs No. 05-005. Open Geospatial Consortium Inc. (OGC).

Sowa, J. F., & Zachman, J. A. (1992). Extending and formalising the framework for information systems architecture. *IBM Systems Journal, 31*(3), 590-616.

Spanoudakis, G., Mahbub, K., & Zisman, A. (2007). A Platform for Context-Aware Run-time Web Service Discovery. *Proceedings of the 2007 IEEE International Conference on Web Services (ICWS 2007),* USA (pp. 233-240).

Spanoudakis, G., Zisman, A., & Kozlenkov, A. (2005). A Service Discovery Framework for Service Centric Systems. *Proceedings of the 2005 IEEE International Conference on Services Computing,* (SCC 2005), USA (pp. 251-259).

Spreitzer, G. M., & Mishra, A. K. (1999). Giving Up Control without Losing Control: Trust and its Substitutes' Effects on Managers' Involving Employees in Decision Making. *Group & Organization Management, 24*(2), 155-187.

Stanoevska-Slabeva, K., Talamanca, C. F., Thanos, G. A., & Zsigri, C. (2007). Development of a Generic Value Chain for the Grid Industry. *Grid Economics and Business Models, 4th International Workshop, GECON 2007.* LNCS 4685/2007, 44-57. Rennes, France: Springer Berlin.

Stewart, J.-A., Silburn, N. L. J., & Birchall, D. W. (2007). *Survey into the Finding, Use and Sharing of Information Within Organizations.* Henley-on-Thames: Henley Management College.

Stöhr, T., Märtens, H., & Rahm, E. (2000). Multi-Dimensional Database Allocation for Parallel Data Warehouses. In *Proceedings of the 26th international Conference on Very Large Data Bases* (pp. 273-284).

Stoica, I., Morris, R., Karger, D., Kaashoek, M. F., & Balakrishnan, H. (2001). *Chord: A Scalable Peer-to-Peer Lookup Service for Internet Applications.* Paper presented at the ACM SIGCOMM, San Diego, CA.

Storey, J., Emberson, C., Godsell, J., & Harrison, A. (2006). Supply chain management: theory, practice and future challenges. *International Journal of Operations & Production Management, 26*(7), 754-774.

Sulistio, A., Cibej, U., Venugopal, S., Robic, B., and Buyya, R. (2007). *A Toolkit for Modelling and Simulating Data Grids: An Extension to GridSim*. Retrieved March 2008, from http://www.gridbus.org/gridsim/

Sun Microsystems, Inc. (2002). *Sun™ ONE Grid Engine Administration and User's Guide*. Santa Clara, California, U.S.A.

Swain J. J. (2005). Gaming reality: biennial survey of discrete-event simulation software tools. *OR/MS Today (December 2005)*. Institute for Operations Research and the Management Sciences (INFORMS), USA. Retrieved June 28, 2008, from http://www.lionhrtpub.com/orms/orms-12-05/frsurvey.html

Swain J. J. (2007). INFORMS simulation software survey. *OR/MS Today*. Institute for Operations Research and the Management Sciences (INFORMS), USA. Retrieved June 28, 2008, from http://www.lionhrtpub.com/orms/surveys/Simulation/Simulation.html

Sydow, J., & Windeler, A. (2003). Knowledge, Trust, and Control. *International Studies of Management and Organisation, 33*(2), 69-99.

Takizawa, S., Takamiya, Y., Nakada, H., & Matsuoka, S. (2005). A Scalable Multi-Replication Framework for Data Grid. *Proceedings of the 2005 Symposium on Applications and the Internet Workshops (SAINT-W '05)*. IEEE.

Tan, K. C. (2001). A framework of supply chain management literature. *European Journal of Purchasing & Supply Management, 7*(1), 39-48.

Taylor, I., Shields, M., Wang, I., & Rana, O. (2003). Triana Applications within Grid Computing and Peer to Peer Environments. *Journal of Grid Computing, 1*(2), 199-217.

Thain, D., Tannenbaum, T., & Livny, M. (2004). Distributed computing in practice: the Condor experience. *Concurrency and Computation: Practice and Experience, 17*(2-4), 323-356.

Tiampo, K. F., Rundle, J. B., Mcginnis, S. A., & Klein, W. (2002). Pattern Dynamics and Forecast Methods in Seismically Active Regions. *Pure and Applied Geophysics, 159*(10), 2429-2467.

Tomov, N., Dempster, E., Williams, M. H., Burger, A., Taylor, H., King, P. J., & Broughton, P. (2004). Analytical response time estimation in parallel relational database systems. *Parallel Comput. 30*(2), 249-283.

Torrington, D., Hall, L., & Taylor, S. (2002). *Human Resource Management*. Essex: Pearson Education.

Townsend, A. M., Demarie, S. M., & Hendrickson, A. R. (2000). Virtual teams: Technology and the workplace of the future. *IEEE Engineering Management Review, 28*(2), 69-80.

Tran, P., Greenfield, P., & Gorton, I. (2002). *Behavior and performance of message-oriented middleware systems*. Paper presented at the International Conference on Distributed Computing Systems Workshops, ICDCSW.

Trim, P. R. F. (2003). Disaster Management and the Role of the Intelligence and Security Services. *Disaster Prevention and Management, 1*(12).

Tripathi, U. K., & Hinkelmann, K. (2007). Change Management in Semantic Business Processes Modeling. In *Proceedings of the Eighth international Symposium on Autonomous Decentralized Systems* (pp. 155-162). IEEE Computer Society.

Trumba, C. (2007). *Five Benefits of Software as a Service*. Trumba Corporation.

Tserpes, K., Kyriazis, D., Menychtas, A., & Varvarigou, T. (2008). A Novel Mechanism for Provisioning of High-Level Quality of Service Information in Grid Environments. *Special Issue on Performance Evaluation of QoS-aware Heterogeneous Systems, European Journal of Operational Research, 191*(3), 1113-1131.

Tsoumakos, D., & Roussopoulos, N. (2003). *Adaptive Probabilistic Search for Peer-to-Peer Networks*. Paper presented at the Third International Conference on Peer-to-Peer Computing, Linköping, Sweden.

Tuckman, B.W. (1965). Development Sequence in Small Groups, *Psychological Bulletin*, *63*(6), 12-24.

Turi, D., Missier, P., Goble, C., Roure, D. D., & Oinn, T. (2007). *Taverna Workflows: Syntax and Semantics.* Paper presented at the 3rd IEEE International Conference on e-Science and Grid Computing (e-Science'07), Bangalore, India.

Turoff, M. (2002). Past and Future Emergency Response Information Systems. *Communications of the ACM, 4*(45).

Turoff, M., Hiltz, S. R., Bahgat, A. N. F., & Rana, A. (1993). Distributed Group Support Systems, MIS Quarterly, *17*(4), USA: Carlson School of Management, University of Minnesota, Minneapolis.

Tyler, T., & Degoey, P. (1996). Trust in Organizational Authorities: Frontiers of Theory and Research. In T. Tyler (Ed.) *Trust in Organizations.* Thousand Oaks: Sage.

Ulijn, J., O'Hair, D., Weggeman, M., Ledlow, G., & Hall, H. T. (2000). Innovation, corporate strategy and cultural context: What is the mission for international business communication?. *The Journal of Business Communication, 37*, 293-316.

Ullman, J. (1997). Information Integration Using Logical Views. In *Procs. 6th International Conference Database Theory (ICDT '97)*, Delphi, Greece. LNCS, *1186*, 19-40.

United Nations (2004, January). *Hyogo Framework for Action 2005-2015: Building the Resilience of Nations and Communities to Disasters.* Paper presented at the World Conference on Disaster Reduction, Kobe, Hyogo, Japan.

United Nations Educational Scientific and Cultural Organization (UNESCO) (2006). Retrieved July, 05, 2008 from http://portal.unesco.org/en/ev.php-URL_ID=29008&URL_DO=DO_TOPIC&URL_SECTION=201.html

Van Dyne, L., & Pierce, J. L. (2004). Psychological Ownership and Feelings of Possession: Three Field Studies Predicting Employee Attitudes and Organizational Citizenship Behavior. *Journal of Organizational Behavior, 25*, 439-459.

van Winkelen, C. (2003). *Inter-organizational Communities of Practice.* ESeN EU funded E-Action project. Henley-on-Thames: Henley Management College.

Vassileva, J. (2002). *Motivating Participation in Peer-to-Peer Communities.* Paper presented at the Workshop on Engineering Societies in the Agent World, Madrid, Spain.

Venugopal, S., Buyya, R., & Ramamohanarao, K. (2005). *A taxonomy of data grids for distributed data sharing management and processing.* Retrieved August 17, 2008, from http://arxiv.org/abs/cs.DC/0506034

Venugopal, S., Buyya, R., & Ramamohanarao, K. (2006). A Taxonomy of Data Grids for Distributed Data Sharing, Management, and Processing. *ACM Computing Surveys, 38*(1).

Viceconti, M., Taddei, F., Petrone, M., Galizia, S., Van Sint Jan, S., & Clapworthy, G. J. (2006). Towards the Virtual Physiological Human: the Living Human Project. Paper presented at *7th International Symposium on Computer Methods in Biomechanics and Biomedical Engineering (CMBBE 2006)*, Antibes Cote d' Azur, France.

Viceconti, M., Taddei, F., Van Sint Jan, S., Leardini, A., Clapworthy, G. J., Domingue, J., Galizia, S., & Quadrani, P. (2007). Towards the multiscale modelling of the musculoskeletal system. In *Y. González & M. Cerrolaza* (Eds.) *Bioengineering Modeling and Computer Simulation*, CIMNE, Barcelona, Spain.

Viceconti, M., Zannoni, C., Testi, D., Petrone, M., Perticoni, S., Quadrani, P., Taddei, F., Imboden, S., & Clapworthy, G. J. (2007). The Multimod Application Framework: A rapid application development tool for computer aided medicine. *Computer Methods and Programs in Biomedicine, 85*(2), 138-151.

Virtual Data Toolkit. (2007). *What is in VDT 1.6.1 (supporting platforms)?* Retrieved June 28, 2008, from http://vdt.cs.wisc.edu/releases/1.6.1/contents.html

Vlaar, P. W. L., Van den Bosch, F. A. J., & Volberda, H. W. (2007). On the Evolution of Trust, Distrust, and Formal Coordination and Control in Interorganizational Relationships: Toward an Integrative Framework. *Group & Organization Management, 32*(4), 407-429.

Vretanos, P. A. (2002). *Web Feature Service Implementation Specification.* Reference Document No. 02-058). OGC.

Vuong, S., & Li, J. (2003). *Efa: an Efficient Content Routing Algorithm in Large Peer-to-Peer Overlay Networks.* Paper presented at the International Conference on Peer-to-Peer Computing, Linköping, Sweden.

Walker, D. W. (2001). *The Grid, Virtual Organizations, and Problem-Solving Environments.* Paper presented at the International Conference on Cluster Computing, Brisbane, Australia.

Wang, Y., Scardaci, D., Yan, B., & Huang, Y. (2007). Interconnect EGEE and CNGRID e-Infrastructures through Interoperability between gLite and GOS Middlewares. In the *Third IEEE International Conference on e-Science and Grid Computing* (pp. 553-560). Bangalore, India.

Waters, G., Crawford, J., & Lim, S. G. (2004). Optimising Multicast Structures for Grid Computing. *Computer Communications, 27.*

Watson, P. (2002). *Databases and the grid.* Technical Report. Retrieved August 17, 2008, from http://www.cs.ncl.ac.uk/research/pubs/books/papers/185.pdf

Watson, P., Fowler, C. P., Kubicek, C., et al. (2006). Dynamically Deploying Web Services on a Grid using Dynasoar. In S. Lee, U. Brinkschulte, B. Thuraisingham, et al. (Eds), *Proceedings of the Ninth IEEE International Symposium on Object and Component-Oriented Real-Time Distributed Computing (ISORC 2006).* Gyeongju, Korea, April 24-26 2006 (pp. 151-158). IEEE Computer Society Press.

Watts, D. (2005). *The Dynamic of Networks Between Order and Randomness.* Princeton: University Press.

Watts, D. J., Dodds, P. S., & Newman, M. E. J. (2002). Identity and Search in Social Networks. *Science, 296,* 1302-1205.

Watts, D., & Strogatz, S. H. (1998). Collective Dynamics of Small-World Networks. *Nature 393,* 440-442.

Wehrle, P., Miquel, M., & Tchounikine, A. (2007). A Grid Services-Oriented Architecture for Efficient Operation of Distributed Data Warehouses on Globus. In *Proceedings of the 21st international Conference on Advanced Networking and Applications* (pp. 994-999). IEEE Computer Society.

Weishaupl, T., & Schikuta, E. (2004). *Dynamic service evolution for open languages in the grid and service oriented architecture.* Paper presented at the Fifth International Workshop on Grid Computing, Pittsburgh, USA.

Welsh, M., Culler, D., & Brewer, E. (2001). SEDA: an architecture for well-conditioned, scalable internet services. *SIGOPS Operating Systems Review, 35*(5), 230-243.

Wetzstein, B., Ma, Z., Filipowska, A., Kaczmarek, M., Bhiri, S., Losada, S., Lopez-Cobo, J. M., & Cicurel, L. (2007). Semantic Business Process Management: A Lifecycle Based Requirements Analysis. In M. Hepp, K. Hinkelmann, D. Karagiannis, R. Klein & N. Stojanovic (Eds.), *Semantic Business Process and Product Lifecycle Management. Proceedings of the Workshop SBPM 2007,* CEUR Workshop Proceedings.

Williams, R., Ochsenbein, F., Davenhall, C., Durand, D., Fernique, P., Giaretta, D., et al. (2002). *VOTable: A Proposed XML Format for Astronomical Tables* (Standard Specification). US National Virtual Observatory.

Winton, L. J. (2005). *A Simple Virtual Organisation Model and Practical Implementation.* Paper presented at the Australasian workshop on Grid computing and e-research, Newcastle, Australia, 2005.

Wognum, P. M., & Faber, E. C. C. (2002). Infrastructures for collaboration in virtual organisations. *International*

Journal of Networking and Virtual Organisations, 2002, *1*(1), 32-54.

Wohrer, A., Brezany, P., & Janciak, I. (2004). *Virtalisation of heterogeneous data sources for grid information systems.* Retrieved August 17, 2008, from http://www.par.univie.ac.at/publications/other/inst_rep_2002-2004.pdf

Wolski, R. (1997). Forecasting network performance to support dynamic scheduling using the network weather service. In *Proceedings of the 6th IEEE international Symposium on High Performance Distributed Computing* (pp. 316). IEEE Computer Society.

Wombacher, A., Fankhauser, P., Mahleko, B., & Neuhold, E. (2005). Matchmaking for Business Processes based on Conjunctive Finite State Automata. *International Journal of Business Process Integration and Management, 1*(1), 3-11.

Wright, A. R., & Smith, R. (2007). *Virtual Organisation Design and Application: A Chemicals Industry Case Study.* Paper presented at UK e-Science All-Hands Meeting, Nottingham, 2007.

Wright, B. M., & Barker, J. R. (2000). Asserting concerting control in the team environment. *Journal of Occupational and Organisational Psychology, 73*(3), 345-361.

WS-I. (2002). *Web Service Interoperability.* Retrieved April 23, 2008, from http://www.ws-i.org/

Wulf, W. (1989). SIPP ACCESS, an Information System for Complex Data: a Case Study creating a Collaboratory for Social Sciences. *Internet Research: Electronic Networking Applications and Policy, 5*(2).

Wustenhoff, E. (2002). *Service Level Agreement in the Data Center.* Sun Professional Services. Sun BluePrints™ OnLine.

Xu, M., Hu, Z., Long, W. & Liu, W. (2004). Service Virtualisation: Infrastructure and Applications. In I. Foster, & C. Kesselman (Eds.), *The Grid 2, Blueprint for a New Computing Infrastructure.* CA, USA: Elsevier.

Yang, B., & Garcia-Molina, H. (2002). *Efficient Search in Peer-to-Peer Networks.* Paper presented at the International Conference on Distributed Computing Systems, Vienna, Austria.

Yang, X., Chohan, D., Wang, X. D., & Allan, R. (2005). A web portal for the national grid service. *2005 UK e-Science All Hands Meeting,* (pp. 1156-1162). Retrieved June 28, 2008, from http://epubs.cclrc.ac.uk/bitstream/1084/paper05C.pdf

Yasuda, N., Mizumoto, Y., Ohishi, M., O'Mullane, W., Budavári, T. A., Haridas, V., et al. (2004). *Astronomical Data Query Language: Simple Query Protocol for the Virtual Observatory.* Paper presented at the Astronomical Data Analysis Software and Systems XIII. ASP Conference Series. Retrieved July 15, 2008 from http://www.adass.org/adass/proceedings/adass03/reprints/P3-10.pdf

Zachos, K., Zhu, X., Maiden, N., & Jones, S. (2006). Seamlessly Integrating Service Discovery into UML Requirements Processes. In *International Workshop of Service Oriented Software Engineering (IW-SOSE 2006),* Shanghai (pp. 60-66).

Zakaria, N., Amelinckx, A., & Wilemon, D. (2004). Working together apart? Building a knowledge-sharing culture for global virtual teams. *Creativity and Innovation Management, 13*(1), 15-29.

Zhang, J., Mustafee, N., Saville, J., & Taylor, S. J. E. (2007). Integrating BOINC with Microsoft Excel: a case study. *29th Information Technology Interfaces Conference* (pp. 733-738). Washington, DC, USA: IEEE Computer Society.

Zisman, A., Spanoudakis, G., & Dooley, J. (in press, 2008). A Framework for Dynamic Service Discovery. To appear in the *23rd IEEE International Conference on Automated software engineering (ASE 2008).*

Zolin, R., & Hinds, P. J. (2004). Trust in context: The development of interpersonal trust in geographically distributed work. In R. M. Kramer, & K. Cook (Eds.), *Trust and Distrust in Organizations.* New York: Sage.

About the Contributors

Nik Bessis is currently a senior lecturer and head of postgraduate taught courses, in the Department of Computing and Information Systems at University of Bedfordshire (UK). He obtained a BA from the TEI of Athens in 1991 and completed his PhD (2002) and MA (1995) at De Montfort University, Leicester, UK. His research interest is the development of distributed information systems for virtual organizations with a particular focus in next generation Grid technology; data integration and data push for the creative and other sectors.

* * *

Giuseppe Andronico received his degree on theoretical physics with his thesis on the methods in Lattice QCD on July 1991. Since 2000, he is working in Grid computing collaborating with EDG, EGEE and other projects. In 2006 and 2007 was technical manager in the project EUChinaGRID where started his work with interoperability between GOS and EGEE.

Vassiliki Andronikou received her MSc from the Electrical and Computer Engineering Department of the National Technical University of Athens (NTUA) in 2004. She has worked in the bank and telecommunications sector, while currently she is a research associate in the Telecommunications Laboratory of the NTUA, with her interests focusing on the security and privacy aspects of biometrics and data management in Grid.

Nick Antonopoulos is currently a senior lecturer (US associate professor) at the Department of Computing, University of Surrey, UK. He holds a BSc in physics (1st class) from the University of Athens in 1993, an MSc in information technology from Aston University in 1994 and a PhD in computer science from the University of Surrey in 2000. He has over 9 years of academic experience during which he has designed and has been managing advanced Master's programmes in computer science at the University of Surrey. He has published over 60 research articles in distributed systems, peer-to-peer networks and software agents.

Chimay J. Anumba is a professor and department head of Architectural Engineering at The Pennsylvania State University, USA. His research interests include advanced engineering informatics, concurrent engineering, intelligent systems, and project management. He has over 400 publications in these fields and has received over £15m in research funding from a variety of sources. Professor Anumba is co-editor of the *International Journal of Information Technology in Construction*, ITCon. He has

Copyright © 2009, IGI Global, distributing in print or electronic forms without written permission of IGI Global is prohibited.

recently held/holds visiting professorships at numerous prestigious universities including Stanford University and MIT (USA). He has also received several awards for his work, including a Doctor of Science (DSc) from Loughborough University (UK) and an honorary Doctorate from Delft University of Technology in the Netherlands.

Eleana Asimakopoulou has a first degree in architecture and a PhD in managing natural disasters using Grid technology. She is currently teaching in the Construction Department of Barnfield College, an associated College of the University of Bedfordshire. Eleana is a reviewer in several international conferences and her research interests include Grid technology, emergency response and planning for natural disasters, business continuity, construction and risk management.

Roberto Barbera is a professor at the University of Catania. His research fields are nuclear and particle physics and he is involved in the ALICE Experiment at CERN. Since 1999 he is interested in Grid computing. He is currently an executive member of INFN Grid with coordination responsibilities in many EU funded projects worldwide.

David W. Birchall is an emeritus professor at Henley Business School, University of Reading. David's research interests are in the area of management learning and innovation practices in organizations. He has particular expertise in the development of systems to support remote learners. David has consulted and lectured throughout the world on aspects of innovation, technology and organization capabilities, organizational learning and knowledge management.

Dino Bouchlaghem is a professor of architectural engineering at Loughborough University. His research interests include collaborative visualization, design for safety and security, disaster management, construction information technology, and design management. He is the coordinator of the CIB International Task Group in Architectural Engineering (TG49) and editor-in-chief of the *International Journal of Architectural Engineering and Design Management.*

Tatiana Bouzdine-Chameeva is a senior professor in BEM Management School Bordeaux (France). She holds a PhD in applied mathematics from Moscow State University (Russia). She has worked for Medtronic, consulted for Northwest Airlines, Sogerma, Ford Aquitaine, Legrand. Her research is in decision-making and decision support. Her articles were published in internationally recognized journals including *Decision Science, European Journal of Operational Research*; she is an editor-in-chief of the *International Business Management Journal.*

Marina Burakova-Lorgnier holds a PhD in social psychology from Rostov-on-Don State University, Russia. She is a lecturer at the École de Commerce Européenne, INSEEC group, France. Her research interests cover such areas as gender identity, social network, social capital, leadership and knowledge management. Currently she seeks to bring together the issues of trust and control in organizational knowledge sharing in a cross-disciplinary perspective. Dr. Burakova-Lorgnier has served as a conference, textbook and journal reviewer and an expert for the Russian local government councils and NGO's and the Embassy of France in Russia.

Yun-Heh Chen-Burger is a senior researcher in informatics, University of Edinburgh. Her research areas are knowledge management and intelligent systems. Dr Chen-Burger specializes in semantics and knowledge based techniques; and automated support for enterprise and process modeling methods. Her book "Automated Business Modelling" was published in "Advanced Information and Knowledge Processing" series, by Springer in 2005.

Gordon Clapworthy is a professor of computer graphics at the University of Bedfordshire (UK). He has a BSc (Class 1) in mathematics and a PhD in aeronautical engineering from the University of London, and an MSc (dist.) in computer science from City University (London). He has been involved in 18 European projects, coordinating 7 of them.

Rogério Luís de Carvalho Costa is a PhD student at the University of Coimbra – Portugal and aggregate professor at the Pontifícia Universidade Católica do Rio de Janeiro (PUC-Rio) – Brazil, where he teaches undergraduate curricula. His research interests include data warehousing, parallel and distributed database systems, database self-tuning and bioinformatics.

James Dooley received his BSc in robotics and intelligent machines from the University of Essex (UK). Since then he has been studying for his PhD in computer science from the same university with funding from the British Telecom. Currently he is completing his PhD part-time, whilst working separately on European projects with City University (UK).

Marco Fargetta graduated in computer engineering in 2002. In 2006, he received his PhD from Catania University, in Italy, with a thesis on advanced Grid scheduling. Since then, he has been involved in several Grid projects. Currently he works with the Consortium COMETA and his activity focuses on the support of HPC applications on Grid computing.

Geoffrey C Fox is a chair of the Indiana University Department of Informatics and director of the Community Grids Laboratory. He holds a PhD in physics (high energy) from Cambridge University (1968). His research interests include parallel computing models on multicore systems, Web service architectures, distributed messaging systems, and cloud computing.

Pedro Furtado is an assistant professor and senior researcher at the University of Coimbra, where he teaches both undergraduate and postgraduate curricula. His research interests include data warehousing, parallel and distributed database systems, performance and scalability, distributed data intensive systems. He received a PhD in computer science from the University of Coimbra, Portugal in 2000.

Genoveffa Giambona is a research manager at the Research Institute for the Built Environment, University of Reading. Jeni's research interests are in the area of leadership development, management learning, virtual teams and trust. She also researches meta-evaluation and the study of how learning mechanisms work in different contexts and cultures. She has published and presented at different conferences on these topics and on the subject of meta-evaluation of e-learning programmes.

Emidio Giorgio received his MSc computer science degree, cum laude, in 2003; he begun its collaboration with INFN on computational grids in 2004, joining the EGEE project in NA3 area, related to users training. In the context of the ICEAGE project, he has been the manager for WP4, concerning the operations for its multi-middleware Infrastructure.

Dimitrios Halkos is a research associate in the Telecommunication Laboratory of the National Technical University of Athens (NTUA), Greece. He graduated from the Department of Electrical and Computer Engineering of NTUA (2001) and obtained his PhD (2008) in the area of maritime operational research focusing on cargo ships routing and scheduling.

Magdalini Kardara has obtained a Diploma in electrical and computer engineering in 2004 from the National Technical University of Athens (NTUA) and an MSc in advanced computing from Imperial College London (2006). She is a PhD candidate in the Department of Electrical and Computer Engineering of NTUA and has a significant expertise on Web services and Grid technologies.

Dimosthenis Kyriazis received his diploma from the Department of Electrical and Computer Engineering of the National Technical University of Athens (NTUA) in 2001, a MSc in techno-economic systems (MBA) and his PhD from the Electrical and Computer Engineering Department of NTUA (2007) where currently he works as a researcher in the area of Grid computing, scheduling, QoS provision and workflow management in heterogeneous systems and SOA.

Maozhen Li is a lecturer in the School of Engineering and Design at Brunel University, UK. His research interests include grid computing, intelligent systems, service-oriented computing, and semantic web. He has over 50 scientific publications in these areas. He is on the editorial boards of *Encyclopedia of Grid Computing Technologies* (IGI) *and Applications*, and the *International Journal of Grid and High Performance Computing* (IGI).

Wen-Yang Lin is a professor of Department of Computer Science and Information Engineering and the director of Library and Information Center in National University of Kaohsiung. He received his PhD in computer science and information engineering from National Taiwan University in 1994. Dr. Lin has co-edited several special issues of renowned international journals, (co-)authored more than 100 refereed publications, served as co-chair, program chair, program committee member, and session chair for many international conferences. His research interests include data warehousing, data mining, evolutionary computation, sparse matrix technology, and large-scale supercomputing.

Enjie Liu is a senior lecturer in computing at the University of Bedfordshire (UK). She has a BSc in computer science from Southwest University in China and a PhD in telecommunications from Queen Mary, University of London. She has been involved in one previous European project and is currently participating in 4 EPSRC/European projects.

Lu Liu is a research fellow in the School of Computing at the University of Leeds. He received his MSc degree in data communication systems from Brunel University and PhD degree from University of Surrey. He has worked on peer-to-peer networking for five years and published a number of papers on peer-to-peer networking.

Areti Manataki is a PhD student in informatics, the University of Edinburgh. She has received a BSc in management science and technology from the Athens University of Economics and Business, and an MSc in artificial intelligence with a distinction from the University of Edinburgh. Her research interests include knowledge management, semantic web and supply chain management.

Navonil Mustafee is a research fellow in Warwick Business School. He received an MSc in distributed systems and a PhD in Grid computing and simulation from Brunel University. His research interests are in grid computing, parallel and distributed simulation, healthcare simulation, bibliometric analysis and interdisciplinary research in operational research, information systems and applied computing.

Gayathri Nadarajan is pursuing a PhD on semantics-based workflow composition for automatic video processing at the University of Edinburgh. Her research interests include Grid workflows, automated planning and ontological systems. Prior to this she obtained an MSc in artificial intelligence, has taught in a technical university in Malaysia and worked in the software industry in Ireland.

Salvatore Marco Pappalardo is a professor at the University of Catania. He graduated in software engineering in 2001 and became an informatics trained teacher in 2007. He collaborates with INFN since 2001 on computational grids as a member of middleware development groups in several projects. He designed and developed request brokering, network and trasport layers components for the European Grid Middleware.

Iain Phillips is head of computer science at Loughborough University. With a PhD and BSc from Manchester University Computer Science, he has worked Loughborough University Electronic and Electrical Engineering from 1992 and Computer Science from 1999. His research interests are in networking, specifically Internet performance, ad-hoc and wireless sensor networks.

Marlon E. Pierce is an assistant director of the Community Grids Laboratory at Indiana University. He has a PhD in physics (condensed matter) from Florida State University (1998). His research interests include computing environments and Web portals for computational Grids, Web service architectures, and the application of Web technologies to problems in scientific computing.

Antonio Puliafito is a full professor of computer engineering at the University of Messina, Italy. His interests include parallel and distributed systems, networking, wireless and GRID computing. He is currently the director of the RFIDLab, a research lab on RFID and wireless, the director of the Centre on Information Technologies Development and their Applications (CIA), the vice-president of the Consorzio Cometa whose aim is to enhance and exploit high performance computing. He is actively working in grid computing and virtualization in the projects TriGrid VL, PI2S2 and RESERVOIR.

Alain Roy is currently an associate researcher with the Condor Project at the University of Wisconsin-Madison in the US. He received his PhD in computer science from the University of Chicago in 2001, where he did research about advanced reservations for quality of service across heterogeneous resources. Today, Alain is the Open Science Grid Software Coordinator, where he guides the creation, deployment, and support of the VDT, a grid software distribution used by OSG, EGEE, and other grids.

Ahmet Sayar is a PhD candidate at Indiana University Computer Science Department. He holds a Master's degree in computer science from Syracuse University and a BSc degree in management engineering from Istanbul Technical University. His research interest is applications of Web technologies to problems in scientific computing and performance problems in distributed systems.

Diego Scardaci was born in Catania, Italy, the 11th September, 1975. Since 2006 he is working as Researcher for the INFN involved in Grid computing activities. He worked on Grid interoperability, Grid security and Grid API development. Moreover, he has been involved in the dissemination of advanced Grid knowledge activities, organizing many induction courses.

Nicholas L. J. Silburn is a research fellow at the Henley Business School, University of Reading. Nicholas's background is in engineering and information management within the utility and construction industries. This experience has centered on the design, implementation and management of distributed content management systems to support collaborative engineering design, construction and asset records management. He is currently carrying out research into what factors might influence professional information workers' information behaviors.

Richard O. Sinnott is a professor at the Glasgow University. He was awarded a BSc (Honours) in theoretical physics from the University of East Anglia, Norwich, England in 1988; an MSc in software engineering from the University of Stirling, Scotland in 1983 and a PhD also at Stirling in 1997 in the area of formal modeling of distributed systems. He has worked across a wide range of computing science research areas both in academia and in industry. He has over 100 publications across a range of computing science and application oriented fields, most recently in the area of Grid security and usability especially in the life sciences. He has edited several ITU-T/ISO international standards.

Rob Smith is a principal research associate in the School of Chemical Engineering and Advanced Materials at Newcastle University. He is a former technical director of the North-East Regional e-Science Centre and an experienced software developer and consultant in the IT and telecommunication industries.

George Spanoudakis is a professor of software engineering in the Department of Computing of City University London. He has more than 15 years of research experience in this area and has managed several R&D projects in it. Over the last few years his research focuses on service-oriented systems engineering and runtime service based systems verification and adaptation.

Simon J. E. Taylor is the founder and chair of the COTS Simulation Package Interoperability Product Development Group (CSPI-PDG). He has served as the chair of ACM's Special Interest Group on Simulation (SIGSIM) 2005 to 2008. He is a reader in the School of Information Systems, Computing and Mathematics at Brunel University, UK.

Theodora Varvarigou is a professor at the National Technical University of Athens (NTUA). She obtained her diploma from the NTUA (1988), the MS degrees in electrical engineering (1989) and in computer science (1991) and the PhD degree (1991) from Stanford University. She has great experience in semantic web technologies and Grids with more than 150 papers in leading journals and conferences and participation and coordination of several EU funded projects.

Rob Wilson is a senior lecturer in management at the Newcastle University Business School, deputy director of the Centre for Knowledge Innovation Technology and Enterprise, and leader of the Social and Business Informatics (SBI) group. Rob's research interests are in public service innovation: the role that IS plays in organizational change and partnership working.

Yong Yue BSc, PhD, CEng, MIMechE, is a principal lecturer at the University of Bedfordshire. He has been in academia since 1990 following his eight years experience in industry. His current research interests include geometric modeling, computer graphics, virtual reality, robot planning and AI applications. He has published over 90 refereed journal and conference papers and led a number of research and consultancy projects.

Xia Zhao is a research assistant at the University of Bedfordshire (UK). She has a BSc in computer science & education from Liaoning Normal University (Dalian, China) and an MSc (dist) in software engineering for the e-economy from the University of Leicester (Leicester, UK). She is currently working on 3 European projects.

Andrea Zisman is a reader in the Department of City University. She has been research-active in the areas of automated software engineering and service oriented computing where she has published extensively. Andrea has been principal and co-investigator of various research projects in these areas.

Index

Copyright © 2009, IGI Global, distributing in print or electronic forms without written permission of IGI Global is prohibited.